Abba Eban

Abba Eban

A BIOGRAPHY

ASAF SINIVER

Overlook Duckworth
New York • London

This edition first published in hardcover in the United States and the United Kingdom
in 2015 by Overlook Duckworth, Peter Mayer Publishers, Inc.

New York
141 Wooster Street
New York, NY 10012
www.overlookpress.com
For bulk and special sales, please contact sales@overlookny.com,
or write us at the above address

London
30 Calvin Street
London E1 6NW
info@duckworth-publishers.co.uk
www.ducknet.co.uk

Library of Congress Cataloging-in-Publication Data
Siniver, Asaf, 1976- author.
Abba Eban : a biography / Asaf Siniver. -- First edition.
pages cm
ISBN 978-1-4683-0933-1
1. Eban, Abba Solomon, 1915-2002. 2. Statesmen--Israel--Biography. 3.
Israel--Foreign relations. I. Title.
DS126.6.E2S55 2015
327.56940092--dc23
[B]
2015027836

Book design and typeformatting by Bernard Schleifer
Manufactured in the United States of America
ISBN US: 978-1-4683-0933-1
ISBN UK: 978-0-7156-5007-3

FIRST EDITION
2 4 6 8 10 9 7 5 3 1

To the memory of my mother,
Sara Siniver, 1943–2015

Contents

Preface

THE PROVENANCE OF THIS BIOGRAPHY IS A LETTER OF PROTEST. IN 1984 Abba Eban was Israel's elder statesman: he had been there at the nation's birth in 1948, serving as Israel's first representative to the United Nations and its second ambassador to the United States, holding both positions simultaneously until 1959. He held ministerial positions as education minister, deputy prime minister, and foreign minister until his dramatic ousting from the cabinet by his great nemesis, Yitzhak Rabin, in 1974. On the global stage, Eban had cemented his place in history as one of the greatest statesmen of his generation, a master diplomat, and an incredible orator. He was still a leading figure in the Israel Labor Party, with twenty-five years in the Knesset behind him, and was widely recognized at home and abroad as a vociferous political dove. Now, at the age of sixty-nine, Eban was jostling for a top spot on his party's ticket for the general elections, and he felt that his best years were certainly not behind him. "There is evidence that the year 1983 was my *annus mirabilis*," Eban wrote to Amnon Abramovich of the Israeli daily *Maariv*; "I was elected into the international hall of fame of the modern era's greatest orators, America's Jews expressed their unreserved confidence in me, I led the public polls for the post of foreign minister, and my book *The New Diplomacy* was widely acclaimed even by [former U.S. Secretary of State Henry] Kissinger, who had never praised anyone but Kissinger."[1]

"Now here is the problem," Eban continued. "Why does all of this carry so little weight in interparty contests where there are people who lack any international resonance? Is this indifference unique to the Labor movement, which devours its people, or is it a sign of Israeli parochialism? Or perhaps I am responsible for it due to insufficient concern for 'public relations.' In any case, the problem is a problem, even if it did not concern me personally. I believe that this is a unique phenomenon and therefore deserves attention."[2]

Abba Eban was, and remains, a unique phenomenon. There is no modern comparison to the huge dissonance between the utter reverence that Eban enjoyed abroad and the travails he endured at home. The qualities that led Conor Cruise O'Brien to eulogize Eban as the greatest diplomat of the second half of the twentieth century—his exceptional eloquence and oratory, enviable wit, nuanced understanding of diplomacy as a vocation, fluency in ten languages, and moderate worldview—were frowned upon in Israel as inanely foreign, elitist, and full of pomposity. Eban's friends and critics alike often noted that he would have been a wonderful prime minister—in any country but Israel. Born in Cape Town in 1915 and raised in England, a Cambridge don by the age of twenty-three, and a major in the British Army during World War II, Eban was always destined to be greeted with suspicion and distrust from his contemporaries in Israel, many of whom settled in Mandatory Palestine as teenagers in the interwar period, where they toiled the land, dried swamps, fought the Arabs, and harassed the British authorities. In many respects, Eban was an antihero to the early Israeli generation of land-working pioneers who were audacious, resourceful, and battle-scarred. Abroad, Eban was lauded as Israel's Cicero; at home, Prime Minister Levi Eshkol called him "the wise fool," and when Eshkol's successor, Golda Meir, heard that Eban was considering running for the premiership, her bemused response was "in which country?"

But Eban's urbane internationalism and perceived elitism alone do not capture the essence of his uneasy relationship with his compatriots. Eban was a voice of reason and moderation in a country that spoke with hyperbolic anxiety. As Israel's ambassador to the United States in the 1950s, he berated his government's military adventurism and political intransigence. As its foreign minister he bemoaned the messianic territorial obsession that engulfed the nation following the 1967 Six-Day War. Eban urged the revival of a "peace mystique" in Israeli society, but his stirring rhetoric was trounced by the cold pragmatism of Meir and the political opportunism of her defense minister, Moshe Dayan. Following Eban's shocking exit from the cabinet in 1974, his criticism of the country's militant obduracy continued to grow both in frequency and ferocity. Israel's disastrous invasion of Lebanon in 1982 and its heavy treatment of the Palestinians in the West Bank had led him to conclude in 1987 that "frankly, when I look back at the speech I gave at Israel's birth to get us into the United Nations, I would not dare make that same speech now . . . I would definitely not use the phrase that we will be 'a light unto the nations.'"[3]

Eban's life, achievements, and failures cannot be narrowly defined by the formal titles of ambassador, foreign minister, political dove, or even the Voice of Israel—the moniker accorded him as Israel's ambassador by Prime Minister David Ben-Gurion. Eban was also a polyglot, an orientalist, the most brilliant debater of the Cambridge Union, the author of countless books, a professor of international affairs at Columbia, Princeton, and George Washington Universities, and the presenter of *Heritage: Civilization and the Jews*, one of the most critically acclaimed and commercially successful TV documentary series ever broadcast. Above all, Eban was a humanist, a universalist, and an intellectual: the challenge for Israel, he told his compatriots in 1973, was how to put "the emphasis on freedom, tolerance, equality, social justice, spiritual and intellectual creativity, and human brotherhood as the salient characteristics of a strong and confident Israeli society."[4]

It is precisely this defense of universal values against the rise of national chauvinism that captures much of the Eban story and points to the dichotomy of global veneration and domestic skepticism he encountered for much of his life. As the distinguished American historian Arthur M. Schlesinger Jr. noted in lamenting this tragic discord in his friend's life, "His courage in pressing for reconciliation . . . along with his ironical British style, denied him the political success in Israel to which his dedication and talent entitled him."[5] According to the theorist and literary critic Edward Said, intellectuals like Eban are guided by universal values that necessarily clash with national narratives. At the same time, the means of effective communication is the intellectual's currency; he is used to polish and justify national policies. But if the intellectual exposes the truth or departs from the narrative, his existence becomes a lonely one.[6] In this respect, Eban's somewhat lonely existence in Israel resonates with Heinrich Heine's depiction of the lone intellectual in his introduction to *Don Quixote*: "Society is a republic. When an individual strives to rise, the collective masses press him back through ridicule and abuse. No one shall be wiser or better than the rest. But against him, who by the invincible power of genius towers above the vulgar masses, society launches its ostracism, and persecutes him so mercilessly with scoffing and slander, that he is finally compelled to withdraw into the solitude of his own thoughts."[7]

ABBA EBAN HAD A TREMENDOUS SENSE OF HIS PLACE IN HISTORY, AND THIS IS partly reflected in the stupendous volume of works he left behind. Few, if any, Israeli leaders gave more interviews and press conferences or wrote more books, journal articles, and newspaper op-ed pieces; there are even vinyl records and CDs featuring Eban's most famous speeches before the United Nations. For decades his wife Suzy compiled a library of scrapbooks filled with news clippings from around the world in which her husband's name was mentioned.[8] The Ebans saved everything: copies of letters sent and received, fan mail, transcripts of radio and TV interviews, drafts of speeches, and one-line notes—altogether, thousands upon thousands of documents, most of which are kept in hundreds of boxes in the archives of the Abba Eban Centre for Israeli Diplomacy at the Hebrew University of Jerusalem. According to Professor Michael Freedman of George Washington University, where Eban served as professor of international affairs in 1993, this voluminous bibliography is easily justified: "Every once in a while if we're lucky we encounter somebody who has an aura about them. Eban had an aura around him. He was a person of history. You knew it when he walked into the room."[9]

And yet, the only biography ever written on Eban was published back in 1972, by the syndicated journalist Robert St. John, though it sits more comfortably in the company of unapologetic hagiographies than emphatically detached scholarship. In 2008, six years after her husband's death, Suzy Eban published her memoir, *A Sense of Purpose: Reflections*, in which she staunchly defended her husband's legacy. In between St. John's biography and Suzy Eban's memoir, Abba Eban's two dense memoirs, *An Autobiography* (1977) and *Personal Witness: Israel through My Eyes* (1992), were both published to wide acclaim. But these four accounts encounter certain difficulties in merging the two faces of the art of biography: the writing of a life story and the writing of a history. As the Israeli historian and biographer of Ben-Gurion, Shabtai Teveth, pointed, all biographers face a similar dilemma: the chronicling of which events must gain prominence—those that influenced the life of the hero or those that affected the life of a generation. There is no easy answer here. According to Teveth, the biographer will face the wrath of the critics regardless of the path he has chosen: a pithy literary page-turner will be condemned by historians for scholarly brevity, while a heavily footnoted tome of painstakingly assembled moments in time will scare away a general readership.[10] St. John's biography of Eban and Suzy Eban's memoirs cannot be accused of excessive deference to historical truths or of being an objective portrayal of the hero. Eban's two memoirs are as close as an autobiography of a diplomat and a politician can be a page-turner: they are rich in historical detail and full of mouthwatering observations of some of the greatest leaders of the last century;

unfortunately, however, they also contain too much self-congratulation and not enough self-introspection.

Eban himself alluded to this basic deficiency in the autobiographical tradition—in his distinctively loquacious and falsely self-deprecating style—when he addressed the National Press Club in Washington, DC, in May 1994. Before delivering his talk on the relationship between diplomacy and the media, Eban took the time to thank the chairperson for his generous introduction, saying, "I'm very grateful to you, Mr. Chairman, for what you have said. You have achieved generosity without any marked departure from precision. [*Laughter.*] The only objective things written about me have been in introductions by successive chairmen, and of course in my autobiography. [*Laughter.*] Autobiography is an excellent device for telling the truth about other people; but sometimes they do reveal something about oneself. [*Laughter.*]"[11]

THIS BIOGRAPHY DOES NOT PURPORT TO BE AN OBJECTIVE STORY OF ABBA EBAN'S life because—simply by choosing to write a biography—the author already has a sense of the importance (if not greatness) of his subject. Moreover, given the time and energy invested in studying the life of another human being, it would be impossible not to develop certain feelings toward that person, be they apologetic compassion or intense repulsion. The surest way to prevent such feelings from corrupting the scholarly and literary value of the biography is for the biographer to base his verdict on rigorous historical research that draws on as many sources as are available and take into account as many sides of the story as possible. This Eban biography is the result of six years of extensive archival research, interviews with dozens of individuals, and, perhaps most dauntingly, reading (almost) every word ever written or spoken by the man himself, from his Cambridge University notebooks in 1934 to his unpublished notes about Benjamin Netanyahu's leadership nearly six and a half decades later. My basic approach is one of sympathy to Eban, if not empathy. This biography highlights some of Eban's acute shortcomings as a man, a politician, and a leader, but it is most definitely not a pathography either. Ultimately it is a story of a man who defined and defended a nation to the world, but never felt at home among his compatriots.

I

The Making of a Zionist Wunderkind

YANISHKI WAS A TYPICAL JEWISH TOWN IN THE KOVNO PROVINCE OF Lithuania. At the end of the nineteenth century, more than half of its 4,500 inhabitants were Jews who made a living from trading in livestock, cloth, and grain. The Age of Enlightenment brought emancipation and prosperity to the Jews of western Europe, but for the Jews of Yanishki and other shtetls in eastern Europe the future looked as bleak as the past. A century earlier, Empress Catherine the Great, determined to limit the rapid growth of the Jewish middle class across Russia, forbade the residence of Jews outside the boundaries of the Pale of Settlement—an area comprising 4 percent of imperial Russia and running from the Baltic Sea in the north to the Black Sea in the south. Amounting to 40 percent of world Jewry at the time, the four million Jews of the Pale were destined to die impoverished or be slain in a pogrom.[1]

When Czar Alexander II was assassinated in 1881 by a group of young revolutionaries, the Jews were immediately held responsible, even though only one of the eight conspirators was Jewish. The Pale was soon swamped by a wave of pogroms, and with new anti-Jewish legislation imposing further restrictions on Jewish movement and participation in society, life for the Jews of the Pale had become more insufferable than ever. Some attacks were organized by the authorities and editorials in local newspapers; some were spontaneously instigated by drunken mobs with the tacit support of the police. The result was invariably similar: countless bodies of dead Jews, their businesses looted and their houses set on fire. There were more than two hundred pogroms across the Pale between 1881 and 1884; the Odessa Pogrom of 1905 alone claimed the lives of some 2,500 Jews.[2] Desperate to escape persecution and discrimination, hundreds of thousands of Jews fled czarist Russia in search of a better life. By the turn of the twentieth century, fewer than a thousand Jews remained in Yanishki.[3] The vast majority of those who fled the town chose to settle in South Africa, a particularly favorite destination for Lithuanian Jews, which was hailed as the "golden land."[4]

Abraham Meir Solomon left Yanishki for the golden land in 1897. Fondly called Avromeir by his friends, the eighteen-year-old was accompanied by his father, Samuel (Reb Shmuel) Solomon. The father and son settled in Cape Town and hoped to save enough money to bring out Avromeir's mother, Rilka, and his fourteen-year-old sister, Celia. But their fortunes were mixed: Reb Shmuel found it difficult to adjust to life in the new country and failed to make financial headway during the Second Boer War (1899–1902) and the subsequent economic depression. In 1904 he left his son in Cape Town to join relatives in America, and five years later he returned to Yanishki to reunite with his wife and daughter. Meanwhile, the young and exuberant Avromeir had done considerably better. He learned the language and soon became a successful "commercial traveler," venturing as far as the German colony of South-West Africa (present-day Namibia). But Avromeir's real passion was Zionism— the nascent idea that Jews needed their own homeland to protect them from persecution and physical destruction. He was one of a small group of devout Zionists who attended the first general meeting of the Dorshei Zion society (Seekers of Zion) in Cape Town in September 1899, and six years later he became its president. Avromeir was also a founding member of the New Hebrew Congregation, which actively supported the Zionist cause of Jewish self-determination. He frequently contributed articles to the *Zionist Record*, and traveled extensively to found Zionist societies in little towns and villages across the Western Cape. By 1905 there were sixty Zionist societies throughout the country, and the South African Jewish Federation even established a trust to purchase land and set up farms in Ottoman Palestine for Jewish immigrants.[5]

In 1910 Avromeir worked as a bookkeeper for Elihau Velva (Wolf) Sacks, a London-based manufacturer's agent and distributor who had business in Cape Town. As fate would have it, Avromeir's boss was a fellow Yanishki expatriate. Back home, Sacks worked as a merchant, trading from his small quarters in anything from silk and silverware to garments and cloth. He traveled on business around Russia and later went to South Africa several times, where he established a commission house that traded mainly in imported eggs from China and Denmark. However, Sacks's real interest lay in Jewish scholarship particularly in the revival of Hebrew as the national language of the Jews. He had been given advanced religious education in a yeshiva in Neustadt as a young boy, but he chose not to enter the life of religious zealotry. As a sign of respect for his father, however, he never took his yarmulke off, not even when he went swimming.[6] Sacks was intuitively a *maskil*, a disciple of the Jewish Enlightenment movement, which advocated the modern study of Jewish texts such as the Mishnah and the Talmud, as opposed to religious orthodoxy. He saw the study of Hebrew and Jewish heritage as a humanist pursuit rather than a religious tool, and he taught his four children Hebrew literature and tradition, as well as English, the language he had come to master on his business trips. Indeed, many in Yanishki agreed that Sacks was a better scholar than businessman: much to the chagrin of his wife Bassa, he was habitually seen in his shop engaged in drawn-out philosophical discussions or a game of chess with a customer, invariably forgetting to take payment. But business was nevertheless thriving, and in 1903 the family moved to London, where Sacks opened a new local branch. Together with Bassa, their two daughters, Lina (nineteen) and Alida (twelve), and two sons Ben (eleven) and Sam (seven), they settled in the northern London suburb of Stoke Newington. They bought a three-story, twelve-room house, where one of the attractions was a dining table that could sit twenty-eight people. They also employed a live-in housemaid, Jessie Blayney, from Hackney.[7]

At the end of 1912, Sacks returned to London from a business trip to Cape Town, accompanied by his new business associate, Avromeir Solomon. "I have found you a husband," he announced to his daughter Alida. She was not overly excited by the news, as she later recalled: "I was not impressed, even though Avromeir was handsome with his brown hair and eyes, whose whole face smiled when he talked. He was thirty-four, I was only twenty-two, so I did not immediately accept his proposal of marriage." But Sacks asked her to think it over, and soon Avromeir began wooing Alida with a barrage of love letters. "I am sure they were the most beautiful love letters any man ever wrote to a woman," Alida recalled. "It was his letters I fell in love with."[8]

Alida Sacks and Avromeir Solomon married in London on April 23, 1913, soon after Avromeir returned from a trip to Germany and Poland. They left for South Africa aboard the *Edinburgh Castle*, and after three weeks at sea they arrived at Cape Town, where they were welcomed at the docks by a party of Avromeir's fellow Zionists. The next night the Dorshei Zion organized a welcome party. Alida was excited by her first encounters with the

Zionist spirit, but her father, though a great admirer of Jewish scholarship and heritage, did not believe that a Jewish state could ever be a reality. "Can you see hair on the palm of my hand?" he jibed whenever the subject came up in conversation.[9]

Alida and Avromeir were financially comfortable, but they were not affluent. Their home on Hofmeyer Street in Cape Town's upscale Gardens suburb was always open to a large circle of friends, where conversations invariably revolved around Zionism. In December 1913 their first daughter was born and named Ruth after her paternal grandmother, Rilka Solomon. Shortly after her birth, Avromeir became seriously ill, but the doctors in Cape Town could not agree on a diagnosis and recommended that he seek expert medical opinion in London as a matter of urgency. On February 2, 1915, the couple had their second child. The boy weighed only five pounds at birth and had a very small body, "but a beautiful large head and twinkling brown eyes," according to Alida, who insisted that her son was born with a great sense of humor. The little boy was named Abba, after Alida's favorite grandfather, Abba Tobias Sacks. But fearing that little Abba would be taunted by other children and called "Abie-baby" at school, Avromeir chose Aubrey as an alternative to the Hebrew-sounding Abba.[10]

"As a baby I emigrated from South Africa because I couldn't stand Apartheid!" foreign minister Abba Eban would wryly recount decades later about his family's exodus from Cape Town.[11] In August 1915, when Aubrey Abba Solomon was six months old, the family traveled to London to get the best medical treatment for Avromeir's undiagnosed illness. But with the world at war, the journey was not an easy one; all the available ships had been transformed into troop carriers, transporting South African soldiers to the British Isles to protect against an expected German invasion. With the help of Avromeir's friend, Morris Alexander, a fellow Zionist and a member of the South African Parliament, Avromeir, Alida, and their two toddlers were allowed to join more than five hundred soldiers on board a troopship headed for the southern English seaport of Portsmouth. Alida could never shake off the memories of the terrifying four-week journey with her ailing husband and two babies in a crowded, sweaty troopship, traveling through rough seas infested with mines and enemy submarines.[12] Upon their arrival at the train station in London, the family was greeted by Elihau Sacks. Before embracing his daughter or checking on Avromeir's health, he rushed to examine little Aubrey, whom Alida described in her letters from Cape Town as frail and delicate.

Holding the baby close to his face, Grandpapa Sacks scolded Alida: "Why did you write me such nonsense? *Mein Kind is a prince!*"[13] Everyone knew that Aubrey was the favorite grandchild of Grandpapa Sacks, but soon this love would turn into obsession, as the grandfather would make it his life mission to teach his little prince everything that he had ever known.

The family settled in London with Alida's parents. Avromeir, by now alarmingly pale and thin, seemed remarkably unfazed by the news that his illness was diagnosed as terminal cancer of the liver and pancreas. "There are soldiers dying every day, every minute. What right have I to grumble?" he muttered from his sickbed. On January 25, 1916, one week before Aubrey's first birthday, Avromeir passed away. "I was destined to live without any recollection of my father beyond a few faded photographs from family albums and Zionist photographs," Eban would later write in his memoirs.[14]

Several months after her husband's death, Alida found a job as a secretary and translator in the new Zionist offices at 175 Piccadilly Street in London. The job was not particularly interesting or well paid, but in November 1917 Alida found herself playing an active, if modest, role in one of the most momentous episodes in Jewish history. She worked for Nahum Sokolow, a prominent Zionist leader who had previously served as secretary-general of the World Zionist Congress and who was also a prolific writer and linguist. But the real driving force behind the Zionist movement in Britain was Chaim Weizmann, who although lower in rank than Sokolow in the Zionist hierarchy possessed tremendous amounts of charisma and vision in his pursuit of the Zionist program. Born in Russia and graduated as a biochemist in Geneva, Weizmann moved to England in 1905, where he taught biochemistry at Manchester University. He was a renowned chemist, considered the father of industrial fermentation, and during World War I served as director of the British Admiralty's laboratories. Weizmann rapidly became known in British and European Zionist circles as a powerful public speaker and an indefatigable lobbyist for the Jewish cause. His scientific assistance to the Allied forces during the war, which included the development of a method for making acetone—an essential ingredient in the production of artillery shells—from maize, brought him into close contact with British leaders, including Minister of Munitions David Lloyd George. According to the popular fable, when Lloyd George became prime minister in December 1916, his thank-you gift to Weizmann was the promise of a Jewish homeland in Palestine once it was liberated from the Turks.[15]

Weizmann's lobbying for a national home for the Jews in Palestine at the height of the Great War was as counterintuitive as it was unrealistic. The British historian and diplomat Sir Charles Webster noted that Weizmann's campaign was "the greatest act of diplomatic statesmanship of the First World War. The people for whom he strove were dispersed over all five continents. The home which he sought to create was in a country whose inhabitants, except for a small and all-important body of pioneers, belonged to another people. He had to go back nearly 2,000 years to establish a claim upon it. There was no precedent for what he asked."[16] In reality, more strategic calculations drove Britain to support Zionist aspirations during the war, and eventually the efforts of Weizmann, Sokolow, and others bore fruit in early 1917, when official negotiations took place in London to outline a program for Jewish resettlement in Palestine.

On the evening of November 1, 1917, the telephone rang at the Sacks house. On the line was Sokolow, who urged Alida to come to the office to help translate into French and Russian an official document that had just been transmitted by the British Foreign Office. Aubrey, who was not yet two years old, lay in his cradle fretting, and Alida grappled with the dilemma of whether to attend to her vexing toddler or play a small part in a momentous event. It was an easy decision to make: she left Aubrey with his grandmother and rushed to the office. When Alida saw the short document she knew that she had made the right decision. Signed by Foreign Secretary Arthur James Balfour and addressed to Lord Rothchild, one of Britain's leading Jewish entrepreneurs and philanthropists, the short statement represented the British government's official commitment to support the establishment of a Jewish homeland in Palestine. The declaration was purposely vague on important issues such as the proposed borders and whether a homeland equated to statehood, though it was more explicit in asserting that the pursuit of a Jewish homeland should not jeopardize the rights of the indigenous communities in Palestine. The significance of this sixty-seven-word text could not be overplayed: for the first time in history the Jewish people were brought into the law and politics of nations via the commitment of a great power to Jewish self-determination. Or, in the words of British novelist Arthur Koestler, in this declaration "one nation solemnly promised to a second nation the country of a third." A copy of the document was duly smuggled into Palestine by the British Secret Service Branch (forerunner of MI6) in order to encourage Jews to support the Allied war effort against the Turks.[17]

Alida accompanied her father to a crowded gala at London's Kingsway Hall, where Zionist delegates from all over the world gathered in celebration. Wolf Sacks never hid his disparaging views of Zionism's aspirations, but now he seemed visibly shaken by the historic occasion. Sitting rigidly at the back of the hall for much of the evening, he suddenly put his head in his hands and began to weep. For Alida the remarkable accomplishment of the Balfour Declaration tasted bittersweet: her thoughts were with her late husband, Avromeir, who had made it his life's mission to found Zionist societies wherever he went but was not with her now to celebrate the realization of his dreams.[18]

Alida found it increasingly difficult to raise her two children and keep her job during the war. In addition to her work in the Zionist office, she also helped her brother, Sam Sacks, who was a successful physician and used part of the Sacks house as his clinic. Dr. Sacks was also a successful eater—weighing nearly three hundred pounds, he was rumored to know the contents of the refrigerators in all his patients' houses.[19] As many doctors were drafted into the armed forces during the war, the practice soon became overcrowded with patients, and Sam had to plead with his sister, "You must come! There are a hundred patients—more or less—and I can't possibly see them all and handle the dispensing, too." When Alida replied that she was needed at the Zionist office, her brother shouted into the phone, "Tell them they'll get Palestine just as quickly without you!"[20] As if her struggle to give Ruth and Aubrey the attention they needed while juggling her two jobs was not enough, Alida feared for the very survival of her family too. With almost daily German Zeppelin raids claiming the lives of hundreds of East Londoners, Alida decided to send Ruth, Aubrey, and their grandmother to stay with the Elliott family, relatives in Belfast, until the war ended. As fate would have it, living next to Aubrey at Clifton Park Avenue in Belfast was a small baby named Chaim Herzog, who decades later would become Israel's sixth president and a brother-in-law to Aubrey through their marriages to two sisters, Suzy and Aura Ambache.[21]

At the end of the war Ruth and Aubrey returned to their mother in London, but soon the hardship of single parenthood and work around the clock resurfaced. Once again, something had to give, and Alida reluctantly heeded her father's advice when he asked, "Don't you think you had better send one of the children back to Ireland?" Everyone knew that Alida would send Ruth, who was boisterous and more of a nuisance than her brother. Aubrey, meanwhile was about to begin his formal education and learning of the Hebrew language.

As soon as Aubrey turned four he was sent to Kent Coast College, a Jewish boarding school at Herne Bay in southeast England, whereas Ruth, who spent the holidays in Belfast, was sent to Brunswick College for Ladies in Hove, near Brighton on the southern coast. Thc siblings struggled to adapt to their new surroundings, and found this period of their lives so traumatizing that even late in adulthood they reflected with some sadness on their upbringing. "Nobody ever told us anything that was going on," Ruth recalled. "If only we had been kept together! There was total fragmentation in our life." Even in their eighties, the brother and sister still found it difficult to come to terms with what they remembered as an emotionally deprived childhood. "We never lacked food but we were emotionally starved," Ruth observed, whereas Aubrey simply refused to share his childhood memories and feelings with anyone, not even his wife, Suzy. All he could say to her was, "It was not the kind of home I fancied."[22]

In February 1920 Alida went back to South Africa for a year to settle some legal issues and other minor business that had been left behind when she had hurriedly departed Cape Town with her family four years earlier. Alida found it too difficult to leave Aubrey behind for such a long period of time, and told him that she would be back in a few days. His mother's departure left Aubrey more pensive than usual, while Ruth, on the other hand, had settled well in Belfast with the Elliott family and had even made a friend: Dr. Isaac Eban, who often came to the house to help with the medical training of Ruth's two cousins, who were studying medicine at Queen's University.

On her return home from Cape Town, Alida's first stop was at Aubrey's school in Herne Bay. She found her six-year-old son sitting atop a radiator to keep warm and reading a book aloud to a group of boys who were huddled together at his feet. Looking up to see his mother after her year of absence, Aubrey quietly remarked, "your hair looks different."[23]

Meanwhile, Sam Sacks desperately needed assistance in his clinic to combat an outbreak of scarlet fever, and he found help in Dr. Isaac Eban, who was recommended by the Elliott twins in Belfast. Isaac was immediately liked by the Sacks family, who found his Scottish vernacular so incomprehensible that they nicknamed him "the goy," even though he was Jewish. Alida initially toyed with the idea of going to medical school, but she eventually followed the encouragement and advice of her young daughter, as well as her father ("we won't study medicine, my child, we will marry medicine!"), and in June 1921 she married the young doctor, who at thirty-one was one year her senior.

Neither Ruth nor Aubrey remembered their biological father, and both were fond of their stepfather—though Aubrey was more reserved than Ruth toward the man he now called Daddy. The Eban family moved to a three-story house at 12 Kennington Park Road, in the Elephant and Castle area of south London, a neighborhood that was both busy and decaying, where grime and poverty were ever present. It was a strange place for Jews to live, south of the River Thames and the Jewish immigrants' natural habitat of the East End, but the reason for Dr. Eban's choice of residence was that Health Services rules dictated that general practitioners must live no more than two miles away from their patients, and so the first floor of the house was transformed into Dr. Eban's surgery, waiting room, and dispensary. Soon Alida and Isaac had two more children, Carmel and Raphael, but it was Aubrey who was coming to be known as the family prodigy.

AT THE AGE OF SIX AUBREY BEGAN TO ATTEND ST. OLAVE'S AND ST. SAVIOUR'S Grammar School for Boys in the South London borough of Southwark. Chosen by Aubrey's grandfather, St. Olave's was considered one of the most demanding and highest-achieving state schools in the country. The school's surroundings were hardly inspiring or conducive to academic excellence, however; it was situated in the dockyards near Tower Bridge, where the disconsolate landscape comprised cranes, factories, and warehouses. Against this dreary backdrop Aubrey was taught in the classical tradition of British education, focusing primarily on Latin and Greek literature as well as English poetry and biblical studies. He soon became fascinated by the rhetorical power of the ancient civilizations, and later in life he would trace the roots of his legendary oratory skills back to this classical education.[24]

Grandpapa Sacks was not content with Aubrey's rigorous scholarship at St. Olave's, however. From the age of six to fourteen Aubrey spent his weekdays at school in the company of Homer, Vergil, Thucydides, and Plato, but whereas his classmates were allowed to unwind on the weekend, he spent the next forty-eight hours at his grandfather's home in Hackney for equally rigorous private tuition in the fields of Jewish philosophy, biblical literature, the Talmud, and modern Hebrew. During those eight years Aubrey did not enjoy a free weekend. He was not allowed to play outside with his sister Ruth and cousin Neville Halper; from Friday afternoon to Sunday night, and sometimes until Monday morning, he experienced "an almost brutally intensive immersion" in the curriculum his grandfather had designed for him, for the sole purpose of turning Aubrey into an exceptional Hebrew scholar.[25] His grandfather's mission to leave a legacy through his grandson's education proved to be the most formative experience in Aubrey's life. Decades later when he was asked about his childhood, Eban admitted that it was "not normal." He did not enjoy life's little pleasures; he did not play football with the boys or get into trouble at school. He recalled, however, being moved by his first book, one of Charles Dickens's novels, and how its social undertones left a poignant impression on his young mind.[26] More than anything else he would go on to study in later life, the "brutal" weekends with his grandfather, as he later described them, would predestine him to embark on a path of exceptional scholarly and diplomatic career. It was only following the death of his grandfather of pneumonia, shortly after Aubrey's fourteenth birthday, when the gifted teenager finally tasted a free weekend. Not surprisingly, his obvious grief was accompanied by a sense of guilty relief, but his love of the written word and of Jewish history and scholarship did not abate. For the rest of the young boy's life, his most cherished possession was the vast library of Hebrew and Talmudic texts that Grandpapa Sacks had bequeathed him on his deathbed. These books accompanied him on his future diplomatic missions to London, New York, and Washington, DC; later they found a prominent place in his own enormous library at his home in Israel.

Aubrey's relationship with his parents ran counter to the family life that evolved with the arrival of Carmel and Raphael. He failed to form a strong bond with his stepfather, and his relationship with his mother was painfully emotional and tainted by a strong sense of separation anxiety. The early death of his biological father, together with his mother's remarriage and her frequent absences from his life—Alida even missed Aubrey's bar mitzvah because she had to attend to his measles-stricken half-siblings—had scarred him so badly that he later lamented that he grew up as an orphan.[27] But Alida was immensely proud of her son, and their emotional attachment was so strong that decades later he never missed an opportunity to pay her a short visit whenever he stopped in London during his many transatlantic flights between Israel and the United States. Ruth, on the other hand, was very fond of her adoptive father but was scornful of Alida's maternal makeup, undoubtedly owing to her mother's decision to send her to Ireland during the war while keeping Aubrey close to her in London. Unlike his two sisters, Aubrey was very reticent and less adaptive to his environment—even though, as his younger brother Raphael later observed, the emphasis and attention of the family were always directed toward Aubrey, leaving the others somewhat in his shadow. Alida herself made no secret of her special bond with Aubrey, declaring decades later, "I am proud of all my children—my son the doctor (Raphael) and my married daughter, but I was always especially proud of Aubrey, as was the entire family. He was just something special."[28] Unsurprisingly, it was at St. Olave's where Aubrey felt most at home. In addition to academic excellence, the school provided the teenager not only a comforting sense of belonging but also a refuge from what he felt was a dysfunctional home.

The Ebans did not struggle in poverty, as had the previous generation of immigrants. In 1930 the family acquired a holiday cottage, in the seaside village of Birchington on the Kent Coast, that provided the setting for some of Aubrey's happiest family memories. Isaac and Alida were both nonobservant Jews, and they brought up their four children in a secular, social-democratic Zionist environment. A Jewish Agency collection box for Palestine was permanently on display in the living room, and the family often engaged in discussions about Jewish philosophy, the Bible, history, and ethics. With the passing of his grandfather, Aubrey could now enjoy the free weekends, but his sharp intellect and thirst for knowledge drew him to the Orthodox Brixton Synagogue, where he spent his Friday evenings expanding his knowledge of Hebrew law and classics. There he formed a symbiotic relationship with Rabbi Arnold Mischon, whose passion for Zionism and command of Greek, Latin, and English literature inspired the teenager; at the same time, the rabbi was impressed with Aubrey's logical reasoning and love of the written word and invited him to join his young Zionist society He'Atid (The Future), of which Aubrey was later elected chairman.

Whereas Aubrey was introverted and pensive in his personal relationships, he seemed to find his gregariousness in Zionist activities, his shyness turning to exuberance whenever he stepped onto a podium to argue the Zionist case. An added benefit to his newfound vocation was the discovery of the opposite sex. After spending eight years in an all-boys school during the week, and in the company of his grandfather every single weekend, he now had a new group of friends who shared his interest in Zionism. He was introduced to the world of dancing, partying, films, and even cricket. While his voice had not fully matured yet, his tall and slim frame gave the impression of a young university don. He was a leader in the young Zionist movement, and by the age of sixteen became an editor of *The Young Zionist* magazine as well as a regular contributor. Aubrey also took part in the association's annual summer school, where young Zionists not only absorbed the intellectual and political foundations of Zionism but also were taught valuable presentation skills, including professional elocution and techniques for handling hecklers. The practical assessment of the course involved the mounting of a soapbox in London's Hyde Park to address an importunate audience. Aubrey's orations were so eloquent and skillful that he was soon asked to train the youngsters himself. Still a teenager, Aubrey also helped establish a new Zionist society for seventeen- to twenty-five-year olds, Avodah (Labor), and spent his school holidays running errands for the Zionist offices at 77 Great Russell Street near the British Museum. Before long he caught the attention of Chaim Weizmann and other Zionist leaders who were looking for young talent to recruit to their campaign for a Jewish state.[29]

The intensity of Aubrey's passion for Zionism was matched only by his outstanding grasp of languages. At fifteen he received the annual English prize at St. Olave's, and the following year he passed his exams with such success that he was excused from taking any future examinations. In his senior year he won a prestigious prize for writing Latin hexameters, and his grasp of German was so exceptional that his teacher took Alida aside and told her, "Frau Eban, a new star has risen in the Jewish firmament." The proud mother was not surprised. "We knew that he would go very far since he was a little boy," she announced. Aubrey's love of books was so absolute that he had no other hobbies, and he was soon diagnosed as having nearsightedness; the family doctor ordered the teenager to abstain from school for a while and go to the countryside in order to rest his eyes. But young Aubrey was soon bored of the rural serenity and demanded a return to his studies.[30]

The financial burden of educating the Ebans' four children meant that Aubrey would have to take an exam to win a fully funded scholarship to go to university. There was no real discussion about which university was the right one for Aubrey; for the headmaster at St. Olave's, no other university existed but Cambridge. Its faculty in the 1930s included such luminaries as the economist John Maynard Keynes and the philosophers Bertrand Russell and Ludwig Wittgenstein, who did not hide their contempt for Oxford's frivolous devotion to politics. The Cambridge ethos of logical reasoning and critical inquiry seemed a natural fit for the boy who was blessed with an unusually analytical mind and excellent grasp of languages.[31] In preparation for his exam, Aubrey received private tuition from Nackdemon Doniash, a close friend of the Ebans who had a distinguished career in Oxford and would later compile the *Oxford English–Arabic Dictionary*. Alida's instructions were simple: "Just teach him anything and everything he might need to know to take the scholarship examinations a year from now for Cambridge." But Doniash soon found that there was very little he could teach the prodigy Aubrey, who already excelled in English, Hebrew, Latin, German, French, Greek, and biblical studies. He thus decided to teach him Arabic, which the teenager tackled with remarkable ease.[32]

There was no surprise in the Eban household when, in the summer of 1934, news arrived announcing that Aubrey had been awarded the Kennett Scholarship in Hebrew and Classics at Queens' College, Cambridge.

II

At the Cradle of British Oratory

AUBREY EBAN ENTERED QUEENS' COLLEGE IN OCTOBER 1934. FOUNDED in 1448 by Margaret of Anjou (wife to Henry VI) and refounded in 1465 by Elizabeth Woodville (wife of Edward IV), the college was known for its exquisite architecture; this and its majestic provenance provided an inspirational environment for Aubrey that made it feel much more distant than the short hour-and-a-half trip from the humdrum of South London. Its academic environment made Cambridge a comfortable place for Aubrey due to his years of arduous scholarship at St. Olave's and dedicated tutelage under his grandfather. During his time there he collected every prize and scholarship that stood before him: the Jeremy Septuagint Prize, the Stuart of Rannoch Hebrew Scholarship, the Syriac Prize, the Tyrwhitt Hebrew Scholarship, the Mason Prize, and the Wright Arabic Scholar Award were ultimately capped by an extremely rare triple first in classics and oriental languages (Hebrew, Arabic, and Persian). He also found the time to translate *Times* newspaper articles into classical Greek and developed into one of the finest speakers of the famed Cambridge Union. After his graduation Aubrey went on to win the E. G. Browne Scholarship at Pembroke College in Persian studies. He was a Cambridge don at the tender age of twenty-three, with a phenomenal academic career on the horizon.[1]

Aubrey's time at Cambridge continued to be divided between scholarship and Zionism. He delivered lectures to the local communities, his letters and articles appeared in the *New Statesman* and the *Spectator*, and he was elected member of the executive body of the British Zionist Federation. He also served as president of the university synagogue, the Jewish Society, and the Zionist Group. His early days in the Young Zionists and his mother's work for

Nahum Sokolow made him a familiar figure among the Zionist leadership in London, but it was his encounters with Palestine's Labour Zionist leaders at his mother's house that excited him the most and stirred his socialist conscience; they represented a different brand of Zionism, one that gave "scent of Palestinian soil and sun." Suddenly the Zionism of the Diaspora felt too synthetic, too sterile, and too declaratory in essence. Aubrey's meetings with Dov Hoz (a founder of the Haganah, the Jewish paramilitary organization in Palestine, and Ahdut Ha'Avoda, one of the main socialist movement in Palestine and later Israel), Moshe Shertok (head of the Jewish Agency, the diplomatic arm of the Jewish community in Palestine), and Berl Katzenelson (the intellectual mastermind of Labour Zionism) convinced him that his future lay not in academia or at the hands of the Russian-born immigrants of world Zionism but with the young, hardworking pioneers in Palestine. In 1935 Aubrey joined the ranks of Poalei Zion (Workers of Zion); at the time it was only a marginal group in London but it became the predominant force among the Yishuv, the Jewish community in Palestine. Shertok and Katzenelson were searching for new talent and invited Aubrey, then barely twenty, to join them. He agreed to do so as soon as he completed his studies.[2]

Alongside his rare academic achievements at Cambridge, Aubrey gradually immersed himself in another arena of excellence: debates in the Cambridge Union. The Cambridge Union Society had been founded on February 13, 1815, after a drunken brawl between members of the debating societies of three Cambridge colleges. Five decades later the society had purchased a plot of land for £925 from St. John's College and commissioned the renowned architect Alfred Waterhouse to design a new building, which had been the site of weekly debates ever since. The debating chamber was built as an almost exact replica of the House of Commons. The president of the society sat on an elevated throne, much like the Speaker of the House, and across the gangway the debaters took turns speaking at the dispatch box. On the opposing sides of the room there were black-leather-covered benches that could seat up to seven hundred Union members, with additional seating available in the balcony above.[3]

Equipped with superb erudition and enviable wit, members of the Union were destined to furnish the top echelons of British politics, business, and academia, thus earning the society the moniker "the nursery of statesmen." The Union gained reputation as the social and political barometer of not only Cambridge undergraduates but of the nation as a whole. It was even reported that the Union's overwhelming vote of October 1938 against conscription, and a similar motion by the Oxford Union not to fight for King and Country five years earlier, convinced Joachim von Ribbentrop, the German ambassador in London (and later Adolf Hitler's foreign minister) of the degeneracy of Britain's youth.[4] Often the student debaters on each side would be paired with renowned public speakers from the worlds of politics, business, journalism, and diplomacy. These invited dignitaries, many of them alumni, not only added to the prestige of the Union but also served to educate the young Cantabrigians in the art of public speaking. Over the years some of these distinguished guests would include Prime Ministers Winston Churchill, Clement Attlee, and Harold MacMillan; U.S. presidents Theodore Roosevelt and Ronald Reagan; Indian prime minister Jawaharlal Nehru; and Nobel Peace Prize winners Desmond Tutu and the Dalai Lama, as well as more unsavory characters such as Libya's Muammar Gaddhafi and the right-wing French politician Jean-Marie Le Pen.

The Union's popularity reached a zenith during the interwar years, with the exchanges often cited in the London and national presses. These debates reflected the preoccupations of Britain and Europe in the 1920s and 1930s, such as the 1933 motion "This House prefers Fascism to Socialism," which was defended masterfully by Sir Oswald Mosley but eventually won by Clement Attlee. Other pressing issues of the time that were debated at Chamber Hall included "This House considers the League of Nations to be worthless as a guarantee of international peace, and to be a radically unsound and dangerous project"; "the chimera of female control is an absurdity as great as that of women entering men's colleges"; "the great fallacy of modern times is that armaments are the real cause of war"; and the idea that the Union had "no faith in the conception of a strong and united British Empire as the mainstay of world peace." The Union chamber was less populated during the summer vacations, and this allowed for more frivolous motions to be debated, though still with much eloquence and potency: "The House decided that it was not glad it was born when it was"; "it was not yet tired of books"; and "work was the curse of the drinking classes."[5]

But it was the gathering storm over Europe that dominated the debates in the second half of the 1930s. The tragedy of the Spanish Civil War and Hitler's steady march across Europe brought to the fore real divisions among the Union members, mirroring the national confusion and trepidation about the future. Communists argued with liberals, nationalists squabbled with republicans, and advocates of appeasement quarreled with critics of the government of Prime Minister Neville Chamberlain. Aubrey was one of the rising stars of the Left in these debates. By his twentieth birthday his hierarchy of loyalties was clearly defined: he was a Zionist, democratic socialist, advocate of resistance to fascism, supporter of the Spanish republicans against Francisco Franco, and advocate for the League of Nations. These ideas would form an ideological basis for the rest of his life.[6]

Aubrey delivered his maiden speech at the Union in October 1935, and his task was not easy—to defend the right of female students to join the Union. Whereas the society was founded in 1815 to promote free speech and the art of public speaking, it was not until 1946 that women were permitted to attend the debates, and another seven years passed before the Union finally admitted female members; it was not until 1967 that it would elect its first female president, Ann Mallalieu.[7] Aubrey spoke for five minutes in support of women's rights, but the vote at the end of the night read 193 ayes and 274 nays. The following year he attended nearly all of the Union debates, and by his final year he was widely praised for his "creative and entertaining wit" and his "rapid sentences and dialectical style." One Cambridge newspaper reporter went as far as to declare, "I am getting tired of repeating all the time that Mr. Eban is the best speaker in the Union." A more critical reporter noted that "Mr. Eban has a genius for misquotation and secures his effects by exaggeration," but he too conceded that "his speeches always have a number of neat cracks and I would sooner listen to him than most speakers at the Union. He just drips wisecracks . . . the most flexible use of language of anyone I know."[8] Arthur M. Schlesinger Jr., who spent a year at Peterhouse College in 1938–39 and went on to become one of America's most eminent historians and a Pulitzer Prize winner, remembered his close friend as an impressive figure at the Cambridge Union who would later use his intelligence and wit "to astonish and persuade the diplomatic world."[9] On January 18, 1938, Aubrey addressed the Union in opposition to the following motion: "That this House will not accept Socialism as a desirable form of government for the United Kingdom." The debate also featured Leslie Burgin MP, the British minister of transport, and Professor Harold Lasky of the London School of Economics, a Marxist and founder of the Left Book Club, who later served as chairman of the Labour Party. Aubrey's opening remarks brilliantly captured his eloquent style of delivery and polished wit; he began by congratulating the newly elected president of the Union, John Mellor Simonds, who was the son of the lord chancellor, Gavin Simonds:

> Mr. President, Sir,
> We on these benches are happy to join in congratulating you on your well merited accession to the Electric Chair. If—as rumour and heredity suggest—it is but a prelude to a career on the judicial bench, you will no doubt find useful training in the two chief requisites of that vocation—an aspect of vigilant boredom and a capacity for inspired irrelevance. Our only regret is for your enforced silence, for we may no longer expect lurid confessions of a repentant Conservative.
>
> The duty of producing the customary light banter about our two distinguished visitors weighs heavily upon me. The only funny thing about the Rt. Hon. Gentleman, the Minister of Transport, is his predecessor in office.[10]

Three months later Aubrey delivered his most powerful speech. On April 26, 1938, he defended the motion "That this House condemns His Majesty's Government for their failure effectively to uphold the interest of this country in preserving the freedom of Czechoslovakia and of other independent and non-German nations of Central and South Eastern Europe." The debate came on the heels of the recent Sudeten Crisis in which Hitler declared himself the defender of the German minorities in Czechoslovakia, and two weeks after a referendum in Germany and Austria that officially approved the Nazi Anschluss and the single-party system in the new Reichstag. Whereas on matters of triviality members of the Union were expected to argue opposing views with equal conviction, when it came to motions of political or ideological nature those voting aye or nay chose their sides very carefully. At 8:15 p.m. Aubrey opened the debate and attacked the government's policy of the previous five years, which had allowed for Nazi expansion across central Europe and made the incorporation of the Sudetenland into Germany inevitable. Moreover, he argued prophetically that "eastward expansion would mean westward expansion for self-protection's sake: Holland and Belgium would be in danger." Facing brigadier general Sir Henry Page Croft, a leading Conservative Party member of Parliament and undersecretary of state for war from 1940 to 1945, Aubrey summed up, "We invoke the self-interest of the House as well as its idealism; and we accordingly ask for the condemnation of a policy which in Europe's most critical hour keeps open the floodgates of war."[11] It was 11:48 p.m.

when the debate was concluded and the votes were counted; the ayes won, 143–79. Three days later the *Cambridge Review* reported on the event: "Mr A. S. Eban made the brilliant speech which we are used to hearing from him. Hitting hard on his opponent's ground and at the same time forcing home his own point of view, he scored many good points." Another of the Cambridge magazines, the *Granta*, praised Aubrey's sober deliberation, which "immensely enhanced the overwhelming case presented by the Union's most fluent debater."[12]

Yet not everyone was enamored of Aubrey's distinct way of communicating. It was during the Cambridge years that those who did not know Aubrey particularly well first described him as aloof and condescending. These labels were so successfully imbedded in future depictions of him that they became part of his public persona. Whereas his close acquaintances at Cambridge described him as reserved, proper, and weighty, those who viewed Aubrey from a distance tended to label him as arrogant and pompous. He was certainly fastidious—about his appearance, his behavior, and his relationships with others—but the quality that contributed most to his image as aloof was his enduring absentmindedness. Aubrey was often forgetful, invariably late, and hopelessly shy. The famous neurologist and author Oliver Sacks, son of Dr. Sam Sacks and nephew of Alida, described his cousin as "very shy with three people, but he was at ease with an audience of thousands. I can see how he might have been seen as aloof, but I think he was painfully shy, except with people he knew well. He was capable of great warmth and I think aloofness is a misunderstanding. He wasn't a deeply social man. His inner life and thinking preoccupied him. . . . It is simply absentmindedness."[13]

The effects of Aubrey's emotionally deprived childhood were still visible into his twenties; he often compartmentalized his relationships, and, with the exception of his future wife Suzy, his friendships tended to be one-dimensional and based on some specific need, be it intellectual, political, or vocational. One of his closest friends at Cambridge, Eileen Alexander, who had a reputation for being "slightly exotic," observed that "it was difficult to imagine Aubrey as ever having been subjected to the normal indignities of infancy."[14]

Aubrey prospered so much at Cambridge, both in personal relations and in intellectual fulfillment, that he was content on settling there. The *Olavian*, school newspaper of St. Olave's, mused in its July 1937 issue about its alumnus's progress at Cambridge: "For Eban Cambridge has come to be as vital a part of his existence as is the huge pipe which always droops from his mouth, emitting the most pungent odors. No doubt he will soon be resigning himself to a lifetime to be spent in this burgh."[15] And, like many other Cantabrigians, Aubrey went on to take great pride in his alma mater—years later, as Israel's foreign minister, he was praised in an interview for his polished "Oxford" accent. "Sir, I would have you know that I went to Cambridge," Eban replied indignantly, "but in public life you must expect to be smeared!"[16]

During his final year of studies at Cambridge, Aubrey focused on the literature and history of the Arab peoples. Beyond the fulfillment of his intellectual curiosity he found some pragmatic benefits in studying these subjects. True to his Zionist credentials, he hoped to settle in Palestine one day, but knowing that a future Jewish nation would not be wholly welcomed by the indigenous Arabs, he felt that it was imperative for the Jews of Palestine to understand and respect their neighbors—their traditions, their culture, their history, and their language. As he later recalled in his memoirs, this cultural appreciation of the Arab world was rarely shared by his contemporaries: "My deep immersion in that legacy made it impossible for me thereafter to adopt the routine Zionist stereotype that regarded the Arab nation with intellectual condescension."[17] Had it not been for his strong Zionist convictions, Aubrey would have most probably settled at Cambridge or entered British politics as a Labour Party member of Parliament. But by the autumn of 1938, as he entered Pembroke College as a research fellow and a tutor in oriental languages, the unfolding events in Palestine and Europe convinced him that his loyalties rested not with academic pursuit at Cambridge but with the struggle for a Jewish homeland in Palestine.

In 1920 the principal victors of the Great War had met in San Remo to carve up the spoils; Britain was awarded administrative responsibility over Transjordan, Iraq, and Palestine, and two years later it was granted the Mandate for Palestine by the fledgling League of Nations. While Palestine held some strategic importance to the British Empire, owing to its close proximity to the Suez Canal, this small piece of land turned out to be a poisoned chalice. During the next quarter century the British authorities in Palestine concentrated much of their efforts on balancing the nationalistic aspirations of two communities at loggerheads. Whereas the Balfour Declaration of 1917 pledged the establishment of a Jewish homeland in Palestine, previous British communiqués, such as the 1915 Hussein-McMahon Agreement and the 1916 Sykes-

Picot Agreement, had promised independence to the Arabs of the land in return for their help in the war effort against the Turks. "All we have to do is not to mix ourselves up with religious squabbles," declared British diplomat Sir Mark Sykes rather naively during the war.[18] But getting mixed up with the contending claims of Jews and Arabs for land and liberation was exactly what the British ended up doing for most of the mandate years. The steady increase in Jewish emigration from Europe to Palestine, coupled with the Zionist purchase of Arab land to accommodate the burgeoning Jewish community, led to sporadic Arab riots against the Jewish settlers and the British authorities in 1920, 1921, and 1929. But it was the Nazi rise to power in 1933 that led to unprecedented waves of Jewish emigration to Palestine, which in turn led to new levels of violence on the part of the Arab communities, most notably during the Great Arab Revolt of 1936–39. In 1918 the 60,000 Jews in Palestine constituted 10 percent of the population. Between 1919 and 1929 more than 120,000 Jews emigrated to Palestine, and between 1933 and 1935 alone a further 130,000 entered Palestine, mostly from Germany. On the eve of the Second World War in 1939 there were nearly 450,000 Jews in Palestine—now constituting nearly one-third of the entire population. For the Arabs of Palestine, the threat to their diminishing demographic majority was compounded by the effective political and social mobilization of the European settlers. Under the terms of the mandate and with the active support of the Jewish Diaspora and the World Zionist Organization, the Yishuv established a semiautonomous government led by David Ben-Gurion's Mapai (the Workers' Party), which provided education, health services, and social services, as well as a paramilitary force, the Haganah, to defend the Yishuv from Arab attacks.

Compared to the highly organized Yishuv, the Arab population was fragmented and suffered from weak leadership. The Arab response to the record levels of Jewish immigration became known as the Great Revolt, targeting first the Jews and then the British mandatory authorities in Palestine. By October 1936, more than 20,000 British troops were stationed in Palestine, and with 10,000 more on their way, the financial burden of keeping the order in this small territory at a time of increasing tension in Europe made it necessary to find a political solution.[19]

In November 1936 a Royal Commission of Inquiry arrived in Palestine, headed by William Robert Wellesley Peel, former secretary of state for India. The Peel Commission looked into the causes for Jewish–Arab tensions and published its findings eight months later, noting that the roots of the conflict were not related to the British Mandate or indeed other causes such as Jewish immigration or land acquisition. There were two national communities fighting over the same small land, and there was no common ground or prospect of peaceful cohabitation between the two clashing civilizations: Jewish-European and Arab-Asian. Given the incompatibility of their national aspirations, the Peel Commission pointed to an unavoidable conclusion: "The disease is so deep-rooted that in the Commissioners' firm conviction the only hope of a cure lies in a surgical operation." In other words, the British Mandate ought to be terminated and the land of Palestine must be partitioned into two independent states. In place of British rule, the Peel Commission recommended "independent sovereign Arab and Jewish States, covering roughly two-thirds and one-third of Palestine respectively"—with the Arab portion annexed to Transjordan under King Abdullah. Britain would then amend the mandate to govern Jerusalem, Bethlehem, and Nazareth only, with a corridor from Jerusalem to the sea. Lord Peel had no illusions about the dramatic ramifications of the commission's recommendations but concluded that "the problem cannot be solved by giving either the Arabs or the Jews all they want . . . while neither race can fairly rule all Palestine, each race might justly rule part of it."[20]

The immediate effect of the Peel Commission's recommendations was the resumption of the Arab revolt with greater intensity against the British authorities as well as Jewish targets. With the exception of King Abdullah of Transjordan, whose emirate was set to increase in size according to the Peel recommendations, Arab leaders across the region flatly rejected the idea of partition. This was a matter of principle and justice: Britain did not possess the legal or moral authority to decide on the future of their homeland, or indeed to give parts of it to the Jews.

The Zionist response to the Peel Commission's recommendations was less visceral and more calculated. In August 1937 the Twentieth Zionist Congress met in Zurich to debate the most controversial proposal since 1903, when Theodor Herzl had suggested Uganda as a temporary refuge for the pogrom-stricken Jews of Russia. The opponents of partition included the leaders of American Jewry, the religious parties, and the revisionists, who opposed any territorial concession. Facing them were Weizmann, who was overjoyed by the prospect of Jewish sovereignty, and the labour movement headed by Ben-Gurion and Shertok, which was not content with the territorial boundaries proposed by the Peel Commission but accepted the idea of partition as a first step toward a more viable future Jewish state. The heated debate ended with a face-saving resolution that neither rejected nor endorsed partition but allowed for the Jewish Agency to explore with the British the precise terms of the proposal.[21]

Among the hundreds of spectators at the assembly was twenty-two-year-old Aubrey Eban. Leaving the assembly after the dramatic exchanges between the delegates, he felt strongly aligned with Weizmann, Ben-Gurion, and the labour movement. Like them, Aubrey felt that the choice between partition and nonpartition was no choice at all. It was clear that Jews and Arabs could not coexist in a united Palestine and that the continuation of the British Mandate would hinder any prospect of Jewish independence. As the violence in Palestine was soaring, it seemed that Britain could no longer fulfill its commitments under the terms of the mandate. And as a Nazi march over Austria and Czechoslovakia was looming on the horizon, the military and financial burden of maintaining a large garrison in Palestine became an acute concern for the British government. Partition was therefore the inexorable conclusion.

In the autumn of 1938 Aubrey made the transition from student life at Queens' College to the position of tutor and research fellow in oriental languages at Pembroke College. By then the prospect of Jewish sovereignty in Palestine, as well as Aubrey's own destiny, seemed to have changed irrevocably. Shortly after his graduation he received a call from the Zionist headquarters on Great Russell Street. Arthur Lourie, the political secretary of the Jewish Agency, had to depart unexpectedly to the United States due to his wife's illness, and Chaim Weizmann was looking for an interim substitute. Weizmann knew Aubrey well as Alida's son and as a promising Young Zionist at Cambridge. Although this was only a temporary position, Aubrey readily accepted the opportunity to work closely with Zionism's most iconic leader because he admired Weizmann's power of persuasion and his ability to command the deference of world leaders. Operating out of his suite at the Dorchester Hotel in London, Weizmann adopted all the mannerisms and rituals of a head of state so effectively that, as Eban saw it, "nobody at high levels of authority in the world considered that he had received a primary contact with Zionism unless he had heard from Weizmann at first hand."[22] According to David Ben-Gurion, who often chastised Weizmann for his indefatigable belief in the alignment of British and Jewish interests, Weizmann was "the greatest Jewish emissary to the Gentile world. He was an ambassador to the Gentiles, the most gifted and fascinating envoy the Jewish people ever produced."[23] British leaders such as Clement Atlee, Ernest Bevin, Winston Churchill, Lloyd George, Lord Halifax, and Malcolm MacDonald behaved toward Weizmann as though "he were already president of a sovereign nation, equal in status to their own. The Jewish people had produced a president before it had achieved a state."[24]

The gathering storm over Europe led to a reversal of the British commitment to a Jewish homeland in Palestine. As control over the Suez Canal and the eastern board of the Mediterranean became paramount in the event of war, and since Jewish support was guaranteed in a war against Nazi Germany, it made more sense to placate Arab states such as Egypt, Saudi Arabia, and Iraq; as Prime Minister Chamberlain candidly told his cabinet, "If we must offend one side, let us offend the Jews rather than the Arabs."[25] Following the appeasement of Hitler in Munich, the British now turned to appease the Arabs over Palestine. Two months after the Munich Crisis, the Chamberlain government rejected the Peel Commission's recommendation for the partition of Palestine and instead invited Jewish and Arab delegations to a conference to determine the future of the land. The St. James Conference was held in March 1939 but failed to make headway, and the British declared that in the absence of an agreeable solution a unilateral one would have to be imposed. Colonial Secretary Malcolm MacDonald authorized further repressive measures to quell the remnants of the Arab rebellion in Palestine, though privately he rejected Britain's previous overtures toward the Jews, stating that "it would be wholly wrong to suggest that this large Arab population should one day in their own native land and against their will come under the rule of the newly arrived Jews."[26]

In conjunction with the British Foreign Office under Anthony Eden, MacDonald presented Britain's new Palestine policy in the White Paper of May 1939: with 450,000 Jews now settled in Palestine, the government concluded that Britain's pledge for a Jewish National Home had been met, and that the aim was now to establish within ten years an independent Palestine state as a response to Arab fears over Jewish immigration and domination. The immediate implications of the new policy were the prohibition of the sale of Arab land to Jews and, more crucially, the restriction of Jewish emigration to Palestine to no more than 75,000 people over the next five years, with Arab consent required to allow for additional immigration after that period. Britain also pressured Romania, Bulgaria, Yugoslavia, and Greece to prevent Jews from making their way by land or sea to Palestine, and in July 1939 MacDonald announced in Parliament that due to the increasing number of Jews entering Palestine in "illegal ways," legal emigration to Palestine under the White Paper quota would be suspended for six months. With the growing persecution of Jews in Germany and central Europe, the White Paper was interpreted by the Yishuv as nothing short of a death certificate to the millions of Jews trapped in Europe. Members of the Peel Commission, which had recommended partition two years earlier, lambasted the White Paper for simply transferring Arab anxieties over Jewish domination to Jewish anxieties over Arab domination, and in the House of Commons Winston Churchill criticized Prime Minister Chamberlain for striking the Jews this "mortal blow."[27]

In August 1939 Aubrey traveled with his mother and sister to Geneva to attend the Twenty-First Zionist Congress, this time as a full-fledged member of the British Zionist delegation. The proceedings were naturally dominated by the reverberations from the MacDonald White Paper. On one side stood the labour delegation, led by Katzenelson, calling for Jewish immigration to Palestine to continue regardless of British quotas. Against him stood the American delegates, led by the outspoken rabbi Abba Hillel Silver, who warned that illegal immigration was bound to provoke the British. The atmosphere in the assembly hall was already dark and foreboding, but it soon turned positively bleak. On August 24 the delegates heard the news from Moscow that the Soviet and German foreign ministers had signed a nonaggression agreement. The Molotov-Ribbentrop Pact meant only one thing: war in Europe was imminent. The following day Britain signed a common defense pact with the Polish government, thus pledging its military support if Poland was attacked by another country. Certain desolation and destruction awaited the continent, but for the millions of European Jews the future looked particularly precarious: there was nowhere to run or hide because the British were closing the gates of Palestine. The delegates in the hall sank in to their seats and held their heads in their hands as Weizmann, visibly shaken, rose to deliver the closing remarks of the Congress: "There is darkness all around us and we cannot see through the clouds. The remnant shall work on, live on, until the dawn of better days. May we meet again in peace."[28]

Aubrey returned to the family's holiday cottage in the village of Felcourt in Sussex, where on September 1 he heard the news of the German onslaught across Poland. Two days later, shortly after 11:00 a.m., Prime Minister Chamberlain informed the nation that his attempts to reach a peaceful settlement with Germany had failed and that Britain was now at war with Germany. Like the reaction of many young men on that day, Aubrey's was almost visceral: he volunteered for military service, sending numerous applications to different branches and units. His efforts were wholly unsuccessful, however; as he wrote to a friend, "The Empire has so far turned a deaf ear . . . I have yielded up all my secrets to the penetrating glare of Whitehall. They know all about me except my abnormal hatred of spinach and cinema organs. My grandfather's birthplace was a genuine surprise to the Ministry of Information, who had never heard of Yanishki. I am not really expecting officialdom to show any haste to utilize me or anyone else. Dash it, war or no war, decencies much be preserved."[29]

Aubrey returned to Pembroke College—now occupied by troops and expectant mothers who had been evacuated from other parts of Britain—fully intending to resume his research and teaching duties. But the exigencies of Zionism and the empire brought his academic career to an abrupt halt. In December 1939 Chaim Weizmann asked the master of Pembroke College to extend Aubrey's leave of absence from Cambridge until his work at the Jewish Agency was completed. "I am writing on behalf of the Executive of the Jewish Agency for Palestine to ask a favour of the College," Weizmann wrote to Sir Montagu Butler. "[Eban] came here on the understanding that the work for which he was required would not extend beyond January 15th, so that he was fully intending to return to Cambridge at the beginning of next term. Circumstances have now arisen, however, which make it extremely desirable that he should continue here for several weeks longer. . . . The work he is doing here is of real importance and value, and we should deeply appreciate your assistance in enabling him to continue here for the time being."[30] Aubrey soon returned to his work at the Zionist offices, only to receive the news weeks later that the British Empire had found some use for him after all: his application for a commission in the Intelligence Corps had been successful. In February 1940, on his twenty-fifth birthday, Aubrey wrote to a friend, "Next week I become a number; a mere mass of Potential Officer Material realizing its potentialities. *Tempora mutantur*."[31]

The times were indeed changing.

III

Aldershot, Cairo, Jerusalem

AUBREY FOUND HIS INITIAL ENCOUNTER WITH THE MILITARY WORLD DOWNright depressing compared to the reassuring tranquility of academic life. "So I have now become a cog in a machine," he wrote to a friend. "I endured the ignominy of squad drill, shot at moving targets, marched six miles to Aldershot and listened to a lecture on the grim and mysterious functions of Military Intelligence officers. Thus from day to day a routine of soul-killing tedium and extreme physical activity lies ahead; the contrast after Cambridge is disconcerting."[1]

Located less than forty miles to the southwest of London, the town of Aldershot houses the largest training camp in Britain, Aldershot Garrison, which has been the home of the British Army since 1854. It was from there that the British Expeditionary Force set out to France to face the Germans in the two world wars, and it was the Ramillies Barracks there—named in commemoration of the Duke of Marlborough's victory at the Belgian village of Ramillies in May 1706 during the War of the Spanish Succession—that was home to the 168th Officer Cadet Training Unit. Between February and May 1940 Aubrey and other promising linguists from Oxford and Cambridge underwent basic infantry training before their commission as intelligence officers. It soon became apparent that the cadets' academic credentials stood in direct contrast to their physical abilities. "Between the lot of you, you know fifty bloody languages!" shouted the sergeant major, "but, Jesus, you can't march fifty bloody steps!"[2]

Aubrey's disconcerting experience in Aldershot was compounded by a similarly bizarre national mood. These were the last months of the Phoney

War, a term allegedly coined by the isolationist U.S. senator William E. Borah to describe the lull in military operations between Adolf Hitler and Joseph Stalin's dismemberment of Poland in September 1939 and the Battle of France in May 1940. As the journalist E. S. Turner vividly described it, the Phoney War was played in three acts: "Act One saw the nation keyed up for instant horrors. Act Two saw it fussing and fumbling, wondering what had gone wrong. Act Three saw it roused by a great blow between the eyes."[3] Following Britain and France's declaration of war on Germany on September 3, 1939, the British government sent an expeditionary force and thirteen Royal Air Force (RAF) squadrons to the French–German border, but this was too little and too late, as by then not much was left of prewar Poland. What followed across the French–German border was not the great cataclysm that everybody expected, but a nine-month stalemate, with the opposing forces observing each other from their defensive positions across the Maginot and Siegfried Lines. At the same time, people in Britain experienced all the sensations of war except the fighting. Although not a single bomb had fallen from the sky, the anticipated upheaval engulfed everyone: Teenagers were filling sandbags, and office workers were busy crisscrossing building windows with tape to prevent their shattering. Museums and city halls were requisitioned and transformed into mass mortuaries. The newspapers stopped publishing weather forecasts for fear of abating the enemy. Children were evacuated from London and other major cities to the countryside (among them was Aubrey's brother, Raphael). The public had been issued gas masks, and was ordered to carry them at all times in the event of a German gas attack. The National Canine Defence League offered specially designed gas-proof kennels, which were no more than steel cylinders with glass doors to accommodate small dogs and cats. For months the victims of the Phoney War were not the British soldiers sitting patiently across the Maginot Line but motorists and those who fell prey to petty criminals as a result of the total blackout imposed on the country. But eventually the anxious preparation for war was replaced by a general atmosphere of indifferent complacency. Gas masks were left behind on buses and train stations in increasing numbers. Evacuated children returned to their families, despite the Ministry of Health's warnings, and fussiness was replaced by frivolousness. The patriotic car stickers that proudly declared JOINED THE NATIONAL DEFENCE TRANSPORT GROUP were discarded in favor of more puerile slogans such as PRIORITY—JUST MARRIED and ONLY A TAXPAYER. And in the absence of dramatic developments on the western front, satirical cartoons mocking the Phoney War began to appear in newspapers, such as the one depicting a family seated around a table wearing gas masks with the caption, "We had Haricot beans for dinner today!"[4]

The Phoney War ended on May 10, 1940. Hitler's forces invaded Holland, Belgium, and Luxemburg by land and air, outflanking the Maginot Line from the north on their way to France. In Britain Prime Minister Chamberlain stepped down, as his majority in the House of Commons had plummeted in a no-confidence vote on the government's mishandling of the situation. On June 25, France signed a humiliating armistice agreement with Germany, leaving Britain's new all-party coalition, led by Winston Churchill, as the only major Western power to fend off the Nazi conquest of Europe. A week later the first daylight bombardment of British cities took place, as the German Luftwaffe bombed Hull in northeast England and the city of Wick at the northeastern tip of Scotland. Within days the Luftwaffe began bombing British convoys in the English Channel, RAF airfields, and major cities across Britain. The Battle of France was over, Churchill famously declared in his "Their Finest Hour" speech at the House of Commons, and the Battle of Britain was about to begin.

Aubrey completed his officer training in Aldershot in May 1940 and was commissioned as a second lieutenant, but the vagaries of military bureaucracy brought his career in the Intelligence Corps to an unexpected end before it had even started. New regulations from the War Office dictated that officers of non-British lineage should be prevented from dealing with classified documents. Since Grandpapa Sacks had not naturalized early enough, it followed that his grandson could not be trusted with confidential material. Aubrey was transferred to the Fourteenth Battalion, South Staffordshire Regiment, which was based in Hereford, and in October 1940 he was sent to Great Yarmouth, which, as the most easterly point in the British Isles, turned out to be the target for a planned German crossing of the English Channel and the North Sea that winter.

Aside from the frequent visitations of German bombers, Aubrey found his time on the Norfolk coast as the regiment's intelligence officer rather tedious; as he wrote to those back home, "I found a German plane in my sector and its occupants patiently awaiting disposal. I stopped them playing poker with our guard, relieved them of documents which were so informative they must have been planted, and went to the pictures to see *The Great Dictator*." By July 1941 the monotonous cycle of counting bomb fragments and craters, charting the direction of the wind and coming aircraft, and never-ending nocturnal jaunts to the countryside had brought Aubrey to the brink of deression. It seemed that even the attention bestowed on him by the female population of Great Yarmouth, which was positively impressed by his possession of a motorcycle and a green intelligence armband, did little to uplift his spirits, as he told a friend: "I meet nobody, read only military manuals and the *New Statesman* and *Nation* and think practically of nothing. . . . I remember no period in my life of equivalent monotony and frustration."[5]

Aubrey's salvation from the prospect of endless vigil in a cold fishing village in East Anglia came from none other than Field Marshal Erwin Rommel, whose Seventh Panzer Division defeated British counterattacks from within Egypt, though it failed to defeat the British forces in the Libyan port city of Tobruk. After the fall of Western Europe in the summer of 1940, the empire's attention now turned to the oil fields of the Middle East and the shipping routes of the Suez Canal, and it suddenly dawned on the War Office that it would be useful to have orientalists and linguists in that part of the world.

When Aubrey finished his basic training in late May 1940—days before Italian forces began their advance in North Africa—he asked Chaim Weizmann to use his powers of persuasion to help him be reassigned to the Middle East. Weizmann appealed to the secretary of the colonies, Lord Lloyd, and he received the following reply: "But, Dr. Weizmann, there isn't going to be any war in the Middle East."[6] By December 1941, however, with the British forces pushing hard to break the siege of Tobruk in Operation Crusader, Aubrey was finally granted his wish and was heading to the Middle East. On December 16, nine days after the Japanese attack on Pearl Harbor, he boarded the SS *Orcades*. Five weeks later First Lieutenant Eban arrived in Cairo.

EGYPT HAD GAINED ITS INDEPENDENCE FROM THE BRITISH EMPIRE IN 1922 AFTER four decades of colonial rule, though the British maintained a military presence in the country to protect the strategically important Suez Canal. In 1940, as Italy launched its first offensive in North Africa, the British Army moved its Middle East headquarters from Malta to Cairo, and a steady stream of British and Commonwealth forces began to arrive in the city. With the German and British forces locked in a stalemate in the Libyan Desert four hundred miles to the east an incongruous atmosphere of hedonism and self-indulgence descended on Cairo. As the celebrated war correspondent Alan Moorehead vividly recalled his time in the city in the *Desert War* trilogy, "The Turf Club swarmed with officers newly arrived from England, and a dozen open-air cinemas were showing every night in the hot, brightly lit city. . . . We had French wines, grapes, melons, steaks, cigarettes, beer, whisky, and abundance of all things that belonged to rich, idle peace. Officers were taking modern flats in Gezira's big buildings looking out over the golf course and the Nile. Polo continued with the same extraordinary frenzy in the roasting afternoon heat. . . . Madame Badia's girls writhed in the belly dance at her cabaret near the Pont des Anglais."[7]

Cairo's exuberant social scene did not appeal to Lieutenant Eban, nor was he particularly enjoying his new post in the Arabic Censorship Department, where he was tasked with the tedious job of reading Arabic newspapers and letters that had been intercepted by the British forces. But his biggest grievance was not being able to visit the Holy Land, even though Jerusalem was only an hour's flight from Cairo. "Like our illustrious forefather, Moses, I am within sight of the Promised Land yet am unable to get there; can't you do something about it?" he asked Moshe Shertok, his former mentor at Weizmann's office and secretary of the Jewish Agency's political department.[8] His plea was answered with remarkable expediency; a week later he was visited by Reuven Zaslani, who headed the Jewish Agency's relations with the Allies' intelligence services and happened to be a friend of the Eban family in London. Sitting on the balcony of the Continental Hotel in Cairo, Zaslani gave Aubrey an overview of Britain's fortunes in the various theaters of war. It was February 1942: Europe was under Nazi occupation, and, in the Far East, Britain had lost Hong Kong and Singapore to Japan and Burma was about to be evacuated. In North Africa, Benghazi was captured by the Axis forces and Rommel was in the midst of his second offensive on Tobruk. There was growing anxiety about the possibility of a British retreat from Egypt and Palestine should Rommel's forces continue their eastern push toward the Suez Canal and then north to the Levant.

Zaslani continued with his *tour d'horizon*, still offering Eban no clue as to its purpose. Given the obvious motivation of the Jews of Palestine to fight Hitler, he explained, the Jewish Agency made contact with MO4, the Middle East branch of the Special Operations Executive (SOE), Britain's wartime espionage organization, to explore the possibility of setting up and training special forces in Palestine that would operate behind enemy lines there as well as in Europe should Palestine fall to German hands.[9] The scheme was approved on February 18, 1942, and was given an initial budget of £19,250 to run to the end of 1944. According to SOE headquarters in Cairo, the objective of the Palestine scheme was to "raise a small force of Jews who are willing to undertake the tasks of attacking enemy communications, installations, headquarters and personnel in the event of Palestine being occupied by the Axis powers." It was to include about 400 Jews, comprising 153 instructors and leaders and 250 volunteers trained "in elements of demolition and use of all toys." They were given some 200 rifles with 250,000 rounds, 160 pistols with 8,000 rounds, 26 light machine guns with 500,000 rounds, 5,000 hand grenades, and hundreds of pounds of explosives. The SOE was not concerned with the future of Palestine as such, and it certainly did not try to bring about Arab–Jewish reconciliation; the objective of this collaboration was simple: "to endeavor to promote the will to resist invasion during a preoccupational period, and to unite and direct resistance to the occupying forces when the country has been invaded."[10]

Finally Zaslani turned to Aubrey and told him that this covert operation required a liaison officer who could be trusted by both the Jewish Agency and British intelligence; Shertok had recommended Eban as the perfect candidate. Aubrey needn't take too much time to mull it over—the new assignment would not only rescue him from his boring job as a censor but would also take him to the Promised Land, make a contribution to the Allied war effort, and help Zionist interests. Within days he left Cairo by train across the Sinai Desert.

When Mark Twain visited Palestine in 1867, he was overtaken by the uninterrupted desolation of the place; he described the soil as "rich enough, but . . . given over wholly to weeds—a silent mournful expanse." He added, "A desolation is here that not even imagination can grace with the pomp of life and action. . . . We never saw a human being on the whole route. . . . There was hardly a tree or shrub anywhere. Even the olive tree and the cactus, those fast friends of a worthless soil, had almost deserted the country."[11] Three quarters of a century later, Aubrey's first impression of Palestine through his train window was of the contrast between the Jewish and Arab settlements, the latter seemingly unchanged since Twain's visit: "The hard truth is that when the early Zionists arrived, the country was a neglected estate. . . . [It was] a land that seemed to reject human settlement. In many areas stagnant pools of water hissed and buzzed with the fever of malaria. The first impact of Jewish settlement on the landscape was one of gentle rehabilitation. . . . Zionists across the world were particularly obsessive about trees, [and] by the 1930s the boundary between a Jewish and an Arab area could be discerned by color. It was simply the line dividing the green from the yellow."[12]

Aubrey's new job title of "Liaison Officer between SOE and the Jewish Agency for Palestine on Special Operations" was as impressive sounding as it was technically illegal. Under the British Mandate regulations, Palestinians—Jews and Arabs—were not allowed to carry arms. However, in response to the Arab riots of 1920, the Yishuv had established the Haganah, an underground military organization to defend the Jewish population from further attacks. Throughout the mandate years, leaders in the Haganah were routinely arrested by British police and its stacks of weapons were confiscated from hidden caches across the country. Now Prime Minister Churchill, the War Office, and the SOE wanted not only to arm special units of the Haganah's striking platoons (Palmach) but also to provide financial assistance and train them in guerrilla warfare, sabotage, and sharpshooting with the help of British instructors. In doing this London was effectively defying the mandatory authorities, leading to an absurd situation in which one arm of the government was financing, training, and arming members of the Yishuv while another arm was arresting them and confiscating their weapons.

Operating out of the SOE headquarters in the Talbieh neighborhood of Jerusalem, Aubrey's main job was to solve problems. The SOE's bizarre decision to supply him with a white Plymouth convertible rather than an army vehicle was a source of simultaneous consternation and enjoyment: as the liaison officer to a clandestine organization, Aubrey soon found that his mode of transport made his business anything but covert, though he drew some comfort in the knowledge that in a country with few asphalt roads and even fewer cars, his well-appointed Plymouth paled in comparison only to the Palestine high commissioner's Rolls-Royce.[13] He had to keep the clandestine program going while at the same time displaying his loyalty to the British Army and the laws of the mandatory authorities. When Palmach trainees were arrested by the police for possession of arms, he arrived in prison armed with an impressive catalog of official documents and demanded their release; when the Palmach needed money, cars, or fuel, they turned to Aubrey to produce for them the necessary permits. He was apparently the only person in possession of the accurate register of trainees in the forested training camp near Kibbutz Mishmar Ha'emek in the Jezreel Valley. Under the terms of the Palestine Post-

Occupational Scheme, the British agreed to train four hundred Jewish guerrillas, but the Haganah kept rotating its men so that every few weeks a different group of four hundred trainees would report to camp; thus, within a few months more than six thousand Palmach fighters had been trained by the SOE. Aubrey also used his time in Palestine to acquaint himself with the Yishuv's top political and military echelons. Many of them would become his colleagues in the Israeli Labor Party years later: David Ben-Gurion, Moshe Shertok (later Sharett), Moshe Dayan, and Yigal Paicovitch (later Allon). He was also invited by the British Council to deliver three public lectures as part of a lecture series on international politics. These winter of 1942–43 lectures, on such topics as "Britain's home and foreign policy and the war" and "controversies on post-war reconstruction," were not only well received but were also attended by high-ranking officials in the region's military, political, and diplomatic circles. After he delivered his first lecture Aubrey excitedly wrote to a friend about the experience, "I have been doing propaganda as a sideline and had a successful show last week when the Chief Secretary, the Attorney-General, the Chief Justice, the Mayor and Counselors attended a lecture I gave to six hundred people in the town. You get such a mixed and at the same time selective sort of audience here that the psychological kick of holding forth is vastly greater than usual."[14]

In October 1942 the Nazi threat to Palestine was effectively removed following Montgomery's decisive victory in the Battle of El Alamein, and as a result the SOE brought to an end the covert cooperation with the Jewish Agency in Palestine. The training camp in Mishmar Ha'emek was disbanded, and the flow of British arms to Palmach units ceased almost overnight. Aubrey's job was now surplus to requirements, though he remained in his position until the spring of 1943. He certainly did not look forward to returning to Cairo, and noted so when writing to his family: "I won't deny that it is a bit depressing leaving here after such a happy and fruitful year, despite all the vicissitudes and 'headaches' which made it anything but a restful period. However, the last word is not yet written in my connection with this country. I hope."[15]

Aubrey's only solace in that period was his burgeoning romance with Shoshana Ambache. In October 1943 he was invited to a tea party in Jerusalem at the home of his friend, Dr. Julius Kleeberg; there he met Simcha Ambache, a Jewish businessman who worked in Egypt as a consulting engineer to the Suez Canal Company. Kleeberg had been the Ambache family physician in

Egypt but had maintained a good friendship with Mr. Ambache after he moved to Jerusalem. During their conversation Eban discovered that he shared several acquaintances with Mr. Ambache, such as Moshe Shertok and Ambache's son, Nachman, who had studied at Trinity College in Cambridge while Aubrey was lecturing at Pembroke College. Ambache explained to Aubrey that he came to Jerusalem because he was feeling lonely in Cairo. The house he stayed in belonged to the uncle of Eileen Alexander, Aubrey's close friend from Cambridge. He also learned that Ambache, fearful of a Nazi sweep through Egypt, had decided to send his wife and three daughters out of the country—to South Africa, of all places.[16] At the end of the evening Ambache invited Aubrey to visit him in Cairo once his mission in Palestine was over. And six months later, when Eban turned to Shertok for help with expanding his social contacts in Egypt, Shertok suggested a meeting with Simcha Ambache, not knowing that the two had previously met in Jerusalem.

"Dear Mr. Ambache," Eban wrote, "May I have the pleasure of calling upon you? I was a lecture in Arabic literature at Cambridge. I recall meeting you in Palestine at the home of my friend, Dr. Kleeberg. Flying officer Ellenbogen, who is the fiancé of Eileen Alexander, is also anxious to make your acquaintance."[17] Ambache asked his daughter Shoshana (Suzy), who had by now returned with her mother from South Africa, to invite the two young officers to the family house in Cairo. One evening in April officers Eban and Ellenbogen arrived at the Ambache villa at 12 Kamel Mohammed Street. The house was in fact a grand old mansion in the affluent district of Zamalek on the Nile island of Gezira. Overlooking the banks of the River Nile and set amid lush gardens dominated by rose bushes, the Ambaches' grand villa was whitewashed and decorated with French windows; majestic magnolia and honeysuckle bushes adorned the entrance.[18] The ladies of the house—Mrs. Ambache and her three daughters, Tsilla, Aura, and Suzy—were sipping iced tea on the lawn while the men drank whiskey and soda and discussed Egyptian politics. "At one point, Aubrey looked at me; he simply looked," Suzy later recalled. "I still remember the stare. I knew he had taken special notice in me." The courting continued for more than a year after that encounter, in Jerusalem and in Cairo. The twenty-two-year-old was flattered by Aubrey's persistent persuasions, but she felt that married life was not yet for her—at least until she completed her degree in French literature at American University in Cairo. She was puzzled by his unusual intellect and stupendous knowledge of history and politics, and soon grew accustomed to his absentmindedness and moments of prolonged silence, during which he would appear oblivious to his surroundings. When Mrs. Ambache asked her husband what he thought of Suzy's suitor, he replied, "I have no opinion. The man can't talk!"[19]

Whenever Aubrey passed by the Ambache residence he signaled to Suzy to come outside by whistling the Egyptian national anthem—an inconspicuous signal guaranteed not to raise the suspicion of her parents. While they were courting they always went out in groups with other British officers, as was the custom in those days. Suzy soon discovered that Aubrey had a particular weakness for all things sweet, and introduced him to Groppi, Cairo's legendary tearoom, which would later prepare a three-tiered cake for their wedding. "Aubrey was always crazy about sweets. I courted him with Groppi's cakes," she recalled. Over the years Aubrey's weakness for sweets became legendary in diplomatic circles, with one report by the U.S. Department of State describing the Israeli ambassador as "a man of medium height, inclined to heaviness from lack of exercise and a predisposition for sweets."[20]

While Aubrey was preparing for his return to Cairo in April 1943, the SOE headquarters offered his services to the Inter-Service Liaison Department, the cover name for the Secret Intelligence Service (later MI6): "Are you interested in taking over the above? He is the neighborhood of 30, of Jewish persuasion, and speaks Arabic, French, Italian and Hebrew fluently. Moreover, he is an expert lecturer, and I have a report to the effect that at a recent lecture he gave under the auspices of the British Council in Jerusalem, the High commissioner and various other Palestinian dignitaries honored him with their attendance."[21]

Aubrey's new assignment in Cairo was as adviser on Jewish affairs at the office of the minister of state in the Middle East, Lord Richard Casey. His immediate superior was Casey's deputy, brigadier Iltyd Clayton, who headed the Middle East Intelligence Centre in Cairo and now served as political adviser to Casey. After the war, Clayton played a key part in the formulation of Britain's Middle East policy and was involved in the formation of the Arab League in 1945. Aubrey shared an office with Clayton's adviser on Arab affairs, the Lebanese-British Albert Hourani, who would later become one of the world's most prominent historians of the Middle East. The Oxford University–educated Hourani shared Aubrey's intellectualism and interest in history, but his intense support for Arab nationalism stood in stark contrast to Aubrey's Zionist fervor. A rumor was soon circulated in Clayton's office that "Hourani, the Arab, is supposed to keep his eye on the Jews, while Eban, the

Jew, is supposed to keep his eye on the Arabs. All for the benefit of Clayton and the Empire."[22]

Following the victory at El-Alamein, Casey and Clayton began planning the future of British rule in the Middle East, and the need for adequately trained personnel to manage the affairs of the region was a top priority. In May 1943 Casey submitted to the War Office his proposals for the establishment of a center for Arab Studies somewhere in the Middle East. The aim of the center was to provide "a body of young men with some knowledge of the Arabic language and an adequate background of Arabic, Islamic and Middle Eastern history as well as the problems with which His Majesty Government is faced now in the Middle East and which will become more acute in the future. . . . These officers, when trained, will provide a pool from which military, diplomatic and administrative demands for personnel may be met." The preliminary plans for the center were drawn up by Colonel Bertram Thomas, an experienced civil servant and an avid explorer who in 1931 won fame as the first Westerner to cross the Arabian Peninsula's Rub' al Khali (Empty Quarter).[23] The Middle East Centre for Arabic Studies (MECAS) was established in the Austrian Hospice in January 1944, amid the buzzing and noisy streets of the Old City of Jerusalem, not far from the Damascus Gate. Five months later the center welcomed twenty students to its first course, under the directorship of Colonel Thomas, and with Aubrey—now Major Eban—acting as its chief instructor.

The course was demanding: mornings were taken up by Eban's language classes, and evening lectures covered the history, present-day politics, and cultures of the region. Whereas in England these topics were often taught by academics who had rarely come in contact with the people of the Middle East, here these courses were delivered by instructors who were actually responsible for the administration or representation of the countries and societies in the region. They included Sir Kinahan Cornwallis (ambassador in Baghdad), Sir Reader Bullard (ambassador in Tehran), Sir Walter Smart (oriental minister in Cairo), and Nuri Pasha (prime minister of Iraq), as well as Chaim Weizmann and Judah Magnes, the first chancellor of the Hebrew University in Jerusalem.[24]

All this time Eban continued to court Suzy, in Cairo and in Jerusalem, the latter being where the Ambaches spent the summer months. "I did not want to be rushed, although I understood very well that he was in love," she recalled, "and I was beginning to be so myself and ever more dependent on him." Much like Alida Solomon in Yanishki three decades earlier, Suzy Ambache fell in love with her suitor's adoring letters, such as this one from April 1944:

> Sweet darling,
>
> You know me well be now, Suzy dear one; so it is necessary to say again how ardently I seek your happiness and satisfaction and I'm not going to be a hypocrite about it—in seeking your happiness and satisfaction I find my own. It is a selfish unselfishness. For my heart and interests are indivisible and if you divide them I tell you simply and honestly that my heart must break.
>
> I have reached a point in my life where I can see no horizon ahead of me in which I can be happy alone without love, by which I mean your love, dear Sue—things are too big for me now, I can't achieve them without happiness and support. . . . You are in fact necessary to me in what I do. Is that not good, Sue? . . . Think of that Sue, when you are worried about what you call my intensity about you. It means that I need you which is different from "needing a woman."
>
> Why not, Suzy, sweet gentle lady—for Heaven's sake, why not? Say it to yourself with a vision of our common future before your eyes—is it a bad vision, Suzy—and ask yourself, "Why not?" I tell you with the painful ecstatic certainty of my love that there is no answer.[25]

The couple was engaged on New Year's Day 1945. The wedding date had to be deferred until Suzy was formally "approved" by the British Army, as officers were discouraged from the frivolous act of marrying indigenous women whose lineage or intentions were unknown. When Eban asked the headquarters in Cairo for permission to marry Suzy, who was of Egyptian birth, a rumor soon spread in regimental circles that he was engaged to a peasant woman draped from head to foot in black. But the empire's doubts were allayed when the officer sent by the general staff to "inspect" Suzy reported back that, far from being a peasant, Major Eban's fiancée could read and write four languages; she was cultured and mingled with Cairo's high society, and even knew the royal family! Meanwhile, in Palestine, the Zionist establishment was reassured by Moshe Shertok's declaration that he knew the Ambache family well and that Eban was not marrying into anyone with an anti-Zionist background. The couple married on March 18, 1945, at the Ambache residence. The chief rabbi of Egypt conducted the ceremony, which was attended by 120 guests, including Egyptian notables and senior British officers, as well as David Ben-Gurion and his wife Paula, Theodor Kollek of the Jewish Agency, who succeeded Reuven Zaslani as liaison officer to British intelligence; Brigadier Clayton; and Eban's cousin, Neville Halper, who was now a captain in the Medical Corps. The two met fortuitously at a Cairo bookstore the day before the wedding, and Neville readily accepted the role of best man. After the wedding Eban wrote to a friend, "I enjoyed it far more than any other wedding that I had ever attended. It was the first time I have been near enough to the center of the proceedings to hear and see what was going on. Suzy looked radiant. Her white *tulle* quite overshadowed my khaki barathea, and she undoubtedly looked the better of the two of us."[26]

Aubrey and Suzy spent their honeymoon sailing the Nile to the ancient sites of Luxor and Aswan. After a brief stop in Cairo to celebrate Pesach they made their way to Jerusalem en route to the Galilee, in the north of Palestine, but Suzy's contracting mumps ended their honeymoon rather prematurely at the Hadassah Hospital on Mount Scopus.

They settled in a small apartment at the American School of Oriental Research in Jerusalem, near Herod's Gate in the Old City and a short distance from Eban's work at MECAS. It was there in May 1945 that they heard of the unconditional surrender of Nazi Germany. The war in Europe was over, but only then, with the liberation of Poland's death camps, did the full scale of the systematic extermination of Europe's six million Jews come to light. As Eban later lamented, some things in Jewish history were too terrible to be believed, but nothing in Jewish history was too terrible to have happened.[27]

THE LABOUR PARTY IN BRITAIN WON A LANDSLIDE VICTORY IN THE GENERAL elections of July 1945, leading many in the Yishuv's leadership to believe that Britain would now quash Malcolm MacDonald's draconian White Paper of 1939 and allow the free immigration of the hundreds of thousands of displaced Holocaust survivors into Palestine. During the war there were many voices from the British Left who openly endorsed the moral imperative of a Jewish state in Palestine or at least the urgent need to lift the restrictions on Jewish immigration to Palestine in the face of the unfolding catastrophe of the Holocaust. The national executive of the British Labour Party exceeded even the most maximalist aspirations of Zionism's right-wing revisionists when it declared in a conference a year earlier, "Let the Arabs be encouraged to move out as the Jews move in. Let them be compensated handsomely for their land and let their settlement elsewhere be carefully organized and generously financed. The Arabs have many wide territories of their own; they must not claim to exclude the Jews from this small area of Palestine less than the size of Wales."[28] However these encouraging signals were soon upended, thanks to a single act that an editorial in the *Economist* described as "the greatest disservice to official Zionism, which naturally condemns any deed so wanton and so politically stupid."[29]

On November 4, 1944, Chaim Weizmann was invited for a talk with Churchill at the prime minister's official residence in Chequers. "It would be wonderful if you could get the whole of Palestine," Churchill said, "but I feel that if it comes to a choice between the White Paper and partition you should take partition." The prime minister did not recoil when Weizmann envisaged a mass emigration of one and half million Jews to Palestine in fifteen years. Churchill reassured the ebullient Weizmann that he had "many friends in the Labour and Liberal camps" and urged him to go and see Walter Guinness, Lord Moyne, who had "changed and developed in the last two years."[30] Ten months earlier Moyne had succeeded Richard Casey as the minister of state in Cairo, making him Britain's most senior official in the Middle East. But Moyne had previously been accused of anti-Semitism by those in revisionist circles in Palestine for his refusal in 1942 to allow the SS *Struma*, an inoperable ship carrying hundreds of Jewish refugees from Romania, to enter Palestine. Moyne, then colonial secretary, ordered the ship back to the Black Sea, where it was torpedoed by a Russian submarine and sunk with all its passengers on board. Two years later he turned down an opportunity to negotiate with Adolf Eichmann a deal to save one million European Jews in exchange for the delivery of ten thousand trucks and goods to Nazi Germany. He was alleged to have said, "What can I do with this million Jews? Where can I put them?"[31]

Now, however, Moyne endorsed a plan that was approved by a cabinet subcommittee concerning a long-term solution for Palestine, based loosely on the 1937 Peel Commission recommendations. A close friend of Churchill, Moyne was in fact in the minority in his views on Palestine. According to foreign secretary Anthony Eden, who opposed the plan, "Moyne's position differed from that of nearly all the British civil and military officials in the Middle

East: the consensus of British official opinion in the area opposed partition and opposed a Jewish state; Moyne supported both."[32]

On the afternoon of November 6, 1944, two days before Moyne was due to present his plan for cabinet approval, the news arrived from Cairo that he had been shot at close range outside his official residence by two assassins; he died at a Cairo hospital later that evening. The following day a mournful Churchill reported to Parliament that the Jews in Palestine "had rarely lost a better or more well-informed friend."[33] The assassins were two young members of the underground group Lehi (Lohamei Herut Israel—Fighters for the Freedom of Israel), commonly known as the Stern Gang after its founder Avraham Stern, who was killed by British police in Tel Aviv in 1942. Eliyahu Bet-Zuri and Eliyahu Hakim were tried in January 1945 in Cairo and were found guilty. They were hanged in the morning of March 22, after Churchill rejected several pleas for clemency from Jewish groups. Churchill's response to the murder of his longtime friend was almost visceral, and the partition plan that was about to be approved by his cabinet was now shelved. Speaking at the House of Commons eleven days after the assassination, Churchill's message was exceptionally ominous to Zionist aspirations, and seemed to mark a real tilt in the prime minister's commitment to Jewish statehood in Palestine: "If our dreams for Zionism are to end in the smoke of assassins' pistols, and our labors for its future to produce only a new set of gangsters worthy of Nazi Germany, many like myself will have to reconsider the position we have maintained so consistently and so long in the past."[34]

Churchill was wary of a sweeping British retribution against the Yishuv that would lead to more terrorist acts against British mandatory authorities. But he needn't have worried, as the Jewish Agency and Yishuv leadership themselves launched an unprecedented campaign against the right-wing groups in Palestine. The *saison* (hunting season) lasted from November 1944 to February 1945: hundreds of members of Lehi and Etzel (Irgun Tzvai Leumi—National Military Organisation, commonly known as the Irgun), were hunted down by the Haganah and were turned over to the British. Others were kidnapped and detained by special Haganah units. Those suspected of membership in the Lehi and Irgun were expelled from schools, lost their jobs, and were denied shelter. The Moyne assassination was merely the last straw in a series of attacks on British targets by Lehi and Irgun members that the Jewish Agency viewed as harmful to the efforts to reach a negotiated solution over Palestine.

In September 1939 David Ben-Gurion famously called the Yishuv to fight the war against Nazi Germany as if there were no MacDonald White Paper, and to fight the White Paper as if there were no war, leading to a period of truce between the various Zionist paramilitary organizations and the mandatory authorities. But following the removal of the Nazi threat to Palestine, the Irgun's new leader (and later Israel's sixth prime minister) Menachem Begin declared in February 1944 the resumption of the revolt against the British Mandate over the policies of the White Paper. Lehi and Irgun began to attack symbols of British rule in Palestine, such as police stations, immigration offices, and radio stations, but it was nothing compared to the audacious assassination of Britain's most senior official in the Middle East.[35] The *saison* that followed simultaneously brought the Yishuv to the brink of civil war and cemented the central authority of the Jewish Agency over the Jewish population in Palestine. By late 1945, however, as it became evident that the new Labour Party government in London was in no hurry to lift the restrictions imposed by the White Paper, the Haganah, Irgun, and Lehi joined forces against British rule in Palestine. Thus began the most violent episode yet in British–Zionist relations, forcing Major Eban—still chief instructor at MECAS—to declare his allegiances.

IV

Choosing Allegiances

THE BRITISH LABOUR PARTY'S ELECTION VICTORY IN JULY 1945 WAS greeted by a wave of optimism among Zionist circles that the new government would reverse Malcolm MacDonald's White Paper's restrictions on Jewish emigration to Palestine, especially following the horrors of the Holocaust.[1] But only a month later the Colonial Office informed Chaim Weizmann that the White Paper's immigration quota of fifteen hundred Jews per month would not be increased. Prime Minister Clement Attlee and Foreign secretary Ernest Bevin could not ignore the new geopolitical realities of the postwar environment. With a bankrupt economy devastated after six years of war, it was more important than ever for Britain to maintain good relations with the Arabs and their oil fields. They also feared that a pro-Zionist policy in Palestine might have a spillover effect in India where, as foreign secretary Bevin admitted, "the cause of the Palestinian Arabs . . . has become a matter of keen interest to their 90,000,000 co-religionists."[2]

The Yishuv's response to the government's refusal to revoke the White Paper was immediate and unprecedented. George Hall, the colonial secretary, warned the cabinet in September 1945 that the Jews of Palestine were gearing up for battle: "On the Zionist side emotions have been deeply stirred by the appalling sufferings of the Jewish communities in Central Europe and the wretched plight of their survivors, while exaggerated hopes have been excited by the change of Government . . . apart from the terrorist organizations, material preparations for an armed revolt by the Jewish community in Palestine are proceeding on a formidable scale."[3]

In October the leaders of the Haganah, Irgun, and Lehi agreed to form a united front against the British, known as Tnu'at Ha'Meri Ha'lvri (Hebrew Resistance Movement). Their maiden operation was very successful: Haganah units sabotaged 153 sites in the rail network across the country, while Palmach units damaged two British launches in Haifa Harbor and sunk a third in Jaffa Harbor to prevent them from intercepting ships carrying illegal immigrants from Europe. A joint Irgun-Lehi unit attacked the main rail station at Lydda and destroyed several locomotives and adjunct buildings, while another Lehi unit attacked the oil refineries at Haifa.[4]

Locked between its prewar promises to the Zionists and its postwar dependency on Arab cooperation, the British government's response to the Jewish insurgency campaign in Palestine was initially restrained and limited to curfews and searches for arms; the notion of declaring war on the Jews in Palestine was morally and politically inconceivable after the Holocaust. The British were also mindful of the rising global power of the United States in the aftermath of the war. The Foreign Office calculated that Britain would have to accept the role of junior partner to the United States, but it hoped that the British "superior wisdom" would help guide the "lumbering giant" toward British interests in the Middle East.[5] Attlee and Bevin were particularly angered by the demand of U.S. president Harry Truman that they allow the immediate entry to Palestine of 100,000 of Europe's displaced Jews. Truman was moved by the ill fortunes of those Holocaust survivors who ended up in squalid camps across Europe with nowhere to go, but the boorish Bevin suggested that the Americans supported Jewish resettlement in Palestine because they "did not want too many Jews in New York."[6] Rather than accepting the American demand, in November 1945 Bevin invited the United States to cooperate in a joint Anglo-American Committee of Inquiry "to examine the question of European Jewry and to make a further review of the Palestine problem in the light of that examination."[7]

The Hebrew Resistance Movement continued to attack British targets in Palestine. Between November 1945 and July 1946 it carried out seventy-seven operations, which included raids on the British intelligence offices in Jerusalem, the sabotaging of more than twenty aircrafts at three Royal Air Force airstrips across Palestine, and even the kidnapping of four army and five air force officers by the Irgun in response to the British sentencing to death of two of its members.[8] At the same time the Jewish Agency continued to cooperate with the inquiry of the Anglo-American Committee.

Major Aubrey Eban received his opportunity to contribute to the Zionist struggle for independence in March 1946. Still an instructor at the Middle East Centre for Arabic Studies (MECAS), he drafted for the Jewish Agency the case for Jewish statehood in Palestine. He presented a two-pronged argument of territory and sympathy: the Arabs had vast territory that was sparsely populated, whereas the Jews had no territory of their own; and following the catastrophic destruction of Jewish life in the Holocaust, it was impossible to ignore the very real need for Jewish statehood, whereas a similar case for Arab independence could not be made:

> It is not easy for the Arab world to appear in the guise of an aggrieved or oppressed party. Thirty years ago all Arabs were subject to the ultimate sovereignty of a foreign ruler. Today their area of independence stretches almost without interruption from the Taurus Mountains to the Gulf of Aden and from the Persian Gulf to the Western Mediterranean. The Arabs indeed are the godchildren of modern history, born with a silver spoon in their mouth. Independence has been lavished upon them—as soon as, or usually before, they could comprehend its full meaning and responsibility. . . Whatever the definition of a sated power, the Arabs must surely fulfill it in the highest degree. For, as though this were not enough, they have now emerged from a war which devastated and starved great centres of human habitation without suffering any loss of life or damage to property, enjoying a gross financial advantage from the fact of their strategic and commercial position. It is grotesque to imagine that their position today gives them any right to compete with the Jews on the grounds of need and suffering. Sympathy belongs to those who suffered: and not merely sympathy, but redress. Against the background of Arab sovereignty, territorial abundance and vast economic opportunity, all obtained at little loss and little sacrifice, we have the somber picture of the Jewish people, with no voice in international councils, its manpower reduced by a vile and sadistic massacre and its one avenue of potential national opportunity besieged, attacked and almost nagged out of existence by an Arab nationalist movement which could surely find more constructive and liberal things to do. For the idea of a Jewish Palestine threatens neither the existence nor the welfare of the Arab world.[9]

The committee published its report on April 30, and recommended the abrogation of the White Paper and to allow the immediate entry of 100,000 Jewish refugees into Palestine; but it also rejected the idea of a Jewish state in Palestine in favor of a binational state. Truman, particularly sensitive to the refugee question, accepted the report as a whole. The British response was much more lukewarm, however; as Prime Minister Attlee leveled at Richard Crossman, a member of the Committee: "I'm disappointed in you, Dick. The report you have produced is grossly unfair." Crossman asked if Attlee meant unfair to the Jews or to the Arabs, and Attlee responded that he meant unfair to Britain, adding, "You've let us down by giving way to the Jews and the Americans."[10] Bevin also rejected the report's recommendations and suggested continuing with a vague timetable for negations "in return for concessions from the Jews toward the Arabs."[11]

But the Jews were not in a conciliatory mood. Chaim Weizmann's measured and collaborative approach gave way to David Ben-Gurion's more confrontational and activist alternative. By the end of 1945 even Weizmann had become increasingly disillusioned by the paralysis that characterized British postwar policy, and while he did not share Ben-Gurion's refusal to cooperate with the British, he gradually acknowledged that the tide was turning against him, as the Yishuv's orientation toward the mandate authorities moved from cooperation to confrontation.[12] The most daring step yet in that direction took place on the night of June 16, 1946, when Palmach units destroyed ten of the eleven bridges linking Palestine to the neighboring countries. In response to what became known as the Night of the Bridges, the government in London concluded that "the situation called for firm action. We could no longer tolerate a position in which the authority of Government was set at nought."[13]

THE TURBULENCE IN PALESTINE, THE HORRORS OF THE HOLOCAUST, AND THE plight of Europe's Jews after the war forced Eban to think over his career choices. Before the British general elections in July 1945, he had received an offer from Harold Lasky, the chairman of the Labour Party and an old Cambridge University friend, to run for Parliament out of the Aldershot constituency, a traditional conservative stronghold. He had no chance of winning, though he was promised an easier constituency in the next elections in return for this act of political suicide. Eban also received a visit from Colonel

Thomas, the MECAS director, who pleaded with him to remain in the army and extend his service at the center, pointing to the desolateness of London after the war and the high price of whiskey in the city's black markets. A third offer came from Montague Butler, the master of Pembroke College, who asked Eban to return to Cambridge and resume his research and teaching duties en route to a professorship.

Eban shared his dilemma with his Cambridge friend Bernard Lewis. "Do you think my style of oratory would be suited to the House of Commons?" he asked. Lewis's reply was, "No, I think it would be more suited to the House of Lords."[14] Despite his enduring loyalty to the Labour Party, the thought of running for Parliament with no hope of winning did not appeal to Eban, who, in any case, preferred to stay close to Jerusalem. He did not wish to remain at MECAS, either, and in fact he had regretted extending his service there the previous year. As an officer in the British Army who was also Jewish and an ardent Zionist, he found his position at MECAS increasingly difficult to reconcile. When one of his officer students was shot dead by the Irgun, he could feel the accusing looks of the British officers directed at him. Yet returning to a life of academic tranquility in Cambridge seemed like a frivolous alternative in the face of the unfolding Jewish drama in Europe after the war and the struggle for statehood in Palestine. The Zionist route was the most precarious and least certain of all his options, but he had made up his mind.[15]

On Saturday, June 29, 1946, Eban invited Moshe Shertok to his apartment in the North Talpiot neighborhood in Jerusalem to tell him of his decision. But Shertok never arrived. In the early hours of the morning the British launched Operation Agatha against the Haganah, Palmach, and Jewish Agency in response to Night of the Bridges. During what became known as Black Saturday, Shertok and other Yishuv leaders were arrested and sent to the Latrun detention camp near Jerusalem; altogether more than 2,700 members of the Yishuv were arrested. The British police and army also raided the Jewish Agency's headquarters in Jerusalem and confiscated thousands of documents. A large depot of Haganah weapons was uncovered in Kibbutz Yagur near Haifa, and curfews were imposed in Tel Aviv, Jerusalem, and Haifa. Operation Agatha quashed the campaign of the Hebrew Resistance Movement, but it also closed the lid on any hopes for Zionist-British cooperation in the future. Ending the British Mandate and fighting for Jewish independence in Palestine was now the ultimate goal of the Yishuv.

Several weeks later, Aubrey and Suzy were due to meet at the King

David Hotel in Jerusalem, as they had many times before. But on that particular afternoon they were both late. Suzy decided to stop at the bakery to buy some pastries, and Aubrey—true to his well-earned reputation for tardiness—was also not there on time, though as he later recalled, he had no cause to regret that weakness on that particular occasion. As he walked toward the hotel he saw a huge explosion that completely destroyed the south wing, which housed the headquarters of the British military and the central offices of the mandatory authorities. The bombing was carried out by the Irgun in reprisal for Operation Agatha and resulted in the death of ninety-one people, including Brits, Jews, and Arabs.[16]

The audacious attack on the King David Hotel convinced the British that stronger measures had to be taken against the Yishuv. On July 30, 1946, some 20,000 British troops descended on Tel Aviv in Operation Shark, which was described by major R. D. Wilson, who served with the Sixth Airborne Division, as "the largest scale operation of its type ever to take place in Palestine." The extent of the operation was evidenced by the divisional operational order: "6 Airborne Division and attached troops, in conjunction with the Palestine Police, will cordon Tel Aviv and the Jewish quarter of Jaffa, and will thoroughly search every house and building with a view to checking up on all inhabitants and detaining any suspects." Four army brigades divided the city into sectors with barbed wire and guard posts, and screened more than 100,000 residents, two-thirds of the city's population. But their most important target—Menachem Begin, leader of the Irgun—escaped the British; he hid in a secret compartment in his small apartment while British forces set up camp in his garden. The British also dealt more forcefully with the issue of illegal immigration, deporting thousands of Jewish immigrants to internment camps in Cyprus.[17]

Rather than installing order in Palestine, Britain's new approach led to more violence. In a space of a year the Irgun and Lehi were responsible for 286 attacks on British targets, resulting in more than six hundred British casualties.[18] Incidents such as the Irgun's hanging of two British sergeants and the subsequent booby-trapping of their bodies in response to the execution of two Irgun members by the British, and the Irgun's whipping of British soldiers to reciprocate a similar British punishment of Irgun members, were received with shock and outrage by the British public, which began to see Palestine as a lost cause. In a desperate final attempt to restore order, the British launched Operations Hippo and Elephant in March 1947 and imposed martial law on Tel Aviv and Jerusalem—an unprecedented measure that put all civilian affairs under the jurisdiction of military courts. All commerce, transportation, postal, and taxation services were suspended, and food was distributed by the army. This imposition of martial law on effectively half of Palestine's Jewish population of 600,000 was not only designed to interrupt the activities of the underground movements but, just as important, was aimed at what British intelligence referred to as targeting the Achilles heel of the Yishuv: "The making of money is almost a second religion with the Jewish race. . . . [The Jewish community] would be forced to go on a manhunt to save themselves and their pockets." Despite these coercive measures, the Yishuv did not capitulate, and martial law failed to achieve the desired results. It was lifted after two months.[19]

Britain was clearly no longer in control of the situation in Palestine, as Winston Churchill, then leader of the opposition, observed during a House of Commons debate on March 3, 1947: "How long does the Secretary of State for the Colonies expect that this state of squalid warfare with all its bloodshed will go on, at a cost of £30 million or £40 million a year, keeping 100,000 Englishmen away with the military forces? How long does he expect that this will go on before some decision is reached?"[20] Soon there were anti-Jewish riots across the country. A blood-red graffito on a Manchester synagogue read HANG THE JEW TERRORIST BEGIN, while a synagogue in Derby was burned down; large crowds smashed the windows of hundreds of Jewish shops and properties in Glasgow, London, and Manchester; gravestones in a Jewish cemetery in Birmingham were uprooted; slogans such as HITLER WAS RIGHT and JEWS—GOOD OLD HITLER were painted on buildings in Cardiff and North Wales. As the headline of the *Sunday Express* angrily demanded, Attlee's government had two clear options: "Govern or Get Out!"[21]

LOCKED IN THE LATRUN DETENTION CAMP, SHERTOK HAD NO IDEA WHETHER EBAN had made up his mind. One day Eban received a letter from David Horowitz of the Jewish Agency bearing a one-word message from Shertok in Yiddish: "Nu? [So?] M.S." Despite his internment Shertok was able to communicate with the outside world freely and without the censorship of his guards, thanks to a very reliable underground postal service, which delivered his mail punctually every day at 11:00 a.m.; as he pointed out after his release, the British were quite unfit to run a police state.[22] Eban's response to Shertok's monosyllabic message was as short as it was life-changing: "Certainly. AE."[23] With this dull exchange he formally committed himself to the Zionist cause, not knowing for sure what job awaited him in an organization that was besieged by the British authorities, a job that would carry no personal status akin to that of a major in the British Army or a distinguished professor at Cambridge. Some of Eban's friends and family were dismayed by his decision, while some were puzzled. But to those who warned him that if he joined the Jewish Agency he would never be heard of again, he replied that this was "a tragic hour that demanded an assertion of conscience. . . . The other possibilities were more tranquil and serene. It is a poetic rather than a prosaic decision, romantic than pragmatic. It is a decision I know I shall never regret." Eban was strengthened by the support of Suzy and her parents, who, upon sensing that their son-in-law was seriously considering a Zionist career despite the meager pecuniary rewards it attracted, promised him that should he struggle financially at the beginning, they would help the young couple out for a year or two "while you find your way to other things."[24]

Eban's final act at MECAS was proof of where his allegiances now lay. A few days after the King David Hotel bombing he saw on the notice board at the center an order by general Evelyn Barker, commander of British forces in Palestine. Barker, who was in his office at the King David Hotel when the southern wing collapsed, and was known for his support for harsher measures against the Yishuv including the enforcement of the death penalty and collective punishment, wrote to the British troops in Palestine,

> I have decided that with effect on receipt of this letter you will put out of bounds to all ranks all Jewish establishments, restaurants, shops, and private dwellings. No British soldier is to have social intercourse with any Jew and any intercourse in the way of duty should be as brief as possible and kept strictly to business in hand. I appreciate that these measures will inflict some hardship on the troops, yet I am certain that if my reasons are fully explained to them they will understand their propriety and will be punishing the Jews in a way the race dislikes as much as any, by striking at their pockets and showing our contempt of them.[25]

This operational order of Operation Shark was classified as merely "restricted," and Eban decided that it was important enough for the world to see. After passing by the notice board inconspicuously several times and memorizing the wording of the order, he passed the text to leftist British-Jewish journalist Jon Kimche. Barker's contemptuous order soon appeared in newspapers across the world and further intensified the calls in Britain and abroad to leave Palestine. Attlee's government criticized the language of the order but supported its content. The order was rescinded two weeks later, but the damage to Britain's mandate policy was irreversible.[26] As Leslie McLoughlin, Eban's successor in MECAS and its future director, recalled, "Eban left MECAS with some éclat."[27]

In September 1946 Eban made the short journey from the Austrian Hospice in Jerusalem's Old City to Camp Allenby near Talpiot to surrender his military credentials. He then proceeded to the Jewish Agency offices in the leafy neighborhood of Rehavia to offer his services. His assignment was to head the agency's Information Department in London, a position Shertok thought he was eminently qualified for. As an expert orientalist of Zionist lineage, and with experience as liaison officer between the Jewish Agency and the Special Operations Executive (SOE) during the war and later as chief instructor at MECAS, Aubrey's reputation preceded him among British officials, Arabs, and Jews. He also possessed the necessary linguistic and rhetorical skills to convince his interlocutors that their interests lay parallel to those of Zionism's. In many ways Aubrey embodied the necessary qualities and attributes of a Zionist diplomat at a time when Zionism did not have a diplomatic corps—a problem of which he was well aware. In November 1944, during his first year in MECAS and shortly after his twenty-ninth birthday, Eban had outlined the urgent need for the establishment of a Zionist diplomatic corps; his unpublished document set the guiding principles of Zionist diplomacy and the kind of diplomatic training that would be required of future diplomats. Many of his reflections on the intertwining of policy, diplomacy, and Zionism were prophetic, still ringing true to this day—particularly in view of the conduct of Israel's public diplomacy in subsequent decades:

Diplomacy and Zionism

> Zionism emerged from the turmoil of [World War I] in the shelter of a great alliance and the security of international support. That alliance and support were obtained by a process of diplomacy. *Diplomacy is the technique whereby the aims of a foreign policy are represented, portrayed and advanced in such a way as to enlist support in their behalf. Diplomacy, in brief, is a means, whereas policy is an end.*

The Death of Isolationism

Nations, like individuals, live partly by their own exertion; but in the final issue, men live by the cooperation and tolerance of their fellows. They are inter-dependent, and isolationism is invariably their death. . . . As yet no such community has existed on earth, though some have aspired to this condition and others have been deluded into thinking that they had achieved it. Neither Russia nor America nor the British Commonwealth can even survive, let alone flourish, without being sustained and supported by external forces. That the Jewish people is in need of external support in an infinitely greater degree is so axiomatic that it be unnecessary to affirm it, were it not that the sterile and fatal delusion of "self-reliance" as an alternative to diplomacy has won credence in some sections of the Yishuv, just when it has been discarded by powerful societies which would afford this delusion more easily.

The underlying motive of this training is that the prospects of Zionism depend upon its ability to win first the tolerance and then the active support of external forces—especially those forces which are most in a position to affect the future of Palestine. This prospect in turn, depends on two factors, firstly the strength and resources of Zionism itself; and secondly its ability to convince external forces that they have an interest, or duty, in supporting it, and that the motive of interest or duty is more valid and potent than any motive that may be invoked in hostility to Zionism.

Existence of Diplomatic Science

This training is concerned primarily with the external intercourse and relationships affecting the destiny of Zionism. It is clear that this aspect of policy requires a special set of attributes and a special technique. To represent a cause to the outside world does not necessarily require the same qualities as the task of mobilising and organising national resources. *Therefore effective national leaders are not necessarily or usually the most efficient diplomatic representatives.*

There is a diplomatic temperament which is international. There is a diplomatic code which goes far beyond the trivialities of etiquette. Men who represent their nations outside their frontiers move in a society and atmosphere of their own, develop special instincts and capacities, and are often bound by a common professional solidarity. Diplomacy is a craft and a technique. *It can no more be practiced by men who have not studied its principles than a bridge can be constructed by a man untutored in the science of engineering.* In both instances the amateur can build something, but the prospects of stability are remote.

Corps Diplomatique in Zionism

The task then is to train specialists, men skilled in the profession of international relations, attuned to their atmosphere, adept in their procedures. It is not a question of giving any key a certain mass of knowledge; it is a question of introducing a certain type of man: a type unknown to Jewish life, because the Jewish people has hitherto not been involved in direct and normal national intercourse. The fact the Jewish people does not exercise sovereignty is irrelevant here; or, if anything, it reinforces the need for training a body of specialist diplomats; for they have the task of creating, not merely maintaining, a new unit in the international society of peoples. . . .

Qualities of Diplomacy

We are concerned here with certain initial attributes—and then with a certain type of training. A diplomat must be immersed in the historic personality of his nation and yet be able to contemplate his nation from outside. He must have an instinct for the impact of policy on external forces. He is concerned with reaction more than with action. He must see himself as others see him and yet retain his natural character. He must, in fact, be given a glimpse of his nation from a special vantage point outside himself. Not all men are temperamentally fitted for this particular process of contemplation. In Jewish life the ghetto has been the great destroyer of the diplomatic outlook and attributes. Insularity, self-sufficiency, seclusion, self-assertion—these are luxuries which a diplomat cannot afford. He cannot afford the casual prejudices, the current phobias, the transient excitements. He must, to that extent, at least, be intellectually ascetic and stand in a detachment which makes him a stranger to his community.

Our candidates, then, must be unprejudiced, un-embittered men with no particularism; they must have a sense of the romance of international relations, a bias for history, a gift of expression, a knowledge and interact with a world beyond their own, men who feel no torment or tension outside their fold, who are prepared intellectually to forego the home comforts of parochialism and move, with a sense of adventure, into a wider older world. . . . Not all people, and not even all talented people, are fitted for this particular range of public duty. Initial selection must be careful and exacting.

The main elements of a diplomatic training need not be improvised here, for they are known and tried as a result of long traditions of specialised diplomatic training in sovereign states. They are:

(a) History of one's own nation, with special emphasis on its foreign relations.
(b) History of international relations since 1789, with special reference to the periods 1900–1941.
(c) Political science and economy.
(d) Linguistics, with special phases on the language of allies and neighbours.
(e) Modern economic history, finance and commerce.
(f) International law and constitutional law.
(g) Military, naval and aerial strategy.
(h) Diplomatic procedure, terminology, precedence and etiquette.

Of this, (a), (b), (e) and (g) have a special (regional) application, determined by the main orientation and commitments of the national policy; or by the destination of the future diplomats.

For Jewish diplomats the orientation of training must be towards:

(a) the British world, and
(b) the Arabic speaking world,

since these two spheres of interest most closely affect the situation and prospects of Zionism.[28]

The image of the Zionist diplomat that Eban portrayed in this document is self-referential, if not autobiographical. In later years Ambassador and Foreign Minister Abba Eban would invariably be described—often derisively—in the same terminology that he himself applied to this ideal image of the diplomat. His support for multilateralism against the popular Israeli delusion of self-reliance, his romantic notion of diplomacy as a noble vocation and the appreciation of etiquette and subtleties of communication, his insistence that national leaders do not necessarily make for the most effective diplomats, his call to engage with the Arab world and understand its history and culture rather than adopting a prejudiced and embittered foreign policy—all led to a common view of Eban in Israel as detached and a stranger to his own community, an attribute he considered—rather ironically—to be the essence of diplomacy.

V

London, Palestine, New York

Aubrey and Suzy found postwar London to be poor and dejected, its landscape still dominated by the skeletal remains of buildings that served as painful reminders of Adolf Hitler's V1 and V2 rockets, which had killed more than 30,000 Londoners during the war. Though the Allies emerged from the war victorious, Britain's economy and industry were ravaged; there was a lack of raw materials and a drastic fall in production and exports, while basic commodities such as bread, potatoes, milk, and tea had to be rationed. And as if the general temperament of postwar London was not somber enough, the winter of 1946–47 was among the harshest ever recorded, making life in the capital downright miserable. Between January and March 1947 snow fell somewhere in the United Kingdom every day, and the sun was seen for only six days out of the entire month of February. This general atmosphere of gloom could only be matched by the misery that accompanied the work of a Zionist agent in London at that time. "If I had to condemn an adversary to cruel and unusual punishment," Eban recalled, "I would sentence him to be an official of the Jewish Agency in London in the winter of 1946."[1]

Eban joined the Information Department of the Jewish Agency at 77 Great Russell Street, and occupied the office from which, nearly three decades earlier, Nahum Sokolow called upon Alida Eban to come and translate the Balfour Declaration into French and Russian, leaving baby Aubrey fretting in his cradle. Eban's starting salary was £900 per year, which was rather less than what he would have earned at Cambridge University or as a Labour Party member of Parliament.[2] His first task was to survey the list of potential contacts in British politics, media, academia, and other sectors that had influence over or access to Britain's Middle East policy. He found that those on the left who already supported Zionism's aims needed little persuading, whereas any efforts at directing Zionist propaganda at the pro-Arab conservative press or the orientalists who advised the government were doomed to fail. The head of the Information Department, Maurice Rosette, was rather doubtful of Eban's potential to transform the work of the department. "The arrival of Aubrey was intended to revolutionise the whole situation," Rosette noted. "Still, the big man has arrived and no great change has taken place. I have the greatest respect for his abilities, I think he can do tremendous work, but as for the reorganization of the Department as a result of his arrival, up to the time of writing this has not happened." Rosette was impressed, however, by Eban's ability to access the policy world: "There is, however, one gratifying change. Aubrey is in close touch with the inner circles, he attend [*sic*] the meetings, and there is no difficulty now in securing information. One simply go [*sic*] down to him or to Teddy [Kollek] and gets the whole story, so that at any rate one does not look to [*sic*] foolish in the eyes of the press who always know everything in advance."[3]

It didn't take Eban long to identify a particular weakness in the working of the department, one that was indicative of Zionism's historical deficiency in the arena of public diplomacy: the "tendency to claim a total rectitude for its views and to be based on the assumption that nobody else has any case at all. I thought that the Jews and Arabs were behaving more or less as each of them would do if their situations were interchanged. Since the decision makers in the world are people of sophisticated temperament, I believed that the rights and claims of Zionism had to be interpreted in terms of broader interests and relative values."[4] His concerns were shared by Walter Eytan, the spokesman of the Political Department of the Jewish Agency and head of its public relations office. Eytan, an Oxford University don who was recruited by British intelligence during the war to help break coded German messages at Bletchley Park, placed great emphasis on understanding the nuances of public diplomacy and matching the content and tone of the message to the intended audience. Eytan and Eban noted that traditional Zionist propaganda failed to distinguish between Jewish and non-Jewish audiences, delivering the same material despite the palpable gaps in the cultural and emotional attachments of these groups to the Zionist message. For a good propagandist, according to Eytan, "it is not enough that he looks at his issue through his own eyes. He must present it in a way which will convince others and win their support."[5] A generation later, when Eban would serve as Israel's foreign minister, he explained his people's enduring lack of objectivity to U.S. secretary of state Henry Kissinger. "Well, Abba Eban once told me that Israelis saw objectivity as being a hundred percent in agreement with them. I thought that was a joke until I met [Prime Minister] Golda Meir," Kissinger recalled. "On one occasion she had eleven demands, and I only agreed to ten of them. She thereupon turned to Eban and said, 'Why is Henry betraying us again?'"[6]

In November 1946 Eban visited David Ben-Gurion at the Hotel Royal Monsue in Paris, where he remained in exile while the mandatory powers were besieging the Jewish Agency in Palestine. Ben-Gurion showed Eban an exchange of letters with Chaim Weizmann. While the tempestuous relationship between the two great leaders of Zionism was marked by differences in temperament as well as views on the nature of British-Zionist relations, they seemed to be in agreement that the partition of Palestine into Jewish and Arab states was the only viable option left on the table. This was a dramatic departure from the hitherto official Zionist line adopted at the Biltmore Conference in 1942, which called for the whole of Palestine to be established as a Jewish commonwealth. The events of the postwar years, however, had forced the two to adopt a more pragmatic line. Ben-Gurion conceded to Weizman that an "enlightened compromise" should not be ruled out "even if it gives us less in practice than we have a right to in theory," and Weizmann concurred: "I am in cordial agreement with the main lines of your policy. . . . I can't help feeling that the inexorable logic of facts will drive [Foreign Secretary Ernest Bevin and U.S. secretary of state James Byrnes] towards partition."[7]

But Weizmann and Ben-Gurion grossly underestimated the British government's principled objection to partition. For Bevin and the vast majority of the Foreign Service establishment, Britain's position in Palestine was inseparable from the empire's strategic dependence on Arab oil. In January 1947 Bevin warned the cabinet about the grave risks of offending the Arabs "by appearing to encourage Jewish settlement and to endorse the Jewish aspiration for a separate state" given the "vital importance for Great Britain and the British Empire of the oil resources of this area." Bevin had no doubt about the Arab hostility to partition and feared that it would "contribute to the elimination of British influence from the vast Moslem area between Greece and India . . . it would also jeopardize the security of our interests in the increasingly important oil production in the Middle East," while the cabinet secretary, Sir Norman Brook, summed up succinctly Britain's position in the region: "Our influence in the Middle East depends on retaining the friendship of the Arab peoples."[8]

The Twenty-Second Zionist Congress opened in Basel on December 9, 1946. It was the first meeting since the last congress on the eve of World War II seven years earlier. The war wiped out a third of the world's Jewish population, but the proportion of registered Zionists in this period had tripled from 6.2 percent in 1939 to 19.6 percent in 1946. In absolute terms there were more than two million registered Zionists, twice more than before the war. Weizmann arrived at the conference in poor health, partially blind from glaucoma, and under increased attacks on his leadership. The American Zionists, led by the combative Abba Hillel Silver and representing half of the organization's membership, rejected Weizmann's support for partition and his call for continued engagement with the British. The Palestinian Zionists noted that Weizmann visited Palestine only rarely, and they declared their support for Ben-Gurion's more bellicose approach toward Zionist–British relations. Against the vigorous Ben-Gurion, Weizmann's poor health and near blindness made him a very fragile and vulnerable figure in Basel. According to Blanche "Baffy" Dugdale, Weizmann's loyal aide at the Zionist offices on Great Russell Street, he encountered opposition wherever he turned:

> It seems that Chaim's chances of re-election to the Presidency are almost nil! This was a great shock to me, and I think it will be to him. But it is all bound up with the question of partition, and even Chaim's most faithful adherents do not think him a good negotiator. Of the whole American Delegation he will only get eight votes (led by Rabbi Wise, who is Silver's enemy). General Zionists and Mapai may be split. Revisionists may be split on some questions but united against Chaim. It seems that many of Chaim's best friends in all parties feel that the British connection means too much to him that [His Majesty Government] might get the better of him.[10]

Weizmann was too ill to write his own opening address and asked Eban to draft it for him. Eban did not travel to Basel, but he later noted that "the draft that I had helped him write was well received."[11] Those who were in Basel felt differently, however, as Dugdale noted in her diary: "I am *not* happy about Chaim's reception. There was no fire in it. He read his speech, a tremendous effort, gallantly carried through, but of course it was not very effective to listen to, and it took an hour and a half. There was hardly any applause but I *hope* that was due to English not being very well understood, for if it were otherwise the reception would be decidedly cold."[12] A week later Weizmann delivered his closing address. Having been attacked for being pro-British, for supporting partition, for calling to accept Bevin's invitation to participate in the London Conference on Palestine, for not visiting Palestine often enough, and for being the face of yesterday's Zionism, he rose to reclaim his reputation and authority. Addressing the hall in Yiddish, Weizmann showed the energy and passion that had made him the undisputed leader of the Zionist movement for three decades. According to Dugdale, this was the "greatest speech of his life. Perhaps the greatest I have ever heard. . . . He showed, physically and mentally, all the fire and vigor of fifteen years ago. His voice was strong."[13]

Weizmann rebuked the American Zionists who called for resistance in Palestine from the comfort of their diasporic existence. The final insult came when Emmanuel Neumann, a member of the Jewish Agency and a Silver supporter, shouted at Weizmann, "Demagogue!" After a week in which his policy, leadership, and dignity came under incessant assault, and now stunned by Neumann's affront, Weizmann stood in silence, taking his glasses off before delivering his reply:

> Somebody had called me a demagogue. I do not know who. I hope that I never learn the man's name. I—a demagogue! I who have born all the ills and travails of this movement. The person who flung that word in my face ought to know that in every house and stable in Nahalal, in every little workshop in Tel-Aviv or Haifa, there is a drop of my blood. You know I am telling you the truth. Some people don't like to hear it—but you *will* hear me. . . . If you think of bringing the redemption nearer by un-Jewish methods, if you lose faith in hard work and better days, then you commit idolatry and endanger what we have built. . . . Go and re-read Isaiah, Jeremiah and Ezekiel, and test that which we do and wish to do in the light of the teachings of our great prophets and wise men. . . . *Zion shall be redeemed in Judgment*—and not by any other means.[14]

Rapturous applause followed. With the exception of the Revisionist and Mizrachi delegates, everyone in the hall stood on their feet and applauded the exhausted and half-blind seventy-two-year-old statesman. But as Weizmann himself cautioned, speeches carry less weight than actions. A week later, back in England, he heard the news that a proposal by Golda Meirson for Mapai (the Workers' Party) to allow the executive of the World Zionist Organization the freedom to discuss partition with the British was rejected by the Zionist Congress by a narrow majority of 171–154. This was tantamount to a vote of no confidence in Weizmann himself. Out of respect to the aged leader, the executive decided not to elect a president. Weizmann refused Ben-Gurion's offer to accept an honorary presidency unless the congress agreed unconditionally to his demand to accept partition and to participate in the London conference. But Ben-Gurion urged the congress's political committee not to accept Weizmann's demands, as they would bind the executive's negotiating position should it participate in discussions in London. There was also little support for Weizmann's position among American Zionists, who were fuming at his attack on them during his address: "This unparalleled imputation has caused a feeling of outrage among the American delegates to the Congress and evoked expressions of protest and indignation at the sessions Monday evening and subsequently. We regret that contrary to reasonable expectations, Dr. Weizmann has not taken the occasion to withdraw his offensive remarks or to correct the painful impression they create."[15] At the end, it was Ben-Gurion's final address at the congress that decided Weizmann's fate. While the heir to the throne avoided attacking Weizmann himself, his ferocious criticism of Britain stood him in direct opposition to Weizmann's conciliatory approach: "We do not turn to England as beggars seeking a kindness. We demand that it is ours by right. Eretz Israel does not belong to England, nor is it part of the British Empire. England has no right to do whatever it wishes there, like someone handling his own property."[16]

There was no way back for Weizmann. Ben-Gurion's takeover was completed, and the relations between the two continued to grow sour. Two years later, when the State of Israel was established, Ben-Gurion rejected a nearly unanimous call to allow Weizmann to add his signature to the Declaration of Independence, insisting on the technical detail that Weizmann was abroad when the declaration was signed. When Weizmann became Israel's first president in 1949, he resented the fact that Prime Minister Ben-Gurion imbued the presidency with no executive power of any kind, and he accused Ben-Gurion of "imprisoning" him at his residence in Rehovot.[17]

Ben-Gurion's style of leadership was hardly palatable, but his charisma and iron will made him irreplaceable among the majority of the Labor Party members in Basel. He was elected chairman of the new executive and also received the newly created defense portfolio, which until then was under the responsibility of the Political Department of the Jewish Agency. Silver was elected chairman of the Jewish Agency in the United States; Moshe Shertok remained head of the Political Department of the Jewish Agency, but also assumed responsibility for Zionist activity in the United States—another sign that the fate of Palestine was no longer at the hands of Britain. Zionism had entered a new era, as Blanche Dugdale pointed out bitterly: "It is an age of pygmies, and so much squalor, spite, folly, and party hatreds seem to be devouring Zionist politics. I think the day is done for Zionism of the old school."[18] Weizmann tried to organize a group of moderates in Britain and America to bring about a change in Zionist leadership. "I have emerged from the slime of the Basel Congress in firm ground," he wrote in January 1947 to his friend, Justice Felix Frankfurter of the U.S. Supreme Court, but his efforts to persuade prominent Zionists such as Selig Brodetsky, Berl Locker, Simon Marks, Leonard Stein, and others to resign from their positions en masse and create a new leadership ended in failure. Reluctantly, he turned to offer his services to the Zionist leadership under Ben-Gurion and Silver—the latter was candidly described by Weizmann as "the filibustering Rabbi from Cleveland"—a rather affable epitaph compared to the British view of Silver as "vain" and "something of a megalomaniac . . . all he needs is to be smiled at and jollied a little."[19]

The drama in Basel left Eban bitter and disillusioned. Since his Cambridge days he had been a devout disciple of Weizmann and Weizmannism, and as the elder statesman's health deteriorated, Eban felt that his relationship with his mentor had become more personal and profound.[20] Now that Weizmann's Zionist career seemed to be over, Eban felt that his own career was nearing its end. How could he continue to serve the Jewish Agency when it seemed to reject the principles that he so passionately believed in? As he had often done in the past, he turned to Shertok. "You can't make the beginning of your career dependent on the end of his," Shertok advised Eban. He heard the same message from Weizmann himself at his Dorchester Hotel suite in London: Weizmannism was not dead yet, and there was plenty of work ahead. Eban acquiesced, promising Weizmann that he would carry on with his work for the Jewish Agency in London.[21]

In line with the resolution passed at the Basel Congress, the Jewish Agency officially boycotted the London Conference on Palestine, which took place on January 27, 1947. The declaration of the leader of the Palestinian-

Arab delegation at the conference, Jamal al-Husayni, that the Arab world would forever oppose partition as the solution to the Palestine problem, was evidence that participating in the conference was futile. Nevertheless, two days later a ten-member delegation of the Jewish Agency, which included Ben-Gurion, Shertok, David Horowitz, Nahum Goldman, Emanuel Neumann (Weizmann's heckler in Basel), and Eban, among others, arrived in London to attend "informal" discussions at the Colonial Office with Bevin and the colonial secretary Arthur Creech Jones. In early January Ben-Gurion had asked Sir George Gater, the undersecretary of state for the colonies, why the British were so anxious to invite the Jewish Agency for talks in London given the obvious divergence of opinions on Palestine, and was unanswered: "the British believed in Conferences and wanted discussion." Indeed, Bevin and other officials met with the Jewish Agency no fewer than five times between January 29 and February 13, but by the end of the talks they were no closer to reconciling their positions.[22]

These were Eban's first personal encounters with Bevin, and the experience left him underwhelmed. "Bevin's humor was heavy," Eban would later note. "When he was told that the lights had gone out, he said, 'Except the Israelites,' and then fell into a paroxysm of husky laughter in which nobody else joined." When Ben-Gurion suggested that social and economic cooperation between the Arabs and Jews of Palestine was still possible despite their political differences, Bevin interjected that "strikes always united all religions—even in Belfast." When Ben-Gurion discussed the expected rate of Jewish immigration into Palestine, Bevin interrupted crassly that "owing to recent events in Europe they were now expecting 100,000 a minute." At one point Bevin wished out loud that the Americans had the Mandate for Palestine.[23]

The Jewish delegation reiterated its demand for the abrogation of the 1939 White Paper and declared readiness to accept a Jewish state in part of Palestine, but Bevin attacked partition as "counsel of desperation," adding that Britain had no intention of imposing a solution that would result in it taking up arms against the Arabs. When Ben-Gurion asked if Britain would consider returning to the pre-1939 regime and carry out the mandate, Creech Jones replied "with vehemence" that the British government was no longer prepared to maintain an administration in Palestine that was perceived by world opinion as an autocratic alien government; Britain was "determined to set up self-governing institutions in Palestine with independence as its ultimate aim." But Bevin's suggestion that in a unitary state, "not everyone would vote as Arab or as a Jews. After a few years they would vote as Socialists, Communists, etc.," was further proof of his naive grasp of the conflict in Palestine.[24]

Bevin tried one last time to break the impasse. On February 7 he presented to the cabinet his very own plan: Palestine would be placed under a five-year trusteeship of the United Nations (UN), after which it would become an independent binational state with noncontiguous cantons determined by the size of Arab and Jewish majorities. Self-government would be restricted, and Jewish immigration would be limited to 96,000 within a period of two years. Further immigration after this period would be decided by an international tribunal. As Bevin himself expected, the plan was swiftly and vigorously rejected by both sides.The government continued to look for other ideas, but there weren't any; there were no more policies, proposals, or options for Palestine, and against the imminent withdrawal from India in five months—the jewel in the empire's crown—the squalid situation in Palestine shed an unflattering light on the demise of Britain's global stature. As ever, Winston Churchill, now leader of the opposition, summed up the state of affairs most eloquently during a debate in the House of Commons: "To abandon India, with all the dire consequences that would follow therefrom, but to have a war with the Jews in order to give Palestine to the Arabs amid the execration of the world, appears to carry incongruity of thought and policy to levels which have rarely been attained in human history."[25]

On February 14, 1947, the British government resolved to transfer the Palestine issue to the United Nations (UN) without any specific recommendations regarding its future administration or governance. The cabinet resolved that the government would not be under an obligation to enforce whatever solution the United Nations might approve: "If the settlement suggested by the United Nations were not acceptable to us, we should be at liberty then to surrender the Mandate and leave the United Nations to make other arrangements for the future administration of Palestine." Bevin noted that he had the impression that the Jews did not believe that Britain would in fact refer the issue to the UN, and that both Jews and Arabs were anxious to avoid discussion of the problem in that forum; perhaps this move would now bring them "to a more reasonable frame of mind."[26] Four days later Bevin made the unavoidable announcement to the House of Commons: "His Majesty's Government have of themselves no power, under the terms of the Mandate, to award the country either to the Arabs or to the Jews, or even to partition it between them. We have, therefore, reached the conclusion that the only course now open to us is to submit the problem to the judgment of the United Nations."[27]

The deference of the Palestine question to the UN was received with mixed emotions in Zionist circles. On the one hand, it would allow the Jewish case to be heard, for the first time, at the highest forum of international diplomacy, where considerations of justice and proportionality ought to weigh more heavily than the narrow calculations of a single power. On the other hand, that single power carried considerable influence in the nascent organization; there was danger that UN member states that belonged to the British Commonwealth would follow the empire's edict at the UN General Assembly. In addition, the five Arab member states of the UN (Egypt, Syria, Iraq, Lebanon, and Saudi Arabia), together with other Muslim countries, were certain to join in alliance against partition or other solutions that might award the Jews a legitimate foothold in Palestine. The historic and ideological aversion of Bolshevism to Zionism also guaranteed that the Soviets and their Communist satellites would vote against any resolution in support of the Jewish case in Palestine. Then there were the Catholic states—one-third of the UN members—who were likely to oppose the idea of Jewish sovereignty in the Holy Land. Finally, western-Europe bloc was largely social-democratic, with close ties to the British Labour Party, leading some British officials to boisterously warn Eban that the Zionists would live to regret the transfer of the Palestine question to the UN. Even the Americans were not overjoyed by the prospect of a British withdrawal from Palestine which might lead to a power vacuum in the region, following the British decision in March 1947 to terminate aid to Greece and Turkey and to pull its forces out of the former. There were thus no grounds for optimism in the Zionist leadership about the likelihood of securing a favorable two-thirds majority among the fifty-five members of the General Assembly. A somber omen for the forthcoming decades of discordant relations between Israel and the United Nations, the Jewish people's first presentation before the organization seemed to be condemned to failure by simple arithmetic. The British intelligence community, however, was evidently more confident than the Jewish Agency about the power of Jews in Palestine to carve for themselves a state—if not a whole empire in the Middle East:

> [It would] be a mistake to look as yet for any finality in Jewish aims. It would certainly be a mistake to expect them to be satisfied with autonomy in a part of Palestine, or even with a fully-fledged Jewish State. They already have a monopoly of brain-power in the

> Middle East (not excluding the representatives of His Majesty's Government). Their position will be strengthened with every breach in the barrier against immigration, and our evidence suggests that they may attempt to get as many as 30,000 illegal immigrants into Palestine between now and . . . September. Militarily, the Arabs are a negligible quantity in comparison with them. In intelligence and propaganda, the same applies. The extent of Zionist financial resources requires no emphasis. It may be early to talk of a prospective "Zionist Empire," but there is no doubt at all that Zionists of the stamp of Ben-Gurion are ambitious politicians first, and humanitarians only for the purpose of propaganda.[28]

In 1947 the United Nations was still a fledgling organization, barely into its second year, and the various clauses and procedures enshrined in its charter were largely unfamiliar to Zionist officials, who until then had focused their attention on London. Eban's first reaction on hearing Bevin's statement was to purchase six books about the organization and its procedures, which instantly made him an expert on the subject among his colleagues. All efforts were now directed at enlisting international support ahead of the General Assembly's session on Palestine, which was scheduled for April 28. The Zionist office in London presented a map of the world and divided areas of responsibilities among its officials. After three decades of Zionist diplomacy aimed solely at Great Britain, the officials on Great Russell Street confronted the ocean of fifty-five member states of the UN, many of which were unfamiliar by name or geographical location, as Weizmann challenged his colleagues who were hovering over the map: "I defy you to find Uruguay, Paraguay or Shmaraguay on this map."[29]

These officials soon turned into the most gifted group of individuals ever assembled in the short history of Zionist diplomacy. Under the leadership of Moshe Shertok, soon to be Israel's first foreign minister, they would go on to form the backbone of the Israeli Foreign Ministry for more than a generation: Walter Eytan (first director-general of the Foreign Ministry and ambassador to France), Arthur Lourie (Eban's deputy at the UN and ambassador to Canada and the United Kingdom), Michael Comay (Eban's successor as ambassador to the UN), Avraham Harman (Eban's successor as ambassador to the United States), Gideon Rafael (ambassador to the UN and director-general of the Foreign Ministry), Eliahu Elath (first ambassador to the United States and ambassador to the United Kingdom), and Moshe Tov (ambassador to Latin America). All but the last two formed the "Anglo-Saxon clique" in the Foreign Ministry either by birth, education, or service in the British Army during World War II.[30]

Eban's command of French earned him the first diplomatic mission of his career: the task of lobbying the governments of France, Belgium, the Netherlands, and Luxemburg ahead of the debate at the UN General Assembly. That he received polite yet noncommittal reassurances from Prime Ministers Paul Ramadier of France and Paul-Henri Spaak of Belgium was an immense achievement given that Eban relied mostly on ingenuity and tact to gain access to these leaders. In Belgium, for example, the Jewish Agency had done no preparatory work, and the lack of a single Jew in Brussels with access to the government meant that Eban had to pretend to be his own secretary when he called on Spaak's *chef de cabinet* to arrange a meeting with the prime minister. He was reassured by Spaak's message that independence was "a popular slogan at the UNO [United Nations Organization]" and that "it was not in the spirit of 1947 to keep mature communities under tutelage, however benevolent." While Eban was in Amsterdam he received an urgent cable from Shertok in New York: "Please wind up as soon as possible and come to New York." Shertok enlisted the assistance of several legal experts to write a document that would sum up the Jewish case before the General Assembly; he was content with the document's coherence and legalistic base, but thought that it lacked "the authentic Zionist passion and the authentic Zionist knowledge."[31] Eban came to mind as the ideal candidate for the job.

Eban did not ask how long his mission would last; nor did he know where he and Suzy would stay in New York. All he knew was that Suzy would have to pay her own way there and that this could be the big break for his career. After only eight months in London, Eban and his wife cleared their flat in Highgate and crossed the Atlantic for the first time in their lives. Compared to the gray glum of postwar London, New York in the spring was a kaleidoscope of colors and sounds, with an un-European medley of cultures and ethnicities that had evidently not experienced the travails of food rationing. But some signs of postwar shortage were still visible, no more so than among the city's hotels, which refused to offer reservations for any period longer than three days. For some time the Ebans had to move from one hotel to another, all of which were rather rudimentary in style yet given ambitious names like Paramount or Empire. Luckily, the couple was not overburdened by possessions, as Suzy believed that they would not stay away for more than six weeks.[32]

THE SIX WEEKS EXTENDED TO TWELVE YEARS, DURING WHICH EBAN WOULD become the fledgling State of Israel's first representative to the United Nations and then simultaneously act as ambassador to the United States. While Eban reached these elevated positions on the merit of his unique qualifications and skills, he owed much of his meteoric rise to Moshe Shertok, who was always present at the most crucial junctions in his career. It was Shertok who had proposed Captain Eban as liaison officer between the Special Operations Executive (SOE) and the Jewish Agency during the war and then enlisted his service to the Jewish Agency after the war. Shertok had even played matchmaker between Aubrey and Suzy thanks to his acquaintance with Suzy's father in Cairo. Now Eban was in New York on Shertok's request, and about to play a historic role in turning Zionist aspirations for statehood into reality.

VI

We Live on the Mistakes of the Arabs

In turning over the question of Palestine to the United Nations, the British government brought to an end a generation of sisyphean efforts to reconcile the demands and aspirations of two peoples over one land. "An empire can permit itself to be unjust, even tyrannical and terrifying," noted Colonel Nichol Grey, the last inspector of the Palestine Police. "It can permit itself defeats on the battlefield or in the diplomatic arena; but it cannot allow itself one thing: to lose prestige and become a laughing stock. . . . Our choice was obvious. Either total suppression or get out, and we chose the second."[1] Even Prime Minister Clement Attlee conceded that Britain could no longer hold on to Palestine: "It was no good our holding the baby any longer with everybody gunning for us. It was one of those impossible situations for which there is no really good solution. One just had to cut the knot."[2]

On April 28, 1947, the first special session of the UN General Assembly opened in Flushing Meadows, New York. It ended just over two weeks later, with the recommendation to set up the UN Special Committee on Palestine (UNSCOP). The Jewish Agency scored some early victories during the special session, in part due to the self-defeating performances of the Arab delegates. First Iraqi foreign minister Fadil Jamali defended the mufti of Jerusalem, Haj Amin al-Husseini, whose picture with Adolf Hitler in 1941 (where he urged the führer to solve the "Jewish problem" in the Arab world, as elsewhere), appeared in all the newspapers that morning. Then Emil Ghouri, secretary of the Arab Higher Committee, compared the mufti with Generals George Washington and Jan Smuts, adding that the Jews had no right to criticize the mufti since they had crucified Jesus. He was soon upstaged by Jamali, who this time declared that the Arabs would take up arms against any General Assembly resolution that they did not deem favorable. On the penultimate day of the special session, Eban reported from New York that the general feeling in the hall was that the Arabs of Palestine "have not vindicated their maturity for independence if these are their views and inclinations."[3]

The special session concluded with a dramatic statement by Andrei Gromyko, the Soviet representative, who spoke of the tragic fate of Jewish displaced persons across Europe and voiced his support for the Jewish case for self-determination in Palestine—either in a binational state or via partition. Gromyko even endorsed the American demand to allow for the emigration of 100,000 Jews to Palestine, given the Jewish suffering during the war and the plight of Jewish refugees across Europe. The Arabs were as fuming at the news from New York as the Jews were thrilled with the unexpected support from Moscow. It mattered little that the Soviet change of heart did not follow a genuine departure from anti-Zionist ideology. In one of many examples of geopolitical calculations overriding ideological loyalties at the United Nations, Moscow's chief ambition was to uproot the presence of a Western power in the region by ending the British Mandate for Palestine.[4]

ON MAY 15, 1947, THE UN GENERAL ASSEMBLY CONCLUDED THE SPECIAL SESSION by resolving that UNSCOP "shall have the widest powers to ascertain and record facts, and to investigate all questions and issues relevant to the problem of Palestine."[5] UNSCOP received no specific guidelines about the desired solution other than the caution that "most careful consideration" should be given to the religious interests of Islam, Judaism, and Christianity in Palestine. The committee's composition reflected the geopolitical balance in the organization: at least notionally, Australia and Canada were aligned with the British Commonwealth; Czechoslovakia and Yugoslavia represented Eastern Europe; the Netherlands and Sweden represented Western Europe; Guatemala, Peru, and Uruguay represented Latin America (the largest group in the UN, comprising twenty countries); while India and Iran represented the Asian bloc.

Eban noted that none of the delegates of these eleven countries was an expert on Palestine, nor was any known for a distinguished diplomatic career: "Not one of them had ever been involved in any decision as momentous as that in which he would now have to participate. . . . [None] of them had ever made any study of Jewish history or of the Palestine problem."[6] This much was evident when, while touring Palestine, one of the committee members wondered if he would get the chance to visit an Arab kibbutz. Other observers noted the committee's lack of professionalism; the district commissioner of Galilee reported to London that "the general impression created by the Committee was one of muddle and second-rateness," while the district commissioner of Lydda reported that, during the committee's visit to Jaffa, "after a bathe and lunch only the Chairman and one delegate left on time for the afternoon tour. The remainder were admonished by telephone at the direction of the Chairman and two more delegates caught up with the programme in time to leave Jaffa."[7]

Ralph Bunche, who served as assistant to UNSCOP, lamented that the committee's fifty-seven-member secretariat did not find it pertinent to appoint a cartographer: "This could prove to be an embarrassing omission, particularly if the Committee should direct its attention to partition schemes," Bunche warned Victor Hoo, the personal representative of UN Secretary-General Trygve Li. "It is my understanding that the Anglo-American Committee had three cartographers along and that at one time they were engaged in frenzied activity." To get around this difficulty Bunche asked that the Palestine government prepare a digest of all partition schemes—with maps.[8] In a letter to his wife Ruth, Bunche despaired of working with this motley crew: "I am disgusted with the people I have to work with—both Committee members and Secretariat—they are all so petty, so vain, so striving and not infrequently either vicious or stupid." Pointing to the personal qualities of each of the delegates, Bunche noted that the Indian delegate, Sir Abdur Rahman, had "more bark than bite; a likable old fellow"; the Canadian delegate, Supreme Court justice Ivan Rand, was "grumbling, neurotic, egocentric and garrulous . . . a one man sabotage team." Enrique Fabregat of Uruguay was a "Latin buffoon, without trying or knowing," while the Dutch delegate, Nicholas Blom, was a "tight-fisted, not bright Dutchman; rather a lightweight" who even managed to stumble and fall into the tomb of Nicodemus while on a visit to the Church of the Holy Sepulcher in Jerusalem. On the other hand, Alberto Ulloa, the Peruvian delegate, was "quiet, self-effacing, highly intelligent" and someone who "knows what he stands for," while the Iranian Nasrollah Entezam was described as "polished, not deep" but still someone who "has know-how; as a Muslim he is fair but very much on the spot." Valedo Simic of Yugoslavia was "quiet, dignified, good-humored, no temperament, very intelligent and earnest," while the Australian John Hood was described as someone who was "intelligent" but had "no force."[9]

The Jewish Agency appointed Eban and David Horowitz—the bearer of Moshe Shertok's fateful note to Eban from Latrun a year earlier and a future governor of the Bank of Israel—as liaison officers to UNSCOP. Horowitz was charged with addressing the economic viability of a future Jewish state, and Eban was tasked with presenting the political dimension.[10] The British appointed Donald MacGillvray, undersecretary to the Palestine government, who offered mainly technical assistance, while the Arab High Committee (AHC) in Palestine refused to cooperate with UNSCOP altogether. The AHC informed UNSCOP that the rights of Palestine's Arabs were self-evident and, rather than be subjected to investigation, deserved to be recognized on the basis of the United Nations Charter. "We live on the mistakes of the Arabs," Eban observed as the floor was left for the Jewish Agency to fervently lobby its case before members of the committee in New York, Jerusalem, and Geneva.[11]

The British proved to be just as obstinate as the Arabs; they insisted on appearing before UNSCOP in private and wanted to be informed in advance about who would be giving testimony—not least because some Jewish groups and individuals were wanted by the mandatory authorities. The British demand only added to wholly negative impression it left on the committee.[12] There were everyday accounts of the emergency regulations that had been put in place by the British; detentions, confiscations, and even deportations could be carried out without showing due cause. Some emergency regulations were retroactive, meaning that a person could be prosecuted in 1947 for an activity that had been legal the previous year. Defendants appeared before military rather than civil courts, with no right to counsel. One-tenth of the British Empire's armed forces now occupied Palestine, operating out of barbed-wired security zones nicknamed Bevingrads (after Foreign Secretary Ernest Bevin) by the Yishuv. "I had crossed half the world to find myself in the one truly police state remaining in the 20th century," Jorge García Granados of Guatemala observed with outrage.[13]

During UNSCOP's two-week tour of Palestine, Eban and Horowitz acted as incessant lobbyists in the guise of helpful tour guides. In the absence of an Arab liaison officer, the committee insisted that the tour of Palestine be balanced, so the two Jewish liaison officers escorted the group to holy places in Jerusalem, textile factories in Haifa, a kibbutz near the Dead Sea, and schools and hospitals in Hebron, Jaffa, and Tel Aviv as well as Jewish and Arab settlements in the Galilee and the Negev Desert. All the while the subtle persuading, appealing, and influencing went on in French, English, German, and Persian, thanks to Eban's linguistic skills. The Jewish Agency instructed Eban and Horowitz to win the support of the majority of the members of UNSCOP, and by Horowitz's own admission they did a pretty good job. On one occasion the Canadian delegate Ivan Rand "had listened to my explanations and recital for eleven hours, with short intervals, and had been able to grasp the full scope and significance of our position."[14]

Eban developed particularly close relationships with the representatives of Guatemala and Uruguay, who proved to be rather sympathetic to Zionism. García Granados of Guatemala naturally opposed the British, owing to his country's conflict with Britain over Belize, and was "prepared to believe the worst of Britain and the best of anybody seeking to remove British power from anywhere." The sympathy of Professor Rodriguez Fabregat of Uruguay was won over the suffering of Jewish children refugees in Europe's displaced persons camps. Eban and Horowitz also had inside information about the committee's deliberations and the personal views of each of its members—the result of an elaborate operation of the Haganah's intelligence service, Shai, to monitor the committee members and even bribe them with gifts and other indiscretions—much to the chagrin of the committee's chairman, Swedish judge Emil Sandström. Noting the special relationship developing between Eban and García Granados, he noted, "I don't know that he took their money, but he certainly took their girls." The Haganah also listened in on all phone conversations and replaced the cleaning staff at the YMCA building in Jerusalem, where the committee held its daily hearings, with female agents—a move that led another delegate to observe that the cleaning ladies were "too pretty and educated. They are the eyes and ears of the Zionist leaders, who come to hearings with replies prepared in advance." True enough, at the end of each day an intelligence report—codenamed Delphi and bearing the inscription "Read and Destroy!"—was put together and circulated among the Zionist leadership in the Yishuv. During the committee's visit to Jewish settlements in Palestine, the Jewish Agency also arranged for several members of UNSCOP to "serendipitously" meet their own compatriots, who did their best to praise the spirit of the Jewish settlers and convince the delegates about the feasibility and desirability of a Jewish state.[15]

In some cases the incessant Jewish lobbying had adverse effects. According to the district commissioner of Galilee, many members of the committee had grown tired of the Zionist campaign; they were "heartily sick of settlements, speeches, propaganda, lemonade and fruit. The Agency representatives soon began to realise that all was not well, and themselves suggested curtailing or cutting out further visits to Jewish settlements. In this they were too late as the interest of the delegates had flagged beyond revival." This prompted Walter Eytan to warn Eban, Horowitz, and Shertok that it "would be good tactics for us to take it upon ourselves to explain some of the Arab case or at least to show that we fully understand it and take it into account in our plans and proposals. There is a good deal of evidence to suggest that some Committee members are developing what Aubrey calls 'an underdog complex' about the Arabs and are subconsciously rushing to their aid."[16]

THE TASK OF FORMALLY PRESENTING THE CASE FOR PARTITION AND JEWISH STATEhood was given to Chaim Weizmann, now back at his residence in Rehovot, where he dedicated his time to the Sieff Institute of Science, which he had founded in 1934. Though Weizmann no longer held an official position within the Zionist movement after the showdown in Basel, he was still regarded internationally as the embodiment of Zionism itself. He was briefed by a dedicated team that included Eban, Walter Eytan, Mordechai Kidron (future director-general of the Israeli Foreign Ministry), Gershon Agronsky (founder of the *Palestine Post*), and Meyer Weisgal (Weizmann's personal assistant). Working from a room at the Eden Hotel in Jerusalem, Weizmann floated his ideas, Eban polished the phraseology, and the others checked the drafts. When the final draft was ready, Kidron rushed to the *Palestine Post* offices to have the text printed in a half-inch-tall font so the partially blind Weizmann could read it. At 4:00 a.m. on July 8, the day of Weizmann's testimony, the printed text was finally ready. After three hours of sleep the team headed to the YMCA building.[17] As Weizmann took his seat before the committee, he pushed the text in front of him off the table and began his testimony. Partition had two great advantages, he said: it was final, and it helped to dispel the fears of the Arabs over Zionist domination. It also meant equity in status between Jews and Arabs. Turning to the Indian delegate, Weizmann added that partition was "*À la mode.* It is not only in small Palestine; it is in big India. But at least there you have something to partition. Here we have to do it with a microscope. There you can do it with a big knife."[18]

Following his testimony Weizmann invited members of the committee to his private residence in Rehovot, where they held informal discussions over lunch. The delegates left Weizmann's residence with such admiration for his personal story and dedication to the Zionist cause that on the way back to Jerusalem, Sandström and Rand were heard murmuring, "well, that's really a great man."[19] At another meeting Weizmann suggested that it was naive to anticipate that Jews and Arabs would fall on each other's necks with affection once a binational state could be created. He then proceeded to suggest that "a reasonable partition would be something along the lines" of the Peel Report recommendation, together with the Negev and a small corridor, which would provide a solution that "would give the Jews a basis for working out their destiny in the next twenty years. At best this Jewish state would be a small state."[20]

Once the idea of partition was firmly on the table, David Ben-Gurion took the next step to help the UNSCOP members reach a decision in its support; during a meeting with the delegates at Shertok's home in Jerusalem, he took out a pencil and a large piece of paper and delineated a partition map with the potential borders of a future Jewish state. One of the Jewish Agency secretaries in the room anxiously approached him and whispered in his ear something about the resolution from the Biltmore Conference, but Ben-Gurion replied decisively, "Biltmore, shmiltmore, we must have a Jewish state."[21] It was this pragmatic attitude and steely determination that led the American journalist Ralph McGill, four years later, to describe Ben-Gurion, then prime minister of Israel, as

> a rough-and-tumble fighter, barring no holds and asking no quarter. He can gouge and butt in the clinches with any opponent who fights in that style. He has tenacity, courage, ability, vision and a bulldog capacity for holding on. He is a short, stocky man, with a bounce in his walk, a jaw which reminds one of John L. Lewis and Winston Churchill. He wears a wispy ring of white hair which some writers have called a hirsute halo, thin lips often compressed, and a cocky, self-confidence which some of his associates at times find irritating. People, seeing him for the first time, always look twice. He is probably the most eminent Jew of his generation.[22]

Weizmann's compelling testimony, Eban and Horowitz's incessant lobbying, and Ben-Gurion's pragmatism seemed to have left the desired impression on a burgeoning majority of the committee members. "Nobody can convince me that you and Jamal Husseini [vice president of the Arab High Committee] will salute the same flag. It's ridiculous!" one of the delegates told Eban, while Rand pointed out that although it was impossible to force the two peoples to live together without their consent, it was possible to force them to live separately. Nicholas Blom cited the ill-fated unification of the Netherlands with Belgium at the end of the Napoleonic Wars as a historical case against the forced unification of two communities.[23] The notion of complete political separation between Arabs and Jews was far from consensual, however, as the representatives of Iran, India, and Yugoslavia preferred a predominantly Arab federal state as a solution. But if opinions were divided over the nature of the political solution in Palestine, the committee was unanimous in its view that the British Mandate had to be terminated.

The depth of the moral bankruptcy of the Mandatory powers received maximum exposure on July 18 with the arrival of a ship carrying 4,500 Jewish refugees at Haifa Harbor, accompanied by several British destroyers. The SS *President Warfield* was a former Chesapeake Bay excursion steamer designed to carry no more than seven hundred passengers, and was later used as a troopship in the Allied landing at Normandy. The Haganah had bought the ship in November 1946, and after some outfitting in Baltimore to make it seaworthy, it left for the Mediterranean in March 1947, sailing under the Honduran flag. It arrived at the French harbor of Sète on July 9, where Jewish refugees from displaced persons camps in Germany were brought on board. As soon as the ship left the French port, it was escorted by six British destroyers and an additional cruiser, with a Royal Air Force plane circling overhead. The 330-foot, 1,814-ton river steamer was unlike other, smaller immigrant vessels, which carried only a few hundred people and aimed to avoid detection by approaching the Palestine shores in the dead of the night. Renamed Haganah Ship *Exodus 1947* and carrying the Zionist blue-and-white flag with the Star of David, it was a symbol of Jewish defiance, aimed at provoking the British by bursting through the blockade and showing to the world the callous treatment of Holocaust survivors by the Mandatory powers. "The ship must arrive in daylight, since the shores will be packed with crowds of Jews from Tel Aviv," read a crew member's diary that was seized by the British. "We will then try to escape the escort by going between two ships, to enter territorial waters and then: full speed ahead! We shall attempt to beach the boat on the shore. . . . Once we reach the shore our passengers will disperse in the crowd and it will be difficult to find them again."[24]

But the British were determined to make an example of the *Exodus 1947*. Even before the ship reached the territorial waters of Palestine, several British destroyers rammed it, and in the battle that ensued three passengers were killed and dozens more were injured. The crew finally surrendered after a British threat to sink the ship, and the damaged *Exodus* was towed to Haifa Harbor. All the while, Haganah radio broadcast the events to its headquarters in Tel Aviv, with one of its crew members, the Christian Zionist reverend John Grauel, urging members of UNSCOP to arrive at Haifa and witness the drama. Eban duly took Sandström, García Granados, Bunche, and Simic to the harbor, where they arrived just in time to see the battered and overcrowded ship escorted by the cruiser HMS *Ajax* and two destroyers. The British transferred the 4,500 Holocaust survivors, more than 2,000 of them women and children, into three prison ships where the refugees were locked in cages on the lower decks. The British refused to allow Eban to accompany the committee members onto the decks, but his commentary on the scene was unnecessary. Having spoken to the passengers and officers, the four delegates returned to Eban, pale and shocked. One member of the press who followed UNSCOP members in Palestine overheard Simic saying to Eban, "It is the best possible evidence we can have."[25] On their return to Jerusalem, Sandström, and Simic gave the other members of the committee an account of what they had seen in Haifa. The *Exodus* affair did not singly tilt the scale in favor of partition, but it certainly led to a backlash in public opinion against Britain and raised deeper sympathy for the Jewish demand for a homeland in Palestine. "I had a feeling that the British Mandate died that day," Eban recalled.[26]

Rather than deporting the immigrants to the detention camps in Cyprus, where they would await their turn to enter Palestine under the immigration quotas, Bevin ordered the three caged ships to sail to France. But the passengers refused to disembark, and the French authorities refused to force them to do so. On August 22 Bevin's disastrous attempt to make an example of the *Exodus* received its final blow when he ordered the ships to dock in Hamburg, Germany, which had been under British occupation since the end of the war. In full view of the press, the passengers put up a determined fight before they were sent to two refugee camps near Lubeck. The incredulous decision to keep thousands of Holocaust survivors at sea for more than a month, and then to plummeted Britain's reputation—and Bevin's public standing—to an unprecedented nadir.[27]

ON JULY 20, 1947, UNSCOP LEFT PALESTINE FOR BEIRUT, WHERE IT HEARD from Hamid Bay Frangie, the foreign minister of Lebanon, that the Arab states would not tolerate the creation of a Jewish state in Palestine: "The Jewish State which the Zionists are endeavoring to establish in Palestine is not moreover a viable State either from the political or from the economic point of view. . . . Against a State established by violence, the Arab States will be obliged to use violence; that is a legitimate right of self-defence." Other Arab representatives warned the committee that the economic boycott of Jewish goods, which had been in place since December 1945, would cripple the Jewish economy and "pull down [the] Zionist existence," as the Arab nation "[could not] keep patient over humiliation."[28]

Eban took a rather frivolous look at the Arab boycott, pointing to its own inherent absurdity. In an unpublished note, he facetiously offered his help to those Arabs wishing to enforce the boycott of Jewish goods:

> In my past articles, I feel I may have been a bit hard on the Arabs. So . . . in apology, I have compiled a list to help them with their boycott. Since it is imperative that all loyal Arabs avoid any and all contact with Jewish influences, the following must be adhered to religiously:
>
> An Arab who has syphilis must not be cured by salvarsan, because it was discovered by a Jew, Ehrlich. If an Arab suspects that he has gonorrhoea, he must not seek diagnosis, because he will be using the method of a Jew, Neissner. An Arab who has heart disease must not use digitalis, which comes from the Jew, Ludwig Traube.
>
> If he has diabetes, he must not use insulin, because of the research work of a Jew, Monkowsky. If he has a headache he must shun pyramidon and antipyrin because of the Jews, Spiro and Ellege.
>
> Arabs with convulsions must put up with them because it was a Jew, Oscar Leibereich, who thought of chloral hydrate.
>
> Arabs should be ready to die in greater number and not permit treatment by the method of Nobel Prize winner, Robert Baram, whose method of treatment of ear and brain damage has saved millions.
>
> Arabs of all ages must forgo the use of vitamins, because the discoverer of their special nutritional value was a Jew, Kasimir Funk. They should continue to die or be crippled by infantile paralysis because the discoverer of the anti-polio vaccine was a Jew,

> Jonas Salk. They must refuse to use streptomycin and continue to die of tuberculosis, because a Jew, Zalman Waxman, invented the wonder drug against this killing disease.
>
> In short, a good and loyal Arab may fittingly and properly remain afflicted with syphilis, gonorrhoea, heart disease, headaches, typhus, diabetes, mental disorders, brain damage, polio, undernourishment, convulsions, and tuberculosis!
>
> Amen![29]

After hearing evidence in Beirut, UNSCOP traveled to Geneva, where Bunche hoped that "the Committee's genius will reveal itself" as it turned to write its report to the UN General Assembly. Eban, Horowitz, and MacGillvray accepted Sandström's invitation to join UNSCOP in Geneva. En route to Geneva Eban stopped in London to assess British official and public opinion with regard to UNSCOP and the Palestine question in general. In his meetings with the London press he heard that foreign secretary Bevin was "rabid" on the matter of Palestine, "so much so that at the moment he would sooner bring British troops out of Germany than out of Palestine," while public officials told Eban that the Foreign Office's official policy in Palestine was being deliberately provocative and that Bevin's "obsession on this matter" was not shared by other cabinet ministers.[30] One of Eban's most instructive meetings was with Richard Crossman, who had represented Britain on the Anglo-American Committee the previous year. Reporting back to the Jewish Agency on his visit to London, Eban described Crossman's assessment of Bevin's current thinking on Palestine in the most lurid terms:

> Crossman described Bevin's outlook as corresponding roughly with the "Protocols of the Elders of Zion." The main points of Mr. Bevin's discourses were: (a) the Jews had organized a world-wide conspiracy against Britain and Mr. Bevin. When Crossman suggested that Mr. Bevin's Palestine policy was isolating Britain from the world public opinion, Mr. Bevin replied, "that proved my point exactly. They have successfully organised world opinion against me." (b) The whole Jewish pressure was a gigantic racket run from America. When Crossman pointed out that the Irish Republic had also been a racket run from America, but that Britain had been forced to concede a State, Bevin replied "Yes, but they did not steal

> half the place first." (c) In a reference presumably to the latest Irgun outrage, Mr. Bevin said that he would not be surprised if the Germans had learned their worst atrocities from Jews.
>
> From this tirade, Mr. Crossman drew the moderate deduction that Mr. Bevin was insane on this issue.[31]

The termination of the British Mandate and the creation of a Jewish state required not only an unequivocally positive report from UNSCOP, but it would then have to be endorsed by a two-thirds majority of the UN General Assembly. Anything less from UNSCOP would positively end all endeavors on the part of the international community to give serious consideration to the Jewish case. The diligent Zionist lobbying thus continued with even greater intensity. From the outset of its mission, UNSCOP was notionally divided into three groups—the pro-Arabs (representatives of Iran and India), the pro-Zionists (delegates of Czechoslovakia, Guatemala, Peru, and Uruguay), and the neutrals (British Commonwealth and European delegates). But these generic camps did not disclose the delegates' preferences for partition, a binational state, a trusteeship, or any other solution. As García Granados pointed out, it was only upon arrival in Geneva that the delegates finally showed their hands. In Palestine they had discussed almost exclusively questions of procedure, and as representatives of sovereign countries they were cautious about revealing their positions on the substance of the Palestine problem. "We were not so much a committee of eleven men as eleven committees of one man each," García Granados noted.[32]

The "neutral" group of the Commonwealth and European countries became the main target of Zionist persuasion. Eban and Horowitz met with Sandström, who reassured them that he viewed the Arab demands as "no more than a form of Oriental haggling" and expressed his regret that he could not help in the case of the *Exodus 1947*. The Canadian, Rand, emphasized his admiration of the Jewish settlers' dedication and hard work, but the other delegates were less forthcoming and refused to reveal their inner deliberations. Eban and Horowitz also met with Bunche, who again complained about the "absence of outstanding personalities in the Committee," which placed a heavy burden on the UN secretariat and principally on himself. The chief aim of the committee, Bunche told the liaison officers, was that there should never be another Palestine commission. It was thus imperative that they concentrated on the practicalities of the solution rather than merely on its conceptual allure. But,

Bunche added, the committee had not had a single substantive discussion on the solution yet. Yugoslav delegate Simic also told Eban and Shertok that "there was a great deal yet to think about."[33]

The eleven delegates could only agree on one point: the British Mandate must end. Everything else was a matter of dissensus. Bunche, who found the hot weather and general boredom in Geneva unbearable, had serious doubts about UNSCOP's ability to reach a coherent decision, commenting that "the mental strain is the heaviest I have ever experienced. This Palestine problem is so complicated and serious that many of us walk about in a continuous state of frustration. . . . The Secretariat must show more initiative, or this will be a fiasco. . . . [The chairman Sandström] lets the Committee wander in circles and never ties anything up."[34] On August 27, after a month of deliberations and only four days before the deadline UNSCOP had been given by the General Assembly to produce its report, Sandström observed worryingly that there were too many proposals on the table and that "the upshot would be a disjointed, incoherent, and from the point of view of the assembly, largely unintelligible report."[35] The nature of deliberations resembled more political horse trading than an informed discussion dictated by law, morality, or abstract rights. All the while, Eban and Horowitz did their best to persuade the vacillating delegates and ensure that some kind of recommendation would emerge rather than no recommendation at all, which meant the return of the mandate to Britain. With the deadline looming, the delegates were still engaged in quid pro quo negotiations, as the following passage from the memoirs of García Granados reveals:

> I think Mr. Rand's proposal for boundaries and his conciliatory attitude in the matter of Jerusalem is a good one, and I am in complete agreement with him. I subscribe to the idea. . . . Fabregat wanted the Jewish State to include the whole of the Galilee, the Negev west of Beersheba, and a large indentation connecting the coastal plan with Jerusalem. . . . Rand thought Jerusalem and its environs should be an international city, part neither of the Jewish nor the Arab State. My position was the same as Rand's, but I did not agree to his idea of a free city of Jerusalem, keeping that as a future bargaining asset. . . . I spoke first to [Arturo] García Salazar, and offered to drop my opposition to a free city of Jerusalem if he would support my proposal to extend the Jewish State's coastal

strip to the Lebanese border, and then have it run parallel to the Lebanese border until it joined Eastern Galilee.[36]

UNSCOP finally submitted its report to the General Assembly on August 31. Unsurprisingly, the committee recommended unanimously that the Palestine Mandate should "be terminated at the earliest practicable date," citing the fact that Arabs, Jews, and the mandatory powers were in agreement about the need for a change in the status of Palestine. The report also unanimously recommended, "Independence shall be granted in Palestine at the earliest practicable date," but it was followed by two different plans to achieve it: partition and federation. The majority report, supported by seven members (Canada, Czechoslovakia, Guatemala, the Netherlands, Peru, Sweden, and Uruguay), supported partition based on the basic premise that the valid claims of the 625,000 Jews and 1.2 million Arabs in Palestine were irreconcilable and that among all the solutions proposed, partition was the most practical and realistic as to afford both communities the chance to pursue their national aspirations.

The seven members recommended dividing Palestine into three areas: an Arab state, a Jewish state, and the city of Jerusalem, which would be placed under international trusteeship given its religious and historical significance to Christians, Jews, and Muslims. The majority report noted that Jewish immigration was "the central issue in Palestine to-day and is the one factor, above all others, that rules out the necessary co-operation between the Arab and Jewish communities in a single State. The creation of a Jewish State under a partition scheme is the only hope of removing this issue from the arena of conflict."[37] The proposed Jewish state comprised 56 percent of the total area of Palestine, which had a 61 percent Jewish majority, while the Arab state was allocated 42 percent of Palestine. The total population of the Jewish state would be 905,000, which included 498,000 Jews and 407,000 Arabs. The Arab state's population of 735,000 included only 10,000 Jews. The city of Jerusalem, with a population of just over 205,000, had an almost equal distribution of Arabs and Jews.[38]

The minority report, written by the representatives of India, Iran, and Yugoslavia, recommended a federal state solution on the grounds that Jewish nationalism ought to be superseded by the well-being of the country and its people as a whole. With regards to partition, it concluded that, both in principle and in substance, it could only be regarded as an anti-Arab solution, whereas the federal state solution could not be regarded as anti-Jewish. The report rejected the Jewish demand for unrestricted immigration into Palestine, noting that "no basis could exist for any anticipation that the Jews now in Palestine might increase their numbers by means of free mass immigration to such an extent that they would become the majority population in Palestine."[39] Hood, the Australian representative, abstained; in the absence of a "decisive majority" for either of the proposals, he suggested that it should be the task of the General Assembly, rather than the committee, to decide on the future of Palestine. Both reports and the unanimous recommendations were drafted by Ralph Bunche, who worked on them without a break for twelve hours, until the morning of August 28, 1947. He then packed and left Geneva, "totally disgusted" by the incompetence of his colleagues. "I'm not at all satisfied with my scheme [the partition plan]. But this is the sort of problem for which no really satisfactory solution is possible," he wrote to his wife.[40]

At midnight on August 31 the eleven members of the committee emerged out of their chamber at the Palais des Nations and handed the anxious liaison officers copies of the report. "To say the Jews are pleased with the report is an understatement, they are elated," the American consul general in Jerusalem reported to U.S. secretary of state George Marshall.[41] Returning to their room at the Hotel d'Angleterre, Eban, Horowitz, Shertok, Gideon Rafael, and other Jewish Agency officials celebrated with a bottle of champagne. The following day Eban and Horowitz traveled to Zurich to deliver the news to Ben-Gurion, who was there for a meeting of the Zionist Actions Committee. They found him sitting behind an empty desk, preoccupied with the problem of curbing the Irgun in Palestine. "We have come to tell you that UNSCOP has recommended a Jewish state," they said excitedly. "And they have included the Negev," Eban added, still failing to secure Ben-Gurion's attention. In total despair the two turned to leave the room when Ben-Gurion suddenly came rushing after them: "What was that you said? They recommended a Jewish state in the Negev? Why didn't you tell me that before?"[42]

THE ZIONIST JUBILATION DID NOT LAST LONG, AS THE REAL BATTLE FOR STATEhood still had to be fought and won. Attention now turned to the General Assembly deliberations in Flushing Meadows, New York. Eban and Horowitz first stopped in London, where they met with Azzam Pasha, the secretary-general of the Arab League, to see whether a compromise with the Arabs was still possible. Pasha's message was ominous: "The Arab world is not in a compromising mood. The fate of nations is not decided by rational logic. Nations never concede; they fight. You won't get anything by peaceful means or compromise. You can, perhaps, get something, but only by the force of arms. We shall try to defeat you. I'm not sure we'll succeed, but we'll try. It may be that we shall lose Palestine. But it's too late to talk of peaceful solutions." Eban assured Pasha that the UNSCOP report left room for satisfactory compromise and that the Jewish Agency would welcome counterproposals from the Arabs, but Pasha was adamant: "An agreement will only be acceptable at our terms. The Arab world regards you as invaders and is ready to fight you. The conflict of interests among nations is, for the most part, not amenable to any settlement except armed clash. . . . You have no alternative. At all events, the problem now is only soluble by the force of arms."[43] The two liaison officers left London with the grim realization that a successful outcome at the UN General Assembly—which at that stage was by no means guaranteed—would be followed by certain bloodshed in Palestine.

On September 25 the UNSCOP report was tabled for discussion by the UN Ad Hoc Committee on the Palestine Question, which included representatives of all UN member states. Its recommendations then had to be forwarded to the General Assembly, where a two-thirds majority would be required to sanction a resolution on Palestine. Lobbying for support among fifty-six representatives in New York was infinitely more difficult than coaxing and cajoling UNSCOP's eleven delegates in Palestine. The Jewish Agency had its headquarters on East Sixty-Sixth Street in Manhattan, and Shertok assigned specific tasks to each official there. "It was a very exciting period," recalled Gideon Rafael. "We were on the go day and night. . . . There was also an operational division of assignments: 'You work on these delegations,' 'You on those.' We discussed the weak points and where we had to mobilize influence in various capitals."[44] Eban was given the task of liaising with the four Scandinavian countries, the three Benelux countries, and France. On November 25 the Ad Hoc Committee recommended partition to the General Assembly. The vote was twenty-five in favor and thirteen against, with seventeen abstentions. This simple majority was enough at the Ad Hoc Committee, but it was one vote less than the crucial two-thirds majority that would be needed at the General Assembly to pass the partition resolution. Critically for Eban, four of the countries under his watch—Belgium, France, Luxemburg, and the Netherlands—chose to abstain.[45]

The vote at the General Assembly was set to take place on Wednesday,

November 26, 1947, amid intense lobbying by the Arabs and Jews. A Jewish Agency survey of the likely voting behavior of UN delegates revealed that it was a couple of votes short of the required two-thirds majority. The agency desperately needed extra time to persuade the representatives of Haiti, Liberia, and the Philippines, among others, to change their position in favor of the UN resolution on partition. The Zionists were rescued by a number of friendly states who instructed their representatives to filibuster for as long as they could. The president of the General Assembly, Brazil's Oswaldo Aranha, who was a good friend of the Zionists, also helped by bringing the session to a close and postponing the crucial vote by two days, to allow for the celebration of Thanksgiving. The French also lent the Zionists a hand by asking for another day's delay, ostensibly to allow the Jews and Arabs a last-ditch effort to reach a compromise—though in reality the French were struggling to reconcile their interests in the Levant and the wish to avoid an Arab backlash in North Africa with the temptation to humiliate the British and the strong affinity toward Zionism inside the French Socialist Party. According to Rafael, "lobbying during the three-day break reached frantic heights with the realization that a single vote could be decisive. It was not a pretty sight." Horowitz recalled that that "the telephones rang madly. Cablegrams sped to all parts of the world. People were dragged from their beds at midnight and sent on peculiar errands. And, wonder of it all, not an influential Jew, Zionist or non-Zionist refused to give us his assistance at any time. Everyone pulled his weight, little or great, in the despairing effort to balance the scales to our favor."[46] The Zionists prudently rejected an offer by Jewish mobsters in New York to kidnap anti-partition delegates and keep them until after the vote had been taken, but they did decide to bug a limousine that was used by the British delegation. The British seemed to be perturbed by the eloquent deliveries of Zionist officials: "Who is that bloke? Where did he learn to speak the King's English?" one of the passengers asked about Eban's provenance. "He's a bloody don from Cambridge," another replied.[47]

Fortunately for the Zionists, they could count on the support of the two superpowers. By mid-October, Washington and Moscow announced their support for partition, albeit for different reasons: the Soviets wished to humiliate the Western powers by uprooting the British foothold in the Middle East, while U.S. president Harry Truman was moved by the fate of Europe's displaced Jews, though domestic politics also played a part in his calculations, as he pointed out to a group of American diplomats after the war: "I'm sorry, gentlemen, but I have to answer to hundreds of thousands who are anxious for the success of Zionism: I do not have hundreds of thousands of Arabs among my constituents."[48] Truman overruled the U.S. State Department's concerns over American interests in the Middle East, but despite his support for partition he nevertheless found the incessant lobbying in the period leading up to the vote intolerable. "The facts were that not only were there pressure movements around the United Nations unlike anything that had been seen there before, but that the White House, too, was subjected to a constant barrage," Truman later wrote. "I do not think I ever had as much pressure and propaganda aimed at the White House as I had in this instance. The persistence of a few of the extreme Zionist leaders—actuated by political motives and engaging in political threats—disturbed me and annoyed me. Some were even suggesting that we pressure sovereign nations into favorable votes in the General Assembly."[49]

According to the British, the Arabs were "thoroughly depressed" by the developments at UN headquarters in Lake Success, New York, and were "beginning to feel that they may fail in the purely negative aim they have set themselves here of playing out time." Like the Zionists, they turned their efforts to lobbying, persuading, and intimidating the various delegations to the United Nations. As early as July the Arab League appointed a special committee in New York with a budget of $100,000 with the aim of forcing "discussion of Palestine independence irrespective of the proposals of the United Nations Committee." They persuaded the Greeks to change their vote in return for future support from Muslim states in the General Assembly. The Arabs also succeeded in persuading Chile to change its vote, but were told by the Costa Rican delegate that he would not sell his vote or sacrifice his honor. In Canada, the Canadian Arab Friendship League presented the government with an ultimatum of friendship or war between the Canadian and Arab peoples. Less conspicuous attempts at changing voting behavior took place in New York, where the female delegate of a "small country" was sufficiently charmed by the diligent courting of a Syrian diplomat that she promised to vote against partition. But the Zionists, who bugged the delegate's hotel room, informed her government of her mischief and she was duly replaced by a male delegate.[50]

At 4:00 p.m. on Saturday, November 29, the waiting was finally over. Oswaldo Aranha, the president of the General Assembly, instructed the fifty-six representatives, "Those who are in favor will say 'Yes.' Those who are against will say 'No.' And the abstainers always know what to say." Undersecretary-general Andrew Cordier proceeded to read the roll call, which was interrupted by loud cheers from the gallery when the French delegate blurted out "Yes." At the end of the voting and after a brief examination of the tally sheet, Aranha declared, "The resolution of the Ad Hoc Committee for Palestine was adopted by 33 votes, 13 against and 10 abstained." Britain chose to abstain, while all eleven Muslim countries voted against partition, as did Cuba and Greece. But, more important, seven of the seventeen countries that had abstained at the Ad Hoc Committee on November 25 now voted for partition—including the four countries under Eban's watch. The two-thirds majority was secured, and members of the Jewish delegation embraced one another as wild applause and cheers broke out from the public gallery. Driving back to Manhattan after the vote, Aubrey, Suzy, and Moshe Shertok sat in the car in complete silence, visibly overwhelmed by what they had just witnessed. The historic achievement at the General Assembly was almost too powerful to comprehend.[51]

VII

L'Homme du Jour

THE JEWISH JUBILATION OVER PARTITION LASTED LESS THAN TWENTY-FOUR hours. Amid the general euphoria that engulfed the crowds in New York after the passing of UN Resolution 181, Eban was under no illusion that the Jews of Palestine wouldn't have to fight to have their state; the resolution was merely "a scrap of paper unless it was confirmed by sacrifice and toil."[1] On November 30, 1947, five Jews were killed in an Arab attack on a bus near Petach Tikva. Sporadic acts of Arab aggression and Jewish retribution continued, with little effort on the part of the British to prevent the escalating violence. The year ended with an attack on Jewish oil workers at a Haifa refinery; hundreds of Arabs descended on the refinery after the Irgun had hurled two barrel bombs from a speeding car into a group of Arab workers. Troops of the Third Hussars failed to stop the fighting, which left forty-one Jews dead and seven injured, and six Arabs dead and forty-two wounded. The new year saw no abating of the bloodshed. In February, three trucks loaded with dynamite blew up in the crowded Ben Yehuda Street in Jerusalem, leaving 52 Jews dead and more than 120 injured, bringing the number of Jewish deaths since the partition resolution to 969.[2] Robert Macatee, the U.S. consul general in Jerusalem, reported to Washington, DC, that "terror is prevalent and normal life (i.e., normal for Palestine) is disappearing. This phase may continue until the withdrawal of the British is more imminent and until the Arabs have made more definite plans to give effect to their determination to prevent partition."[3]

During this first wave of violence, which lasted until March 1948, the Haganah concentrated its efforts on defending the Yishuv from Arab attacks and maintaining contact with settlements in northern and southern Palestine that were cut off from the center of the country. Assisted by volunteers of the Arab Liberation Army, which came from Syria, the Arabs of Palestine succeeded in blockading the 100,000 Jews of Jerusalem and sabotaging many roads in the Galilee and the Negev Desert. Aid convoys to besieged settlements were routinely ambushed and attacked, resulting in the death of dozens in places such as Kfar Etzion, Hulda, Mount Scopes, and Nebi Daniel. Colonel Roscher Lund of Norway reported on the chaos in April 1948:

> At the present stage the British troops and police have completely abandoned certain areas such as the Jewish and Arab parts of Jerusalem and cities such as Jaffa and Tel Aviv.
>
> Most probable result of an open civil war is that if in the first period no interference from outside troops (Arab Legion, etc.) will take place the situation will, after heavy losses on both sides, end in a stalemate, but if troops of the Arab countries, to any extent worth mentioning, appear in the first stages of the fighting, the Jews may be practically exterminated in Palestine as they have been in many areas of Europe in the last ten years.[4]

The wave of sporadic violence was not confined to Palestine. In Aden, 82 Jews were murdered by a mob and 220 Jewish homes were burned, while in the Syrian city of Aleppo dozens of Jews were murdered and Jewish properties were destroyed. The powers that supported partition were also targeted: a "well organized Syrian mob of about 2,000" first stoned and then broke into the American diplomatic mission, setting fire to three cars, and the American legation in Baghdad was attacked as well. The office of the Russian-Syrian Cultural Society was broken into and looted, while the French legation was stoned and its French flag torn down. The British legation was left untouched, however. In Cairo, King Farouk informed the American ambassador that Egypt, in accord with the other Arab states, intended to resist by force of arms the partition of Palestine, and that he had already dispatched two of his best divisions to El Arish. He promised that the Arab countries would not make a military move until after British forces had left Palestine so as not to create further difficulties for Britain. From Jerusalem, Macatee reported to Washington that in Palestine, too, all signs indicated that the Arabs were preparing for war as soon as the British left the country, just as King Farouk had promised:

> The women of the country are preparing bandages and material for the welfare of the troops. Young men are being recruited and sent to neighboring states to be trained for military service. There is an active market here for all kinds of arms and ammunition. Frequent thefts are made of guns and equipment from the British military. Constant information shows that the Palestine Arabs are relying for considerable assistance, especially in arms, food and training of young men, on the surrounding Arab countries . . . there is a general feeling here that the Arabs will fight.[5]

The chaos in Palestine was mirrored by a diplomatic struggle in New York. In December 1947 the UN Security Council—where, unlike in the General Assembly, Britain held more power as a permanent member with the right to veto—had discussed the issue of Palestine for the first time. Moshe Shertok asked Eban to stay in New York to hold down the fort, while Shertok and David Horowitz returned to London and Palestine, respectively. Eban was permitted to attend the Security Council's open meetings as an observer, but he lacked the diplomatic credentials to make any statements himself. The Jewish Agency's diplomatic battle in New York no longer revolved around foiling the expected Arab initiative to reverse the General Assembly's partition resolution and was now directed at preventing the United States from joining the anti-partition camp. The rise of violence in Palestine and the increasingly belligerent messages emanating from Arab capitals led many in the U.S. State Department to doubt the ability of a nascent Jewish state to survive the combined invasion of several Arab armies. There were additional concerns among the Washington bureaucracy that a Jewish state could be turned into a communist base in the Middle East, compounded by the ubiquitous fears over the continued supply of Arab oil from the region in the event of war.

Meanwhile, the British had given up on quashing the violence in Palestine altogether; as Colonial Secretary Creech Jones explained, "Let no one imagine that the situation is other than grim. . . . Since the General Assembly's decision we have suffered further heavy loss of life and we cannot prolong our commitments in so thankless a task. . . . It is the turn of others now to take up the active part."[6] Faced with these ominous signs at Lake Success, New York, Eban felt it was imperative to defend the partition plan before the Security Council or at the very least the United States. He cabled Chaim Weizmann in London, pleading with him to change his plans to go to Palestine and travel instead to New York and Washington, where "[the most] crucial phase of all now approaches. . . . We surely miss your presence advice activity influence [*sic*]." Weizmann was reluctant to accept Eban's invitation due to ill health and his rancorous relations with the Jewish Agency ("We have just left New York, and the idiots want us to go back!" Weizmann told his wife), but he succumbed to the pressure of his close advisers and arrived in New York in early February 1948.[7] Over dinner at the Waldorf Astoria Hotel, Weizmann scolded his junior associate: "Why in heaven did you drag me to this frozen waste when I might have been in Rehovot?" Eban explained that the situation was so bad that President Harry Truman refused to meet with Zionist leaders, and that only Weizmann could persuade the president to stay on course. But Eban seriously underestimated the problem. As the president told Eddie Jacobson, his old army pal and business associate from Kansas City, who also happened to be a Jew, he was so irritated by the Zionist lobbying that he refused to meet with Weizmann:

> There wasn't anything he could say to me that I didn't already know, anyway. I had also made it a policy not to talk with anyone regarding the Palestine situation. . . . The situation has been a headache to me for two and a half years. The Jews are so emotional, and the Arabs are so difficult to talk with that it is almost impossible to get anything done. The British, of course, have been exceedingly noncooperative in arriving at a conclusion. The Zionists, of course, have expected a big stick approach on our part, and naturally have been disappointed when we can't do that.
>
> I hope it will all work out all right, but I have about come to the conclusion that the situation is not solvable as presently set up.[8]

Though not a Zionist, Jacobson was troubled by the suffering of his people and accepted an appeal from Frank Goldman, president of the American Jewish organization B'nai B'rith, to use his friendship with the president to arrange a meeting with Weizmann. Jacobson recalled that as soon as he mentioned the subject to Truman, the president "immediately became tense in appearance, abrupt in speech, and very bitter in the words he was throwing my way. In all the years of our friendship, he never talked to me in this manner or in any way even approaching it." Jacobson's saving grace was a sculptured model of President Andrew Jackson that adorned the Oval Office. He convinced Truman about the many similarities between their respective heroes—the seventh American president and the ailing Zionist leader—and made an emotional appeal to the president that he meet with his hero, "the greatest Jew who ever lived . . . he is a very sick man, almost broken in health, but he travelled thousands and thousands of miles just to see you and plead the cause of my people." Truman turned away from Jacobson and sank in his swivel chair, gazing out at the Rose Garden. After some moments of silence, he got up to face his friend with the endearing words, "You win, you baldhead son-of-a-bitch. I will see him." Eban was relieved to hear that Weizmann had not crossed the Atlantic in vain, even though he acknowledged that the premise of the Weizmann-Truman meeting rested on shaky ground: "My own view as a student of history is and was that no two human beings who ever walked on earth had fewer common attributes than Andrew Jackson and Chaim Weizmann, but since the establishment of a Jewish state was of higher interest for me than historical accuracy, I was prepared to join the preposterous Jackson-Weizmann analogy for the forty-eight hours necessary for the crucial visit to take place. I told Jacobson that if anyone met Weizmann and Andrew Jackson together, he would find it hard to tell them apart."[9]

On March 18 Weizmann arrived in Washington. On Truman's instructions he entered the White House through the East Gate rather than the front entrance to avoid any detection by the press. Even though this was not their first meeting, the president struggled to pronounce Weizmann's first name properly, which the Zionist leader did not seem to mind very much. After forty-five minutes, during which Truman explained with his usual frankness his decision not to meet with Weizmann the previous month, he promised to work for the establishment of a Jewish state that would include the Negev. Truman concluded the meeting with a heartfelt farewell to Weizmann and Jacobson: "All right, you two Jews had pulled it over on me, and I'm glad you have, and I like you both."[10]

The following day both Truman and Weizmann were astounded to hear that under the instructions of Secretary of State George Marshall, Ambassador Warren Austin declared before the UN Security Council that the U.S. government had decided to shift its position from support of partition to a temporary UN trusteeship in Palestine, under a joint British-American leadership. "How could this have happened?" Truman wanted to know. "I assured Chaim Weizmann that we were for partition and would stick to it. He must think I am a plain liar." But Weizmann remained sanguine about the president's will and ability to deliver on his promise. The notion that the General Assembly would reverse its own resolution on partition in response to the threat of violence in Palestine was unpalatable not only to the Jewish Agency but to many members of the United Nations, including the Soviets, who bitterly resisted the American attempt to fill the vacuum left by the British with another international regime in Palestine led by the Western powers.[11]

Eban played his part in the diplomatic efforts to kill off the idea of trusteeship. In his autobiography he proudly recalled that "most people's lives have their turning point, and this was mine." Though he had been in New York for nearly a year, he remained an unknown figure among the diplomatic community. Weizmann, Shertok, and Abba Hillel Silver were the primary expounders of Zionist aspirations on the world stage, and Shertok's early efforts to expose his junior associate to the scene were met by some resistance. On one such occasion came the response, "We know that [Shertok] speaks English quite fluently. How do we know that this Eban knows the language at all?"[12]

Any such doubts about Eban's abilities were consigned to history on May 1, 1948. The previous night he had been drafting an anti-trusteeship address for Shertok, to be delivered before the General Assembly, when the phone suddenly rang. Shertok was on the line. Since you've written the speech, he told Eban, why won't you deliver it too? Shertok's magnanimous gesture reflected the high esteem in which he'd held Eban since mentoring him in the summer of 1937 at the Zionist offices in London; it also followed the unspoken Zionist tradition whereupon public speakers usually wrote their own speeches. Eban's drafting of Weizmann's speeches was the exception given Weizmann's stature and poor health. But Shertok had always written his own speeches, and as he explained to Eban over the phone, ghostwriting was not an established Zionist vocation. Still, Eban was convinced that very few Zionist leaders, if any, were capable of such generosity. Exhilarated and moved by this unexpected opportunity, he spent the remainder of the night polishing the speech, and then submitted it to Shertok for approval.

The next morning Eban took his seat as the representative of the Jewish Agency for Palestine at the General Assembly, waiting to be called to address the representatives of fifty-seven countries. Less than two years earlier Eban had been teaching Arabic in Jerusalem, and now, at the age of thirty-three and with practically no diplomatic experience, he was making his first presentation before the highest international tribunal. "All I remember is looking around the table and feeling much younger than anybody else in sight," he later recalled. At thirty-eight, Andrei Gromyko was, aside from Eban, the youngest representative at the assembly. Warren Austin was seventy; Britain's Alexander Cadogan was sixty-three. "I also recall the curiosity of many delegates when I finally took the floor," remembered Eban. "I was a stranger to them. . . . I knew that I wanted intensely to succeed." In his address, Eban challenged the trusteeship proposal as impractical and immoral, as not only could it not stop the de facto partition of Palestine into two communities as soon as the British left on May 15, but the proposed reversal of UN Resolution 181 also challenged the moral basis of the organization itself. As soon as Eban finished his speech, Shertok left the hall to send a congratulatory, if shorthand, telegram to Eban's family in London: "Happy be able congratulate on Aubrey's striking speech in appearing as official spokesman Jewish people in international council. His extraordinary brilliance in thought and expression powerful cogency of reasoning dignity of presentation did outstanding credit to our cause . . . many characterizing it as one of the highest watermarks of entire session."[13] One foreign delegate remarked after Eban's maiden address that "what he sold was made in Israel, even though the wrapping might be from Cambridge."[14] That evening Eban and Shertok were invited to a dinner reception at Trygve Lie's residence in Forest Hills, Long Island. Eban was greeted by a beaming Gromyko, who warmly congratulated him on his maiden address and exclaimed, "Good! Good! You have killed trusteeship!"[15]

As the crucial date of May 15 approached, the Jewish Agency came under intense pressure from the U.S. State Department to postpone a declaration of independence, or at least accept a truce, in order to avoid a full-on war in the Middle East. The issue came to a head at a tense meeting between Secretary Marshall and Shertok on May 8 in Washington. "Don't rely on your military advisers. They have just scored some success," Marshall cautioned Shertok. "What will happen if there is a prolonged invasion? It will weaken you. . . . However, if it turns out that you're right and you will establish the Jewish State, I'll be happy. But you are undertaking a grave responsibility."[16] U.S. intelligence also feared that the new Jewish state might not make a natural ally to the Western bloc. The Central Intelligence Agency (CIA) estimated that any general war before 1953 was likely to result from Soviet aggression, which would translate into major offensive operations in Europe and the Near East.

Assessing the likely political alignments in such scenario, the CIA placed Israel in the "probable neutral" camp, together with countries such as Sweden, Yemen, Afghanistan, Pakistan, and India.[17]

At 4:00 p.m. on Friday, May 14 (10:00 a.m. in New York), David Ben-Gurion proclaimed the establishment of the State of Israel. He cited the Jewish people's natural and historical right over the land, as well as the UN General Assembly's partition resolution, as the moral and legal foundations of the new state. But there were still eight hours left until midnight, when the British Mandate would officially expire. In New York, Eban's task for the ensuing hours was to prevent any last-minute Arab maneuvers to delay the inevitable. He went around and urged several delegates to filibuster in order to kill off any chance of the trusteeship idea tresurfacing on the agenda. Ambassador Enrique Fabregat of Uruguay, who had served on the UN Special Committee on Palestine (UNSCOP) the previous year, was more than happy to indulge Eban's request that he make a one-hour speech; "for me one hour is not a short speech, it is simply a few words," Eban was told by the veteran diplomat, who could always be relied upon to give free rein to his tongue.[18] At 6:00 p.m. the Iraqi representative stood up and declared that the game was up; the British Mandate had officially ended and the partition of Palestine became a reality. Eleven minutes later President Truman sent a telegram to Eliahu Elath, the Jewish Agency's representative in Washington: "The United States recognizes the de facto authority of the new State of Israel." When Philip Jessup, the U.S. delegate to the UN, read Truman's proclamation to the assembly, an atmosphere of chaos and surprise descended on the delegates.[19] At the end of that eventful day at the General Assembly, Eban—physically exhausted and emotionally drained—paid a visit to Weizmann at his hotel suite, and then took Suzy out to dinner. Two days later, the provisional government of the new state announced that Weizmann had been elected the first president of Israel.

On May 20, Shertok—Israel's new foreign minister—informed Eban that he had been appointed the government's representative to the United Nations. Eban was now in charge of the country's most important diplomatic delegation, which operated out of a five-story brownstone at 16 East Sixty-Sixth Street in Manhattan. Arthur Lourie, whose job Eban was asked to fill temporarily in the summer of 1937, was appointed consul general.[20] Eban's most pressing task at that period was to fight for the diplomatic survival of the infant state, first by defending its actions before the UN's General Assembly and Security Council, and then by proposing Israel for admission to the UN as a full member. The two tasks were interconnected, and as Eban pointed out, a full Israeli admission to the UN was not a foregone conclusion: even long-established states such as Italy, Romania, Bulgaria, Ireland, and Austria were not yet members of the organization. Even some Jewish leaders, including Nahum Goldman, chairman of the World Zionist Congress, questioned Shertok and Eban's eagerness to accomplish this, and the right-wing Herut Party opposed the idea to avoid the indignity of failure.[21] For Israel, however, membership was a vital matter at a time when it was fighting for its very survival. It was essential to eliminate from the Arab mind the idea that Israel was a transitory or an unlawful entity, and membership in the United Nations provided that much-needed certificate of legitimacy.

Ben-Gurion's declaration of independence was followed by another, though slightly more prosaic, announcement. Since the early days of the Yishuv in Palestine, there had been a significant movement to Hebraize the names of the Jewish immigrants in order to form a collective modern Jewish identity to replace the diasporic symbols of the old, passive and prosecuted generation. Now that a Hebraic state had been born, this sentiment was given even greater impetus. Ben-Gurion (who himself Hebraized his surname from Green back in 1910) maintained that the State of Israel could not be led and represented by individuals who carried "foreign" names. The officers of the Israel Defense Forces, as well as the government's ministers, diplomats, and other senior officials, were duly ordered to change their names accordingly. Moshe Shertok was now Moshe Sharett, Golda Meirson became Golda Meir, and one morning Aubrey Eban discovered—apparently unbeknownst to him while he was in New York—that his name had been changed to Abba Even (literally, "father" and "stone," respectively).[22] But while his diplomatic passport carried his new Hebraized name, to the world he remained known as Eban, and until his death in 2002, none of those who were close to him had ever called him Abba. The names Abba and Aubrey were used interchangeably in official correspondence until 1950, and it was not until March 1954 that the government's Portfolio of Notifications officially announced the change.

Eban's name was the only one on that list not to be accompanied by a national identification number, because he was never issued one. He was also listed under the municipality of Jerusalem even though he had no residence there— or anywhere else in Israel.[23] He renounced his British citizenship shortly after Israel's independence ("you just write the Home Office and tell them that you're leaving; that it's been nice knowing them," he told a friend who inquired about the procedure), even though British law permits British citizens to have dual nationality.[24] Even so, for many years Eban was not considered an Israeli citizen by law.

THE WAR IN PALESTINE HAD ENTERED A NEW PHASE IN APRIL 1948 FOLLOWING Ben-Gurion's order to the Haganah's High Command to execute Plan D—a strategic offensive designed to capture the territory allotted to the Jewish state under the UN resolution, including the Arab settlements in that area. Despite a UN Security Council resolution calling for a general arms embargo on all sides in Palestine and banning fighting personnel from entering the country, the fighting continued with the same intensity. In taking the initiative on the battlefield from the Arabs, Haganah brigades managed to capture Jaffa, Haifa, Safed, Acre, and Tiberias in order to create territorial continuity from the north to the edge of the Negev. While Plan D enabled the soon-to-be-declared Jewish state to consolidate its territorial gains, it also resulted in the Palestinian Nakba (catastrophe)—the mass exodus of more than 700,000 of Palestine's Arabs from their homes and the destruction of some five hundred Arab villages.[25]

Beyond the creation of territorial contiguity, the Haganah gained valuable military experience and self-confidence in preparation for the anticipated invasion of the Arab armies following the departure of the British from Palestine. On May 15 the armies of Egypt, Syria, Jordan, Lebanon, and Iraq attacked the embryonic state from the south, north, and east. Egyptian forces advanced into the northern Negev and within a week were only thirty miles south of Tel Aviv. A Syrian armored brigade attacked the Jewish settlements around the Sea of Galilee and captured several of them. The Jordanian Legion attacked Jerusalem and besieged the Jewish quarter. An Iraqi column advanced from within Jordan to take the road leading to the coastal town of Netanya, while two brigades of the Arab Liberation Army and the Lebanese Army advanced into northern Galilee.[26]

At the United Nations, all efforts were directed at achieving a truce. The General Assembly appointed Count Folke Bernadotte of Sweden as the UN mediator in Palestine, with the unenviable task of promoting "a peaceful adjustment of the future situation in Palestine." The fifty-three-year-old president of the Swedish Red Cross had no experience with the Palestine question, and the height of his diplomatic career involved the managing of several exchanges of prisoners of war with Germany during World War II. His chief qualification for the job of Palestine mediator was his expected neutrality.[27]

Eban was called to assert Israel's sovereignty and legitimacy several times during this period. On May 18 he criticized before the UN Security Council the British and Arab efforts to pass a resolution that forbade the entry of fighting personnel to the country. He reminded the council that Israel was now a sovereign state, and that under Article 2(7) of the UN Charter the organization had no mandate to interfere in the domestic affairs—such as immigration—of sovereign states. As Eban later pointed out, on that day he became the first Jewish spokesman in centuries to utter the words "none of your business" to external powers.[28] Four days later the Security Council called for an unconditional cease-fire, which Israel accepted but the Arabs rejected; instead, they demanded that the "Jewish authorities" declare the State of Israel null and void, and insisted on the indefinite halt of Jewish immigration as the basis for a truce. In response, on May 26 Eban took the floor to make one of his most potent statements in defense of Israel:

> The answers received from the Arab States are more significant for what they omit than for what they contain. They contain a remarkable array of violent threats. But they omit any sign of willingness to stop making war. . . . Israel is asked to yield her integrity and independence in return for a cessation of the assault upon her.
>
> Here is a flat and defiant rejection of the Security Council's cease-fire resolution. In its place, we have a proposal for revoking Israel's statehood and independence. The sovereignty regained by an ancient people after its long march through the dark night of exile is to be surrendered at pistol-point.
>
> It becomes my duty to make our attitude clear. If the Arab States want peace with Israel, they can have it. If they want war, they can have that too. But, whether they want peace or war, they can have it only with a sovereign State of Israel.

Eban later admitted that this was "dramatic stuff with a flamboyant touch about it," but nevertheless proportionate to the occasion.[29] The Arab threat to delegitimize the integrity of the infant Jewish state was a serious one and required this kind of response, which would soon become an Eban hallmark—eloquent, somewhat hyperbolic, and always framed in reference to universal principles.

The failure to impose a cease-fire led the UN Security Council to issue a more robust resolution on May 29. It called for a four-week truce, with the explicit threat of invoking Chapter VII of the UN Charter, which authorized the imposition of sanctions and even the use of UN forces in the case of non-compliance by either of the parties. The cease-fire came into effect on June 11, and two weeks later Bernadotte submitted his first peace plan to the Security Council: the area of Transjordan and Palestine was to comprise Arab and Jewish entities, with common economic services and coordinated defense and foreign policies; Arab refugees would be allowed to return to their homes, and Jerusalem would be incorporated into the Arab territory. The plan was swiftly rejected by the Arabs and the Israelis, as well as the international community, on the grounds that it was too impractical. The Israelis claimed that Bernadotte ignored UN Resolution 181 and the fact that a sovereign Jewish state already existed, while the Arabs refused to acknowledge any Zionist entity in their midst. The Soviets supported the Israelis and accused Bernadotte of colluding with the British to protect Britain's strategic and political interests in the Arab world. Such sentiments were shared by many on the Israeli right, especially the underground Lehi (Lohamei Herut Israel—Fighters for the Freedom of Israel), which was particularly militant in its opposition to Bernadotte's mission. The group declared that there remained "only one way open to counter Bernadotte's tactics: to force the issue. . . . The task of the moment is to oust Bernadotte and his observers. Blessed the hand that does it."[30] The Israeli government continued to deal with the UN mediator, but as Ralph Bunche, Bernadotte's deputy, noted in his diary, the independence of the Jewish state had some undesirable effect on its representatives: "Shertok's reply re demilitarization of Jerusalem enigmatic and obscure. Israelis now swashbuckling and Shertok pompous. Jewish imperialism rampant already."[31]

The four-week truce ended on July 9. In the next ten days the Israelis consolidated their military positions and took control of several areas assigned to the Arab state in the partition resolution: they captured Nazareth and strengthened their control of the Lower Galilee, conquered Ramla, took Lydda and its airport, and expanded the corridor to Jerusalem. On July 13 Eban appeared before the Security Council once more, this time to denounce with great conviction the aggression of the Arab states and their continued refusal to accept Israel's sovereignty and legitimacy. Once again he rested his case on the judicial provenance of the Jewish state and the morally egregious actions of the Arabs. In a prelude to what would evolve over the years into an Eban trademark, the address was rooted in legal reasoning cushioned by the indignant depiction of Israel as the perpetual victim of Arab aggression:

> There is not a single person in this room or outside it who does not know in the depths of his heart that the Arab States, by resuming their attacks on Israel, have committed an act of aggression. . . . Their violence is directed against the recommendation of the General Assembly, against the appeal of the Security Council, against the call of the Mediator, against the very life and survival of the State of Israel, against the principle of world peace.
>
> No elaborate evidence is needed to prove the aggressive character of these warlike movements upon which the Arab States have embarked—with welcome lack of success—since Friday last. Neither Article 51 which allows members of the United Nations the "right of self-defence" . . . nor the preamble of the Charter which lays it down that "armed forces shall not be used save in common interest," can possibly be invoked in support of these attacks. For Egypt, Transjordan, Syria, Lebanon, Saudi Arabia and Yemen have not been individually or jointly attacked; and they have certainly not been invited by the United Nations to storm into territory not their own for purposes of havoc and murder.
>
> The State of Israel is an immutable part of the international landscape. To plan the future without it is to build delusions on sand. Everything that contributes to an Arab belief in the stability and permanence of Israel brings the prospect of harmony nearer. That is why every recognition of Israel, every voice uplifted against aggression, every manifestation of sympathy for our republic in its gallant fight, is a milestone on the road which may lead us to peace, perhaps more rapidly than we can now expect.[31]

Two days after Eban's address, in its ninth resolution on Palestine in just four months, the Security Council explicitly laid the blame for the resumption of fighting on the Arab states and noted their successive rejections of appeals to extend the cease-fire. Invoking once more Chapter VII of the UN Charter, the Security Council resolved that a truce should remain in place until the conclusion of a peaceful settlement in Palestine. This time the Arabs acquiesced, and a second truce was announced on July 18. Two months later Bernadotte submitted to the Security Council his second peace plan: Jerusalem would remain an international city; there would be territorial exchanges so that Israel relinquished control over the Negev for sovereignty over the Galilee; the towns of Lydda and Ramla, which Israel captured in July, would be included in the Arab territory; the Palestinian refugees would be allowed to return to their homes in the territories conquered by Israel; and a UN Palestine Conciliation Commission would be set up.[32]

At 5:30 p.m. on Friday, September 17, Bernadotte left Government House in Jerusalem at the back of a three-car convoy. As the convoy crossed Ben-Zion Guini Square in the Katamon neighborhood, it was stopped by a jeep occupied by four men wearing the khaki uniform of the Israeli Army. Assuming they had stumbled onto a routine checkpoint, the passengers in Bernadotte's convoy reached for their passes. Three men emerged out of the jeep. One of them briefly inspected the first two cars before proceeding to the third. Bernadotte sat at the back of the sedan, next to colonel Andre Serot, the chief UN observer in Jerusalem. When the man in the uniform recognized the Swedish mediator, he thrust his German Schmeisser submachine gun through the open rear window and squeezed the trigger. The first six bullets hit Bernadotte in the chest, throat, and left arm. Another eighteen bullets ended in the head and body of Colonel Serot. The assassin had mistaken Serot for the Swedish general Aage Lundstrom, head of UN truce supervision in Palestine and Bernadotte's personal representative, who was the second target of assassination. Before the convoy left Government House, Lundstrom had agreed to swap places with Serot, who wanted to thank Bernadotte for helping rescue his wife from the Dachau concentration camp in 1945. Bernadotte and Serot were dead before their car arrived at Hadassah Hospital in Jerusalem.[33]

The following day Bernadotte's body was flown back to Sweden, where an apprehensive Eban represented the State of Israel at the funeral. The attack had been ordered by Lehi's High Command and its leader, Yitzhak Shamir, who thirty-five years later would be sworn in as the seventh prime minister of Israel. Eban held a dim view of what many Israelis—including Shamir himself, as late as 1988—romanticized as heroic resistance to a foreign power. As Eban would later recall in an unusually laconic tone, the assassination was "neither useful nor well guided."[34] On September 20 Ralph Bunche was duly appointed as Bernadotte's successor. Along with the rest of the world, the provisional government of Israel expressed its shock and indignation at the attack; it promised to bring the culprits to justice, not least out of concern that its pending application for full membership in the United Nations might be rejected because of this episode. The Lehi was promptly disbanded, but nobody was charged with the murder of Bernadotte and Serot. In February 1949 two of the Lehi leaders, Natan Yellin-Mor (who by then had been elected to the first Knesset) and Mattityahu Shmuelevitz would be convicted of membership in a terrorist organization and sentenced to eight and five years in prison, respectively—but they were almost immediately released through political amnesty in celebration of the election of the new Knesset.[35]

THE FIGHTING RESUMED ON OCTOBER 5, 1948, WITH A RENEWED EGYPTIAN attack on Israeli settlements in the Negev, but an Israeli counteroffensive captured the Arab towns of Isdud and Majdal, north of Gaza. In the northern part of the country the Israeli Army was in complete control of Upper Galilee, an area that had been allocated to the Arab state in the UN partition resolution. The UN Security Council passed several more resolutions on the conflict, the most significant one calling on the parties to withdraw beyond the positions that they held on October 14. Eban attacked the resolution, which allowed the Egyptians to restore their positions to the point from which they had been ejected after invading Israeli territory. Israel, he argued, was being ordered to retreat from its own territory "for no other reason than that an invading army had challenged unsuccessfully its internationally sanctioned rights by force of arms."

On December 11 the UN General Assembly passed its most important resolution since it had endorsed the partition of Palestine the previous November. Resolution 194 called for the repatriation of refugees to their homes and the establishment of the UN Conciliation Commission to facilitate negotiations between the parties over the implementation of previous Security Council resolutions; it also reaffirmed the designation of Jerusalem as an international city. Meanwhile, in the Negev, Israeli forces succeeded in crossing the international border into Egypt and captured the town of Auja and the airfield at El-Arish at the north of the Sinai Peninsula. In response the British invoked the 1936 Anglo-Egyptian Treaty and sent the Royal Air Force to support the Egyptian ground forces. Eventually British and American pressure brought Israel and Egypt to agree to enter armistice negotiations under the auspices of the United Nations. The war officially ended in March 1949 after Israeli forces crossed the Negev Desert to capture the Red Sea port of Umm Rashrash (Eilat).[36]

Arab-Israeli armistice negotiations commenced in January 1949 on the island of Rhodes under the auspices of Ralph Bunche. Unlike Bernadotte, Bunche was immensely familiar with the intricacies of the conflict and was personally acquainted with many of the characters involved owing to his rich experience in Palestine and in Arab capitals during the UNSCOP mission. He was also a far more able communicator and a better negotiator than Bernadotte had been. Between January and July 1949 Bunche mediated four bilateral agreements between Israel and Egypt, Lebanon, Jordan, and Syria. The armistice agreements delineated the cease-fire borders that had since become known as Israel's Green Line. Jerusalem became a divided city, with Jordan controlling the Old City in the eastern part, and Israel in control of West Jerusalem; Jordan also controlled the West Bank of the River Jordan, while Egypt was in control of the Gaza Strip at the north of the Negev. As a result of the armistice agreements, Israel increased its territorial control from 55 to 78 percent of Mandatory Palestine. While the armistice lines differed considerably from Israel's boundaries as outlined in the partition resolution, they have since acted as the de facto borders between Israel and its neighbors.[38]

While the Israeli delegation to Rhodes was negotiating the armistice agreements, in New York Eban turned his efforts to securing Israel's admission to the UN as a full member. A first application was submitted immediately after Israel's declaration of independence in May 1948, but it was not even considered by the UN Security Council. A second attempt failed that December due to the ongoing fighting in the Negev.[39] Eban submitted a third application on February 24, 1949, the day the Israeli-Egyptian armistice agreement was signed, and ten days later it was approved by a majority of 9–1 in the Security Council, with Britain abstaining and Egypt opposing. On March 9 the president of the Security Council, Alberto Alvarez of Cuba, transmitted to Secretary-General Lie the message that the council considered Israel to be "a peace-loving State . . . able and willing to carry out the obligations contained in the Charter."[40] The following month Israel's application was debated at the Ad Hoc Political Committee of the General Assembly, where the Arab delegates attacked Israel's refusal to allow the return of Arab refugees to their homes and its continued flaunting of UN resolutions.

At noon on May 5 Eban rose up to deliver a forty-six-page response to the Arab objections to Israel's application for UN membership. As he reached the one-hour mark of his address he was suddenly interrupted by the chairman of the committee, Carlos Romulo of the Philippines. In a crude demonstration of the vagaries of UN proceedings, Romulo informed the members of the committee that Eban had delivered a third of his address, and that if they wished to hear the rest of it, they would have to remain in their seats until 3:00 p.m., thus committing the unfathomable sin of missing lunch. To avert this egregious offense he proposed to adjourn the session at once and reconvene the next day at 8:30 p.m., when the representative of Israel would be allowed to continue with his address. Eban's surprise at the discourteous behavior of the chairman was instantly overshadowed by the unexpected retort of Charles Malik, the representative of Lebanon and the only Arab ambassador with whom Eban had something resembling a mutually respectful relationship. Malik pointed out that Eban had in fact already delivered about half of his address and there was no danger of missing lunch; besides, he was actually quite interested in hearing the rest of Eban's speech. The Polish representative was outraged at the prospect of reconvening at the most uncongenial time of 8:30 p.m., while Warren Austin of the United States insisted that hearing Eban's address in its entirety would be the fair thing to do—provided that a short recess for lunch would be made available. Ten minutes and several exchanges later the matter was brought to a vote, and to the relief of the visibly perplexed young Israeli diplomat, he was permitted to carry on with his address by the narrow majority of 19–18, with 9 abstentions. Before returning to the weighty issue of the Arab refugees, Eban felt obliged to open with a conciliatory note: "Mr. Chairman, this particular statement was not written with a hungry audience in mind, and I hope that the Committee will bear with me."[41]

Turning to the status of the Arab refugees and their right of return, Eban set out what had since become Israel's official position on the issue: the problem was exclusively of the Arabs' own making, first by starting a civil war against the Yishuv immediately after the UN partition resolution, then by attacking the one-day-old Israeli state with a coalition of five Arab states, and finally by the refusal of the Arab states to accommodate the refugees in their own vast territories. Eban reminded the Committee that

> all the outstanding political problems between Israel and its neighbours only exist as a direct consequence of the fact that a war was

> launched for the purpose of overthrowing the General Assembly's Resolution by force. Of no problem is this more true than the refugee question. . . . Every disturbance of the 1947 plan is a plain result of the fact that a war was launched. The Arab States are responsible for every modification of that Resolution; responsible for every death, for all the bereavement and for all the panic and exile which has resulted from this futile and unnecessary conflict.

As for Israel's proposed solution to the refugee problem, Eban maintained that in the absence of peaceful contacts and recognized borders, ongoing security consideration had to take precedence; a solution to the problem thus could only be found within a final peace settlement between Israel and its neighbors. On borders, too, Eban declared Israel's commitment to pursue previous Security Council resolutions that called on all parties to settle their territorial claims through peaceful negotiations. The absurdity of the Arab claims, Eban mused, resembled a situation in which "one who, having been attacked in a dark street by seven men with heavy bludgeons, finds himself dragged into court only to see his assailants sitting on the bench with an air of solemn virtue, delivering homilies on the duties of a peaceful citizen. It is essential for the dignity of international institutions that such a device should not succeed."[42] After nearly two and a half hours, Eban finally concluded his address, noting, "A great wheel of history comes full circle today as Israel, renewed and established, offers itself, with its many imperfections but perhaps with a few virtues, to your common defense of the human spirit against the perils of international conflict and despair." With equal vigor and less prose the exasperated chairman hurriedly concluded the session by thanking "the members of the Committee for their patience, the speaker for his endurance, the interpreters for their industry and fortitude. And now the Committee will apply for admission into the restaurant. Committee is adjourned!"[43]

Six days later, on May 11, 1949, Israel became the fifty-ninth member of the United Nations. Resolution 273 of the General Assembly admitted Israel by a majority of 37–12, with 9 abstentions. Tumultuous applause greeted Sharett as he led the Israeli delegation to take its seat at the General Assembly. For Eban, Resolution 273 was far more significant than Resolution 181 eighteen months earlier; that earlier resolution had not been followed by international recognition; it had no legal basis, but instead had been a recommendation that could be either accepted or rejected (and the Arabs chose to do the latter).

But on the morning of May 12, 1949, when Eban—at the young age of thirty-four—hoisted the Israeli flag on the flag pole in the circle of banners, he considered it to be the proudest moment of his life. For Eban, the raised flag symbolized Israel's sovereignty and equality among all other nations on Earth, and with it came the realization that the status of the Jewish people in history was being irreversibly changed.[44]

It did not take long for the newest member of the UN to challenge the organization's views on the thorny issues of the status of Jerusalem, the future of the Palestinian refugees, and the demarcation of Israel's borders. Prime Minister Ben-Gurion's famous boast that "what matters is not what the Gentiles will say, but what the Jews will do" epitomized this defiant attitude, and even Eban, who had been accused in Israel of displaying unnecessary deference to world public opinion, occasionally followed suit. In December 1949 he declared, following a UN vote in favor of internationalizing Jerusalem, "Israel does not have to surrender to every decision by the United Nations if it deems it unjust. As long as Israel does not resist UN resolutions by force, it does not contravene the Charter."[45]

Before long the Israeli stand on these issues brought it into conflict with the United States. In May 1949, only three weeks after Israel's admission to the UN, President Truman warned Ben-Gurion,

> The government of the U.S. is seriously disturbed by the attitude of Israel with respect to a territorial settlement in Palestine and to the question of Palestine Refugees. . . .
>
> The Government of Israel should entertain no doubt whatever that the United States government relies upon it to take responsible and positive action concerning Palestine Refugees and that, far from supporting excessive Israeli claims to further territory within Palestine, the United States Government believes that it is necessary for Israel to offer territorial compensation for territory which it excepts to acquire beyond the boundaries of the November 29, 1947 resolution of the General Assembly.
>
> If the government of Israel continues to reject the basic principles set forth by the resolution of the General Assembly of December 11, 1948 and the friendly advice of the United States

> Government for the sole purpose of facilitating a genuine peace in Palestine, the United States Government will regretfully be forced to the conclusion that a revision of its attitude toward Israel has become unavoidable.[46]

THE STRONG AMERICAN REBUTTAL PROMPTED EBAN TO FORMULATE "WITH THE utmost frankness" a coherent Israeli position on the complex issues of Jerusalem, refugees, and borders. The entire emphasis of Israel's case, Eban wrote to Walter Eytan on June 8, should not rest on the partition resolution of November 1947 ("I sometimes fear that our romantic attachments to the November 29th Resolution make it difficult for us to resist reference to it"), but on Resolution 194 of December 11, 1948, which called upon the parties to negotiate their outstanding differences. Accordinglh, he said, count on the support of the two superpowers any calls by the Americans or others in the international community for Israel to make unilateral concessions had no legal basis. Moreover, the recently signed armistice agreements were endorsed by the General Assembly, meaning that "every inch of soil now occupied by Israel is lawfully occupied from the viewpoint of the United Nations. Wherever Israeli soldiers are, they are there by virtue of armistice agreements." Eban concluded that Israel's position was therefore politically and legally unassailable, as any change to the armistice agreements required the consent of the parties to the conflict, and if the Arabs did not wish to sign peace treaties with Israel then the boundaries as delineated in the armistice agreements would remain unchanged.[48] Ben-Gurion concurred with Eban's assessment about the relative stability that the armistice agreements provided Israel. As the prime minister wrote in his diary, it was better to maintain the current frontiers than to enter a risky peace initiative with the Arabs that would involve an Israeli withdrawal to unsecure boundaries: "[Eban] sees no need to run after peace. The armistice [agreements] are sufficient for us. If we run after peace—the Arabs will demand of us a price—borders or refugees or both. We will wait a few years."[49]

While Eban's note to Eytan was important in formulating a coherent basis for Israel's negotiating position, it also revealed the importance he attached to the role of language in formulating policy. "The events of the past year had taught me," he wrote to Eytan, "I confess somewhat to my surprise, that formulations by themselves are influential and sometimes decisive in a political struggle. Thus by defining our position on Jerusalem in a slightly different form, we were able to affect the votes and attitudes of States on a matter of principle. I believe that here too an advantageous formulation may transform the prospects of our territorial struggle both on the international arena and in the field of public opinion."[50] Exactly two decades later, Eban's talent for formulation and reinterpretation would become the heart of Israel's policy toward negotiations with the Arabs under UN auspices.

Eban's formulation was the basis of Sharett's reply to Truman's telegram: so long as the Arab states refused to discuss peace with Israel, any talk of repatriation of refugees or the compensation of territories was "clearly impractical." In response to Sharett's letter, J. W. Rockwell of the Near East Division at the U.S. State Department sent President Truman a memo concerning the future course of U.S.–Israeli relations. The proposals included the "immediate adoption of a generally negative attitude toward Israel: maintenance of no more than a correct attitude toward Israeli officials in this country . . . and failing to support the position of Israel in the various international organizations," as well as the holding up of the allocation of $49 million to Israel via an Export-Import Bank loan, and the reconsideration of the provision of tax exemption to American Jewish organizations.[51] The first rift in U.S.–Israeli relations seemed inevitable. Truman, Eban wrote to Sharett, believed that he had "done more for the Jews than anyone since Moses." Given that his attitude to Israel was informed mostly by State Department officials who highlighted Israel's objections and rejections and ignored similar practices on the part of the Arabs, Eban was fearful of a "far-reaching rift" with Washington. The fact that "we are right, U.S.A. wrong, has become irrelevant in plain issue of political interest," he concluded.[52]

The final setback to Israeli diplomacy in 1949 came on December 9, when the UN General Assembly passed a resolution on the internationalization of the city of Jerusalem, whereby the city would be divided into demilitarized Arab and Jewish zones, with a UN administrative authority over all municipal affairs. Sharett described the resolution as a "black day" for the organization and its moral authority, while Ben-Gurion's response was decidedly less diplomatic and more defiant: he ordered that the government offices and the Knesset building be moved from Tel Aviv to Jerusalem. On January 23, 1950, the Knesset proclaimed the Israeli part of Jerusalem as the capital of the country. In the run-up to the December vote, Ben-Gurion told Sharett that he intended to tell the Knesset that Israel would never agree to any form of foreign rule in Jewish Jerusalem, and that if the choice was between leaving Jerusalem or leaving the UN, Israel would opt for the latter. Sharett strongly objected to this combative message, which he thought was unnecessarily belligerent. But Sharett failed to stop Ben-Gurion telling the Knesset, following the resolution, that the transfer of government offices to Jerusalem would continue as normal. Only the Ministries of Defense and Foreign Affairs remained in Tel Aviv, the former for security reasons and the latter due to Sharett's fears that foreign diplomats would refuse to visit Israel. Sharett even questioned whether the decision to declare Jerusalem the capital was premature.[53] The British *Observer* reported on Eban's efforts to reverse the resolution, noting the insurmountable challenge that he faced at the General Assembly: "When he goes to Lake Success it will be to argue Israel's case for holding the New City of Jerusalem before the very Assembly which voted to internationalize it. This tall, cool, and laconic young man will have to bring all the fluency of his Cambridge Union days to withstand the united arguments of the Soviet, Catholic, and Arab blocs, and overcome the muteness of America and Britain."[54]

Ultimately however, as Eban and others predicted, the General Assembly recommendation on the internationalization of Jerusalem did not materialize. The Jordanians, in control of East Jerusalem and the Old City, also rejected the attempt to internationalize the city, and as U.S. secretary of state Dean Acheson told Eban, the General Assembly resolution was "only recommendation without legislative effect." Ralph Bunche also argued that an international regime for Jerusalem "simply wouldn't work"—there were no clear divisions of sectors and there were no armed forces to enforce the arrangement—as was the case in Berlin, for example.[55] Eban's impression that "Israel could do just as it liked in Jerusalem and that the new 1949 resolution would have no effect on our international position" was only partially accurate: while the resolution was indeed not enforced by the UN, to this day none of the countries with which Israel holds diplomatic relations maintain their embassies in Jerusalem.[56] At the same time Eban, like Sharett, did not agree with his government's combative response to the UN resolution and its hasty decision to relocate the government offices. He told Eytan of his dismay over the "overdramatizing" of the Israeli reaction: not only was the tone of "defiance and desperation" that came out of the government uncalled for but it was particularly regretful that the Israeli government portrayed the Soviet and Latin blocs as enemies because of "temporary disagreement on one abortive resolution."[57]

EBAN HAD MADE A VERY POSITIVE IMPRESSION ON HIS AUDIENCES DURING HIS first eighteen months at the United Nations. Following one of his early appearances before the Security Council he was approached by a jubilant Texan lady who exclaimed, "Israel is a wonderful country, you've only existed three weeks and you already speak English!" While President Truman was reported to have been deeply impressed by Eban's performances.[58] Soon enough, rumors of Eban's meteoric rise in New York had reached Israel too. In September 1948 the daily newspaper *Maariv*, under the headline "The Successful Choice: Abba Eban," introduced to its readers the country's hitherto unknown youngest and brightest diplomat:

> He was not raised in this country. He did not make a career for himself at the Jewish Agency's headquarters in Rehavia. He did not engage himself with our bureaucracy or party politics. Even when he was based in Jerusalem during the war and with UNSCOP, he was noticed by only a few. It appears that he had never made a public speech or sat on the rostrum for us. And all these "shortcomings"—are his advantages . . . his horizons are wider, his demeanor is more modest. . . . Because of his obscurity, many—especially among the revisionist press—highlighted his English name and upbringing, his service under Clayton in Cairo. This is preposterous. Even if his name is not Abba Even but Aubrey Eban—he is the most successful choice that Sharett had made throughout his diplomatic service.
>
> He is without doubt one of the most talented individuals in our foreign service. He is the master of languages—not only English, French, German, etc.—he is internationally renowned scholar of Arabic and Farsi, and he is only in his thirties. He supersedes many of our diplomatic representatives. With no nervousness, without deference to the Gentiles or condensation over the Jews—quietly, with light humor and constant vigilance, he walks among world statesmen as seasoned veteran. As if we have had a long and established diplomatic tradition; not at all like the first representative of the youngest nation; not at all like the youngest diplomat to have sat among the world's statesmen before the Security Council.[59]

Another Israeli newspaper described Eban in January 1949 as "L'homme du jour"—the man of the moment. It reported on talks within the higher echelons of the Israeli Foreign Ministry that Eban was destined to take over from

Sharett as foreign minister. Even though "Dr. Eban" was not a member of the ruling Mapai (the Workers' Party) like Sharett, he was better educated than his mentor: "after all," the reporter exclaimed, "he is an Oxford Man!"—thus achieving the distinction of erroneously awarding Eban a doctorate *and* smearing him with the indignity of an Oxford education in the same paragraph.[60] The Israeli daily *Davar* described Eban to his readers in similarly glowing terms: "Together with the birth of the State of Israel, another star is born: the young Jewish statesman, Major Aubrey Eban, who at 33 is the youngest among the 58 delegates at the General Assembly." The reporter, S. N. Schneiderman, cited one veteran UN diplomat's impression of Eban's early performances: "He fuses knowledge of British diplomacy with a sense of Jewish morality, and most importantly—he utilizes his wonderful English and deep convictions for a just cause." In describing the unfamiliar Eban to the people of Israel for the first time, the reporter noted the young diplomat's "slightly downward-tilting head and squinting eyes, who seems to be invariably preoccupied with reading and studying—a genuine man of words, as evidenced by his rare triple-first at Cambridge and his fluency in Hebrew, Arabic, Farsi, French, German and Yiddish, and of course his masterful command of the English language." Eban's previous lectures and publications on Middle Eastern affairs, including his 1947 translation to English of leading Egyptian writer Tawfiq al-Hakim's *A Maze of Justice: Diary of a County Prosecutor*, were cited as evidence of Eban's conciliatory approach to Arab-Jewish relations. But, most tellingly, the article concluded, "Major Aubrey S. Eban is not an ambitious professional diplomat. He considers himself first a man of science and a scholar."[61]

VIII

He Looks Remarkably Like a Wise Owl

In December 1949, two and a half years after leaving London, the Ebans still had no place to call home. Having stayed at the Sulgrave Hotel on Park Avenue in New York City for six months, the couple moved into a more commodious location, a rented two-bedroom penthouse in an apartment building at 241 Central Park West. A month later, on the evening of January 17, 1950, in the middle of a snowstorm, Aubrey rushed from a United Jewish Appeal fund-raising event to Columbia Presbyterian Medical Center in upper Manhattan just in time to witness the birth of his son Eli, who was named after his maternal grandfather, Elihau Sacks.[1] A few days later Eban boarded a plane to Israel for consultations and from there he continued to Geneva to attend the UN Trusteeship Council meetings over Jerusalem. He did not return home for two and a half months. "The apartment seems dead without you," Suzy wrote in one of the many letters she sent him during this period. In another letter to her husband in Geneva, she confessed, "I don't know how this separation has worked out for you, but for me it is one big dreadful bang in my emotional life. I shall never forget the lonely days and nights alone, just watching tenderly and sadly over our little Eli. When I lecture myself and tell myself that this will probably have to happen again and again in our lives, my courage fails me at the thought."[2]

But even Suzy could not imagine how much harder things would become. One night in August 1950, after delivering an address in Atlanta, Eban received another of Moshe Sharett's enigmatic cables: "Can you do both?" Five months earlier Mordechai Eliash, Israel's ambassador to the United Kingdom, had passed away suddenly, and Sharett and David Ben-Gurion decided to move

Eliahu Elath from Washington to London. Sharett persuaded Ben-Gurion that Eban was the perfect man for the Washington job, having already made a name for himself not only among the diplomatic circles in New York but among the American administration as well. Eban was not deterred by the prospect of simultaneously holding the two posts. By his own admission he was beginning to begrudge the confinements of his UN role and wished to do more than conduct "a permanent rhetorical contest with Arab representatives . . . [and argue] endlessly about ourselves in United Nations debates." Now that Israel's main political and military aims had been satisfied, he wished to make a more constructive contribution and felt rather envious of his colleagues in the world's capitals.[3] With Suzy's consent he accepted Sharett's offer, and in early September 1950 the couple relocated from their Manhattan apartment to a three-story residence at 1673 Myrtle Street in northwest Washington, DC, which had been donated to the State of Israel by one of the city's prominent Jewish families. Before long, however, the house was too small to accommodate the Ebans' social needs. Luckily the Israeli government was given another gift by another prominent Jewish family in Washington: a fourteen-room Tudor mansion at 1630 Juniper Street, only a few blocks from the Myrtle house. This four-story residence had extensive grounds, and its exterior was rather appealing, but Suzy was concerned that its relatively small rooms made it a difficult place to entertain. With the help of Theodor Kollek, who had recently been appointed minister at the Embassy, as well as some dedicated bricklayers, carpenters, and decorators, the house was suitably transformed: the new furniture was custom-made in Israel and the oyster-white walls were adorned with many paintings by modern Israeli artists. When Suzy invited the Washington press for a viewing, there was a unanimous reaction of surprise and admiration at the daring combination of traditional exterior and modern interior. One reporter observed, "For a poor country, how did [they] dare spend [so much] money on decorating the house?" while another wondered, "How come there are no crystal chandeliers and dark red velvet curtains as would be expected from an ambassadorial residence?"[4]

The ambassadorial job in Washington was far more demanding than the New York post, but Eban, who at thirty-five was the youngest ambassador in town, was also one of the most well informed and connected diplomats in Washington. His frequent appearances before the UN Security Council and his high profile in the national media had placed him on an elevated position in his discussions with the White House and the State Department, while his ambassadorial duties in Washington had made him one of the most respected delegates at the UN General Assembly. In both cities the degree of deference accorded Eban was patently out of proportion to the size of the country that he represented or its political leverage in the international arena. It placed him in a most opportune position to harness public opinion to Israel's advantage in order to pursue closer relations with the United States, as well as to generate sympathy (and donations) among the five million U.S. Jews toward the Israeli state. Eban also had the foresight to cultivate personal relationships with American politicians who he thought would one day be in a position of power to make important decisions about U.S.-Israeli relations. "Most ambassadors concern themselves only with Presidents and Secretaries of States and neglect whosever may be Vice-President," he later recalled. "My strategy was to be in touch with everyone who might ever become President or Secretary of State. . . . I wanted whoever might become President to be a man who had once dined in my house during his humbler days and would be able to recall that I had not sought his aid only when he became eminent."[5] Thus, when John Foster Dulles returned to practice law in New York after a one-year spell as a senator in 1950, Eban took the time to go up to Wall Street and call on him. The future secretary of state appreciated the ambassador's time and effort to keep him abreast of Middle Eastern developments, and two years later, before the 1952 Republican Party Convention, he sought Eban's advice about formulating the Middle East policy plank in the party's platform. Eban also cultivated long-lasting acquaintances with Illinois governor Adlai Stevenson, vice president Richard Nixon, and senators John F. Kennedy and Lyndon Johnson; they all received personal invitations to attend dinners at the ambassador's residence and were kept informed of recent developments in the Middle East.[6]

On September 15, 1950, Eban arrived at the White House to present his credentials to President Truman. Mindful of protocol and dressed formally in a morning suit and a black homburg hat, Eban was ready to deliver his carefully prepared statement. But as he entered the Oval Office his nerves gave way to surprise. The president of the United States sat behind his desk, wearing a plain white shirt and no jacket, with glaringly red suspenders and a pair of two-tone brown-and-white shoes. "If you passed him in the street of a small town," Eban later recalled, "you would imagine that he was on the way to an office in a central part of a moderately sized building. If there was such a thing as an 'imperial presidency,' nobody had broken the news to Harry S. Truman of Independence, Missouri."[7] Then, before Eban had the opportunity to read out his formal letter of credence, the president snatched the leather-bound document from his hands and said, "Let's cut out all the crap and have a real talk!" But Truman's informality did little to alleviate Eban's awe at the occasion, as he noted some years later: "It occurred to me that I was sitting a few yards away from the most powerful leader in the history of mankind. More powerful than the Babylonian and Persian emperors, than Alexander the Great, Julius Caesar, Napoleon, the rulers of the British Empire at its zenith, or the Russian and German dictators of the twentieth century."[8]

Soon after Eban's ambassadorial appointment, the *Saturday Evening Post* told its readers that he looked much younger than his age, and that with his brown eyes hiding behind those shell-rimmed spectacles, he looked "remarkably like a wise owl."[9] But Eban's youthful looks could barely mask his hectic lifestyle. "The ambassador has no typical day," the article explained, "Some weeks ago he talked with a reporter at his house at 6:30 one evening. At 7:30 he was host at a dinner party for a group of congressmen. The next morning he was on the 9:30 plane to New York, met with his associates at the Israeli delegation to the United Nations at 11:00, had lunch with Sir Gladwyn Jebb, of the British delegation, at 1:00, held conferences at 2:30 and 4:00 o'clock at the United Nations and took a 5:30 plane back to Washington. At 7:30 he was entertaining at another dinner in his home."[10] Eban's legendary absentmindedness was not helped by his busy schedule and multitude of duties. "If you see a man who has forgotten his brief case, his passport or his tickets, that will be Eban," remarked a fellow delegate at the UN, while one of Eban's secretaries added, "There isn't an airline in the world that I haven't chased trying to get something he forgot on one of their planes."[11] It was for this reason, Eban later mused, that he also switched from pipe smoking to cigars soon after his arrival in New York: "I found that I could never bring all the various elements of pipe smoking together at the same time: the pipe, the tobacco, the pipe cleaner, the matches. There was always at least one of them missing."[12] Eban's relationship with his staff was always congenial, though bereft of personal friendships. Those who worked close to Eban were extremely devoted to him and were keenly aware of his inability to engage in mindless small talk. They attributed it to his innate shyness and absentmindedness rather than to an ingrained sense of superiority or aloofness on his behalf. Eban often shied away from confrontations and was even reluctant to chastise those subordinates who underperformed; sometimes it meant that he preferred to take additional work on himself rather than ask somebody else to do it. "It is difficult to help him, because he knows everything," said one of his aides at the embassy.[13]

Despite his agreeable public demeanor, in private Eban proved to be a tough interlocutor, as the Americans soon found out. The U.S. State Department's aptly named Biographic Information Division provided a particularly incisive account of Eban's personality traits during his time in Washington and New York: "He is not considered a warm or easily approachable person, and speaks pedantically. He is extremely tenacious in arguments, and often assumes a cold and dialectic manner with U.S. officials but with those he likes is quite friendly and open. Much of his time is spent in public speaking before various Jewish groups in the United States, where Eban has been an active and ardent worker for the Israel Bond Drive and the United Jewish Appeal (UJA). He can be eloquent or sarcastic in six languages, English, Hebrew, Arabic, Persian, French, and German."[14]

Eban dispensed his eloquence freely. Whatever the issue was, his defense of Israel was always grounded in historical perspectives and legal precedents, while his overbearing message was that justice and morality both emanated from Jewish provenance and stood on Israel's side in the conflict with the Arabs. Fighting against the internationalization of Jerusalem, Eban cautioned the United Nations that

> A devotion to the Holy City has been a constant theme in the history of our people for three thousand years. In our generation we have seen the ancient link between Israel and Jerusalem fully restored. Assaulted by the violence which threatened their total destruction two years ago, the State of Israel and the New City of Jerusalem have emerged together from mortal danger to deliverance.
>
> There is no example in history of a people, having once achieved union with its own natural and kindred government, voluntarily turning back to semi-autonomy under outside control. The Charter provides for no contingency whereby a self-governing community can become a dependent territory.
>
> The spiritual ideals conceived in Jerusalem are the moral basis on which modern democracy rests. Would it not be incongruous if the United Nations were to advance the course of democratic liberty

> everywhere, and yet prevent self-government from taking root in the very city where the democratic ideal was born? Out of Biblical ethics came the Declaration of Human Rights proclaiming in its 21st Article that "the will of the people shall be the basis for the authority of government." Less in Jerusalem than anywhere else on earth can this principle be denied fulfillment or set aside.[15]

Similarly, Eban's defense against the wholesale repatriation of the Palestinian refugees had since become the backbone of Israel's official policy: "Once you determine the responsibility for that war, you have determined the responsibility for the refugee problem. Nothing in the history of our generation is clearer or less controversial than the initiative of Arab governments for the conflict out of which the refugee tragedy emerged."[16]

EBAN'S EXHAUSTING SCHEDULE AND THE DEMANDS OF SIMULTANEOUSLY CARRYING Israel's two most important diplomatic posts inevitably took their toll. On May 17, 1951, Eban fought hard before the Security Council to avert a resolution condemning Israeli military actions against Syria. For over a month Israeli and Syrian forces were engaged in skirmishes across the demilitarized zone north of the Huleh Valley, where Israeli attempts to turn the malaria-infested swamps into an irrigated farmland were taken as an act of provocation by Damascus. Eban denounced the proposed resolution against Israel as an appeasement of Syrian aggression that ignored Israel's legitimate claims in the area. Later that evening he returned to his hotel room to prepare his address, to be delivered before the Security Council the following afternoon. With no food and little sleep, he finally completed the address in the early hours of the morning. In his hourlong, impassioned address, Eban rebuked the four sponsors of the resolution for ignoring the nature of the dispute: when one group of people was busy drying swamps and another group was opening fire on them, shouldn't the UN be responsible for stopping the latter rather than the former?

Eban did not wait to hear the Security Council unanimously adopting the resolution ordering Israel to stop the work in the Huleh Valley. As he left the council chamber he suddenly collapsed and fell face down on the floor. Eban's doctor concluded that he was generally in good health but on that occasion he was the victim of nervous exhaustion—an obvious symptom of the almost inhumane physical and mental pressures he had been placed under since assuming his dual ambassadorial role nine months earlier.[17] Two weeks later, Lillie Shultz, the director of the American Jewish Congress, shared with Eban her concerns over his emotional and psychological well-being:

> Because I can imagine what a great "mortification" it must be to you that the flesh should have seemed so weak, I am taking the liberty, as your friend, to say a few things based on my own experience:
>
> People like you with enormous mental and physical resiliency find doing things so easy that they accept all kinds of responsibilities without measure, and without anticipating their toll. What I think you have overlooked, in relationship to your own make-up, is the fact that you are a profoundly emotional person. And what has happened to you, without your conscious awareness of it, is a series of profound emotional shocks as a result of the intimate contact into which you have been placed with the top level of diplomacy. The process of being stripped of every illusion, as you have been, is most unpleasant when it relates to the world at large. Add to it the cynical ricocheting on Israel over a period of four years, and you need to be made of stone not to react.
>
> These emotional shocks, combined with the physical load—which would have been the undoing long before this of ten people—have been responsible, I think, for producing your condition. . . . What has happened to you is a warning—not of any inherent physical weakness—but that you are a *human being* and that you must live like one. Which is to say, the physical burdens must be lightened to the measure of one human being—which automatically means a lessening of the emotional stress as well. But much more important, in order to cushion you against the tensions of the world at large, and of your special world, you'vc got to take the time to do and enjoy the things you do enjoy when you have leisure, plus some things you've never done before. And, remember, you are indispensable only to yourself, Susie [*sic*] and Elie—with due apologies to the government of Israel and no reflection on the important work you do.[18]

Ten days later Eban responded to his friend's concern in typical Ebanesque fashion—a concoction of sincerity and cynicism that all but confirmed her assessment of him as a profoundly emotional man in denial: "Thank you very much for your very moving letter of friendship during my recent indisposition. Suzy and I not only appreciate your kind thought; we also fully concur in your psychoanalytical conclusions."[19] Eban, who never had a hobby and whose only recreations included cigar smoking and reading, was forced to adjust his work and life balance, at least in the immediate period after his collapse. He took a three-week break, assumed a perfunctory interest in golf, and even indulged in motorboating with Arthur Lourie in the resort town of Lake Placid in upstate New York.[20] But the pressing matters of the time did not allow for prolonged relaxation, and soon personal tragedy added to Eban's woes.

In December 1952 Suzy gave birth to a second child, a daughter named Meira. Three weeks later Aubrey was called out of a meeting in New York with UN secretary-general Trygve Lie. On the line from Washington was Suzy with the devastating news that baby Meira had died in her sleep of crib death. Overcome with grief, the couple left Washington for Florida to recuperate, but they never recovered from the tragedy that rocked their life. They never talked about it at home, though decades later Suzy acknowledged that her husband's demanding diplomatic duties in Washington and New York did not allow them the necessary time and privacy to go through the grieving process.[21] Eighteen months later, when Suzy was carrying their third child, Aubrey requested Sharett's permission not to attend the forthcoming opening session of the General Assembly in September 1954. "We had undergone through this process last year and the year before. I could not do it in 1952," Eban wrote to Sharett. "I shall never forget for the rest of my life that winter and its bitter end. It was unjustly burdensome and under brutal personal circumstances. . . . I made a promise to Suzy. . . . Please understand this sacred promise and my strong wish for you to help me carrying it."[22]

In December 1954 the Ebans celebrated the birth of another daughter at George Washington Hospital in Washington, DC. Suzy decided to name her Gila, Hebrew for "joy," because "she was consolation for the child we had lost."[23] But Suzy also felt "completely overloaded" by the demands of her job as an ambassador's wife. Looking over her husband's hectic schedule for the coming year and fearful of another long spell of separation, she felt trapped.

In March 1955 Suzy left Washington for six weeks in London and Israel, leaving three-month-old Gila and four-year-old Eli in the trusted hands of her mother-in-law, who came to stay with her son and two grandchildren in Washington. Despite his demanding schedule in Washington and New York, Eban found the time to take his son for his first train ride and to his first circus, but that was not enough. In one of his many letters to Suzy during this period, Eban confessed, "At lunch today Eli broke the wishbone of the chicken and said he wished *Ima* [mother] to come back yesterday, or this afternoon, or not in three weeks, so you can work out the psychology."[24]

Apart from the constant shuttling between New York and Washington and the frequent absences from home, Eban's least favorite part of his job was the social life of an ambassador. Luckily Suzy was always there by his side, ready to save him from the awkward but obligatory idle chitchat about the Washington weather or the local schools with some senator's wife. Informally known as "the most beautiful woman in Washington's diplomatic colony," Suzy's aristocratic upbringing in Cairo between the wars helped her to master the art of being the perfect hostess while teaching her husband some basic social skills along the way. Family life and privacy were the immediate casualties of those years. Even when Aubrey and Suzy were in the same city, their only private time together was in the chauffeur-driven limousine from the ambassador's residence to another reception or a fund-raising gala. Once there they would move in different circles and mingle with different people. Saturday evening was the only time when the family sat together for dinner—other engagements permitting. Aubrey and Suzy's frequent absences from home also meant that they had to pay for private tuition to teach their children Hebrew. "I do not separate between my mission and my personal life," Eban once observed. He then pointed to Suzy and added, "but I am not the only one."[25] Decades later Suzy lamented with some regret that "the mission" always came before the children—but this sacrifice was not unusual among the Zionist leaders of that generation. Golda Meir's two children were so excited when their mother fell ill because it meant that they could spend time with her at home, and as one of them admitted years later, she felt she was "orphaned of my mother."[26]

The future of U.S.-Israeli relations had preoccupied Eban from his first day in Washington. On the one hand, Israel was condemned by the White

House and the State Department over its position on the issues of Jerusalem, refugees, and borders; at the same time, Israel was in desperate need of foreign aid to support its nascent economy, crippled by the influx of 600,000 Jewish immigrants, which almost doubled the country's population. The Israeli economy was in such a dire state that Ben-Gurion told Eban, "By the end of February there will be no bread. By the end of January there will be no supplies for poultry runs."[27] U.S.-Israeli relations were further soured by Israel's declared policy of "nonalignment" or "nonidentification" between the Eastern and Western blocs: since the UN resolution on the partition of Palestine in November 1947, and the immediate recognition of the State of Israel in May 1948 by both Washington and Moscow, Israel held on to a principled foreign policy that foreign minister Moshe Sharett described as navigating "safely between Scylla and Charybdis," leading the Israeli government to declare its "loyalty to the principles of the United Nations Charter and friendship with all freedom-loving States, and in particular with the United States and the Soviet Union."[28] The reasons for this policy were manifold, and included a sense of responsibility for the fate and welfare of Jews around the world; the fact that Israel owed its birth to both superpowers; a principled concern for international peace, which might be jeopardized by geopolitical rivalries; and domestic political considerations, such as the reluctance of the ruling Mapai (Workers' Party of the Land of Israel to alienate the country's hundreds of thousands of new immigrants by declaring an allegiance to one of the blocs.[29] Israel wanted Moscow to allow free Jewish immigration from Eastern Europe, and at the same time it wanted American capital to absorb the new immigrants; declared neutrality thus seemed both inevitable and logical.[30] Yet by declaring its commitment to democratic values and liberal ideals, and at the same time refusing to ally itself officially with the West, Israel was soon treated with some suspicion and even irritation by Washington. In January 1950 senior officials at the Israeli Foreign Ministry met to review the state of U.S.-Israeli relations and consider ways to improve them. Sharett identified three such areas:

1. The broad context of political relations between the countries; how to bring the United States to develop closer relations with Israel, and to understand that Israel's democratic outlook places her in the Western camp. This includes the issue of arms supplies.

2. How to increase U.S. economic aid to Israel via private investments, public appeals, etc.
3. Israeli public diplomacy (*hasbara*) towards the American public.[31]

Eban pointed out that the crux of the strained relations between the countries was not Israel's stated neutrality on global affairs but instead its regional standing: so long as Israel failed to integrate in the Middle East, any friendly gesture by the Americans was bound to be interpreted as an act of provocation by the Arabs. The State Department, Eban added, was guided by the principle that Israel should be an integral part of the area and must live in peace with its neighbors; any step in this direction would lead to a favorable change in U.S. attitude toward Israel.[32] The Israeli mission in Washington was particularly stymied by what it viewed as a myopic rigidity on behalf of the government in Jerusalem. Moshe Keren, the chief diplomatic officer at the embassy, expressed these concerns to Walter Eytan, director-general of the Israeli Foreign Ministry. The staff at the embassy, Keren wrote, felt that the government was vacillating. It was unnecessarily preoccupied with a policy of "mathematical neutrality" between Washington and Moscow when it was clear that Israel was naturally predisposed toward the West, and especially the United States. There was no need to make a dramatic departure from the stated policy of nonalignment, but it was nevertheless important to signal to Washington Israel's de facto association with the West. If nothing else, there were obvious practical reasons for such a move, such as Israel's almost absolute dependence on American aid: the Jewish Appeal, the main fund-raising organization for Israel in America, practically prevented the young state from going bankrupt, as did Washington's $100 million loan, while the largest Jewish community in the world—the American Diaspora—was shown to be overwhelmingly supportive of Israel. Yet the government in Jerusalem refused to publicly declare its affinity to the United States; it even asked the Soviets for a loan, knowing that it would not be granted, only to demonstrate to the world Israel's pious neutrality.[33]

The outbreak of the Korean War in June 1950 forced Israel to make a choice: either declare allegiance to the United Nations and the international force that was soon assembled under American leadership to repel Soviet- and Chinese-backed North Korean aggression, or stand by the Soviet Union and the forces opposing the intervention of the international community. On July 2 the Israeli government declared its support for the UN Charter and the Security Council's efforts to restore international peace.[34] The immediate reward from Washington was the promise to supply half-tracks, PIAT bombs, radar equipment, and eighty-six training aircraft.[35] James McDonald, the U.S. ambassador in Tel Aviv, suggested that perhaps Israel's leaders had finally recognized the "ultimate folly of pursuing a strict East-West neutrality . . . it has resulted from the ultimate realization that the hand that feeds will not submit indefinitely to being bitten."[36]

On July 7, 1950, the UN Security Council passed Resolution 84, which called on all member states to repel the attack by North Korea on its southern neighbor and to restore the peace by providing military forces and other assistance under the Unified Command led by the United States. Israel responded by contributing medical aid and food supplies worth $100,000—a significant contribution from a small country close to bankruptcy and still recovering from its violent birth two years earlier. At the General Assembly, Eban introduced a statement of principles and then formulated a resolution that served as the basis for the subsequent negotiations over an armistice agreement between the two Koreas. This was Israel's first attempt at drafting and presenting a resolution to the United Nations, and it taught Eban a valuable lesson about the precedence of politics over morality at the world organization. Eban's draft resolution called for, among other things, an immediate cease-fire, the withdrawal of foreign troops, the independence of Korea guaranteed by the UN and China, and the beginning of UN-China dialogue over outstanding issues. The Israeli draft resolution received the enthusiastic support of India, Mexico, Canada, Norway, and other countries, as well as the more reserved backing of the American delegation, which found the proposed inclusion of China in UN activities too radical. But the strongest objection to Eban's document came from the Arab countries, which, while in support of the substance of the draft resolution, refused to vote for it at the General Assembly as long as the records showed that it was proposed by the representative of Israel. The Arab position was hardly surprising given the declared Arab boycott of anything that bore relation to Israel, but even so Eban was outraged by the implication. "This is petty nonsense!" he protested before the Canadian foreign minister Lester Pearson and Norway's representative to the UN, Hans Engen.[37] Eban's colleagues agreed, but it was also clear that securing the Arab votes and passing the resolution were more important than the scoring of personal points. To bypass the Arab boycott of the Israeli proposal, Eban agreed that the draft resolution would be sponsored by the Norwegian delegation without any substantive changes in language. Eventually the Norwegian draft resolution was duly adopted with a majority of 45–5, with 8 abstentions.[38]

Eban also assisted with the legal framework for the U.S.-sponsored Uniting for Peace resolution. Frustrated by the Soviet veto of Security Council resolutions on the Korean issue, the American delegation sought to empower the General Assembly to act on matters of international security and breach of peace when the Security Council became deadlocked owing to the exercise of the veto power by one of its five permanent members. The draft resolution was controversial, for it appeared to be in breach of Chapter VII of the UN Charter, which defined the primacy of the Security Council in all matters relating to international peace and security. Eban proved instrumental in devising the political and legalistic language to address these potential problems, and the resolution was passed by a majority of 52 to 5, with 2 abstentions.[39]

While the Korean War pushed Israel toward a de facto alignment with the West, other factors also contributed to Jerusalem's reorientation toward Washington. The magnitude of Israeli dependence on American aid for its very existence could not be exaggerated. At the end of June 1950, leaders of American Zionism and the United Jewish Appeal arrived in Israel to negotiate with the Israeli government an aid plan: American Jewry would contribute $500 million through the issuance of bonds and through charitable donations, while another $500 million would come from other sources within the U.S. government.[40] A month later President Truman delivered to Abe Feinberg, a prominent Jewish lobbyist and a chief financier of the president's election campaign in 1948, his commitment to strengthen Israel as a bulwark of democracy and to support its ambitious campaign of absorbing hundreds of thousands of immigrants, for failure to do so would invite the spread of communism. Truman also indicated that he would "consider favorably" a support program of $500 million, but he cautioned that it would be necessary to enlist congressional support while it was preoccupied with the Korean War. After his talk with the president, Feinberg reported back to the Israeli embassy in Washington that he would turn to mobilizing senators and congressmen to sponsor the aid program.[41] Eban assumed a leading role in this mobilization; he reported to Walter Eytan in Jerusalem that he had "concluded discussion with leaders Jewish organizations with following results on U.S.A. government aid Israel: (1) All organizations . . . agreed cooperate concerted effort influence Congress, public opinion, in favour inclusion Israel American aid allocations generally aiming at half billion over three–four years."[42] Israel's third source of economic aid from the United States, in addition to the government's $500 million aid program and the raising of a similar sum by various Zionist groups, was the Export-Import Bank, which in December 1950 had agreed to loan the Israeli government $35 million for agricultural projects on top of the $100 million already delivered the year before.[43] By the end of the decade the U.S. government was directly responsible for about 55 percent of capital imported to Israel. It is no surprise that Israel sought to develop "special political ties and bonds" with Washington.[44]

THE INAUGURATION OF DWIGHT D. EISENHOWER AS PRESIDENT IN JANUARY 1953 began a new era in U.S.-Israeli relations. In contrast to Truman's emphatic support for the establishment of Israel and his intimate familiarity with the Jewish problem, Eisenhower had never held a political position in his life, and his long and distinguished military career did not make for a natural springboard to the wheeling and dealing of Washington's lobbying. Eisenhower had no experience with Jewish political pressures, and he certainly did not owe his electoral victory to the Jewish vote (two-thirds of the Jewish vote went to Adlai Stevenson, the Democratic candidate). While Truman was surrounded by several Jews or pro-Israel individuals in key posts in his administration (such as David Niles and Clark Clifford) as well as outside it (such as Eddie Jacobson, Abe Feinberg, and Jacob Blaustein), there was not a significant presence of Zionist sympathizers in the Eisenhower administration who had the president's ear. During a meeting with Governor Theodore McKeldin of Maryland and Judge Simon Sobelhoff, a prominent Jewish leader, in February 1953 the president confessed that "he had no idea [of] there being different Jewish organizations, or that they represent different groups or hold different points of view"; in July 1954 he would tell the National Security Council that he was "astounded" to learn from an Israeli visitor that the "government in Israel was thoroughly unreligious and materialistic," thinking instead that "a good many of the Israeli government were religious fanatics."[45] Given Eisenhower's complete ignorance of Israel and the American Jewish community, it was not surprising that he did not feel obliged to listen to pro-Israel groups in Washington. At the same time, Eisenhower and his secretary of state, John Foster Dulles, wished to court the Arab states in order to ward off Soviet interest in the Middle East and secure access to the region's oil fields—a policy that was described as "friendly impartiality."[46]

On a personal level, Eban found Eisenhower a decidedly less impassioned and emotional character than Truman. He later recalled his first meeting with Eisenhower in February 1952, when the future president served as supreme commander of NATO in Europe: "I remember that he spoke the whole time we were in his office with the utmost fluency, and when we came away we couldn't remember a single thing he had said. He had the gift of being extremely articulate without being coherent. His thoughts were always ahead of his capacity of expression."[47] Moshe Sharett's impression after his first meetings with Eisenhower and Dulles was of "inferior intelligence and ability" and of "confusion and blundering." Sharett concluded that while, like Truman, Eisenhower was graced by simplicity of manners, he lacked his predecessor's "moral weight and rectitude."[48] American Jews were also troubled to find that the new president "rarely spoke about their favorite subjects: Israel and the Holocaust," even though he oversaw the liberation of the Nazi death camps as the supreme commander of Allied forces in Europe.[49] Ben-Gurion summed up Israel's anxieties about the new administration in the clearest terms: "Until now there was only one conduit to the White House—the Israeli; from now on there will be an Arab one as well."[50]

In May 1953 Secretary Dulles embarked on a twenty-day tour of the Middle East and East Asia. His impressions from this fact-finding mission planted the seeds of what would become the administration's official Middle East policy, and for the most part this presented more disadvantages than opportunities for Israel. During his visit to Israel, Dulles expressed his admiration for the fledgling nation's history and creativity, but he also complained to Ben-Gurion and Sharret about the undue influence of American Jewry on domestic politics and the formulation of U.S. Middle East policy. He believed that the Eisenhower and Truman administrations had been "so subject to Jewish influence that Arab viewpoint [was] ignored." The unavoidable implication was that from now on America's policy toward Israel would be taken as part of a broader policy that took into account U.S. relations with the Arab world and the global conflict with the Soviets. He emphasized that the administration would not be able to play a useful role in the area without the goodwill and confidence of the Arabs in the United States, but also reaffirmed his country's sympathy for Israel.[51] Ironically, Dulles's irritation with Jewish groups in the United States, "which felt they had right [to] exercise influence because of contributions to election victory," was shared by Eban, who often complained that "the constant demand by individual Jewish leaders to see the President and the secretary of state leads to negative results. . . . their frequent intercession harms Israel's interest and is unwarranted. . . . Israeli officials in Washington must be given priority in presenting the country's case before the American policymakers."[52] Eban identified Golda Meir, then Israel's minister of labor, as one of the chief culprits in a campaign designed to stir up support for a more emboldened and "heroic" Jewish effort in the United States. He complained to Sharett that Meir publicly criticized the work of the embassy in Washington as naive and cowardly and in so doing undermined the authority of the embassy in Washington as well his own position as ambassador.[53] This was the first round in the Eban–Meir duel that would see them trade blows over personal and political affairs for the remaining of their public careers.

On June 1, 1953, Dulles delivered an address to the American people on his Middle East mission that confirmed the Israeli anxieties of recent months: "The United States should seek to allay the deep resentment against it that has resulted from the creation of Israel. In the past we had good relations with the Arab peoples. . . . Today the Arab peoples are afraid that the U.S. will back the new State of Israel in aggressive expansion. They are more fearful of Zionism than of Communism and they fear lest the U.S. become the backer of expansionist Zionism."[54] Only a month passed before Washington's new policy was put to the test by the Israeli government. During Dulles's visit to Israel he was informed by Sharett of the Israeli government's intention to move its Foreign Ministry from Tel Aviv to Jerusalem; the foreign and defense ministries were the only government ministries to have remained in Tel Aviv following the government's decision to move its offices to Jerusalem in 1949. "Don't do it while I am around," Dulles warned Sharett, who interpreted the message as acquiescence to the idea once Dulles had left the region. On Friday, July 10, the Israeli government informed the U.S. State Department that the Israeli Foreign Ministry would be transferred to Jerusalem the following Sunday. Perhaps more than the decision itself, it was the timing and manner in which the Israeli decision was conveyed that angered the State Department. Francis H. Russell, the chargé d'affaires at the U.S. embassy in Tel Aviv, reported to Washington that the Israeli decision caused "deep resentment" among the majority of his colleagues at the embassy, while Harold B. Minor, the ambassador in Lebanon, suggested that this was the first real test of the new American foreign policy in the region and that the administration must show the Arabs that it was capable of saying no to political Zionism; otherwise all the efforts of the previous six months would "have been for naught." An official statement by the State Department to Israel certainly satisfied these concerns: it declared that the United States had no plans to transfer its embassy to Jerusalem, and that such a move would be inconsistent with UN resolutions dealing with the international nature of Jerusalem, or indeed with Secretary Dulles's own position on the issue. The secretary himself described the Israeli decision as regrettable and an embarrassment to the United Nations.[55]

The controversy over the relocation of the Foreign Ministry was but a prelude to the most troubled period in the short history thus far of U.S.-Israeli relations, one in which Israeli adventurism was met by decisive and at times coercive American response. In late July 1953 the Israeli government approved a project to divert the route of the River Jordan near the B'not Yacov Bridge in northern Galilee in order to generate hydroelectric power to direct the river's flow southward to irrigate the arid Negev Desert. The diversion project was to take place on Israeli-owned land inside the demilitarized zone, but on September 23 General Vagn Bennike, chief of staff of the United Nations Truce Supervision Organization (UNTSO), ruled that the project would alter the strategic balance in favor of Israel and thus violated the terms of the 1949 armistice agreements. Israel was ordered to stop the work until it obtained Syrian consent to the project. Eban advised Sharett that the political situation did not necessitate a "head-on collision with incalculable effects," especially with regard to relations with the United States. Sharett and Gideon Rafael recommended to Ben-Gurion that Israel halt the work for a week so as to not violate UN resolutions, but Ben-Gurion, claiming the matter was vital to Israel, ordered that the work should not be interrupted.[56] Meanwhile, in Washington, the State Department moved swiftly to reprimand Israel. On September 18 Henry Byroade, the assistant secretary of state for the Middle East, had informed Eban that the forthcoming $26 million in economic aid allocated to Israel under the Mutual Security Act of 1953 would be suspended until the issue was resolved.[57] Beyond the fear of military escalation between Israel and Syria, Washington viewed the Israeli project as an act of defiance of UNTSO that turned a local dispute in the demilitarized zone into an Israeli challenge to the authority of the world organization, which necessitated a tough response. A week later Eban protested to Dulles the American linkage between political action and economic aid. The secretary, however, reminded Eban that in the aftermath of the relocation of the Israeli Foreign Ministry to Jerusalem it was difficult for the administration to pursue an even-handed policy in the region if the Israeli government "appeared to be disrespectful of United Nations decisions while we continued to furnish aid which from our point of view was discretionary."[58] Two weeks later he warned Eban that Israel had to stop the work in order to avoid the "awkward position" of being in contempt of the United Nations.[59]

Throughout this episode Eban disagreed with his government's intransigence. After the crises over the Huleh Valley work two years earlier and the Foreign Ministry's relocation to Jerusalem in the summer, he warned Sharett against another "first-rate crisis" with the United States and pointed out that the entire Israeli delegation in New York agreed that Israel must be in "complete compliance" with Bennike's ruling as a first step.[60] Eban was evidently irritated with his government's indifference to or ignorance of the many challenges that faced the mission in New York and brought the Washington embassy to the verge of "general collapse." The beginning of the water project, for example, coincided with the opening of the eighth session of the UN General Assembly in September 1953 and added unnecessary burden to an already trying agenda for Israel, which included the status of Jerusalem, the status of refugees, the supply of Western arms to the Arabs, and Washington's decision to withhold aid from Israel.[61] Eban went as far as accusing the United States division of the Foreign Ministry in Jerusalem of misreading the political situation and of "an appalling lack of self-criticism"; the current crisis was not the result of the U.S. State Department's recent critical mood toward Israel, he said, but of Israel's intransigent actions and defiance of the United Nations. This international sentiment was more prevalent than Jerusalem realized, Eban added, and even American Jews were openly saying that Israel had scarcely allowed one crisis to die down before generating another.[62]

In the midst of this turmoil Eban was elected vice president of the UN General Assembly. It was a testimony to the high regard in which he was held, and all the more extraordinary given Israel's rocky relationship with the UN at that time. Together with the other six vice presidents, Eban now served as ex-officio on the General Committee, which helped the president of the General Assembly determine the agenda and conduct business. Walter Eytan wrote to Eban that everyone at the Foreign Ministry in Jerusalem was "naturally all still suffering from the thrill" of his election, before adding, "You are entering a new procedural world from which we have hitherto been excluded, and it will help us for the future if we know what happens on the inside." Eytan's assessment that "it will presumably be years before we again get a place on [the General] Committee" was a colossal understatement—more than five decades would pass before the honor was accorded to another Israeli representative at the UN.[63]

If the River Jordan water crisis placed Israel on a collision course with the United States and the United Nations, the inopportune outbreak of another international crisis over Israeli actions all but relegated the country's international standing to that of pariah. While the 1949 armistice agreements concluded the official hostilities of the first Arab–Israeli war, they provided less than adequate security to Israel or its Arab neighbors. Israel's border with Jordan—devoid of natural obstacles and with close proximity to concentrated areas of population on both sides—proved particularly porous: in June 1953 the Israeli government had complained to Washington that in the previous year alone there had been 3,714 cross-border infiltrations into Israel, which included 874 cases of theft, 43 cases of robbery with violence, 1,395 cases of attempts to steal, and 395 attacks on military personnel, resulting in 59 people killed, 74 wounded, and 35 taken prisoner and approximately $3 million worth of damage to property.[64] The question of adequate response to Arab infiltrations had preoccupied the Israeli government for several years. On the one hand, Ben-Gurion and the defense establishment advocated a "two blows for one" policy against the Arab towns and villages the suspected marauders came from. On the other hand, Sharett and other moderates in the government (as well as the vast majority of the Foreign Ministry) maintained that acts of retribution should be used sparingly, and only after due consideration of the diplomatic repercussions. In most cases Ben-Gurionism defeated Sharettism.[65]

On the night of October 12, 1953, the Israeli settlement of Moshav Yehud became the latest target of cross-border attacks: a mother and her two children were killed by a grenade thrown into their bedroom. The Jordanian government joined Israel in condemning the attack and vowed to track down the perpetrators and bring them to justice, but Israel's security chiefs were bent on retribution. Although the perpetrators' tracks did not lead to their home base, the village of Qibya, which was the base of previous attacks, was chosen as the target. The operation, which was carried out by the 890th Paratroop Battalion and Unit 101, a commando unit that had been founded and commanded by Major Ariel Sharon two months earlier, was an act of vengeance as much as it was an act of deterrence. Israeli Central Command's operational instructions were clear: "to attack and temporarily to occupy the village, carry out destruction and maximum killing, in order to drive out the inhabitants of the village from their homes."[66] Two days later the troops carried their orders to the letter, leaving behind sixty-nine dead villagers, two-thirds of them women and children, and forty-five houses blown up.[67]

The unprecedented magnitude of this reprisal was matched by a similarly unprecedented wave of international condemnation. On October 17 the president of the UN Security Council received three identical letters from representatives of the United States, the United Kingdom, and France requesting an urgent meeting of the council to consider the Israeli operation. The next day the U.S government expressed its "deepest sympathy for the families of those who lost their lives" in Qibya and added its conviction that those responsible "should be brought to account," and Secretary Dulles followed with a public statement confirming the State Department's decision to suspend aid to Israel. He emphasized that the decision had been made three weeks earlier in response to the crisis over the River Jordan water project, but the timing of his announcement was calculated to bring the utmost pressure on Israel over the Qibya raid.[68] American Jewry also strongly condemned the operation, with Jacob Blaustein, president of the American Jewish Committee, denouncing it as a "tragic and clearly reprehensible affair . . . under no circumstances can it be condoned. The claim that this act was retaliatory, no matter how well substantiated, does not excuse it."[69] The British also condemned the Israeli government in the strongest terms, noting that the reprisals policy put in jeopardy the relations between the two countries and adding, "In the light of the attack on Kibya [*sic*], which was clearly a planned military operation . . . Her Majesty's Government find it hard to accept protestations of Israel's peaceful desires as sincere. Such actions as that at Kibya indeed render them empty and meaningless."[70] Prime Minister Winston Churchill described the affair as the most shocking incident connected with Israel since the assassination of Walter Guinness, Lord Moyne in 1944 and that as a Zionist he regretted the Israeli action since there was nothing Israel needed more than a good reputation.[71] The British Ambassador in Tel Aviv, Sir Francis Evans, expressed his puzzlement over the "mystery that such intelligent people as the Israel leaders can be so blind to the consequences of their violent actions, and so deaf to the advice of their friends."[72]

Sharett was particularly incensed by the turn of events. Three months earlier Ben-Gurion had taken an extended vacation and appointed him acting prime minister and Pinhas Lavon acting defense minister, but Ben-Gurion had refused to detach himself from matters of government and continued to exert influence from the outside. The decision to raid Qibya had been taken on the morning of October 13 by Lavon, Chief of General Staff Mordechai Makleff, Chief of Operations Moshe Dayan, and a vacationing Ben-Gurion; Sharett, the acting prime minister, was not invited to the meeting. When he heard of the impending retaliatory operation, Sharett demanded from Lavon that the order be rescinded, but Lavon refused, invoking Ben-Gurion's authority.[73] Ben-Gurion ended his vacation on October 18, only to announce his decision to formally resign from his posts as prime minister and defense minister two weeks later. (On December 6 Sharett would become prime minister, and in January 1954 he would present his new government to the Knesset.) On Ben-Gurion's resignation, Sharett wrote in his diary that "perhaps it is best if he left so for the first time there can be a real effort to align the security policy with foreign policy considerations."[74]

Eban was one of the most vocal critics of his government's actions, describing to Rafael his astonishment over the perpetration of such a "cruel reprisal" that could not be excused by previous Arab attacks—though in his memoirs he merely noted that "the Israeli reaction was regarded by most Israelis as excessive."[75] Rafael himself lamented to Eytan that Israel had turned from a sylph into a monster overnight and rued the fact that Israel's diplomats had failed to impress upon the government that the country's international standing was an integral part of its security. The government's pathological disregard of this principle, he added, "could well bring the state to the brink of the abyss." Herzl Berger, a member of the Israeli delegation to the UN, warned the Foreign Ministry in Jerusalem that the Qibya operation was but the latest in a series of issues that created an impression at the UN of Israel as a repeated provoker and violator of the organization's directives. Another Israeli diplomat, David Hacohen, was particularly acerbic in his criticism of the Israeli government: "This murderous frenzy that has seized our people—this Deir Yasin incident under the aegis of the authorities, at their full responsibility, carried out by the IDF [Israel Defense Forces]—literally freezes my blood"; he could not look into the eyes of colleagues at the UN who expressed their astonishment "at the Nazi actions of my colleagues and myself."[76]

Eban and Sharett's anger at the Qibya operation was public knowledge. Morris Fischer, Israel's counsel in Ankara, told his British counterpart that "certainly Sharett was against these tactics and so, above all others, was Eban, the ambassador in Washington," whereas Evans, the British ambassador, noted,

"I daresay, too, that Eban doesn't like such a policy: certainly he cannot like having to defend Israel when she is so utterly in the wrong, and when he knows his defence, however clever, must fail."[77] Eban's outrage at the reprisal soon turned to anger at his government's decision (in which Sharett again found himself in the minority) to altogether wash its hands of the operation. On October 19 Ben-Gurion announced that the perpetrators of the Qibya raid were in fact frontier settlers whose patience over the incessant murderous attacks from Jordan had finally become exhausted. He added that after an investigation by the government it was "clear beyond doubt that not a single army unit was absent from its base on the night of the attack on Qibya."[78] Eban told Sharett that Ben-Gurion's statement was neither courageous nor truthful and did not gain any credence given the evidence to the contrary. When Sharett (who helped draft the statement despite his strong reservation to its content) showed Ben-Gurion the cable from Eban, the fuming prime minister told Sharett that "Eban is a child" if he thought that a vigorous Israeli rejection of the Qibya operation would blunt the international condemnation, and even added that Bennike's version of events (that the raid was carried by IDF units) was "a fantastic lie."[79]

Handling the repercussions of the Qibya affair as well as the American pressure over the River Jordan water crisis proved to be impossible. Despite the government's decision on October 18 not to stop the water diversion project (against Sharett's recommendation), it was only a matter of time before it was forced to reconsider its position.[80] Luckily, however, Dulles inadvertently provided Israel with a face-saving opportunity. His statement on the withdrawal of aid from Israel on October 20, while designed to pressure Israel to abide with the UN ruling on the water diversion project, also put him on a collision course with Jewish leaders and congressmen from both parties who protested the suspension of aid and the broader unbalanced attitude of the State Department toward Israel. With the adroit coordination of Eban and the Israeli Embassy behind the scenes ("we are shooting our arrows carefully but with precision," he reported to Jersualem)[81], the domestic criticism over the aid suspension put the State Department in a "prestige deadlock." Byroade confessed to Eban that the department had made a mistake on that issue and he now sought ways to get Secretary Dulles, who was "personally disconcerted at the great internal storm," off the hook.[82] Dulles proposed a compromise solution that would help both sides: if Israel accepted the UN Security Council's invitation to suspend its works on the water project "courteously and without prejudice" to enable a more calm discussion on the issue, the United States would lift the aid suspension.[83] Within days the crisis was over; on October 27 Eban informed the Security Council of his government's willingness to suspend the project in the demilitarized zone while the issue was being considered by the council. The council noted its "satisfaction" with Eban's statement, and the following day Secretary Dulles announced the lifting of the suspension of aid to Israel. On November 4 the withheld $26.5 million was made available to Israel.[84]

But with the abating of one crisis there was little respite before the culmination of another. Turning to the issue of the forthcoming debate on Qibya, Eban insisted that when the question was brought before the Security Council he would be unable to personally praise the operation or defend it unreservedly. As far as forming a public position on the matter, Eban suggested that Israel could only adopt a "candid and self-confident position" that placed the operation within the broader context of the problem of Jordanian infiltration into Israel, though the act itself could not be justified.[85] But as Rafael noted, even Eban's "masterful oratory, incisive logic and persuasive argument . . . [his] mightiest flow of rhetoric, though evoking admiration," could not turn the tide at the UN in favor of Israel.[86] In his address to the Security Council on November 12, Eban described Israel's security problems since the signing of the armistice agreements of 1949, stating that Israel was within easy reach of its hostile neighbors and pointing to the consistent Arab refusal to negotiate a peace agreement with Israel. Turning to the tensions along the Israeli–Jordanian border, he gave a detailed background of the history of cross-border infiltration into Israel and reiterated the circumstances that had led to the Qibya raid. He expressed his government's "profound and unreserved regret for the loss of innocent life," stating that it was an unfortunate explosion of pent-up feeling and a tragic breakdown of restraint. Attempting to draw attention away from Qibya, Eban suggested a meeting at UN headquarters between senior political and military officials of Israel and Jordan to discuss armistice problems and ways to prevent further border incidents. He concluded that the primary cause of tension in the area was the absence of peaceful relations between Israel and the Arab states, and that the signatories of the armistice agreements (Israel, Jordan, Egypt, Syria, and Lebanon) should be called upon to enter into direct negotiations for a final peace settlement.[87] Though Eban reported to Sharett that his address managed to embarrass some members of the Security Council who wished to focus the debate on Qibya rather than the broader security context in the region, there was no way for Israel to win the debate. Four days later the Jordanian representative flatly rejected Eban's proposal for an Israeli-Jordanian meeting at UN headquarters and added, rather convincingly, that there was a difference between individual Jordanian infiltration and the aggression carried out by organized units of the Israeli military.[88] On November 24 the Security Council passed a resolution expressing its "strongest censure" of the Qibya action, while it only took note of the substantial evidence of the crossing of the armistice line by unauthorized persons into Israel and completely ignored Israel's request to insert a call for the parties to enter negotiations.[89] Sharett described the resolution in his diary as "worse than anything we had imagined," while Eban condemned the resolution's strong language, which he described as "without precedence in the UN history even in events of far greater severity" compared to the "lightness and gentility" with which the incursions from Jordan were treated.[90] Two days later Eban sent Sharett his assessment of the Qibya affair: it plunged Israel's international standing into the abyss, involving mishaps, dangers, and blunders the likes of which had not been made since the establishment of Israel:

1. Sending regular armed forces across an international border, without the intention of triggering a full-scale war, is a step that distinguishes Israel from all other countries. No other state acts in this way. It was this, rather than the heavy casualties, that shocked the world.
2. Another blunder was the number of victims and the wild and unrestrained nature of the operation. But the world would have tolerated atrocities and murder, as it often does elsewhere, had they not involved violation of an international boundary.
3. This operation was the first since the establishment of Israel with which world Jewry refused to identify, viewing it instead as a blow to the good name of the Jewish people.
4. Dulles viewed the raid as a deliberate and insolent response to his personal request that Israel review its defense policy. World opinion, too, was revolted. Even Deir Yasin had not prompted such horror, because there is no similarity between action undertaken by dissidents during a struggle for national liberation and an operation mounted by a sovereign state that enjoys international recognition.

5. One must certainly assume that a similar incident in the future would trigger military intervention by the British and Americans, and might even lead to a UN-mandated operation, as in Korea. Such an Israeli operation could bring the country to the threshold of foreign occupation and loss of independence. Hence the Qibya operation must be defined as the greatest threat to national security since the end of the War of Independence.
6. Reports coming out of Israel confirm the assumption that Israel obtained no local military advantage to offset these international disadvantages: infiltration continues. The assault on Qibya solved nothing.[91]

On the basis of these assumptions Eban concluded that Israel desperately needed a respite from military actions: "Any initiative that could be interpreted as a confrontation with the West or the UN must be postponed or cancelled. Even if this entails restraint unjustified by the facts of a case, Israel must bow to circumstances out of global considerations."[92]

Eban found a natural ally in Sharett on the issue of public diplomacy (*hasbara*). Both men attached great importance to the role of public opinion in attaining Israel's legitimacy in the eyes of the world. The psychological makeup and diplomatic disposition of Sharett and Eban were very similar. In 1952 the London *Observer* had published a profile of Sharett that could easily describe Eban too: "He has been criticized for his loquacity, and some visitors have been dumbfounded by the irresistible stream of what tends to be, perhaps, too one-sided conversation. . . . Yet it is unlikely that anyone could be seriously offended, for there is a disarming *naiveté* about the joy he takes in talking, and particularly in talking a language which a visitor could not have expected him to know."[93]

Sharett and Eban also shared a certain diplomatic outlook. "His qualities and his inherent ideas are those which Israel must acquire if that disturbed and uneasy community is to achieve political and psychological stability," the *Observer* wrote about Sharett. Only weeks earlier Eban had annunciated these very sentiments; while lecturing on the subject of Arab nationalism, he declared that Israelis should not begrudge the spread of nationalist movements sweeping the Middle East despite the likely detrimental ramifications to Arab-Israeli relations: "It would be utterly incongruous for the State of Israel to approach the national movements, which now agitate our area, with anything but a basically sympathetic spirit," he noted before adding an important caveat: "I suggest to you in all seriousness that not every student in Cairo who throws a stone through the window of a foreign establishment, is necessarily the spiritual descendent of Thomas Jefferson or of Robespierre."[94]

In his seminal study of Israeli foreign policy, Michael Brecher—a former research assistant to Eban at the UN in 1948—described the two as "men of words" whereas all their leading contemporaries (Ben-Gurion, Dayan, Lavon, Sharon, and Rabin) were "men of deeds." Both Eban and Sharret were distinguished by their bearing, manner, dress, and speech. They were more formal and showed greater deference to world opinion, but displayed poorer understanding of domestic politics and were slower to make decisions. Both distrusted the generals and military experts whose self-reliance and swagger were at odds with their inherently internationalist and measured outlook.[95] Surprisingly, however, Eban himself shied away from the popular depiction of himself as the natural heir to Sharett. In a 1976 interview, two years after he was ousted from government by Prime Minister Yitzhak Rabin, Eban not only rejected this automatic affiliation with Sharettism but also objected to the dichotomous treatment of Sharettism versus Ben-Gurionism—the first defined as the search for reconciliation through moderation and the latter through the application of force. Eban dismissed the differences between Ben-Gurion and Sharret as "microscopic . . . subsidiary, individual and temperamental." He acknowledged that he followed Sharett's international line, but added that he found Sharett "excessive in his deference to what he called world opinion, or rather static and unwilling to accept that opinion could be changed. So I would say the distance between them is very small and I would be in the middle, somewhere nearer to Ben-Gurion than Sharett."[96] Eban's criticism of Sharett's deference to world opinion was particularly telling, as it was this attribute more than any other that Eban's critics—and even his friends—habitually used against him. Ironically, it was Sharett himself who noted in his diary his agreement with Rafael's assessment that the tone of Eban's cables from New York and Washington was overly anxious and that while Eban took notice of international and American practices, he ignored domestic processes within Israel.[97]

Eban's dismissal of the perceived wisdom concerning the polarization between Ben-Gurionism and Sharettism is not wholly accurate, according to Brecher, who has pointed out that beyond the temperamental differences, the two had opposing views of substance: "in summary, there were *more* shared themes in the *global* system images of Ben-Gurion and Sharett, but the points of divergence were *more serious*. . . . Yet even in these [shared] components there were *differences* in *tone*, *stress*, and *nuance*. And their basic difference in outlook—the place of the UN in global politics, and, particularly, in the Middle East conflict, as well as in Israeli foreign policy—overshadowed all the points of convergence."[98] More recent studies, however, find greater nuance in this debate than Brecher's: "Without denying the general usefulness of such contrasts, there is much evidence to suggest that these analyses tend to exaggerate actual *policy* difference between Ben-Gurion and Sharett and their respective supporters."[99] In the final analysis, however, it is evident that during Eban's ambassadorial years his views were almost always in sync with Sharett's, and at times even more critical than Sharett's regarding the tone and substance of Ben-Gurion's policies. This was the case over the timing of Ben-Gurion's decision to preempt the General Assembly's resolution on the internationalization of Jerusalem, the Jordan River water crisis and, of course, the reprisals policy, which would intensify when Ben-Gurion would return to the prime minister's office in November 1955. Eban's view of the reprisals policy was as critical as Sharett's, as evidenced by his outrage after Operation Black Arrow in Gaza in February 1955, which left thirty-eight Egyptian and eight Israeli soldiers dead: "[H]ow absurdly the Gaza episode had worked out," he wrote. "The international and Jewish disappointment is extreme where no advantage of a local military character has been secured. It's just 100 percent loss. We must draw the conclusion that to send armies across a frontier losing eight boys to avenge the four killed in five months is just ridiculous. Retaliation is just *finished* as a policy and our people should get used to obeying the same rules, even under provocation, as other governments when provoked."[100]

But Eban's principled objection to his government's adventurist spirit was matched by equally vigorous defense of the same actions he personally found so objectionable. Nowhere was this attribute, one that led Ben-Gurion to describe Eban as the "Voice of Israel" abroad, demonstrated so perfectly as in the aftermath of another controversial reprisal raid orchestrated by Ben-Gurion, Dayan, and Sharon that was fiercely criticized by Sharett and Eban. In December 1955, following Operation Kinneret's botched military raid on Syrian military positions which led to fifty Syrian and six Israeli deaths and jeopardized Sharett's efforts to secure an arms deal with Washington, Eban wrote Ben-Gurion a long letter in which he listed his strong reservations over the conduct and timing of the raid. Ben-Gurion's reply, which Eban described as "somewhat mischievous" and "as close to repentance as I was likely to secure," was testament to Eban's prowess as a diplomat as it was to the folly of his government's pathological infatuation with the use of force: "I fully understand your concerns about the Kinneret operation," Ben-Gurion wrote. "I must confess that I, too, began to have my doubts about the wisdom of it. But when I read the full text of your brilliant defense of our action in the Security Council, all my doubts were set at rest. You have convinced me that we were right, after all."[101]

THE YEAR 1955 ENDED WITH NO NOTICEABLE IMPROVEMENT IN ISRAEL'S RELATIONS with the United States and the United Nations. The Eisenhower administration refused to supply arms to Israel following the Kinneret operation, last in a succession of reprisal raids by the IDF that left Israel more isolated internationally than ever before.[102] Operation Black Arrow in February that year (shortly after Ben-Gurion had returned to the post of defense minister) had led not only to another round of international outrage against Israel but was also used as an excuse by the Egyptian leader, Colonel Gamal Abdel Nasser, who had seized power in a military coup three years earlier, to sign an arms deal with the Soviets the following September. The $250 million deal, which included 150 MiG-15 jet fighters, 50 long-range bombers, 230 T-34 tanks, and hundreds of artillery pieces, changed the course of the Arab–Israeli conflict irrevocably. Beyond the immediate threat to Israel's security, it also had instant implications for France and Britain's strategic interests in the region.[103]

With a feeling of siege and isolation engulfing Israel, Eban found some minor personal solace in the news of the admission of Ireland and Italy to the UN in December 1955. Having been wedged between the representatives of Iraq and Lebanon for more than six years, the alphabetical order of seating at the General Assembly meant that Eban would now be wedged between the Irish and Italian delegates. As they took their places on each side of the representative of the Jewish state, Eban turned to welcome them: "I believe the three of us together account for the whole of New York City and most of Massachusetts."[104]

IX
Suez

EVER SINCE THE ESTABLISHMENT OF ISRAEL, ABBA EBAN HAD REPEATEDLY complained before the United Nations Security Council about Egypt's denial of Israeli shipping through the Suez Canal. The Israeli case rested on the convention on the free navigation of the Suez Canal that was signed in 1888 by the great powers of the time, and declared that the canal should "always be free and open, in time of war as in time of peace, to every vessel of commerce or of war, without distinction of flag."[1] Egypt, however, maintained that owing to the state of belligerency between the two countries, it was entitled to deny Israeli shipping on the grounds of self-defense—an argument that was flatly rejected by the Security Council in its resolution of September 1, 1951, which called upon Egypt "to terminate the restrictions on the passage of international commercial shipping and goods through the Suez Canal wherever bound and to cease all interference with such shipping." Yet no effort was made by Egypt—or indeed by the UN or Britain, the official guarantor of Egypt's adherence to the 1888 treaty—to implement the resolution.[2] Six months later the Soviets vetoed a Security Council resolution directed against the Egyptian blockade, leading Israel to ponder other means to secure free shipping through the canal.[3] Six months later Israel attempted to break the Egyptian blockade, for the first time since 1948, by sending the freighter *Bat Galim* through the canal. The ship left Eritrea en route to Haifa, carrying food and hides, when it was seized by Egypt. Once again, no action was taken by the UN to sanction Egypt; by September 1956 more than a half dozen ships en route to Israel had been blocked or seized by the Egyptians.

The Soviet shift from support of the 1947 partition resolution and the recognition of Israel six months later to a more invested involvement in Egyptian affairs was made manifest by several acts of friendship toward the Egyptian leader, Colonel Gamal Abdel Nasser, who seized power in a military coup in 1952, championing Arab nationalism and escape from the country's colonial past. Israel's raid on Gaza in February 1955, which left thirty-eight Egyptian soldiers dead, and the formation of the military security organization known as the Baghdad Pact the same month by the United States, Britain, Iraq, Turkey, Pakistan, and Iran, led Nasser to ditch his hitherto nonaligned policy and to seek military arms from the Soviet Union. The arms deal of September 1955 threatened to change not only the balance of military power in the region but also the course of superpower relations more broadly. As U.S. secretary of state John Foster Dulles pointed out to Eban, it was one of the gravest developments in recent years, as it opened a new era of Soviet "mischievous activity" and was likely to transform the military balance in the area within twelve to fifteen months.[4] The arms deal led the Americans to withdraw their funding for the construction of the Aswan High Dam on the River Nile, which led Nasser to announce in July 1956 his decision to nationalize the Anglo-French Suez Canal Company in order to fund the ambitious project. In so doing Britain and France became interested parties in the conflict between Egypt and Israel. The French were also angered by Nasser's material and financial support of revolutionary groups in North Africa—not least the Algerian Liberation Front, which fought for independence from France, while the British, beyond the projected loss of enormous revenue, also feared the immediate threat to Western oil interests in the Middle East, since the canal was the principal gateway to Europe for oil coming from the Persian Gulf.

The Israeli government built its case against Egypt over not only the closure of the canal to Israeli-owned and Israeli-bound shipping but also the increasing cross-border raids of Egyptian *fedayeen* (armed militias) into Israel that had claimed the lives of dozens of civilians since 1948. As discussions in the Security Council to adopt a resolution favoring Western interests and against Egypt were thwarted by the Soviets, the convergence of Israeli, French, and British aspirations gradually led to a tripartite collusion designed to bring about the downfall of Nasser.

Before Prime Minister David Ben-Gurion could convince his cabinet of the need for a military action against Egypt, he had to get Moshe Sharett out of the way. The indefatigable foreign minister was a formidable opponent of Ben-Gurion and was highly respected by his colleagues, and after his fierce

Above, five-year-old Aubrey in London, 1920. The death of his biological father before his first birthday and his mother's frequent absences from home made Aubrey feel like an orphan.

Left, as a pupil at St. Olave's School. He passed his exams with such success that he was excused from taking any further examinations.

Left, aged 10, with sister Ruth, brother Raphael and a nurse, 1925. "We never lacked food but we were emotionally starved," Ruth lamented years later.

Above, Lieutenant Eban in 1941, as intelligence officer of the South Staffordshire Regiment. "I remember no period in my life of equivalent monotony and frustration," he wrote to a friend.

Above, during his first year at Cambridge University, with Ruth and Raphael at the Ebans' holiday cottage in Birchington, 1935

Right, Major Eban in Jerusalem, 1944, where he served as Chief Instructor at the newly established Middle East Centre for Arab Studies (MECAS).

Below, With the officers at MECAS, 1945. Eban is third on the right, front row.

Aubrey with, from left to right, his parents Sam and Alida, Raphael and Ruth, London 1947. "I am proud of all my children," Alida stated, "my son the doctor and my married daughter, but I was always especially proud of Aubrey, as was the entire family. He was just something special."

Sitting behind Chaim Weizmann during a UNSCOP meeting in Jerusalem, 1947. Partition was *À la mode,* Weizmann told the committee. "Not only in small Palestine; it is in big India. But at least there you have something to partition. Here we have to do it with a microscope. There you can do it with a big knife."

Eban's first appearance before the United Nations Security Council, May 14, 1948. The plaque in front of him reads "Jewish Agency." Seated to his right (from right to left): Warren Austin (U.S.), Alexander Cadogan (UK), Andrei Gromyko (USSR)

Left, arriving with Israel's Foreign Minister Moshe Sharett at the UN General Assembly in New York before the vote on Israel's admission to the UN, May 11, 1949

Below, with Sharett and David Hacohen, raising the Israeli flag at the circle of banners following the country's admission to the UN, May 12, 1949

As Israel's ambassador to Washington, with wife Suzy and the sailfish they caught on a fishing trip in Florida, November 1951

Presenting a Menorah with Israel's Prime Minister David Ben-Gurion to U.S. President Harry Truman, May 1951. Ben-Gurion described Eban as the Voice of Israel and the "admired emissary of all Jewry."

With Sharett and U.S. President Dwight Eisenhower, April 1953. "He had the gift of being extremely articulate without being coherent," Eban said of the president.

With Truman at a dinner in honor of Chaim Weizmann in New York, December 1953. "Let's cut out all the crap and have a real talk!" Truman told Eban at their first meeting.

objection to the military reprisals policy led by Ben-Gurion and Moshe Dayan, the prime minister had every reason to fear that Sharett might foil his war plans against Egypt too. After a quarter century of political partnership, the dismissal was bound to be brutal. On June 5, 1956, following days of speculations and interparty wrangling, Sharett was given an ultimatum: resign by five o'clock that afternoon, or Ben-Gurion would quit the government and return to his home in Sde Boker. Six days later Sharett handed his resignation letter to Ben-Gurion, wary of plunging the party and the country into turmoil if Ben-Gurion resigned instead. Sharett's trusted aides and closest allies were outraged by the affair. Gideon Rafael, Arthur Lourie, and Yaacov Herzog offered to resign in protest, but Sharett stopped them.[5] On June 11 Eban wrote a letter of support to his friend, mentor, and ally, noting that the crisis was entirely unnecessary. Any suggestions by Ben-Gurion that the decision was intended to strengthen the government and party were not taken seriously by anyone in Washington, DC.[6] Sharett thanked Eban for his support and added that their relationship defied "any framework of work relations. It is the fruit of deep friendship and years of spiritual bond." As for Ben-Gurion, Sharett added, he alone was responsible for the crisis.[7] Reuven Shiloah (formerly Sazlani) also comforted Sharett, and noted that the injustice done to Sharett, and Ben-Gurion's leadership style, had prompted some to fear that Israel would soon have its own Nasser.[8]

Sharett's bitterness at his dismissal was matched only by his outrage at Ben-Gurion's decision to appoint the faithful but diplomatically neophyte Golda Meir as his successor at the Foreign Ministry. By her own admission, Meir was "a novice among experts. Many of the more senior ambassadors and officials had been educated at British universities, and their particular brand of intellectual sophistication, which Sharett admired so much, was not always my cup of tea."[9] An early clash with the Cambridge-educated and intellectual Eban was unavoidable. Compared to Eban's view of the art of diplomacy as a noble vocation, Meir's assessment of her own role was rather more rudimentary, noting that "all a foreign minister does is talk and talk more."[10] But Sharret did not consider Eban suitable for the job either. Following Sharett's succeeding Ben-Gurion as prime minister in 1953, the question of Sharett's replacement at the foreign ministry was floated. Sharett dismissed Eban's candidacy for the following reasons, which were still valid in 1956: "He is brilliant to the outside world, but lacks roots and weight at home, and his non-membership of the party will also cause difficulties."[11]

A few days after Meir took office, Ben-Gurion recalled Eban to Jerusalem. Very much aware of Meir's lack of diplomatic prowess (which made her the perfect candidate for the job, in Ben-Gurion's eyes), he proposed that Eban give up his ambassadorial duties to act as a foreign affairs adviser to the prime minister, while Meir would act as a figurehead. In one of the first—and last—displays of harmonious relations between the two, Meir and Eban flatly rejected Ben-Gurion's proposition. According to Eban, the proposal was "an infallible prescription for antagonistic explosions."[12]

On October 24, 1956, after three days of secret negotiations in a private villa in the town of Sèvres on the outskirts of Paris, David Ben-Gurion, French foreign minister Christian Pineau, and assistant undersecretary at the British Foreign Office Patrick Dean signed a war plan against Egypt. Kept out of public knowledge until 1996, the seven articles of what became known as the Protocol of Sèvres laid down the chain of events: on the evening of October 29 Israel would launch a large-scale operation with the aim of reaching the Canal Zone the following day. The British and the French would then appeal to Israel and Egypt to stop fighting and to withdraw their forces to a distance ten miles from the canal. The Egyptians would also be asked to accept "temporary occupation" of key positions on the canal by Anglo-French forces to guarantee freedom of passage. The anticipated Egyptian refusal to comply would serve as the pretext for Anglo-French forces to conquer Egyptian positions along the canal the following day.[13]

The following day Ben-Gurion set in motion one of the best-kept military secrets in history by ordering a word-of-mouth mobilization of the Israeli Army, with only a handful of people fully aware of its ultimate aim. The same day Eban—oblivious to Ben-Gurion's carefully planned ruse—declared at the United Nations that "Israel will start no war. It will initiate no violence." The next day officers of the Israel Defense Forces (IDF) Southern Command were told of the plan and were given seventy-two hours to make the necessary preparations. On October 27, Chief of Staff Moshe Dayan approved the operational plans, and later that day Ben-Gurion shared the secret with the Mapai party members of his cabinet. The aim of the large-scale military operation against Egypt was threefold: to destroy bases of Egyptian aggression in Sinai, to expel the Egyptians from the Gaza Strip, and to safeguard the freedom of navigation of Israeli and Israeli-bound shipping through the Egyptian-controlled Straits of Tiran, which commanded the southern entrance to the port of Eilat in the Gulf of Aqaba. On October 28—twenty-four hours before the launch of the campaign—Ben-Gurion, now feverish with viral infection, broke the news to the non-Mapai members of the cabinet, and a public announcement of the mobilization was authorized with a vague reference to the recent events in neighboring Arab states as the pretext.[14]

A few hours later, in Washington, Eban was called out of a round of golf with congressman Sidney Yates and journalist Martin Agronsky at the Woodmont Country Club. Unaware of the fact that a second Arab–Israeli war was only a day away, Eban was summoned by Secretary Dulles to explain the growing number of intelligence reports about the mass mobilization of Israeli forces, seemingly without Arab provocation.[15] Unfamiliar with the full facts, Eban elegantly but unsuccessfully reassured Dulles that Israel might have been "wrong" in calling up some reserve battalions, but it had very good reason to fear that the Arab countries were gearing up toward war, especially following the recent tripartite agreement of Egypt, Jordan, and Syria that placed the armed forces of the three countries under Nasser's command.[16] Dulles contested Eban's reference to "several battalions" and pointed out that U.S. intelligence concluded that Israel was being "totally mobilized," but he concurred that ultimately the question was whether Israel's intentions could be described as offensive or defensive. Having been briefed by Ben-Gurion earlier in the month about the growing tension along the Israeli–Jordanian border, and kept in the dark over the design against Egypt, Eban offered Dulles his frank impression that if and when Israel acted out of self-defense, the likely target would be Jordan and not Egypt. Dulles conceded that he did not know what the Israeli government had in mind, and pointed out that Israel had never been safer. Immediately after the meeting Dulles received a call from President Dwight D. Eisenhower, who wanted to know if Eban had divulged any significant information. With the presidential elections due to take place the following week, the president was busy entering the final stages of his reelection campaign against Adlai Stevenson. Not reassured by Eban's assertion to Dulles that the mobilization was merely defensive, Eisenhower pondered canceling his trip to Florida the next morning in anticipation of a burgeoning crisis in the Middle East.[17]

That evening in Tel Aviv, U.S. ambassador Edward Lawson heard from Ben-Gurion a "self-exculpating" explanation of Israel's position: since the government did not know where an attack was likely to come from, it decided to mobilize a "few battalions" as a "purely precautionary measure" to the borders with Syria, Jordan, and Egypt. Though Ben-Gurion assured Lawson that he "will be happy as President if things remain quiet," the ambassador was struck by the prime minister's "considerable and deliberate caution" and his ineffective attempt to create a "feeling of assurance there will be no hostilities."[18]

The next day, October 29, 1956, at 4:59 p.m. local time, four platoons of the 890th Paratroop Battalion under the command of major Raphael Eytan parachuted out of sixteen DC-3 Dakota planes near the Mitla Pass in the Sinai Peninsula, less than thirty miles east of the Suez Canal. In accordance with the Protocol of Sèvres, the following day British prime minister Anthony Eden announced that the British and French governments had sent a twelve-hour ultimatum to Israel and Egypt "to stop all warlike action by land, sea and air forthwith and to withdraw their military forces to a distance of 10 miles from the Canal." Eden then declared that in order to separate the belligerents and to guarantee the freedom of shipping through the canal, they had asked the Egyptian government "to agree that Anglo-French forces should move temporarily . . . into key positions at Port Said, Ismailia and Suez."[19] Having been the victim of an Israeli surprise attack, Egypt refused to comply with the ultimatum, and this surprised no one—not least the French and the British, who were about to begin the next stage of the operation, the bombing of Egypt's airfields. The Anglo-French demand of Egypt to withdraw from its own territory after being attacked, while allowing Israel to advance its forces to the Suez Canal (the IDF had not even captured the Sinai Peninsula at that point) crudely unmasked the British, French, and Israeli charade. The Americans were outraged by the setup. In a typical British understatement Sir Anthony Nutting, who served as minister of state at the Foreign Office during the crisis, recalled that Eisenhower "had been duped in an unforgivable way, and both he and his Government colleagues were very angry indeed."[20] According to the *New York Times*, Eisenhower was so angry when Dulles broke the news to him on the telephone that "[t]he White House crackled with barracks room language the likes of which had not been heard since the days of General Grant."[21]

Throughout this period Eban, like the rest of Israel's diplomats abroad, was left completely in the dark about his government's aims. Immediately after his meeting with Dulles on October 28, he cabled Ben-Gurion and Meir to demand some clarifications in the most undiplomatic language: "For the rest of my life I shall never understand how it was possible to cause such frightening military commotion without a modicum of guidance to myself and other missions on how to explain, act, and respond. I am obliged, and in my opinion entitled to ask: 1) what is really happening? 2) how to respond?"[22] It took two more days before the government finally issued guidelines to its missions abroad about the aims of the operation (the destruction of the fedayeen bases), its scale ("under no circumstances should it be described as 'war'"), and its provenance ("If asked, you must deny vehemently that there was some collusion between ours and the Anglo-French action").[23]

By then all hell had broken loose in Washington and New York. The U.S. State Department stopped all economic assistance to Israel, including a proposed $75 million loan by the Export-Import Bank, negotiations over a new grant-in-aid, and the provisions of the Food Surplus Law.[24] Eden and his French counterpart, Guy Mollet, pleaded for a meeting with Eisenhower but were told that the president's diary was full for at least a week. At the United Nations, the American ambassador Henry Cabot Lodge Jr. ignored the British pleas for time and called an urgent meeting of the Security Council. As expected, Britain and France exercised their power of veto as permanent members of the council to block an American proposal for an immediate Israeli withdrawal behind the 1949 armistice lines. The impasse at the Security Council was bypassed by the Uniting for Peace procedure, which was first used in the Korean War to enable the General Assembly to act on matters of international security in such circumstances where the council was deadlocked.[25] On November 1 the General Assembly sat its first emergency special session. By the time Eban arrived in New York from Washington late in the evening there was no time to work out a carefully prepared speech. Israel's critics were already making their case at the assembly hall, and it was crucial to achieve maximum exposure for Israel's case. Given that TV and radio networks ended their normal programming at 11:00 p.m. and then broadcast live the proceedings from the General Assembly, the Israeli delegation asked their dependable Latin American colleagues to occupy the floor until that hour. Meanwhile, Eban, accompanied by the embassy's legal adviser Jacob Robinson, sat down to work on the address at the restaurant in the Westbury Hotel on East Seventieth Street opposite the delegation's residence. After discussing with Robinson Israel's right to act against Egypt under Article 51 of the UN Charter, which sanctioned the right of self-defense, Eban borrowed a pencil and a few pieces of paper from the waiter and scribbled some notes. With this hasty preparation over, Eban arrived at the assembly hall ready to address a TV and radio audience of tens of millions of Americans and many more millions abroad. This audience did not include any Israelis, however, as the government-run radio network did not broadcast the speech live and another decade would pass before the country enjoyed its first television broadcast. Unsurprisingly, in 1956 Eban was far more recognizable in the United Stated than in Israel.[26]

Biting his nails nervously while reciting in his head the impromptu address he was about to deliver, Eban stood up to take his place at the podium, clutching an impressively thick batch of papers. The stakes were painfully high: facing the uproar of the international community and an unprecedented reprimand from the United States, Eban's task was not only to advocate his country's right to defend itself against Egyptian belligerency but also to persuade the world organization that international law and morality were on Israel's side. The military campaign against the fedayeen bases in Sinai and Gaza must not be studied outside its historical context, Eban began, for it was the inevitable and legitimate result of years of Egyptian violence against Israel: "Not for one single moment throughout the entire period of its modern national existence has Israel enjoyed that minimal physical security which the United Nations Charter confers on all member states, and which all other member states have been able to command." Turning to the legal justification of Israel's actions, Eban highlighted Egypt's successive failures to apply its obligations under the UN Charter to its relations with Israel:

> Whatever rights are enjoyed by other members of this Organization belong to Israel without addition or diminution. Whatever obligation any member state owes to another, Egypt owes to Israel and Israel to Egypt.
>
> What are the obligations which Egypt owes to Israel under the Charter? Under the Charter, Egypt is bound "to practice tolerance and live together in peace" with Israel as a good neighbor. Under the Charter, Egypt is bound to "unite its strength" with Israel "to maintain international peace and security." Under the Charter, Egypt is bound to regard Israel as a state endowed with sovereignty equal to its own. Under the Charter, Egypt is bound to respect the "territorial integrity and the political independence" of the State of Israel, and especially to refrain from the use of force against that integrity and that independence.
>
> To these broad obligations, derived from the Charter, there must be added to Egypt's account other obligations of a more spe-

> cific nature, based on the Armistice Agreement of 1949. Under that Agreement, Egypt is bound to respect the demarcation line between Israel and Egypt; to prevent any illegal crossings of that line; to abstain from the threat or use of force from its own side of the line against Israel's side, . . .
>
> Is there any resemblance whatever between this list of obligations and Egypt's actual conduct of its relations with Israel? Can anyone imagine that, if Egypt had been willing to carry out this system of relations with Israel, we should have been assembled here on this tragic and solemn occasion?
>
> What we confront tonight is a point of explosion after eight years of illicit belligerency. Belligerency is the key to the understanding of our problem tonight. Egypt has practiced belligerency against Israel by land. Egypt has practiced belligerency against Israel by sea. Egypt has established belligerency as the judicial basis of its relations with Israel. Egypt has held belligerency to be the spiritual and emotional mainspring of its conduct toward Israel.[27]

Having provided the historical background of the Sinai campaign and the international legal basis for Israel's actions, Eban moved to the third leg of his argument, which had since been uttered by every single advocate of Israel at home and abroad: Israel's unique place among the nations meant that while it was an equal member of the UN, it rarely enjoyed the freedoms and rights bestowed upon it by the UN Charter:

> If we have sometimes found it difficult to persuade even our friends in the international community to understand the motives for our action, this is because nobody in the world community is in Israel's position. How many other nations have had hundreds of their citizens killed over these years by the action of armies across the frontier? How many nations have had their ships seized and their cargoes confiscated in international waterways? How many nations find the pursuit of their daily tasks to be a matter of daily and perpetual hazard? . . . It might perhaps require an unusual measure of humility and imagination for others to answer the question how they would have acted in our place. Nobody else is in our

> place and is therefore fully competent to equate the advantage and the disadvantage of our choice.
>
> The Government of Israel is firmly convinced that it has done what any other nation would have done in our place, with the reservation that many would have done it earlier and with perhaps greater impact of resistance.[28]

Yet despite of the tumultuous character of Egyptian-Israeli relations in the past eight years, Eban concluded, Israel's hand was still reaching out for peace:

> Israel has no desire or intention to wield arms beyond the limit of its legitimate defensive mission. But whatever is demanded of us by way of restoring Egypt's rights and respecting Egypt's security under international law must surely be accompanied by equally binding Egyptian undertakings to respect Israel's security and Israel's rights under the identical law. Egypt's obligation to abstain from acts of hostility, to liquidate its commando activities, to abolish its illicit discrimination against Israeli shipping in the Suez Canal and in the Gulf of Aqaba, is equal and identical in law to Israel's obligation to respect the established Armistice lines.
>
> Our signpost is not backward to belligerency, but forward to peace. Whatever Israel is now asked to do for Egypt must have its counterpart in Egypt's reciprocal duty to give Israel the plentitude of its rights.
>
> Egypt and Israel are two people whose encounters in history have been rich and fruitful for mankind. Surely they must take their journey from this solemn moment towards the horizons for peace.[29]

Eban's "Horizons of Peace" address was the biggest news story that night, and the effect on his audience was immediate. "It's a pity we can't have him instead of you as our delegate here," Dulles was heard remarking to his ambassador, Henry Cabot Lodge; and the *New York Times* waxed lyrical about the performance of the forty-one-year-old Eban: "Arising from a rolling sea of oratory and invective, the words and manner of the young Mr. Eban defending the actions of his young country made him one of the television heroes of the United Nations. Housewives set down the vacuum cleaners when his unmistakable accent was heard." Within minutes of Eban concluding his address in New York, the small staff at the Israeli embassy in Washington became inundated with congratulatory telegrams and requests for copies of the speech. More than five thousand letters arrived in the first two days. "My dear Mr. Ambassador," one American wrote to Eban the following day, "'Great' is a word I have taught myself to use sparingly, but I think its use is more than justified in describing your speech at the United Nations on Thursday night . . . the diction you employed; the unusual facility of putting your thoughts into words; the construction; and the deep eloquence that emanated the effort. Yours was a noted performance." Ben Raeburn, the owner of Horizon Press, offered to have Eban's speeches published in a book. Yet when the first secretary at the embassy asked Eban for the bundle of papers he carried with him to the podium, she discovered to her horror that they were all blank. "Ah yes," Eban explained casually, "I did not write my address, but I thought that it would look more impressive if I carried with me some papers when I addressed the Assembly." Some requests for copies of the unscripted address came from less conventional bases of support, such as a prison warden in Ohio who asked for 120 copies for his Jewish inmates, or a Chicago schoolteacher who confessed that "in as much as I disagree with everything the ambassador said, he said it so beautifully that I humbly request that 30 copies of his address be sent to my school."[30]

Eban later recalled enjoying the "cascades of applause" that broke around him as soon as he finished his address, "growing in intensity, sometimes accompanied by emotional stamping of feet," but the subsequent voting at the General Assembly displayed the UN's "sharp dichotomy between its reaction and its conclusion."[31] There was little appetite for understanding Israel's action, no matter how brilliant Eban's speech was. The Sinai campaign was seen as the last in a chain of unilateral adventures that seemed to defy the letter and spirit of the UN Charter. The following day the Americans introduced a resolution that called for all the fighting parties to agree to an immediate ceasefire; for Israel and Egypt to withdraw their forces behind the armistice lines; and to take steps to reopen the Suez Canal and restore the secure freedom of navigation. The resolution was passed with an overwhelming majority of 64–5 (the dissenters being Israel, France, Britain, Australia, and New Zealand).[32] That same day Canada's Lester Pearson introduced the novel idea of an international force as an instrument that would separate the fighting forces and ensure the free navigation in the Suez Canal—thus removing the need for

Anglo-French intervention. Pearson's proposal to create what came to be known as the United Nations Emergency Force (UNEF) was approved in the early hours of November 4 by an impressive majority: 57–0, with 19 abstentions.[33] By then Israel had completed the occupation of the Gaza Strip, and the following morning the entire Sinai Peninsula was under IDF control. That night, British and French forces landed at Port Said and took positions along the Suez Canal. But before they achieved their objectives Prime Minister Eden succumbed to the intense pressure at home and abroad and announced Britain's acceptance of the cease-fire. Unable to carry on the operation alone, the French reluctantly followed suit. For the Western allies, Operation Musketeer had been a total disaster. Not only had they failed to secure the objectives that were set in Sèvres, but the episode marked the ignominious swan song of the British and French influence in the Middle East.

For Israel, the speedy and impressive military campaign was followed by four disputatious months over the terms of its withdrawal, interspersed by half a dozen condemnations by the General Assembly, the threats of sanctions, and the souring of relations with the United States to a historic low. These international pressures put Eban squarely in the center of the drama: working opposite UN secretary-general Dag Hammarskjöld and Secretary of State Dulles; consulting with his government in Jerusalem and formulating frameworks of negotiation; directing public diplomacy efforts out of the embassy in Washington and leading the mission in New York; meeting with other congressmen, public officials, and Jewish leaders; and appearing before the media and the General Assembly. It is not surprising that years later Eban recalled that he "never felt a greater sense of personal excitement or fulfillment than during the four months between November 1956 and March 1957."[34] His laborious schedule led the *New York Times* to note that his days "have become a succession of quick dashes by train or plane between his offices in New York and in Washington. . . . But he has not visibly lost either weight or sleep, although for the last few months he has been involved in negotiations so sensitive that relatively few diplomats would expect to emerge without at least a case of ulcer." As a negotiator, Eban was recognized "as one of the most eloquent pleaders any country has sent to the United Nations. In United Nations circles he is considered a 'tough diplomat,' invariably defending his Government's actions and policies with marked vigor. There is reason to believe, however, that he thinks Israel should abstain from over-provocative gestures towards her Arab neighbors."[35]

ISRAEL ACCEPTED THE UN CEASE-FIRE RESOLUTION ON NOVEMBER 5, 1956, BUT two days later Ben-Gurion signaled that the government was in no hurry to withdraw its forces. In a particularly emboldened speech to the Knesset, the prime minister announced that the armistice agreement with Egypt was dead and could not be restored, and that under no condition would Israel agree to the stationing of foreign troops on its territory or in a territory under its occupation. The backlash was immediate. An irate Hammarskjöld told Eban that he considered Ben-Gurion's statement to be in contradiction to the legal stand of the UN on the armistice agreements and that Israel's refusal to withdraw would lead to armed Soviet intervention and a third world war. The situation was so grave that the current question was "will there be an Israel two months from now" and the answer was in Ben-Gurion's hands.[36] The secretary-general also asked Lodge to request that Eisenhower personally press Ben-Gurion to order the immediate withdrawal of the IDF from Sinai and to accept the presence of UNEF there. Later that evening the General Assembly passed a resolution by a vote of 65–1 (Israel being the dissenter) that called on Israel to withdraw its forces immediately.[37] Ben-Gurion suggested a meeting with Eisenhower at the White House to explain Israel's position, but after winning reelection by a landslide majority, Eisenhower was in a combative mood and had no desire to grant the Israeli premier a presidential audience. Instead he sent him an ominous message: "Statements attributed to your Government to the effect that Israel does not intend to withdraw from Egyptian territory, as requested by the United Nations, have been called to my attention. . . . It would be a matter of the greatest regret to all my countrymen if Israeli policy on a matter of such grave concern to the world should in any way impair the friendly cooperation between our two countries."[38] When the Israeli cabinet met the following day, the atmosphere was of impending cataclysm. Several ministers feared that anything short of unconditional surrender to the international demand of immediate withdrawal would bring a Soviet attack on Israel, following a threat by the Soviet premier Nikolai Bulganin three days earlier that Moscow was "fully resolved to use force to crush the aggressors and to restore peace in the Middle East."[39] Eban, however, argued that this course of action would see Israel "emerge from the war humiliated and with no gain from much effort and sacrifice." Instead he proposed to make the withdrawal conditioned on the arrangement of the international force, which would buy time to secure Israel's war aims and to launch an effective diplomatic campaign. Some ministers in the room muttered, "Eban must be out of his mind." Two of Mapai's heavyweights, Pinchas Sapir and Zalman Aranne, feared that Eban's formula would lead to a world war and that Israel was in no position to haggle. But Ben-Gurion decided to put his faith—and the fate of the country—in the ambassador's hands. "If you take the responsibility that it is feasible, then I agree," he told Eban.[40]

Eban was enthralled by this unusual granting of executive authority; it was "one of the most extraordinary situations that I, or for that matter, any other ambassador had ever confronted," he later recalled. "In an age in which heads of government have usurped the negotiating functions of ambassadors to the vogue of summitry . . . the idea that an ambassador can decide between sensitive and potentially explosive courses seems unreal even in retrospect.[41] Ben-Gurion's confidence in his ambassador was absolute: "Nobody appreciates more than me your intellectual efforts to explain our behavior," he wrote to Eban during the crisis, "and I do not know of anyone who could do it better than you."[42] After some drafting by Eban, the government announced that it would "willingly withdraw its forces from Egypt immediately upon the conclusion of satisfactory arrangements with the United Nations in connection with the emergency international force."[43] While in spirit the Israeli statement showed some deference to world opinion, the stipulation concerning the "conclusion of satisfactory arrangements" as a condition of withdrawal was in effect the critical hinge around which a bitter diplomatic struggle revolved for the next four months. The Israeli about-face certainly did not translate immediately into any actions on the ground; after General Assembly resolutions on November 2 and November 7 failed to bring about the withdrawal of Israeli, French, and British forces, on November 24 the assembly noted with regret that "two-thirds of the French forces remain, all the United Kingdom forces remain . . . and no Israel forces had been withdrawn behind the armistice lines although a considerable time had elapsed since the adoption of the relevant General Assembly resolutions."[44]

A few weeks later, on December 22, 1956, the last of the Anglo-French forces finally left Egypt, but the withdrawal of Israeli forces from the canal area and the Gaza Strip would take another three months of tough bargaining. The issues to be negotiated were the very same reasons Israel had gone to war in the first place: a stop to the fedayeen attacks on Israel from the Gaza Strip, and an Egyptian commitment on the freedom of navigation through the Suez Canal for Israeli and Israel-bound ships. Without firm guarantees from the UN on these issues, Israel refused to commit to any future withdrawals; meanwhile, Hammarskjöld, while naturally sympathetic to Israel's moral case, was bound by previous UN resolutions that demanded unconditional Israeli withdrawal from Egyptian territory it had occupied by force.[45] In the north of the Sinai Peninsula, Israeli forces were still more than fifty miles west of the 1949 armistice lines, and more than 120 miles inside Egyptian territory to the south, adding more tension to an already explosive situation. On January 5, 1957, Hammarskjöld complained to Eban about the slow rate of the Israeli withdrawal: Israeli forces were still in control of 40 percent of the Sinai Peninsula, including almost all the intersections. The following day Eban advised Ben-Gurion that the delaying tactics had now been exhausted: "The period of playing for time has come to an end. It has become clear that holding on to Sinai weakens, and does not strengthen our stand in the battle for freedom of shipping and over Gaza."[46]

On January 14 Eban held another tough meeting with Hammarskjöld and Ralph Bunche, the undersecretary-general for political affairs.[47] An impatient man by nature, Hammarskjöld had now become irate with Eban's meandering, but he still admired his integrity and intellect. Both men were great talkers and sometimes tended to digress to a point of exasperation in their meetings, but at this particular meeting Hammarskjöld demanded a straight answer: "[These] problems should be handled and studied and, if possible, solved, but they are no excuse for either delay or deviation from decisions which have expressed the principle for which the United Nations not only wishes to stand but, to my understanding, simply has to stand. That is, of course, a worry, and that is something on which I need not in any way elaborate, because it must be just as clear to you as it is to me."[48] Five days later the General Assembly passed its fourth resolution in demand of Israel's immediate and unconditional withdrawal beyond the armistice lines, by a vote of 74–2 (with Israel and France dissenting).[49]

The news from Washington was equally ominous: On February 3 Eisenhower threatened Ben-Gurion that Israel's "continued ignoring of the judgment of nations as expressed in the United Nations Resolutions would almost surely lead to the invoking of further United Nations procedures which could seriously disturb the relations between Israel and other member nations including the United States."[50] Faced with such strong censure from the White House, Eban took an indirect approach to enlist American support for Israel, calculating that even a recently reelected president had to pay heed to public opinion. Eisenhower, having lost control of both houses of the U.S. Congress to the Democrats, was particularly vulnerable on Capitol Hill, and Eban, who for years worked hard to cultivate personal relations with key leaders in both houses, as well as the media and American Jewry, now seized the opportunity to launch a carefully crafted public campaign designed to explain Israel's position to the American public and in turn bring about pressure on the president to moderate his attitude. The scale of this public relations campaign was without precedent. Between November 1956 and March 1957 there were on average two hundred public appearances in twenty-five to thirty states per month by Meir, Eban, staffers at the Washington embassy and the New York consulate, and other lecturers who were brought especially from Israel to meet the demand. National news programs such as *Meet the Press*, *Face the Nation*, *United Nations in Action*, and *Youth Wants to Know* featured the Israeli foreign minister or ambassador on an almost weekly basis. Jewish and pro-Israel organizations played a crucial part in the successful dissemination of information to policy makers, the media, and the general public. The Presidents Club met eighteen times during the crisis and held national and regional conferences. The American Zionist Council, the American Zionist Committee for Public Affairs (forerunner of the American Israel Public Affairs Committee), the American Christian Palestine Committee, the Anti-Defamation League, and other groups helped to mobilize public, congressional, and media support for Israel.[51]

The result of this campaign of public diplomacy was very encouraging. On Capitol Hill, forty-two Republicans and seventy-five Democrats declared their support of Israel's demand to condition the Gaza withdrawal on direct peace negotiations with Egypt. The Senate submitted a resolution calling on the U.S. government to provide Israel the necessary guarantees against the resumption of fedayeen attacks from Gaza or of the maritime blockade. There was also criticism of the administration's double standard in its condemnation of Israel while it refused to demand that the Soviets withdraw their forces from the recently occupied Budapest. Senate majority leader Lyndon Johnson wrote to Dulles, "To put it simply, the United States cannot apply one rule for the strong and another for the weak," while Senators William Knowland (Republican) and Hubert Humphrey (Democrat) threatened to resign from the American delegation to the UN if the administration carried out the threat of sanctions.[52] Eban was quite sanguine about the changing tide in the American sentiment; he reported to Ben-Gurion that discussions at the U.S. Senate reflected the growing public concern for Israel's security, and there were signs that the U.S. government was becoming disillusioned with Nasser, not to mention the strong aversion to bend vital American interests to fit Hammarskjöld's agenda. It now became clear, Eban concluded, that Eisenhower and Dulles were determined to "take matters into their own hands before they lose domestic and international trust."[53]

On February 11 Eban received an aide-memoire from Dulles that had been approved by Eisenhower. In effect a policy paper, the document urged Israel to withdraw "promptly and unconditionally" from the Gaza Strip, the future of which was to be worked out through the offices and efforts of the UN. The United States supported the presence of UNEF in Gaza and in the Straits of Tiran following the withdrawal of Israeli forces. In return, the U.S. government confirmed that it viewed the Gulf of Aqaba as an international waterway that no country had the right to prevent the free passage of other countries thereto and, moreover, it expressed willingness to join with other maritime powers to guarantee such passage. In essence the American position now moved closer to the Israeli position on free navigation, though it remained unchanged on the question of Gaza. Eban praised the aide-memoire as "very important" but emphasized the "illegal" situation that existed before Israel went to war on October 29 and outlined four steps to solving the current crisis: an Egyptian commitment to nonbelligerency; the securing of effective measures to prevent the reblockading of the Straits of Tiran by Egypt; an Israeli withdrawal from Sharm el-Sheikh after the implementation of such measures; and an IDF withdrawal from the Gaza Strip following negotiations with the UN over the civilian administration of the strip. Dulles responded that the United States government was sympathetic to Israel's aims, as indeed it was before the war, but he stressed that the way that Israel, Britain, and France went about achieving their aims was wrong. The secretary assured Eban that he was not a pacifist, but the three countries should not have gone to war against Egypt when the world saw their case for war as unjust. With regards to Israel's demands, Dulles explained that the American commitment to upholding the right of free navigation was far more important than securing a commitment to nonbelligerency from Nasser, who could not be trusted anyway. Dulles also dismissed any rumors of impending sanctions on Israel as "not serious" and detrimental to the collective efforts to reduce the tension in the region.[54]

Following his meeting with Dulles, Eban reported to Ben-Gurion enthusiastically about the encouraging change in atmosphere and the need to respond positively and swiftly— "within hours."[55] Ben-Gurion, however, was more cautious than his ambassador, who had gained a reputation as overly optimistic in his assessment of American attitudes toward Israel.[56] While Ben-Gurion acknowledged the importance of the American commitment to free navigation, he demanded more formal and comprehensive guarantees. He also reminded Eban that the American promise was conditioned upon an Israeli withdrawal from the Straits of Tiran and the Gaza Strip, which would bring Israel back to the situation that had existed before October 29. For Israel's security and very existence Ben-Gurion insisted on reversing the conditionality element: the Israeli withdrawal should be conditioned on securing the guarantees, rather than the other way around, "even at a cost of threats and sanctions."[57] Ben-Gurion's refusal to accept in principle the American memorandum put the Eisenhower administration in a predicament: on the one hand, it could not accept Israel's flaunting of several UN resolutions that called for its withdrawal from Egyptian territory without endangering relations with the secretary-general and the Arab world; on the other hand, Israel's very effective public diplomacy campaign meant that the growing sympathy to the country's position in the media and on Capitol Hill severly constrained the power of the president to punish Israel. The atmosphere at the next meeting between Dulles and Eban, on February 17, was one of impending crisis, as the secretary of state expressed his sadness and depression over the Israeli response. Anticipating "great troubles" ahead, Dulles added that this missed opportunity for Israel to work with the United States might damage relations between the two countries and the two peoples, and that the Soviets might use the opportunity to intervene in the region as the defenders of the authority of the United Nations.[58] Eban, disappointed by Ben-Gurion's rejection of the February 11 aide-memoire and desperate to break the deadlock, told Dulles that he would have to return to Jerusalem "to carefully explain [Dulles's] views to the authorities."[59] In the meantime, he asked Dulles to hold off any action against Israel in the General Assembly. Eban's brinkmanship worked. As he expected, later that day he was ordered by Ben-Gurion to return for consultations. In Jerusalem he succeeded in pressing the urgency of the situation on the government and managed to secure a concession from Ben-Gurion on Gaza in return for American guarantees for navigation in the Suez Canal. Meanwhile, bipartisan congressional support in Washington for Israel convinced Eisenhower and Dulles that sanctions would be unworkable.[60] On February 22 the African-Asian bloc at the UN General Assembly introduced a resolution that condemned Israel for non-compliance with earlier UN resolutions and called upon all member states to deny all military, economic, and financial assistance to Israel. The widespread condemnation of Israel as an aggressor at the UN was by no means a novel feature, but Israeli aggression on its own was not the sole reason for the cool attitude displayed by an increasing majority of member states. Of the twenty countries that were admitted to the UN between 1955 and 1956, more than two-thirds were communist, African, or Asian. The dramatic shift in the composition of the UN toward a Muslim and nonaligned majority meant that Israel was increasingly viewed as a base of Western imperialism in the Middle East through which the American and European powers sought to protect their strategic and economic interests in the region—or worse, as an imperialist and belligerent state in its own right. This new reality led Eban to muse some years later about Israel's perilous position in the UN, where it invariably found itself in the minority: "If Algeria introduced a resolution declaring that the earth was flat and that Israel had flattened it, it would pass by a vote of 164 to 13 with 26 abstentions."[61]

On February 24 Eban arrived in New York with instructions and clarifications that, he told the press, were aimed at bringing about a "constructive and fair solution." At his meeting with Dulles the same day, Eban presented an eleven-point memorandum: ten clarifications concerning the freedom of navigation in the Straits, and one demand that there be no Egyptian presence—military or civilian—in the Gaza Strip following Israel's withdrawal. Instead, Israel proposed that following the entrance of UNEF into the Strip a UN committee would investigate and produce a plan for the administration of the area. The last point suggested a considerable shift in Ben-Gurion's position on Gaza. Dulles welcomed the Israeli proposal, but maintained that Egypt still had legal rights over Gaza based on the 1949 armistice agreements and, accordingly, American interest in the plan was conditional on its acceptance by the United Nations.[62] When Ben-Gurion received Reuven Shiloah's report of Eban's meeting with Dulles he was so outraged he reprimanded Eban over his "catastrophic error"—the government instructions that had been given to him outlined that under no circumstances would Egypt be allowed to return to Gaza, and no agreement had been reached concerning the entry of UNEF before or after the establishment of the UN committee. Fearing "an immediate crisis with unknown consequences" if Eban's commitment to Dulles became public knowledge in Israel, Ben-Gurion ordered Eban to explain the misunderstanding to Dulles.[63] Eban was so infuriated by the prime minister's charge that he offered his resignation on the spot, in his usual verbose and acerbic manner: "I do not believe that such 'catastrophic' hands should be allowed to handle a vital struggle for the freedom of navigation, border security, mending relations with the United States, mobilizing public opinion around the world and freeing Israel to deal with central tasks which had been neglected owing to our preoccupation with this crisis over four months. Therefore if the 'catastrophic' assessment is accurate, the government should be allowed the opportunity to draw a conclusion if it so wishes."[64]

In testimony to Eban's indispensable position, Ben-Gurion apologized for the "misunderstanding" and tried to appease his indignant ambassador, concluding his telegram with, "Be strong and courageous!" Once the government received the full protocol of the meeting between Eban and Dulles (rather than Shiloah's report of the meeting), the impression of Eban's "error" was not considered to be so serious, and the order to inform Dulles of the misunderstanding was rescinded.[65]

But the talks between Dulles and Eban were suddenly stopped in their tracks by Hammarskjöld, who was furious at being left out of the bilateral negotiations. He refused to concede on Egypt's right to return to the Gaza Strip and was adamant that it was legally impossible to separate the Straits of Tiran from Gaza—all previous UN resolutions referred to "Egyptian territory" as a whole. He also warned that a U.S.-Israeli understanding did not oblige the UN to take action.[66] The impasse was broken on February 26, at a meeting between Dulles and the French Foreign Minister Christian Pineau. Dulles presented to Pineau a draft proposal and asked him to comment on it. First, Israel would announce at the United Nations its willingness to withdraw completely from the Gaza Strip, with the assumption that UNEF would take administrative responsibility in the area. Should Egypt resort to violence, Israel would be free to defend its rights. Second, the United States and other states who wished to do so would "take note" of the Israeli statement at the United Nations, thus according international recognition to Israel's right of self-defense, while future Egyptian resorting to arms would prompt UN action. Pineau endorsed the proposal, and with Dulles's encouragement later read it to Eisenhower as a "French proposal." But Dulles kept from Pineau one vital point, designed to allay Arab fears of a secret American undertaking with Israel: the United States itself would not state publicly what the "French proposal" clearly stated—namely, Israel's right to defend itself should the Gaza arrangement break down.[67] While the plan required additional drafting and refining, Eban—who was also unaware of Dulles's cunning move—recommended that the Israeli government accept the plan, which would enable Israel to comply with the UN demand to withdraw without preconditions, though the acknowledgment of the United States, France, and other friendly states of Israel's right of self-defense provided it with the much needed (albeit informal) guarantees. Finally, the proposal bypassed the need for discussions at the General Assembly with its automatic majority against Israel. But the most important reason to accept the proposal was that cooperation with the United States and France over such a critical question was a "security and international asset in itself." Ben-Gurion was forced to acknowledge that neither Israeli presence in the Sinai nor UN guarantees could secure the freedom of Israeli navigation. Under the present circumstances, the French plan promised to rescue Israel from certain international isolation, maintain the flow of French arms, and—perhaps most important—begin to restore relations with the United States.[68]

Eban and Dulles turned to drafting two speeches to be delivered before the General Assembly: one by Foreign Minister Meir stating Israel's willingness to withdraw based on several "assumptions," and another by U.S. Ambassador Lodge, reaffirming these assumptions. On March 1 Meir, faithful to the understandings between Eban and Dulles, announced that Israel was prepared to withdraw completely from the Gaza Strip and the Gulf of Aqaba based on the expectation that UNEF would assume full responsibility for the civil and military functions in those areas and that the Suez Canal would be open to Israeli navigation; any future blockade would entitle Israel to act again in self-defense under Article 51 of the UN Charter. She was followed by Lodge, who reiterated her points on the issue of the Straits of Tiran; but when he turned to Gaza, rather than recognizing Israel's right to defend itself should Egypt violate its international obligations, he stated Egypt's legal rights in the area under the armistice agreements. The French and Israelis were equally outraged by the "deceitful and untrustworthy" Dulles, who that morning had reassured a group of Arab ambassadors that the U.S. government did not acquiesce to Israeli demands and that Israel must withdraw unconditionally from Gaza.[69] Embarrassed by Lodge's statement, the government in Jerusalem asked Eban to demand from Dulles clear reassurances about the nonreturn of Egypt to Gaza and Israel's right to self-defense. Meanwhile, the French, who had stood firmly by Israel since the beginning of the crisis, pleaded with Israel not to create a new crisis in the wake of Lodge's statement. After several reassurances from Eisenhower, Dulles, and others that "the President and the Government of the

U.S.A. have undertaken a moral obligation which they definitely intend to fulfil," on March 5 Ben-Gurion announced the Israeli government's decision on the final withdrawal from Sinai and Gaza.[70]

Three days later the Israeli withdrawal was complete, and by March 12 UNEF assumed complete control of these areas, but within days the American commitment to Israel's security was put to the test. In response to violent protests in the Gaza Strip in support of Nasser, UNEF opened fire and imposed a curfew on the area. Egypt responded by dispatching a civil governor to restore its control over the Gaza Strip. Ben-Gurion protested and demanded that Eisenhower and the U.S. State Department take action against the Egyptian move, yet all he received was a presidential call to Israel to refrain from taking precipitate action.[71] But Ben-Gurion himself was in no mood to spark another international crisis; he rightly recognized Nasser's move as no more than a symbolic dare, which indeed was not followed by another provocation. While Israel's stunning victory on the battlefield did not yield the cast iron diplomatic guarantees that Ben-Gurion hoped to secure, Israel enjoyed a decade of relative calm along its southern frontier. Fedayeen attacks were not resumed and Israeli ships enjoyed free navigation through the Suez Canal. Egypt, Syria, and Iraq nailed their colors to the Soviet mast, and amid a wave of radical Arab nationalism and political instability Israel had emerged as the only stable democracy in the region. The most testing period in U.S.-Israeli relations had come to an end.

Israel's relations with Hammarskjöld also improved over time. On May 9, 1957, Hammarskjöld and Bunche arrived in Jerusalem to meet with Ben-Gurion, Meir, and other officials from the Foreign Ministry. Ben-Gurion and Hammarskjöld talked alone for almost two hours before the formal meeting. The talks revolved around some of the underlying causes of tension in the area, as Bunche later noted:

> BG, as usual, in open-necked shirt. He has aged greatly since I last saw him in Feb. 1953. Pleading, almost whining note in his voice. Admits that he has no fear that Arabs can drive Israel "into sea" or that there is imminent threat of Arab attack. BG rambles, invents his own distorted history, rants in a semi-buffoonish way, laughs childishly at his own humor, and shows distressing signs of acute senility. Golda is remarkably friendly and relaxed; pompous, of course, but not hostile. Both parties agreed that the Secretary-

> General's visit had been valuable, even indispensable, since it had gone a long way in restoring confidence between the UN and Israel, and between Hammarskjöld and Ben-Gurion which had been lost during past nine months. Even Golda has been relaxed and cordial and had avoided her typical emotional, accusatory outbursts.[72]

Eban, having been given an almost executive authority by Ben-Gurion to negotiate the terms of Israel's withdrawal, emerged during the crisis as no less than "the advocate, negotiator, and implementer of Israel's foreign policy par excellence."[73] Others observed that Eban's appearances in the General Assembly and his negotiations at the U.S. State Department were worth "a division of soldiers to the Israeli army, if not more"; without Eban, Israel's fate after Suez would have been far worse.[74] But there were also reports in the press that some in Israel were disappointed with Eban's soft handling of the crisis. This call, which originated in Jerusalem and may have come from the foreign minister's office, demanded that Eban be replaced by someone favoring a "tougher Israeli foreign policy."[75] Eban's exercise of authority and his close working relationship with Ben-Gurion exceeded the normal arena of operation of most ambassadors—a fact that did not go unnoticed by Meir. The foreign minister strongly opposed Ben-Gurion's agreement to withdraw from Gaza and resented being sidestepped by Eban throughout the negotiation process. She reached a boiling point when U.S. ambassador Lodge failed to stick to Dulles and Eban's agreed-upon points in his address to the General Assembly on March 1. She called Eban and Rafael to her hotel suite and told them of her intention to ask Ben-Gurion to rescind the order for the evacuation of the Gaza Strip. Eban explained that Israel could not go back on its commitment to withdraw without irreparable harm, and suggested instead that she warn Dulles of the consequences of the American failure to stick up to the agreement. Meir's response was a visceral attack on Eban, as Rafael later recalled: "'Now you want me to repair the mess,' she fumed, 'after you have confronted me with a *fait accompli*.' Her pent-up frustrations erupted like a geyser. Her ambassador, she charged, had not deigned to report to her personally on all stages of his negotiations with Dulles and Hammarskjöld, let alone consult her. Of course, he was covered by the instructions of the Prime Minister, but after all she *was* the Foreign Minister." Eban was "stupefied and speechless" at the unprecedented and unprofessional tirade. He refused Meir's order to cable Ben-Gurion forthwith to postpone the Gaza withdrawal, and told her that if she felt so strongly on the matter she should send the telegram to Ben-Gurion herself. Eban's defiant response enraged Meir even further; as Rafael recalled, "She was beside herself and cried that she would jump out of the window. In her state of mind, I feared it was not just a figure of speech. I tried to calm her down but to no avail. She raised her voice from demand to command level. Without saying a word Eban got up, marched out and shut the door behind him with audible emphasis."[76] After some cajoling by Rafael, Meir eventually agreed to drop the issue and decided not to send the telegram to Ben-Gurion after all. But she refused to forgive or forget Eban's disobedience. Her revenge would be served cold more than a decade later.

X

There's Nobody Like Our Abba

In May 1957 Horizon Press published *Voice of Israel*, a selection of Eban's addresses from nearly a decade of service in Washington, DC, and at the United Nations. While some in Israel thought that the title of the book—and its author—were rather egotistical, the reception abroad was wholly positive. One reviewer noted that the title of the book "would have seemed presumptuous in any one but Eban. And it is just this which his critics in Israel should ponder,"[1] while another pointed out that Eban's "language of dignity, race, logic, force and wit is often compared by diplomats with that of Winston Churchill. . . . Only 42 years old, he is considered one of the most popular figures at the United Nations and his addresses always attract utmost attention because of their eloquence. . . . He is also the most eagerly listened-to speaker at any public function in this country." The *New York Times* celebrated Eban's "equal facility with the majestic phrase, the mild word and the blunt rejoinder," adding that whereas Churchill was eloquent in one language, Eban was eloquent in at least four. The book sold 30,000 copies in the United States alone—a remarkable feat for a collection of diplomatic speeches.[2] Two years later Eban's analysis of the current geopolitical trends in the Middle East and the Arab world was published as *The Tide of Nationalism*, also by Horizon Press. "It is an example of that cadency and cogency for which the author's name has become a synonym," one reviewer noted. Surveying the history of the region and Gamal Abdel Nasser's recent efforts at pan-Arabism, Eban observed in the book that "nothing has divided the Arab world more fiercely than the attempt to unify it." He challenged the assumption that Arab hostility to the West was derived solely from Arab–Israeli tensions and the myth that the

Middle East had ever been a homogenous, exclusively Arab domain. Eban was critical of Arab nationalism, for it failed to recognize the equal rectitude of Israeli nationalism; neither had Arab leaders successfully introduced to their peoples the social and economic conditions necessary for national freedom, instead leaving them in an anguished existence of exploitation, illiteracy, and poverty. But he also acknowledged the enduring qualities of Arab culture: "There is an Arabic literature of such versatility and range as to constitute a full humanistic education in itself. Apart from its contributions to the humane arts and to philosophy, the Arab mind has achieved radiant insight into the natural sciences."[3]

Although Eban was critical of Arab nationalism's refusal to acknowledge Israel's right to exist, he maintained an unusually effusive optimism about the chances of Arab-Israeli peace. All the Arab leaders had to do was recognize Israel's right to exist; after all, Eban maintained, there was no objective obstacle to Arab-Israeli peace: "It is not that the Arab peoples lack territory or that Israel seeks any. It is not that there do not exist, in the Middle East, the possibilities for solving all the problems bequeathed by this conflict, including the desperate refugee problem. . . . It is a small refugee problem in proportion to other refugee problems already solved. Therefore we do not have to look to the objective complexity of the problems, but rather to the absence of a will to solve them." But unless the obstacle of Arab nonrecognition and belligerency toward Israel was removed, Eban concluded, none of the subsidiary elements of the conflict could be resolved.[4] This narrative of "there is no partner for peace on the other side" had since become the most oft-cited Israeli alibi for the continuation of Arab–Israeli hostilities.

Eban also emerged as the most lucid expounder of his generation in the spheres of Jewish identity and the Israeli spirit. One of his most evocative defenses of Jewish heritage came in January 1955 in a rebuttal of the work of the eminent British historian Arnold J. Toynbee. In his eight-volume tome *A Study of History* (which would grow to twelve volumes by 1961), Toynbee charted the rise and fall of the major civilizations throughout the world. While he had been criticized before for confusing myths with facts and for making sweeping generalizations, it was his reference to Judaism as a "fossil" that vexed so many scholars and commentators. According to Toynbee, Jews were the followers of a Syriac civilization, and the greatest event in their history was the rise of Christianity, after which Judaism became a mere sterile fossil. He also equated "the evil deeds committed by the Zionist Jews" against the Arabs with the crimes committed against the Jews by the Nazis. Despite his busy schedule that month, Eban accepted an invitation by Yeshiva University in New York to give his thoughts on Toynbee's thesis. Titling his address "The Toynbee Heresy" and dubbing its author a "heretic," Eban dismantled his adversary piece by piece and declared him a charlatan and an anti-Semitic: "Here we have no partial or selective criticism of the Jewish historic performance. We have an almost total negation of anything affirmative in the entire record. The attack is not alone upon the credit of contemporary Israel. There is a vehement assault on the antecedents of modern Israel reaching back into the mists of antiquity. Rising up in revolt against orthodox history, Professor Toynbee . . . presents the story of Israel over thousands of years as a grotesque psychic aberration leading to a squalid tragedy of historic injustice." Eban lambasted Toynbee's "cardinal omissions of fact" in his treatment of the birth of Israel and ridiculed his regard of national sovereignty as obsolete. He concluded that Toynbee's thesis was "an analysis in which an inaccurate and hostile passion smothers any spark of human sympathy." Toynbee's reputation never fully recovered after Eban's address, which, according to the *New York Times*, was a "piece of scholarly demolition"; Toynbee's biographer described Eban's lecture as "a vigorous, shrill polemic."[5]

Three years later, appearing on the *Mike Wallace Interview*, Eban again defended the nexus of Judaism, Israel, and Zionism and countered the challenge that the emergence of Israel and Zionism imposed a status of dual loyalty on America's Jews: "We ask no allegiance, we seek no loyalty from anyone who is not a citizen of Israel. . . . If American Jews wish to express that kinship, it is for them so to do; if not, then that also is their decision. We, as a free nation speaking to a free nation, set forth the reasons why we believe they will find it infinitely rewarding to draw upon our common heritage and to sustain us in our great historic enterprise, but it is their decision and we impose nothing on them at all." Yet could a Jew be a good Jew and still be opposed to Zionism and to Israel? Wallace inquired. Eban answered, "In my own personal interpretation, I would say that a man who opposed the State of Israel and the great movement which brought it about, would be in revolt against the most constructive and creative events in the life of the Jewish people, and it's a fact that the great majority of our kinsmen everywhere, are exalted and uplifted by these events." Wallace did not relent: "But Judaism is a religion, sir," he responded, to which Eban retorted, "It is a religion, and it is a peoplehood, and it is a civilization, and it is a faith, and it is a memory; it is a world of thought and of spirit and of action and it cannot be restrictively defined." Eban's performance on the night was warmly received by American Jews, with hundreds of congratulatory letters flooding the embassy in Washington. "Congratulations on the superb handling of Mike Wallace's questions on Israel!" one of them read. "It was a privilege and pleasure to listen to your calm, thorough answers to the type of questions he asked. . . . I hear Jews everywhere singing your praises."[6]

In the aftermath of the Suez Crisis, the mythology surrounding Eban in the United States—that of the eloquent and indefatigable Voice of Israel, adulated by schoolchildren and seasoned diplomats alike, whose Shakesperean English could only be understood by a handful of people—had reached unimaginable proportions. In one of the wittiest and most incisive accounts of the Eban phenomenon, Ephraim Kishon, Israel's most brilliant satirist, described the magnitude of Eban-mania in New York:

> Abba Eban's prestige with American Jewry is comparable only to Albert Schweitzer's with the jungle aborigines. He is the omnipotent White Man, the miracle-working medicine man who utters words nobody quite understands—except the specially engaged interpreter from Stratford-on-Avon.
>
> It had been a run-of-the-mill day at the U.N. . . . And then, in a hall hushed with expectation, the Chairman of the Council invited Mr. Abba Eban of Israel to take the floor. The gallery filled up in anticipation of the great linguistic event. Attendants distributed the text of Eban's speech among the delegates, who immediately started marking in red pencil the words that called for further study at home . . . Hammarskjöld inconspicuously opened the Big Webster lying on his knees.
>
> Abba kicked off in splendid form. His third sentence effortlessly combined "maeruesse" and "gastlicim," last used by King Alfred. Then came a rolling masterpiece of linguistic architectonics: "Thrummed periapts orgulous of their gules, fordid ronyons and bona-robas affied to their cheveril fitchens, dearn gallimaufries and obidicuts, to you all I say: 'Avaunt nuthooks, stop pheezing and sneck-up'!" Next was a word which visibly electrified the whole Council: "Disexposticulation." The delegates feverishly thumbed through their dictionaries.

> The interpreters were sweating profusely in their booths, with the expression of hunted deer in their eyes. And American Jewry on the gallery sighed raptly and breathed with difficulty, in the throes of ecstatic pleasure: "Where on earth does he find such words?!"
>
> The speech had its content, but who cared? What mattered was to rake up the largest number of points during the quiz show. The Turkish delegation, for instance, was willing to wager that "syphogloom" meant "a missing vertebra in a fossil-toothed cetacean" whereas the Latin American delegates were convinced that it simply referred to "a copper pan for frying snails."
>
> As Abba sensed his audience warming up, his sentences became more flowery and he switched to Classical Gaelic. The Belgian diplomat had not yet discovered that by mistake he had been listening to the Chinese translation all the time. Hammarskjöld gave up, snapped the Webster shut and went out for a breather. The British delegation demonstrated its superiority in listening to Abba's words without the benefit of earphones and dictionaries; everyone knew that they were simply showing off, and that they would later receive the speech translated into everyday English.
>
> The speech ended with a winged appeal to the world's conscience to improve its English. The interpreters collapsed in their booths; the delegates were white and exhausted; Hammarskjöld returned; the delegates were crowded around. The gallery broke into spontaneous cheers; "Whole sentences!"—one of them shouted, his face transfigured with adoration, "whole sentences I didn't understand! There's nobody like our Abba!"[7]

Kishon's parody was not so far from the truth. While Eban's face and voice were well known to tens of millions of Americans through his frequent TV and radio appearances, he had a special place in the hearts of American Jews. His contribution to the development of a solid American-Israeli relationship and his conviction about the common spiritual and moral affinity between the peoples of the two countries were intimately linked to his representation of the inseparable kinship between the State of Israel and America's Jews. For Israelis and Americans alike, Eban was more than just Israel's representative to the United Nations and to Washington; he was the most revered spokesman of the Jewish people around the world.

This was the most enduring aspect of Eban's legacy. When he presented his credentials to President Harry Truman in September 1950, he was not well known in the country, relations between Israel and the United States were not yet institutionalized, and the leadership of American Jewry was fragmented. At the end of his mission nine years later, U.S.-Israeli relations were stronger than ever, the pro-Israel lobby had turned into the most effective and mobilized pressure group on the land, and Eban was honored with an unprecedented farewell tour organized by the aptly named National Testimonial Committee for Ambassador Abba Eban, comprising distinguished Americans such as vice President Richard Nixon, Chief Justice Earl Warren, former Presidents Harry Truman and Herbert Hoover, Senators Hubert Humphrey and John F. Kennedy, and the publishing magnet William Randolph Hearst.

The gradual yet steady evolution of U.S.-Israeli relations in the 1950s was first and foremost the result of geopolitical developments in the Middle East that no ambassador, no matter how brilliant, could delay or hasten. A diplomat does not make policy but executes it, and Eban's execution was second to none; even when the policies of his government caused much irritation in the White House or the State Department, his ability to win support for Israel's case in the U.S. Congress, the media, and among American Jews had translated over time to a certain popular and bipartisan sentiment that endorsed the alignment of American national interests with those of Israel. Thus, following Eisenhower's 1952 landslide victory over Adlai Stevenson and the Republican takeover of both houses of Congress, Eban, concerned about the loss of Democratic friends in the Senate and the House of Representatives, began searching for suitable Republican replacements. One of his most prominent targets was New York representative Jacob K. Javits, who agreed to work with the embassy and the lobby. Over the years Javits would become one of Israel's most ardent supporters in Congress.[8]

At times the Israeli government feared that Eban's enthusiasm for the development of strategic relations with the United States may have clouded his judgment. But while some of his reports to Jerusalem were certainly overoptimistic, his long-range view of the necessity to develop such relations with the United States was ultimately vindicated. The development of a special U.S.-Israeli relationship cannot be attributed to Eban alone, but there is little doubt that had it not been for his decade-long successful tenure as the voice and face of Israel in the United States, the natural affinity between the two peoples would not have bloomed into one of the most enduring alliances of modern times. The *Washington Post* pointed out the key to Eban's success on this front: "It is probably Abba Eban's supreme achievement that he always judges the grievances and rights of Israel against the ennobling perspectives of history and conscience. He is a people's advocate—but his theme is universal justice."[9]

The fact that U.S.-Israeli relations did not result in total implosion after the crises of the water diversion project, Qibya, and the Sinai campaign was perhaps Eban's greatest achievement, not least through his public representation of Israel as a country that was far less intransigent and defiant than it really was. None of the critical episodes in U.S.-Israeli relations reached the point of irreparable damage, due to the effective Jewish lobbying on Capitol Hill or due to a popular sentiment in support of Israel's case. While geopolitical changes of that time, such as the rise of radical Arab nationalism, certainly contributed to the warming of relations between the United States and Israel, had it not been for Eban's actions over a decade a certain vacuum in this relationship would probably have developed.

From his first day in Washington, Eban focused his efforts on securing economic aid to Israel, and in particular he directed the efforts to include Israel in the Mutual Security Act (the U.S. overseas aid program) and the extension of the Export-Import Bank's credit to Israel. In Eban's estimation he had negotiated no less than $700 million worth of economic agreements during his ambassadorial years.[10] But in the face of a U.S. State Department bent on not antagonizing the Arabs, Eban had to direct his efforts at Capitol Hill to promote the necessary legislation. His "technique," as he later explained, was "to generate a bipartisan proposal in each house of Congress in favor of a special dimension of aid for Israel in view of our special role in the absorption of refugee immigrants."[22] But American law prohibited the agent of a foreign country for engaging in lobbying, so Eban recruited for this job Isaiah L. "Si" Kenen, a Jewish journalist who had been lobbying for American support for Palestine's Jews and Israel since the 1940s and was now working at the Israeli embassy. Eban conceded that this method of winning support "deviated from traditional routines," but it was nevertheless strictly legitimate in a pluralistic democratic system; As Secretary of State Dean Acheson once told Eban rather indignantly, "You are theoretically presenting your case to us today. But I know as well as you do that you have already seen [Presidential Adviser] Dave Niles, [and Senators] Paul Douglas and Robert Taft [who cosponsored the Appropriation Bill]."[12]

In January 1951 Kenen left the embassy and registered as a lobbyist so he could represent the American Zionist Council in Washington. He enlisted the support of major groups, such as B'nai Brith, Hadassah, the Jewish War Veterans, the Anti-Defamation League, and the American Jewish Committee in lobbying Congress to authorize a $100 million to Israel in grant rather than as a loan. In less than two months Kenen and his colleagues persuaded thirty-six senators to act as cosponsors of a foreign aid bill and thirteen leading representatives to sign a joint endorsement of it (representing an almost even split of twenty-six Democrats and twenty-three Republicans in the two houses of Congress). After much wheeling and dealing with the House and Senate committees, which included several amendments and counteramendments to the bill, as well as the posting of one thousand letters to Jewish leaders urging them to "unleash a flood of telegrams" on members of Congress, in October 1951 Israel received $65 million in economic assistance.[13] The following year the lobby fought hard to ward off cuts in aid to Israel. Despite a horizontal cut in the U.S. government's Mutual Security Act in 1952, Israel was allocated more money than the previous year—just over $70 million for the relief and resettlement of Jewish immigrants, and an additional $2.7 million in technical assistance.[14]

According to Suzy Eban, the idea of consolidating various Jewish, Zionist, and pro-Israel groups into one organization was born in her husband's mind out of sheer exasperation of having to appear before countless Jewish bodies across America and talk about "the situation," often as the last speaker at the end of a five-hour formal dinner. After one such event he suggested to Nahum Goldman, president of the World Jewish Congress, "why don't we collect all the organizations into one and then I'll come and speak to them?"[15] On February 19, 1953, following the news of anti-Semitic campaigns in Eastern Europe organized by the Kremlin (the Prague Trials and the Doctors' Plot), Eban invited the presidents of some of the leading Jewish organizations in America to the embassy residence on Juniper Street to consult with him "informally and confidentially" on the international and American aspects of the affair, and "especially on the means of enabling Israel to meet those serious developments."[16] This meeting was the bedrock of what two years later became the Conference of Presidents of Major Jewish Organizations; "I'm still waiting to hear of a minor Jewish organization," Eban remarked wryly.[17] Rather than engaging in the practicalities of lobbying, the Presidents' Conference was designed to bring together the views of the leading Jewish organizations in the country (representing Zionist and non-Zionist, as well Reform, Orthodox, and Conservative groups) and to present a coherent voice with which the White

House, the State Department, and other government officials could consult. According to another account, it was Dulles who "urged Jewish leaders to unite in one group rather than having competing Jewish organizations repeatedly call on him," whereas Si Kenen points to a meeting between Nahum Goldman and Henry Byroade, Dulles's undersecretary for Near Eastern affairs, in which the latter complained that he had "received representatives of Jewish organizations five times in five days during one week," and that as a result Eban and Goldman joined forces to create the Presidents' Conference.[18] For Eban, Kenen, and other Jewish leaders, the important lesson from episodes such as the Jordan water diversion project and the Qibya conflict was that more effort should be directed at improving pro-Israel mechanisms of influence. In early 1954 a new lobbying committee was formed, the American Zionist Committee for Public Affairs, with the aim of promoting an American foreign policy favorable to Israel's interests. In order to include non-Zionist groups and enlarging its membership, in 1959 it was renamed the American Israel Public Affairs Committee (AIPAC).[19] The rest was history: while this consolidation of Jewish influence in America's political and economic centers did not contribute on its own to the development of "special" relations between the two countries, it served as a key agent of cooperation and advice during critical moments in U.S.-Israeli relations.

Whereas Eban's effective skills as a negotiator and mobilizer of public support were instrumental in the development of bilateral relations during the 1950s, his numerous personal interactions with hundreds of communities across the country and his frequent media appearances were equally important in developing public affinity toward Israel. This aspect of Eban's mission was so exhausting that the physical strains were soon evident. Harold Freed, a physician and a Dallas Zionist, pleaded to Si Kenen to give Eban a break from his hectic schedule; after all, he said, Eban was "truly irreplaceable in whatever capacity he may serve the Jewish people, and Israel would need him for a long time to come."[20]

The popular affection for Eban came from a wide cross-section of American society, and was evidenced by the thousands of letters of adulation he received personally and through the Israeli embassy. Paula Shuster, an eleven-year-old schoolgirl from Pennsylvania, explained to Eban why she wrote him: "My teacher [has] thought of the idea of writing to famous people. Some of my classmates are writing to [famous pianist] Van Cliburn, Queen Elizabeth, and well known authors. I wrote you because I admire your great ability. It would be a great honor if I ever saw anyone who is known over the whole world."[21] Bert Eaton, a California teenager and an avid follower of political personalities, wished to include Eban in his collection: "I have devoted a page in my album devoted to your public career. . . . I am addressing this letter to you because of my sincere admiration for you as a man and a leader. It would be pointless to try to enumerate the many reasons I have for wishing to include you in my album. Abler writers than I have already acknowledged your stature in our great society of nations."[22] Fifteen-year-old Judy Simons from Massachusetts shared with Eban her impression of his talk at her school: "I have never heard a lecturer who is so explicit, but yet not boring in his choice of words as you."[23] Mrs. Isaacs from Long Beach, New York, wrote to Eban that her friend recently told her, "Eban—pearls fall from his lips," and that after his recent performance on television opposite the Syrian ambassador she felt that he was indeed "the only one that is capable to come up against what I call those suave slinky Arabs."[24] Sydney Theille from the Bronx also felt obliged to congratulate Eban after that broadcast. His letter, and many like it, is proof of Eban's power to mobilize support for Israel simply by the power of his words:

> I have listened to you whenever I can, for I consider you one of, if not the top statesman in the world today. I never realized how truly great you were, what agility of mind, and real dignity you have. The ambassador from Syria was like a juvenile delinquent beside you. . . . For the first time in my life I got a slight inkling of the real hate that exists for the Jew. It made me ill. Although I am an American by birth, I am a Jew by religion. Your talk made me realize, once and for all, that just because I was born in this country, does not give me the right to just sit by. It is not enough that my son is preparing for the Rabbinate, I must do something constructive for Israel. May God bless you and keep you so that you may continue to represent the people of Israel.[25]

Eban did not resist too vigorously his remarkable transformation from one of the back-room boys of the Jewish Agency in 1947 to a household name in America a few years later. Despite his reputation for being aloof and introverted, in the company of news reporters and camera crews Eban's innate shyness readily gave way to a more relaxed and humorous disposition. The abundance of such flattering stories in the press in the mold of "that witty young man from Israel" was not an end in itself for Eban but instead a means toward creating a positive attitude toward Israel in the American psyche, one that could in turn lead to stronger relations between the White House and Jerusalem. In this respect Eban's ambassadorial years were the pinnacle of his career: his growing reputation as one of the most eloquent and adroit diplomats of the century reached global proportions; he was courted by the international press and was revered by his peers in New York and Washington. His public appearances represented for many Americans an image of Israel that may not have existed in reality, but was instead an inspiring entity that Eban successfully used to develop an enduring kinship between the peoples of the two countries; Eban's Israel was always virtuous, yet spirited; besieged, yet heroic; a perpetual victim, and rarely an aggressor.

In every public introduction of Eban the word *eloquent* popped up, often two or three times, along with other chestnuts about his wit, linguistic skills, and Cambridge University education. He soon grew tired of such clichés, but he did little to discourage them. Yet Eban's loquacity and supreme confidence in his abilities sometimes failed him.[26] On occasions where he felt prompted to respond in writing to what he considered unjust criticism—of himself or of his country—a petty, less convivial and more bellicose mood would take over. One of his colleagues at the UN once remarked that "Eban suffers from low blood pressure and high indignation," and this latter attribute was viscerally displayed when he put acerbic words to paper. On one such occasion Eban took time out of his busy schedule to express to the editor of the *Herald Tribune* admonishment over the publication of an article by William Ernest Hockin, a Harvard University philosopher and a prolific anti-Zionist: "It is not easy to write calmly of Dr. Hocking's intemperate assertion in your July 20 issue that 'Israel was the aggressor in the armed conflict of 1947–8' and that 'the documented facts leave no doubt on that point.'" In his five-page letter Eban debunked every single claim made in the original article, citing UN Security Council and General Assembly minutes as well as the conclusions of the UN Special Committee on Palestine report and his own conversations with Arab leaders during that period. Eban's rebuttal was adorned with a tirade of eloquent insults, such as, "Dr. Hocking's assault upon my country's honor is a painful offense to international courtesy and to objective truth"; "he clearly reveals himself as an advocate of no ordinary daring"; "I must assume that Dr. Hocking was not aware of the confessions, determinations and verdicts which I have quoted here; for any other assumption raises implications which I prefer not to face"; and "It matters little that men's opinions differ. But it matters greatly if they do not tread gently and humbly in the ways of the truth."[27]

General Moshe Dayan was another casualty of Eban's tongue-lashing. After reading a report in the press of criticism leveled by Dayan against the New York consulate's work with America's Jews, Eban felt compelled to reprimand Dayan in a typically scornful style:

> Dear Moshe,
>
> You will easily understand why I respond to your words and opinions on Israel and the Jewish diaspora. The issue has fascinated and occupied me for years. In its name and for its sake I have travelled almost a million kilometers in recent years over hundreds of Jewish communities in this continent—which are the majority of the entire Jewish people. A man does not go to such lengths and performs this task unless he has passion for it to begin with, and certain familiarity post factum.
>
> I hope, therefore, that you will kindly accept my first remark—a kind of "welcome" to you for your concern for this matter whose vitality is beyond any doubt and refutation.
>
> But showing an interest in a subject is one thing—and knowing it is something else. I think that you have not yet passed the threshold leading from a welcome interest to serious knowledge—and hence some of your inaccuracies which reported in the above-mentioned newspaper. . . .[28]

EBAN WENT ON TO PROVIDE A DETAILED AND INCISIVE RESPONSE TO EACH OF Dayan's alleged assertions, always peppered with sarcastic, personal insinuations: he did not believe that Dayan actually made a reference to the consulate's "courting" of only the rich and the Yiddish-speaking Jews, but he nevertheless felt compelled to note that from his own "humble experience" he found a number of opportunities to speak English to a few millions of people; he did not recall a time when a civil servant publicly criticized an officer in the Israel Defense Forces, and thus did not expect an IDF officer to do the same; perhaps the fact that Dayan did not know the name of the general consul in New York had less to do with the consul's poor performance and more with Dayan's ignorance. Dayan's rejoinder arrived ten days later in the form of a single paragraph: he saw no point in providing a detailed response, as Eban was due in Israel shortly, but had he done so, he would have highlighted three points: those things on which Eban was right and he was wrong; those things that the press distorted; and those things on which the two men disagreed.[29]

Of Golda Meir, Eban famously said that she chose to use only two hundred words, although her vocabulary extended to five hundred.[30] After Eliezer Livne, a member of the Knesset's Foreign Affairs and Defense Committee, met with a Pakistani diplomat during a visit to the United Nations, he received the following dressing-down from Eban: "The purpose of this letter is to express protest over your unauthorized interference in matters which are not within the remit of your responsibility and authority, and which you cannot assist with advancing, as you are detached from the familiarity of, and ongoing authority over our international relations. . . . I also must express the discomfort caused to myself by the private meeting, which demonstrates your contempt towards my authority and position."[31]

Eban also held a contemptuous attitude to those matters that he considered unimportant or simply inane—such as the Foreign Ministry's request that all employees fill out a four-page questionnaire detailing their personal details, including places they had visited abroad and membership in any professional and social organizations. Eban was so outraged by the attempt to invade his privacy that he refused to complete the form and wrote an indignant letter to the prime minister's office: "I cannot find the words to describe this worthless document—its vulgar interference in one's private domain and his conscience and thought, its insulting intimations and its disregard of all rules of respect and courtesy. The heart shrivels in the face of this bureaucratic rampaging, which is infused with an obvious totalitarian attitude. I have no intention to fill in this questionnaire. I do not know of any biographical or other fact about me which is not already registered and known in the office."[32]

It is little surprise, then, that by time Eban landed in Israel in 1959 to enter politics, these exchanges and others, together with tales of his Cambridge education and urbane demeanor, yielded the following associative words in the press and the political landscape: *arrogant*, *aloof*, *pompous*, *condescending*.

Eban had made his decision to return to Israel as early as May 1957. After a decade of incessant diplomatic activity abroad, the Ebans were tired of the demanding lifestyle. They also wanted Eli and Gila, now seven and three, to grow up and be educated in Israel. The ruling Mapai party, headed by Ben-Gurion, was the obvious home for Eban, given his Zionist socialist upbringing, his intimate links with Berl Katzenelson and Moshe Sharett, and his work for the Jewish Agency, which was headed by leading Mapai figures. Prime Minister Ben-Gurion welcomed Eban's move, but he thought that Eban's desire to return as early as March 1958 was premature. There were no obvious candidates to replace him in Washington and New York and, more important, Ben-Gurion feared a party backlash if Eban joined the government immediately after arriving in Israel. Instead he proposed that Eban join Mapai and participate in the general elections, scheduled for November 1959. This would allow Eban the time to familiarize himself with the party and the electorate and remove any accusation that he was parachuted into government as a Ben-Gurion lackey.[33] Ben-Gurion did not promise Eban a particular portfolio in his cabinet, but told him cryptically that he would play some role in the "international affairs" of the country.[34]

At the same time, Eban received an enticing proposition from Meyer Weisgal, the chairman of the board of the Weizmann Institute of Science in Rehovot. Since the passing of Chaim Weizmann in 1952, the position of president of the prestigious institute had remained vacant out of respect for the great man. Now Weisgal asked Eban whether he, as a man of intellect and reason and one of Weizmann's most ardent disciples, would agree to serve as the institute's second president. With the support of Ben-Gurion, who thought that Eban's affiliation with the prestigious institute would boost the party's standing in the forthcoming elections, Eban accepted the offer. Owing to Eban's political commitments, however, his presidency was largely symbolic and devoid of administrative responsibilities.[35]

On February 11, 1959, days after his forty-fourth birthday, Eban formally informed Ben-Gurion of his desire to be relieved of his ambassadorial role in Washington, and in a separate letter the following day requested to be relieved of his post in New York as well. He recalled, in his usual verbose way, conversations in Jerusalem in which he had discussed the prospect of "entering the public life of the country in the framework of its parliamentary institutions," and expressed his deep appreciation for the support accorded him by Ben-Gurion and Foreign Minister Meir in pursuing this aspiration. At Ben-Gurion's request, his three-page response to Eban was read out to a crowd of eighteen thousand people at New York's Madison Square Garden. Ben-Gurion confirmed to Eban that the cabinet decided—"not with a light heart"—to respect his wish, and with the knowledge that it would be difficult to fill the void he was leaving behind in New York and Washington. He congratulated Eban on his extraordinary talent and the magnetism of his exposition, which captured the hearts of his listeners. He praised the ambassador's tact, wisdom, and efficiency in his negotiations with the U.S. government, which translated to the development of a special bond between the two countries and their peoples: "you raised our nation's prestige, strengthened its security, reinforced its economy and increased its welfare. In strengthening the link between these two countries you skillfully drew on spiritual values and political interests that are common to the two nations. . . . " In his successful mission in Washington, Ben-Gurion continued, Eban had become no less than the "admired emissary of all Jewry."[36]

The special reverence accorded Eban in America reached unprecedented proportions in a farewell tour under the aegis of the National Testimonial Committee for Ambassador Abba Eban, which included no fewer than 164 leading Americans, from former presidents and justices of the Supreme Court to senators, industrialists, and media moguls. In its tribute to Ambassador Eban, the committee explained the reasons for this unusual gesture:

> Ambassador Abba Eban's contributions to American-Israel relations and to international comity and diplomacy in the United Nations have been of historic proportions. By his brilliant articulation of the tradition of his people, he has become a truly memorable figure in hundreds of American communities as well as in the diplomatic world and in the council of nations.
>
> It is, of course, the duty of every ambassador to represent the policies of his government in the country of his accreditation, and Ambassador Eban indeed has been an effective advocate of his country's interests. . . . But Ambassador Eban has done much more than that. He has been an inspired spokesman for the cause of world freedom and for those values and traditions which are common not only to Americans and to the people of Israel but to all people everywhere who cherish freedom and seek the paths of world cooperation toward peace.
>
> Because of the impact he has had upon American understanding of Israel, the Middle East and world events generally and because of our own deep respect and affection for him, which is shared by so many Americans, this Committee of distinguished Americans has been formed to pay tribute to Ambassador Eban on the occasion of his departure from these shores.[37]

During his six-week farewell tour Eban stopped at dozens of cities and was honored in scores of luncheons and fund-raising dinners, from a community meeting at Pimlico Junior High School in Baltimore and a luncheon at the Denver Chambers of Commerce to an address before the Massachusetts State Senate and TV appearances in Louisville, San Francisco, and Los Angeles. He was made a Kentucky colonel, and an honorary citizen of Philadelphia and Maryland. He was awarded the Freedom of the City award in New York by Mayor Robert Wagner, an honor placing him in the company of former presidents Hoover and Truman, and a forest bearing his name was planted in the western hills of the city of Jerusalem in honor of his work with American Jewry.[38] On May 11, 1959, a special gala dinner was held at the United Nations in honor of Eban and the tenth anniversary of Israel's admission to the organization. It was attended by some 450 people from forty-one countries, including thirty ambassadors. The guests were treated to the very first kosher dinner ever served at the UN. Sir Pierson Dixon, the British representative at the UN, said that Eban was one of the few men he was envious of; it wasn't Eban's grasp of diplomacy he envied, Dixon explained, but the fact that they had both attended Cambridge, but Eban had received a triple first.[39]

The *Washington Post*'s review of Eban's achievements summed up neatly his ambassadorial years: "The Cambridge-trained diplomat has presented the cause of the young Jewish state with great oratorical brilliance and intellectual agility, and sometimes he has overwhelmed others by the sheer force of his eloquence. If American and Israeli interests have not always coincided objectively in every particular, Mr. Eban has nonetheless done his best in official representations and in his talks through the country to make them appear identical."[40] Lawrence Spivak, a journalist and the face of the current affairs program *Meet the Press*, bid Eban farewell, noting, "In all the years I have been in Washington I have known no other Ambassador who has been listened to with so much interest, pleasure and profit. . . . I am sure, also, that I shall interview you one Sunday in that not too distant future as prime minister of Israel." Spivak's estimation of Eban's political destiny was shared by most foreign observers, though they did not seem to appreciate that attaining the highest position in Israeli politics required an altogether different set of abilities and attributes from those Eban had commanded so admirably in New York and Washington.

XI
Into the Fray

THIRTEEN YEARS AFTER LEAVING JERUSALEM FOR WHAT WAS SUPPOSED TO be a brief mission in London, the Ebans arrived at Lod Airport at midnight on July 2, 1959, together with more than four tons of baggage, the majority of which was Eban's books. As a testament to the genuine curiosity and interest that Eban's arrival stirred in the country, they were greeted by a press frenzy and an official reception by a welcome group from Mapai.[1] The Weizmann Institute of Science provided the Ebans a house on its landscaped grounds, at 19 Neveh Weizmann Street. Within days their home turned into a popular tourist destination, as Eban explained in a letter to Meyer Weisgal, the chairman of the institute: "[It] is becoming like a mad-house with a constant incursion of uninvited pilgrims, some of whom come to stare with awe at the living Shrine, while others actually come in to remind me that they attended a meeting where I spoke at Madison Square garden—and therefore I surely must remember them." On one occasion Eban spotted an intrepid journalist in the back garden, taking photos of the inside of the house—presumably, in Eban's words, to gather "all possible evidence of orgiastic opulence. He dully photographed the Regency façade of 19 Neveh Weizmann, the rear end of the Rambler and an amiable but decrepit group of Yemenite gardeners."[2] The incident resulted in Eban lodging a formal complaint to the Association of Israeli Journalists and the posting of NO TRESPASSING signs in the vicinity of the Eban residence.[3]

Eban was surprised and shocked by the affectionate welcome he received from his compatriots.[4] But there was an early indication that his assimilation into this new environment would not be as smooth as he had hoped. Because

Eban had never resided in the State of Israel, he was not registered as a citizen of the country. Despite his best efforts to persuade the Israeli bureaucracy otherwise, he had to arrive in Israel with the status of a naturalized immigrant and then apply for citizenship—a legal prerequisite to enable him to run for public office.[5] As holder of an Israeli diplomatic passport Eban had simply never thought that he would need to apply for citizenship. Lacking this most basic token of affiliation to his home country, Eban found it "psychologically difficult to admit" to himself that despite all his work for his country and the personal sacrifices he had made over the past twelve years he could not be regarded as a fellow citizen.[6]

Eban's place near the top of the Mapai list for the fourth general elections in 1959 was guaranteed. Whereas the candidacy of Moshe Dayan and Shimon Peres—the other rising stars who were promoted by prime minister David Ben-Gurion—was met with some disgruntlement among the party's ranks, no one disputed the value of placing Eban in one of the top places on the ticket; there was wide consensus among the press and the general public that Eban was capable of making a real contribution to political life in Israel. Yet whereas the coverage of Eban in Israel featured the usual glowing accolades he had become accustomed to during his twelve-year tour of service in the United States, the Israeli press also asked one question that had never been asked of him in America and was of no relevance to his ambassadorial duties: Would his demeanor become more Israeli-like and less foreign? Would he be willing and able to connect with the average Israeli, the sabra? Eban was apparently one of the few men in the United States who did not succumb to the informal custom of tapping on one's shoulder; would he try to lend his shoulder for tapping in Israel? Similar questions were raised in the press with regard to Eban's uppity image and his overly eloquent way with words. Other people chiseled their words out of stone, whereas Eban was depicted in one caricature chiseling his words out of marble; the contours were more refined and elongated.[7] *Herut*, the leading daily of the right-wing opposition party led by Menachem Begin, carried personal attacks against Eban simply because he was "foreign." In its Rosh Hashanah issue of October 1959 the paper published a sensationalist exposé of Eban under the provocative heading "A Proletarian in a Cadillac"; among the sources it used to discredit Eban's socialist provenance, the paper quoted a gardener at the Weizmann Institute who complained that Eban never said hello to the grounds staff. According to the report, Eban was a fraud, for he clearly did not lead the life of a Labor Party leader: he earned too much money (as president of the Weizmann Institute and as a prolific writer), he lived in a "luxurious" and expensively decorated four-bedroom villa on the grounds of the institute, and owned not one but two cars, including a "grand" Cadillac, which carried a foreign license plate. The story dripped of personal and political animosity, claiming that Eban brought with him from America an exquisite lifestyle that was foreign to the Israeli scene; he insisted on bringing with him his children's Christian nanny, and his villa was equipped with—lo and behold!—air conditioning; he never picked up soldiers or hitchhikers in his Cadillac, as was the custom in the days when there were more roads than cars in Israel. His privileged education enabled him to join the British military, "but only the Intelligence Branch—not one of the most respected services"; Eban was proficient in Hebrew, "but not the one spoken in Israel"; even as a baby Aubrey was "chubby" and his name "was not very Hebraic"; Eban "lived like a millionaire" and "drank wine while preaching the working class to drink water."[8]

Notwithstanding such anecdotal antagonisms toward Eban, the vast majority of the press was very welcoming, though there was genuine curiosity about his ability to adapt to an environment that was unfamiliar; after all, the Ebans' "return" to Israel in 1959 was not really a return, as they had never resided there. In a country of immigrants from the four corners of the world, Eban's bombastic and long-winded oratory, always delivered in a perfectly punctuated Hebrew, was so unintelligible to its listeners that Ben-Gurion asked him to tone it down a bit. After hearing Eban speaking at a memorial to Chaim Weizmann, the prime minister—himself a great admirer of the Hebrew language—noted in his diary, "In the afternoon at the Weizmann memorial Eban gave a speech. . . . He spoke with clear, crisp and polished Hebrew—though somewhat foreign." Others in the party, like Yosef Almogi, also advised Eban to change his style and speak a more colloquial Hebrew.[9] On some occasions when Eban appeared before oriental Jewish immigrants he would address his audience in Arabic, French, Persian, or Spanish. (Eban taught himself Spanish after he came across a Spanish edition of his book *Voice of Israel*. He spent the next year studying the language on airplanes and at the UN General Assembly, where he would listen to the proceedings via the Spanish translation on his headphones.) The Jerusalem branch of Mapai was particularly jubilant about the arrival of the young polyglot; finally there was someone in the party, which was composed almost entirely of eastern Europeans, who could speak to the large Farsi community in the city.[10]

Jokes about the pompous Eban soon followed: "Abba Eban is so good, he is incomprehensible in ten languages!"; "Eban can explain in seven languages why proportional representation is appropriate, and why it is inappropriate in eight languages"; "Abba Eban is the only politician in Israel who can finish a sentence—but when!?"; "At the end of Eban's thirty-minute address before a crowd of immigrants in a development town, someone shouted to the speaker: please, can we now hear it in Hebrew!" These jokes masked an ugly truth that Eban could not ignore: despite his admirable service abroad to his country, from the moment he set foot in Israel he was considered an alien, a stranger in his own country. "So what if he speaks six languages," his new colleagues snorted, "what about the ones that count here—Russian and Yiddish?"[11]

There was more in this offhanded jibe than meets the eye: astonishingly, of the eighteen politicians who composed Israel's high policy elite from 1948 to 1968, only Eban was not born in Poland, czarist Russia, or Palestine. He was the only one who counted English as his mother tongue, and he settled in Israel in 1959 at the grand old age of forty-four—making him the oldest and last to do so compared to his peers, most of whom arrived in Palestine in their teens or early twenties, during the first three decades of the twentieth century. Eban's agony over what he perceived as unjust criticism by his compatriots was particularly acute because his roots in Zionism were deeper and stronger than those of the majority of his critics. He was also dismayed by the blatant anti-intellectualism that accompanied the criticism against him, as if he was ought to be ashamed of his sharp mind and quick wit. "Intellectuals generally don't fare well in politics in Israel," he lamented bitterly to a *New York Times* reporter, before adding hopefully that perhaps the Israeli public would soon grow tired of old-style politics and wouldn't mind "hearing a problem intelligently analyzed." It was precisely these kinds of comments that made Eban seem big-headed and condescending in the eyes of his colleagues.[12]

But in some quarters the misgivings about Eban went beyond the trivial idiosyncrasies of his elitist education and accentuated vernacular. He had no roots in the party, or in Israeli politics for that matter. Worse yet, he was not a pioneer (*halutz*) who had dried swamps and fought malaria, but instead enjoyed an idyllic existence at Cambridge University. Most perplexing however, was the fact that Eban could speak ten languages, but Yiddish was not one of them. Nobody doubted that his global prestige was a huge addition to the Mapai ticket, but at the same time his ingrained internationalism, suave demeanor, and ubiquitous intellectualism were the least relevant attributes to success in the rough and tumble of Israeli politics. Eban also did not look and behave like his peers: whereas Golda Meir and Yitzhak Rabin were heavy cigarette smokers, Eban opted for imported Montecristo No. 3 cigars.[13] His mild obsession with golf further contributed to his elitist image; he was the captain of the golf club in the coastal town of Caesarea, the first (and only, even today) eighteen-hole golf course in Israel. The exuberant membership fees ($55 a year), the peculiar clothes, and the flocks of rich American Jews who crowded the hundred-acre course were as alien to the austere Israeli society as was Eban's witty self-deprecation. "It was much below my usual form!" he announced to the thousand spectators who inaugurated the course to see him slice neatly into the rough 150 yards away.[14] In his perceptive study of the foreign policy system of Israel, Michael Brecher pointed out those qualities in Eban that made him an outsider in this arena: "He is more formal than his peers in bearing, dress, manner and speech. He is less quick to make decisions, more inclined to delay while the complex forces at work. . . . As a diplomat, with a donnish air, he has a basic mistrust of "the generals" and their *bitzuist* [doer] mentality, with the strong taint of chauvinism, total self-reliance, isolationism and disdain for 'the world.'"[15]

Mapai's Nominations Committee placed Eban twelfth on the party ticket for the general elections, one above Moshe Dayan and twelve ahead of Shimon Peres. In the November 1959 elections the party won a record forty-seven of the Knesset's 120 seats. With seven seats more than at the previous Knesset, and with the departure of several members of the party's old guard, attention now turned to the suitably named Seating Committee. After some wrangling, it was agreed that Eban, Dayan, and Giora Yoseftal, another member of Ben-Gurion's "young Turks," be seated at the front row of the party's bloc at the Knesset because they were destined to join the cabinet.[16] But Eban's first taste of disappointment in politics arrived soon after: whereas Dayan was appointed as minister of agriculture, Yoseftal became minister of labor, and Peres was appointed Ben-Gurion's deputy minister of defense, Eban was awarded the utterly useless title of minister without portfolio—a popular tool used most often in coalition governments to allow an individual to sit at the government's table but without possessing any responsibility or authority. Eban's surprised disappointment at his new situation reflected his political naiveté. He was clearly out of his depth. "The Israel Cabinet is a busier beehive than I ever imagined," he admitted to the British historian Rushbrook Williams.[17] The marriage between the astute Eban and his hollow title proved an irresistible target for jokes. As one joke went, a man asks his friend, "Have you heard that

Abba Eban has been appointed Minister without Portfolio?" The friend answers "Yes, and he will be the first minister without portfolio who knows exactly which portfolio he will be without." Eban, too, managed to see the humorous side in his idle governmental position. "Believe me when I say that I wholly sympathize with your unfortunate situation!" he once said before the unemployed residents of a development town, "after all, I am the minister without portfolio!"[18]

Eban's desire to succeed Golda Meir as foreign minister was common knowledge. As early as June 1958 there were rumors in the press that Meir would soon retire due to ill health and that Eban was the front runner to replace her.[19] Five months later Eban discussed his future position in government with Ben-Gurion and came out of the meeting with the understanding that he would have some role to play in the international affairs of Israel. Sources close to Ben-Gurion, however, emphasized that the prime minister had no desire to replace Meir.[20] Eban was disconsolate; he desperately wanted the job, but had no leverage to pull against such heavyweights as Meir and Ben-Gurion. "It's important for you to understand my personal situation, which is not simple at this time," Eban wrote to Reuven Shiloah. "Because I am anxious for my relations with G.M. and for simply official reasons, I decided to refrain from making any comment which may be interpreted as if I have already assigned myself a responsibility which is not mine."[21] Ben-Gurion's motives to keep Meir in place were purely personal—compared to his bitter working relations with Moshe Sharett, he got very little trouble from the subservient Meir, who on more than one occasion remarked that she would jump out of the window if Ben-Gurion asked her to do so. Replacing her with Sharett's greatest disciple was only certain to create turmoil among the party's old guard and bring personal discomfort to Ben-Gurion himself. But despite her blind loyalty to Ben-Gurion, in November 1959 Meir threatened to stay out of the new government unless he put a stop to what she described as the usurpation of the Foreign Ministry's operational and administrative powers by the Defense Ministry. Unlike Sharett and Eban, Meir agreed with Ben-Gurion that Israel's security needs should dictate its foreign policy, but she refused to tolerate a situation in which the Defense Ministry led its own diplomatic initiatives. She and her aides were particularly perturbed by the rise of Ben-Gurion's exuberant protégé and director-general of Defense Ministry, Shimon Peres, who was now also acting as deputy secretary of defense.[22]

When the party refused to accept Meir's resignation, Eban sensed an opportunity. He approached the disgruntled foreign minister and offered her, based on his understanding with Ben-Gurion from November 1958, his full cooperation to work toward the promotion of Israel's international affairs. He stressed that he would fully accept her authority and would not take any action without her and Ben-Gurion's prior approval. Unburdened by the capacity to forgive or forget, Meir's response was decisive and brutal; recalling her record of working relations with Eban during the Suez Crisis, she flatly rejected Eban's overture, adding that while he was able enough to be "a superb and a successful foreign minister" his continuous engagement with international affairs might interfere, in the present circumstances, with her own authority. It was thus better if he attended to "other matters" and detached himself as much as possible from international affairs. Shocked at Meir's response and generally frustrated by his superfluous ministerial position, Eban sent Ben-Gurion a four-page letter detailing his recent exchange with the foreign minister: "I am obliged, regretfully, to ask for your immediate attention to the grave situation created by this unpredictable and unjust response. Tonight I was a victim of a bitter insult and severe offence, for no need or reason." After begging Ben-Gurion to meet with him and Meir to resolve the conflict, Eban concluded with an explicit yet long-winded threat to resign—the second since his warning to do so following the "catastrophic error" episode during his meeting with Dulles in March 1957: "It is not my wish or intention to 'interfere' with anyone, and if a decision is taken about my expulsion from the arena of action which is so precious and close to my heart, then I shall draw the natural conclusion. But such decision, if taken at all, must be taken with full responsibility and judgment."[23]

Eban received no reply from Ben-Gurion, and he did not follow through on his threat to resign. As the new kid on the block he was no match for the seasoned foreign minister, and it was inconceivable for Ben-Gurion to side with him in this quarrel. As he noted in his diary, he was keenly aware of the disgruntlement among the party's veterans about his decision to promote youngsters such as Eban, Dayan, Peres, and Yoseftal: "Talked to Golda Meir. . . . As soon as I mention the young ones she becomes stubborn, her mood changes. . . ." A few weeks later he added, "I told [Eban] that in the past 11 years he worked on the international level, and now he needs to learn the country: not the geography, but the nation and the people inside it . . . for now he will be minister without portfolio . . . perhaps over time Golda Meir will change her mind and attitude, and maybe not."[24]

Ironically, and unbeknown to Eban, soon after his appointment as minister without portfolio in December 1959 Meir expressed her concern to Ben-Gurion that Eban might begrudge his new post; perhaps he should be offered the Health Ministry, she suggested. Ben-Gurion agreed with Meir's assessment of Eban's irritation, but insisted that Eban must first familiarize himself with the country and its people before taking on a "proper" ministerial post.[25] Another seven years would pass before Eban finally got his dream job. According to one newspaper editorial, Ben-Gurion never intended to appoint Eban as his foreign minister—not because he thought Eban was incapable but because of what "Ebanism" represented:

> a. Abba Eban is a certified intellectual, and Ben-Gurion has an inferiority complex towards highly educated individuals . . . b. and this is the main reason: Eban is a Weizmannist, not only in his training and education, but in his nature and character. And Ben-Gurion hates all those who were Weizmann disciples . . . and Abba Eban has made another fatal mistake: when he settled in Israel six months ago he declared in public that Weizmann and Sharett were his main Zionist teachers. . . . It is clear therefore that [Ben-Gurion] will not give the foreign ministry portfolio to Eban; even during the election campaign he publicly criticized his Weizmannist-Sharettist political outlook; this is sufficient evidence that [Eban] is staring at the foreign minister job in vain."[26]

Eban was crushed. He felt that he was used by Ben-Gurion as a campaign tool before the elections, and wondered whether he had made the right decision to enter politics. His longtime friend Gideon Rafael recalled that, "[for] a time he was almost in a state of shock over what seemed to be happening to his career. It took him a long time to rally and get over it."[27]

Eban spent the first half of each week in Jerusalem, trying to heep himself busy as a member of several Knesset committees and carrying the occasional tasks delegated to him by the government. The second half of the week was dedicated to thinking, writing, and carrying his formal duties as president of the Weizmann Institute. In May 1960 Eban was tasked with representing the government at Argentina's 150th anniversary celebrations in Buenos Aires. In lieu of the more frugal option of placing Eban on a commercial flight, he was told that in order to honor the occasion he would fly with a special chartered

El Al flight, even though the national carrier did not operate flights to that destination. The true reason for that decision became apparent days later, when the world press reported excitedly that among the plane's passengers on its return to Israel was Adolph Eichmann, one of the chief perpetrators of the Nazi extermination of Europe's Jews, who had been captured in his hiding place by Mossad agents. Pressed by the inquisitive news reporters to provide an explanation for this audacious operation, the usually long-winded and loquacious Eban replied curtly, "I know nothing about it."[28]

The same month the education and culture minister, Zalman Aranne, stepped down over the growing power of Mapai's newcomers and Ben-Gurion's refusal to support him over a bitter dispute with the teachers' union. Arrane suggested as his successor Yigael Yadin, the former chief of staff who was not a Mapai member, as a countermeasure to Dayan, Peres, Eban, and Yoseftal. Ben-Gurion reluctantly accepted Aranne's resignation but offered the post to Sharett, who was offended by the gesture and turned it down. He then invited Yadin to join the government, but Yadin, now a world-leading archeologist, also refused the invitation. For two months Aranne's deputy, Ami Assaf, held the post. In July Ben-Gurion finally offered the portfolio to Eban, though he still hoped that Arrane would come to his senses and return to his beloved ministry. Succumbing to the fact that Meir was going nowhere and desperate to escape his vacuous post of minister without portfolio, Eban readily accepted the post. While the prospect of being further removed from the international arena and concentrating solely on domestic issues did not appeal to Eban, the post of education minister was nevertheless a more attractive proposition than his current post or Ben-Gurion's other offer to him—that of minister of postal services. Eban welcomed the opportunity to engage with his "natural" constituency—academics, teachers, intellectuals, and people of culture—a refreshing change from his experience at the government table. But Eban's critics maintained that he was not the most suitable candidate for the job: the education of the young generation should not be entrusted to the hands of an immigrant who had never lived in the country and who during his short eleven-month residence in Israel had not yet absorbed the nation's spirit and psychological climate. Other critics pointed to Eban's lack of familiarity with the historical settings of the Yishuv and the maze of problems engulfing the Israeli education system: "the minister of transportation does not need to be a driver, and the minister of postal services does not need to be a postman. But the minister of education must be a teacher and an educator, a man who personally experienced the education problems, unlike Mr. Eban who says: 'I shall now study the problems.'"[29] Eban, in return, charged that the public mind in Israel had failed to fully embrace the scientific revolution of the twentieth century: "People here still think of an academic as nothing more than a fine decoration or a luxury toy!"[30] As if to confirm the impression that Eban did not move in the same circles as his compatriots, in May 1960 he was elected as a foreign honorary member of the American Academy of Arts and Sciences, together with Pablo Picasso, Jean-Paul Sartre, and prima ballerina Sergeyevna Ulanova.[31]

Eban was able to draw some minor consolation from the fact that the personal attacks on him paled in comparison to the calls for Moshe Dayan's resignation over his "Marxist and totalitarian" conduct as agriculture minister. Shimon Peres, meanwhile, was noted with some sarcasm for his activism and unusual talent for public relations.[32] Eban found it hard to form alliances in his party—the bedrock of every successful political career. Mapai's "youngsters" never considered Eban one of their own and did not accord him the respect or collegiality he expected; they mocked his meticulous elocution and did not see him as a valuable political ally.[33] On the other hand, members of the party's old guard, known as the Gush (Bloc), which included heavyweights such as foreign minister Golda Meir, finance minister Levi Eshkol, Education minister Zalman Aranne, and former defense minister Pinchas Lavon,—opposed in principle Ben-Gurion's elevation of the young guard. The Gush maintained that while these youngsters had their qualities, they should await their turn for a seat at the government table. Eban lacked the political nous and sufficient leverage to be considered a valuable asset to the old guard or its younger challengers. And since he couldn't change his biography or master enough allies within the party, he was viewed as somewhat of an outsider.

Eban's ordeals in Israeli politics were oceans apart from the personal and professional excitations of his ambassadorial years. He drew some comfort in being placed ahead of Dayan and Peres on the Mapai ticket for the general elections, but the ultimate prize—the Foreign Ministry—remained tantalizingly out of reach.[34] On the long wait to succeed Meir, Eban wrote to Meyer Weisgal at the Weizmann Institute that he was "simply sitting tight awaiting developments, abstaining from initiative and giving clear impression that I could hardly care less. That, incidentally, is a true impression." But this was a false impression, as Eban's overture to Meir in 1959 indicated. Eban cared very much about both his reputation and his image abroad, and he felt that his appointment as education minister did little to enhance either. He confessed to Ben Raeburn of Horizon Press that "my Cabinet activities have for the time being taken a different course from that which I originally expected."[35] Replicating in Israel the phenomenal highs that he had experienced in Washington and at the United Nations was always going to be Eban's greatest challenge; doing it from the position of a minister without portfolio or education minister would be downright impossible. Eban was well aware of his predicament, not least because he was continually reminded of it by others. Esther Herlitz, first secretary at the Washington embassy, recalled years later the advice Eban received soon after arriving in Israel: "We told him: 'you will crash in the party on your own. You don't have friends there, you will be isolated.' It's impossible for someone as intelligent as Eban not to have understood what he was getting himself into."[36] Weisgal was equally frank with Eban, writing, "You were the first to admit in our conversation that the experience of political and governmental life which you have had the past eighteen or twenty months has not been exactly exhilarating. Politics at best is a rough-and-tumble game and invariably deteriorates into a rat race. You have been running that race since you came back to Israel. Much as I regret saying this to you, your prestige in Israel has suffered considerably following your acceptance of government office."[37] Eban did not disagree with such gloomy assessments. He was bored, depressed, and disillusioned, though in public he insisted that the rumors of his demise had been greatly exaggerated. He often rebutted such concerns with the same jibe: "many of my friends bade farewell to me very much in the mood that the friends of Daniel must have seen him off into the lions' den, expecting him to be torn to pieces without a trace. Well, this hasn't happened. I am here, as you can see, completely intact."[38]

Eban found some refuge from the rough and tumble of Israeli politics in his work at the Weizmann Institute. His chief achievement was the convening of an international conference in Rehovot, "The Role of Science in the Advancement of New States." The aim of the conference was to examine ways by which new states could be aided by modern science and technology to address their social and economic problems.[39] The ten-day conference opened in August 1960 and was an impressive gathering of renowned scientists and statesmen from across the world. It resembled a session of the UN General Assembly on a smaller scale: more than a hundred delegates representing forty-one countries, half of them from Africa and Asia.[40] Eban embraced the opportunity to fraternize once more with statesmen and to engage in international affairs.

In particular, he wished to explore two themes of independence: first was the recent experience of many Asian and African states of political independence from colonial rule; the second was the challenge of achieving independence from want, hunger, and disease. As a young state not blessed with natural resources or vast geography, Israel demonstrated how science and technology could be harnessed to achieve social, economic, and spiritual freedoms. In bringing to Israel for the first time a large group of political leaders and scientists from new and developing countries, Eban also succeeded in portraying a different, positive image of his country to the international community: Israel was not merely a belligerent, conflict-ridden country but a society at the forefront of technological and scientific innovation that could assist the advancement of human endeavor. Testament to the international acceptance of Eban's vision were two further annual Rehovot conferences, which by 1963 inspired the United Nations to hold its own conference in Geneva, "The Application of Science and Technology for the Benefit of Less Developed Areas." Heading the Israeli mission, Eban was among 2,500 delegates, including thirty Nobel Prize winners.[41]

After the Rehovot conference Eban turned his attention to the new "empire of staggering dimensions" under his watch: 600,000 pupils and students, a million parents, 20,000 teachers, a limited budget (133 million Israeli pounds) and no previous knowledge or experience of dealing with any of these components.[42] He was thrown into the deep end only days into his new post, trying to mediate among teachers who were fighting for improved working conditions and better pay, parents who demanded smaller class sizes and free secondary education, and a Finance Ministry that could not afford to subsidize either. While Eban relished the opportunity to introduce his own vision and make policy in such an important area of Israel's life, he soon became frustrated by the bureaucracy that seemed to engulf every aspect of his job. The endless meetings over what he thought were tedious issues, the incessant demands of teachers and parents to meet with him in person and, most of all, the daily working with people whom he considered to be his intellectual inferiors made him both irate and bored. From his first day in office Eban also had to deal with the constant threat of a teachers' strike, and in March 1961 the threat became a reality: fifteen hundred high-school teachers went on an eight-week strike that affected 30,000 pupils.[43] According to one of Eban's colleagues, his problem was that "he was a university man dealing with primary and secondary problems."[44] But once he cast aside his personal frustrations and concentrated on the job at hand, Eban drew enormous satisfaction from setting priorities and introducing new projects.

He oversaw the diversification of the national curriculum, which now included classic literature, the arts, French, and new English prose (and less Shakespeare, whose works Eban thought were unsuitable for the rudimentary level of English displayed by Israeli pupils).[45] One of Eban's greatest achievements as education minister was truly historic: he ordered the integration of children of oriental families (Mizrachi or Sephardic Jews) into the education system in effort to balance a historical injustice. The ethnic cleavage between the European Jews who formed the majority of the Yishuv in Palestine and had engineered the founding of Israel and the Jewish immigrants from North Africa and the Middle East who had arrived in the country in the early 1950s had been one of the most enduring and prickly challenges facing the young state. The gap in the fortunes of the two communities was stark: only two of the government's seventeen ministers were of oriental origin (minister of religious affairs Yaacov Toledano and minister of police Bechor-Shalom Shitrit), while the Supreme Court and the general staff of the Israel Defense Forces (IDF) were populated solely by Ashkenazi Jews. Most Sephardic Jews lived in squalid development towns in the periphery and felt disenfranchized against and discriminated by a ruling European elite that did not do enough to help their social, economic, and political mobilization. This grim reality was directly linked to academic attendance and performance: half of Israel's population was of Sephardic orientation, but it comprised only 5 percent of students at the Hebrew University in Jerusalem, 4 percent at the Technion (the Israel Institute of Technology), and 0 percent at the Weizmann Institute of Science, of which Eban was still president; one-third of oriental children who completed primary education could not read or write.[46]

Eban recognized that new priorities in education were a vital first step to rectify the socioeconomic inequalities in Israel. Under his reform, 30,000 Sephardic pupils at primary education enjoyed longer school days, while a further 20,000 received a month's worth of extra tuition during the school holidays in order to help them catch up with their more privileged peers. A new category of pupils was developed—those "in need of special studies"—to address their specific difficulties. In secondary education the proportion of Sephardic pupils had risen during Eban's term in office from 11 to 20 percent—a modest but nevertheless impressive result given the abysmal opening conditions.[47]

Eban's other historic legacy as education and culture minister was his insistence in bringing educational television to Israel. The idea of inflicting this modern contraption on the impressionable Israeli youth horrified many and was the subject of intense debate in the Knesset. Even Ben-Gurion objected to Eban's proposal on the grounds that it would open the door to the broadcasting of mind-corrupting entertainment programs, while the religious parties denounced the sacrilegious machine in principle. Eban retorted, "I do not see any reference in the Bible or the Talmud to any prohibition against television."[48] The resistance to Eban's revolutionary idea was typical of the austere and pioneering spirit of the country at the time—the same sentiment that in 1964 would lead an interdepartmental government committee to ban the Beatles from performing in Israel for fear of corrupting the country's youth.[49] Eban was amazed by the magnitude of the opposition to his initiative, but he was adamant: "Despite herself Israel is going to be pulled, kicking and screaming, into the twentieth century."[50] After nearly two years of proposals, deliberations, and debates, in January 1963 the Knesset finally endorsed Eban's proposal to accept an offer by the wealthy Rothschild family to finance the establishment of an educational television network in Israel.[51] Three years later the dream became a reality, with the first broadcasting of classes in mathematics, biology, and English. By the time Eban stepped down as minister of education in June 1963 the press took note of the teachers' "excellent" relationship with him, as opposed to their sour relations with Zalman Aranne, his predecessor and successor.[52] Still, some suggested that Eban did not leave a discernible legacy as education minister: one of the longest teachers' strikes in the country's history took place under his watch, and he failed to fully grasp the workings of this complex system. Even Ami Assaf, his much respected deputy, complained to Ben-Gurion a year after Eban's appointment that his boss didn't do very much and that he, Assaf, had to carry the heavy burden of the office alone. Many years later, reflecting in his memoirs on his tenure as education minister, Eban answered his critics: "It would require a sharp degree of churlishness to call this an undistinguished harvest for an incumbency of less than three years."[53]

The reason for Eban's short incumbency as education minister was Ben-Gurion's resignation as prime minister on June 16, 1963, and the formation of a new government headed by Finance Minister Levi Eshkol a week later. The seeds of this upheaval had been sowed nine years earlier, and its historic ramifications saw the end of the Ben-Gurion era and the realignment of the political system in Israel. In the spring of 1954 Britain and Egypt were negotiating the withdrawal of British forces from the Suez Canal Zone, which would have left Egypt in possession of new bases and airfields. At the same time Colonel Gamal Abdel Nasser was being courted by the administration of U.S. president Dwight D. Eisenhower, which saw the Egyptian leader as the lynchpin of its New Look policy in the Middle East. These developments gave Israel's military chiefs sufficient motivation to act against what they viewed as a dangerous tilt in the regional balance of power in favor of Egypt.

Operation Susannah was carried out by Unit 131 of Aman, the Israeli Military Intelligence Directorate—an underground sabotage and espionage network of Egyptian Jews that had been set up a few years earlier. Its task was to sabotage Nasser's rapprochement with the West by planting bombs in several British and American institutes in Cairo and Alexandria with the hope that the two countries' outrage at Egyptian terrorism would lead them to reassess their policies in the region. The plan was audacious, but the execution was amateurish. On July 2, 1954, small firebombs went off in several mailboxes in Cairo and Alexandria but caused no damage, and twelve days later several bombs, hidden in books, exploded in the U.S. Information Agency libraries in Cairo and Alexandria, but there were no casualties and no damage was caused to the buildings. Later that month members of the network carried firebombs to Cairo's railway station and cinemas in Cairo and Alexandria, but one of the bombs went off prematurely in the pocket of one of the perpetrators as he entered the Rio Cinema in Alexandria. Within days the entire network was uncovered and arrested. The trials lasted from December 1954 to January 1955, and two men were sentenced to death by hanging, while two others committed suicide in their prison cells; six members of the network received lengthy prison sentences, and two were acquitted. Avri Elad, the Israeli agent who had overseen the operation, had mysteriously disappeared off the face of the earth.[54]

Prime Minister Moshe Sharett, who had no advance knowledge of the operation, was irate when the news unfolded. He had only found out about the network and the failed operation in October 1954, when Radio Cairo announced the arrest of members of an Israeli sabotage network. He told Gideon Rafael, his political adviser, that the story could not be true, as such an audacious operation could not be ordered without the knowledge of the prime minister, and that if a mishap had taken place, he would have been informed about it by now. Upon checking the matter with Defense Minister Pinchas Lavon, Sharett returned to his office "flabbergasted": nobody in the defense establishment seemed to question the basic assumption that Western-Egyptian relations would break down over a few explosions—or indeed what consequences might have resulted if the operation failed.[55] In the days, weeks, months, and years that followed, the affair was reduced to one question that had since gained infamy in Israeli history: Who gave the order?

Uncovering the truth behind what became known as the Lavon Affair and Esek HaBish (The Mishap) involved three commissions of inquiry, accusations of perjury, the resignation of a defense minister and two prime ministers, the implosion of Mapai, and a political legacy that kept historians busy for decades thereafter.[56] Seething beneath the surface—and often even above it—was a tangled web of interpersonal rivalries. From his first day in office as prime minister, Sharett had been undermined by Ben-Gurion in Sde Boker and by his young disciples, Chief of Staff Moshe Dayan and Shimon Peres, the director-general of the Defense Ministry. He was criticized for being too lenient and too afraid to use the military option in response to fedayeen attacks; he was criticized for leading an indecisive and irresponsible security policy, and his relations with defense minister Pinchas Lavon, who was appointed by Ben-Gurion as his successor, were particularly rocky. Sharett did not trust the conspiratorial Lavon, who had not informed him of the Qibya operation in October 1953 and had failed to consult with him on the workings of his ministry. Even Dayan, who did not miss an opportunity to criticize Sharett, shared the prime minister's outrage over some of Lavon's grand designs, such as the bombing of Arab capitals and the spreading of poisonous bacteria in the Syrian demilitarized zone. Ben-Gurion also realized that his appointment of Lavon, which was designed to handicap Sharett, was a mistake. In addition, there was bad blood between Lavon and Ben-Gurion's young disciples: Lavon saw himself as a natural successor to Ben-Gurion, but from his first day in office he felt threatened by Dayan and Peres, who acted in cahoots to usurp his authority and showed no loyalty to their superior. "These two can twist him around their little finger," Minister of Trade and Industry Pinchas Sapir noted one day; "he wouldn't notice if they took his socks and shoes off while he was asleep."[57]

In January 1955 Sharett appointed a commission of inquiry to investigate the affair, but even before the commission published its findings he wanted to dismiss both Lavon and Binyamin Gibli, the head of military intelligence; as for Dayan, who was abroad when the operation was launched, Sharett thought that he was "capable of serving God as well as Satan," but he trusted the chief of staff to regain control of the situation.[58] Gibli insisted that the order for the operation came directly from Lavon, but Lavon argued with equal vigor that he did not give the order. The two members of the commission of inquiry, Supreme Court Justice Yitzhak Olshan and Israel's first chief of staff, Ya'acov Dori, found both Lavon and Gibli's versions to be "poisoned" and concluded that it was impossible to find conclusive evidence that Lavon had indeed given the order to Gibli. Rather than clearing one of the protagonists, the Olshan-Dori Commission effectively tarnished the reputation of both. After reading the material presented to the commission, Sharett was reassured that Lavon, Gibli, and Dayan should go; there had to be a serious reorganization of the IDF, with truth being its principal aim; the defense minister had to be a highly moral person; the chief of staff had to be a regular soldier and not a political dilettante.[59]

In February Lavon stepped down, and the party, fearful of a public backlash in the forthcoming general elections, pressed on Sharett to invite Ben-Gurion back to the Defense Ministry. Sharett knew that Ben-Gurion's return would spell his own inevitable downfall, as he told his aides at the Foreign Ministry—"You understand, my friends, that this is the end of my political career"—but he also appreciated that Ben-Gurion's charisma and gravitas were two qualities which the government could not afford to forego at such critical moment.[60] One of Ben-Gurion's first decisions upon his return to the Defense Ministry was to order Operation Black Arrow against the Egyptian Army in Gaza in February 1955, despite Sharett's reservations. It was clear in which direction the wind was blowing. Ben-Gurion renewed his personal attacks on Sharett: he was a coward; Israel could not rely on the kindness of foreign powers; the government's line under Sharett was irresponsible.[61] With signs of Egyptian belligerency growing by the day and Ben-Gurion positioning himself as Mr. Security, Sharett's reign as prime minister came to its inevitable end. At the July 1955 elections Mapai lost five seats, but maintained its parliamentary hegemony, with forty seats in the Knesset. Sharett continued to lead the government, but his position was so precarious that in November he was replaced by Ben-Gurion. Sharett remained in government as foreign minister, but not for long. Seven months later he was shown the way out, as Ben-Gurion was making preparation to go to war against Egypt.

In 1960 new revelations about the Mishap came to light from an unexpected source: Avri Elad, the agent who had overseen the sabotage operation but managed to escape from Egypt without being caught, was put on trial in Israel on unrelated charges and was jailed for ten years for holding secret documents and making unauthorized contacts with the Egyptian intelligence network. Elad had since been outed by several sources as the double agent who delivered the network to the Egyptians, a charge he would deny to his death. During the trial Elad revealed that he was pressured by Gibli to perjure his testimony before the Olshan-Dori Commission and to lay blame on Lavon. He added that several documents had been forged to make it look as though Lavon had ordered the botched operation. In August 1960, parts of Elad's testimony were leaked to the press, which could only refer to Elad as "Prisoner X." Lavon, now secretary-general of the Mapai-controlled Histadrut, Israel's largest and most powerful trade union, felt vindicated by these revelations and asked Ben-Gurion to release a public statement that would clear his name, but Ben-Gurion refused: "I didn't condemn you then, and I don't condemn you now," he said; he was neither a judge nor an investigator.[62] Ben-Gurion asked the chief of staff to appoint a military commission of inquiry to be headed by Supreme Court Justice Haim Cohen. It was to be a limited military inquiry with no civilian oversight or powers to delve into the wider aspects of the decision-making process among the head of military intelligence, the chief of staff, and the defense minister at the time of the affair. On October 16 the commission concluded that "The head of Aman [Gibli] and the commander of Unit 131 [Elad] suborned their subordinate to commit perjury before the Olshan-Dori Commission." Strict military censorship prevented the press from reporting to the Israeli public about the commission's investigation or its findings. Ben-Gurion, ever so protective of his beloved army and its officers, rejected the commission's findings and did not take any action against Gibli.[63]

Lavon was furious. Ignoring Ben-Gurion's warning not to do so, in October 1960 he took the matter to the Knesset's Foreign Affairs and Defense Committee, where he presented mountains of evidence to clear his name. He described dozens of corruption cases and other irregularities at the defense establishment in which Dayan and Peres played a leading role. Details of Lavon's testimony were soon leaked to the press, and the country was rocked by the scandal. For the first time in the country's history the public was exposed to the ins and outs of such personal rivalries at the highest echelons of government. The exact details of the original affair were still subject to strict military censorship: the public was clueless about the Mishap and the papers were adorned with code words, such as "senior army officer," "the third man," and "Prisoners X and Y," which only added to the drama. Many of Lavon's accusations were baseless, but it did not matter. The Israeli public and most of the press were siding with Lavon, who appeared to be the victim of an unimaginable conspiracy designed to protect Ben-Gurion's protégés. Opposition parties on the left and right seized the opportunity to attack Mapai and Ben-Gurion in the hope of bringing down the government, while Ben-Gurion, who until then had remained resolutely out of the fray, was infuriated by Lavon's smirching of the country's defense establishment. He now wanted to see Lavon crushed.[64]

Ben-Gurion now demanded a judicial inquiry to establish once and for all who had given the fateful order in July 1954. But Mapai's old guard refused, fearing that a full judicial inquiry would reopen old wounds and put the entire party in disarray. Instead, Levi Eshkol, the minister of finance and a master of compromise, suggested that the matter could be investigated more expediently and less formally by a ministerial committee. The cabinet sided with Eshkol. The Committee of Seven, as it was known, aimed to reflect the widest possible consensus and avoid allegations of political bias. It was chaired by the minister of justice, Pihas Rosen, and included senior ministers from the six parties in the coalition government. Limiting the damage to the party and getting the truth out were noble causes, but Mapai's old guard was motivated by another political aim, as Sapir explained: "To stop Dayan, Peres and their friends from taking over the government with the help of Ben-Gurion."[65] Ben-Gurion lost this battle, and would soon lose the war. The commission began its work in November 1960, and consulted all the documents relating to the affair but did not interview any witnesses—except for Gibli's former secretary, who confirmed that she had been asked to forge documents in order to incriminate Lavon. On December 21 the Committee of Seven published its findings: Pinchas Lavon had not given the order to carry out the operation and was not even aware of it in advance. Gibli was forced to resign as head of military intelligence. The unanimous report was endorsed by the government and the Knesset, despite Ben-Gurion's sharp protestations.

The lines in the sand were drawn: On one side stood Ben-Gurion and his young disciples, Dayan and Peres, maintaining Lavon's culpability and demanding a judicial inquiry with the power to summon witnesses and make personal recommendations. Facing them were the stalwarts of Mapai's old guard, who felt that Lavon had been unjustly hounded by Ben-Gurion, whose insistence on a judicial inquiry was obsessive and unnecessary—it did not differ from the cabinet committee that was headed by the justice minister. Ben-Gurion admonished his colleagues—especially Eshkol, who masterminded the committee, and Pinchas Rosen—for corrupting the democratic process and judicial integrity. His critics responded that his personal vendetta against Lavon was upsetting the national priorities. A group of professors from the Hebrew University released a public statement denouncing Ben-Gurion's methods, while crowds of students and teachers protested in defense of democracy and against Ben-Gurion. The majority of the press, the Knesset, and the Israeli public were siding with Lavon and Mapai's veterans, not least because they simply wanted to move on from 1954 and look to the future.[66]

Abba Eban sat on the fence. He thought that Ben-Gurion had a strong case, but rather than voting against the recommendations of the Committee of Seven he chose to abstain. Eban had to play his cards carefully in this melee. Choosing the winning team could help him strike vital strategic alliances in the party, but jumping on the wrong bandwagon could bring his political career to a premature end. But with the stakes that high, Eban could not afford sitting on the fence for long, and he tentatively aligned with Ben-Gurion, Dayan, and Peres—a perplexing choice given his disappointment with Ben-Gurion's refusal to hand him the Foreign Ministry and his strained relations with the other two. Eban was always the weakest side in this triangle of "rising stars" that had entered the Knesset in 1959 under Ben-Gurion's wings; Ben-Gurion admired Dayan's military leadership and heroism and fell for Peres's vision and guile. He respected Eban's eloquence, but was not enamored of his political skills. Eban defended Ben-Gurion's line against Lavon, but he was less vocal than Dayan and Peres in his public support of Ben-Gurion, and he certainly refrained from attacking Mapai's old guard, as Dayan had done so frequently.[67] In effect, Eban refrained from declaring his allegiance to either camp, which did not stop him from rejecting reports that he had chosen to sit on the fence.[68] Eventually, however, Eban's judicious temperament and huge public draw (his public addresses were second in their popularity only to Ben-Gurion's) had led him to align more closely with the veterans of the party, led by Eshkol and Sapir.[69]

Defeated within his own cabinet and incensed by his party colleagues' betrayal, on January 31, 1961, Ben-Gurion announced his resignation. Four days later Mapai's Central Committee voted to dismiss Lavon as secretary-general of the Histadrut, if only to placate Ben-Gurion, who was still an indispensable asset to the party and the country despite his many flaws. Ben-Gurion immediately rescinded his resignation threat but the die had already been cast. Other parties in the coalition government refused to serve under Ben-Gurion without a renewed mandate from the electorate, and in August the Israeli public went to the polls, for the second time in less than two years.[70] Mapai remained the largest party, but its loss of five seats (down to forty-two) was a punishing blow from the public. In November 1961 Ben-Gurion presented his new government, but he was no longer seen as the almighty leader of the nation. It wasn't even his government—Eshkol stepped in to form a coalition with the labor socialist party Ahdut Ha'Avoda rather than with the center-right Liberal Party, against Ben-Gurion's wishes (Ahdut Ha'Avoda strongly supported Lavon in 1960–61).[71] Morale in the party was low, the relationship between Ben-Gurion and the old guard growing more sour by the day. Whatever the issue of the day was, it seemed to be dominated by the intergenerational battle within the party.

After leading his country and his people for more than three decades, the seventy-seven-year-old Ben-Gurion had run out of steam. When he had resigned in 1953, and even in 1961, his party had appealed for him to stay on and lead the nation. When he announced his resignation on June 16, 1963, however, such appeals were not forthcoming.[72]

Ben-Gurion did not pick a successor, but there was little doubt within the party about the identity of the new prime minister. Levi Eshkol lacked the charisma and steely determination of his predecessor, but he cut a more humane, tolerant, and agreeable figure. Having been finance minister from 1952 to 1963, and before that minister of agriculture and director-general of the Defense Ministry, he was a seasoned politician with a judicious mind and excellent skills as a negotiator and moderator. His interchangeable use of Hebrew and Yiddish and penchant for insightful quips also made Eshkol one of the most likable politicians in Israel. ("You want to make a small fortune in Israel?" he once asked foreign investors; "then bring a large fortune!") In style as well as substance, Ben-Gurion and Eshkol were polar opposites, and the Israeli public seemed to embrace the change of personalities at the top. The daily newspaper *Maariv* noted that whereas Ben-Gurion was often irascible and combative, Eshkol was the master of compromise, naturally optimistic and kindhearted—even when he levied taxes. Even Herut party members noted with satisfaction that the political discourse returned to the normalcy of Sharett's days as prime minister.[73]

ON JUNE 26, 1963, ESHKOL PRESENTED HIS NEW GOVERNMENT WITH MINIMAL reshuffling. Following the Ben-Gurion tradition, Eshkol also held the defense portfolio, and he kept Peres on as deputy defense minister and Dayan as minister of agriculture. Sapir replaced Eshkol as finance minister, and Eban was appointed deputy prime minister—a newly created position in Israeli politics. His successor as education minister was Zalman Aranne—who together with Meir and Sapir formed "the Troika"—the core of anti-Ben-Gurionism in Mapai.

Never one to undervalue titles of grandeur and prestige, Eban was elated by his new position. "I have been translated to loftier spheres," he wrote to his friend Adlai Stevenson. "The view, as one gets near the summit, is much broader. The oxygen, however, is more scarce, and one has to expend more energy in order to breathe."[74] In many respects Eban was the Israeli equivalent of Stevenson—an eloquent uberintellectual who was respected for his polished appearance but was ultimately unsuitable for the highest office. "One never remembers what he says, only how well he says it," was the common assessment of Stevenson, who as the Democratic presidential candidate lost the 1952 and 1956 elections to Eisenhower. "The trouble with Stevenson is that he is too much of an intellectual," followed another verdict. "No one in the United States understands his speeches excepting Eban and he hasn't got a vote here."[75]

Eban's whimsical description of his new domain did not hide the fact that he was demoted to a vacuous position to enable Aranne's return to his beloved Ministry of Education. The title of deputy prime minister was a glorified version of a ministry without portfolio. Eban did not have a ministry under his control, and he did not enjoy an autonomous freedom to initiate or influence policy. Instead he was asked to advise Eshkol on foreign policy matters and to act as a liaison between the prime minister and the foreign minister.[76] This was a more benign version of the role that Ben-Gurion intended for Eban back in 1956 as a watchdog over Meir. This time Meir, vastly more experienced as foreign minister and with Eban's star shining a bit less brightly, did not object to this arrangement. But as Eban pointed out, Meir's agreement to this arrangement was "inspired not by sympathy for me but by solidarity with Arrane."[77]

Eban described his new job as having "a fireman's atmosphere about it, with long periods of waiting, but always with the possibility of being called to meaningful action." It was, as his wife Suzy told her parents, a period of "between jobs . . . there is less pressure and less tension. . . . In the morning when one wakes up it is a bit like half working and half being on a holiday."[78] At the end of one government meeting that Eban headed in Eshkol's absence, some ministers asked Eban how he found the experience. "It is not easy being a prime minister," Eban mused, "but one can get used to it!"[79] Over time, Eban asserted himself as a vocal and respected defender of Eshkol's policies against Ben-Gurion's attempts to undermine the new government. He enjoyed a very positive public image and his political stature was rarely questioned. The occasional attacks on his style were now more of a nuisance than subjects for a national debate, and his appearances at the UN General Assembly or reviews of international affairs before the Knesset in lieu of the ailing Eshkol and Meir confirmed his important position in the party and in government. As a result Eban grew in confidence—even daring to publicly attack Ben-Gurion over his crusade against the Eshkol government and Eban personally.[80]

Ben-Gurion's obsession with the Lavon Affair did not diminish once he retired to Sde Boker. The Israeli public wanted to forget the affair and move on, but Ben-Gurion refused to let it go. In October 1964 he submitted to the attorney general a voluminous dossier containing all the material relating to the affair since 1954. In it Ben-Gurion attacked Lavon, Eshkol, the Committee of Seven, and anyone else who stood in his way to establish justice through a full judicial inquiry. By then Eban had sided firmly with Eshkol, Meir, and the other members of Mapai's old guard. In early November the cabinet rejected Ben-Gurion's dossier and voted against launching another investigation into the Lavon Affair, which prompted Dayan to resign in protest from his post as minister of agriculture.[81]

Days later Mapai's Central Committee voted to endorse a political alliance with Ahdut Ha'Avoda, led by Israel Galili and Yigal Alon, under the banner of the Alignment, this time prompting Ben-Gurion to resign in protest from the Central Committee. It came on the heels of Eshkol's invitation to Lavon and his supporters to return to the party.[82] Taken together, these moves were seen by Ben-Gurion and his disciples as an audacious attempt by the old guard to outflank them and even kick them out of the party. The inevitable showdown between the two camps took place at the first session of Mapai's tenth convention in February 1965, in front of the party's 2,200 delegates. The debate was acrimonious, personal, and vehement, and neither side pulled any punches. Even the temperate Eban referred to some of Ben-Gurion's policies as "nonsense" and denounced any further engagement with the Lavon Affair as a waste of the party's energy. Eshkol deplored Ben-Gurion: "You know that I didn't want this job, but once I accepted it following your advice and pressure, give me some credit! That's all I ask, four years at most! Let us do our job!" Meir, for years the most loyal supporter of Ben-Gurion in the party, reminded the audience that it was Ben-Gurion who appointed Lavon as defense minister despite her and others' warnings. She went on to reprimand Ben-Gurion for saying that the party was divided between "those who chased the truth and those who chased government seats." And if one called Eshkol a liar, "then we are all liars!" she thundered. Rachel Yanait, the widow of Israel's second president, Yitzhak Ben-Zvi and one of Ben-Gurion's closest friends, asked him in a quavering voice, "What are you doing to us, David?" But the most poignant address was delivered by a wheelchair-bound Moshe Sharett. Pale and decrepit from a long battle with cancer (he would die four months later), Sharett's final public appearance was his most moving. He placed the responsibility of the crisis on the shoulders of Ben-Gurion, accusing him of lacking humility and loyalty to the truth. Ben-Gurion had lost the pulse of the nation and deceived the public, and it was time for the party to reunite and rid itself of this nightmare. Long and thunderous applauses followed. When Sharett finished, Meir, never one for public shows of affection, leaned down to place a kiss on his forehead—the final act in the night of the long knives. In his own address to the delegates Ben-Gurion reiterated once again his contestations and allegations against Eshkol and the old guard, and did not miss an opportunity to reprimand Eban for his apparent about-face. At the end of the stormy session the party approved the decision not to reinvestigate the Lavon Affair, and supported the new Alignment alliance with Ahdut Ha'Avoda in the run-up to the November 1965 general elections. Ben-Gurion was shown the way out of his party in a most empathetic fashion.[83]

Within days Ben-Gurion formed a new political party, Rafi (Israel Workers' List), and was joined by Dayan, Peres, Theodor Kollek, and Yosef Almogi, among others.

THE CAMPAIGN FOR THE NOVEMBER 1965 GENERAL ELECTIONS WAS THE LONGEST, dirtiest, and most costly the country had seen. Shimon Peres was particularly vocal in his personal attacks on his former colleagues: Eshkol was not a statesman; Meir should have resigned after nine years as foreign minister; Eban's only quality was that "he speaks well, but he only expresses the opinions of others. Not a single word to come out of his mouth expresses his own original idea."[84] Eban was equally vigorous in his attacks on Rafi, calling it the most unfortunate phenomenon that had visited Israel in the past decade, while the justice minister, Yaacov Shapira, called Ben-Gurion a neofascist.[85] Eban, who received that summer his tenth honorary doctorate, this one from the University of Philadelphia, assumed a prominent role in the Alignment's election campaign, alongside Pinchas Sapir and Yigal Alon of Ahdut Ha'Avoda. He was finally recognized as one of the party's leading figures—the more Ben-Gurion, Peres, and their followers attacked him, the more he was perceived publicly as an equal of Eshkol, Sapir, and Meir—even if his own party colleagues continued to view him as somewhat of an outsider.[86]

In the midst of the political acrimony in the summer of 1965, *Foreign Affairs*, the prestigious quarterly publication of the Council on Foreign Relations, published an article by Eban titled "Reality and Vision in the Middle East: An Israeli View." Following two dramatic events that year—the establishment of full diplomatic relations between West Germany and Israel and the pronouncement of President Habib Bourguiba of Tunisia that Israel was a permanent reality in the Middle East—Eban set out to examine the prospects for positive change in Arab-Israeli relations. The piece was classic Eban—effortlessly debunking the Arab aspirations for the liquidation of Israel, followed by equal consternation at Israeli chauvinism, and then a firm grasp of the politics and history of the region, with intellectual inspirations from Alfred Whitehead, T. S. Eliot, and Albert Camus. It demonstrated perfectly Eban's analytical grasp and incurable optimism. "Arab obsession with an Israeli 'threat' runs against all rational evidence," he explained, adding,

> It has won its independence in 4,463,000 square miles. It is far-fetched to believe that it cannot flourish without 8,000 more. Arab freedom in a subcontinent has been qualified, in a small area, by the liberation of another people which had centuries of Middle Eastern history behind it before the Arabic language or the Moslem faith saw the light of day. It has never been possible to convince world opinion that it is right for the Arab world to possess an empire—and wrong for Israel to exercise the peaceful possession of its tiny but cherished home.
>
> There is no greater fallacy than to regard Israel as a "colonial" phenomenon. No state in the world expresses the concept of nationhood more intensely than Israel. It is the only state which bears the same name, speaks the same tongue, upholds the same faith, inhabits the same land as it did 3,000 years ago. . . . Israel is

> not alien to the Middle East, but an organic part of its texture and memory. Take Israel and all that has emanated from Israel out of Middle Eastern history—and you evacuate that history of its central experiences. Arab political and intellectual leaders have never made a serious effort to understand, even in reluctant mood, the tenacity, depth and authenticity of Israel as a national reality with deep roots in the Middle East.[87]

IF SUCH AN INCISIVE ANALYSIS OF ARAB REJECTIONISM WAS EXPECTED FROM THE Voice of Israel, Eban's genuine self-introspection of Israeli follies, made with equal vigor and eloquence, was the quality that set him apart from most other Israeli statesmen who followed him. "I am aware that the Arab-Israel dialogue is not distorted on one side alone," he said in reproach of his compatriots. "Hostility usually evokes an attitude in its own image. The Israeli vision of Arab life and culture has been eroded by years of separation. Israel must try, above the conflict, to see her neighbor as she has been in her greater moments—the heir and author of a rich culture, the bearer of a tongue whose echoes will always fill our region and without which a man is cut off from an inner comprehension of the Middle East."[88]

Eban's solution to this reciprocal Arab and Israeli intransigence was revolutionary. Taking note of examples of regional economic cooperation in Europe, Latin America, and Africa, he proposed that the key to Arab-Israeli peace laid in the potential for economic, scientific, and cultural integration:

> The revolution of which I speak can best be expressed in terms of an Open Region. Israel's land is small but wonderfully central. It is a nodal point of communication. In peaceful conditions we could imagine railway and road communications running from Haifa to Beirut, Damascus and Istanbul in the North; to Amman and beyond in the East; and to Cairo in the South. The opening of these blocked arteries would stimulate the life, thought and commerce of the region beyond any level otherwise conceivable. Across the Southern Negev communication between the Nile Valley and the Fertile Crescent could be resumed without any change of political jurisdiction. What is now often described as a wedge between Arab lands would become a bridge. The Kingdom of Jordan, now cut off from its natural maritime outlet, could freely import and export

Addressing a rally of the American Jewish Congress in Central Park, New York, April 1956

At a "Salute to Israel" rally at Yankee Stadium, 1956. According to the *New York Times*, Eban was so popular with the American public that "Housewives set down the vacuum cleaners when his unmistakable accent was heard."

The Ebans at the Ambassador Ball in Washington, 1957

Eban with (left to right) Eleanor Roosevelt, General Moshe Dayan, and Union Leader George Meany at the Freedom Rally in New York City, April 1958

With Suzy, daughter Gila, and son Eli at a reception for Israel's 10th Independence Day, May 1958

Suzy, Eli, and Gila in Boston, January 1959

Eban during his last year as Israel's ambassador at the UN and in Washington, 1959. Summing up his decade-long ambassadorial career, the *Washington Post* observed "it is probably Abba Eban's supreme achievement that he always judges the grievances and rights of Israel against the ennobling perspectives of history and conscience. He is a people's advocate—but his theme is universal justice."

The Ebans with Kirk Douglas on the set of *Spartacus*, 1959

Leaving America for Israel, 1959

Eban enters the political fray in Israel: here with Shimon Peres, another "rising star" of the Mapai party, during the election campaign of November 1959

Minister without Portfolio Eban and Minister of Agriculture Moshe Dayan, another of Ben Gurion's "youngsters," in the Israeli Knesset, May 1960

Minister Eban in his office, 1960. His new colleagues snorted: "so what if he speaks six languages, what about the ones that count here—Russian and Yiddish?"

Suzy, Eli, Gila, and Suzy's parents celebrate Eban's 45th birthday in Rehovot, 1960

Inaugurating the golf course in Caesara, 1961. His mild obsession with this elitist pursuit further stood him apart from his *sabra* compatriots.

Above, Foreign Minister Eban with UN Secretary General U Thant, 1966. Eban later accused Thant of precipitating the June 1967 War by heeding Egyptian President Nasser's demand to remove the UN Emergency Force from the Sinai Peninsula: "What is the use of a United Nations presence if it is in effect an umbrella which is taken away as soon as it begins to rain?"

Below, with U.S. President Lyndon Johnson in the Oval Office, February 1966. "I think you are the most eloquent speaker in the world today," the president told Eban.

Left, with Senator Edward Kennedy at the foreign minister's office in Jerusalem, December 1966

> its goods on the Israeli coast. On the Red Sea, cooperative action could expedite the port developments at Elath and Aqaba which give Israel and Jordan their contact with a reviving East Africa and a developing Asia. . . .
>
> Thus, in full respect of existing sovereignties and of the region's creative diversity, an entirely new story, never known or told before, would unfold across the eastern Mediterranean. For the first time in history no Mediterranean nation is in subjection. All are endowed with sovereign freedom. The problem is how to translate freedom into creative growth. . . . In the long run, nations can survive only by recognizing what their common interest demands.[89]

The news of Eban's article caused a stir in Israel. Some newspapers accused him of selling Israel to the Arabs, and his political rivals charged him with delusion and naiveté. But the most poignant response came from Ben-Gurion; despite his fierce criticism of Eban and the bitter rivalry between Mapai and the Rafi dissidents, he felt compelled to write Eban a glowing letter in praise of his article's many qualities. Not known for gushing displays of generosity, especially toward his political rivals, Ben-Gurion's declaration that this was the best article that he had ever read on the subject caused widespread speculation about the motives behind his letter. Did his confession that Eban's article made him forget the recent squabbles mean that he wanted to poach Eban from Mapai and recruit him to Rafi? Was he attempting to cause a split in Mapai's leadership? Or maybe, as Eban himself suggested, the old man simply thought that it was an excellent article.[90]

RAFI RAN ITS ELECTION CAMPAIGN ON A STRONG ANTI-MAPAI AND ANTI-ESHKOL ticket, but the public voted with its feet. Despite the public allure of two former chiefs of staff (Moshe Dayan and Yaacov Tzur) and a new generation of political figures such as Peres, Kollek, Yitzak Navon, and Eban's brother-in-law Chaim Herzog, most Israelis were tired of Ben-Gurion's pathological obsession with the Lavon Affair and remained loyal to the party that had been in power since the first general elections in 1949. The Alignment, under Eshkol's leadership, won forty-five seats. Rafi's ten seats made it the fourth largest party, one seat behind the National Religious Party and no less than sixteen seats fewer than Menachem Begin's Gahal party, an amalgamation of Herut and the Liberal Party. In an interview in the French daily *Le Monde*

Eban maintained that these results carried a clear message to Ben-Gurion and his followers: the Israeli public had turned its back on military activism and adventurism.[91]

Shortly after the election results Meir, decrepit with ill health and exhausted by her nine-year stint as foreign minister, informed Eshkol of her desire to step down. Eshkol, who himself suffered from exhaustion and had had a heart attack a month earlier, presented his new government in January 1966.[92] Unlike the previous government, this one certainly reflected more change than continuity—and no change more notable than the appointment of Abba Eban as foreign minister.

XII

Der Klug Na'ar

At the age of fifty-one Eban was the second-youngest member of Eshkol's cabinet, though he felt that his appointment as foreign minister was long overdue. "And so the great opportunity arrives at last," he wrote to his parents in London, while his wife Suzy wrote to hers, "I think this promise of the work that Aubrey loves so much and the new possibility to mold things his way is returning new confidence to him. It will be good for him to be back in his profession, for we all know that he loves that kind of work and has his undeniable talent for it."[1]

Their children Eli and Gila, now sixteen and twelve, respectively, were understandably less happy about leaving behind their friends and a wholly pastoral existence in Rehovot and moving to a new school and a very different environment at the foreign minister's official residence in Jerusalem. There was an endless flow of government officials and foreign visitors into the eighteen-room residence on 3 Balfour Street, and they all wanted to meet with the foreign minister at the most uncongenial hours. There was a constant presence of security personnel in the immediate proximity of the house, which bred a stifling rather than a secure environment for the two youngsters. Both parents were often absent, sometimes for weeks; Suzy usually accompanied her husband on his foreign trips. "When we came home from school we never knew who was going to be there," Eli would later recall, "and when there was a family argument the atmosphere was even worse because we knew that the security guards outside could hear every word. Our childhood had this acute sense of protection and seclusion from the outside world, but at the same time it was devoid of privacy altogether."[2] Suzy was equally overwhelmed by the demands of the new job, as she wrote to a friend: "The life we lead! The tensions in the air! The telephones all hours of the day and night. The constant presence of strangers. The constant presence of staff. The police. The people who watch the children as they come in and out of the house." Eli and Gila's childhood may have been devoid of some privacy and family intimacy, but it was not emotionally deprived—unlike Eban's own childhood, which he never discussed with his children.[3]

The news of Eban's appointment was received with global enthusiasm. His view of diplomacy as a specialized vocation rather than a political exigency, coupled with his moderate outlook and genteel demeanor, fostered an expectation that Israel's international conduct would now be more humble and conciliatory toward its Arab neighbors. From his first press conference as foreign minister it was evident to all that, if given the chance, Eban could herald a new dawn in Israel's relations with the Arab world.

On January 10, 1966, three days before Eban's first day in office, the Soviet Union facilitated in Tashkent a framework for peace to end the war between India and Pakistan over Kashmir. Moscow's constructive engagement with that regional conflict gave Eban hope that the "spirit of Tashkent" could have positive influence on the prospects for an Arab-Israeli dialogue sponsored by the great powers. A few weeks later Eban embarked on a tour d'horizon of Paris, London, and Ottawa, Ontario, during which he explained to his interlocutors that only the Soviet Union could exert a more moderate Arab attitude toward Israel. He then continued to Washington, DC, to meet with President Lyndon Johnson to conclude the sale of A-4 Skyhawk jets to Israel.[4] While Eban's rationale for propagating the spirit of Tashkent was questioned by Israel's hawks as well as by his Western counterparts, who pointed out that Moscow's interests in the Asian subcontinent were markedly different from its Middle East interests, Eban's mere arrival on the scene was greeted with hope and renewed optimism. The German press lauded his plans for a four-power framework (the United States, the Soviet Union, Britain, and France) to facilitate Arab-Israeli dialogue as a welcome "peace offensive" that confirmed Eban's "reputation as an "intelligent man," while Lyndon Johnson's national security adviser, Walt Rostow, told the president that "with Eban's appointment, the winds in Israel might begin to shift away from the old timers' idea of 'fortress Israel' to the younger men's hopes for some kind of break in the impasse." Ephraim Evron, second in command at the Israeli embassy in Washington, thought that "Golda Meir's replacement by Eban would greatly decrease the decibel level of Israeli diplomacy and make things easier all around."[5] The American impression of Meir had changed little since the Suez Crisis a decade earlier, when Edward Lawson, the ambassador in Tel Aviv had suggested that "Golda's bite is worse than her bark and she is disposed to throw tough language around a little more recklessly than one might expect from a Foreign Minister."[6]

Eban himself felt that his arrival at the Foreign Ministry was greeted by the senior officials there—many of them his former colleagues—with relief rather than apprehension. After a decade of serving Meir, a "tough character with a domineering streak" whose talent "lay in the simplification of issues," the Foreign Ministry officials welcomed the opportunity to work under a foreign policy specialist. What Meir and many of her contemporaries failed to appreciate, Eban explained, was that "[the] trouble with foreign ministry is that it is foreign, and it is there that a nation's sovereignty has less influence than in any other field of public policy." Eban, however, had intimate knowledge of the workings of the international system and the kinds of dilemmas and challenges that his staff encountered. "No previous first-name habits were suspended, and team spirit prevailed over hierarchy. The harmony was deep and broad," he recalled with some pride years later.[7] Though Eban lacked the informal style of his predecessor, the atmosphere in the office was very collegial. Emanuel Shimoni, his trusted aide at the Ministry of Education and at the deputy prime minister's office, who now headed the foreign minister's bureau, noted that Eban in the company of friends was very different from Eban in the company of strangers: "He rarely felt comfortable in the company of strangers and would rarely be seen engaging in mindless chitchatting. Rather, he would go over his notes or cast a vacuous gaze toward an obscure point in the distance. He seemed visibly edgy when forced to engage in those harmless though evidently painful social encounters." Others who worked under Eban in the Foreign Ministry similarly portrayed an image of a man who was clueless about how to start a conversation and lacked the basic social skills to make small talk. Eban's door was always open to his staff, but everybody knew that he did not like to be bothered with trivial matters.

Eban's closest confidant, with whom he shared his most intimate thoughts and anxieties, was none of the Foreign Ministry people but instead his personal driver. Described by Eban as "a steadfast counselor and a friend of intense fidelity," Yaacov Markovitch was an Auschwitz survivor who had came to Israel shortly after the formation on the state. Lacking formal education or professional qualifications, he began working in the 1950s as a government pool driver, and in 1959 he was assigned as Eban's personal driver when Eban served as minister without portfolio. Yankale, as he was fondly known, was the exact opposite of his boss—gregarious, street smart, and devoid of inhibitions. He remained with Eban throughout a ministerial career that spanned fifteen years, and during that period this odd couple clocked up thousands of hours together in complete isolation. Yankale would tell his boss all the latest political gossip he heard from the other ministerial drivers and in the Knesset's canteen (Eban preferred to dine at the more refined hotel restaurants in Tel Aviv and Jerusalem), while Eban confided in his driver about personal matters that even Suzy was not aware of. Yankale reached such a legendary status in the political folklore that he was often referred to by the press and the parliamentary aides as the deputy foreign minister. Once Shimoni asked Yankale, who sat idly in the office, to deliver some documents to the Knesset. Both the office staff and Yankale looked at him aghast for having the temerity to even make such a suggestion.[8]

As always, the British were the most incisive in analyzing the Eban phenomenon: The *Observer* reminded its readers of Eban's Cambridge University education and noted, "Cosmopolitan diplomatic experience and a probing mind combine to make him well worth paying attention to: he has a plummy way of speaking and likes to hear himself talk. . . . He isn't all that young, 51, but much more flexible than his rigid predecessor, Mrs. Golda Meir, who typified the missionary zeal of the early Zionist pioneers."[9] The British Foreign Office accurately depicted Eban as more at home in international diplomacy than in Israeli internal affairs, noting that despite his experience and status he has struggled to find his place in his own party. As an individual, Eban was "not an exciting personality, but nevertheless agreeable in conversation."[10] The French were particularly excited by Eban's appointment. The daily *Le Monde* noted that Eban's oriental education, deep knowledge of the Arab world, long experience at the UN, and pleasant temperament as a negotiator would undoubtedly lead him to deal with Israel's problems in a more constructive and delicate manner.[11] His first foreign visit was to Paris, and his hosts did not hide their enjoyment at the noticeable change in style and tone between Eban and his predecessor. A reporter for the daily *Maariv* noted that it was difficult to comprehend how much the French appreciated the ability of a stranger to speak their language, sometimes in ways which were even beyond their own abilities, as Eban had done in his meetings and speeches in Paris: "From the moment he landed at Orly airport to the moment of his departure, Eban had no trouble sharing his opinions in his most grandiloquent French, answering each question in length, even when in fact he said nothing." After years of dealing with Israeli officials who communicated in English, French diplomats were thrilled by Eban's polished style and careful attention to diplomatic protocol.[12]

Eban's early pronouncements stood in stark contrast to Meir's skeptical outlook or the security paradigm that dominated the school of David Ben-Gurion, Moshe Dayan, and Shimon Peres. In September 1966 Eban rebuked the prevalent notion in Israel that the Arabs only understood the language of force: "As Jews we must be sensitive to any national 'typology,' or to attempt to give a whole people a negative appearance. It is our duty to educate the young generation towards an attitude of respect towards this region and its culture. . . . It is our duty to screen public speeches for insulting innuendoes and any derision of Arab culture." It is little surprise, then, that even some in the Arab world congratulated Eban's appointment. The Lebanese daily *Al Hayat* commented on Eban's "flexible realism" and welcomed his vision for a Tashkent-style Arab-Israeli agreement, while the Tunisian weekly *Jeune Afrique* noted that Eban "knew extremely well the psychological motivations of the Arab world, and that he had displayed his flexibility" during his years at the UN, leading to the hope that "Israeli diplomacy under Eban could outline some kind of co-existence with the Arab world, unlike the views of the previous foreign minister . . ."[13]

During his first tour of the ministry's twenty-two operational departments and ten administrative departments in Jerusalem, Eban was noticeably impressed by the sheer size of what he had inherited and expressed his surprise at the extent of his new domain. In 1954 Israel had forty-two diplomatic posts abroad; in 1960 the number jumped to sixty, and by 1965 there were ninety-eight Israeli missions across the globe (including twenty-nine legations in African countries, one of Meir's most important legacies). One of Eban's first tasks as foreign minister was to address the drastic shortage in manpower resulting from this rapid expansion. More than thirty new cadets were recruited to the Foreign Ministry, and several personnel changes were made to ensure the depth—and not just the breadth—of expertise in several critical areas, such as the research department and the newly established Middle East Bureau. After Israel's successful building of relations with several Arican countries through technological and agricultural advancements in the previous decade, Eban now targeted Eastern Europe and Asia. In his first year in office he was the first Israeli foreign minister to have ever visited Poland, Japan, Thailand, Burma, Singapore, and the Philippines, as well as Australia and New Zealand.[14]

Eban was equally interested in pouring a theoretical dimension into the working of the Foreign Ministry. Unlike his predecessor and all of his successors, he was a career diplomat rather than a politician. With two decades of intimate knowledge of the vagaries of Israeli diplomacy, Eban insisted that Israel's foreign policy should learn from its own experience rather than approach new challenges with no reference to historical patterns. Some of the doctrinal elements to guide Israel's relations with the world, Eban maintained, included adherence to the territorial status quo, a view of the Middle East as a multinational region with different centers of power, and the importance of recognizing global trends and striking diplomatic relations with small states. In practical terms, Eban used his own ambassadorial experience in Washington to instill in his colleagues the importance of public diplomacy. The ubiquitous debates by Israel's enemies about the legality and legitimacy of the Jewish state had to be countered by an effective portrayal of Israel as a Middle Eastern country integral to the history, culture, and development of the region. The greatest problem of Israel's foreign policy was the image of Israel itself in the eyes of the world, Eban explained: "they say that we are newcomers, that we do not belong in here, that we should not exist as a state, and if we should—then not here . . . we are like a Middle Eastern Rhodesia, a pronounced colonial entity."[15] Eban's response to these charges was based, as always, on the themes of universal justice, morality, and history. He delivered one of his most poignant defenses of Israel's right to exist before the UN General Assembly at the height of the 1967 Six-Day War: "It would seem to me that after 3,000 years the time has arrived to accept Israel's nationhood as a fact, for here is the only State in the international community which has the same territory, speaks the same language and upholds the same faith as it did 3,000 years ago. . . . How grotesque would be an international community which found room for 122 sovereign units and which did not acknowledge the sovereignty of that people which had given nationhood its deepest significance and its most enduring grace."[16]

EBAN'S POSITION WITHIN THE PARTY, AT LEAST UNTIL JUNE 1967, WAS ALMOST AS comforting as the reception accorded him abroad. His relations with Levi Eshkol were certainly better than the relations he had had with all the prime ministers who had succeeded Eshkol, though they were no less complex. Like others in Mapai, Eshkol admired Eban's eloquence and rhetorical skills, but not a lot beyond that. Though Eban's views were often solicited, he was not as close to Eshkol as other ministers were, such as Israel Galili, Pinchas Sapir, Zalman Aranne, and Yaacov Shimshon Shapira. But unlike Meir, Dayan, and others in the party, Eshkol did not harbor an inferiority complex in the presence of intellectuals. He enjoyed the company of brainy people such as Eban and Yaacov Herzog, the director-general of the prime minister's office and a phenomenally cultured scholar of philosophy and theology. But while Eshkol, like Ben-Gurion before him, often confided in Herzog on foreign and security affairs, he held a more skeptical view of Eban's abilities as a strategist. Eshkol did not trust Eban's judgment, which he thought was clouded by too much idealism and not enough pragmatism. He referred to Eban in Yiddish as *der klug na'ar* (the smart fool), and once noted that "Eban never gives the right solution, only the right speech."[17]

While in many governments the foreign minister's position of influence is second only to that of the prime minister, as an Anglo-Saxon immigrant in a cabinet of Eastern European pioneers, Eban had no political following of his own. In party politics, too, Eban's upbringing and demeanor set him apart from virtually everyone else in Mapai. Israel Lior, Eshkol's military secretary and one of the closest aides to the prime minister, added that alongside the clichés about Eban's qualities as a linguist and his high international standing, some less endearing sides of Eban's personality made his ministerial life rather uncomfortable at times: "Eban was a boring man. His weakness came up during his presentations before the government . . . very detailed, very long, very boring. There were many details that could not influence the decision. . . . He would read every word in the telegram, slowly, with great enunciation, with precision. The ministers would fall asleep." The *New York Times* reported that Eban's colleagues could be heard complaining that he "has no warmth, that he is not a policymaker but a skillful advocate. He has been accused of being slick, crafty, an opportunist."

But Eban also knew better than anyone else in government the workings of foreign governments, and had personal relationships with many leaders abroad. He understood the nature of international developments and could anticipate the reactions of the international community to Israeli policy. He played an important role in the decision-making process, especially until the outbreak of the Six-Day War in June 1967 though, according to Lior, this was sometimes because Eshkol "wanted to prevent emotional misunderstanding" between himself and Eban, who was very proud: "Eban had a special way to express his anger over not being consulted. . . . He would pretend to be surprised and sulk that he did not have sufficient time to make his own view. He would then object almost automatically to every matter of which he did not have prior knowledge, always asking for time to think, check and study." Many discussions were delayed because of Eban's antics, and Eshkol would often send Lior or Herzog to iron things out with Eban on his behalf before the meeting.[18]

Herzog held similar views of Eban. He respected the man's intellect and commended him on his "tremendous stand" during the Suez Crisis of 1956, but he strongly disagreed with Eban's apparent eagerness to yield to international pressure. On a more personal level, Herzog took a dim view of a certain egotistic streak in Eban's personality. On one occasion in October 1966, to mark Ben-Gurion's eightieth birthday, Eban tried unsuccessfully to outwit Herzog into allocating Eban a role in the public committee responsible for the celebrations. Herzog put Eban in his place and noted his surprise and hurt. "I assume that the failure to invite Eban stems not only from BG's contempt of him, but also from the profound hostility between him and Peres," Herzog later wrote in his diary. He also noted the critical impressions of *Maariv*'s editor Arieh Disenchik, who pointed to Eban's declining standing among the country's political establishment "not least because of his boundless publicity-seeking—though his position in the general public remains strong." Disenchik also recorded Eban's boasting that Meir and Arrane could never explain why they hated Peres until he came along to give it the right expression." Eban's contemptuous treatment of Meir began during her visit to the United States at the height of the Suez Crisis: he told diplomats that Meir lacked political understanding, and he even directed the embassy staff in Washington to ensure that he and Meir would not be at the same city on the same day.

Even Suzy Eban did not escape Herzog's critical eye. He wrote that Suzy never let her guard down and kept a distance from those around her, "as though *noblesse oblige*." As for Suzy's sister, Aura, Herzog recorded her remarking that Eban "'[is] a brain but not a man, and lacks character.' She believes he cannot be changed."[19]

WHEN ESHKOL BECAME PRIME MINISTER IN 1963 HE SUMMONED EBAN TO HIS office. "Tell me, *yunger man,"* Eshkol asked his forty-eight-year-old deputy, "what exactly involves being the prime minister of Israel?" In Eshkol's eyes anyone under the age of seventy was a young man; he had been prime minister for only a couple of days and was unsure what he was supposed to be doing. Eban explained that the prime minister's job was akin to that of the conductor of a symphony orchestra: he didn't play an instrument, but his will and personality guided the collective effort. "And you, Mr. Eshkol, are our conductor. Your task is to persuade us, your cabinet ministers, to perform together in a single, harmonious whole in accordance with your program, your vision, and your interpretation." Eban also advised the prime minister that he would probably soon find himself confronted by challenges involving the very existence of Israel. Such an ominous prediction seemed unfounded in 1963, and even as late as November 1966, when Eban would confidently pronounce, "The two least likely things that can happen in the Middle East in the near future are war or peace. We are destined to live for some time in a sort of twilight zone between the two." Yet this serene estimation, shared by many observers of the region inside and outside of Israel, was turned on its head almost overnight by the events of May 1967.[20]

The Suez Crisis of 1956 was followed by a decade of relative calm along Israeli's borders. While none of the parties to the conflict seemed content with the prevailing status quo of a suspended state of war, there was no apparent eagerness to disturb the delicate balance by opening a third Arab-Israeli war. The origins of the 1967 Six-Day War have been the subject of a rich and diverse scholarship. Reciprocal inadvertency, miscalculations, and a series of over- and underestimations by Israelis, Arabs, and Soviets alike are often cited as the most immediate causes of the war.[21] According to Eban, the Six-Day War "was undoubtedly born in Syria," referring specifically to a military coup in the country in February 1966 that bred a more confrontational policy toward Israel under the leadership of general Salah Jadid.[22]

In response to a series of attacks by Palestinian guerrillas against Israel from the Jordanian-controlled West Bank, on November 13, 1966, Israel launched a four-hundred-man military operation against the Arab village of Samu, on the outskirts of Hebron, which reportedly aided and sheltered a group of Palestinian fedayeen. What was supposed to be a limited strike turned into a bloody battle with a Jordanian armored column, resulting in fifteen Jordanian and ten Israeli soldiers dead, three villagers killed and sixty-nine wounded, and more than a hundred homes destroyed. The Israeli government's decision to operate against Jordan—rather than go after Damascus, which instigated the Palestinian infiltrations—prompted some criticism in Israel and abroad, especially following Eshkol's declaration that he hoped that the Syrian authorities would learn the lesson from the Samu raid. But the immediate result of the operation was the undermining of the position of the moderate King Hussein of Jordan, who for the past three years had conducted a secret dialogue with Israel via Yaacov Herzog. Hussein felt betrayed by the Israelis, who previously assured him that they would respect Jordan's sovereignty. He was also criticized by his own people and the Arab states for failing to protect Samu. Although the Israeli government later apologized to Jordan for the incident, Hussein became convinced that what happened at Samu was a prelude to an Israeli invasion of the West Bank. Eban told Walworth Barbour, the American ambassador in Israel, that the operation "merely got out of hand . . . [its effect] was not as anticipated and dangerous situation had resulted."[24] A few weeks later Eban, who supported the operation unreservedly, went even further, admitting to Joseph Sisco of the U.S. State Department that at the time Israel could not link the terrorist attack to Syria. The Samu operation came after two weeks with no signs of terrorist activity inspired by or perpetrated by Damascus; going after the Syrians, Eban explained, would have entangled Israel in an unnecessary conflict. At the same time, Eban insisted that Israel had no ambitions to bring down the Jordanian regime. When asked during an appearance on NBC's *Meet the Press* whether Israel had a Machiavellian design to have King Hussein toppled and replaced by a more radical group in order to foster more sympathy in the United States for Israel's Jordan policy, Eban replied, "I think that to ascribe that sort of doctrine to Machiavelli is an insult to that very interesting Italian philosopher." Ever the harbinger of good news, Eban declared that far from bringing the region to the brink of war, the Israeli operation had actually stabilized the situation.[25]

Worse still, the Samu operation failed to deter the Syrians from instigating further attacks against Israel, so on April 7, 1967, the Israelis turned to punishing Damascus for its continuous support of terrorism against Israel. In a premeditated attempt to draw the Syrians into battle, Israel sent two armored tractors into the demilitarized zone. As expected, the Syrians responded with artillery shelling of Israeli villages nearby. Israeli tanks returned fire, and before long the land skirmish escalated into a dogfight between Syrian MiGs and Israeli Mirages. By the end of the afternoon the Israeli Air Force had downed six MiGs. To make sure that the Syrians got the message, the Israeli jets continued to fly over Damascus, producing shattering sonic booms.[26] From then on events unfolded rapidly, even though it seemed that neither party wanted to see further escalation. Eban reassured the United States that Israel would not react militarily to Syrian aggression without first consulting with Washington; as he put it to Barbour, "there were no automatic switches open."[27] Eshkol also wanted to avoid war at all cost. Addressing the Knesset's Foreign Affairs and Defense Committee on May 17, he was adamant: "We do not want war . . . we must escape now from war and maneuver accordingly."[28]

By now Egypt was already on a war footing. On May 13, Gamal Abdel Nasser received a secret cable from Moscow alerting him to a mass mobilization of Israeli forces close to the Syrian border. According to the Americans, the Soviet message was a fabrication and provided the spark to ignite the third Arab-Israeli war. Drawing on this dramatic message from a medium-level Soviet official, the U.S. Central Intelligence Agency (CIA) concluded that "there had been miscalculations by the Soviets and by the Arabs. The Soviets overestimated the Arabs' ability to employ their substantial military strength against the Israelis while the Arabs overrated their own strength and underrated the Israeli military capability and determination to win." Asked if the Soviets had encouraged the Arabs to up the ante in the weeks before the war, "the Soviet [agent] replied affirmatively, stating that the USSR had wanted to create another trouble spot for the United States in addition to that already existing in Vietnam. The Soviet aim was to create a situation in which the US would become seriously involved, economically, politically, and possibly even militarily and in which the US would suffer serious political reverses as a result of its siding against the Arabs."[29]

Nasser, who had been criticized by Jordan for failing to come to its aid in Samu or to assist Syria when Israel shot down six of its MiGs, feared an irreparable damage to his credibility and leadership in the Arab world if he stood by idly a third time. Despite the erroneous reports about the mobilization of Israeli troops along the Syrian border, the cascade of militant threats by Israeli officials, buoyed by the forthcoming celebrations of Israel's Independence Day, lent some credibility to the Syrian fears of an imminent Israeli attack. On May 9 Eban warned Syria to cease its aggressive policy toward Israel or face another round of retribution. Two days later Eshkol announced that if there was no other way out, Israel would be forced to take suitable retaliatory measures against the saboteurs' nests, adding that Israel might have to take measures "no less drastic than those of April 7." Chief of Staff Yitzhak Rabin added, "Since the Syrian regime is behind the acts of terrorism, it had better take measures to curb these actions, and the sooner, the better." The Syrian Foreign Ministry complained about the "successive Israeli threats" by senior Israeli officials, which were designed to prepare world public opinion for the "forthcoming Zionist aggression."[30] As Eban himself conceded years later about the adverse effect of the Israeli statements, "If there had been a little more silence, the sum of human wisdom would probably have remained intact."[31]

On May 15, tens of thousands of jubilant Israelis cheered on a military parade in Jerusalem—the highlight of the Independence Day celebrations. At the same time in Cairo, another military parade took place, but for a very different reason. Alarmed by the intelligence reports about the massing of Israeli troops on the Syrian front, Nasser began moving an entire division through the streets of Cairo, Ismailia, and into the Sinai Peninsula in a public display of force. Eban instructed Gideon Rafael at the UN to inform Egypt, via secretary-general U Thant, that there was no concentration of Israeli troops along the Syrian border and that Israel had no aggressive intentions against any Arab state. Rafael duly delivered the message and was informed later that day by Thant that Nasser had received it.[32] The following day Eshkol and Rabin decided on a partial mobilization of military reserve units, and that evening Nasser asked Thant to order the evacuation of the United Nations Emergency Force (UNEF) out of Gaza and Sinai, where it had been stationed since 1957. Thant's precipitate response—within one hour of Nasser's request—to order the withdrawal of UNEF signaled the beginning of a tense three-week period known as Ha-Hamtana (The Waiting) in anticipation of a resolution of the burgeoning crisis along the Israeli–Egyptian border. By May 22, when UNEF completed its withdrawal, there were nearly 80,000 Egyptian soldiers and six hundred tanks in the Sinai.[33]

Eban cautioned U.S. ambassador Barbour that in the absence of a clear American commitment to Israel's sovereignty in the face of the emerging crisis, the government in Jerusalem might heed public pressure and take unilateral action. But, Eban continued, Israel had no interest in causing the situation to deteriorate. He told Barbour that he had even asked the editors of the daily newspapers to refrain from highlighting the crisis so as not to provoke Egypt or pressure the Israeli government into action. Throughout this period Washington tried to restrain Israel from taking a military action to solve the crisis, while at the same time acknowledging that Nasser's blockade of the Straits of Tiran was an act of aggression. On May 17, President Johnson—a strong supporter of Israel, who had first learned of the country's problems and challenges at Eban's ambassadorial residence in Washington more than a decade earlier—warned Eshkol that he could "not accept any responsibilities on behalf of the United States for situations which arise as the result of actions on which we are not consulted."[34] On May 23 Johnson declared that the U.S. government considered the Gulf of Aqaba to be an international waterway and added that Nasser's blockade of the straits to Israeli shipping was "illegal and potentially disastrous to the cause of peace." At the same time, he asked Israel to delay any action for forty-eight hours.[35]

The American request for time suited Israel, whose army also needed time, as Rabin informed Eban. For a decade the presence of UNEF along the Egyptian border and the absence of armed infiltrations into Israel from Gaza and the Sinai allowed the Israeli Defense Force (IDF) to concentrate its attention on the Syrian and Jordanian fronts. Now Rabin asked Eban for time to rebuild the army's strength on the southern front and prepare it for battle. At that point in the crisis there was an unusual consensus among Israel's generals and diplomats that war should be avoided.[36]

At 4:30 a.m. on May 23 the telephone rang at the Eban residence in Jerusalem. On the line was Rabin, informing him that the previous night Nasser had announced the closing of the Straits of Tiran to Israeli and Israel-bound vessels. At 6:00 a.m. Eban was already presiding over a meeting at his home with his senior aides. According to Moshe Bitan, the head of the American desk at the foreign ministry, there was very little discussion of substance at the meeting, though Eban was adamant over one thing: he was determined to go to Washington, and perhaps London and Paris too, to enlist diplomatic support to resolve the unfolding crisis. He then rang Barbour and Michael Hadow, the British ambassador in Tel Aviv, asking them to consult the speeches made by their respective governments' representatives before the United Nations on March 1, 1957, on the subject of freedom of navigation through the straits. At 8:00 a.m. Eban left with his closest aides to Tel Aviv for a meeting at the Defense Ministry. An Arabic station on the car radio broadcast Nasser's speech from the previous night, which Eban translated for the benefit of his companions.[37]

Eban was joined at the Defense Ministry's war room by Chief of Staff Yitzhak Rabin, Chief of Operations Ezer Weizmann, Chief of Military Intelligence Ahron Yariv, and all government ministers. Rabin's assessment of the situation was alarming: this round would be much more difficult than the 1956 Sinai campaign. Israel would win the war, but at a much higher cost. None of the generals proposed immediate military action, instead asking for time to build up the army's strength and call up reserve units. Eban proposed granting President Johnson what he had asked for: forty-eight hours to find a diplomatic solution. A clear American commitment to ensure Israel's navigation rights could save Israel from going to war, Eban explained, and anything less than that might require an Israeli preemptive strike against Egypt, in which case Israel needed international support. If Israel went to war without America on its side, the political ramifications might dwarf any military success, he warned: "we may win a war and lose a victory."

At 10:00 a.m. leaders of the opposition joined the meeting: Dayan, Peres, and Menachim Begin were there, as well as Meir, now secretary-general of the Alignment. Eban overviewed the diplomatic situation and explained the international commitments of March 1957 to free navigation. Notably, he added, the question was not whether Israel should resist Nasser's threats by force but whether it should do so alone or seek the support and understanding of others. Nobody challenged Eban's assessment, although Dayan proposed to strike the Egyptians soon after the forty-eight-hour deadline expired. The meeting concluded with decisions to call up 35,000 reservists, to wait a further forty-eight hours, and, should Eshkol and Eban see fit, to allow Eban to travel to Washington to meet with the president.[38]

Later that afternoon Eban informed the Israeli embassy in Washington of his imminent arrival. But Eshkol feared that Eban's nuanced style and high profile would only complicate matters. Sensing that on this occasion the Americans (and not least American Jews, who were expected to yield pressure on Washington) needed to be stirred by emotion and sentimentality rather than coaxed by legal-diplomatic nuances, the prime minister suggested that Meir go instead, believing that the former foreign minister, who had grown up in Milwaukee, Wisconsin, was the right person for the job. Fearing this historic opportunity to meet with the American president on the eve of an international crisis slipping through his fingers, Eban threatened to resign on the spot. Eshkol, who could not afford to lose his foreign minister at such a crucial time and have a political crisis on his hands, had no choice but to acquiesce to Eban's protestations.[39] Eban also wanted to stop in Paris en route to Washington; the French were major suppliers of arms to Israel, and it was important to assess their mood, especially as President Charles De Gaulle had not met with a senior Israeli official for some time. But fearing that receiving the Israeli foreign minister in such a tense atmosphere might be misinterpreted by the

Arab states, De Gaulle agreed instead to meet with Walter Eytan, the ambassador in Paris. When Eytan heard that Eban insisted on meeting with De Gaulle himself, he protested vigorously: it was a mark of distrust in his abilities as ambassador and, after all, De Gaulle had agreed to meet with him and not with Eban. In response Eban instructed Arieh Levavi, the director-general of the Foreign Ministry, to order Eytan to reconsider his position and concentrate instead on facilitating the meeting between the foreign minister and De Gaulle. When Eytan's reply was not forthcoming, Eban sent him a personal note, copied to Eshkol. He asked Eytan to put aside his ego during this impending crisis, "not many like it in severity throughout Jewish history." Eytan capitulated.[40]

Eban left Israel in the early hours of May 24. At the Elysée Palace, accompanied by Eytan, he was warned by a tense and serious De Gaulle not to go to war: "So far as I am concerned, whoever fires the first shot is the one who begins the hostilities." Eban replied that Israel had two options, resistance or submission, and that it had decided to resist, though it first wished to ask the advice of the involved powers. De Gaulle warned Israel again not to fall into Egypt's trap and start a war, and reiterated his statement to Eshkol from 1964 that he wished for Israel to survive and prosper. Eban left the meeting feeling that the president understood his message, although De Gaulle thought that Eban's reference to "resistance" was not the same as "making war," and after the meeting he informed Nasser and Soviet premier Alexei Kosygin accordingly that Israel would not make war.[41] From Paris Eban continued to London, where he met Prime Minister Harold Wilson at 10 Downing Street. He delivered a similar message: Israel could surrender, fight, or work for an international solution to reopen the Straits of Tiran. The first option was out of the question, the second was undesirable but probable, and the third the most preferable. He added that the problem was created by Thant's rush decision to pull UNEF out of Sinai, which was "an error that will reverberate in history." In ten minutes, Eban said, the secretary-general "had undone the labours of ten years." Turning to his impression of De Gaulle, Eban said that "he had achieved nothing by his policy of friendship with the Soviet Union" and that France "had no influence whatsoever" on Soviet policy. Wilson's message to Eban was much more reassuring than De Gaulle's: Britain supported international action to uphold the right of free navigation through the straits and was willing to work under American leadership on the idea of an international flotilla to break the blockade.[42] It was too late to catch a flight to the United States that evening, and Eban took the opportunity to have dinner with his parents in London before spending a sleepless night in a hotel room in preparation for his trip to Washington in the morning.

The following morning Eban and Moshe Raviv, his political secretary, flew to Kennedy Airport in New York. There he met Gideon Rafael, Israel's ambassador to the UN, and asked him to accompany him to Washington. Eban's schedule included meetings with Secretary of State Dean Rusk and his aides that evening, a meeting with Secretary of Defense Robert McNamara and Pentagon chiefs the following morning, and a meeting with the president later the following evening. But his mission was compromised even before he set foot in the White House. Eban and Rafael were greeted at Washington's National Airport by Avraham Harman, the Israeli ambassador in Washington. Harman handed Eban a sealed envelope and asked him to read its contents before he entered into any discussions with White House officials. Eban opened the enveloped at his hotel room and "was extremely angry," according to Rafael, when he read its contents. He threw the telegram at Rafael and asked him to read it: Israeli military intelligence reported that there were now six Egyptian divisions in the Sinai and that the Arabs were planning an all-out general attack. The blockade was no longer the main issue; now it was the very existence of Israel. Eban was asked to press Johnson to clarify what concrete measures he was willing to take to avert the impending explosion. The Israeli High Command, led by Rabin and Yariv, pressed Eshkol not only to order Eban to convey this intelligence assessment to the Americans "in the most urgent terms" but also to ask Eban to make an unprecedented request: that President Johnson issue an official American statement that an attack on Israel was equivalent to an attack on the United States.

It was a complete change of course for Eban's mission: the issue was no longer the need for multilateral action to reopen the Straits of Tiran, but a demand that the United States come to Israel's help if war broke out—in effect, a request for a formal military alliance. Eban doubted the authenticity of the intelligence assessment; there was no indication of such immediate danger when he had listened to the generals' assessment in Tel Aviv only twenty-four hours earlier. Rafael, too, thought that the content of the telegram was "utterly implausible" and that "somebody must have gone mad or have no explanation," and he urged Eban to disregard it and continue as planned. But Eban could not do so, despite his evident irritation with the telegram's instructions. "How can I, I'm a foreign minister, my Prime Minister sends me instructions," he told Rafael.[43]

Later that afternoon at the State Department, Rusk, a man of great composure, was visibly annoyed as Eban read out to him the English translation of the urgent telegram he had received from Jerusalem. "Did you give me that information in order to justify a preemptive strike by Israel?" Rusk asked the foreign minister. Eban himself was angry at the position he had been placed in by the generals in Israel; "I feared that the Jerusalem cable had caused me to lose the first round," he would later recall. This was exactly the intention of Rabin and Yariv, who the following day admitted at a government meeting that in fact they had no way of knowing what the Egyptians were planning; a few days later Eban received a halfhearted apology from the two.[44] According to Undersecretary of State Eugene Rostow, who attended the meeting, there was "terrific tension. . . . It was a very sinister and tense atmosphere, and it showed with both Eban and Rafael. Rusk too was so perturbed that he went up to his liquor cabinet and poured himself a whisky, too distracted to offer his guests a drink."[45] Rusk decided to break the meeting in order to inform the president of the Israeli message and to corroborate thc report with America's own intelligence agencies. At 8:30 p.m., over a working dinner, Rusk transmitted to Eban a message from the president: "The information available to us does not really support the belief that an attack by [Egypt] and Syria is imminent." He added that the president "particularly wanted Eban to understand" that the U.S. government could not give assurances along the lines of "an attack of you is an attack of us." Eban, so upset that he barely touched his food, explained that the atmosphere in Israel was "apocalyptic" and that Israel required firm reassurances about the American commitment to open the straits, but he also showed appreciation of the domestic constraints placed on the president by the U.S. Congress and the Constitution as far as striking a NATO-like military alliance with Israel. Eban was clearly embarrassed by the incident. According to Undersecretary Rostow, Eban told him later that evening that had he been in Tel Aviv he "never would have phrased the message as it was written. He realized that such a commitment would be beyond the constitutional power of the president to make."[46] Eban himself later described the telegram as "an act of momentous irresponsibility" that "lacked wisdom, veracity and tactical understanding. Nothing was right about it."[47]

The following morning Rusk delivered more troubling news to Eban: the president was too busy and would not be able to meet with him. The truth was that Johnson did not know what to say to Eban. The idea of sending an international flotilla through the Straits of Tiran to break the Egyptian blockade was still in its infancy, and he did not wish to commit the United States to any concrete course of action at this stage. Furthermore, a meeting of the president with the high-profile and media-savvy Israeli foreign minister at the height of an international crisis was bound to complicate an already delicate situation. Washington supported Israel's case for the reopening of the straits, but it did not wish to be seen as pushing Israel to war. Johnson thus made every effort to avoid meeting Eban, instead preferring that lower-level officials iron out the details of an American-Israeli understanding. Rusk told Eban that the president would not be able to see him until Saturday, as he was waiting to hear a report from UN secretary-general Thant, who was due to return from Cairo that weekend. But Eban was adamant: he had to see the president today, Friday, as the cabinet in Jerusalem was scheduled to meet on Sunday morning. It was "perhaps the most crucial cabinet meeting in our history," Eban warned in typical hyperbole, and he had to return to the cabinet with a message from the president. "I understand," Rusk responded, and he went to deliver Eban's message to Johnson. The president was furious. "Tell [Eban] to take a walk, take a nap," he told his aides. "If the gentleman from Tel Aviv is in such a hurry he can go home right away. I don't like anyone to put a pistol to my head. This Sunday cabinet meeting of his to decide on peace or war—it's an ultimatum, and I don't like it."[48]

Eban and Harman arrived at the Pentagon later that morning. They met with McNamara, his deputy Cyrus Vance, chairman of the Joint Chiefs of Staff Earl Wheeler, and several other defense officials. McNamara reiterated the American position that "an Israeli attack under present circumstances would have most serious consequences. We cannot undertake to support Israel if Israel launches an attack." He concurred with the Israeli assessment that Israel would prevail in a conflict even if Egypt were to strike first, but added that the issue was not a preemptive strike by Israel but how to prevent hostilities in the first place. At that point Harman was called urgently to the telephone. He reappeared a couple of minutes later with a note from Tel Aviv: a recheck of Israeli intelligence confirmed the cable that had arrived the previous day and reiterated that a joint Egyptian-Syrian attack was imminent. Once again McNamara and Wheeler discredited the Israeli reports, saying that their own intelligence differed from Israel's not only on some of the facts but also on their interpretation: the Egyptian troop deployment was not offensive but was in fact defensive, in anticipation of an Israeli attack. Eban insisted that the note "was not just an evaluation of intelligence but was concrete 'information'"—a word he immediately replaced with "knowledge." For a man known for his careful choice of words, Eban's rephrasing seemed suspicious, and General Wheeler demanded to know exactly how solid the Israeli "knowledge" was about an imminent Arab attack and the troop dispositions; for example, did it come through an agent? Unable to corroborate the note from Tel Aviv and without intelligence sources of his own, Eban only "reaffirmed the statement that this was knowledge." Unhappy with Eban's response, McNamara interjected by telling Eban that he felt "that there had been inadequate exchanges of intelligence and supply information between us," hoping that they could be improved.[49]

Eban tried to minimize the damage by imploring Eshkol to provide the Americans some clarifications about the nature of the source behind the telegram—an unorthodox request indicating the desperate situation in which Eban found himself. He did not hide his displeasure with the telegram and with his own government, later signaling his hosts not to take the message from Jerusalem too seriously.[50] Instead Eban concentrated on the task for which he had embarked on his mission in the first place—the Egyptian closure of the Straits of Tiran—even though the government in Jerusalem now saw this issue as secondary to the concentration of Egyptian forces in the Sinai.

Johnson eventually agreed to meet with Eban that day, after Evron and Eugene Rostow ironed out the terms of the meeting: Israel would refer to it as a "courtesy call"; the content of the meeting and the president's mood would not be leaked to the press; and Eban would arrive at the White House through the south entrance to avoid contact with the media. The meeting took place at 7:15 p.m. at the Yellow Oval Room in the living quarters of the White House—a beautiful room that looked out on the Jefferson Memorial. Rostow thought it was certainly too elegant and majestic a venue for the kind of meeting that was about to take place; "I felt the weight of history in the room," Eban later recalled.

The differences in style and demeanor between the straight-talking six-foot-four Texan and the Cambridge University–educated Israeli egghead only added to the tense atmosphere in the room. (After the meeting Johnson turned to his aides and mimicked Eban's uppity performance, calling him "a mini-Winston Churchill."[51]) Eban was accompanied by Harman and Evron, while Johnson was joined by McNamara, Walt Rostow and his brother Eugene, Sisco of the State Department, and General Wheeler. There are two documented versions of the meeting: a verbatim record taken by Harman, and a summary drafted by Sisco. According to Rostow, Eban looked "sober and serious but not agitated." He opened with a foreboding message: "There has never been a moment for my country such as at this time. We are on a footing of grave and anxious expectancy."[52] Eban was apprehensive and uncomfortable. The military intelligence cable from Jerusalem threw him off course and set him to fail; if the president refused to entertain a public announcement that committed Washington to view an Arab attack on Israel as an attack on America, then what was the point of the meeting?

Focusing on the problem of the blockade, Eban emphasized that Israel's legal case was sound: it had the firm guarantees of the Western powers to ensure its freedom of navigation in the Gulf of Aqaba, and it was now time to draw on those guarantees—which served as the basis for the Israeli withdrawal from Sinai in 1957—either via a multilateral effort to reopen the straits (based on Harold Wilson's idea to send an international flotilla of the maritime powers through the straits), or failing that, by letting Israel open the straits by force. He thus asked the president two questions: "(a) Aqaba: do we fight alone or are you with us? (b) What is the practical expression of the US commitment to us?" Eban explained that what his prime minister was asking "was essentially very simple—a public statement by you that you stood with us."

Johnson came to the meeting well-prepared, exuding American confidence and power. "We are fully aware of what three past Presidents have said but this is not worth five cents if the people and the Congress did not support the President." All he needed from Israel was a little patience, he told Eban; he needed time to organize an international flotilla to open the straits, and to work with Congress in supporting the Israeli position.[53] "I'm not a feeble mouse or a coward and we're going to try," Johnson said, explaining to Eban the domestic constraints he was operating under. "I'm not a king. How to take Congress with me I've got my own views. I'm not an enemy or a coward." Concerned that such presidential despondency would drive his government to act alone, Eban pushed hard to get a firmer commitment from Johnson.

According to the Israeli record of the meeting, Eban asked whether he could tell his cabinet that Johnson had decided to "pursue every measure" to ensure that the Gulf of Aqaba and the Straits of Tiran would be open to free navigation. According to the American record, Eban asked whether Johnson was disposed to "*make every possible effort* to assure that the Strait and the Gulf will remain open to free and innocent passage." In his memoirs Eban recalled that as Johnson accompanied him to the elevator at the end of the meeting he repeated his question: "Again, Mr. President, can I tell my government that you will take *every measure in your power* to ensure that the Gulf and Straits will be open for navigation by all nations including Israel?" Johnson said yes. The American record also shows that the president also told Eban, "You can assure the Cabinet [that] we will pursue vigorously any and all possible measures to keep the Strait open." The difference between the two versions of the American commitment hinged on the American inclusion of the word *possible*—an important qualification that did not appear in Eban's subsequent report to his government, which seemed to have committed Johnson far more than the American version of the conversation implied.[54]

Twice in the conversation Johnson repeated the enigmatic warning coined by Rusk a few hours earlier: "Israel will not be alone unless it decides to go it alone."[55] Rather than yielding to Eban's gloomy predictions, Johnson pointed out, "All of our intelligence people are unanimous that if [Egypt] attacks, you will whip the hell out of them." Eban tried one more time to get an explicit commitment from the president: "Hasn't Barbour conveyed the mood in Israel?" But he was quickly shot down: "Mood isn't intelligence," retorted Walt Rostow.[56] The Americans were evidently more confident than Eban about Israel's military capabilities; their intelligence agencies concluded, "Israel could almost certainly attain air supremacy over the Sinai Peninsula in less than 24 hours after taking the initiative. . . . Armored striking forces could breach [Egypt's] double defense line in the Sinai in three to four days. . . . Israel could contain any attacks by Syria or Jordan during this period." As one senior U.S. intelligence official later recalled, "rarely has the Intelligence Community spoken as clearly, as rapidly, and with such unanimity."[57]

At the end of the ninety-minute meeting, Eban felt none the wiser about the president's position. Harman conceded that it was "undoubtedly a disappointing conversation. The Israelis were hoping for more." Eban was not persuaded by Johnson's reassurances either: "Whether an international effort to run the blockade would be mounted was in my mind a matter of doubt," he later recalled, and summed up Johnson's attitude, rather unfairly, as "the rhetoric of impotence . . . [of] a paralyzed president."[58] Johnson himself felt that his efforts came up short: "I've failed. They'll go," he told his advisers after the meeting. Rostow, too, was unsure whether the American message "would be sufficiently convincing to deter Israel." To the administration's surprise, Rostow added, "Eban had come to Washington to check on U.S. intentions and promises, rather than to threaten an immediate Israeli strike."[59] But the president was satisfied that he had not fallen into Eban's trap: "They came loaded for a bear, but so was I! I let them talk for the first hour, and I just listened, and then I finished it up the last 15 minutes." According to the president's daily diary, Secretary of Defense Robert McNamara was so pleased with the outcome of the meeting that "he just wanted to throw his cap up in the air, and [White House press secretary] George Christian said it was the best meeting of the kind he had ever sat on."[60]

At the same time, the cabinet in Tel Aviv was split over which course of action to take. Some ministers demanded to go to war immediately, while others doubted the IDF's ability to overcome the Egyptians. It was decided to wait for Eban's report from his meeting with Johnson. But the report did not arrive: Eban instructed Harman not to cable it to Jerusalem. Undoubtedly aware of his central role in this historic moment, he wanted to be the one to present to the government the contents of his meeting with the president of the United States. He took the minutes with him and boarded the plane to Israel, via New York and Paris. Eshkol was fuming, and ordered Harman to cable immediately a telegram with details of the Eban-Johnson meeting. A few hours later the cable arrived.[61]

Eban landed in Israel at 10:00 p.m. on Saturday, May 27. Exhausted and unshaven, he was greeted at the airport by the largest assemblage of news reporters and photographers he had ever seen in the country. A caricature in one of the dailies captured the levels of national anxiety that surrounded Eban's mission. As Eban hurries back home from Washington, puffed-cheek and carrying his briefcase and coat, a fellow Israeli is shackled to the ground, swinging a sledgehammer in the air to smash the padlock. "Did you bring the key?!" he says, turned to Eban.[62] When Eban arrived at the emergency cabinet meeting in Tel Aviv, all of the country's political and military echelons were already there, eager to find out if he had indeed brought with him the key—an explicit American commitment to stand by Israel if it were to strike first. There were eighteen ministers, as well as members of the Knesset's Foreign Affairs and Defense Committee; Generals Rabin, Yariv, and Weizmann (Rabin's deputy); advisers and experts from the foreign, defense, and prime minister's offices; all eyes were on fixated on Eban as he produced notes from his briefcase. With slow and meticulous elocution he reported on his meetings in Paris, London, and Washington. The overall impression he gave was very encouraging: De Gaulle was opposed to war; Wilson supported an international effort to break the blockade; and Johnson promised the United States was committed to open the straits at any cost, even without the help of other nations if it had no choice. Eban's estimation of Johnson's position seemed to be at odds with the American message. He was confident that Johnson would stand by Israel if it continued to pursue its diplomatic endeavors, and repeated Johnson's commitment that he would use "any and all measures in his power to ensure that the Gulf and the Straits are open to Israeli shipping." Eban then went further to quote an explicit commitment from Johnson (which did not appear in the American record) to open the Straits: "What we need is a group, 5 or 4 or less, or if we can't do that then on our own." The cabinet members were evidently impressed by the strongly worded and unequivocal American commitment. Eban's recommendation to the country's leadership was clear: they had to give diplomacy more time to work. He reiterated the U.S. president's warning that Israel would not be alone unless it decided to go it alone, and recommended accepting the American request to postpone military action by a couple of weeks.

Some people in the room were growing restless as they listened to Eban's report. A note signed by several Foreign Ministry officials was handed to Eshkol: Eban is deceiving the government; his report is inaccurate and does not match the reports received from Israeli diplomats who accompanied Eban to Paris and Washington; Johnson promised to make every effort to open the straits, but he did not say that the United States would act on its own to do it. Eshkol read the note but did not question its signatories. After delivering his report Eban moved to a nearby room to meet with the Knesset Foreign Affairs and Defense Committee, where he was overheard telling some of his colleagues, "I would not stay in the government if it decided to make war at once. First, every avenue of diplomacy must be explored."[63]

Nobody in the room imagined that within a year that meeting would become a headline story. From his early days as ambassador in Washington, Eban had been accused of sending overly optimistic reports to Jerusalem about trends in U.S.-Israeli relations. But according to the journalist Michael Bar-Zohar, who broke the story in 1968, on this occasion Eban's tendency to adjust reality to his opinions actually betrayed his integrity. In his book *The Longest Month*, Bar-Zohar referred to the three Foreign Ministry officials who alerted Eshkol to the inaccuracy of Eban's report, but he did not name them, while in a contemporaneous book on the war, Moshe Gilboa identified the three officials as Yosef Tekoah, Moshe Bitan, and Shlomo Argov. Tekoah and Bitan strenuously denied the story, though the latter admitted to his principled aversion to Eban's ways. According to Bitan, who headed the American desk at the Foreign Ministry, Bar-Zohar's book was no more than a sensationalist journalistic account which was full of distortions. The allegations against Eban were so serious that Eshkol had to defend his foreign minister before the Knesset, labeling Bar-Zohar's account "totally fabricated," while Eban himself described Bar-Zohar as "the type of man for whom lying is a profession, a hobby and a custom." Bar-Zohar's reply was equally vigorous: "I will continue upholding what I wrote, and if Mr. Eban wishes to sue me I am willing to go to court."[64] The story eventually dropped from the headlines, but its reverberations continued to haunt Eban. He either misunderstood the president's message or deliberately misrepresented it to the Israeli government. It would seem unlikely, however, that a polyglot like Eban, famous for his pedantic attention to semantics and the power of words, would misjudge the most important message he had ever received in his life.

It was 4:00 a.m. when Eshkol put the vital question to a vote: should Israel go to war at once? The eighteen government ministers—tired and jittery after consuming copious amounts of coffee and cigarettes—were split right down the middle. Nine, including Eshkol, Galili and Allon, were in favor, while nine others, including Eban, Aranne, and Sapir, opposed immediate military action. Eshkol, whose penchant for long consultations became a symbol of hapless indecisiveness in the national folklore, ended the climactic meeting in a typical anticlimactic fashion: "It's late. Let's get some rest. We'll meet tomorrow to make up our minds." The situation had changed dramatically by the time the cabinet reconvened the next day at 4:00 p.m. In a strongly worded cable to Eshkol, President Johnson warned Israel to not make itself responsible for the outbreak of hostilities, and asked the government to give Washington two to three weeks to exhaust all the diplomatic options. The presidential communication changed the mood in the cabinet: the tie from the previous night turned into a majority of seventeen-to-one against going to war; only Moshe Carmel, the minister of transportation, voted in favor.[65]

By then the national mood had turned from resilient preparedness for war to creeping anxiety. There were now 100,000 Egyptian troops and eight hundred tanks in the Sinai, and the Tiran Straits were blockaded. Nasser's public statements became more provocative and emboldened each day. The government was criticized for its failure to pull the country out of a yearlong economic recession, and the opposition parties criticized Eshkol over his lack of leadership during the crisis. The newspapers compared Israel's situation to that of Czechoslovakia in 1938 and painted Nasser as the new Adolf Hitler.

All the signs pointed to an impending war. According to one account, "housewives were storming the groceries to stock up on flour, oil, sugar, and canned goods. . . . Thousands suddenly paid up their taxes, knowing the state needed money. Groups formed of their own accord to dig trenches, act as messengers, build bomb shelters, and operate essential services." Across Europe and the United States there were mass demonstrations of unity with Israel. In Britain, the chief rabbi proposed a poll tax on world Jewry to save Israel from its impending doom.[66] An editorial in the daily *Haaretz* criticized Eshkol's failure to lead the country and called for him to be replaced as defense minister by Moshe Dayan or even the octogenarian David Ben-Gurion. Shimon Peres of Rafi and Menachem Begin of Gahal, both in opposition, even called for Ben-Gurion to return to the helm and for Eshkol to act as his deputy—an idea that an indignant Eshkol flatly rejected: "These two horses cannot be hitched to the same carriage." Ben-Gurion was not interested in sharing power with Eshkol either. Meir, now in her role as the all-powerful secretary-general of the party, also opposed the idea.[67]

But the most intense pressure on Eshkol came from the generals. Lacking the charisma, authority, or strategic military vision of Ben-Gurion, Eshkol was an easy target for this self-assured group of officers, whose substantial experience and soaring public popularity easily trumped Eshkol's image as a weak and indecisive leader. Following the cabinet's decision to postpone military action on May 28, Chief of Staff Rabin invited the prime minister to the Pit, the underground IDF command headquarters in Tel Aviv to meet with the High Command so he could explain the government's decision and listen to the generals' concerns. Eshkol agreed, but on his way to the Pit he stopped to broadcast a live radio message to the nation in order to reassure his agitated compatriots.

Yet rather than reassuring and inspiring the public, Eshkol's hesitant and confused delivery led to national hysteria. Having recently recovered from a cataract operation, the seventy-two-year-old prime minister struggled to read from the heavily edited text before him. At one point he rubbed an eye and displaced his contact lens. The entire nation, holding its breath in anticipation, heard the prime minister stumbling over a few words that had been changed and added to the text minutes earlier. Worse yet, Eshkol, unaware that he was live on the air, asked his military secretary, "What does that mean?" Never in the history of radio had three seconds of hesitation led to such levels of national panic and hysteria. "It is hard to describe the alarm and despondency that swept through the country," Eban later recalled, while Major General Yeshayahu Gavish, commanding general for the southern front, noted, "You felt that the man who was speaking either had no self-confidence or was afraid. It was very depressing." According to the legal adviser of Kol Israel Radio, Eshkol's address was the worst failure in the broadcaster's history.[68]

As the only person in the country who did not hear it, Eshkol had no idea about the depressing impact of his radio address on the nation. He arrived at the Pit, accompanied by Yigal Allon, to meet with the generals; he was upbeat and did not spare them his Yiddish jokes. An hour later he left the place hurt and angry. In what his wife, Miriam, later described as "a real putsch," the generals went for the prime minister's jugular, accusing him of indecisiveness and putting the very existence of the country at risk. General Ariel Sharon complained that the IDF has lost its deterrent power and that the lobbying and Eban's lobbying and pleading in foreign capitals only made Israel seem weak. Brigadier General Avraham Yoffe protested that "as military men we feel that the army is not allowed to fulfill the mission for which it was established" and that the government's indecision would hurt the home front. General Israel Tal, commander of the Armor Forces, also questioned the essence of the government's decision to wait, and demanded that the IDF should be allowed to land the first strike. General David Elazar, head of the Northern Command, cautioned that the IDF could not wait forever before it was called to action, and Uzi Narkiss, head of the Central Command, warned that the "discontent of the IDF is a very serious matter." Eshkol was surprised, hurt, and angered. "Nothing causes me greater sorrow than hearing you talking and expressing your feelings in this way," he rebuked the generals. "In effect you are telling me: 'give us a chance to blow up the Egyptian air force.' Why didn't we attack them two, three months ago? It can still be done in two months' time, just like that." The atmosphere in the room was tense, unbearable; Allon decided that it was time to end the meeting there and then. As Eshkol left the room, Rabin turned to his generals to discuss how to boost the soldiers' morale after Eshkol's now infamous radio address.[69]

These were Eshkol's darkest days as prime minister. The public calls to form a national unity government and for him to be replaced by Moshe Dayan as defense minister grew stronger by the day. Like many of the party's old guard, Eshkol did not trust Dayan. During his short political career Dayan, the war hero of 1956, had earned himself a reputation as an opportunist and an adventurer with loyalties to no one but himself. Eshkol made no secret of his personal loathing of Dayan, observing that "there is Dayan who is a man and there is Dayan who is Abu-Gilda"—a notorious bandit in 1930s Palestine. Mapai floated various ideas designed to satisfy the public demand for a change without appointing Dayan as defense minister: appointing him as "minister of the armies"; forming a war council comprised of former generals of staff; and even appointing Allon as defense minister, giving Dayan the Foreign Ministry, and appointing Eban as deputy prime minister in charge of international affairs. But Eban made it clear that he would rather resign altogether than be moved to another ministry. Eventually Eshkol yielded to the public pressure, telling his party that if Dayan did not join the government as defense minister, he feared that Rafi would send Shimon Peres instead, whom he disliked even more. "I don't want a man [in government] whose sole job is to make my life miserable," he added. On June 1 he presented a national unity government with Dayan as defense minister. Menachem Begin was appointed minister without portfolio.[70]

To add to Eshkol's woes, it now became apparent that Eban's report to the cabinet on May 29 was indeed at odds with President Johnson's message. On May 30 Eshkol sent a telegram to Johnson to thank him for the "remarks and assurances" he gave Eban; in particular, the prime minister welcomed "the assurance that the United States will take *any and all measures* to open the Straits of Tiran to international shipping" and added, "I rely on your . . . assurances that the United States, if necessary, will open the straits on its own." Johnson was furious. Eshkol's message, which relied on Eban's report to the government, did not mention the conditions that underpinned the American commitment and had been clearly communicated to Eban during his meeting with the president: the need to exhaust all avenues at the UN and work within the boundaries of the U.S. Constitution to secure the support of both houses of Congress. "I have no right to make such promises without the consent of Congress!" Johnson exclaimed to Walt Rostow. "This is not what I told Eban. Tell the Israelis so!"[71]

The following day Rostow communicated to Evron the president's "concern" over the fact that the "language in a communication between Chiefs of Government was inexact." On June 3 Johnson formally replied to Eshkol's telegram. He acknowledged the American position that the Gulf of Aqaba was an international waterway, but also qualified the constraints under which he was operating, telling Eshkol rather angrily, "I am sure Foreign Minister Eban has reported to you the written statement which I had prepared and from which Ambassador Harman made notes during our meeting of May 26. . . . As you will understand and as I explained to Mr. Eban, it would be unwise as well as most unproductive for me to act without the full consultation and backing of Congress." Johnson also reiterated to Eshkol his key warning to Eban: "I must emphasize the necessity for Israel not to make itself responsible for the initiation of hostilities. Israel will not be alone unless it decides to go alone. We cannot imagine that it will make this decision."[72]

General Aharon Yariv, chief of military intelligence, maintained all along that Eban's trip to Washington was a mistake and that the IDF should have been allowed to strike first—days earlier. He told Eshkol that Eban's report was "catastrophically mistaken," that he had not interpreted correctly the American position and that he, Eshkol, and Eban placed too much importance on what Washington was saying officially. He suggested that the head of Mossad, Meir Amit, who had good relations with CIA director Richard Helms, would travel to Washington himself to find out exactly what the Americans would do if Israel were to strike first.[73]

Amit flew incognito to Washington on May 31. He was angered by the "helplessness and inaction at the top," and despised the scores of Israelis who left the country in fear of the war: "It's all right—if people want to run away, let them. Whatever we're left with at the end of the war will be healthier."[74] Unlike Eban, who came to Washington seeking reassurance, Israel's chief spy bluntly informed the Americans that he intended to recommend his government to go to war. Whereas Eban had unsuccessfully tried to get a clear message from Johnson, the head of Mossad was more successful in relaying his government's intentions. Amit was convinced that the plan to lead an international flotilla through the Straits of Tiran was not forthcoming.[75] He pointed out to Helms and McNamara that Israel had no choice but to act alone, and accordingly he asked his interlocutors for three things: to continue to supply weapons already arranged for, to provide diplomatic support at the United Nations, and to keep the Soviets out of the fighting. Following the meeting, on June 2 Helms reported to Johnson, "Amit thinks the Israeli decision will be to strike. . . . Amit told one of our senior officers this morning that he felt this must mean the time of decision has come for the Israeli Government. He stated there would have to be a decision in a matter of days." Then, referring to Eban's meeting with President Johnson a few days earlier, Helms continued,

> He said that Eban's mission was seen by him and the Israeli nation as a failure. Here Amit almost certainly shares the views of General

> Dayan, Israel's new defense minister, since Amit and Dayan have been very close for many years. Both are Sabras—men born in Israel—and their past careers have been closely connected. It seems clear from Amit's remarks that the "tough" Israelis, who have never forgotten that they are surrounded by hostile Arabs, are driving hard for a forceful solution, with us and with their own government. Dayan's appointment, combined with Amit's and Harman's recall, can be interpreted as an ominous portent, considering the Israelis' military capability to strike with little or no warning at a time of their choosing.

According to Helms, the substance and tone of Amit's message left no doubt in his mind about the future: "Israel's economy is suffering with each additional day of crisis. There are no workers in the fields, and the harvest is still standing, but so long as 82,000 Egyptian troops remain in the Sinai, Israel cannot demobilize its reserves. . . . It is better to die fighting than from starving."[76] Amit told McNamara that he intended to recommend to the cabinet in Jerusalem to launch a preemptive strike, to which the secretary of defense replied, "I read you loud and clear."[77] After Amit's departure Walt Rostow offered Johnson an illuminating psychological assessment of the recent visitors to the White House: "Evron—like Amit and Dayan—is a born Israeli. This is one reason why he is so much more natural and relaxed than Harman and Eban who must constantly prove their authenticity. These boys are going to be hard to hold about a week from now."[78]

By then Eban was persuaded that all the diplomatic options had been exhausted and that a military action was inevitable. On May 31 the Israeli cabinet received the news that Jordan had signed a defense pact with Egypt, which put Jordanian forces under Egyptian command and completed Israel's encirclement. That same day Secretary Rusk was asked by a journalist whether the United States was restraining Israel from taking military action. "I don't think it is our business to restrain anyone," Rusk replied tersely. The following day, June 1, Eban heard that Supreme Court Justice Abe Fortas, Johnson's informal adviser on Arab-Israeli affairs, reassured Ephraim Evron that "Israelis should not criticize Eshkol and Eban. If Israel had acted alone without exhausting political efforts it would have made a catastrophic error." Eban read the message as a sign that further diplomatic maneuvers were no longer necessary to protect Israel if it did land the first blow. After consulting with his top advisers in Tel Aviv, Eban came to the conclusion that diplomacy had now run its course.[79]

Some of Eban's contemporaries, especially those in the military High Command and in the opposition parties, pointed out that in his visit to Washington he had failed to secure a tangible American commitment to come to Israel's aid, let alone an explicit green light for Israel to fire the first shot. But Eban's insistence on exhausting the diplomatic avenues not only gave the generals valuable time to prepare the army for war but also created an international atmosphere of sympathy to Israel that had not existed ten days earlier. There were now nearly a quarter of a million troops, some two thousand tanks, and nearly a thousand fighter and bomber aircraft encircling Israel from the south, north, and east, with Iraqi, Kuwaiti, and Algerian contingents supporting the standing armies of Egypt, Syria, and Jordan. There were no signs of excessive international commitment to either lift the Egyptian blockade or stop Israel from doing so itself. One hundred thousand Israeli citizens were on reserve duty, placing additional strain on an economy already in recession. Fourteen thousand hospital beds were prepared to receive the casualties, and mass graves were dug in Tel Aviv's municipal park. As Eban explained at a May 30 press conference in Tel Aviv to war reporters from all over the world, first in English and then in French, Israel was like a coiled spring, ready to jump into action. Asked how long Israel would wait, he replied in his clipped Cambridge tone, "You can eliminate years and months from your vocabulary. . . . Israel will open the Straits alone if we must, with others if we can." Eban concluded the press conference with the scornful observation that the United Nations had not emerged from the events of the past two weeks "with brilliance or credit." As one correspondent later reported, Eban's confident performance was everything that Eshkol's radio address was not: "In one of the most brilliant press conferences I have ever seen anywhere, Eban completely transformed the mood of gloomy fear of a Munich-type betrayal which had descended on Israel as a result of the most unfortunate radio speech by Eshkol. . . . Eban was completely relaxed and exuded confidence which appeared too great and too sincere to be acting."[80]

Amit sent a preliminary report from Washington on June 1, claiming that the international efforts to reopen the straits were "running into heavier water every hour" and that there was "a growing chance for American political backing if we act on our own."[81] Fearing for their relations with the Arab world, the vast majority of the countries who were asked to sign a maritime declaration asserting the freedom of passage through the straits refused to do so. Only Britain, Australia, and the Netherlands agreed to send their own ships to break the naval blockade.[82] Convinced that diplomacy had achieved its maximum result, Eban informed Generals Rabin and Yariv and that he no longer opposed military action.[83]

On the morning of Friday, June 2, the ministers and the generals met for the second time that week to assess the situation. The atmosphere at the war room in the Pit was tense, reminiscent of Eshkol's meeting with the generals a few days earlier. It was about to get a lot worse for the prime minister, who was bitter about having had to step down as defense minister. After equipping the army for war for four years and ensuring that the generals had everything they had asked for, he now had to endure the public jubilation over the appointment of Dayan as the country's savior. General Yariv opened the meeting, and his foreboding assessment set the tone for the rest of the meeting: every day that passed significantly reduced Israel's chances of gaining the much-needed aerial superiority and damaged the country's prestige and the credibility of its deterrence. Then Rabin took over; time was working against Israel, he warned, and there was a real danger to the very existence of the country. He added that things would only get worse in the next few weeks. Similar warnings were voiced by chief of the air force, Motti Hod. His revelation that on four occasions in the previous week Egyptian planes had flown through Israel's airspace to photograph "sensitive security installations" shattered whatever shred of confidence the ministers still had. As additional generals took the floor to deliver equally ominous assessments, Israel Lior, Eshkol's military secretary, wondered about their motives: "I asked myself if their intention was to bring the ministers to their knees or to make them burst out crying." The generals' bashing of the government was unrelenting. Brigadier General Yoffe, pointed out that so far the government's only initiative had been to send the "foreign minister to the United States and other places . . . we see the gathering clouds and we sit and do nothing . . . the time has come to take the initiative out of Nasser's hands!" The final blow came from Ariel Sharon, who referred to Eban's diplomatic mission as "running around and kowtowing before the big powers," and Matti Peled, the quartermaster general, who protested, "why does the army deserve these doubts in its ability? What more does the army need to do, after winning every battle, to win the government's trust? . . . we deserve to know why we are suffering this shame!" Eshkol was dumbfounded; his authority and leadership had been challenged once again. As if a father reprimanding his wayward children, Eshkol explained to Sharon that all the material power at the disposal of the IDF had come from "lobbying" and "kowtowing." Israel was a country of two million people, not the Goliath that the generals had made it out to be, he continued. "Suppose we broke the enemy's power today. Tomorrow we will need to rebuild our power, for we will have also lost some of our power . . . and then, if we have to fight every ten years—we shall have to see if we have an ally who will help us, or do we talk with our ally today and tomorrow we say: we don't care about you." He concluded the meeting rather prophetically, noting that "a military victory will resolve nothing. The Arabs are here to stay."

There was no denying the impact of the generals' words on the ministers. War was around the corner, even if the government had not yet sanctioned it. Shortly after the meeting Eshkol called his closest advisers to a consultation in his office. Dayan, Allon, Eban, Lior, and Rafi Efrat, Rabin's bureau chief, were present. They all felt that war was inevitable if not imminent. Dayan reported that the IDF was ready to go as soon as the government voted for war—as early as Monday morning. Eban reviewed the latest diplomatic developments and concluded that he had no doubt that President Johnson was unable to fulfill his commitments. There were no political options left on the table.[84]

Close to midnight on Saturday, Amit, accompanied by Ambassador Harman, arrived at Eshkol's home in Jerusalem. Eban, Dayan, Allon, Rabin, and Yariv were already there, showing visible signs of stress and sleep deprivation. Amit reiterated his early assessment that Johnson seemed to have given up on the international flotilla plan. He concluded that "the United States won't go into mourning if Israel attacks Egypt." Even though Eshkol received a letter from Johnson earlier that day imploring Israel not to be responsible for the initiation of hostilities, the prime minister shared Eban's assessment that Washington would extend diplomatic support at the United Nations even if Israel struck first. Nobody in the room thought that there was a need to wait any longer. The military plans were discussed at length, and there was a unanimous decision to recommend to the cabinet the next day the decision to go to war.[85]

At 8:30 a.m. on Sunday, June 4, the government heard Dayan's survey of the military situation. Then Eban presented a summary of the diplomatic situation. He recounted all the telegrams and messages that were received from the United States and did not leave out a single word. "I lost my mind," Lior recalled. "He kept on talking and I thought that by the time he finished his report the ministers will not be able to decide whether to go to war or not. They will ask for a holiday."[86] Eban expected the Americans to stand by Israel in the aftermath of the war, and stated his support for military action. Ministers Haim Moshe Shapira and Zerach Werhaftig of the National Religious Party were surprised by Eban's apparent about-face and pushed for postponement of military action. Even Menachem Begin suggested sending Golda Meir on another diplomatic mission to London, Paris, and Washington. Dayan, however, pressed his colleagues to authorize the prime minister and the defense minister to put the army into action if necessary, and Eshkol and Eban, neither of whom could be accused of warmongering, reiterated that the political options were now exhausted. When Eshkol called for a vote at 3:00 p.m. all the ministers endorsed Dayan's proposal. Yisrael Barzilai and Mordechai Bentov, two ministers from the left-wing Mapam party, asked for time to consult their leaders first, and returned two hours later with a supportive vote for military action. The Hamtana period, which had begun on May 15, was officially over.[87]

XIII

A Very Foreign Foreign Minister

On Monday, June 5, 1967, at 7:14 a.m., 196 Israeli planes took to the air, leaving behind only six fighter jets to defend the country's airspace. Maintaining complete radio silence and flying at a low altitude—just a few hundred feet—to avoid detection by enemy radar, the Israeli Air Force caught the Egyptians completely by surprise. At dawn the Egyptian Air Force had been at the highest level of alert, but by 7:00 a.m. that level of readiness had dropped. The shifts changed, and most of the aircrews were in the barracks eating their breakfast, while the senior officers were still on the way to headquarters. Those who remained on the ground outside were blinded by the rising sun from the east, which provided the perfect cover for the Israeli planes. Three hours later the war was effectively won, with 309 of Egypt's 340 combat aircraft destroyed on the ground. Buoyed by (false) reports from Cairo about an early Egyptian success, at noon Syrian, Jordanian, and Iraqi planes began bombarding Israel, but with little success. By the evening the Israelis had obliterated the Jordanian Air Force, while Syria lost half of its combat aircraft and Iraq lost ten planes. The magnitude of the Arab catastrophe was startling, with a total loss of nearly four hundred fighter jets, bombers, helicopters, and transportation planes, many of them destroyed on the ground, as well as dozens of airfields and radar stations. The Israeli Air Force lost only twenty-six planes.

Israel's ground forces advanced swiftly through the Sinai Desert, taking over the Gaza Strip and reaching the Suez Canal within four days. On the Jordanian front, despite repeated messages from Jerusalem to King Hussein via American, British, and UN channels that Israel had no offensive designs for the West Bank, on the first day of the war Jordanian forces began shelling Jerusalem's Jewish neighborhoods and other targets along Israel's coastal plain. In response, the Israeli cabinet decided later that night to take over the West Bank and East Jerusalem. By June 7 Israel had captured the entire West Bank, including East Jerusalem and the Old City.

After two UN-brokered cease-fires ended the fighting on the Jordanian and Egyptian fronts, all eyes now turned to the Israeli–Syrian border. Fearful of heavy losses and an armed Soviet intervention, Defense Minister Moshe Dayan was reluctant to engage the heavily fortified Syrian positions along the Golan Heights. But the continued Syrian shelling of Israeli villages and the exuberant support of General David Elazar, head of the Northern Command, persuaded the government to capture the area. The campaign began on the morning of Friday, June 9, and within thirty-six hours the territory was under Israeli control. A third Security Council resolution in as many days ended the fighting on the Syrian front on Saturday, June 10.

In just six days the military balance of power between Israel and its Arab neighbors had changed dramatically, and so had the story of the Arab–Israeli conflict. Israel was now in control of the Sinai Peninsula, the Gaza Strip, the West Bank, and the Golan Heights. Its land mass had more than tripled, but it was now also responsible for the daily administration of the one million inhabitants of the West Bank and Gaza Strip. The Arabs suffered a humiliating defeat, and Israel's military occupation and the plight of 350,000 refugees gave rise to the Palestinian national struggle. The Soviet Union and its East European satellite states cut off diplomatic relations with Israel, not to be renewed until the demise of Communism a quarter of a century later. At the same time, Israel's relations with the United States grew stronger as the Middle East became an active arena of superpower confrontation by proxy. Most important, however, was that while Israel's newly acquired frontiers significantly reduced the national anxiety over the very existence of the state, the stunning military victory did not resolve any of the underpinning causes of Arab-Israeli hostility. If anything, it made Arab-Israeli peace a far more distant prospect than it had been six days earlier.[1]

Even in the midst of the fighting Eban had no illusions about what Israel should do with the newly acquired territories. "We will have to give them back after some frontier adjustments which will be necessary for security," he told his wife, Suzy.[2] On the first day of the war Eban made his way from Tel Aviv to Jerusalem, where the cabinet met in an air-raid shelter in the Knesset building, with the unsettling noise of Jordanian artillery shells landing a few hundred yards away. It was clear that Eban's key task in the next few days would be to ensure that the military achievements would not be squandered under international pressure for a quick Israeli withdrawal, as had been the case a decade earlier. Eban took some comfort in the fact that Israel's bargaining position was much better than it had been in the aftermath of the Suez Crisis: Gamal Abdel Nasser's closure of the Straits of Tiran, his dismissal of the United Nations Emergency Force (UNEF) from the Sinai Peninsula, and the mobilization of 100,000 Egyptian troops toward the Israeli border were viewed by most foreign governments as the triggers of the crisis; Eban's mission to Paris, London, and Washington, DC, had also demonstrated Israel's determination to exhaust all diplomatic avenues to prevent war; and finally, U.S. president Lyndon Johnson was far more sympathetic to Israel's security needs than had been president Dwight D. Eisenhower during the Suez Crisis. This time Israel was not isolated and did not risk a unanimous condemnation at the United Nations.

But Eban still had to convince the international community not to force Israel to return to the June 4, or pre-war lines (the 1949 Green Line) without the conclusion of Arab-Israeli peace. As he heard the news from New York that France and India were already drafting up resolutions calling for an immediate cease-fire and an Israeli withdrawal to the June 4 lines, he felt a sense of a deterministic, historical repetition. Yet again he had to advocate Israel's righteousness before the UN Security Council and the world media. At 8:00 p.m. he went home to pack his suitcase and say goodbye to Suzy and his children Eli and Gila, who were huddled in the air-raid shelter attached to the Foreign Ministry residence. After the surreal experience of attending a government meeting under the target of enemy guns, Eban came even closer to bearing the scars of war as he bid his family farewell. As Abba and Suzy separated from their embrace, a swift gush of wind crossed the gap between them. A policeman standing nearby pointed out to Suzy a piece of shrapnel that had flown between her and her husband's heads.[3]

After a precarious three-hour drive to Tel Aviv via side roads, at 3:00 am on Tuesday, June 6, Eban embarked on a particularly tortuous journey to New York, accompanied by his political secretary, Moshe Raviv. As Lod Airport was closed to international flights, they had to charter a twin-engine plane to Athens from Tel Aviv's domestic airport. Flying at low altitude to avoid detection by enemy radar, they landed in Athens and from there continued on a

KLM flight to Amsterdam, and then on to a transatlantic flight to New York. Three hours before landing at Kennedy Airport, the pilot delivered to Eban a radio message from Gideon Rafael, the ambassador at the UN: the discussion at the Security Council was moving swiftly, and Eban was expected to address the council as soon as he landed. Sleep-deprived for thirty-six hours, Eban asked the air crew for pen and paper and retired to their curtained cubicle to write the most important speech of his life.[4]

The three national television networks canceled their normal programming to broadcast the momentous debate at the UN Security Council. The tension in the gallery was almost tangible following heated exchanges among the Soviet, Iraqi, Syrian, and American representatives. As the *New York Times* reported the following day, fifty million viewers were glued to their television screens, engrossed in the "nuances of debate and oratory, an insight into the shifting tides of political alliances and the numbing spectacle of mankind torn apart."[5] It was nearly midnight by the time Eban addressed the Security Council, carrying with him nothing but his hastily prepared notes and the heavy burden of defending Israel's cause. His dramatic opening sentence set the stage to one of the greatest speeches of the last century: "I have just come from Jerusalem to tell the Security Council that Israel, by her independent effort and sacrifice, has passed from serious danger to successful resistance." He began by charting the three main causes of the current crisis: the sabotage activities perpetrated by Syria, the blockade of the Straits of Tiran and the Gulf of Aqaba, and the military encirclement of Israel. He anchored his case for Israel's right of self-defense in the UN Charter and international law, challenging the council members to put themselves in Israel's shoes:

> Was there any precedent in world history, for example, for a nation passively to suffer the blockade of its only southern port, involving nearly all its vital fuel, when such acts of war, legally and internationally, have always invited resistance? This was a most unusual patience.
>
> There was in [Nasser's] wanton act a quality of malice. For surely the closing of the Strait of Tiran gave no benefit whatever to Egypt, except the perverse joy of inflicting injury on others. It was an anarchic act, because it showed a total disregard for the law of nations, the application of which in this specific case had not been challenged for ten years. And it was, in the literal sense, an

> act of arrogance, because there are other nations in Asia and East Africa, that trade with the Port of Eilat, as they have every right to do, through the Strait of Tiran and across the Gulf of Aqaba. Other sovereign States from Japan to Ethiopia, from Thailand to Uganda, from Cambodia to Madagascar, have a sovereign right to decide for themselves whether they wish or do not wish to trade with Israel. These countries are not colonies of Cairo. They can trade with Israel or not trade with Israel as they wish, and President Nasser is not the policeman of other African and Asian States.
>
> There was another reason too for that shock. Blockades have traditionally been regarded, in the pre-Charter parlance, as acts of war. To blockade, after all, is to attempt strangulation; and sovereign States are entitled not to have their trade strangled. To understand how the State of Israel felt, one has merely to look around this table and imagine, for example, a foreign Power forcibly closing New York or Montreal, or Boston or Marseille, or Toulon or Copenhagen, or Rio or Tokyo or Bombay harbor. How would *your* Governments react? What would *you* do? How long, how long would *you* wait?

Eban's most acerbic rebuke was aimed not at Arab aggression or the apathy of foreign powers, but the incompetence of the United Nations. It was impossible for those in the gallery to ignore the irate face of U Thant, the phlegmatic secretary-general, as Eban scrutinized the hasty removal of UNEF from the Sinai at Nasser's behest:

> I should, however, be less than frank if I were to conceal the fact that the Government and people of Israel have been disconcerted by some aspects of the United Nations' role in this conflict. The sudden withdrawal of the United Nations Emergency Force was not accompanied, as it should have been, by due international consultations on the consequences of that withdrawal. . . . And I confess that my own attitude and those of my colleagues and of my fellow citizens to the peacekeeping functions of the United Nations have been traumatically affected by this experience. . . . People in our country and in many countries ask: What is the use of a United Nations presence if it is in effect an umbrella which is taken away as soon as it begins to rain?

This rhetorical question in particular caused much consternation at UN headquarters for months to come. It also crystallized an Israeli consensus, which had been growing steadily since the Suez Crisis, that the country's vital interests would be best protected through bilateral agreements and regional alliances rather than via vacuous UN assurances.[6] Eban concluded his address by looking to the future. The task of the governments concerned was now to devise new conditions for coexistence, but the question was whether there was any reason to believe that this new era may yet come to pass. Eban's answer to this turned out to be one of his most memorable quips: "If I am a little sanguine on this point, it is because of a conviction that men and nations do behave wisely once they have exhausted all other alternatives. Surely the other alternatives of war and belligerency have now been exhausted. And what has anybody gained from that?"

Eban proposed three principles on which future Arab-Israeli relations ought to be based. The first was an authentic Arab recognition of Israel's deep roots in Middle Eastern reality; after all, he pointed out, "There are not two categories of States. The United Arab Republic, Iraq, Syria, Jordan, Lebanon—not one of these has a single ounce or milligram of statehood which does not adhere in equal measures to Israel itself."

His second principle concerned the peaceful settlement of disputes, but not merely as a reproduction of "the old positions of conflict, without attempting to settle the underlying issues of Arab-Israel co-existence"—a clear indication that Israel sought a comprehensive peace treaty rather than a return to the 1949 armistice regime. "When the Council discusses what is to happen after the cease-fire," Eban cautioned the Arab leaders, "we hear many formulas: back to 1956, back to 1948—I understand our neighbours would wish to turn the clock back to 1947. The fact is, however, that most clocks move forward and not backward, and this, I think, should be the case with the clock of Middle Eastern peace—not backward to belligerency, but forward to peace."

Finally, Eban asked for the rigorous support of the great powers, "not for individual States, but for specific principles; not to be for one State against other States, but to be for peace against war, for free commerce against belligerency."[7]

It was well past midnight when Eban concluded his address to the sound of rapturous applause. President Johnson told his advisers that Eban's address was worth several divisions to Israel, while the *New York Times* reported that Eban "took honors for the mastery of phrase-making and drew applause from the gallery." Three months later Johnson and Eban would meet again in the White House. "I think you are the most eloquent speaker in the world today," the president would then say to Eban. "I try to listen to your speeches on TV whenever I can and I am deeply impressed."[8]

Eban was disappointed to hear upon his return to Israel on June 9 that his address was received with far less enthusiasm or even interest by his compatriots. "All the marvelous exhilaration you felt at Aubrey's appearance before the Security Council was never put across here," Suzy wrote to friends in America. "Here it was only war, life, death, planes, bullets, sniping, the terrible worry about the boys."[9]

Soon enough Eban's name did adorn the news headlines, but not over his triumphant address at the UN. Only two days after the Six-Day War had ended there were reports of heavy political pressure on Prime Minister Levi Eshkol and Eban not to yield to the expected international demands of Israel to return to its prewar borders. Their decision to wait and see if international diplomacy could lift the blockade before the war was cited as a worrying omen of the two men's indecision. Moshe Dayan emerged as the undisputed hero, even though he had taken over the Defense Ministry from Eshkol only a hundred hours before the war. Now some suggested that he was ready to take over as prime minister too. A public opinion poll conducted on June 14 revealed that almost half of those questioned wanted Dayan as prime minister, while less than one-third favored Eshkol. Even though Dayan was not "the most loved of men among politicians or even in the military branch," the *New York Times* told its readers, he was "capable of whatever decisiveness and sternness found necessary. Apparently, most people do not think Mr. Eshkol is." The independent daily newspaper *Haaretz* doubted Eban's abilities to present Israel's case, while other calls demanded that Eban be accompanied to the upcoming UN session by fellow ministers, including Dayan and even Menachem Begin, so they could keep watchful eye on him. Eban's tendency "toward a euphoric approach on many issues"—an accusation that had followed him since his ambassadorial years—was cited as the major reason for the government's misplaced trust in Washington's ability to lift the blockade diplomatically. His critics claimed that just as Israel needed a strong man (like Dayan) to lead it during the war, it now needed a strong man to lead the peace negotiations, and Eban was clearly not that man. Furious about these reports, Eban pointed out to Eshkol that he would not dream of telling Dayan what to do in military matters, and he thus expected Dayan not to hover over him while he led the diplomatic campaign at the United

Nations. Eshkol agreed. Just before his departure Eban told the British *Observer* that even if the General Assembly voted 121 to 1 in favor of an Israeli withdrawal to the 1949 armistice borders, Israel would refuse to comply. This uncompromising message seemed to be aimed at his critics at home as much as it was designed to preempt the debate at the General Assembly.[10]

WHAT AWAITED EBAN AT THE FIFTH EMERGENCY SPECIAL SESSION OF THE UN General Assembly on Monday, June 19, was no less than a duel with Soviet premier Alexei Kosygin before tens of millions of spectators. Before the session opened, Eban received a much welcome show of support from President Johnson, who laid out his vision for Middle East peace in a national television and radio address that morning. He effectively supported Israel's position and rejected in advance Kosygin's anticipated demand for an unconditional Israeli withdrawal. The president's five-point blueprint for peace included the right of national life, progress in resolving the refugee problem, freedom of innocent maritime passage, limitation of the arms race in the Middle East, and respect for the political independence and territorial integrity of all parties to the conflict.[11]

Once again the television and radio networks canceled their regular programming to broadcast the proceedings, the result of which, as U.S. ambassador Arthur Goldberg told Eban, was certain to affect the future course of American policy toward the conflict. At 10:30 a.m. Gromyko rose to speak. For forty minutes, in a brisk and businesslike manner, he read from the script in a monotone, rarely lifting his eyes from the paper. The severity of his criticism of Israel and the United States gave an early indication that the road to a peaceful conclusion of Arab–Israeli hostilities would be long and tortuous. He accused Israel of being the aggressor, responsible for unleashing the war in the Middle East. He condemned the Israeli invaders as committing the kind of heinous crimes perpetrated by the fascists during World War II: they were "burning villages and destroying hospitals and schools . . . prisoners of war and even women and children were shot, and ambulances carrying the wounded were burned." Gromyko also attacked U.S. policy in the Congo, Cuba, and Vietnam, as well as American and British "promotion" of Israel at the UN and an "unbridled anti-propaganda campaign, played up by the press of certain Western countries." As expected, he introduced a draft resolution condemning Israel as the aggressor in the Six-Day War, demanding an immediate withdrawal of Israeli forces from all the Arab territories they had seized and calling on Israel to make restitution for "everything it has destroyed."[12]

Eban's preparation for his appearance was not ideal. As usual, he had left his speech writing until the very last minute. The drafting began only in the early hours of Sunday, June 18, the day before he was to speak. The suite at the Plaza Hotel was stocked with a battery of typists and typewriters and a fresh supply of hot coffee and cold sandwiches. On Sunday evening Eban's aide Emanuel Shimoni and the typists were joined by Gideon Rafael and Avraham Harman, though their contribution was rather superfluous. When Eban took one look at their suggested changes to his draft he turned to Shimoni: "Speeches cannot be written by a committee!" he exclaimed. Amazingly, Eban found the time to write an indignant letter to the editor of *Maariv* in protest over the paper's correspondent's assertion that Eban had misled the government over his conversation with French president Charles De Gaulle before the war: "Never in my public life have I encountered such a blatant example of inaccuracy over such important matters." At 2:00 a.m. on Monday, June 19, Eban finished his final draft and handed it to Shimoni to be typed. He retired to his bedroom, while Shimoni, Harman, and Rafael went over the speech one more time. At 5:00 a.m. Shimoni handed the papers to two typists in the adjacent room and retired for some much-needed sleep. Two hours later he was awakened by the phone; Eban wanted to see the speech. Shimoni delivered it to Eban's suite, then went back to his own room tohave a quick shower and a shave. When he returned to Eban's suite, which also served as the office, he found the foreign minister raging. "Who changed this!?" Eban demanded to know, pointing to the last paragraph. While Eban was asleep Rafael had inserted the words "with the help of God, we shall triumph." Eban insisted that the offending remark be removed and all the copies immediately changed. Shimoni duly complied, and ordered the delegation at the UN to replace the final page with Eban's original version. A few hours later, the fatigue and stress of the past month were cast aside as Eban rose to rebuke Kosygin's accusations and defend Israel's actions. As always, he tensed up just before he rose to the podium at the General Assembly, but he was not nervous.[13]

According to the *New York Times*, at age fifty-two Eban was now in the "solid period of middle age, looking jowlier and less glamorous than 1956. But nothing in his oratory appears to have aged; if anything, solidity has become a virtue."[14] Eban denounced Kosygin's charges against Israel as a flagrant breach of elementary human decency and of international morality, and revealed to his audience that the Soviet ambassador to Israel refused his personal invitation in May to visit Israel's border with Syria to see with his own eyes that there was no concentration of Israeli troops there as Moscow had claimed. But apparently, Eban explained, "the prospect of finding out the truth at first hand seemed to fill him with a profound disquiet." Once again, Eban attacked U Thant's order to remove UNEF from the Sinai, using another colorful analogy: "What is the use of a fire brigade which vanishes from the scene as soon as the first smoke and flames appear? Is it surprising that we are resolved never again to allow a vital Israeli interest and our very security to rest on such a fragile foundation?" Recalling the events of June 5, Eban explained that, faced with Arab encirclement, "our country's choice was plain. The choice was to live or perish, to defend the national existence or to forfeit it for all time." He then defended the inherent righteousness of Israel's actions:

> From these dire moments Israel emerged in five heroic days from awful peril to successful and glorious resistance. Alone, unaided, neither seeking nor receiving help, our nation rose in self-defence. . . . Today, again, the Soviet Union has described our resistance as aggression and sought to have it condemned. There is no foundation for this assertion, and we reject it with all our might. Here was armed force employed in a just and righteous defensive cause, as righteous as the defenders of freedom at Valley Forge; as just as the expulsion of Hitler's bombers from the British skies; as noble as the protection of Stalingrad against the Nazi hordes, so was the defence of Israel's security and existence against those who sought our nation's destruction. What should be condemned is not Israel's action, but the attempt to condemn it. Never have freedom, honour, justice, national interest and international morality been so righteously protected!

A crescendo of applause followed Eban back to his seat after his seventy-two-minute speech. His neighbors, the Irish and Italian representatives, congratulated him warmly. In the usual routine, thousands of congratulatory letters flooded the Israeli embassy in Washington, and the international media showered Eban with adulation. *Maariv* admitted that even by Eban's own high standards, this performance was "truly outstanding. He spoke with a rare mixture of logical reasoning and moving pathos." The American press reported the following day that only the most ardent supporters of Moscow refused to admit that Eban had delivered a knockout blow to the Soviet Premier: "Many diplomats, some Western but some, also, from the nonaligned countries conceded the first round to the Israeli Foreign Minister." Several observers in the General Assembly chambers could not help but draw comparisons between Eban's address and "Winston Churchill sending the English language to war in 1940."[15]

One person who was not so enthralled by Eban's address was U Thant. Visibly fed up with Eban's constant attacks on his precipitous decision to evacuate UNEF from the Sinai three weeks before the war, the UN secretary-general was unusually robust in his rebuke of Eban's address. He told the General Assembly that while he never had to comment on a statement made by a representative of any government, he found it necessary to "restore the balance" because Mr. Eban's "highly critical" remarks were "damaging to the United Nations with regard to its peace-keeping functions, past and present." He revealed that at a recent meeting with Eban on the issue, the Israeli foreign minister raised no protestations over the decision to withdraw UNEF, and that he thus did not accept the validity of Eban's "strictures" before the assembly. Thant concluded his extraordinary address by reprimanding Eban over his "picturesque simile" of UNEF as the fire brigade that vanishes as soon as the first smoke and flames appear; after all, UNEF had done its job effectively for more than a decade, and its mandate did not include fighting an invading Egyptian Army.

Later in the afternoon Eban gingerly delivered a brief conciliatory statement. He clarified that he had only referred to the "legal and practical" situation surrounding UNEF's withdrawal rather than Thant's personal judgment, and that the representatives of Britain, Canada, and other countries raised similar concerns over the withdrawal of UNEF. The president of the General Assembly, Abdul Rahman Pazhwak of Afghanistan, did his best to ease the tension by declaring that "the good faith of the Secretary-General has not been questioned." But others questioned the purpose and benefit of Eban's personal attack on Thant. Notwithstanding Eban's "first-class oratorical act," *Maariv* lambasted his "tactical and principled" mishap: after imploring the Arab countries and the international community to look forward and not backward, he had dwelled for no good reason on an episode that had no present significance. All that Eban had achieved was to create unnecessary tension with Thant at a time when the goodwill of the secretary-general was most needed. Even Gideon Rafael, the head of the Israeli delegation at the UN and one of Eban's biggest fans, distanced himself from Eban's personal attack on Thant, suggesting that the secretary-general was not responsible for the war in the Middle East.[16]

As Eban was fighting Israel's case at the UN, the government in Jerusalem seemed to have finally agreed on a formula for peace negotiations with Egypt and Syria, though it deferred a decision on the future of the West Bank. The government resolution (opposed by Yigal Allon and Menachem Begin) read, "Israel proposes the conclusion of peace treaties with Egypt and Syria on the basis of the international frontiers and Israel's security needs," meaning an Israeli willingness to withdraw from the Sinai Peninsula and the Golan Heights in exchange for full demilitarization of these areas and guarantees of Israeli naval and aerial rights along the Straits of Tiran and the Suez Canal. The government decided that according to the international border (that preceding the armistice agreements of 1949), the Gaza Strip was within Israeli territory. On June 21 Eban conveyed the resolution to U.S. Secretary of State Dean Rusk, though the message was not communicated subsequently to Cairo or Damascus.

Despite Eban's later boasting that the Americans were dumbfounded by Israel's "generous peace offer", and that the Arabs flatly rejected Jerusalem's outreached hand for peace, there is no record of either taking place: Israel never officially presented the offer as such to the Americans, and the Arabs never rejected it because they never received it from the Americans. In any case, a year later the Israeli cabinet effectively rescinded its "peace offer" by deciding to maintain territorial contiguity from the southern port of Eilat to Sharm al-Sheikh at the southern tip of Egypt's Sinai Peninsula.[17]

June 27 the Knesset, despite the strong protest of Eban from the General Assembly, swiftly passed three law proposals that effectively annexed East Jerusalem and the Old City, which had been captured from Jordan during the war. The municipal boundaries of unified Jerusalem were expanded threefold, and Israeli law was applied to all parts of the city. The Knesset also sanctioned free access to the holy places by all religions. Eban supported the unification of Jerusalem, but he implored Eshkol to postpone the Knesset vote at least until after the conclusion of the special session to avoid a likely condemnation of Israel. Even though a majority of nine ministers against seven supported Eban's request, Eshkol insisted that it was better to be condemned after the unification of Jerusalem than to defy an international decree not to do so in the first place. Despite Eban's warnings, the three laws were passed in lightning speed through the relevant committees and approved by the government later that day.

Eban, along with the entire Israeli delegation at the General Assembly, was dumbfounded by the government's hurried decision. "I cease to comprehend developments," he wrote to Eshkol. Jerusalem ordered the missions abroad to describe the unification of Jerusalem "not as annexation but as municipal fusion." Eban presented this formula to his British counterpart, Hugh Foot, Lord Caradon, ("unify the city without annexing it"), but semantic virtuosity could not hide the facts on the ground.[18] As Eban predicted, on July 4 the General Assembly, by a majority of 99 to 0, with 20 abstentions, considered the Israeli measures in Jerusalem to be invalid and called on Israel to rescind them. But more important for Israel, on the broader issue of the withdrawal of its forces the assembly was deadlocked. Neither the Soviet-Arab bloc nor the pro-Western bloc could muster the necessary two-thirds majority. First a Soviet draft resolution (introduced by Kosygin on June 19) that condemned Israel's aggression and demanded the immediate and unconditional withdrawal of Israeli troops from Arab land was defeated by an overwhelming majority of 71–22 (with 22 abstentions). Then a counter draft resolution sponsored by the Latin American states that tied the issue of Israeli withdrawal to the cessation of Arab-Israeli belligerency was defeated 57–43 (with 20 abstentions). With no progress to show for itself, on July 21 the special emergency session adjourned. The General Assembly opened its regular session on September 21, but with little new to be said or agreed on, on October 13 the matter was referred back to the Security Council for informal discussions.[19]

While the stalemate at the UN continued, the Israelis and Arabs did their utmost to make the situation even less amiable to peaceful resolution. In mid-July the first Jewish settlement in the recently occupied territories was established in the Golan Heights. Though not formally approved by the government, it had the firm backing of Yigal Allon, the deputy prime minister. On September 1, the Arab League Summit in Khartoum declared its infamous "Three No's" resolution: no to peace with Israel, no to recognition of Israel, and no to negotiations with Israel. The uncompromising resolution notwithstanding, from the verbatim record of the deliberations at Khartoum that Israeli intelligence was able to obtain, Israeli officials could recognize a certain diversity of opinions among Arab leaders on how to reclaim the territories from Israel. In particular, it was apparent that Egypt's Nasser and King Hussein of Jordan were more inclined to talk (albeit not directly) to Israel than their more resilient counterparts from Syria, Iraq, and Algeria—and particularly Ahmad al-Shukeiri, the chairman of the nascent Palestine Liberation Organization, who demanded the insertion of the Three No's to the resolution. Publicly however, the Khartoum Resolution was greeted in Israeli and Western public opinion as evidence that the Arabs were still bent on pursuing an intransigent policy toward Israel. In response to growing pressure from various religious and nationalistic circles, in mid-September Eshkol's government authorized the first settlements in the West Bank and the Sinai Peninsula—despite the advice of the government's legal counsel that "civilian settlement in the administered territories contravenes the explicit provisions of the Fourth Geneva Convention."[20] Eban was still in New York for the opening of the new session of the General Assembly, and was, according to Eshkol, "really boiling, angry, upset" at having to clean up his government's mess once again.[21]

Back at the UN it was apparent that only the most artfully crafted formula could persuade Israelis and Arabs—and their respective superpower backers—to accept a UN resolution on the peaceful settlement of the Arab–Israeli conflict. From mid-October on there were almost daily negotiations among the members of the Security Council, mostly hinged on the context of the withdrawal of Israeli troops. The Arabs demanded a complete and unconditional withdrawal, while Israel insisted on linking it to an Arab commitment to make peace. There were no fewer than five draft resolutions on the table: the first was submitted by India, Mali, and Nigeria, representing the nonaligned bloc in the council. The second proposal was introduced by the Latin American and Caribbean countries, while the Americans and Soviets submitted their own drafts. It was, however, the British proposal that was finally approved. It was officially presented by Lord Caradon, the British delegate, but many hands were involved in its drafting—chiefly those of Eban and Arthur Goldberg, the American ambassador, as well as the Canadian and Latin American representatives. The resolution might not be perfect, Caradon explained, but it represented "above all an endeavor to be fair, to be just and to be impartial." The final draft was a masterstroke of ambiguity and compromise, designed to satisfy the demands of all parties concerned. Its preamble emphasized the "inadmissibility of the acquisition of territory by war and the need to work for a just and lasting peace in which every state in the area can live in security." The British use of "acquisition" was more palatable to the Israelis than the Soviet draft, which had used the term "seizure," or the nonaligned bloc, which referred to "acquisition or occupation." At the same time, the inclusion of the "inadmissibility of acquiring territory by force" was aimed at satisfying the Arabs.

But it was the first operative paragraph that was the most contentious and has remained so ever since. It called for the "withdrawal of Israeli armed forces from territories occupied in the recent conflict." It was partly based on the American draft, which called for "withdrawal of armed forces from occupied territories" and departed from the Soviet and Latin American proposals, which specifically referred to withdrawal from "positions held before 5 June" and withdrawal from "all the territories," respectively. Similar compromises included the clauses dealing with the "freedom of navigation through international waterways in the area" and the achievement of "a just settlement of the refugee problem." There was no mention of the Palestinians or their right to self-determination because, as Caradon himself conceded, "we all took it for granted that the [West Bank] occupied territory would be restored to Jordan." The third operative paragraph in the resolution asked the UN secretary-general to designate a special representative to establish and maintain contact with the parties in order to achieve a peaceful and accepted settlement.

Throughout this period all members of the Security Council, as well as the Egyptian and Israeli delegates, expressed their concerns over this or that aspect of the draft resolution, especially surrounding the vague reference in the English text to the withdrawal of Israeli armed forces "from territories" (the French and Spanish versions referred to "the territories"). But the resolution contained a very balanced ambiguity, as both parties could interpret it to their liking and declare a diplomatic victory at home: Israel pointed to the resolution's affirmation of its sovereignty, territorial integrity, and political independence, while the Arabs stressed that it did not include a specific demand to recognize the boundaries and legitimacy of the Jewish entity. Israel read the resolution's call for "withdrawal of Israeli armed forces from territories occupied in the recent conflict" as "withdrawal from *some* territories," while the Arabs read it as "withdrawal from *all* territories." Eban was adamant that the absence of the determiner "the" in the resolution meant that there was only one way to read the operative paragraph: "For us, the resolution says what it says. It does not say that which it has specifically and consciously avoided saying." As a whole, both parties found some solace in the carefully balanced resolution. Israel, forever fearful of third-party mediation and insistent on direct negotiations, was satisfied that the UN mediator's role was to be limited to merely promoting agreement and assistance efforts, whereas Egypt and Jordan could claim victory in that they were not required to conduct direct negotiations with Israel, thus remaining faithful to their own interpretation of the Khartoum resolution.[22]

After months of assiduous negotiations the resolution was put to a vote on November 22, 1967. All fifteen members of the Security Council raised their hands in support, to loud cheers from the public galleries. Since then, Security Council Resolution 242 has remained one of the most important resolutions ever adopted by the United Nations, and the single most important cornerstone in every subsequent peace dialogue between Israel and its Arab neighbors. Though Resolution 242 did not end the Arab-Israeli conflict, it laid down a new framework for its peaceful settlement through the formula of "land for peace"—though its ultimate tragedy has been that the question of how much land Israel should return and what kind of peace the Arabs should give remains as unresolved today as it was in 1967.

Eban emerged out of the Suez Crisis as the Voice of Israel, but his legacy in the aftermath of the Six-Day War was rather more checkered. As an ambassador he had been ultimately an apolitical figure; the vast majority of Israelis had never seen or heard him in action, which only added to the mystique of the newspaper reports of his exploits in New York and Washington. But as a foreign minister and with several years of public office in Israel behind him, Eban's biography and demeanor were a matter of intense debate. His diplomatic mission to the Western capitals on the eve of the war gave the generals a much-needed respite to prepare the Israel Defense Forces for war, and his speeches before the UN Security Council and the General Assembly convinced millions around the world of Israel's righteousness, but in the cauldron of Israeli politics Eban was more vulnerable than ever. While he would remain foreign minister for another seven years and a member of the Labor Party for two more decades, Eban struggled to find wide support in Israel for the moral rectitude of his political views. The heroes of the war were Dayan and the generals, whose faces adorned the many victory albums published after the war, while Eban and Eshkol were charged by some sectors in the press and the public with indecisiveness and undue deference to world opinion. Moreover, against a national infatuation with the newly acquired territories and the prospect of the country expanding its borders to biblical proportions, both Eban and his moderate views seemed suddenly irrelevant, as he conceded in his memoirs years later: "I lived in an isolated realm of anxiety while the noise of unconfined joy kept intruding through the window. For me, the Six Day War meant salvation in an hour of peril . . . and the possession of territorial assets that could be transacted in a negotiation for peace. For many Israelis, it was a providential dispensation enlarging Israel's areas of jurisdiction beyond anything that has ever been conceived before."[23]

There was a perverse dichotomy in how Israeli society perceived Eban after the war: while very few doubted his diplomatic forte and standing in the world community, his “foreignness” and uber-intellectualism remained unpalatable, especially to his colleagues and some sectors of the press. According to a public opinion poll conducted for *Haaretz* in July 1967, Eban’s approval ratings as foreign minister were higher than Dayan’s as defense minister and Eshkol’s as prime minister: 47 percent endorsed Eshkol and 81 percent supported Dayan the war hero but, remarkably, Eban enjoyed 82 percent approval. Together with Dayan, Eban was by some distance the most popular politician in Israel, but with one caveat—his arena was clearly foreign affairs. His approval ratings for the premiership were pathetically low, at 4 percent, trailing behind Eshkol, Dayan, Allon, and even the octogenarian David Ben-Gurion and the eternal opposer Menachem Begin. For some Israelis Eban was a *foreign* foreign minister. Only weeks after the Six-Day War had ended, a newspaper caricature depicted an impeccably attired Eban strolling into the UN General Assembly building, only to be blocked by one of his compatriots. Wearing khaki shorts, sandals, and a soiled open shirt, this “typical” Israeli—a sabra—blocks Eban’s way and suggests that he change into similar attire before he enters the building. The message to Eban was clear: you are not one of us. As one of Eban’s colleagues remarked, “he is our attorney, not our representative.”[24]

XIV

The Harbinger of a Vacuous Diplomacy

FOR EBAN THE SIX-DAY WAR AND ITS OUTCOME REPRESENTED AN OPPORtunity, not a solution to Israel's problems. On the surface, the period that followed the war was full of diplomatic initiatives: the appointment of Gunnar Jarring as the UN's new mediator in the conflict; Israel's own peace proposal, which Eban articulated in 1968; an American peace plan, promoted by the new secretary of state William Rogers in late 1969; the secret negotiations between Israel and Jordan over the future of the West Bank; and an Egyptian peace initiative announced by Egypt's new leader, Anwar Sadat, in 1971. But as Eban would lament years later, despite these seemingly luring opportunities for Arab-Israeli peace, this was ultimately a disappointing period for diplomacy, something for which both parties were equally responsible: the Arab leaders refused to adapt to the new reality and kept on demanding "100 percent of the territories and zero percent of peace," while many Israelis who had first viewed the territories as bargaining cards "ended up falling in love with the cards and embracing them so tenaciously as to eliminate their bargaining value."[1] There was evidently too much Arab pride and not enough Israeli humility to break this deadlock.

Amidst the messianic euphoria that engulfed the nation as soon as the guns fell silent, it was impossible to debate seriously the contours of a coherent peace strategy. There was a popular perception that time was working in Israel's favor (a July 1967 poll showed that 71 percent of Israelis favored keeping the West Bank), but Eban maintained that "time does not 'work' at all. Everything depends on what we do and how we act as time passes."[2] With a national unity government comprising a wide spectrum of political views from the labor-socialist Mapam party on the left to Menachem Begin's nationalist Gahal party on the right, a cacophony of opinions about what to do with the new territories—especially the West Bank—began to adorn the newspapers on an almost daily basis. The West Bank and its more than 600,000 inhabitants were naturally the hottest item on the agenda. Drunk on victory and enthralled by the realization of a two-thousand-year longing to return to the Old City of Jerusalem, both left- and right-wing ministers fantasized about a return to the biblical Eretz Israel (Land of Israel). But none was oblivious to the very real tension between the desire to hold onto these areas for security, religious, and ideological reasons and the unsavory notion of becoming an occupying power responsible for administrating the daily lives of the Arab population. Prime Minister Levi Eshkol put this dilemma succinctly to his colleagues: "I get it. You want the dowry, but you don't like the bride!"[3]

Eban apparently wanted neither, proposing an active peace policy that offered a semi-independent Palestinian entity in the West Bank or a return of the area to Jordan. He was firmly against annexing the recently occupied territories and opposed the publication of a specific territorial plan before a firm Arab commitment to enter peace negotiations. Yigal Allon presented his own plan that viewed the River Jordan as Israel's eastern border, thereby annexing most of the Jordan Valley, as well as East Jerusalem and other territorial blocs, while the rest of the West Bank would be returned to Jordan. Minister of Police Eliyahu Sasson proposed the resettlement of the 400,000 inhabitants of the Gaza Strip in the Jordan Valley, while education minister Zalman Aranne warned of the disastrous political, diplomatic, and security consequences of annexing the West Bank. Moshe Dayan vacillated between doing nothing and giving the Palestinians of the West Bank autonomy. "We are quite happy with the current situation," he said in a BBC interview. "If anything bothers the Arabs, they know where to find us." None of these ideas translated into concrete policy in the months following the war, and it seemed that the government settled for indecision—at least for the time being. "Is there a serious split between the hawks and doves in the Israeli government?," Eban was asked again and again. "Israel is not an aviary!" was his custom reply.[4]

At a meeting of the Mapai secretariat on September 14, 1967, Eban summed up to the party the tough choices Israel now faced: "With relation to the West Bank, we've all reached the same conclusion: there is no easy solution; every possible solution has a nasty territorial, demographic, or socio-cultural conclusion. A purely good solution does not exist."[5] Nobody disputed Eban's assessment. Eshkol agreed that "the truth is we don't know so clearly what we actually want," while Golda Meir asserted that "nothing is pressing us to decide now on the borders. . . . God is my witness that I don't want one million Arabs, but what can I do? Shall I ring King Hussein and tell him: my dear king, come and get it? . . . I don't have a solution. I will not come with a proposal."[6] On September 23 Eban communicated to Arthur Goldberg, the U.S. ambassador to the UN, Israel's current thinking:

> [The Israeli government] had decided to take current stands on position of security principle rather than on territorial basis and to keep their options open for future negotiations. If Israel were compelled to state its specific policy publicly at this time they would have to be stated in a maximalist position. Israel's general position was that in the absence of a situation of peace Israel would have to maintain its positions on basis of considerations of national security but in a peace agreement with Arabs they could be in a flexible negotiating position.
>
> West Bank presented particularly difficult problems. Incorporation of West Bank into Israel, with its large Arab population, would completely transform Israel's national existence and reason for being. In any case it would cause a total reshaping of Israeli politics, as Arab votes were sought, and thus produce alterations in structure of Israel that they did not desire. Neither could Arabs be incorporated into Israel without granting them Israeli citizenship. This would not be permitted by international community nor would it be acceptable to Israeli people themselves.
>
> [The Israeli government] had also given thought to establishment of separate, autonomous Palestinian state on West Bank. This also has serious drawbacks. Days of autonomous dependent regions had really passed. Creation of Palestinian state might simply increase irredentist desires. There would be yet another Arab state on Arab scene. In a year or two it would ask for UN membership, and it would be admitted. Such prospects did not look attractive. On the other hand, now that Israelis for first time had opportunity to visit areas of historic significance to them, it would be difficult for their citizens to understand [the government] simply turning the area back.[7]

In the absence of better options or a clear consensus, the cabinet settled for a policy called the Oral Law—a compromise document between the hawks and doves that did not commit the party to strict prescriptions regarding the future borders but instead provided an informal understanding among Mapai, Rafi, and Ahdut Ha'Avoda, the parties that joined forces in January 1968 to form the Israel Labor Party. The Oral Law stated that the Israeli government saw the River Jordan as its eastern border, "fit for the purpose of providing protection from possible invasions." The Golan Heights and the Gaza Strip would remain under Israeli control, while Israeli forces would secure the entrance to the Gulf of Eilat near Sharm el-Sheikh, thereby establishing permanent Israeli control along the eastern strip of the Sinai Peninsula. The Oral Law concluded that Israel would be willing to enter into peace negotiations without preconditions; it was essentially the Allon Plan (control of the Jordan Valley) with the addition of a territorial continuity from Sharm el-Sheikh to Eilat.[8]

Eban had no territorial aspirations, though he did not rule out extending Israel's hold in some unpopulated areas of the West Bank for security reasons. His major gripe was not the act of settling itself but announcing it so publicly as a government policy, which he feared would bring about international condemnation. At the same time, Eban saw every day that passed without an international demand of an immediate and unconditional withdrawal as a victory to Israeli diplomacy. As long as the Arabs refused to negotiate directly with Israel, he reasoned, why should Israel commit itself to a particular peace plan? An overzealous public peace offensive would only tie Israel's hands and increase the Arabs' appetite before negotiations had ever begun: "If an Arab country was curious to know what our peace terms are, we will satisfy its curiosity at the negotiation table," he said to his party colleagues. For Eban, the Israeli insistence on direct negotiations was not a tactical ruse to delay making tough decisions, but a matter of principle: direct negotiations implied Arab recognition of Israel's existence and sovereignty and formed the basis of normal relations between states. For this reason, too, he held a dim view of third-party mediation: it would be absurd for Israel to share its negotiation position vis-à-vis the Arabs with the United Nations, the Americans, or the British when the Arabs refused to sit with Israel: "To negotiate with the United States the fate of Nablus, or to negotiate with Britain over the Jordan Rift, seems to me as supreme folly," he suggested. Israel applauded the efforts of friendly governments to bring Arabs and Israelis into direct and unconditional contact, he continued, but "no peace has ever yet been made if one party refuses to set eyes on the other, which is why we interpret refusal to meet as refusal to make peace. . . . The Arabs meet us face to face on the field of battle. Let them now meet us face to face at the conference table."[9]

Until then, he reasoned, actions mattered more than words:

> If someone proposed to sow, plough and settle in the Golan Heights, I will vote for it. If someone proposed that we declare that the Golan Heights are from this day part of the State of Israel, I will vote against it, because the declaration does not help or advance anything, and it is not necessary for the act itself. . . . I propose that if there is a possibility of settling, of creating facts, we shall have to set out our priorities. There is a clear situation in Greater Jerusalem, and we need to turn the declaration [on the unification of the city] to a fact . . . if it's possible to dilute the Arab population of Gaza, meaning that the bride will be a bit thinner so the dowry is more attractive, then this is excellent."[10]

At the same time, and somewhat incongruously, Eban asserted that he did not believe that creating such facts on the ground predetermined in any way Israel's negotiation position. Speaking before the assembly of the Council of Europe in September 1967, Eban declared that "we do not regard anything done in those places or any other settlements on the West Bank as in any sense excluding the free discussion of the territorial problem in the peace negotiations." He referred euphemistically to the settlement in the Golan Heights as "cultivation" and the settlement in Gush Etzion, south of Bethlehem, as a "military outpost" of the military occupation regime in the West Bank—which, unlike civilian settlements, was permitted under the Fourth Geneva Convention.[11]

For Eban, there was no contradiction between Israel's desire for peace and the burgeoning settlement activity. On the one hand he was concerned that in the absence of peace over time "the very vision of peace will disappear among certain circles in Israel," but on the other hand he insisted that "we have taken a clear decision that the map of 4 June is null and void. Therefore there is no logic in behaving as if we live and will continue to live within the bounds of the map of 4 June." In January 1969 Eban repeated this view—which was shared by the majority of the cabinet and the public—in his typical hyperbolical manner. He told the German weekly *Der Spiegel* that for Israelis, the map of June 4, 1967, was equivalent to insecurity and danger: "I do not exaggerate when I say that it reminds us of Auschwitz." This was perhaps the only statement that Eban had ever come to regret making throughout his illustrious career. His reference to Auschwitz was meant to evoke a metaphor of the existential danger confronting Israel before the Six-Day War, but in subsequent years an endless succession of right-wing politicians readily misused Eban's metaphor as a warning against making territorial concessions in the West Bank and in favor of an expansionist settlement policy. For Suzy Eban, this misquoted statement became such a stain on her husband's legacy as Israel's chief dove that even four decades later she insisted vigorously that he had never said such a thing.[12]

While Eban supported the government's policy of de facto indecision, he was nevertheless perturbed by what he termed as the absence of a mystique of peace in Israel, compared to the omnipresent mystiques of territories and security in the public discourse. But he hoped that this imbalance could change if peace was presented as a credible option. In a February 1968 interview in *Haaretz* he postulated that "[if] you confront the general public with the actual alternative: peace without part of the territories or all the territories without peace, I do not think that public opinion will necessarily be against peace."[13] This carefully worded statement made instant headlines and irked many people in Israel, including his party colleagues. The burgeoning Greater Israel Movement publicly called on the government to denounce Eban's comment, while several Mapai meetings were spent on scrutinizing Eban's statement. The most vocal critic was Shimon Peres, whose dim view of Eban had not diminished following the reunion of Rafi and Mapai under the Labor Party banner only a month earlier. "Why does the foreign minister of Israel have to say, in 1968, that there are mystiques of security and territories in Israel?" Peres demanded to know. "I think it's a mistake and Eban has been repeating it for many years, that the matter of peace or lack of it stems from omissions of the State of Israel." Eshkol wondered whether Eban's "mystique of peace" could be misconstrued as an Israeli desire for peace at all costs. David Hacohen was one of the few party members who congratulated Eban for "daring to speak his mind" against the current trend in the country, where "whenever one speaks his mind he is immediately labeled a 'Chamberlainite.'"[14]

Eban's position in the government became increasingly precarious throughout 1968. Eshkol was ailing, Dayan's popularity was soaring, and the constraints of a broad national unity government made any diplomatic overtures difficult to get off the ground. Harry McPherson, special counsel to Lyndon Johnson, told the U.S. president that the difficulties in the Israeli cabinet stemmed not from the debate over the future of the territories but from the basic disagreement over the merits of talking to UN mediator Jarring. The majority, led by Dayan and Allon, argued that only direct talks with the Arabs would do, as not only did they demand greater accountability from the Arabs, but third parties could not be trusted to represent Israel's interest as well as Israel could. On this point McPherson quoted Ephraim Evron of the Israeli embassy in Washington, DC: "You wouldn't trust U Thant to settle the war in Vietnam; we don't trust him to settle our problem." As for Eban's position, McPherson continued, he "vacillated" and "seemed to encourage Jarring," and as a result he had been censured by the cabinet and was forced to submit his "peace plans" for the cabinet's prior approval.[15] Similarly, the American ambassador in Israel, Walworth Barbour, reported that political parties on the right had attacked Eban for drawing Israel into a trap through his conciliatory and flexible approach to the Jarring mission. He was dubbed "Israel's Chamberlain" by the Free Centre Party for encouraging talks with Jarring.[16]

Evron also pointed to Eban's limited leverage around the government table. The problem with communicating U.S. encouragement for negotiations with the Arabs through Abba Eban, Evron said, was that Eban lacked "the political weight to bring the Cabinet to take a hard decision." Evron suggested instead Golda Meir, who was scheduled to visit New York in the summer, as "an excellent recipient for such a message."[17] The British Foreign Office also pointed out Eban's predicament: "He has no comparable position in domestic Israeli politics. There is a good deal of latent suspicion of him as liable to negotiate away Israel's true interests for the sake of international approval, and he has a number of jealous political enemies. However, his standing in the country, the party and the Government have been greatly strengthened since the immediate afterflow of the war, when his prestige was low, by the brilliant and successful conduct of Israel's case at the United Nations."[18] The Americans, too, were well aware of Eban's precarious position in the cabinet following the war. Alfred "Roy" Atherton, the country director for Israel and Arab-Israel Affairs at the U.S. State Department, noted that while Eshkol may have privately leaned toward the moderate camp in his government (led by Eban), rather than the hardliners (led by Dayan and Allon), his chief concern was to arbitrate between the two groups. As Israel's chief diplomat, Eban's "main card . . . with otherwise negligible political influence in the country, lies in his ability to present the disadvantageous international consequences of the hard line should the Israeli Cabinet adopt it.[19]"

Eban maintained that whether the inhabitants of the West Bank defined themselves as part of a Palestinian entity or part of a greater Arab populace was for them to decide. He was adamant that it would be an act of hubris for the Israeli government to answer these questions for the Arabs; Israel should be concerned with determining its own essence and character and let the Arabs determine theirs. "I recently visited the West Bank town of Jenin," he said, "but found no trace of a Hebrew letter, or Jewish grave, or blood and sweat of pioneers, or a national creation."[20] But on the possibility of an independent Palestinian state in the West Bank, Eban was adamant that it was a nonstarter: "It is not desirable, in my opinion, that the area of the British mandate will contain three states: Jordan, Israel and Palestine. I don't know what will be left for us if we need to crowd together like this, or if Israel shared its borders with five Arab states: Egypt, Jordan, Palestine, Syria and Lebanon. . . . Therefore if such pragmatic processes are not present, I don't think we should have any interest encouraging them." He reiterated this view in May 1969, urging his party "not to be led astray by the idea of a Palestinian State." Eight months later, at a meeting of the senior staff of the Foreign Ministry in Jerusalem, Eban noted that the question was not "whether we recognize the existence of a Palestinian people or not; rather, the legal-judicial framework of its definition. . . . It is a delusion to argue that there is a Palestinian people and a Jordanian people."[21]

Eban was far from the overzealous peacenik who was prepared to sell Israel's security for a piece of paper, as his critics often portrayed him. He did, however, insist that Israel ought to exhaust all avenues for peace even if the chances of attaining it were slim at the present time; the very concept of "peace" must never disappear from the vocabulary simply because of the present difficulties, he told his party in April 1968.[22] The following month Eban told an audience in Finland that the chief obstacle on the path to peace was not Israel's insistence on direct negotiations but the Arab League's "Three Nos" resolution: "The three negatives of the Khartoum Conference are a very big obstacle, perhaps the greatest single obstacle to the promotion of peace in the Middle East. No recognition of Israel, no negotiations with Israel, no peace with Israel. Well, out of such ingredients how do you put together peace?" Still, Eban insisted that Israel must not shut the door to the very slim prospect of peace: "If you don't succeed in April then try again in May, and if you don't succeed in May then try again in June. One must never give up because there is nothing more important than to promote a peace settlement in the Middle East."[23]

Dayan was the most formidable of Eban's political adversaries during this period. Their rivalry was fought in the open, as manifestation of the rivalry between Mapai and Rafi, between doves and hawks in the cabinet, and between different international outlooks. By the end of 1967, as many had feared, Dayan's surging political and popular power threatened to break up the national unity government. He declared at a Rafi convention that he would do his best to topple Eshkol and Sapir, the finance minister and Mapai's stalwart kingmaker, but Eshkol refused to heed the calls for him to sack Dayan.[24] Dayan's public popularity continued to soar as Eshkol's continued to plummet. In June 1968, 48 percent of the public supported Dayan for the premiership, and a month later his support jumped to 54 percent; by the end of the year it increased to 60 percent. In the same period Eshkol's approval ratings as prime minister plunged from 31 to 20 percent. When asked to rank Israel's leaders according to seven leadership traits, Dayan came out on top, scoring 6.5 points. Right behind him, with a score of 5.7 was Eban, followed by Eshkol and Allon. Among the party voters the gap between Dayan and Eban was reduced further, with Dayan scoring 6.4 and Eban scoring 6.1. Both were also the most popular leaders among Israeli Arabs. Such results, which remained consistent in the postwar period, seemed to dispel the myth in Israel at the time that Eban was more popular abroad than in his own country, though at least within the political system he was charged with unwarranted deference to the UN and a ready acquiescence to international demands.[25] Eban's main weakness vis-à-vis Dayan was his lack of security and military kudos, a shortcoming he tried to deflect, not very convincingly, by dismissing his public image as the chief dove in government. "I don't know what my ornithological definition is," he said in February 1969. "I don't see military power as the answer to every situation, but I recognize situations when there is no other answer." Whether he liked the typology or not, Eban certainly considered himself a political dove: "Usually the dove is nicer than the hawk, and Noah had a good use for it. I haven't found any reference in the Bible to a useful mission performed by a hawk."[26]

ON NOVEMBER 23, 1967, IN ACCORDANCE WITH UN SECURITY COUNCIL RESOLution 242, U Thant advised Israel, Egypt, Jordan, and Syria of his decision to designate Swedish diplomat Gunnar Jarring as his special representative to the Middle East. Jarring, at the time Sweden's ambassador to Moscow, appeared eminently qualified for the job. He had a long diplomatic experience as his country's envoy to the United States, the United Nations, Iran, and Iraq, and he acted as a UN mediator between India and Pakistan. And as Sweden maintained strict neutrality in the Cold War and was not allied with any of the parties in the Middle East, Jarring was regarded by all sides as an agreeable and honest broker. For almost four years Jarring held several rounds of talks with Israeli and Arab officials, but his efforts ultimately ended in failure. Israel feared that substantive talks with the Arabs through a third party would significantly reduce its bargaining position, while Jordan and Egypt, who were already criticized by their neighbors for accepting Resolution 242, refused to acknowledge Israel by talking to it directly. Jarring had no choice but to focus on procedural matters, turning his mission effectively to negotiations about negotiations.[27] Despite the inhospitable opening conditions of the Jarring mission, both parties made some minor concessions in response to pressure from the great powers and out of fear of being blamed for failing Jarring. In early 1968 Egypt and Jordan agreed to indirect talks with Israel even before an Israeli withdrawal but on condition that Israel publicly declare its acceptance of Resolution 242 and its willingness to implement it. Israel refused to do so, however, and instead insisted on direct talks over the substantive issues.[28]

Fearing the premature termination of Jarring's mission, on October 8, 1968, Eban outlined his vision in a nine-point blueprint for peace before the UN General Assembly. In the address, Eban declared Israel's readiness to replace the cease-fire lines with permanent, secure, and recognized borders with each of its neighbors. Once these borders were established, Eban continued, Israel would then proceed to implement the "disposition of forces in full accordance with the boundaries under the final peace"—a diplomatic euphemism for "withdrawal." Eban also proposed agreeing to a pledge of mutual nonaggression, and called for a regional conference to solve the refugee problem. On Jerusalem Eban reassured the Arabs that Israel did not seek to "exercise unilateral jurisdiction" over the Muslim and Christian holy places. Perhaps most important, however, was the Israeli government's departure from its earlier demand to only conduct direct face-to-face negotiations with the Arabs. In order to take advantage of the presence of the Egyptian and Jordanian delegates and Ambassador Jarring in New York, Eban announced that Israel was ready to exchange "ideas or clarifications on certain matters of substance through Ambassador Jarring with any Arab Government." He warned against international imposition of a solution to the conflict, and urged the Arabs to respond in kind to his invitation: "Lest the Arab Governments be tempted out of sheer routine to rush into impulsive rejection, let me suggest that tragedy is not what men suffer but what they miss. Time and again Arab Governments have rejected proposals today—and longed for them tomorrow."[29]

The *Baltimore Sun* noted that Eban's proposals provided "a way out of a regional dilemma and a world danger, in reasonable and honorable terms," while the *Washington Evening Star* described the speech as "a determined effort in moderation. Eban specifically rejected polemics against Arab antagonists." The *New York Times* suggested that Eban's peace plan was evidence that Israel was "serious about negotiations. . . . The proposals had a considerable effect on those neutrals who have clamored for action." *The Economist* wrote that "Eban went to Israel's most tolerant limit," and the *Atlanta Journal* reported that Eban's peace plan was "a refreshing breeze in an otherwise hot, explosive atmosphere. . . . Representatives of the Arab world must now be willing to show the same evidence of good faith and trust."[30]

But as Eban himself expected, his plan was flatly rejected by the Arab delegates. Hashid Mourad, the Arab League representative, asked, "What are the secure boundaries he keeps talking about? He never once used the word 'withdrawal,' which comes at the top of the Security Council resolution." The Arab press either ignored Eban's address altogether or criticized it for repeating Israel's old positions, while the Egyptian and Jordanian delegates at the General Assembly broke off the talks they were holding with Jarring in New York and returned home in early November. As Jordan's foreign minister Abdelmunim al-Rifai explained to the press, until Israel explicitly declared its readiness to accept and implement Resolution 242 and to withdraw all its forces from the Arab territories, there was no point in his continued presence in New York. Eban was criticized at home, too: Menachem Begin accused him of deviating from the government's guidelines by expressing Israel's willingness to negotiate with Jarring matters of substance, while members of the opposition charged Eban with adopting a "too apologetic attitude" toward the Arab states.[31]

Eban's "peace initiative" was motivated as much by his fear of Israel being blamed for the failure of the Jarring mission as by his earnest belief in the prospects of Arab-Israeli peace. Since such a peace was not forthcoming under the present conditions, and in order to fend off international pressures to force an unconditional withdrawal to the pre-1967 borders, Eban reasoned that Israel must settle for an interim objective: convincing the world that it was "striving for peace while holding forth." Compared to the two other alternatives of holding forth without striving for peace or withdrawing without peace, he told his colleagues, the proposed policy was by far the most logical. As an ardent student of history, Eban did not want Israel to be depicted as the intransigent party in the conflict. To fend off accusations that Israel's policy was in fact static, if not essentially tactical trickery, Eban set on pouring substance into his "holding forth" policy by bombarding Jarring with procedural queries, itemizations of agendas, and other correspondence for the sake of keeping his mission alive. If Israel's peace efforts were to be compiled by future historians, Eban was confident that the record would show that Israel was actively engaging in peace talks with Jarring while all the Arabs did was ignore or reject Israel's outreached hand: "If there was a comprehensive international inquiry of the peace efforts of the last months it would transpire that against Israel's positive initiatives the Egyptian position was one and only: no negotiations, no agreement, no recognition, no peace." He repeated this mantra at a press conference in New York: "All the initiatives, all the responses, all the formulations designed to advance a dialogue have come from Israel. From the other side has come nothing at all."[32] He likened his role to that of an acrobat standing on a tightrope: there had to be a great deal of movement of the arms and legs in order to stay still.[33]

Eban's strategy worked rather well. In April 1969, after a hiatus of five months, Jarring terminated his mission and returned to his ambassadorial post in Moscow. Keeping the Jarring mission alive for so long by tactical means not only helped preserve the national unity government and cleared Israel of blame for the failure but also prevented the subject of Arab-Israeli diplomacy from returning to the Security Council. Despite the intransigence displayed by Israel, Egypt, and Jordan in the preceding eighteen months, most fingers were pointed at Jarring, rather than the parties, for failing to break the deadlock. In particular, the parties pointed to his tepid personality and unimaginative tactics. Eban believed that Jarring's European humanism was his greatest virtue as well as his major defect, realizing too late that logic played a small role in the politics of the Middle East. All that Jarring could do, according to Eban, was "ask Israel to be less rational and the Arabs less emotional." Gideon Rafael also found the scholarly Jarring lacking in expertise on Arab-Israeli politics, describing him as "a quiet man, more of a scholar than a dashing diplomat. . . . He understood what the contenders said but not always what they meant. . . . Undeniably he was studious and conscientious in his efforts to help clarify the controversial issues, but he lacked the boldness needed to summon Israel and the Arab states to a peace conference. It eluded him, probably because of his inclination to disentangle painstakingly every thread of the Gordian knot, instead of cutting it with one well-aimed stroke."[34] In similar fashion, U.S. secretary of state Dean Rusk once told his British counterpart, Michael Stewart, that both Jarring and his boss, U Thant, were not up to the job: They were not "bold enough in pressing for both substantive and procedural progress. Unfortunately, pushing on U Thant was like pushing on the end of a piece of spaghetti; nothing happens at the other end." Rusk criticized Jarring's passivity in pushing forward his own agenda, stating that he was "inclined to accept suggestions, but then simply pass them along and blame the individual party (i.e., Israel) for rejection." But Eban, ever the optimist, also described Jarring's efforts as "not hopeful but not hopeless."[35] He believed that the Jarring mission was useful so far as it "frizzed other alternatives"—namely, the return of the matter to the UN General Assembly or the superpowers. If peace was unreachable under the present conditions, he continued, it was nevertheless imperative to maintain the Jarring mission, as its termination would create a "dramatization of no solution, of polarization of war and peace as the only two options." His advice to his party colleagues was clear: they must not give up on peace, even theoretically, as a political aim. "I am certain that emphasizing our desire for peace is important, even if there is no chance of peace," he said. "In other words, we should not condition a talk of peace and an initiative of peace on the prospects of an Arab response."[36]

THE JARRING MISSION COINCIDED WITH ANOTHER, MORE SECRETIVE DIPLOMATIC dialogue between Israel and Jordan. A first meeting between King Hussein and Yaacov Herzog, the director-general of the Israeli prime minister's office, had taken place in London in September 1963 under the king's initiative. Over the years a frank and open dialogue was developed between the two, which included some verbal understandings on a range of issues, from the demilitarization of the West Bank to Israel's commitment to lobby Washington to secure aid for Jordan. In October 1967 Eban asked Eshkol to allow him to take part in the secret negotiations with Hussein, but he was told that the king preferred to have a soldier-to-soldier meeting with Dayan, the soldier who beat him in the Six-Day War war. According to the British diplomat Julian Amery, who facilitated the talks, "Hussein said that he has no interest in meeting Eban."[37] Dayan, however, refused to meet with the king, telling Eshkol and Eban that Hussein could not be trusted. "I will blow up the talks," he warned. "I will not maneuver with him like Eban. I don't play games."[38] Eshkol also refused to meet with Hussein, but following American pressure to enter negotiations with Jordan, the government agreed to send Eban to meet with the king. On May 3, 1968, Eban and Herzog met Hussein and his private secretary Ziad Rifai at the London residence of the king's Jewish physician, Dr. Emanuel Herbert. It was the first of a dozen meetings between Israeli and Jordanian officials that year (mostly attended by Herzog and Rifai) and a further ten in 1969.[39]

Despite the pace and intensity of the talks, it soon became clear that the gaps between the sides over the future of the West Bank were unbridgeable.[40] The king was insulted by the Israeli offers, which suggested that Israel retain as much as 30 percent of the West Bank, while the Israelis insisted on holding on to most of the Jordan Valley for strategic reasons. But Eban was not blind to the real value of the dialogue, writing to Eshkol that for the time being Israel should focus on the tactical aim of ensuring the continuation of the talks. Herzog remained suspicious of Eban, telling Allon, "Eban and I disagree. While Eban believes there is a chance [of peace with Jordan], I don't believe in it. I consider [the talks with Hussein] to be purely tactical."[41] The personal relations between the two deteriorated following Eban's decision to recommend Yitzhak Rabin as the next ambassador to Washington despite first promising the post to Herzog. "I was puzzled by Eban's lack of sincerity," Herzog later wrote in his diary. He enlisted the support of Allon, Galili, Meir, and even Begin to persuade Eshkol to allow Allon to join Eban in his meetings with Hussein. So strong was the opposition to Eban's mission among some quarters in the government that Pinchas Sapir, Eban's principal backer in the party, felt obliged to warn Eshkol that a "'blood libel' was being conducted against Eban, that the PM's office must react sharply, and Eban must be given bodyguards to protect him from physical harm."[42]

On February 20, 1969, Eban, Allon, and Herzog met with Hussein and Rifai on board the king's yacht in the Gulf of Aqaba. When Eban searched for a pen to write some notes, Hussein gave him his gold pen, engraved with the emblem of the Hashemite crown. Sensing that Allon also expected a gift, the king gave him a rifle. Eban spent the next few days beaming with glee and brandishing his pen to anyone he had met—and unwittingly exposing the secret talks with the king.[43] The two sides continued to meet sporadically for the next few years, but the resumption of the Jarring mission and the civil war in Jordan in 1970, among other reasons, all but killed the "Jordanian option." In any case, the gaps between the two sides remained as wide as they were in 1967: Israel expected the king to accept a smaller territory under his control—after all, he had started a war and lost—while Rifai explained that "[because] of the war we are now willing to agree to the June 4 lines, which we were unwilling to do before the war."[44] For Israel, compromise meant keeping only those parts of the West Bank that had security and emotional resonance. For Jordan, compromise meant recognizing Israel's existence in the pre-1967 lines.

THE TERMINATION OF THE JARRING MISSION IN APRIL 1969 WAS FOLLOWED BY a hiatus of sixteen months. By the time the mediator returned to the region in August 1970 the conditions had changed dramatically. There were new leaderships in Israel, the United States, and Egypt, and the War of Attrition between Egypt and Israel along the Suez Canal was threatening to get out of control. On the morning of February 26, 1969 Levi Eshkol died of a heart attack, his second in three weeks. His sudden departure at the age of seventy-three marked the end of an era for Israel and its people. Together with David Ben-Gurion, Moshe Sharett, and Golda Meir, Eshkol belonged to the founding generation of the state, the Russian-born pioneers who had risen through the ranks of Mapai to become the ruling elite during the prestate years. Now the door was opened to the next generation of political leaders: Dayan, Allon, Peres, and Rabin: unlike the party's old guard, they were not scarred by anti-Semitism and pogroms in eastern Europe; they were politically ambitious, if not audacious, and had dazzling military careers behind them (except for Peres, who earned his stripes in the Defense Ministry as Ben-Gurion's protégé). They were young, defiant, confident, and ready to take the helm. But Mapai's tight grip over the Labor Party's bureaucracy meant that Eshkol's successor would be chosen by thc inner circle of Mapai's executive and not by members of Rafi and Ahdut Ha'Avoda, the much smaller partners in the Labor Party. All eyes turned to Finance Minister Pinchas Sapir, the Labor Party's secretary-general and its undisputed kingmaker. For most outside observers there seemed to be only two candidates for the job: Dayan, who was riding the crest of a wave of public support but had virtually no support among the party leadership, and Allon ("a pushy type," according to Eshkol), the pensive deputy prime minister and interim caretaker of the government, who had moderate support in the party but fewer followers among the public. Peres remained as always a polarizing figure in the eyes of many Israelis, while Rabin, who retired as chief of staff in 1968 as a war hero, now served as Israel's ambassador in Washington. Sapir, despite wheeling considerable power among the party ranks as a founding member of the ruling troika with Eshkol and Meir, was not interested in the post, while Eban, despite his formal senior role as foreign minister, had no support base in the party and was considered an outside candidate. Assessing the leadership contest following Eshkol's death, the *Daily Mail* of London noted that though Eban was recognized "as Israel's best possible spokesman abroad, he has no party qualifications. Israelis say he lacks *rapport* with simple people, being 'the prototype intellectual devoid of popular humanity.'" Acutely aware of his position in the party, Eban ruled himself out of the race: "If I wanted to be prime minister, I would have had to be reborn," he told a reporter. "You know, I wasn't born in [Kibbutz] Nahalal, Mescha or Eastern Europe."[45]

After weighing old political alliances, personal rivalries and the future of the party, Sapir concluded that only one person could succeed Eshkol: Golda Meir, who had resigned from her influential post as the party's secretary-general six months earlier. Initially the choice surprised many outside observers, but few within the party disagreed with Sapir's logic. If Allon was chosen, his premiership was certain to be undermined by the Rafi faction led by Dayan and Peres, while his political roots in Ahdut Ha'Avoda, a splinter group of Mapai, made his candidacy unpalatable to many in the Mapai leadership. The resistance to Dayan was even fiercer, a mixture of personal detestation and fears that his election would effectively split the new Labor Party. As for Eban and Sapir, while they were the most senior Mapai ministers in the cabinet, Eban could never be elected by his party colleagues, and Sapir didn't want the job.

Meir, on the other hand, had vast political experience that included seven years as labor minister and a decade as foreign minister (the longest in Israel's history). She was the most powerful political personality in the country and represented continuity in the leadership of the old guard, which wished to delay the inevitable and much feared takeover by the young generation. "Golda is unwell," Sapir told Eban, alluding to the seventy-year-old's long battle with lymphoma; "it is only an interim solution to block Dayan and Allon." Ten days after Eshkol's death Meir's candidacy was endorsed by an overwhelming majority in the party's Central Committee. In presenting her government to the

Knesset, the chain-smoking former Milwaukee schoolteacher announced that there would be no change in personalities or policies; her job was to stabilize the ship, not to rock it, ahead of the general elections that were scheduled for October. But the change in the prime minister's office could not be more dramatic: Eshkol had been a mediator, a conciliator, and a coalition builder; Meir was none of those. She was more dogmatic and tough than her predecessor, though like him she was plainspoken and lacked intellectual sophistication. Intransigence and pragmatism best described her attitude to the Arabs and her views of reconciliation. In the biographical profiles of her that followed soon after her election, many in the national and foreign press chose to borrow Ben-Gurion's reference to Meir as the only man in the cabinet.[46]

The change of personalities in Washington was no less dramatic. In January 1969 the Republican Richard Nixon entered the White House after eight years of Democratic rule. During the first year of the administration Middle East affairs were not dealt with by the White House—a sign of the secondary importance Nixon placed on the resolution of the Arab–Israeli conflict compared to other issues. He told Henry Kissinger, his national security adviser, that only matters concerning East-West relations, the Soviet Union, China, Eastern Europe, and NATO be brought to his immediate attention. The relegation of the Middle East to the second tier of foreign policy priorities meant that it would be handled almost exclusively by the State Department—an unappetizing prospect for the Israeli government, whose view of the department as a bastion of Arabists and anti-Israelis went back to the years of president Dwight D. Eisenhower.[47]

The new administration made it clear that after more than a year of the Jarring mission and with virtually no progress, the four powers (the United States, the Soviet Union, France, and Britain) would have to intervene to help Jarring find a way out of the deadlock, or else the situation, which Nixon described as a powder keg, might explode into a superpower confrontation. In March 1969 Eban met with Nixon and Secretary of State William Rogers. The message from the president was clear: if you don't want the negotiations to be internationalized, then you need to show some flexibility in your position, starting by dropping the insistence on direct negotiations over full peace, and agree to a more limited, interim framework.[48] Joseph Sisco, assistant secretary of state for Near Eastern and South Asian affairs, spelled out this new American thinking to Ambassador Rabin: U.S. interests in the region did not center on Israel alone, and if the friendship with Israel was the only thing that the

United States was left with in the Middle East, then it would be a catastrophic setback for American policy. This policy, which Washington saw as decidedly even-handed, was interpreted by Jerusalem as nothing short of disastrous. Both Eban and Rabin expressed to their American interlocutors Israel's apprehension over a possible big power deal at its expense and reiterated Israel's objection to the introduction of outside powers into the negotiating process.[49] Ahead of his meeting with Eban, Secretary Rogers had aptly summed up for the president the challenges which the administration's new policy posed to U.S.-Israeli relations: "It will not be easy to win Israeli confidence in our approach, given the Israelis' deep distrust of [Egypt's Gamal Abdel] Nasser, the Soviets and the French; their uncertainty about British and even US policy; and their lack of faith in the United Nations and in international arrangements and guarantees of any kind. . . . Israel opposes efforts to alter the status quo while it waits for the Arabs to accept the inevitability of negotiating a genuine peace settlement."[50]

The first major Middle East initiative of the new administration was produced by Rogers on December 9, 1969. Following the failure of the Jarring talks and the entanglement of Israel and Egypt in the War of Attrition along the Suez Canal, which mainly involved reciprocal artillery bombardments and air raids, Rogers called on Israel to withdraw to the 1949 armistice lines and for Egypt to agree to a binding commitment to peace. Nine days later Charles Yost, the U.S. representative to the United Nations, presented a similar proposal for an Israeli-Jordanian settlement that required a full Israel withdrawal from the West Bank which included "insubstantial border changes." On December 22 the Israeli government formally rejected the American proposals, describing them as an attempt to impose a solution and to appease the Arabs at the expense of Israel's security. A week later the Knesset followed suit, with a 57–3 vote against the proposals. According to Meir, Rogers was demanding substantial Israeli withdrawals in exchange for no more than the verbal promises of Arab leaders, while Eban told Kissinger during his visit to Washington on December 16 that he didn't know why the United States had to be the "author of a doctrine on precise boundaries." Rogers's allusion to "insubstantial" changes made the whole point of negotiations futile, since "that is precisely what we want to negotiate about. Nobody can replace our sensitivity to our own security needs."[51] On December 23 Egypt also rejected the Rogers Plan, since Nasser insisted on an unconditional Israeli withdrawal and refused to negotiate security arrangements and free passage in the Suez Canal with Israel. The Soviets also criticized the American proposals, terming them one-sided in accepting the Israeli demands for negotiations and ignoring the Arab demand of full Israeli withdrawal.[52] Nixon himself washed his hands of the Rogers Plan altogether and dismissed it as a "State Department initiative." It was a significant first step in the gradual exclusion of Secretary Rogers and the elevation of Kissinger as the chief architect of American foreign policy during the first term of the Nixon administration. Rogers continued to serve as secretary of state until September 1973, when he was replaced by Kissinger, but he was routinely kept out of the loop on important foreign policy initiatives such as the secret opening to China and the negotiations with Hanoi to end the war in Vietnam.[53] The two- and four-power talks continued for another year, but with the Jarring mission at a standstill and with growing internal arguments on how to proceed, they were emptied of any substance and eventually fizzled out. As a triumphant Eban informed Rabin in February 1970, the Israeli tactic had worked pretty well thus far, and since the four-power talks were brought upon Israel despite its strong reservations, there was no need to press for the resumption of a dialogue with Jarring.[54]

EBAN'S LIFE UNDER MEIR WAS STRANGELY SIMILAR TO THAT OF ROGERS UNDER Nixon. Meir's succeeding Eshkol, and the political exigencies of operating within a national unity government, significantly reduced Eban's ability to influence policy issues both within his party and around the cabinet table. Flanked by Dayan and Begin, even Eshkol could not have afforded to give his foreign minister free rein after the 1967 war, as he had done in the previous eighteen months. But under Meir's reign, Eban's position became even more precarious. His shaky relations with Meir had been public knowledge for more than a decade, but he also had to deal with Dayan and Yisrael Galili, the minister without portfolio who enjoyed the support and respect of the prime minister more than any other member of the cabinet.[55] Together with Allon, Galili headed the Ahdut Ha'Avoda faction in the Labor Party, and his political and security orientation was far closer to Dayan and Meir's than to Eban and Sapir's. When Eban arrived in Israel in 1959 he had to wait seven long years before Meir finally vacated the foreign minister post. Now he had to serve under the woman who once boasted to a group of journalists that she had a "fantastic foreign minister . . . he lives in a fantasy land!"[56]

Meir appreciated Eban's rhetorical skills, but she did not respect him. Beyond her ingrained disdain of intellectuals, she detested Eban's inability to stand up to her and fight for his views. Her relationship with Eban stood in sharp contrast to her relationship with Dayan: despite her initial antagonism and suspicion of Dayan, Meir came to rely on his expertise, and she respected his straight talking, a virtue that she could not find in Eban.[57] Moshe Meisels, the political affairs editor of the daily *Maariv*, explained in a conversation at the American embassy in Tel Aviv that Meir's ascendance to power had cut the ground from the two main doves in the cabinet, Eban and Sapir. They had to tread very carefully, Meisels said, "lest they get a rap in the knuckles from Mrs. Meir for appearing too soft."[58]

Meir had many reasons to personally loathe Eban, going back as far as the diplomatic campaign of the 1956 Suez Crisis and as recent as his public backing of Yigal Allon for the premiership following Eshkol's death.[59] Ironically, on the rare occasions when Eban did fight for himself, Meir backed down. One such incident involved Meir's decision to take away the responsibilities for information abroad (*hasbara*, or public diplomacy) from the Foreign Ministry and place them under an autonomous Ministry of Information, headed by her pal Yisrael Galili. Eban was outraged, and threatened to resign in protest. The work of political information abroad could not be separated from other aspects of diplomatic activity, he protested. Rather than branching it out and causing further fragmentation and bureaucratic infighting, he suggested a reorganization of this responsibility within the Foreign Ministry. It was not merely a territorial matter, Eban maintained, but a principled and a personal one. Quite rightly, he argued that had Galili been the foreign minister, Meir would not dream of taking these powers away from the Foreign Ministry. Eventually Meir backed down, and Galili remained minister without portfolio. Eban may have won this battle, but it only made his life more miserable under Meir's reign.[60]

But even Eban's woes under Meir paled in comparison to his relations with Yitzhak Rabin, perhaps his biggest political nemesis for the next two decades. The recently appointed ambassador in Washington could not stand Eban, his direct superior. He did not like Eban's style and demeanor, and accused the foreign minister of smirching him in the press through his clique of journalists, such as *Maariv*'s Yosef Harif and *Yedioth Ahronot*'s Arieh Tzimuki. (According to Moshe Bitan of the Foreign Ministry, whenever Eban encountered a difficult situation his first instinct was "to write something, a speech, a telegram. The main thing is to tell Tzimuki and Harif, even before he writes anything.") Like Meir, Rabin had little time for intellectuals and career diplomats, once commenting that Israel's foreign policy was too important to be left in the hands of the Foreign Ministry's professional diplomats. Yet unlike Meir, Dayan, or Peres, whose disdain of Eban was confined largely to the political realm, Rabin's antipathy for the foreign minister was almost visceral in its brutality.

Eban was far from the innocent recipient of Rabin's attacks, however. He didn't like Rabin's brash style and enjoyed mocking his limited vocabulary, once describing him as "the repelling pole of a magnet." A man of few words, Rabin succinctly described the foreign minister as "worthless."[61] Eban's chief gripe with Rabin was his basic "incomprehension of the ambassadorial role. He considered that the hierarchical principle on which he had relied in the army career was not applicable to the relations between an embassy and a foreign ministry. . . . Rabin clearly had leadership quality. Indeed, it was this attribute that prevented normal cooperation with me in a subordinate capacity."[62]

Devoid of savoir faire and unburdened by excessive familiarity with diplomatic protocols, Rabin had no problem sharing his views on Eban with many people, including Foreign Ministry officials. At a private meeting in Washington with Gideon Rafael, the director-general of the Foreign Ministry and one of Eban's closest friends for over two decades, Rabin launched into a typical tirade of abuse against the foreign minister. Rafael was astounded by the sheer malice of Rabin's words. "Rabin opens the conversation by criticizing stupid Eban, idiotic Eban," he noted of the meeting. "I call him to order and say that I could not speak to him like this. . . . There is a recurrent theme of blind hatred of Eban." Rafael pointed to the stark difference in personalities: "Rabin is explosive, he is impatient, righteous and decisive; Eban takes a deep breath and tackles the issues with intellectual discipline. . . . I demanded Rabin to stop these uninhibited attacks and to cultivate an atmosphere of trust. . . . In my opinion the man is seriously disturbed, suffers from insecurity, negative characteristics, unfriendliness, an almost chronic stress." Rafael also cited Moshe Raviv, Eban's political secretary, who said that Rabin "hates the foreign minister but stands back if he is reprimanded, he respects power." On some occasions even Meir felt that Rabin had crossed the line, and ordered him not to comment "directly or indirectly to the press, the radio or the television about the conflict with the foreign ministry, a matter which has already brought damage and shame to the country."[63]

Such hostile views of Rabin were countered by Moshe Bitan, the head of the American desk at the Foreign Ministry, whose blind admiration of Rabin was matched only by a pathological antipathy toward Eban and Raphael. Bitan acknowledged that Rabin was "really allergic to the foreign ministry, the minister [Eban] and the director-general [Rafael], and so his every argument becomes even more aggressive," but Bitan's diary is also littered with references to a narcissist and egocentric Eban who frequently twisted reality to suit his ego and his overoptimistic worldview. Bitan conceded that Eban was hardworking and a gifted orator, and perhaps he could have been an excellent foreign minister in an "unproblematic" country like the Netherlands or one of the Scandinavian countries, but he lacked the strong character and resilience needed to fight for himself in an embattled country like Israel. Bitan also accused the working of the Foreign Ministry under Eban as lacking systematic analysis and collective thinking, whereby policy making was dictated by semantic formulations and an anarchic deference to the UN rather than a rational calculation of the available options. Eban himself conceded that he suffered from "controlled impulsivity" and that he preferred to "leap rather than slouch" toward a decision; he had little patience for lengthy or large meetings and preferred to reach decisions quickly and efficiently. "Consulting with three people is preferable to consulting with four, and consulting with four is better than consulting with five," he said in an interview. Nevertheless, those who worked closest with him—such as Raviv, Shimoni, Eytan Bentsur, Mordechai Kidron, Arthur Lourie and, of course, Raphael—took pains to emphasize the collegial atmosphere in the office and Eban's methodical approach to foreign policy making.[64]

Beyond the clash in personalities and styles, at the heart of the Eban-Rabin rivalry was a struggle for power and influence. During her first visit to Washington as prime minister in 1969, Meir and Nixon agreed to bypass Eban and secretary of state Rogers by setting up a back channel via Rabin and Kissinger. The president's national security adviser—a professional back-channeler—admired Eban's eloquence and professionalism. "I have never encountered anyone who matched his command of the English language," he recalled in his voluminous memoirs. "Eban's eloquence—for those who had to negotiate with him—was allied with first class intelligence and fully professional grasp of diplomacy. . . . I was not always sure whether Eban's more matter-of-fact colleagues in Jerusalem appreciated his eloquence as much as I did."

Kissinger's impression of Rabin was altogether different: "Except for his intelligence and tenacity, he was an unlikely ambassador. Taciturn, shy, reflective, almost resentful of small talk, Rabin possessed few of the attributes commonly associated with diplomacy. . . . He hated ambiguity, which is the stuff of diplomacy. I grew extremely fond of him though he did little to encourage affection."[65] In his memoirs Rabin insisted that the idea to bypass Eban—and his American counterpart William Rogers—was Nixon's, and the inevitable result was the souring of relations between himself and Eban. "[If] that suggests a lack of confidence in Rogers by Nixon and in Eban by Golda that's hardly my fault, is it?" Rabin explained to Menachem Begin in December 1969. "The trouble is, I'm caught in the middle, and have to take the brunt of eban's umbrage." The Americas were, of course, aware of the Eban-Rabin rivalry, which sometimes manifested itself in Eban's insistence on excluding Rabin from his official talks with Kissinger. On one such occasion Harold Saunders of the National Security Council reminded Kissinger of "Rabin's sensitivity to being asked to wait outside while you talk with Eban since there is an active rivalry there."Kissinger knew very well that Eban carried little favor with Meir and he gradually became exhausted with his clever equivocations. Rabin made no secret of his back channel to Kissinger, and was not afraid to reprimand those who dared to bypass it. In March 1971 On his part, he scolded Simcha Dinitz, the director-general of the prime minister's office and one of Meir's golden boys, for arranging a meeting between Meir and a Kissinger envoy without informing him first. "Of course you can do as you wish on these issues," Rabin cabled Dinitz, "but don't kid yourself that we won't find out."[66]

On another occasion that month, Rabin wrote to Dinitz, in his typical blunt manner, of his and Kissinger's (code name Cardinal) irritation with Eban: "When I told Cardinal that Eban will arrive [in Washington] he asked, 'why is he coming just now.' I replied that it was arranged months ago. Cardinal was puzzled. . . . I added that the foreign minister wished to see him. Cardinal asked if the foreign minister knows about his conversation with me. I replied that I cable the prime minister via special mail and I presume that the foreign minister sees some of the cables. Cardinal grimaced. I want you to understand that there is some degree of mistrust by Cardinal in the foreign minister. He is not happy that [Eban] is part to the negotiations between him and me. Please bear in mind that the foreign minister is a terrible gossipmonger." The following year, after a sensitive meeting with Sisco in October 1972, Rabin wrote to Dinitz: "I ask again in every possible way not to transmit Sisco's report to the foreign ministry and the foreign minister." A couple of weeks later, after Rabin updated Eban on his latest conversation with Kissinger, he found the story in the pages of the Washington Star. Kissinger angrily demanded from Rabin "clarifications" and threatened to sever the backchannel as it became clear that Eban was the source of the story.[67] On another occasion Shlomo Argov at the Israeli embassy in Washington. Kissinger "actually yawned" when Eban spoke and that it was clear that "in any case Kissinger underrates our dear minister."[68]

Eban did not hide his frustration with his exclusion from the inner circle of policy making, but his options were limited and he gradually became foreign minister by title only. He continued to meet with Jarring, make policy statements, and make his views heard around the government table, but outmaneuvering Meir, Dayan, Allon, and Galili was an impossible task, certainly for someone like Eban. He acknowledged that he did not agree with every policy adopted by the government, but he dismissed suggestions that he should resign in protest. He refused to accept the common wisdom about his "alienness" in the party, blaming the media for inflating this image, though he conceded that "there are alien phenomena in the party. There are certainly many differences in background. There are certainly not many cycles in the party whose ideational and temperamental origins are similar to mine. First of all, unfortunately, the academic public is insufficiently represented. There is also a lot more representation of Eastern European Jewry than that of Western Europe." As far as Israel's attitude to the Jarring talks and the broader question of peace were concerned, Eban cited the political exigencies of maintaining a national unity government with Begin's Gahal party as the main reason for the Israeli inability to make substantive progress: the ruling Labor Party was tied down by too many voices and ideas around the coalition table, and was too weary of breaking the delicate balance in government. "I assume that in a different composition we would have achieved a freedom of expression at an earlier point," he conceded in an interview, "and then we could have minimized the potential for collision with public opinion abroad." It was simply too hard to run a government when foreign policy formulations had to satisfy those who advocated Israeli withdrawal from the West Bank as well as those who demanded the exact opposite.[69] But even the withdrawal of Gahal from the national unity government in August 1970 did not lead to a more moderate policy, and Eban's position at the cabinet table remained precarious. He could rarely muster a majority against the hard line led by Meir, Dayan, and Galili, and even in his natural area of operations, that of U.S.-Israeli relations, he was routinely bypassed by the Rabin-Kissinger back channel.

In November 1971 Eban decided to fire Rabin—in one of the most acerbic and poignant letters he had ever composed. The last straw for him was a series of cables by Rabin in which he demanded in an undiplomatic language that Yoseph Tekoah, the ambassador to the UN, not be allowed to deal with American Jewry without his prior approval, and that David Rivlin be removed from his post as consul general in New York. Having consulted with Meir, Sapir, Allon, and Galili, and after reviewing the many cables received from Rabin, Eban wrote to him that it was evident that despite repeated warnings he continued to be dismissive of the foreign minister and other Foreign Ministry officials, and that the "psychological conclusions were worrying. From the many occurrences it is clear that the fabric of your social and personal relationships is damaged." Eban also criticized Rabin for displaying hostility toward U.S. congressional Democrats and for failing to cultivate a bipartisan and trustworthy relationship with all segments of American policy. "You continue to spread negative publicity about the government, the foreign minister, the representatives at the United Nations and others," Eban concluded. "Accordingly I announced that I rescind my recommendation to extend your tenure in Washington by a year, and that in my opinion your tenure as ambassador in Washington should be shortened. . . . There are colleagues in the foreign ministry whose judgment I appreciate, especially those working in the area of U.S.-Israeli relations, who feel that I cannot accept your attitude and behavior. . . . I see it fit to inform you that it is my intention to recommend the government another candidate for the embassy in Washington, for I cannot see any way of working with you since you have no intention to work with me in a civilized and proper manner."[70] But Rabin was not fired, and his tenure was not cut short. Despite his many shortcomings, he was admired by his American interlocutors for his military expertise and sharp analytical mind, and Meir certainly did not want a domestic crisis over the firing of the ambassador in Washington by her foreign minister.

Eban did not resign in protest over his shrinking influence around the cabinet table. He simply plowed on and kept praising the mystique of peace, though his calls fell on deaf ears. On February 8, 1970, Eban proposed a unilateral Israeli call to a cease-fire with Egypt for a limited period, backed by an open appeal to enter peace negotiations. Supported by Sapir and other doves, he claimed that Israel had nothing to lose by launching this "peace offensive": given Israel's overwhelming military superiority Nasser was unlikely to make the first step toward a settlement; at best, the proposal could edge the parties toward ending the War of Attrition; at worst, Nasser would be criticized for rejecting Israel's call for negotiations. But Meir would have none of it, as Eban recalled in his memoirs; she "wanted to give expression to the bitterness that had accumulated in her heart toward me." Meir denounced Eban's proposal as a sign of weakness and a contradiction of Israel's stated policy. Shocked and humbled by her response, Eban asked to withdraw his proposal, but Meir insisted on putting it for a vote so she could formally raise her hand against it. As she anticipated, the proposal was duly defeated, with only the members of Mapai supporting Eban's rescinded proposal, while Eban himself chose to abstain in protest over the absurdity of the procedure. There seemed to be no reason for Meir's insistence other than the sheer humiliation of her foreign minister. "The episode highlighted the centrality of personal rancor in the general system of her thought and emotion," Eban later recounted. Though he rarely discussed politics at home, he simply couldn't mask his long and turbulent relationship with Meir. One day his daughter Gila came home from school carrying a ceramic dish engraved with the ancient symbol of a blue eye, "to protect you from Golda's evil eye, Daddy!"[71]

During that fateful meeting with President Johnson in the yellow Oval Office on the eve of the June 1967 War, May 26, 1967. "I felt the weight of history in the room," Eban later recalled.

Consulting with Gideon Rafael, Israel's representative to the UN, during the fifth emergency session of the UN General Assembly, June 19, 1967. Golda Meir is behind Eban.

Above, touring the Golan Heights, shortly after the June 1967 war; Chief of Staff Yitzhak Rabin to his left

Left, with Suzy in the Golan Heights after the June 1967 war. He told his colleagues: "If someone proposed to sow, plough and settle in the Golan Heights, I will vote for it. If someone proposed that we declare that the Golan Heights are from this day part of the State of Israel, I will vote against it, because the declaration does not help or advance anything, and it is not necessary for the act itself."

A cartoon in the Israeli daily *Haaretz* from October 9, 1968, portraying Eban's sisyphean efforts at the UN General Assembly to defend Israel's position in the aftermath of the June 1967 war

With President Richard Nixon at the White House, March 1969

With Israel's Prime Minister Golda Meir and UN Mediator Gunnar Jarring in Jerusalem, January 1971. Eban worried that the replacement of Jarring by a more vigorous and talented mediator might bring Israel more harm than good.

At a press conference in Jerusalem with Meir and Deputy Prime Minister Yigal Allon, January 1973. Eban said of Meir that she chose to use only two hundred words, although her vocabulary extended to five hundred.

At a press conference in Tel Aviv during the Yom Kippur War, October 1973. Eban was routinely bypassed by Meir and Simcha Dinitz, the ambassador in Washington. "The foreign minister calls from New York all the time and asks to know the situation. Please instruct urgently what to tell him and what part of the picture to share with him," Dinitz asked Meir.

With U.S. Secretary of State Henry Kissinger and Israel's Defense Minister Moshe Dayan in Jerusalem, January 1974. Three months later Eban was ousted from the new government led by Rabin.

On the David Frost Show, October 1976

The Ebans in their living room in a shoot for *Monitin* magazine, 1979. True to his aristocratic image, Eban is portrayed as an English butler.

With Rabin, perhaps his greatest nemesis, in the Knesset, February 1983. Their rivalry began in 1968 when Rabin was appointed ambassador to Washington while Eban was foreign minister, and lasted for a generation. Eban described Rabin as "the repelling pole of a magnet," while Rabin described Eban as "stupid," "idiotic," and "worthless."

Eban during his brief spell as Knesset Speaker, September 1984. "Every time I open my mouth they expect me to tell a joke," he complained about his colleagues.

As Chairman of the Knesset Foreign Affairs and Defense Committee with Prime Minister Shimon Peres at his office, March 1986. Eban felt that Peres helped to end his political career, describing him later as "a medieval pope who believed himself infallible," and "strident to the point of vulgarity."

In the aftermath of Eban's dramatic ousting from his party in the 1988 primary election, a cartoon in the Israeli daily *Yediot Ahronot* depicted the party's elder statesman making room for a new generation of Labor politicians. June 16, 1988.

The Ebans in New York, 1989, where they spent most of their time following Eban's exile from Israeli politics

The dissonance between the “aristocratic” Eban and the symbols of the “typical” Israeli—a prickly sabra plant and a tembel hat. This iconic picture appeared on the cover of *The Israelis,* a book by the Israeli photographer Micha Kirshner, in 1997.

XV

Against the National Style

THE WAR OF ATTRITION ALONG THE SUEZ CANAL CONTINUED TO ESCALATE in the early months of 1970. Casualties were mounting on both sides as the Israeli Air Force pounded targets deep inside Egypt while Egyptian artillery barraged Israeli outposts along the canal. By May there were more than ten thousand Soviet personnel in Egypt, and Soviet pilots were flying Egyptian planes. Against this spiraling escalation the United States undertook a new initiative to stabilize the situation before an Israeli–Soviet military confrontation led to a direct superpower confrontation in the Middle East.[1] On June 19, Secretary of State William Rogers presented the American plan, which called for a ninety-day cease-fire, a thirty-mile standstill zone on either side of the canal, and a resumption of the talks under Jarring based on Resolution 242. On July 23, Egypt accepted the plan, and Israel did the same eight days later following intense deliberations and a personal pledge by U.S. president Richard Nixon to Golda Meir that there would be no American pressure on Israel to withdraw against its will. The immediate cost of this decision was the departure of the Gahal party from the national unity government, with its leader, Menachem Begin, comparing Israel's fate following the acceptance of the plan to that of Czechoslovakia in 1938.[2]

The cease-fire went into effect on August 7, but it was violated almost immediately by the Egyptian movement of antiaircraft missiles into the standstill zone. Not wishing to restart the war, the Israeli cabinet sided with Eban's call for restraint and against Moshe Dayan's demand for military retribution. But, taking Israel Galili's suggestion that something had to be done nonetheless, on September 3 the Israeli government announced its refusal to return to the Jarring talks, which had just resumed, until the full observance of the cease-fire was assured and Egypt withdrew its batteries from the standstill zone.[3]

Meanwhile, an emerging crisis in Jordan threatened to destabilize the region even further. On September 6 members of the Popular Front for the Liberation of Palestine hijacked four commercial airplanes, three of which were flown into Jordan while the fourth was redirected to the Cairo airport, where it was destroyed on the runway once all the passengers had disembarked. The ensuing emergency evolved into a bloody civil war between the Jordanian Army and armed Palestinian guerrillas, and a Syrian intervention in Jordan that nearly drew Israeli forces into battle in aid of Jordan's King Hussein. Constantly hovering above the crisis was the prospect of a superpower confrontation to protect their respective interests in the region; as Secretary of State Henry Kissinger warned Nixon early on in the crisis, "It looks like the Soviets are pushing the Syrians and the Syrians are pushing the Palestinians. The Palestinians don't need much pushing."[4] By September 23 the Jordanian army finally managed to regain control of the country and repel the invading Syrian forces; the Jordanian Crisis was over, and the political landscape in the region changed dramatically. The Palestinian rebellion was quashed and the Syrians (and their Soviet backers) were defeated. Israel emerged from the crisis as a valuable strategic asset to the United States, the immediate result of which was a presidential and congressional pledge to ensure Israel's qualitative military superiority vis-à-vis the Arabs. In Washington, Ambassador Yitzhak Rabin's military experience and sharp analytical mind made him a valuable asset to American intelligence during the crisis, which further strengthened his position as the key foreign policy link to Jerusalem at Eban's expense.[5]

Only days after the ending of the Jordanian Crisis, President Gamal Abdel Nasser of Egypt died of a heart attack and was succeeded by his deputy, Anwar Sadat, whose tepid demeanor was in almost direct opposition to Nasser's vigor. U.S. Undersecretary of State Elliot Richardson estimated that Sadat wouldn't last more than four to six months, while Kissinger believed that he was little more than an interim figure. Eban publicly described Sadat as an example of "anti-charisma." The restoration of calm in Jordan, the improvement of relations with Washington, and now the arrival of a seemingly weak Egyptian leader to the scene all led to certain Israeli complacency, if not altogether arrogance, which soon caught on with the Americans. Three years after the Six-Day War, Israel was still in control of all the territories and was stronger than it had ever been in terms of both sheer military power and its relations with Washington. Dayan's brazen remark immediately after the war—that if the Arabs wanted to change the situation they could pick up the phone and get in touch—now became the de facto Israeli policy.[6] According to U.S. Ambassador Charles Yost at the UN, Jarring was left "fed up, frustrated [and] bitter" by the ongoing deadlock and blamed the situation on the Israelis, who made him "eat dirt." Israel was under no tremendous pressure from the White House to talk to Jarring. It did receive, however, a delivery of twenty A-4E Skyhawk and twelve F-4 Phantom jets, as well as the promise of a further two hundred M-60 tanks, and 175-millimeter long-range artillery and electronic systems, all designed to ensure Israel's military edge over its neighbors.[7]

In December 1970, having received reassurances from the White House, and weeks before Jarring was due to publish a report on his failed mission, Meir announced that Israel agreed to resume the talks. This was nothing more than a blatant tactic to keep Jarring in his comatose state, since there had been no discernible change in the Israeli position other than semantic gestures. As Gideon Rafael explained to Yosef Tekoah at the United Nations earlier in the year, "I agree that we currently have no use for Jarring but let's not forget that our shrewd use of this instrument has given us mileage for two years. We must not break this tool ourselves or bring it to submit a final report which could serve our adversaries later on. Therefore our policy towards Jarring must remain as before: Handle With Care."[8] After a sixteen-month hiatus, on January 5, 1971, Jarring returned to the region to resume his mission. In Jerusalem he received from Meir and Eban a lengthy document on "the essentials of peace" that did not offer any substantive changes in the Israeli position, while in Cairo he heard once again that complete Israeli withdrawal must come before peace.

Frustrated by the futile shuttling, the lack of progress, and the imminent failure of his mission before it had even left the ground, Jarring made a surprise move to regain the initiative, a final "take it or leave it" offer to the parties. On February 8, without prior consultation or notification, Jarring presented his own peace initiative. Since the key obstacle seemed to be the refusal of both parties to take the first step—namely, an Israeli commitment to withdraw and an Egyptian commitment to peace—Jarring asked both parties to make "parallel and simultaneous" commitments. Israel was asked to withdraw its forces from Egyptian territory to the international border that existed before the June 4, 1967, lines, subject to necessary security adjustments and in exchange for freedom of passage in the Suez Canal. Egypt was asked to enter into a peace agreement with Israel and to undertake the commitments explicit in Resolution 242, including an end to the state of war; mutual recognition of sovereignty and political independence; and respect for each side's right to live in peace within recognized and secure borders.[9]

The Israeli government was furious with Jarring's audacious move. Not only had he failed to consult with the parties before publishing his proposal, but his interpretation of Resolution 242 concerning Israeli withdrawal from "the" rather than "some" of the territories made him a dishonest broker; his mandate was to facilitate talks between the parties, not to offer his own interpretation of Resolution 242. Egypt found no such principled objections to Jarring's initiative. On February 15 it responded favorably to the proposal, announcing that it would enter into a peace agreement with Israel if the latter publicly committed to fully implementing Resolution 242.[10] Egypt's positive response to Jarring followed another surprising offer from Sadat. On February 4, four days before Jarring presented his own initiative, the Egyptian president announced before the People's Assembly his willingness to enter negotiations with Israel over an interim settlement. In exchange for a limited Israeli withdrawal of up to forty kilometers east of the Suez Canal, Egypt would open the canal to free shipping. The evacuated Israeli zone would be demilitarized, except for a token Egyptian police presence. Sadat viewed the limited Israeli withdrawal as the first in a process that would eventually lead to a complete Israeli withdrawal to the June 4, 1967 lines. He also offered an unconditional extension of the cease-fire by thirty days with future cease-fires conditional on Israeli commitments to withdraw from Sinai. Sadat did not offer peace or even the normalization of relations with Israel, but taken together with the encouraging reply to Jarring's initiative eleven days later, it was hard to ignore the change in the Egyptian tone. In several speeches that year Sadat declared 1971 to be "the year of decision"—whether the region would be heading toward war or peace. For the first time since the beginning of the conflict, Egypt had publicly and formally agreed to enter into negotiations with Israel over substantive issues that might, over time, lead to a full peace settlement.[11]

The Israeli government took a dim view of Sadat's overtures. On February 9 Meir told the Knesset that an Israeli withdrawal could only come about in the context of a peace settlement with Egypt. Two days later Eban expressed his own doubts about the recent initiatives by Jarring and Sadat. Speaking before the Central Committee of the Labor Party, the foreign minister said that for the negotiations to be conducive, the parties should not be constrained by preemptive definitions from which they might want to deviate during negotiations. Regarding Jarring's proposal, Eban reiterated the position he had held since November 1967—the UN mediator was not the key to peace but it was nevertheless important to keep his mission alive to deflect international pressure. Keeping the mission alive for three years was "an achievement," Eban continued, even if the Jarring framework was "merely a tool, a tool which could not open the gate without the mutual desire of the sides to reach peace."[12]

After a protracted debate between the doves and the hawks around the cabinet table, on February 26 the government finally delivered its response to Jarring's initiative and Egypt's reply to it. Eban wanted an Israeli commitment to withdraw its armed forces to "secure, recognized and agreed borders, to be determined in a peace treaty." Galili objected to this vague phrase and demanded an explicit reference to Israel's refusal to withdraw to the June 4, 1967 lines. Eban protested this inclusion, arguing that it would kill any chance of negotiation, but he was duly defeated by a coalition of Meir, Galili, and Dayan, as well as Rabin, who had been invited by Meir to take part in the meeting. The official Israeli response thus said that while the government viewed "favorably" the Egyptian readiness to enter into a peace agreement, Israel insisted that it would not withdraw to the June 4, 1967 boundaries. As Eban predicted, Sadat totally rejected the Israeli message, although as Eban also added that had Sadat been fully committed to a settlement the wording of the Israeli reply to Jarring should not have been a deal-breaker. In any case, this was the death knell of the Jarring mission. The resolute Israeli response convinced Jarring that the deadlock would never be broken until Israel modified its position on borders, and on March 25 he returned to his ambassadorial post in Moscow. The following day Meir told the Knesset that peace could only be established through direct negotiations between the parties and without preconditions—before adding Israel's own precondition concerning its refusal to withdraw to the June 4, 1967 lines.[13]

Although Jarring made his services available to the parties for another year, his mission never officially resumed. After more than three years on the Jarring rollercoaster, the Middle East entered a more sedate period of diplomatic activity. The relative calm along the Suez Canal and the overwhelming military superiority against the Arabs gave the Israeli government little reason to change the status quo by making tough decisions about war and peace. Even during the height of Jarring's mission Meir refused to engage with such questions. "What is the pressure to decide right now?" the prime minister asked her party in May 1970. "I don't want to. If I knew that it would bring peace a day or an hour sooner I would say, we have no choice. Now? Why? What is it on the horizon that forces us to decide now among ourselves?" Almost exactly a year later, after the death of the Jarring mission, Meir explained Israel's refusal to rush into Jarring's arms and offer concessions. There was one Jewish flaw, she told her party: memory. "And the world should understand that . . . we remember. We remember not what happened hundreds and thousands of years ago, but in our lifetime, and not just in our generation, but in the second generation too. We remember the 1930s, Hitler's first years." She then went on to deliver a stern warning to Sadat: "We have a cease-fire. As far as we're concerned—may it continue. But if not—there is no fear. There is total confidence. I would really like to say, if I could, to Sadat and his friends in Egypt and the Arab countries: You shouldn't, you really shouldn't. . . . " Dayan was equally vigorous. "I know there is Resolution 242, and there is a Rogers Plan and there is a Dayan Plan and an Allon Plan and there will be many more plans," he said. "But there is one thing much bigger and stronger than all of these, and it is the return of the Jewish people to its homeland. The IDF is sitting on the River Jordan!"[14]

Propelled by such hubris and obduracy, Israel fiercely opposed the return of Jarring to the region. Mordechai Gazit, who succeeded Gideon Rafael as director-general of the Foreign Ministry, wrote to Eban in December 1971 that since Jarring "has shown very little diplomatic skill (and this is an understatement) . . . [if] this man returns to action we will soon have to deal with a mediocre diplomat who lacks imagination . . . my proposed solution for the future is to fight Jarring every step of the way (by way of 'preventative diplomacy'). Under no circumstances should we maintain passivity and an attitude of trust Jarring.'" The Americans also gave up on Jarring, telling Rabin in Washington that the best way forward was through an interim agreement and that it was "desirable" that the Jarring mission was not renewed.[15] A few weeks later Meir explained her views on Jarring to Gazit: He "will not bring us peace. Knowing that, we are not expecting miracles from him and so we should not encourage him or give the impression that we encourage him." At the same time, Meir warned, it was important not to give Jarring a reason to blame Israel for his failure. "We should accept his invitations, converse with him politely but without discussing the essence or substance of things. This is the line and there is nothing else to add to it."[16]

In the summer of 1972 Israel was presented with an unexpected opportunity to not only terminate the Jarring mission once and for all but to bring Jarring to retract his February 1971 document *and* claim the moral high ground over the UN mediator in the process. In early May, under the headline "Sensational Revelation," one of Sweden's largest papers, the *Aftenbladet*, disclosed that from 1926 to 1939 Jarring was an active member of Sweden's National Unity Party, and that in 1936, at the age of twenty-nine, he was the party's parliamentary candidate. He left the party three years later to enter the Swedish Foreign Ministry. Jarring's party opposed Jewish emigration to Sweden and later forged strong links with the Nazis. In response to these reports, a UN spokesman dismissed the charges as "trivial"; Jarring had merely joined the youth organization of the Conservative Party in 1926 "when it was considered respectable," and he left it in 1937, which may have been before or after the party "veered far right."[17] Though Jarring did not respond publicly to these allegations, sources close to him accused Israeli reporters at the United Nations of "harping on the issue" for the sole purpose of discrediting Jarring and forcing him to resign.[18]

Two weeks later, on May 30, 1972, Eban told foreign reporters in Jerusalem that Israel "has made no independent investigation of reports that United Nations peace emissary Dr. Gunnar Jarring belonged to a Nazi-affiliated party in Sweden in the 1930s."[19] But Eban was lying. The political and public significance of this story was potentially earth-shattering. Exposing Jarring as having former links to the Nazi Party could provide Israel the perfect excuse to denounce the mediator as an anti-Semite and discredit his entire mission. The Foreign Ministry immediately opened an investigation into the matter, and informed the ambassador in Stockholm that there were ongoing preliminary discussions about how to manage the affair with its "historical, personal, political and tactical considerations." The ambassador was ordered to gather "maximum information. At this stage we do not want your act of probing and investigating to be made public, however this restriction does not prevent a thorough collection of all the material that can be gathered." This included, among other items, "any other information which could be used to complete the 'case.' Please consider the matter a top priority."[20]

Even the Mossad was brought in to investigate Jarring's past; on June 19 David Kimche, its deputy director, submitted an interim report to the Foreign Ministry noting that in the 1930s Jarring articulated his racist views in the party's publication. The merchants of the Kashmir city of Srinagar, Jarring wrote, "are said to belong to the most devious and deceiving race. In the east it is known that they surpass the Jews, the Armenians and the Greeks, who habitually cheat their neighbors." Nevertheless, Jarring continued, there still lived in Kashmir "better people, who are true Arian, who personify the qualities of the Arian race to such an extent that they could serve as specimen in every 'race institute' which is founded by our southerly neighbours [Nazi Germany]." In 1936, when Jarring presented his candidacy to the Swedish parliament, his party—which ideologically identified with Vidkun Quisling's Norwegian pro-Nazi party—demanded that Sweden withdraw from the League of Nations and established a Nordic bloc based on the Arian race in order to prevent the arrival of "foreign elements" and the "Jewish danger" into Sweden. Jarring was also tasked by his party to compile a register of all Jewish students in Swedish universities. It did seem, however, that Jarring decided to leave the party when it sought to establish more formal links with the German Nazi Party.[21]

On July 10 Yosef Tekoah, the Israeli ambassador to the UN, suggested to Eban that a decision needed to be made on how to use the information before Jarring's arrival in New York in early August to meet with the parties. If Israel announced that for obvious historical and moral reasons Jarring could no longer be trusted and that his 1971 document should be rescinded, some would no doubt accuse Israel of tactical maneuvering, but even Israel's enemies would find it hard to dismiss its sensitivity on this issue.[22] Four days later Eban resolved the issue: Jarring's forthcoming visit to New York was unlikely to result in a breakthrough as long as he continued to use his February 1971 proposal as the frame of reference for negotiations. The Americans and the Soviets were also tired of his mission. Since nothing dramatic was going to happen in New York, Eban concluded that it would not be necessary to blow up the talks over Jarring's past, although he added that he "would not regret it" if Israel's independent investigation came up with decisive findings that would call for such action. Eban added that it was equally important to consider the options following Jarring's departure, as the replacement of the "dwindled and devoid of prestige" Jarring by a more vigorous and talented mediator might bring Israel more harm than good. After all, Eban said, Israel "will not benefit from these mediations and the more the UN activity is feeble and monotonous the better."[23]

Eban's protest against the prevailing mystique of security in Israeli society and the absence of a parallel mystique of peace had not diminished in the aftermath of the Jarring mission; if anything, he became more disillusioned about some of his colleagues' attitudes toward peace. Perhaps peace was distant and negotiations were equally remote, he told the Labor Party secretariat in November 1972, but he was saddened to see that the party's response to that reality was one of relief rather than disappointment. For Eban, the Labor Party's indifference toward peace was only a symptom of society, of the Israeli national style; Eban lamented that it was too hyperbolic, too indignant, too vulgar, and insufficiently inattentive to the suffering of others. He told a Haifa University audience in March 1973 that, in essence, the Israeli national character lacked humanity. The national style was nothing less than "a defensive attitude which would be suitable for a weak country subjected to perils and threats. . . . The question that is now asked everywhere concerning Israel is not about its courage and resourcefulness, which are everywhere taken for granted, but about its human quality." Eban was especially critical of his country's belligerent style, which seemed to have replaced tangible, visionary policy in recent years: "A strong nation does not have to shout or to beat drums in nervous agitation in order to make its voice heard. On the contrary; a confident and balanced national style is perfectly reconcilable with an alert security consciousness and a rational and firm political line." The challenge for Israel, Eban concluded, was how to put "the emphasis on freedom, tolerance, equality, social justice, spiritual and intellectual creativity, and human brotherhood, as the salient characteristics of a strong and confident Israeli society."[25]

The Labor Party was confronted with more prosaic challenges in the run-up to the general elections, scheduled for October 1973. For months there was mounting pressure to resolve the differences between the doves and the hawks in the party over the policy toward the occupied territories. On the one hand Dayan grew increasingly vocal in his demand to expand the settlements in the territories not just for security reasons, while Eban, Sapir, and other members of the Mapai faction continued to warn against the long-term consequences of such policies; Yitzhak Ben-Aharon and Arie Eliav maintained that what was west of the Green Line (the 1949 armistice lines, or borders that existed before June 4, 1967) was Israel, and to its east was Palestine. Meir concluded the debate with her trademark fatalism: as peace was not on the horizon, there was no urgency to resolve these internal differences. She received unexpected support from Eban, who maintained that the Labor Party was large enough to accommodate all those different views; after all, he said, that was the reason for the Oral Law of 1969.[26]

On June 17, 1973, Meir announced that she would continue to lead her party into the next general elections, scheduled for October that year. Dayan welcomed her decision but demanded that fundamental changes be made in the party's ticket. He composed a ten-point document that presented a new policy of creating facts on the ground in the occupied territories. These were not abstract principles but a plan of action: among other points, Dayan called for further urbanization and industrialization of East Jerusalem and beyond the Green Line; the establishment of an urban industrial center in the Golan Heights; the development of the town of Yamit in the Sinai Peninsula as a regional and urban center; the establishment of a deep-water seaport south of Gaza; the continued funding of existing settlements and the development of new ones; and the acquisition of lands in the occupied territories by companies and individuals.

In response, Sapir and Eban threatened to withdraw from the party's list for the general elections if such a document was forced on the party against their wishes.[27] Meir herself was reluctant to acquiesce to Dayan's demands, but fearing a split of the party and a possible coalition between the Rafi and Gahal parties before the general elections, she asked her trusted ally Galili to compose a compromise document that would appease Dayan and maintain the unity of the party. The Galili Document as it came to be known, set the party's policy on the territories for the next four years. Galili managed to meet most of Dayan's demands without spelling them out explicitly: future settlements were to be established according to government decisions, and that subject to government regulations there would be some scope for nongovernmental development of the settlements. It added that the government would purchase all land necessary for "settlement, development, housing and industrial purposes" in accordance with its policies. The Galili Document received an almost unanimous approval by the party members. But Eban viewed it as no more than an extension of the Allon Plan and the Oral Law: an agreeable compromise to find a common ground among the Labor Party ranks. He received the document while on an official visit to Peru, and was underwhelmed by its content: "Is that it? I can certainly live with it!" he told Galili. "But Dayan could have achieved all this without all the noise!" But other doves, such as Eliav, opposed the document and denounced it as a "strangulation of Zionism."[28]

However the prospect of a personal confrontation with the prime minister compelled the critics to toe the line. When the hands were raised, the vote showed 78–0 in support of the Galili Document. In a subsequent foreign press briefing Eban tried to dispel the confusion surrounding the document, claiming that even Eliav's views were not that far from his own. The document did not offer any departure from the party's stated policies on the territories and, Eban added, that this "should be evident to anyone who can read or write." Asked if all the leaders of the party shared his views on the document, he replied that those who could read and write shared his views, then succumbing to an irresistible dig at Dayan and his iconic black eyepatch, the result of a battle injury in Syria in 1941. "Different people may read the same thing differently," Eban added, "and it also depends on whether you read with one or two eyes."[29] In private however, Eban was furious. "What are you doing? This document will have terrible significance abroad!" he said to Sapir in September 1973. "[I]t allows for more settlements!" But Sapir reassured his ally that this was a watered-down document and that the alternative—a Dayan withdrawal to establish an independent list that would cost the Labor Party twelve to fifteen seats in the Knesset—would be far more disastrous.[30]

A month later, on October 4, 1973, Eban met with Kissinger in Washington. Kissinger, who recently had replaced William Rogers as secretary of state, asked Eban about the Galili Document: "Seriously, why was it necessary? The Arabs suffer from a frustration complex and they see the new document as a decision to see the present situation as permanent." Eban explained that the document did not mark a shift in the Israeli position, but Kissinger remained unconvinced: "It's possible to prove what you say with your great intellectual prowess. I'm prepared—with my even greater intellectual prowess—to accept your explanation. But the fact remains that the consequences for Israel's position will be negative."[31] Two days later, the Yom Kippur War broke out.

XVI

A Superfluous and Disgruntled Foreign Minister

THE ROOT CAUSE OF THE ISRAELI SURPRISE AT THE OUTBREAK OF THE YOM Kippur War was the national security doctrine that took hold shortly after the 1967 Six-Day War. It was based on a concept that Israel had sufficient preponderance to deter an Arab attack, and that even if an attack took place it would be defeated with lightning speed and at minimal cost which would further bolster Israel's strategic deterrence. In operational terms, Israeli intelligence was confident—even as late as two days before the war—that there was a low probability of war and that it would remain so until the Arabs improved their airpower capabilities and acquired more effective ground-to-air missiles, which, according to this concept, was unlikely to happen before 1975.[1] Despite the growing reports in the months preceding the war about the mobilization of Egyptian troops along the western bank of the Suez Canal, both Israelis and Americans seemed confident that the Arabs were not foolish enough to start another war.

In May 1973 the U.S. National Security Council (NSC) submitted to Henry Kissinger a report about Egyptian moves that could be interpreted as "a pattern of action that could be preparation for hostilities against Israel." These actions included the mobilization of Soviet surface-to-air SA-6 missiles, bombers, and jet fighters. Nevertheless, the report concluded that "whatever the Egyptian and Arab leaders intend at this stage, the pattern of their actions thus far does not provide the Arabs with a rational basis for an attack at an early date."[2] Kissinger, too, did not expect Sadat to go to war, telling Eban on May 12 that the Egyptian leader "shows no capacity for thinking moves ahead."[3] Even hours before the joint Egyptian-Syrian attack on Israel, American intelligence refused to question the Israeli assessment of the likelihood of war. William Quandt of the NSC reported to Brent Scowcroft, Kissinger's deputy, that the intelligence services "have continued to downplay the likelihood of an Arab attack on Israel and still have no signs that such action is imminent. They appear to favor the alternative explanation of a crisis in Arab-Soviet relations."[4]

Having rejected Anwar Sadat's and Gunnar Jarring's initiatives in 1971, the Israeli government chose to ignore two more signals that Sadat was eager to break the status quo. In July 1972 Sadat expelled more than ten thousand Soviet personnel from Egypt and returned some Soviet military equipment to Moscow in protest over the growing Soviet interference in domestic Egyptian affairs.[5] In taking this dramatic step Sadat hoped to make the United States take a more active role in Middle East diplomacy, not least by getting Israel to enter into negotiations with Egypt. But rather than seize the opportunity, the response in Jerusalem and Washington, DC, was a mixture of suspicion of Sadat's motives and satisfaction that Israel's current policy was working.[6] Following president Richard Nixon's landslide reelection victory in November 1972, Kissinger opened a back channel to Hafiz Ismail, Sadat's national security adviser. But with Kissinger busy nailing down the final details of a political settlement to end the Vietnam War, this channel took secondary precedence. Following the conclusion of the Paris Accords in January 1973, which ended the Vietnam War, Nixon and Kissinger turned to coaxing Israel into presenting a peace plan and entering a process of negotiations with Egypt. Meir, however, told them that Israel "never had it so good," and that it would be unwise to make such commitments before the general elections in October of that year.[7] All the borders were secure and quiet, new settlements were popping up in the West Bank and the Golan Heights, the political pressure on Israel to withdraw had gradually abated, and relations with the United States were stronger than ever; why risk all of that for an unwarranted process of negotiations that entailed more pitfalls than possibilities?

Sadat made no secret of his frustration with the Americans and Israelis, who did not seem to take his recent moves seriously. In an April 1973 interview in *Newsweek* he delivered his most poignant warning yet, that in the absence of a diplomatic breakthrough war was only matter of time: "Everyone has fallen asleep over the Mideast crisis. But they will soon wake up to the fact that Americans have left us no way out. . . . Everything in this country is now being mobilized in earnest for the resumption of the battle—which is now inevitable."[8]

Eban readily accepted the assessment of the military intelligence about the low probability of war with Egypt. Addressing the U.S. House of Representatives' Middle East Subcommittee the following month, he flatly dismissed Sadat's most recent threat: "There was nothing in Egyptian military disposition or general behavior to indicate Egypt intended to resume hostilities in the near future. The evidence was to the contrary; when one saw Egyptian soldiers in ragged uniforms playing cards near the Canal, it was difficult indeed to believe Sadat's rhetoric."[9] Eban's disparaging assessment was a shade paler than the boastful declarations of the generals: In July former Chief of Staff Yitzhak Rabin asserted that Israel's present defense lines were sufficient to frustrate the Arab armies, and that there was "no need to mobilize our forces whenever we hear Arab threats, or when the enemy concentrates his forces along the cease-fire lines." He even miscalculated, with an almost prophetic accuracy, the thrust of the Arab offensive that would soon surprise Israel: "The Arabs have little capacity for coordinating their military and political action. To this day they have not been able to make oil an effective political factor in their struggle against Israel." But even Rabin's gross misreading of the situation was no match for the sheer hubris of General Ariel Sharon, commander on the southern front, who declared in August: "The armies of the European countries are weaker than ours. Israel can conquer in a week the land from Khartoum to Baghdad and Algeria—but it's not necessary."[10]

During the summer of 1973 Sadat rebuilt his relations with Moscow, and the supply of Soviet weapons to Cairo resumed to such levels that Sadat boasted to Ismail Fahmi, his deputy foreign minister, that the Soviets were "drowning" him in new arms. He also coordinated his war plans with Syrian president Hafez al-Assad and King Faisal of Saudi Arabia. The offensive was set for Saturday, October 6, which fell on Yom Kippur—the most solemn day in the Jewish calendar, when all public services would be closed and many military posts undermanned to allow soldiers to return home to pray with their families. The Arab leaders agreed to use oil as an economic and political lever to bring American pressure on Israel to withdraw from the occupied territories. On September 22 Sadat informed Soviet premier Leonid Brezhnev of his decision to attack Israel and received his blessings. On October 4, Soviet diplomats and their dependents were evacuated from Cairo and Damascus. The following day, Ashraf Marwan, a Mossad agent and the son-in-law of the late

Egyptian president Gamal Abdel Nasser, warned Zvi Zamir, the head of Mossad, that Egypt and Syria would strike Israel on Yom Kippur, October 6. The Israeli government received the message at 2:45 a.m. Less than twelve hours before the outbreak of war, Israel finally woke up from its six years of exuberant immobilism.[11]

At exactly 2:05 p.m. Egyptian artillery began to barrage the undermanned Israeli posts along the east bank of the Suez Canal, while commando units crossed the canal. At the same time, the Syrians launched a massive military and air bombardment in the Golan Heights that lasted fifty minutes. Israeli forces were heavily outnumbered on both fronts: 8,500 Israeli infantrymen, 276 tanks, and 48 artillery guns faced 100,000 Egyptian infantrymen, 2,200 tanks, and 1,848 artillery guns in the Sinai, while on the northern front Israel's 5,000 infantrymen, 177 tanks, and 44 artillery guns faced a 45,000-strong Syrian army, 500 tanks, and 690 field guns. The Israeli Air Force, which six years earlier had pummeled the Egyptian and Syrian Air Forces before they even took to the sky, was outnumbered by three to one and had no answers for the new and deadly effective Soviet SA-6 surface-to-air missiles.[12]

Eban was forced to play only a modest role in the diplomatic activity during the war. Having had his wings clipped by the prime minister's office and the embassy in Washington for the past four and a half years, this was neither surprising nor avoidable. It is clearly reflected in Eban's own writings: in his expanded second autobiography, he devoted more than one hundred pages to the diplomatic activities that preceded and followed the Six-Day War; he dedicated just a third of that to the Yom Kippur War, which lasted three times longer. These three weeks in October 1973 encapsulated the essence of Eban's five years as foreign minister under Meir. As the Israeli journalist Matti Golan noted in his explosive book on the war, "routinely, and particularly during emergencies, Eban was the last person the prime minister would turn to. She made it a custom, enforced on her own staff as well as personnel in the Washington embassy, that Eban was the last person to be informed of anything important." It is no surprise, Golan concluded, that during the war Eban was a "superfluous and disgruntled foreign minister."[13]

When the war broke out, Eban was in New York, heading the Israeli delegation at the annual session of the UN General Assembly. Rabin's departure from the Washington embassy earlier in the year would have been a welcome relief for Eban had Rabin not been replaced by Simcha Dinitz, the former director-general of the prime minister's office and one of Meir's most trusted confidants. The new Washington ambassador continued to serve as the main source of information and consultation between Kissinger and Meir. During the war scores of telegrams between Dinitz and Mordechai Gazit, the new director-general of the prime minister's office, were exchanged without the knowledge of the foreign minister. On the second day of the war Gazit instructed Dinitz that any "delicate" discussions with Kissinger should be sent to the prime minister's eyes only. Two days later Dinitz asked Gazit for clarifications, noting that "the foreign minister calls from New York all the time and asks to know the situation. Please instruct urgently what to tell him and what part of the picture to share with him."[14] Having already endured four years of this charade, but oblivious to its true extent, Eban threatened to resign. "Go ahead," Meir replied curtly. But Eban stayed at his post.[15]

Twenty-four hours before the outbreak of the war, Eban was instructed by Meir to cancel his scheduled meeting with Kissinger and instead transmit to him the latest Israeli appraisal of the situation in writing—even though they were both in New York. In his autobiography Eban rationalized the instruction from Jerusalem as a reasonable desire not to trouble Kissinger, "a busy man whose close friends have never praised him for monumental patience" with another meeting. In private conversations at the time however, he was fuming about the request to cancel the meeting with Kissinger, describing it as a move "to prevent me from taking a step which may have emphasized my position too much." It was "the bitter continuation" of the prime minister's dislike of him, he added. He was so upset that he decided to skip the Kol Nidrei prayer at the synagogue on the eve of Yom Kippur. He shut the curtains in his suite at the Plaza Hotel, took the phone off the hook, and settled in for the night.[16]

Eban was awakened by a loud knock on the door at 6:20 a.m. (1:20 p.m. in Jerusalem). His aide, Eytan Bentsur, delivered a telegram from Jerusalem signed by Galili, and Eban sat on the sofa in his pajamas to read it: "According to authentic intelligence sources the Egyptians and Syrians will launch a coordinated attack this evening."[17] At 8:25 a.m. Eban telephoned Kissinger, who had already spoken to the Soviet ambassador Anatoly Dobrynin (twice), the Egyptian foreign minister Muhammad al-Zayat (three times), and Mordechai Shalev at the Israeli embassy in Washington (Dinitz was in Israel on October 6 to mourn the death of his father). Kissinger updated Eban on his efforts thus far. Twenty-five minutes later Eban telephoned Kissinger again with the message that the Syrians had launched an artillery attack on the Golan Heights. Kissinger cited an Egyptian report claiming that Israel fired first with a naval attack near some oil fields. Eban doubted its authenticity, and Kissinger concurred: "I don't believe myself that you would start a general war with a naval attack in one place, but you always do surprising things." Speaking to Dobrynin, Kissinger said that the Egyptian claims were "baloney."[18]

Heavy losses on both fronts in the first days of the fighting prompted Israel to launch a two-pronged campaign in Washington: diplomatically, Eban asked Kissinger to delay any moves in the UN Security Council toward a cease-fire resolution before Israel had a chance to recapture the territory it had already lost, while militarily, Dinitz urged Kissinger to supply Israel with more arms to help turn the tide on the battlefield. Throughout these crucial days Dinitz kept Eban—his direct superior—in the dark about his talks with Kissinger over the airlift of arms to Israel. Beyond the need to exclude Eban from such sensitive matters, per Meir's orders, Dinitz also suffered from a mild infatuation with the secretary of state and refused to "share" him with anyone else. According to one account, this was a one-way relationship that Kissinger had groomed from the outset: "Kissinger, supreme artist of personal diplomacy, sensed what Dinitz was like from the moment he arrived in Washington. He started massaging his ego. Dinitz surrendered completely to Kissinger's solicitations and personal charm. He was flattered that the powerful, brilliant Kissinger called him frequently, consulted him, and invited him to official and private social events. Without desiring it, without even being conscious of it, Dinitz turned into a Kissinger man."[19]

Kissinger reassured Eban that he would call a meeting of the UN Security Council to preempt the Soviets from doing so, and that he would not push for a cease-fire quite yet. "We will not indicate today," he told Eban on the second day of the war, "whether we will table a resolution or what it will be. Don't want to get too much . . . generated." Eban was scheduled to address both the General Assembly and the Security Council the following day, October 8. Determined to prevent any diplomatic movement at the early stages of the war, both men agreed that delaying tactics were called for. "We will count on your eloquence . . . and in this case wouldn't mind if you sacrificed eloquence to length," Kissinger told Eban. "Oh yes, I agree it often happens in reverse relation," Eban replied.[20] He opened his address at the General Assembly with a typical appeal to international consciousness: "There is not a single man or woman in this hall or outside it who does not know, in the depths of his heart, that Egypt and Syria have dealt a heavy and sudden blow to the most cherished of human causes—the cause of international peace." He went on to describe the joint Egyptian-Syrian "premeditated and unprovoked assault" as an act that "will surely rank in future history as one of the basest and most odious acts for which Governments have ever been responsible." After chronicling the record of Arab violations of Resolution 242 in the run-up to the war, Eban turned to trounce the Egyptian claim that Israel had started the war:

> There is also the evidence of normal common sense. Across the world, people must be asking themselves this question: How idiotic would a man have to be to believe that on a day when there were no communications, no activity, no radio, no ability to summon reserves, when the vast majority of our soldiers were in their homes or synagogues, when even forward posts were manned at minimal level—that precisely on that day Israel would launch a war, on the day holiest to all those who cherish Jewish solidarities, in order to invite thousands of Egyptian and Syrian tanks to attack across a relatively undefended and totally quiescent line?[21]

ON OCTOBER 12, AFTER FOUR DAYS OF FRUITLESS DISCUSSIONS, THE UN SECURITY Council ended its deliberations and agreed to reconvene at an unspecified date after further consultations.[22] Ten more days would pass before a joint Soviet-American resolution ended the fighting. The atmosphere in New York in that period was far from tranquil, but it was markedly better than the wall-to-wall condemnation of Israel in 1956 or the high drama of 1967—both of which Eban had been a central player in. This time he struggled to keep abreast of developments on the ground and of the American position, being at the mercy of Meir and Dinitz for whatever information they chose to share with him.

There was greater urgency on the military front. Heavy losses on the battlefield made Israel desperate for new arms, but there was little movement in Washington. On Tuesday, October 9, Kissinger told Dinitz that the American strategy "was to give you until Wednesday evening, by which time I thought the whole Egyptian army would be wrecked." In Jerusalem that morning, Meir made a dramatic decision. After consulting with Dayan, Allon, Galili, Chief of Staff David Elazar and General Ahron Yariv, she decided to fly to Washington incognito to meet with Nixon in order to press on him the urgency of the situation and to speed up the delivery of arms to Israel. Gazit instructed Dinitz to set up the meeting through Kissinger, and reiterated that Eban must not know about it. Neither was Eban informed of the Israeli Defense Forces' decision to bomb strategic targets deep inside Damascus that day.[23] Unaware of these developments, on October 11 Eban suggested that he would meet with the president, but Meir flatly rejected the idea. "Kissinger is doing a terrific job and keeps in close contact with Simcha, as you must know from the current reports," she told Eban, knowing full well that he only had partial knowledge of what was going on. "In the current situation it is unlikely that the president will want to see any of us," she continued, without mentioning her own plan to see Nixon. To add insult to injury, Meir then "comforted" Eban: "Surely Dinitz asks for your opinion and shares with you everything that happens."[24]

By then the situation on the battlefield had turned from bad to worse. An Israeli counteroffensive in the Sinai failed, and in the north, Israeli tanks were down to their last shells; pilots were ordered to conserve fuel and ammunition. The cabinet, which only days earlier instructed Eban to delay any movements in the UN Security Council toward a cease-fire resolution, was now prepared to accept a cease-fire, thus leaving Egyptian troops on territory that was held by Israel before the war. At this point Meir finally relented and decided to send her foreign minister—accompanied by Dinitz and Shalev—to meet with Kissinger in Washington. Kissinger blamed the delay in the airlift to Israel on the Pentagon. He then picked up the phone and ordered Brent Scowcroft, his deputy at the NSC, to make sure that ten C-130 transport aircraft would take off to Israel that day, or else "we will send [Deputy Secretary of Defense William] Clements back to Texas."

Evidently impressed by Kissinger's impromptu display of leadership, Eban and Dinitz were convinced that the delay in the delivery of arms was indeed the Pentagon's fault.[25] In reality, however, the delay was part of Kissinger's greater strategic vision of postwar diplomacy. It was a straightforward calculation of achieving the perfect equilibrium of leverage on the parties at the end of the war, as he had told the administration's crisis management group only hours earlier: "Our problem is to get the war over in a way the Arabs have to come to us, and then turn on the Israelis. If Israel feels we have let them down and the Arabs think they have done it themselves, we are sunk." Kissinger warned Clements that if a massive airlift got underway and Israel won the war too decisively, "we will lose our Arab friends." He then told Secretary of Defense James Schlesinger that he had to take the blame for the delay because the White House could not be viewed as the problem while negotiations were underway with the Israelis.[26] With Nixon's intervention, the following day, October 14, the massive American airlift to Israel finally got under way. Neither Eban nor Dinitz were aware of Kissinger's ploy, and as Eban recalled years later, there was no question in his mind of who saved Israel in its darkest hour: "Our heroes were Nixon and Kissinger. Our enemies were the Pentagon and Schlesinger."[27]

The new arms made an immediate impact on the battlefield. Two days later, Israeli troops completed a successful counteroffensive in the Sinai and crossed the Suez Canal. The change in fortune on the battlefield was followed by a similar reversal of initiatives at the UN Security Council.[28] This time it was the Soviets who enquired on behalf of their clients whether Israel would accept a cease-fire. Kissinger and Eban were enthusiastic, but Meir demanded the exclusion of any reference to Resolution 242 from the proposed cease-fire resolution. Eban wished to meet with Kissinger in Washington, but Dinitz cabled his strong objection to Meir: "I request that the foreign minister will be clearly instructed not—repeat not—to come to Washington. It is essential that we do not launch a diplomatic move at the foreign ministers level before we decide that the time is ripe. . . . It is better to carry all preliminary discussions with the White House in secrecy as we have done so far."[29] Meir sided with Dinitz and refused Eban's request to travel to Washington. Dinitz also refused to travel to New York to meet with Eban, asking Meir, "how could I excuse my refusal to travel?" and "should I tell Eban [about a previous meeting with Kissinger] beyond what I have already cabled? Should I inform him of the Soviet proposal?"[30] As Shalev explained to the prime minister's office in a separate cable, handling Eban had become as delicate a matter as the tantalizing negotiations with Kissinger: "I request that the prime minister's instructions to the foreign minister will not refer to Simcha's cable or to mine, and refer only to Eban's cable to her. She must understand that among other things we also have to keep the house in order and maintain correct relations."[31]

Meir's solution to the problem was simple: she ordered Eban to return to Jerusalem "for consultations"—a ludicrous pretext given her habitual exclusion of Eban from consultations in Jerusalem. "He will cause less danger here than in the United States," she told Dinitz, referring to Eban's support for the inclusion of reference to Resolution 242 in the UN cease-fire resolution.[32] Grudgingly Eban returned to Israel, leaving Dinitz alone at the helm. Before his departure Eban asked Dinitz to keep Yosef Tekoah at the UN informed of developments. The next morning Dinitz informed Meir of Eban's request. "Keep Tekoah in the frame but don't pass him any material," the prime minister instructed.[33] Back in Jerusalem, Eban appeared before the Knesset's Foreign Affairs and Defense Committee. As more tough questions were leveled at him about the diplomatic movements during the war, the more it became clear to him how much had been kept from him by Meir and Dinitz. He ordered his aides at the Foreign Ministry to put together a dossier about the contacts between the prime minister's office and the Washington embassy dating back to October 5. He was stunned to discover that Dinitz had objected to his arrival in Washington and had persuaded Meir to return him to Israel.[34]

The cabinet decided to delay the diplomatic moves to allow the military time to finish its business. By October 21 both Egypt and Syria were desperate for a cease-fire, and the following day the UN Security Council passed Resolution 338, calling for a cease-fire and the implementation of Resolution 242. But the Israeli encirclement of the 20,000-strong Egyptian Third Army on the east bank of the Suez Canal delayed the implementation of the resolution by two further days, which further tested the détente between Washington and Moscow.[35]

Militarily the war ended in a draw, with the Arabs winning the first round and the Israelis the second, but as far as the Israeli public was concerned, it was a monumental disaster. Israel was not defeated on the battlefield, and its territory was not conquered by the attacking Egyptian and Syrian armies; in fact, at the end of the war Israel was in control of more Arab territory than it had been after the Six-Day War. When the guns fell silent on October 25, Israeli forces were on the western bank of the Suez Canal for the first time, and only sixty miles from Cairo, while on the Syrian front Israeli troops were less than thirty miles from Damascus and in control of territory beyond the Golan Heights. Israel lost more than 2,600 soldiers—nearly four times more than during the Six-Day War, but less than half of the casualties of the first Arab-Israeli War in 1948. Psychology, rather than territory, dictated the Israeli mood in the weeks, months, and years following the war. Eban recalled it as a "victory without celebration," while Kissinger noted during his visit to Israel shortly after the war that "Israel was exhausted, no matter what the military maps showed."[36]

The war woke up the nation from its apathy. It turned out that Israel was not as invincible and the Arabs were not as pathetic on the battlefield as the public had been led to believe by its self-assured leadership ever since the end of the 1967 war. Five weeks after the war ended, Eban returned to offer some much-needed introspection before the Presidents Club in Washington, the powerful lobby group that he had helped establish two decades earlier: "The extent of our 1967 triumph—a hundred percent Israeli victory and a hundred percent Arab defeat—was not an authentic or permanent reflection of the real military balance." For six long years, Eban continued, Israelis had lived with certain endemic illusions that stood at odds with the very ethos of the Jewish state:

> I mean the illusion that cease-fire could exist indefinitely in a diplomatic vacuum with no constancy of political activity.
>
> I mean the illusion that a million Arabs would be kept under Israeli control forever provided that their economic and social welfare was impressively advanced.
>
> The illusion that Zionism forbade a sharing of additional sovereignty between two nations in former Palestine mandate area.
>
> The illusion that Israel's historic legacy was exclusively a matter of geography and not also, and principally, heritage of prophetic values of which central value was peace.
>
> The fallacy that to see anything temporary in some of Israel's positions west of the Jordan was tantamount to alienation from the biblical culture.
>
> The fallacy that a nation could not be strong unless it demonstrated its toughness in every contingency.[37]

THIS POTENT ANALYSIS WAS A NATURAL SEQUEL TO EBAN'S DENUNCIATION OF THE Israeli national style at Haifa University eight months earlier. Now that the fallacy of the government's prewar policy had been exposed, Eban became even more vocal on the need to resuscitate a process of negotiation with the Arab world. Revisiting his old appeal to reinstate a mystique of peace into the Israeli psyche, he declared that a peace conference "does not make peace inevitable, however it makes it less improbable. Peace conference must be approached as opportunity and not only as danger."[38]

The idea of a Middle East peace conference sprouted in Kissinger's mind even before the war had ended. It was to be the cornerstone of a new American foreign policy in the region, one that convinced the parties to the conflict that they would be better off with an agreement than without one, and that Washington's involvement in the process was absolutely essential to its successful implementation. By making American mediation an essential ingredient on the road to Arab-Israeli reconciliation, Kissinger hoped to achieve several strategic aims: mending relations with the Arab world following Washington's support for Israel during the war; lifting the Arab oil embargo that had been imposed during the war and paralyzed the global economy; reducing Soviet influence in the region to a minimum; and cementing America's role, for the first time in the Cold War, as the principal external power in the Middle East. As a first step in this ambitious plan he proposed to hold a peace conference in Geneva as soon as possible, but Meir was worried that he was moving too fast. "It is absurd how little we know about the conference, but absurd can turn into disaster," she warned Dinitz on November 16. It seemed that Kissinger had already arranged everything without consulting anyone, maybe he should go ahead and appoint the Israeli delegation too, she complained.[39]

Kissinger did not relent. He insisted that it was important to keep the momentum going and launch a peace process while both sides were still recovering from the ruins of war and were susceptible to external pressure. On November 20 he discussed with Eban the details of the conference. Eban hoped that Geneva would be the venue for comprehensive and meaningful negotiations; he instructed the Foreign Ministry to prepare draft peace treaties with Egypt, Jordan, and Syria. The Israeli delegation was bolstered by an auxiliary of journalists, academics, and public relations experts. Anticipating the meeting in Geneva to be a thorough affair, the Foreign Ministry did not book hotel rooms for a few days but instead rented a whole building headed by a permanent representative. Israel's was without doubt the most organized delegation in town.[40] But Kissinger had different plans: Geneva would be no more than a ceremonial launching pad for America's own new peace strategy—an incremental approach aimed at securing limited agreements that would help build trust between the parties and in an American-led peace process.

Having first rejected the convening of the Geneva conference at an early date, the government in Jerusalem changed its tune and proposed holding it on December 18. The reason was not a newfound desire for peace but the prosaic realization that holding a peace conference in close proximity to the general elections, scheduled for December 31, could give the Labor Party a much needed boost at the polls.[41] The conference at the Palais des Nations eventually opened on Friday, December 21, after a three-day delay caused by quarrels over the phrasing of the invitation letters. The opening ceremony, scheduled for 10:00 a.m., was then delayed by another hour due to disagreements over the seating arrangements. The Egyptians did not want to sit next to the Israelis and demanded that the empty seat reserved for the Syrians (who refused to attend the conference) would be placed between them. Eban refused to sit next to an empty seat, which would visually signal to the world Israel's isolation. Finally Kissinger proposed a compromise: Egypt and Israel would sit on either side of UN secretary-general Kurt Waldheim, the Americans would sit to the right of the Egyptians, and the Soviets would flank the Israelis on the left. Waldheim spoke first, followed by Kissinger, Egyptian foreign minister Fahmi, and Jordanian prime minister Zaid

Rifai. At 12:30 p.m. Waldheim suggested concluding the public proceedings for the day to allow for private discussions in the afternoon. Eban protested indignantly. Having his speech delayed until the next day would give the Arabs all the attention of the international media at Geneva and an unfair advantage in the propaganda war. It also meant that the public at home could not watch his address on the evening news. He consulted briefly with Meir, who felt that an immediate and vigorous reply by Eban could boost the Labor Party's dire state at the polls.[42] Eban's request to deliver his address there and then was granted. Nearly three times longer than the other speeches, Eban's had all the usual ingredients: it began with a universal appeal to banish any doubts over Israel's right to exist in the Middle East, followed by a chronology of Arab hostility toward Israel, and then concluded with Israel's desire for peace:

> Its meaning is not exhausted by the absence of war. It commits us also to positive obligations which neighbouring States owe to each other by virtue of their proximity and of their common membership in the international community. Above all, a durable peace must create a new human reality. It does not rest on the cold formalism of documents alone. Nations at peace are not separated from each other by hermetically sealed boundaries guarded by international police forces. . . . It may take time to achieve that full objective. But does not every serious architect design a vision of the finished structure before anybody begins to face the prosaic difficulties of construction?[43]

FAHMI FELT OBLIGED TO RESPOND TO EBAN'S ACCOUNT OF ARAB-ISRAELI RELAtions. His own speech, unlike Eban's, was based only on facts, he said, and that was because "I do not have any problem of speaking here for home consumption and I do not have any election campaign which is going to take place in a few days in my country."[44]

Fahmi was not wrong. The electoral pull of the sight of Foreign Minister Eban in Geneva delivering one of his masterpieces in three languages and sharing the platform with Arab foreign ministers for the first time could not be underestimated. According to Pinchas Sapir, "The Geneva conference gave us four [to] five seats." But Eban alone could not prevent the party's worst electoral result in history. From the outset, no one expected another Labor Party landslide. There was public outrage at the government's failure to prepare the country for war, and the party itself was torn by infighting and soul-searching. The Galili Document was history. Yigal Allon was at the forefront of those calling for Meir and Dayan to take responsibility and step down. Eban did not mention Dayan's name, but everyone present knew of whom he spoke when he attacked "the charismatic form of power exercised by some persons in government" and noted that prewar "statements within our own camp" had weakened Israel's credibility as a peace-seeker. Meir and Sapir exchanged verbal blows at a charged party's Central Committee meeting. Other party members cited a crisis of confidence in the leadership and called for a changing of the guard. The sense of utter disarray in the party was only slightly mitigated by the images from Geneva; without the peace conference, the Labor Party may well have lost the elections. It won fifty-one seats, down from fifty-six, while Menachem Begin's recently amalgamated Likud party shot up from thirty to thirty-nine seats. The gap between the two blocs had never been narrower. "One more election campaign and we will find ourselves in opposition," was the pessimistic if prophetic conclusion of one party leader.[45]

A month before the elections the government heeded the public demands to investigate the failings leading up to the war, and appointed a commission of inquiry led by Shimon Agranat, the president of the Supreme Court. Luckily for the Labor Party, the Agranat Commission did not release its interim report until April 1, 1974. It recommended the dismissal of the chief of staff, the head of military intelligence, and several other senior officers. Those at the political helm—especially the prime minister and the defense minister—were let off the hook, as the commission judged the investigation of the political decisions leading to the war to be beyond its remit and something that should instead be judged in the court of public opinion. That is precisely what happened: outraged that Meir and Dayan came out unscathed while the military was hung out to dry, the public demanded Meir and Dayan's resignations. Weighed down by the toll of the war and its aftermath, nine days later Meir announced her resignation. "I can no longer carry this burden, I have reached the end of the road," the seventy-six-year-old told her party. "I have no regrets in my life. I did not betray my conscience," she added, in a vain effort to absolve herself of any responsibility for the war. The usual Mapai ritual of pleading and begging the leader to reconsider the decision to resign would not work this time. There was finality in her tone when she said, "I've had enough."[46]

XVII
Dismissal

FOLLOWING MEIR'S RESIGNATION ALL EYES TURNED ONCE AGAIN TO PINchas Sapir, her presumed successor and the kingmaker of Mapai. Once again the powerful finance minister was adamant that the job was not for him. In the absence of an heir apparent for the first time in the party's history, the new prime minister had to be elected by a vote in the party's Central Committee. Eban considered running for the top job, but he backed down after Sapir refused to support his candidacy. Sapir, who was the one person in the party whom Eban truly respected, knew that Eban had no chance of garnering sufficient support at the Central Committee, and didn't want to see him get hurt: "You missed the train. Don't run, and save yourself the disgrace of getting no more than 90 votes [in the 615-member Central Committee]." Sapir also explained to Eban that nobody who was unacceptable to Meir could be regarded as her successor. When Sapir told Meir that Eban was considering running for the premiership, she wryly replied, "in which country?"[1]

What Sapir did not tell Eban, however, was that he had decided to support Yitzhak Rabin, who emerged as a strong candidate, together with Shimon Peres of the Rafi faction of the Labor Party. Still a political neophyte after fifteen years in the party, Eban did not understand the basic logic behind Sapir's decision. A three-horse race with Rabin, Peres, and Eban would not only have fragmented the party, but Eban's candidacy would have taken sufficient votes from Rabin to hand the premiership to Peres, the one person that both Mapai and Ahdut Ha'Avoda members were united in opposition against. Although Rabin nailed his flag to the Ahdut Ha'Avoda mast rather than Mapai's, Sapir and Meir saw him as the most agreeable candidate for the job: a former general, a war hero, a successful ambassador to Washington, a sabra, a fresh face who was not tainted by the Yom Kippur War.

Eban heard about Rabin's nomination on the radio. This was a double blow for him: not only had his most trusted ally in the cabinet lied to him (Sapir had previously told Eban that Eban would succeed Meir), but Sapir's choice turned out to be Eban's greatest nemesis. Eban's response was visceral: first he severed his friendship with Sapir, telling reporters, "what is the point in friendship if it is not reciprocal?" Then, he announced his unconditional support for Peres—a surprising though somewhat inevitable choice, given Eban's abysmal relations with Rabin. Peres was a Rafi man who was a vocal supporter of the settlement project in the West Bank, whereas Rabin was positioned closer to Eban's views on the need for territorial compromise with the Arabs as a necessary ingredient in a future peace settlement.[2] Years later Eban admitted that he made a fatal mistake by heeding Sapir's advice not to run. "Had I presented my candidacy and got, say, only 25 per cent, I would still be on the map. . . . I was wrong on this matter. A person with ambition would have entered the race."[3]

On April 22, 1974, Yitzhak Rabin, who had entered the Knesset only three months earlier and had served as minister of labor for four weeks, was elected as Meir's successor, winning 298 votes to Shimon Peres's 254. One of his first and least pleasant tasks was to negotiate the composition of the government with his coalition partners. His chosen man for the defense portfolio was Yigal Allon, his longtime friend and a Palmach commander during the 1948 war, but he had to yield to an ultimatum from the Rafi faction to appoint Peres instead or risk the collapse of the new government. Rabin offered Allon the Foreign Ministry as a consolation prize; he also asked him to remain as deputy prime minister, a position Allon had held since 1968. After eight years as foreign minister Eban was ousted. In his memoirs Rabin was adamant that this was not a personal vendetta against Eban and that after eight years as foreign minister it was time for Eban to move on, but in private conversation he made it clear that after Eban's "campaign of mudslinging against me I couldn't include him in my government."[4]

On May 25 Rabin presented his proposed cabinet to the party. Sensing the brewing storm surrounding Eban's dismissal, he preempted the announcement of the new ministerial positions by noting that "every man naturally holds himself in high regard" and that the cemeteries were full of indispensable people. He then read from his notes an alphabetical list of the nineteen ministerial appointments, but two in particular dominated the subsequent discussion: "Information minister—turned down by Abba Eban. . . . Deputy prime minister and foreign minister—Yigal Allon." Members of the Mapai faction were outraged—Rabin and Allon came from Ahdut Ha'Avoda, and Peres was a Rafi man—and for the first time in Israel's history the leadership of the country was no longer a Mapai prerogative.

Mapai members implored Rabin to reconsider his decision and protested his casual dismissal of Eban. How come the prime minister could not find a seat for Eban at the government table? Why was Eban the only member of the previous government who was shown the way out? (Meir, Dayan, and Sapir had resigned from their posts.) Why did Allon have to be foreign minister *and* deputy prime minister? Why couldn't Rabin do the collegial thing and offer Eban the latter post? Beba Idelson, the party's longest-serving member, articulated those views most passionately:

> I do not accept and I cannot accept this behavior towards Eban. We do not have many like him. I never heard once during the 26 years of this country's existence that Abba Eban had damaged the policies of the State of Israel. I saw him abroad, I saw him in this country, I sat in the Knesset for 18 years, and I know what I'm talking about. I don't know if everybody thinks the same about the other ministers. The behavior towards Eban in this case is not correct and is not just. . . . I see it as a dismissal. Nobody should be treated like this. . . . I know that Abba Eban can get a job. I'm not worried that he will become jobless. I am worried about the composition of the government. I know who Abba Eban is. I know *what* Abba Eban is.[5]

Buoyed by such a compelling display of empathy from his colleagues, Eban took the floor. He was particularly angry with Allon's behavior. A few days earlier Allon had dismissed before Eban the widespread rumors that he had been offered the Foreign Ministry by Rabin. But Eban told his colleagues, "Since I regularly listen to the radio it so happened that I heard of the appointment of another comrade to the post which I have fulfilled for seven years." Only then did Allon confirm to Eban that he would indeed be the next foreign minister and deputy prime minister. In response, Eban announced on the radio that he would not join the Rabin government under any circumstances. He certainly refused to accept Rabin's offer of the recently created post of information minister—the very same post that Eban had urged Meir to kill in its infancy three years earlier. He was infuriated that Rabin offered him a post that both of them knew Eban would reject out of hand for reasons of prestige and reputation. "I didn't think I had any reason to accept a position that I thought was not compatible with my capacities or my prestige or my dignity," he later explained. And Rabin certainly never intended to ask Eban to be his deputy, even if Allon were to do the honorable thing and relinquish the post. Both men knew very well that their reciprocal antipathy was not conducive to harmonious working relations; as some insiders explained, for Eban the prospect of working under Rabin was as perilous as waving a red cape in front of a charging bull.[6]

Three days later, and only two hours before he was due to present his new cabinet before the Israeli president, Rabin told the party that Eban alone was responsible for ending his fifteen-year ministerial career. "I offered him alternative ministerial posts but he was not interested in any of them," Rabin said. There was nothing else that could be done to keep him in government. Rabin's halfhearted affirmation did not convince many in the room. Israel Kargman, one of the party's veterans, lamented that the dismissal of Eban significantly weakened the government's standing, and he blamed the "egocentric" Allon for blocking Eban's prospects for joining the new government. Pinchas Sapir also came to Eban's defense. The manner in which Eban was shown the way out was wrong, Sapir said; he himself would have resigned from government in protest over Eban's treatment had he not announced his own resignation for personal reasons some time ago. Another party member, Yehoshua Rabinowitz, went even further, declaring that had it not been for the political and security exigencies engulfing the country at the time (including the negotiations with Egypt over a phased Israeli withdrawal from the Sinai Peninsula), Eban's dismissal ought to have been a sufficient reason to disband the new government.[7]

Several lamentations later it was Eban's turn to speak. Bitter and indignant, he seized the opportunity to settle the score. "Perhaps I could ask Yitzhak Rabin to stop saying that he wanted me to join the government but that he was unsuccessful, because this is only formally true," Eban began, "since his will was accompanied by moves which in fact rendered my joining the government essentially impossible." In his usual verbose style, Eban then turned to Allon, deliberately choosing not to refer to the deputy prime minister by his name.

Here was the most painful issue, Eban said, as it pertained to the most basic human, collegial, and educational values that determined the ethical character of public life. Allon had every right to accept Rabin's offer to appoint him as foreign minister, but then, Eban accused, neither Allon nor Rabin took the initiative to inform him of the decision before it was made public. What then followed, he continued, was an "anonymous initiative" to appoint Allon as deputy prime minister as well; and apparently nobody stopped to ask how would that affect the "standing, desire, and the work environment at home and abroad of another individual. There is no evidence that the thought had come up in somebody's mind that perhaps somewhere in the Jewish world there is a wish for that other individual to continue his mission in one form or another." Eban plowed on, full of pathos: the prime minister had sealed his ears to the "profound public and party demand" to reinstate Eban. He had sealed his ears to a "civilized request, not an ultimatum, of 60 per cent of the party members"; he had even refused to confront Eban directly until that very afternoon. Turning to Allon, Eban protested his absence from the meeting: "I thought that Yigal Allon would explain to us here why he thought that the move was justified or collegial. His absence perturbs me, and I protest against it."[8]

Thirty-four years after this episode, Suzy Eban published her memoirs. Always fiercely protective of her husband and his legacy, she refused to either forgive the culprits or forget their actions. "I wondered in my heart, was it jealousy?" she wrote. "Was it sheer headiness at the approach of power? . . . I leave it to historical interpretations and will only add that party pride and collegiality had reached murky waters. Perhaps mine is not the most gracious way of accepting defeat, and yet why should I, when speaking now for Abba who has gone from us, dismiss a gross abandonment and add a congratulatory smile to the two generals' achievement when it was not occasioned by any political failure?"[9]

For the first time in his political career Eban was now an ordinary member of the Knesset, with no ministerial responsibilities or intimate dealings with questions of national security. The wilderness of parliamentary life scared and depressed him. He was only fifty-nine, a juvenile in political years, and his career seemed to be over. Only months earlier Gideon Rafael had asked Eban if he considered taking a "sabbatical from politics," to which the foreign minister replied irately, "I'm used to better advice from you." Didn't Rafael know that once a minister gave up his cabinet post he rarely returned to it?[10] Now Eban was about to live out his own wisdom.

But just as this door seemed to close on his political career another one opened, offering him a propitious opportunity to revive his real passion, the one he had passed on to join political Zionism nearly three decades earlier. In the summer of 1974 Eban accepted the position of Distinguished Visiting Professor of International Relations at Columbia University in New York. He and Suzy settled in an apartment overlooking Central Park that belonged to the Weizmann Institute. Suzy studied art at Columbia, and for the first time in many years they could enjoy some private time, sampling the many cultural gems that the city had to offer. Surrounded by awestruck students and the millions of American Jews who retained an infantile infatuation with "Ambassador Eban," New York was always Eban's favorite arena of action. He may have lost ground in Israel, but in America they could never get enough of him: he was still the phenomenal Voice of Israel, the eloquent defender of a besieged and righteous country. They knew him as the brilliant diplomat of 1948, 1956, and 1967, and not as the disgruntled and marginalized figure of the more recent past.

The Columbia professorship was but one of dozens of offers that flooded in as soon as the news of Eban's dismissal broke. Random House offered to publish his memoirs and another book on diplomacy, with a hefty advance, and there was an endless stream of requests for public appearances on campuses and contributions to various media outlets. Following the historic yet controversial appearance at the UN General Assembly of Palestine Liberation Organization leader Yasser Arafat, Eban wrote in a *New York Times* op-ed piece, "Of all recent offenses against peace and international civility, the most astounding is the decision of the United Nations General Assembly to bring an Al Fatah terrorist leader to its rostrum. It is one thing to confess impotence before the gun of the assassin. It is quite another to give him obsequious deference. . . . In its present mood and structure, the United Nations would refuse to endorse the Ten Commandments on account of their Israelite origin." A few years later Eban told his party that "those who think that Martin Luther King and Yasser Arafat are the same, insult both Martin Luther King's followers and the victims of Arafat's violence."[11]

After decades of bureaucratic struggles, political infighting, and high levels of stress, Eban now enjoyed a more a comfortable and tranquil existence, though his daily schedule was rarely empty. On Tuesday evenings he delivered a seminar on multilateral diplomacy, and on Wednesday afternoons he taught the course "Case Histories on War and Peace in the Middle East."

The rest of the week saw him shuttling around the United States giving public lectures—altogether more than forty of them during his four-month stay in New York, each earning him $3,000 plus expenses. All the while he kept a watchful eye on political developments back home and insisted that he had not retired from politics but was simply pausing; this was why he turned down Columbia's invitation to stay for the full academic year. He admitted that the trauma of being "thrown out and abandoned" was impossible to shake off.[12] Nevertheless, unburdened by false modesty and conveniently overlooking the fact the American Jews did not vote in the Israeli elections, Eban insisted that he was the logical choice to succeed Rabin as prime minister: "Whether I like it or not, most people, and especially Jews, still think that I'm responsible somehow for the destiny of Israel and that I articulate its visions. People still stop me in the streets—what do I think, what do I not think, what's going to happen—half the people who speak to me don't even know that I've left office. Abba Eban is a kind of institution . . . and they ask me why I am not in charge."[13]

EBAN RETURNED TO ISRAEL IN DECEMBER 1974 AND POSITIONED HIMSELF IN direct opposition to Rabin. On May 9, 1975, he criticized the prime minister for his lack of leadership and for plunging U.S.-Israeli relations to their lowest ebb following the breakdown in negotiations over a second Israeli-Egyptian disengagement agreement in Sinai. Two days later he described the Rabin government as a drifting ship without a compass or an anchor, in trouble over the direction of its rudder. Eban's acerbic attacks were reciprocated by equally barbed rebuttals from Rabin and the party's secretary-general, the first describing Eban's statements as "irresponsible, even though they were made by a man who formerly held responsible office," while the latter remarked that Eban's style did not measure up to the level of responsibility expected from someone of his stature. The exchange caused such a stir that even members of the left-wing Mapam faction in the Alignment cautioned against the transformation of legitimate political debate into "personal vendetta."[14] A few months later Eban accused the government of pursuing a policy of stagnation and urged it to present a peace initiative that would include the Palestinians of the West Bank. He charged that the sum total of Israel's obstinate policies toward further agreements with Egypt, Jordan, and Syria meant "explaining why every door is closed and every window is bolted."[15] There was a degree of churlishness in Eban's incessant attacks on the government—after all, he had spent five years as foreign minister in Golda Meir's government, explaining to the world why it was only Israel who truly desired peace while the Arabs could not be trusted until they dropped their preconditions for negotiations.

But now, unshackled from the burdens of defending a government policy with which he did not agree, Eban finally spoke his mind. He lobbied to change the Alignment's platform before the next general election in such a way as to reflect a clear ideological position toward peace and the territories. He wished to replace vague statements about "territorial compromise" with specific references to "significant territorial concessions" and even "far reaching" concessions. He even did not rule out the establishment of another state between Jordan and Israel.[16] On negotiations with Palestinian leaders, Eban wanted the Israeli government to get rid "of its inhibitions of refusal, lack of competence to withdraw" and to lay down affirmative conditions; "I am saying to the Palestinians, if you want to talk to us, then pick up the telephone and dial Geneva 242-338. I'm afraid if they got the Israeli system, it would probably say "'All lines are busy,' but eventually they would get through."[17]

For years Eban had been the Voice of Israel, but not its mind. He presented to the world in the most palatable way possible ideas he sometimes found unpalatable himself. It was, in the words of Hal Saunders, a member of the National Security Council during the administrations of Presidents Lyndon Johnson and Richard Nixon, deception in its purest form—but that was Eban's job, and he did it beautifully.[18] Now, just as lucidly, Eban presented his own coherent pathway for the future of the Labor Party. "It was like having an intellectual shower . . . an intense mental pleasure," was one *Jerusalem Post* correspondent's impression of an Eban article denouncing any attempts to annex the West Bank as folly.[19]

Eban's chance to test his premiership credentials came earlier than he or anyone else expected. In December 1976 Rabin called for early elections to be held in May 1977 over a no-confidence vote in the government by the religious parties. The prosaic reason for that vote was the desecration of the Sabbath: On a Friday afternoon a formal ceremony was held to accept the first shipment of F-15 fighter jets from the United States, and several cabinet ministers failed to return to their homes before sunset. Although the government survived the vote, Rabin decided to use the opportunity to go to elections and form a new government without the religious parties.[20] Rabin's gambit was misjudged, however. For the first time in the country's history the Labor movement was ousted from power as Menachem Begin's Likud party emerged victorious.

The political upheaval of May 1977 had its roots in the trauma of the Yom Kippur War and the moral bankruptcy that engulfed the Labor Party in the run-up to the elections. In January 1977 Minister of Housing Avraham Ofer committed suicide following allegations of embezzlement. Two months later Asher Yadlin, a senior member of the party who was about to be appointed governor of the Bank of Israel, was imprisoned over charges of corruption and bribery. Still reeling from the trauma of 1974, this time Eban resolved to throw his hat into the ring. On January 24 he formally announced his candidacy for the leadership of the Labor Party, but in the eyes of the press and the general public the real contest was still between Rabin and Peres. The American embassy in Tel Aviv reported to Washington in the run-up to Eban's announcement that "Eban is regarded as little more than a stalking horse for Peres while the latter considers his strategy and seizes up the new situation. . . . " In a later cable the embassy pointed out that "Eban clearly has not succeeded in convincing most observers that his candidacy is serious. Many believe he has made a deal with Peres and that his candidacy is intended to draw votes from Rabin." And indeed, only ten days after he formally declared his candidacy for the top job, Eban removed himself from the race and pledged to support Peres. He invited eighty former Mapai members to his house to explain this quick volte-face: he did not believe that he had sufficient time to gather enough votes at the party's Central Committee, and that by joining forces with Peres he would be able to have more of a say in the party's political agenda while presenting a united front against Rabin. Peres warmly thanked Eban for his brave decision and for putting the national interest above his own. His reward to Eban for his unselfish act was a promise to reinstate him as foreign minister in the new government.[21]

In April 1977, a month before the elections, Rabin himself stepped down as leader of the party after it was discovered that he and his wife held two foreign currency accounts in Washington in contravention of the Israeli law at the time, which prohibited Israeli citizens from holding unauthorized currency accounts abroad.[22] He was replaced at the helm by Peres, while Eban, who had received more votes than Allon in the party's Central Committee, found himself third on the ticket after Allon threatened to resign were he to be placed behind Eban.

Only two weeks after Rabin announced his resignation over the foreign currency accounts scandal, Eban found himself in the spotlight for the very same reason. The news caused added embarrassment for the party, and amid fears of a public backlash many of Eban's scheduled public appearances were canceled. The facts were incontrovertible and dwarfed the Rabin affair: Eban held not two but five foreign currency accounts—four in the United States (a savings account, a checking account, and two deposit accounts) and another in London, to which some of the money from the American accounts was transferred. The total amount of Eban's foreign currency accounts was also unprecedented—$351,000 of which $121,500 was withdrawn abroad and $112,000 was transferred to Eban's bank accounts in Israel. The remaining $117,500 was transferred to Israel only after the revelation of these accounts. According to the reports, as soon as Eban heard the news of the Rabin scandal he transferred from one of his accounts $18,000, leaving only $5,000, the maximum amount that did not automatically trigger an investigation by the authorities. Eban's accounts were discovered by Moshe Eliaz, a New York–based Israeli businessman and former Foreign Ministry employee who had left his post after a dispute with his superiors. Eliaz spotted a check by Eban in a New York store drawn from Citibank.[23]

In response to these allegations, Eban maintained that in 1967 he received a permit to hold foreign currency from Yossi Katz, the former comptroller of foreign exchange at the Finance Ministry. Eban had good reasons to hold a foreign account: he received royalties and honorariums as an internationally renowned author, a public speaker, and, most recently, as a visiting professor at Columbia University, which naturally necessitated dollar and sterling bank accounts. Eban's fourth book, *My People: The Story of the Jews*, which was published by Random House in 1968, had sold 40,000 copies in its first year. Eban's fifth book, *My Country: The Story of Modern Israel*, had also became a best seller following its publication in 1972. According to one popular joke in Israel at the time, Eban was already working on the third book in his trilogy titled *My Bank Account: The Story of My Growing Wealth*.[24] Some of that wealth had to be available to Eban in the United States to pay the salaries of a secretary, a research assistant, and his literary agent, not to mention the living expenses during his frequent and lengthy visits to New York.

Unfortunately for Eban, Katz passed away in 1976 and the permit could not be retrieved by the Finance Ministry. Moreover, even if such permit had been issued to Eban, it would have expired in 1975, and Eban had failed to renew it. Eban insisted that what mattered was his letter to the Finance Ministry in 1967 (which could not be found) in which he asked for a permit to be issued. He was also supported by Zvi Dinstein, the former deputy minister of finance, and four Foreign Ministry secretaries, who confirmed that the permit had indeed been granted in 1967. As for his failure to renew the permit before 1975, Eban dismissed it as no more than a "technical error" that could be explained by his residence in New York at the time as a visiting professor at Columbia.[25]

Two weeks after the general elections, two opposing recommendations emerged following the investigation of the Finance Ministry: to close the case and issue Eban a retroactive permit, or to charge him.[26] The person charged with making that fateful decision was Attorney General Aharon Barak. On July 7 Barak decided not to charge Eban and closed the case. He ruled that Eban "genuinely believed" that the permit issued to him in 1967 allowed him to keep unlimited funds abroad, and there were therefore no grounds on which to issue criminal proceedings. Eban was elated with the news, which he described as "predictable, natural and inevitable, since I acted flawlessly." When the dust settled, he turned to thank his lawyer, Yaakov Ne'eman (who happened to be Barak's own lawyer and his former law lecturer). "He saved me a million pounds in fines," Eban said of Ne'eman, "but then took it in fees."[27]

In 1977 Eban's autobiography was published by Random House to glowing reviews. "If any 628-page memoir of a statesman and scholar can be called a page-turner, this is it," was the verdict of *Newsweek,* while the *New York Times* opined, "Statesmen rarely write memoirs that are memorable. Abba Eban . . . proves the exception to this cautionary rule. He has written an autobiography that makes compelling reading."[28] Others, however, pointed to Eban's reluctance to delve into the personal domain and his unusual laconic treatment of some of the controversies surrounding his ministerial career, such as that concerning his fateful meeting with Lyndon Johnson two weeks before the Six-Day War.[29]

Eban concluded the Hebrew edition of his memoirs with the assertion that he had not been traumatized by his new position as an ordinary politician.[30] In reality, however, the defeat of the Labor Party in the general elections of May 1977 made Eban's return to the front row of Israeli politics a remote possibility. His disdain for the backstabbing, arm-twisting style of Israeli politics did not suit him, and he did not hide his boredom with the humdrum of life in opposition. As foreign minister Eban had once remarked before an academic forum, "I spent most of the last twenty-four hours in the Knesset where systematic thinking is not forbidden but nobody would say that it is a condition of membership."[31] Now, as an ordinary Knesset member, he scolded his peers:

"If we could harness all the energy produced by gossip at the Knesset canteen every week, maybe we could substitute it for our power stations and other sources of fuel and electricity. Perhaps one of the Knesset's weaknesses is that the canteen is overpopulated and the library is underpopulated."[32]

The Knesset was clearly not Eban's natural habitat. When *Reader's Digest* asked twenty famous people to list their "5 events in history I would most like to have seen," Eban was noted for his original answer:

1. The return of the Jews from Babylon to dedicate the Second Temple (515 B.C.).
2. Pericles's funeral speech about the virtues of Athens after the war with Sparta (431 B.C.).
3. The signing of the American Declaration of Independence in Philadelphia (July 4, 1776).
4. The First Performance of Beethoven's Ninth (Choral) Symphony (1824).
5. Winston Churchill's speech in the House of Commons (May 13, 1940).

"I CAN DECLAIM PERICLES'S SPEECH IN CLASSICAL GREEK," EBAN REMINDED one television interviewer, "and of course Cicero's Latin, but I shall not bore this audience with it."[33]

Eban spent weeks—sometimes months—in New York, lecturing and writing, often at the expense of attending sessions of the Knesset. (In 1977 he accepted a position at the Institute for Advanced Studies at Princeton University.) He was undoubtedly the best-paid member of the Knesset: in the autumn of 1979 he charged a nonnegotiable $3,500 fee for each of the thirty public lectures he delivered in the United States, not including expenses. (Moshe Dayan charged $2,500.) His lecture fees for the period April 1985 to March 1986 alone stood at $49,325, and his royalty payments in this period from his most recent books came to more than $210,000.[34] Eban left a less indomitable imprint as a parliamentarian: in the Knesset records there is not a single bill attached to his name, and he consistently held one of the worst records of attendance. As a member of the prestigious Knesset Foreign Affairs and Defense Committee, Eban attended only sixteen of forty-seven meetings in the first half of 1979, while two years later he attended only twenty-three of forty-nine meetings; during the first fifty-five sessions of the Knesset in 1985 Eban spoke only once, and did not ask the government a single question.[35] Even as foreign minister he did not see himself as an integral player in the political game. Once a journalist opened an interview with "Mister foreign minister, you as a politician. . . ." but Eban curtly stopped him. "I would prefer it if you address me as a statesman," he said, correcting the nervous journalist.[36]

Following the signing of the Israel-Egypt peace treaty in March 1979, Prime Minister Menachem Begin invited the Ebans to join him on his visit to Egypt. It was their first visit to the country since their honeymoon on the River Nile exactly thirty-four years earlier. Soon there were rumors that Eban had been offered the post of the first Israeli ambassador to Egypt—an inspiring prospect given his obvious linguistic skills and diplomatic nous. But Eban was adamant that his ambassadorial days were behind him: "Ambassadors no longer have the great amount of influence that they had in my early days. When I was ambassador in Washington for 10 years, my Prime Minister came to Washington once in 10 years, so that I did the negotiations. Now the Prime Minister comes 10 times in a single year." But more importantly, Eban pointed to the unpalatable prospect of defending and explaining the policies of an expansionist right-wing government. "I saw Adlai Stevenson end tragically because he accepted the idea of being a spokesman for views that were not his own," Eban noted, recalling his old friend's experience as U.S. ambassador to the United Nations under presidents John F. Kennedy and Lyndon Johnson, "and I don't intend to be a spokesman for views that are not my own."[37]

Having narrowly won the 1981 general elections by forty-eight seats to the Alignment's forty-seven, Begin soon gave Eban an excellent reason to speak his mind—against the government's haphazard decision to invade Lebanon. The roots of Israel's invasion of Lebanon in 1982 went back to the 1970 Jordanian Civil War, which had led to the expulsion of the Palestine Liberation Organization (PLO) from Jordan to southern Lebanon. Torn by a civil war in 1975 and plagued by violent struggles for power between Shias, Sunnis, and Maronite Christians that dated back to the 1940s, Lebanon proved to be a fertile ground for PLO operations. During the 1970s the group steadily increased its cross-border incursions into northern Israel, which culminated in the massacre of twenty-two schoolchildren in the northern town of Ma'a lot in May 1974, and a deadly attack on a bus on the Haifa–Tel Aviv road in March 1978 that left thirty-seven passengers dead and a further seventy-eight injured. In its search for a grand strategy for Lebanon, the Begin government formed an alliance with the country's minority Maronite Christian community, which sought to free Lebanon from the PLO and the increasing intervention of Syria. On June 3, 1982, Shlomo Argov, the Israeli ambassador to the United Kingdom, was shot outside the Dorchester Hotel in London by members of the Abu Nidal Organization. It seemed like the perfect pretext for Israel to eradicate the PLO threat once and for all (even though the assassins belonged to a group that opposed Arafat's leadership). The plan was the brainchild of Defense Minister Ariel Sharon, who promised the government a swift and limited ground operation to push the PLO back forty kilometers from the border in order to eliminate the threat of its rockets and cross-border infiltrations. It soon became clear, however, that Sharon's real design for Lebanon far exceeded the declared aims of the operation. By June 14, eight days into Operation Peace for Galilee, the Israel Defense Forces (IDF) and Christian militias (the Phalanges) were laying siege to the capital Beirut and engaging Palestinian and Syrian forces. Menachem Begin likened the Israeli invasion of Lebanon to the Allies' just war against the Nazis, and Yasser Arafat was deemed to be Adolf Hitler reincarnate. The prime minister wrote to U.S. president Ronald Reagan in August 1982 that he felt "empowered to instruct a valiant army facing 'Berlin,' where, among innocent civilians, Hitler and his henchmen hide in a bunker deep beneath the surface. My generation, dear Ron, swore on the altar of God that whoever proclaims his intent to destroy the Jewish state or the Jewish people, or both, seals his fate, so that what happened from Berlin—with or without inverted commas—will never happen again."[38] Begin's resurrection of Hitler to justify Israel's heavy-handed intervention in Lebanon (on the eve of the war he told the Knesset, "The alternative to this operation is Treblinka") angered many Israelis. Eban described Begin's letter to Reagan as "a dark and macabre fantasy" and "one of the most bizarre documents in recent diplomatic history," suggesting that the Israeli prime minister was "losing touch with reality."[39] Reagan himself later described Begin as a leader who believed in the biblical maxim of an eye for an eye, while Ariel Sharon, the godfather of invasion, was described by the American president as "a bellicose man who seemed to be chomping at the bit to start a war."[40]

The siege of Beirut continued for nearly two months and was accompanied by intense Israeli bombardment of the city. On August 12 American mediation finally succeeded in negotiating a cease-fire, and the PLO agreed to leave Beirut to a host of Arab countries. On September 2 the last of its besieged six thousand fighters left the city, and PLO headquarters were relocated to Tunis. At that point, in strict military terms and notwithstanding Sharon's political deception, the operation was a resounding success: the PLO was banished from Lebanon, and with it disappeared the threat to Israel's northern towns, while the Syrians were also humbled by the superior Israeli Air Force and armored divisions. But the military success came at a heavy price. Some 20,000 Lebanese civilians were killed and more than half a million were made homeless as many villages and towns in southern Lebanon were deserted at the sight of the advancing columns of Israeli tanks. Large parts of Beirut were reduced to rubble from the incessant Israeli artillery, air, and naval pounding of the city, and its people were cut off from electricity, water, and food for weeks. Hundreds of Israeli soldiers also died in the fighting, and as the IDF closed in on Beirut in July, many Israelis began to question the morality versus the utililty of the war. Eban was among the most vocal and critical voices of this movement. He pointed out that Israel's image in the eyes of the world had been rightly tarnished, and it was now portrayed as "an aggressive and arrogant country which inflicts suffering on besieged children."[41]

With the departure of the PLO and Syrian forces from Beirut, the road was open for the Phalanges, Israel's Maronite Christian allies, to take control of the city. But on September 14 Bashir Gemayel, the Phalange leader who had won the presidential elections three weeks earlier, was killed when a 450-pound bomb exploded in the headquarters of the party in East Beirut. Eban's old quip that in the Middle East "no situation is ever so bad that it cannot get significantly worse" became a tragic reality in the following days. Fueled by primordial vengeance against the Palestinian Muslims, the Christian Phalanges entered Sabra and Shatila, two refugee camps in West Beirut that were under the full control of the Israeli Army. Despite early intelligence warnings of the likelihood of Phalangist retribution in the aftermath of Gemayel's assassination, IDF commanders allowed these units to enter the camps to search for and arrest any remaining terrorists. But what followed was as harrowing as it was predictable. In a bloody orgy of violence that lasted from the evening of September 16 to the early hours of the morning of September 18, between eight hundred and two thousand men, women, and children were massacred (the numbers are disputed to this day) by the Christian militias while the Israeli Army illuminated the camps at nighttime with flares and manned all the exits to prevent anyone escaping.[42]

The news of the Sabra and Shatila massacre shocked the world and the Israeli public. A week later 400,000 Israelis (10 percent of the total population) participated in the largest political rally in the country's history, demanding the resignation of defense minister Sharon and the establishment of a commission of inquiry to investigate how the massacre was allowed to take place. Eban berated some voices who argued that the massacre was unexpected: "It is akin to saying 'I let the fox into the henhouse but I had no idea that it might slaughter the hens.'"[43]

Three days after the mass rally in Tel Aviv, Begin finally bowed to public pressure and instructed the government to establish a judicial commission of inquiry. On February 7, 1983, the three-member commission, led by the president of the Supreme Court, Yitzhak Kahan, published its report. It attributed direct responsibility for the massacre to the Phalangists, but added that several Israeli officials bore indirect responsibility for what had happened. Unlike the Agranat Commission, which had investigated the failings leading up to the Yom Kippur War nearly a decade earlier, the Kahan Commission decided not to distinguish between military and political leaderships. It attributed to Begin responsibility for failing to prevent the entry of the Phalangists into the camps, even though he did not receive an early warning from Sharon or Chief of the General Staff Rafael Eitan that the militias were about to do so. Sharon, however, was found to bear "personal responsibility" for ignoring the signs pointing to the potential for Phalangist retribution and for failing to inform Begin of his decision to allow the Phalangists to enter the camps. The report called on Sharon to "draw the appropriate personal conclusions" and, if necessary, the prime minister was called to exercise his authority "to remove a minister from office." Sharon initially called on the government to reject these recommendations, but on February 14 he finally bowed to public pressure and resigned. In October, gnawed by the mounting antiwar protests outside his residence and depressed by the death of his wife, Aliza, a year earlier, Begin announced his resignation. He was replaced by Yitzhak Shamir, his foreign minister and old comrade-in-arms in the underground fight against the British Mandate.[44]

Eban was one of the fiercest critics of the war and the Likud government that instigated it. The only thing that the Begin government had achieved in the war was uniting the fragmented Lebanese society against Israel, he thundered from the podium of the Knesset.[45] He lent his support to the war's opponents at home and abroad, describing the war as "the most miserable war in the country's history, with the dubious honor of being listed alongside the greatest failures and disgraces of the twentieth century, such as the Vietnam War."[46] He teamed up with the Committee of Concerned American Jews, a nonpartisan group, in a mass mail appeal to "restore the image of a Jewish democratic state."[47] Addressing a Houston synagogue, Eban charged that the Begin government could only be compared to "some parts of South Africa" and that the PLO threat did not justify the military invasion of Lebanon—"in the year before the war the PLO killed only two people," he said, "and because of this government's decision the PLO has now killed 500 people in this war."[48] Eban even wrote the introduction to the published Kahan Commission report, in which he blasted the "inhibited" design for the Lebanese frontier adopted by Begin and Sharon and described the Sabra and Shatila massacre as the "terrifying ordeal . . . of the Nazi-like sadism with which the Phalangists did their work, of the vain effort of women and children to escape from the camps, which were surrounded by Israeli troops."[49]

Eban's reputation abroad as Israel's elder statesman, if not its moral compass, grew steadily alongside his strident attacks against the tragedy of the Lebanon war and the Likud's expansionist designs in the West Bank. In August 1983, nearly a decade after his ousting from government and a generation after his heyday as the Voice of Israel at the UN, Eban was inducted into the International Platform Association's Orators Hall of Fame as one of the modern era's "ten greatest orators in the English language"; the other nine were Daniel Webster, Abraham Lincoln, William Jennings Bryan, Franklin Delano Roosevelt, Winston Churchill, Martin Luther King Jr., Adlai Stevenson, Douglas Macarthur, and John F. Kennedy. "I'm the only one who's alive in that hall," he later wryly exclaimed, "which they seemed to resent when I called out to thank them."[50] The same year Eban's new book, *The New Diplomacy: International Affairs in the Modern Age*, was published to unanimous acclaim. The *Guardian* of London described Eban as the "Rolls-Royce of the diplomatic circuit," and "as urbane, fluent, thoughtful and surefooted as ever."[51] Conor Cruise O'Brien, one of Ireland's greatest public intellectuals, gave Eban perhaps the greatest accolade by naming him "the modern diplomatist who has best earned the right to be considered [Charles-Maurice de] Talleyrand's heir," referring to the astute French diplomat who served under Louis XVI and Napoleon Bonaparte. Whereas Henry Kissinger was more in the class of Otto von Bismarck or the post-1814 Klemens von Metternich, who always negotiated from a position of strength, Eban—like Talleyrand—"has held some mighty poor cards, and played them mighty well."[52]

Yet undoubtedly Eban's crowning achievement came the following year, with the broadcast of the television series *Heritage: Civilization and the Jews*, which he hosted and narrated. The nine-part series charted three thousand years of Jewish civilization and was the product of six years of planning and production. It was filmed in eighteen countries across four continents, and cost more than five million dollars—a staggering budget for a documentary series.

The series won three Emmy Awards and a Peabody Award. It was shown on 275 PBS stations in America and reached an audience of more than fifty million. The series was subsequently used as course material by more than 150 universities and colleges in the United States, and the accompanying book became an instant bestseller, with 150,000 copies sold in the first eight weeks of publication. The screening of the series was so successful that PBS aired it again in 1985. *Heritage* was a resounding triumph—though as one *New York Times* TV critic pointed out, "Mr. Eban recites history, often with great insight, but sometimes it is rather like an electronic yeshiva. . . . This viewer found himself wishing, respectfully, that Charlton Heston were around."[53]

THE POLLS LEADING UP TO THE JULY 1984 GENERAL ELECTIONS LOOKED VERY promising for the Alignment under Shimon Peres—and for Eban personally. There was real optimism that the travails of the Lebanon war and the plummeting economy under Likud would catapult the Labor Party back into power. Eban, who as the public's favorite choice for foreign minister consistently dwarfed any other candidates, was reassured by Peres that the job was his. Peres had truly valued Eban's support of him ever since 1974 and considered him a senior member of his political team. But unlike Eban, Peres was a political animal whose survival instincts trumped tentative alliances and personal relationships. When Yitzhak Navon, the Israeli president, returned to the Labor Party in May 1984, Peres sensed an immediate threat to his leadership; Navon was an old hand in Israeli politics, having served as David Ben-Gurion's political secretary and bureau chief in the 1950s, and later joining Rafi following the 1965 split from Mapai. He was a natural ally of Peres and a counterforce to Rabin, and as a former president who returned to the political game he had a certain public aura that neither Peres nor Rabin could match. Fearful of losing to the new contender in the battle for the party's leadership, Peres, who at that time led thc polls, moved quickly to neutralize the potential threat. He offered to Navon whatever portfolio he wanted in the future potential government in exchange for the promise not to run against him. Three days later Navon returned with an answer: he demanded not one but three posts: foreign minister, deputy prime minister, and acting prime minister—the latter being the highest rank in the order of succession, whereas the title of deputy prime minister was more honorary than a statutory provision.[54] Peres accepted Navon's extortionist demand with a heavy heart, but he was elated about removing the threat to his leadership.

Peres then met with Yossi Beilin, the party's spokesman, in order to determine what to do with Eban. He sent Beilin to Eban's house to deliver the news. Upon hearing it, Eban did not flinch; he merely collected himself. He didn't say anything, but his face said everything. Sitting next to him on the sofa, Suzy—forever her husband's outspoken defender—gave Beilin a piece of her mind: "How could Peres do this to Aubrey!? I've never trusted this man! He tricked him!" Beilin's gallant efforts to explain some simple truths about Israeli politics fell on deaf ears. Suzy would have none of it, and she never forgave Peres. Eban was the party's spokesman on foreign affairs at the time, and the recipient of successive promises from Peres that he was his chosen foreign minister, dating back to 1977. He was naturally devastated by the news but he was hardly surprised, knowing very well that without political backing of his own in the party his position was more precarious than that of other members.

Eban's global reputation as Israel's brightest and most experienced diplomat was his chief obstacle at home: while he topped every opinion poll as the public's favorite for the post of foreign minister, that same public could not imagine him at any other post—and neither was he interested in doing anything else. Peres, for example, had served as minister of immigration and absorption, minister of transportation, minister of communications, minister of information, minister of defense, and briefly as acting prime minister following Rabin's resignation in 1977. Even Moshe Dayan, who was so intimately associated with the Defense Ministry, had served as foreign minister in Begin's first government. Eban, whose early spell as education minister had never become attached to his legacy, insisted that for him it was either the Foreign Ministry or political wilderness. A few days after the meeting with Beilin he formally responded to Peres in a well-composed letter: "I do not agree that there is no choice. Let's win first and then divide the areas of responsibility." He flatly rejected any offers to act as deputy prime minister with "political responsibilities," and demanded that Peres stand by his earlier promises to him. Accepting Navon's "excessive" demands, he warned Peres, would therefore lead to his dismissal and to a new probing into Peres's widely acknowledged "credibility gap." Eban would have no choice but to blame Navon for his dismissal, he told Peres, and the whole episode would do nothing but damage the party's chances of winning the elections.[55]

Eban was fighting a losing battle. Later that day he discovered that he was placed fifth on the party's ticket, behind Peres, Navon, Rabin, and former chief of staff Haim Bar-Lev. This ranking was not accidental: these four men comprised the newly established Organizing Committee, which aimed to replace the rancorous party leadership battles of the previous three election campaigns. Meeting in room 772 at the Dan Hotel in Tel Aviv, the committee did not take long to allocate the first four places on the party's list to themselves. The problems started from the fifth place down. Eban, who was placed third in 1981, of course had no idea about the meeting and did not expect to drop down to fifth.[56] At sixty-nine, Eban was the oldest member of the party and the only senior remnant of the historic Mapai; even Peres acknowledged Eban's status as the elder statesman of the Labor Party. But Eban did not buy Peres's explanation that Navon's popularity was the reason to offer him the Foreign Ministry post. If Navon was indeed so popular, Eban retorted, then perhaps Peres should have offered him the prime minister's post.[57]

History was made at the general elections, which took place in July 1984. For the first time neither political bloc could form a majority coalition. Though the Alignment won 44 seats compared to the Likud's 41, it could only muster a 60-seat coalition in the 120-seat Knesset, and Likud couldn't do any better either. After weeks of intense negotiations, conducted under an atmosphere of mutual suspicion and apprehension, the leaders of the two blocs agreed on a unique compromise: a national unity government would operate for fifty months. Shimon Peres would act as the prime minister during the first half of the period, while Yitzhak Shamir, the Likud leader who succeeded Begin, would serve as acting prime minister and foreign minister. After twenty-five months a "rotation" would take place, whereby Peres and Shamir would exchange posts. In September 1984 the mammoth government, which included twenty-five ministers and five deputy ministers and rested on a coalition of ninety-seven members of the Knesset, was sworn in. Peres described it as the most interesting government in the history of Israel, whereas Eban was typically perceptive in his assessment: "This government, the like of which has never been seen in any parliamentary democracy, allows each of the big parties to stop the other from doing what it wants. . . . This government is so inconceivable that it may even work."[58]

Despite the unprecedented size of the coalition government, Eban found himself left out once again. He took no comfort in the fact that Yitzhak Navon, to whom Peres had promised three posts before the elections, was "relegated" to the post of education minister. Eban wanted to remain relevant, but the more he flagged his successes abroad the more he looked foreign to the political game at home. This unmistakably Ebanesque pursuit of recognition reached a somewhat absurd level in an interview with an Israeli daily three months after the new government was sworn in:

Q: Abba Eban, let's start with a question on . . .
A: Excuse me. I would like, with your permission, to define some of the topics of which I would like to express my opinion. I have a special interest to talk about the withdrawal from Lebanon, the American aid and my special television series in the United States, which has been seen by 50 million viewers so far. I would also like to mention the fact that my name continues to top public opinion polls for the post of foreign minister, for the 20th consecutive time.
Q: Then perhaps you should write an article . . . it seems that despite the polls you gradually disappear from the political map.
A: I do not feel that a political person must act and create only out of the minister's seat. . . . I continue to act on the international level, I am a member of 10 Knesset sub-committees, I write books, and take part in the recording of television productions, and draw comfort in the fact that my latest book, *Civilization and the Jews*, became a bestseller in the United States. More than one hundred and fifty thousand copies to date.
Q: Which means about one million dollars, sir.
A: Perhaps a bit less.[59]

EBAN'S PARLIAMENTARY STATURE WAS BRIEFLY RESURRECTED WHEN THE KNESSET opened its eleventh seat in August 1984. Until the Knesset elected its new speaker, it was customary for its eldest member who was not a minister to carry out this duty, and at sixty-nine, Eban was handed the job of presiding over the sessions of the parliament, albeit temporarily. Armed with his enviable eloquence and acerbic humor, Eban turned the humdrum proceedings into the best show in town, if only for a short few weeks. His fellow parliamentarians and the reporters at the gallery gulped down with glee his funny witticisms. "Only Eban's humor saved the Knesset's first day," read one headline, while even his political adversaries admitted that "a Knesset headed by Abba Eban would have attained a worldwide prestige which it has hitherto lacked."[60]

In fact, Eban was so successful at his new job that he sought a way out. "Every time I open my mouth they expect me to tell a joke," he told Uri Raday, the director of the Knesset's Foreign Affairs and Defense Committee. "Now I have to wrack my brains about what new witticism I'm going to tell them when I open the next session. What am I, a clown? I've had enough!" Eban revealed to Raday that Peres offered him the post of minister without portfolio in the new government, or the chairmanship of the Foreign Affairs and Defense Committee, of which he had been a member since 1974. He quizzed Raday on what it was like to be the chairman of a committee. "Nobody expects the chairman of the Foreign Affairs and Defense Committee to tell jokes," Raday reassured him.[61]

Eban concluded his final appearance as speaker of the Knesset in typical form. "What awaits me now reminds me of Exodus 2:11," he announced before an enchanted plenum. "And it came to pass in those days, when Moses was grown, that he went out unto his brethren, and looked on their burdens. . . ." He then stepped down from his rostrum to take his seat among his suffering colleagues.[62]

The chairmanship of the Knesset Foreign Affairs and Defense Committee seemed to be the one parliamentary job that most suited Eban's experience, interests, and qualifications. He now had the power to oversee the workings of the intelligence, security, and foreign services, and had the authority to undertake personal hearings of the country's top policy makers. Two factors determined the gravitas of the committee—its members and, even more so, its chairman. The committee's reputation as ruthless or toothless was often a direct consequence of the chairman's own standing in the eyes of his parliamentary colleagues. Eban was respected by his peers, but he certainly did not instill fear in those who were invited to appear before the committee. He read all the material presented before him and rarely missed a meeting, but it was clear to the other members of the committee that he did not immerse himself in the specifics of the issues. Despite the enviable reputation of the committee he was heading and the fact that he was privy to the same sensitive material as the prime minister, Eban did not particularly enjoy the job. It was painfully obvious to those who worked with him that he still resented his party's failure to give him the one thing that he felt befitting his national and global stature: a return to the Foreign Ministry.[63] And, as he was soon about to discover, his new post was a poisoned chalice: it would allow him to return to the center stage of Israeli politics and enjoy the glowing limelight of the international media but, almost simultaneously, it ended his political career in a most brutal manner.

XVIII

How Terrible Is This Place

On November 21, 1985, FBI agents arrested Jonathan Pollard, a civilian U.S. Navy intelligence analyst, outside the Israeli embassy in Washington, DC, charging him with spying for Israel. It emerged that Pollard, an American Jew and a devout supporter of Israel, had offered his services to Aviem Sella, a brilliant Israeli Air Force colonel who had studied for a doctorate at New York University. Sella had forwarded Pollard's offer to his contacts at a shadowy intelligence unit in the Israeli Defense Ministry, euphemistically called the Bureau of Scientific Relations and known by its Hebrew acronym LAKAM. It was headed by Rafi Eitan, a celebrated spy chief who had masterminded the capture of Adolf Eichmann in Buenos Aires in 1960. Pollard quickly became one of Israel's most productive intelligence assets. He delivered more than a thousand classified documents, providing valuable information on the military capabilities of Arab states on a weekly basis, in exchange for a monthly stipend of $1,500 plus bonuses—though he always maintained that he was motivated by a love for Israel rather than money.

Allies aren't supposed to spy on one another, and the news of Pollard's arrest rightly shocked and angered the Americans. The Pollard affair soon brought U.S.-Israeli relations to their lowest point in history, surpassing even the tumultuous years of the administration of President Dwight D. Eisenhower. The Israeli government's hasty announcement that the affair was a "rogue operation" rather than a government-sanctioned one did little to appease the Pentagon and the intelligence community. The Israeli government was naturally embarrassed by the affair, as it was caught red-handed betraying the trust of its most important ally. And it vexed America's Jews, who were always sensitive to accusations of double loyalty. The damage to U.S.-Israeli relations, especially in the field of intelligence cooperation, was not rectified until the First Gulf War in 1991, while Pollard himself was refused pardon by four successive presidents, until his mandatory parole in November 2015; to this day he remains the longest-held spy in an American prison.[1]

Pollard began spying for Israel in May 1984, the twilight months of the Likud government under the premiership of Yitzhak Shamir, with Moshe Arens as defense minister. But following the electoral draw at the general elections of July and the rotational national unity government that had formed two months later, Shimon Peres assumed the premiership until October 1986, when he swapped posts with Foreign Minister Shamir. Throughout this period —from September 1984 onward—Yitzhak Rabin held the defense portfolio. On the night of November 30, 1985, nine days after Pollard's arrest, Prime Minister Peres was awakened by the telephone at 3:00 a.m. On the line was an incensed secretary of state, George Shultz. What could Israel do to improve the situation? Peres asked. "Apologize, and promise to cooperate fully with us," was the terse reply. The magnitude of the affair and its potential implications for U.S.-Israeli relations were palpable to Peres even at that uncongenial hour. He assured Shultz that the Israeli government would fully cooperate, and promised to retrieve every single one of the documents that Pollard had stolen.[2]

On March 4, 1987, Pollard was convicted of spying and was sentenced to life in prison. In response to the mounting pressure from American officials, a week later two separate commissions of inquiry were set up in Israel to investigate the events leading up to Pollard's recruitment, the nature of ministerial knowledge of his activities, and the actions taken after his capture. The first commission was appointed by the government, and was composed of Yehoshua Rotenstreich, a prominent Tel Aviv attorney, and Zvi Tsur, a former chief of staff. The second commission was the Knesset's Foreign Affairs and Defense Committee's Subcommittee for Intelligence and Secret Services, headed by Eban. Neither committee enjoyed the executive powers of a national commission of inquiry, such as the Agranat Commission in 1974 or the Kahan Commission in 1982. The Rotenstreich-Tzur Commission's mandate was limited by the inner cabinet that established it, while Eban's commission was essentially a parliamentary commission led by politicians to investigate politicians. The reports of the two commissions were therefore not binding, and they could not make personal recommendations; Rotenstreich and Tzur could not even decide which parts of their report, if any, would be made public, whereas the Eban Commission drew on the judgment of the Agranat Commission, stating that any conclusions to be drawn from issues concerning ministerial responsibility were not a matter for a commission of inquiry but for public opinion.[3]

Reflecting the exigencies of the national unity government, the seven-member parliamentary committee was split down the middle: three members from the Alignment (Eban, Micha Harish, and Simcha Dinitz, whose relationship with Eban remained courteous but not overly friendly—a legacy of the Yom Kippur War),[4] three from the Likud (Ehud Olmert, David Magen, and Eliyahu Ben-Elisar), and Yosef Burg from the National Religious Party. From the outset political loyalties dictated much of the calculations of the committee members: Olmert was Shamir's man, Ben-Elisar was in Moshe Arens's camp, and Magen was loyal to Ariel Sharon, who as defense minister in 1981 had appointed Rafi Eitan as head of LAKAM. Harish and Dinitz were supporters of Peres, while Burg had made as little effort as possible to lead an independent line of inquiry, and as the commission reached the final and decisive stages of deliberation he conveniently ventured off on a tour of Latin America. Eban, meanwhile, showed no signs of a political or a personal agenda, even though he had many reasons to use this fortuitous opportunity to settle some old scores with Rabin and Peres.[5]

The committee sat for nearly two months, held dozens of meetings, and questioned twenty-five witnesses. Rabin and Peres had good reasons to fear the outcome of the Eban inquiry. They suspected that he might use the opportunity to exact revenge—on Rabin for bypassing him as foreign minister while he was ambassador in Washington and then for kicking him out of government in 1974, and on Peres for lying to him repeatedly and gradually excluding him from the party leadership. Determined to preempt Eban's expected act of revenge, both Rabin and Peres launched a smear campaign against him, his commission, and its anticipated recommendations. Rabin reminded everyone that Eban's commission was no more than a parliamentary subcommittee devoid of any executive powers, while Peres described the members of the committee as pompous peacocks, a description widely understood to be pointed directly at Eban. The other two Alignment members in the committee, Harish and Dinitz, were expected to counteract Eban's independent line and dilute whatever the recommendations against Peres and Rabin might be. At the same time, Olmert and Magen tried to shift the focus of the committee from the period leading up to Pollard's recruitment (May 1984) to the period following his discovery (November 1985)—thus deflecting attention from Shamir and Arens to Peres and Rabin. In the midst of it all was Eban, trying to balance the opposing agendas of his colleagues on the committee while still presenting a consensual report, but not so politically balanced as to be devoid of all substance; it was an unwanted realization of Eban's old adage that "consensus means a lot of people saying collectively what nobody believes individually." At the same time "too much" substance in highlighting ministerial responsibilities was certain to put Eban on a collision course with Rabin and Peres.[6]

As expected, the work of the Eban Commission was the subject of intense media scrutiny and the source of incessant leaks on an almost daily basis. After more than a decade of diminished political activity in Israel, Eban was quite amused to find that he had become a cause célèbre almost overnight. Suddenly everybody was talking about Eban again—his ambassadorial years, his rifts with Rabin and dismissal from government, his topsy-turvy relations with Peres, his unusual fit in Israeli society. After such a long time, they asked, how did he feel to be in a position of political power once again? ("I am not the country's hangman, such epithets do not fit my standing nor my temperament.") After such a long time in politics, why did he still project a certain alienation from his environment? ("If an Israeli citizen is accused of that it means that he was not born in Eastern Europe.") Did he see himself as a political leader? ("I didn't see any desire in my party to put me in a position of leadership.")[7]

The task of drafting the commission's report fell into Eban's hands, but some of his colleagues soon regretted it; they simply could not understand Eban's ornate expressions, not to mention the sheer length of his creation—all three volumes of it. "What does he think he's doing, writing another *Heritage*?" they moaned.[8]

The sensitivity of the material and the danger of leaks convinced Eban of the need to conduct the final deliberations in a secure place, away from the prying eyes of the media. Upon Olmert's recommendation, on Sunday, May 24 the members of the committee arrived at the gates of the Neurim police facility near the coastal town of Netanya—only to be greeted by a crowd of reporters and photographers. Accompanied by Uri Raday, the committee's secretary, and retired general Aharon Yariv, its intelligence adviser, they spent the next two days and two nights at the secure facility until the all-important recommendations were finalized. The setting was hardly regal: Eban had a room to himself, but the others had to share three bedrooms. They had access to only one telephone, and they had to share their meals with the police officers in the facility.[9]

The basis for the discussions was a questionnaire compiled by Eban and submitted to the members of the committee. Each was asked to respond directly to the sixteen questions in Eban's document (Burg did so in writing from Argentina). The discussions were tense, at times explosive, and included quite a few outbursts, especially between Olmert and Harish. The pressure on Eban was tremendous. He made it clear from the outset that he would not put his signature to an official document that could be read as a whitewash. At the eleventh hour, with the report all but written yet the crucial preamble still elusive, Olmert gave Eban the reassurances he evidently needed. He appealed to Eban's conscience and sense of history, noting that "your brilliant career is behind you. What is left is your magical name in the world and especially in the United States—are you going to tarnish all you have achieved by defending these two people who never respected you and let you down time after time?" There was only one conclusion from the investigation, Olmert said: in a parliamentary system Peres "must bear preponderant responsibility as prime minister" during the scandal, whereas the ministerial responsibility of Rabin, under whose watch Pollard continued to spy for Israel for a period of fourteen months, must "stand beyond any doubt." Eban swallowed Olmert's cheap psychological trick. He insisted, however, that the report refer to Peres's "decisions" rather than "mistakes." "What have I done to deserve this?," Eban later bemoaned, "managing an enquiry commission of politicians led by politicians?"[10]

On the morning of May 27, 1987, Prime Minister Shamir received the report of the Rotenstreich-Tsur Commission, and that evening Eban presented at a press conference the report of his commission. There were basic similarities as well as some very important differences between the reports. Both concluded that the government did not know of Pollard's activities, and laid the direct blame for the scandal on Rafi Eitan. Both reports concluded that it was up to the Knesset and the Israeli public to determine whether individual cabinet members should be reprimanded for their actions and decisions. The Eban report accused Eitan and Sella, the Air Force colonel with whom Pollard had made the initial contact, of exceeding their authority and of failing to inform their superiors of their activities. Eitan, the veteran spy master, was particularly criticized for plunging the country into a serious crisis with its most important ally and into violation of official state guidelines that prohibited spying on the United States.

The major difference between the two reports concerned the proportioning of ministerial responsibility: the Rotenstreich-Tsur Commission concluded that rather than specific cabinet members, "the government must shoulder all the responsibility since every minister fulfils a certain function, but is part of the government. There is no possibility of imposing a sanction on a particular minister." The Eban Commission, however, was much more critical in placing responsibility on individual ministers. It stressed that the Pollard affair was not a rogue operation, as the government initially announced, but noted that none of the ministers concerned knew that Pollard existed until he was arrested in November 1985. Nevertheless, the report added, "asking a lot of irritating questions is the very essence of the ministerial function," and none of the four individuals chose to question Eitan about this remarkable intelligence source. Moshe Arens, the defense minister at the time, was blamed for not supervising Eitan's activities, while Shamir, as prime minister until September 1984, was reprimanded for a certain laxity. But it was the two Labor Party leaders who received most of the blame. Rabin, who had succeeded Arens in September 1984, was accused of failing "to maintain procedures of scrutiny or to tighten control, as he was duty-bound to do so." It was under Rabin's watch that the Pollard affair became protracted, and he should have asked where the intelligence on his desk came from. But crucially, Harish and Dinitz added their reservations to Eban's wording, noting that Rabin's responsibility was no greater than that of Arens. As for Peres, who served as prime minister from September 1984 to October 1986, the report found him to carry "preponderant parliamentary responsibility" during the unmasking of the Pollard affair. Once again, Harish and Dinitz noted their reservations from this conclusion in the report, thus creating the impression that Eban sided with the Likud members of the committee to single out Rabin and Peres. Eban did his best at the press conference to praise Peres, Rabin, and Shamir for saving U.S.-Israeli relations from collapse by their decision to cooperate fully with the American investigation of Pollard and noted that Peres in particular deserved most of the credit for doing the right thing during his nocturnal telephone conversation with Secretary Shultz.[11] But such praise left little impression on Rabin and Peres. Eban didn't know it yet, but that evening his political career was over.

The following day the government publicly accepted the findings of the Rotenstreich-Tsur Commission, noting, "In our system, the whole government as one body bears responsibility before the Knesset." But it completely ignored the Eban report, and for good reason. "When everyone is guilty, no one is guilty," the press said about the whitewashed findings of the Rotenstreich-Tsur Commission. Even some cabinet members objected to the formulation of collective responsibility when it was clear that the affair was dealt with exclusively by a handful of ministers. "How can you expect the minister of agriculture or the minister of religious affairs to share responsibility on this kind of security matter?" asked one minister; another complained, "I found it very difficult to accept responsibility for issues which were never discussed in the Cabinet, and now, because some of our colleagues are pressed, we are obliged to take responsibility."

By comparison, the Eban Commission's report seemed egregiously vindictive because, as one senior official explained, "You don't punish people here, you don't execute people here." The report was criticized for blaming two ministers from each party—Shamir and Arens from the Likud, Peres and Rabin from Labor, thus appearing eager to lay equal blame but without calling for individual resignations. William Safire, the influential syndicated columnist, lambasted the Eban Commission for flinching at the sight of its duty, claiming that Eban himself "evaded his duty in a fog of red-faced rhetoric." One Israeli political commentator summed up succinctly the general feeling about the two reports: the two-man inquiry was "a joke," and "the only reason the Eban report looked brave was because it was compared to that." Another commentator described the Eban Commission's ruling as *parve*—"not really meat and not really milk, but something in between." But all of these critiques paled in comparison to what awaited Eban at the hands of Rabin and Peres. "No one in the States cares about this subject anymore," said one of Rabin's people. "Now is the time for Mr. Eban to be worried."[12]

This was an understatement. "Party Flays Eban for Pollard Report: Peres, Rabin Lead Labor's Attack on Israeli Elder Statesman," read a *Washington Post* headline two days later. Fuming over Eban's "act of disloyalty," Peres and Rabin ordered Uzi Baram, the party's secretary-general, to convene a special meeting of the Central Committee to discuss Eban's unacceptable behavior. The elder statesman was now a troublesome senior citizen. Baram knew that Eban's report was not a matter for discussion or approval by the party's Central Committee, but he yielded to the relentless pressure from Rabin and Peres. "It was one of the biggest failures in my political career," he later admitted.[13] The highly charged meeting took place on May 28, and Eban had no idea what was awaiting him. Rabin and Peres—the longtime party rivals whose mutual antipathy went back as far as 1974—joined forces to humiliate and crush Eban in front of hundreds of party members. Rabin went first, and without mentioning Eban's name even once, accused him of playing politics and betraying the party by siding with the Likud members on the committee.

Shocked by Rabin's attack and the hostile environment at the densely packed Ohel-Shem Auditorium in Tel-Aviv, Eban demanded the right to retort—amid heckling and catcalls from the crowd. There was not a grain of precision in Rabin's accusations, he declared, as shouts of "Traitor!" echoed across the hall. He insisted that he stood by his commission's report and that he would not be pressured by the party to change his mind; he had not invested ten weeks of hard work in the report "in order to be someone else's echo." He was applauded by some members of the party when he demanded "the right to differ with leaders with power and responsibility," and was then booed by others when he noted that one could be a party member without being forced to accept the party's line.

Then Peres took the stage. Speaking for nearly an hour, he was much more personal, more vehement, more visceral than Rabin in his attack on Eban:

> What are you complaining about!? Has anyone asked you to go against your conscience!? . . . You are the one under pressure!? You are the one who deserves pity? For months on end our names have been besmirched by the committee which you headed. . . . Abba, go your own way and take your conscience with you, nobody is pressuring you here . . . nobody attacked you. If anyone was hurt, it wasn't you. If anyone was hurt, it was because of your report . . . you sit on the Foreign Affairs and Defense Committee not as a judge but as the representative of the party.

At this point Peres was interrupted by two shouts from the crowd: "You don't need to lynch Abba Eban!" and "When can he respond to you?" But Peres did not relent. "Was your name besmirched or mine!?," he retorted, attacking Eban's anonymous defender.[14]

It was the most traumatic and humiliating evening in Eban's political career, and one of the most disgraceful episodes in the Labor Party's history. "It was very, very ugly," said one party veteran. "Here you had the number one and number two in the party publicly lambasting an elder statesman. It will play abysmally here as well as in the States." The next morning Baram was asked about the fallout from that dramatic meeting. "Let's just say that there are no lingering queues outside our offices of people wishing to join the party," he said wryly.[15]

Eban was upset but not surprised by Rabin's attack. Peres's assault, however, really hurt him. Unlike his long and tumultuous history with Rabin, he had always stood by Peres, even in the early days when many Mapai members doubted the young Rafi leader. "Maybe I'm spoiled," Eban said in an interview a few days later, "but I'm not used to being spoken to like that . . . my first thought was: why the hell do I need all this?"[16] He received unexpected encouragement from an unlikely ally, Ariel Sharon. "Now you know what he's like," Sharon said of Peres to Eban at a state dinner. "He's really a terrible person." Eban seemed to agree, describing Peres as "strident to the point of vulgarity" and "like a medieval pope who believed himself infallible." Eban also went beyond his commission's report and accused the ministers involved in the scandal of "hair-raising neglect . . . grave dereliction . . . and contemptuous disregard for one of our allies."[17]

Despite that traumatic experience and his rancorous relations with the party's two powerful leaders, Eban refused to declare his political career over. He drew strength from the party's new process for nominating its candidates for the next general elections. After two stunning defeats in 1977 and 1981 and an electoral tie with the Likud in 1984, the party had dropped its old habits of trusting a handful of leaders to draw up the entire slate behind closed doors and instead opened the process to the 1,260-member Central Committee. Eban also found solace in the fact that in the public eye he continued to be associated with the foreign minister's post more than anyone else—a remarkable record that had remained unbroken ever since his ousting from government thirteen years earlier. At the beginning of 1987 he led the polls with 21.1 percent approval, with Shamir (13.3 percent) and Peres (12.5 percent) trailing behind; by July his approval rate of 31.8 percent dwarfed Peres's second place, with 12.1 percent.[18]

There was, however, one major drawback for Eban in this new party primary system—ever since 1959 his place in the party's top echelon was secured by virtue of his ministerial positions and the backing of the party's leaders. But now his fate rested in the hands of 1,260 people who were complete strangers to him. Most party leaders enjoyed an established support base and a well-oiled lobbying machine, the result of years of handshaking and chitchatting with the rank and file, the foot soldiers of the party. They went to their weddings and helped their cousins get jobs. This was an alien experience to

Eban; realizing the enormity of the task before him, he asked Peres and Baram if he should run. Both thought that it would be an uphill struggle, but promised to support him.[19] Armed with a long list of the names and telephone numbers of all the Central Committee's members, Eban sat down to call on them and solicit their support. It was a bemusing and utterly frustrating experience, he later admitted: "Every time I said 'hello, this is Abba Eban speaking,' the voice on the other line would say 'Ok, and I'm Napoleon.'" Nobody believed that Abba Eban himself would pick up the phone to call on them. Begrudgingly, he spent the majority of the conversation persuading the person on the line that he was indeed speaking to Abba Eban.[20]

The party elections took place on June 15, 1988, at a conference center in Ramat Efal, an upscale municipality near Tel Aviv. A carnival-like atmosphere, with barbeque stands and live music, greeted the candidates and the hundreds of party members. Accompanied by his wife Suzy and wearing a suit jacket, Eban stood out from the crowd for reasons beyond his sartorial elegance. As Thomas Friedman had pointed out in the *New York Times* almost exactly a year earlier, by now Eban was looked on by many in the party as a fringe radical. His vocal criticism of Israel's military occupation of the West Bank and the Gaza Strip (it was "deforming and defacing our society" and "wasting our resources, and it is not necessary for our security") and his public lynching by Rabin and Peres further sharpened his image as an alien to the local scene. "When I go abroad I still can speak for Israel in terms of its achievements," Eban said, "But, frankly, when I look back at the speech I gave at Israel's birth to get us into the United Nations, I would not dare make that same speech now. The rhetoric was too utopian. Now I would be much more reserved. I would definitely not use the phrase that we will be 'a light unto the nations.'"[21]

Such statements did not chime well with the mainstay of Israeli politics—especially when they came from the chairman of the Knesset's Foreign Affairs and Defense Committee. Eban had no qualms about publicly criticizing his own government's treatment of the Palestinians, for example, writing in a November 1986 op-ed piece in the *New York Times*, "The Palestinians live without a right to vote or be elected . . . exposed to restraints and punishments that could not be applied against them if they were Jews, permitted to cross into Israel to work, but without permission to sleep overnight. It is a bleak, tense, disgruntled, repressed existence, with spurts of violence always ready to explode. There is no precedent for believing that this condition can long endure without explosion."[22]

Eban's first battle in Ramat Efal was to get into the top ten on the party's list for the general elections. But the first seven spots were reserved for Peres, Rabin, Navon, Israel Keysar (secretary-general of the powerful workers' union Histadrut), Ezer Weizmann (whose three-member Yahad party had merged with the Labor Party), Shlomo Hillel (speaker of the Knesset) and Baram. Eban had no chance of competing for the remaining three spots with party members whose expansive political nous stood in direct contrast to their years of ministerial experience or global reputation. Of the seventeen candidates fighting for those places, he came in sixteenth, receiving the support of only 480 of the 1,260 members of the Central Committee.[23] He now faced a dilemma—risking his pride and fighting for his place in the top twenty, knowing that he might not be successful, or saving himself the humiliation and bowing out of the race there and then. Once again he asked Peres and Baram for their advice. Once again they encouraged him to run, and he did. It was a pitiful scene to see thc party's elder statesman hopelessly chasing around for support. He was sweating, pale, helpless and anxious. "Suzy, Suzy, come on, we need to discuss, to carry on or not," he whispered to his wife by his side, "is there a chance? And what if I don't win it in the second round?"

After nearly three decades of parliamentary life, Eban still did not understand Israeli politics. No member of the party could sit on its ticket without at least tacit approval from Rabin and Peres. Eban could not emerge unscathed from the fallout of the Pollard inquiry. He was a marked man; from the outset of the investigation Rabin had promised that "no heads will roll," thus dissolving himself and his colleagues from any ministerial responsibility. The only politician's head that did roll was Eban's. But even if there wasn't an institutional anti-Eban design among the party ranks, then his personal tragedy was even greater: so many people assumed that someone of Eban's stature would find his place near the top of the list that they simply didn't bother voting for him.[24]

Regardless of the causes of Eban's ousting, if there was an atom of doubt in anyone's mind that Eban was out of his depth in the backstabbing and arm-twisting arena of Israeli politics, the scenes at Ramat Efal were a painful reminder. He did his best to mingle and solicit support, but it was too little, too late; he should have heeded David Ben-Gurion's advice to him nearly three decades earlier: "Eban, stop writing books and go talk to the comrades!"[25] Having been placed fifth, third, and third on the party's list for the previous three elections, Eban felt that a failed attempt to make it into the top thirty—

or perhaps worse, to actually being elected *only* in the third tier of the party—would be the sort of a humiliating blow that did not befit the status and reputation he had labored to build in the course of four decades. Eban decided not to abase himself further. “Come on Suzy, let’s go home,” he said before the results of the second round were even announced. This time he received even fewer votes—only 398. He went home to shower and change his suit, and then returned to Ramat Efal to thank those who did vote for him. Even Peres was surprised by the drama. “This is democracy,” he said to someone who protested Eban’s exclusion.[26]

The British politician Enoch Powell once observed that all political lives end in failure, for that is the nature of politics and of human affairs. Eban’s story was no different. It was long after midnight when the Ebans returned to their home after that torturous day. Exhausted, he sank into the sofa and turned to Suzy. “Ma norah ha’makom hazeh,” he grumbled. How terrible is this place.[27]

XIX

Will I Be Remembered?

EBAN'S SHOCKING EXIT WAS FOLLOWED BY AN OUTPOURING OF POLITICAL eulogies. His ousting received so much coverage in the press that it seemed to overshadow the other news from the primaries—there was a dramatic generational change in the party's list for the Knesset, with no fewer than eighteen members giving way to younger contenders. Shimon Peres was excited by the new list, describing it as "the best ever," one that would give the party "more public support and a victory over the Likud." Both predictions proved to be hollow within months.[1] A *Los Angeles Times* editorial suggested that Eban "fell victim to the kind of political deal-cutting from which he had always held aloof, and indeed scorned."[2] The *Miami Herald* told its readers, "If Israel is very lucky, Mr. Eban will continue to try to serve it, speaking out more freely than before, unencumbered by political constraints."[3] Some members of the Labor Party described Eban's exclusion as "our own intifada," though others pointed out that the party was looking to the future, and Eban represented the past. "But what about Peres, Rabin and Navon, all pensioners?" Eban retorted. "[E]ach of them is a grandfather in his own right."

Peres wrote a very personal letter to Eban, describing him as a "master statesman" and the "leading spokesman of thc Zionist revival and the Labor movement before the world," adding that "neither the people nor the party can afford to let go of your services." Addressed to "Dear Aubrey," it was a very warm and moving letter that left Eban bewildered; if Peres truly felt like this about Eban, why hadn't he tried harder to include him on the list?[4] Even Eban's political rivals on the right were shocked by Eban's ousting, with Ehud Olmert describing him as a "Gulliver in Lilliput." The Israeli public was also on

Eban's side; even after the ending of his political career he continued to be the most popular choice as foreign minister, with a 29 percent approval rating—double that of Peres.[5] In another poll, 64 percent of Labor Party supporters said that it was wrong to dump Eban, while 57 percent of Likud voters also felt that the Labor Party had blundered. Only 5 percent of those polled thought that the decision to keep Eban off the Labor list would help the party win the next general elections.[6]

When the dust settled a bit, Eban turned to record his indignation in a three-page letter to Peres and Baram. The voting in Ramat Efal had not happened overnight, he said, but was a direct result of the party's leadership's attitude toward him since 1974—an attitude that gave rise to a tradition he termed "the exclusion of Abba Eban as one of the cornerstones of the movement." He bemoaned the humiliation that he and Suzy had endured that day, adding that in his "wildest dreams" he had not imagined that he would be "a victim of such humiliation and disgrace." This was all the more shameful given his long list of literary, academic, and media achievements for many years, he said, adding, "It turns out that for ten and a half years the party had been using only ten per cent of my talents. . . . The purpose of my letter is not only archival. It suggests that among its other qualities our party does not excel at maximizing its resources." Looking to the future, Eban referred to "speculations in the national and international press that I shall express my opinions more candidly. I believe that this is a reasonable expectation."[7]

And Eban did just that. He was now even more candid, more outspoken, and more critical, and he had many reasons to be so. From the Labor Party's narrow electoral defeat to the Likud in the November 1988 general elections (which gave rise to another national unity government), through to the diplomatic deadlock on all fronts, to the raging Palestinian intifada against the Israeli occupation in the West Bank and Gaza: wherever Eban turned he saw doom and gloom. He blasted the permeation of superstition, intolerance, and xenophobia in Israeli society and politics.[8] He warned that the continuing occupation of 1,500,000 Palestinians weighed no less heavily on the rulers than on the ruled: "The present situation endangers our national and individual security, our economy, our international relations, our democratic principles, our Jewish majority, our image in the eyes of the world, our prospect of attaining peace, our probability of avoiding war, our universal Jewish unity, our national consensus and, above all, our most cherished values." Eban insisted that there was "no need of many words to explain why the 1,500,000 Palestinians under military rule have an interest in a different condition. They do not have a single one of the conditions that give fulfillment or dignity to a nation's life." The only solution was therefore partition of the land—it was the solution in 1947, and it remained the only feasible solution today: "The idea that one of the two nations in the area between the River Jordan and the Mediterranean Sea can permanently hold 100 per cent of the territories and their effective sovereignty is doomed to replacement, because it offends all the laws of political and human nature."[9]

Eban also chastised the Israeli government's refusal to negotiate with the Palestine Liberation Organization (PLO), despite Yasser Arafat's historic declaration in December 1988 that the PLO accepted UN Resolution 242, recognized Israel's right to exist, and renounced terrorism: "We refuse to negotiate with those who are willing, and are ready to negotiate with those who don't exist," Eban said. "Can anyone seriously believe that a Palestinian organization which can get 160 states to affirm its representative status can be totally and permanently excluded from the negotiation process?"[10] He laughed off the commonplace wisdom depicting the PLO as an existential threat to Israel. On the one hand, Eban explained, was the notion "that Israel is a demilitarized land like Iceland or Monaco, Lichtenstein or Costa Rica. The P.L.O. forces, by contrast, are depicted as the lineal descendants of Alexander the Great, Genghis Khan, Napoleon and the Hitler and Stalin dictatorships, able to exterminate Israel. . . . This is drastically opposed to reality. The Israeli defense system is one of the wonders of the world. Never in history has so small a community been able—and ready—to yield such vast capacity of defense, deterrence and reprisal."[11]

If Eban's words were not enough to embarrass the government, his actions certainly did. In January 1989 he accepted an invitation from the Netherlands-based Middle East Dialogue organization to attend an Israeli-Palestinian symposium in the Hague, which was also attended by senior PLO officials. At the time an Israeli law forbade Israeli citizens from meeting PLO members face to face, a ban that Eban thought was ludicrous: "There is nothing like it anywhere in the world. Even [U.S. senator Joseph] McCarthy would not dare introduce a law such as the law against meetings with the PLO! I am not allowed to meet with [senior PLO official] Nabil Shaath face to face, but if there are 100 people around us, it's OK. Laughable! . . . I do not believe that we can work toward peace without making a contact or without listening. The means of diplomatic contacts is not a grace to be awarded, but an opportunity to be seized."[12]

Though Eban was careful not to break the law by holding private conversations with PLO representatives, the mere presence of Israel's elder statesman in the company of senior PLO members such as Shaath, Bassam Abu Sharif, Hanna Siniora, and Sari Nusseibeh was seen as just short of treason in the eyes of the Israeli establishment. Benjamin Netanyahu, the deputy foreign minister, immediately ordered the cancellation of an official dinner in honor of Eban that was scheduled to be held at the residence of the Israeli ambassador in the Hague. Explaining his decision to the Knesset, Netanyahu said that Eban chose to attend the conference despite being advised not to do so by the Foreign Ministry, and that as an experienced diplomat with unique sensitivities to such matters he must have known that his presence there would significantly erode the stated policy of the Israeli government against such contacts. Other Knesset members accused Eban of "harnessing his talents for the Palestinian issue" and lobbying against his own government, while one member of the government demanded that Eban return his diplomatic passport, since by his incessant attacks against his own country he was serving the Palestinian cause. But others pointed sarcastically that "Abba Eban is the only Israeli who can travel around the world without a passport!" Eban's own response to the whole affair was typically acerbic. Jibing Netanyahu's unusual intervention, he mused, "The word 'deputy' has certain superfluous resonance. Bibi's actions remind me that we are not a banana republic but a republic of banana peels."[13]

It did not take Eban long to appreciate that his forced exile from politics was actually a blessing in disguise. "I now realize that not possessing the title of Member of the Israeli Knesset has no impact on status or prestige," he remarked in an interview. He and Suzy relocated to New York, where they spent up to eight months a year in their nineteenth-floor apartment of the Delmonico Hotel on Park Avenue and Fifty-Ninth Street. Eban was now a resident alien in Israel, meaning that he was exempt from paying income tax, though he insisted that he left the country simply because there was nothing left for him to do there. "The party retired me against my wishes," he said in 1991, "and I found it mentally difficult to be there with no reason to wake up in the morning. Nothing was offered to me. They thought that I should retire, and that's it. I had nothing to contribute, and nobody asked me to, either. . . . If I had stayed there, I have no doubt that I would have suffered, mentally and physically. It was a tragic situation."[14]

There was certainly nothing tragic about Eban's new life in New York, where everyone still addressed him as "Mr. Ambassador." He worked fourteen hours a day, dividing his time between writing books, frequent media appearances, guest lectures (for which he was paid $15,000 each), and the production of a new five-hour TV series, *Israel: A Nation Is Born* (for a fee of $2,000 per day of filming). He was invited to join (free of charge) the Harmony Club and the Metropolitan Club, two of the oldest and most exclusive private clubs in the country, though he could certainly afford their princely membership fees: his books have sold more than a million copies around the world, with *Heritage: Civilization and the Jews* alone selling up to 200,000 copies. "I have earned more money in the past two years than I have throughout the rest of my life," he boasted in 1991, "though even then I did not live in hardship."[15] But even his idyllic existence in Manhattan did not mask the scars of 1987–88. He described Peres's subsequent apologies as "the hollow talking of a politician," while Rabin "was in no position to look down at me. This is a man whose every role in his career was too big for him." As for the choice between the two to lead the party into the general elections of 1992, Eban described it as "a choice between the unpleasant and the intolerable."[16]

As a testimony to Eban's continued relevance on the world stage, in 1990 Henry Kissinger hosted a party for him at the United Nations to celebrate his seventy-fifth birthday. President George H. W. Bush and former presidents Ronald Reagan, Jimmy Carter, Gerald Ford, and Richard Nixon attended, along with King Juan Carlos of Spain and many other dignitaries who paid tribute. "How can one not give Abba Eban his due?" British prime minister Margaret Thatcher asked rhetorically in a telegram from London. "Actually, there are quite a few people in Israel who think it's possible," was Eban's wry reply. Flanked by Henry Kissinger and Jacqueline Kennedy, Eban could be excused for feeling a little smug. As one reporter observed, what on earth had the Labor Party been thinking when it ousted him two years earlier? Nobody in Israel could ever match Eban's international magnetism. "He was, and remains the greatest spokesman the Jewish people had ever had," Kissinger said, as old footage of the young Eban at the UN General Assembly was screened behind him.[17]

Two years later, in 1992, Eban's second autobiography, *Personal Witness: Israel through My Eyes*, was published to critical acclaim across the world. "Unfortunately, Eban was never fully appreciated in Israel," read the *Financial Times* review. "Perhaps the reason is that his moderation flowed from an alien rationality. His book, rich in insights, resonant in language, is the story of the Jewish state told by Cicero, not Thucydides."[18] Later that year the Hebrew University in Jerusalem dedicated the Abba Eban Centre for Israeli Diplomacy. In his address, Eban explained that the motivation for opening the center was to dispel the "conventional Israeli belief that diplomacy can do little more than ratify military success." Turning to Israeli-Palestinian relations, Eban reiterated his long-held belief that Israel "will not be able to claim to be the 'only democracy in the Middle East' if it remains one of the diminishing number of states in which a large proportion of the people under its jurisdiction . . . have no control over the government that rules their lives, may not compete freely in the market and are subject to collective rigors and penalties that are not applicable to their Jewish neighbours." Yet Eban's solution to this problem was not a full-blown Palestinian statehood, but a European or Benelux model of economic federation—a vision he had first proposed in 1967 in the aftermath of the Six-Day War before the Council of Europe in Strasburg: "A Palestinian state that could do exactly as it liked would arouse the most serious reservations in all sectors of Israeli opinion, but a self-governing Palestine, confederated with Jordan, that would accept community restraints and a co-ordinated security policy would pose a much lesser threat than Israel would face by maintaining the present volcanic status quo."[19]

In 1993 Eban joined George Washington University as its first J. B. and Maurice C. Shapiro Professor of International Affairs, which included an endowment of $100,000. During his one-year appointment he taught graduate and undergraduate courses in international affairs and delivered a number of public lectures. He then accepted a four-year term as George Washington University's first James Clark Welling Professor of International affairs. He also collected his twenty-first honorary degree, from Aberdeen University.[20] But Eban's most joyous cause for celebration that year was not his academic achievement but the news of the conclusion of the Oslo Accords between Israel and the PLO. He praised the courage and vision of Prime Minister Rabin and Foreign Minister Peres, and even admitted that his earlier criticism of the duo following his ousting from the party may have been unwarranted.[21] As expected, Eban was full of scorn for Netanyahu, the young Likud leader, describing his fierce attacks on the government as falling "far short below the traditions of truth and civility upheld by former opposition leaders."[22] Eban mourned Netanyahu's rise to power in the 1996 general elections, less than a year after Rabin's assassination at a Tel Aviv peace rally. In electing Netanyahu, Eban wrote, the Likud party has given Israeli society "a relatively youthful political leader and a totally antiquated political doctrine. . . . He supports indefinite Israeli rule over a disenfranchised Palestinian people in Gaza and the West Bank. . . . His worship of the status quo ignores the awkward fact that the status quo is in a terminal condition of disintegration."[23]

Eban's last book, *Diplomacy for the Next Century*, was published in 1998, and was based on a series of lectures he delivered at Yale University's Program on Ethics, Politics and Economics in 1993 and 1994. The *New York Times Book Review* praised Eban for his distilled views of world affairs and nominated the book to join the very short list of readable introductions to realism in foreign policy, alongside Walter Lippmann's *U.S. Foreign Policy*, Martin Wight's *Power Politics*, and George F. Kennan's *Realities of American Foreign Policy*.[24] Of all of Eban's books, this 191-page semiautobiographical primer on contemporary diplomacy provides the most compelling testimony to Eban's rare ability to infuse facts with wit. Eban laced his analysis of the many faces of the diplomatic practice through the ages with his own rich experience: "No situation is so bad that a badly conceived summit meeting cannot make it worse." "The United States has not been more virtuous than other nations. It has only been more fortunate." "All governments take their decisions individually in the name of national interest and then explain their decisions in terms of self-sacrificial altruism."[25] Eban dedicated the last two chapters of the book to the Israeli-Palestinian dialogue of the 1990s. He was an avid supporter of the Oslo peace process, and praised the Israeli, Palestinian, and Norwegian architects of the Oslo Accords. But by 1998, two years after Netanyahu swept Likud into power, Eban was downright disillusioned by the future prospects of the peace process. He thus concluded his analysis with a prophetic warning: "I do not say that the success of the peace process will lead to utopia. I do, however, declare that the failure of the peace process would lead to an inferno of explosive antagonisms and volcanic hatreds. Generations might have to pass before anybody would attempt such a peace project again."[26]

IN 2001, DURING A RAGING SECOND INTIFADA AND A MOTHBALLED PEACE PROCESS, Eban received the highest honor bestowed by the State of Israel—the Israel Prize for Lifetime Achievement. The judging panel praised the eighty-six-year-old Eban's diplomatic achievements at a time when Israel faced its toughest challenges at the United Nations. After decades of being labeled an alien in Israel, the award brought a sense of closure—not least to Suzy, who was always fiercely protective of her husband and his legacy. "We finally feel that people here understand what he has done," she said in an interview. "It would have been a shame for us if only the world but not Israel understood it. Now it balances it and completes the picture."[27]

Suzy's only regret was that she had to accept the award on behalf of her husband, who was by then housebound. A few years earlier he had fallen off a platform and broken his thigh after delivering a speech in San Francisco. He made full recovery, but soon after he was diagnosed with Parkinson's disease and aphasia, a particularly cruel neurological disorder that affects a person's ability to communicate. Eban's mind remained perfectly clear, and he understood what people said to him, but he could not express himself coherently. He was painfully conscious of this terrible affliction, which naturally caused him and those around him great anguish. The measured and poised Voice of Israel was frustrated and tormented by the loss of the power that had made him one of the greatest communicators of his century.

Eban's frail health did not slow his curious mind. Every day, Suzy and members of the household staff would read him the daily newspapers to keep him abreast of the political events of the hour, and he rarely missed the evening news on television. The unprecedented violence of the second intifada that erupted in October 2000 particularly vexed Eban. He would wave dismissively at the television screen, signaling to Suzy to turn it off. He was now a shadow of his old plump and witty self, but he refused to give up. One day Suzy sat with him in his bedroom on the first floor, which had been converted from his grand study, and showed him an old photo album. "Captain!" he muttered with a boastful smile, as he recognized himself in the uniform of the British Army. Another time he sat in the garden, wheelchair-bound, listening intently to a CD collection of his greatest speeches at the United Nations. "Darn good! Darn good!" he congratulated his young self. During those twilight years he would sometime ask those around him, "Will I be remembered?" and one time his cousin, Oliver Sacks, asked him in turn, "How would you like to be remembered, Aubrey?" He surprised Sacks with an instant answer: "As a teacher." Not as a diplomat or a statesman, but a teacher. Eban always saw himself as a Cambridge University don, despite—and perhaps because of—four eventful decades of public service.[28]

In the early hours of Monday, November 18, 2002, Eban passed away at the Rabin Medical Center in Petach Tikva, Israel, after coming down with pneumonia for the second time in eight months. He was buried at the Kfar Shmaryahu Cemetery near his home in Hertzliya. Shimon Peres, Foreign Minister Benjamin Netanyahu, and President Moshe Katzav were among the hundreds of people who paid their respects. Former president Ezer Weizmann, a man unburdened by excessive tact, eulogized Eban: "I respected Abba Eban very much as a highly intelligent man with tremendous linguistic skills—but he was not Israeli. In our eyes he was always a newcomer. He represented the Jewish-Zionist kind which was unfamiliar to us, the Israelis." At a special session of the Knesset in honor of Eban, Peres lauded Eban's place in the "gallery of remarkable people who left their mark on the entire world and were a lifeline for their own people. . . . From Moses to Moshe [Sharett], from [Theodor] Herzl to [David] Ben-Gurion . . . in this gallery Abba Eban's place is guaranteed." The speaker of the Knesset, Reuven Rivlin, described Eban as "the most eloquent spokesman of the Zionist movement, and the most polished ambassador who rightly found his place in the Pantheon of the greatest statesmen of the twentieth century." Ehud Olmert remembered Eban as a comet who lit the Israeli skies: "Never in the history of Israeli politics has anyone been able to carry the country's message to more people, in more languages, in more countries across the globe, than this gifted man." But the most poignant tribute to Eban and his legacy came from the chief rabbi of Israel, Meir Lau: "When I heard on the phone that Abba Eban had died I had to come to say sorry. We never appreciated him as much as we should have."[29]

XX

Legacy

Legacy IS A TERM OFTEN USED, BUT SELDOM DEFINED. CAPTURING THE essence of what it means to leave a legacy is akin to U.S. Supreme Court justice Potter Stewart's definition of hard-core pornography: "I know it when I see it."[1] I presented this question to almost every one of the thirty-nine individuals I interviewed for this book: "Is there such a thing as an Eban legacy?" Some of those who worked closest to him described him as the founding father of Israeli diplomacy. Others mentioned his famous speeches and UN Resolution 242. For some, it was Eban's strategic outlook on Israel's relations with the United Nations and the United States during his ambassadorial years, while others cited the outspoken dovish views of his postministerial years.

Yet for others there was an altogether different answer to my question: "There is no Eban legacy, but which political leaders *did* leave a real legacy behind them?" If a legacy is an interminable footpath on which successive generations tread, then perhaps the first prime minister David Ben-Gurion and the revisionist leader Zeev Zabotinsky are in a league of their own. One cannot speak of Ebanism, just as there is no Dayanism, Rabinism, Allonism, or Eshkolism. Eban was a political dove, but so were other leftist politicians such as Uri Avneri and Yossi Sarid, and they were more outspoken than him; Eban advocated an alternative pathway to the Ben-Gurionist pursuit of the national interest, but he lacked the political gravitas of Moshe Sharett, his mentor; he was the Voice of Israel, but not its mind; he was the most globally revered Israeli of his generation, but back home he was viewed as an alien.

Despite an illustrious diplomatic, political, and academic career that stretched over half a century, Eban's story is ultimately one of failure, but the onus of this failure lies with his compatriots as much as it weighs on Eban's own shoulders. Like his friend Adlai Stevenson in America, Eban represented—for better or worse—the antithesis of the political domain. Both men are contemporary victims of anti-intellectualism—a pervasive social phenomenon unbound by national or cultural strictures. Intellectuals are essentially "dealers in ideas"; they are individuals who are dedicated to the "life of the mind." In his seminal study of anti-intellectualism in American life, Richard Hofstadter defined this phenomenon as "a resentment and suspicion of the life of the mind and of those who are considered to represent it; and a disposition constantly to minimize the value of that life."[2] Israeli anti-intellectualism dates back to the provenance of the Jewish state. The ideal image of the "New Jew" was that of the "young intellectual or professional who left a promising career in order to redeem the land and build a moral society."[3] As audacity, impudence, and self-help came to embody the image of the young state, the pursuit of purely intellectual vocations was largely undervalued. Anti-intellectualism had become an Israeli tradition.[4]

As a Cambridge don, an orientalist scholar, a diplomat, and a polyglot who translated ancient Greek into Latin in his spare time, Eban was—and remains—the archetypical intellectual in Israeli life. As long as he spoke of the abstract notions of peace, justice, and equality before the world gallery, his peers embraced him as the Voice of Israel, the brilliant orator who with the power of his words defended a nation during its hours of peril. But once Eban arrived in Israel and entered the political arena, those qualities that had made him one of the most revered statesmen of his generation—the exuberant intellectualism, urbane demeanor, and utter reverence to the written and spoken word—now made him an easy target for ridicule and suspicion; simply put, Eban was alien to the Israeli ethos and its political landscape. This dissonance was perfectly visualized by the famed Israeli photographer Micha Kirshner, who in 1996 shot Eban as part of *The Israelis*, his weekly photography column in the daily *Maariv*. Wearing a *tembel* hat and holding a sabra plant, the suited Eban looked grotesquely at odds with these enduring symbols of the typical Israeli. The photo was so iconic that it adorned the cover of Kirshner's book of the same title the following year.[5]

Eban's temperament and natural arena of action prevented him, almost ipso facto, from leaving behind a tangible political legacy; as a true intellectual he believed that "the actions of men are ephemeral but noble ideas are immortal."[6] Therefore, what Eban bequeathed to posterity is more acute than a war legacy, a peace plan, a political strategy, or one of his famous witticisms, such as "the Arabs never miss an opportunity to miss an opportunity." He was much more than the eloquent defender of a nation; what he did was to *define* a nation and its zeitgeist. Eban created in the mind of the international community a certain image of a resilient, besieged young nation, and he did so more brilliantly and more persuasively than anyone else who had ever presented Israel's case to the world.

If there is thus an Eban legacy, it is this: Abba Eban was, and remains, the most brilliant articulator of the symbiosis between Zionism and peace. Nobody in the history of the Zionist movement or the State of Israel on which it was founded has balanced so eloquently the right of Jewish self-determination in the heart of the Middle East with the just claims of another people over the same land. Nobody in the past century has so vigorously defended Israel's many virtues while simultaneously alerting others to its many faults. Eban's most important addresses were thus not the ones broadcasted to tens of millions of people in 1956 or 1967, but the two speeches he delivered shortly before and after the 1973 Yom Kippur War. First was Eban's "national style" address before a modest audience of Haifa University graduates in March 1973, where he declared, "A strong nation does not have to shout or to beat drums in nervous agitation in order to make its voice heard." It was followed eight months later by the equally poignant attack before the Presidents Club in Washington, DC, on the "illusions" to which his compatriots subscribed so fiercely following Israel's victory in the Six-Day War:

> I mean the illusion that a million Arabs would be kept under Israeli control forever provided that their economic and social welfare was impressively advanced.
>
> The illusion that Zionism forbade a sharing of additional sovereignty between two nations in former Palestine mandate area.
>
> The illusion that Israel's historic legacy was exclusively a matter of geography and not also, and principally, heritage of prophetic values of which central value was peace.
>
> The fallacy that to see anything temporary in some of Israel's positions west of the Jordan was tantamount to alienation from the biblical culture.
>
> The fallacy that a nation could not be strong unless it demonstrated its toughness in every contingency.[7]

Such introspections were born out of sheer humanism and concerns for the moral character of the Jewish state, but they also reflected Eban's vision of the national interest. That Eban failed to persuade his compatriots to endorse his worldview is indicative of the man's incompetence as a national leader as much as it is the story of a nation that continues to believe that diplomacy must be subordinate to militarism.

In the end, the most honest assessment of Eban's legacy comes from the man himself. Two years before his death he gave his last interview, to the veteran journalist Dov Goldstein. "Don't push him too much, it's hard for him," Suzy cautioned Goldstein, but her husband, crippled by Parkinson's disease but still with lucid mind, surprised her. He finally made his peace with his own legacy and wanted it recorded: "Publish it only after my death," he said to Goldstein in a feeble but determined voice. "I was wrong all along. I have nothing to say in my defense. I was wrong when I did not fight for my positions. I was wrong when I didn't contest the premiership. I never felt inferior to any of the prime ministers in Israel, but I didn't have the courage. I failed to convince the public and the politicians that only Israeli concessions and recognition of the right of the Palestinians to live independently will bring peace and prosperity to Israel. And now my time is running out. Soon I will say goodbye."[8]

Acknowledgments

THIS BOOK WOULD NOT HAVE BEEN POSSIBLE WITHOUT THE SUPPORT OF many individuals and institutions, though I am mindful of one book reviewer's caution that authors, like Oscar winners, should keep their acknowledgments short. In this spirit, my first debt is owed to all the interviewees who agreed to share with me their recollections and impressions of Abba Eban, with special thanks to his family members: his late wife, Suzy, and son, Eli, his brother Rafael and cousin Oliver Sacks, and nephews Jonathan Lynn and Yitzhak Herzog. I am also grateful to Yael Student, who cared for Eban in his twilight years, for her extreme dedication and support in the early stages of my research, as well as Cecile Panzer and Marc Sherman at the Eban Archives in Jerusalem. I was fortunate to receive generous funding for this project from the Department of Political Science and International Studies at the University of Birmingham; the British Academy; and the Harry S. Truman, the Dwight D. Eisenhower, and the Lyndon Baines Johnson presidential libraries. I am particularly grateful to the Leverhulme Trust for awarding me a precious two-year research fellowship (RF#2011-222) that provided cover for my normal teaching and administrative duties at the University of Birmingham while I was working on his book. I also owe thanks to my indefatigable agent, Lisa Adams of the Garamond Agency, and the team at Overlook Press who believed in this project from the outset. My biggest thanks, as always, are to my wife, Alison—for holding down the fort while I was away from home doing research for the book, for sacrificing many weekends and evenings while I raced against various deadlines to bring it to fruition, and for generally keeping me sane throughout this journey.

Notes

Preface

[1] A. Eban to A. Abramovich, April 2, 1984, C-121/F-1315, AEA.

[2] Ibid.

[3] "Eban in '87: On fringe of politics," *New York Times*, June 14, 1987.

[4] Abba Eban, "The National Style," *New Outlook* 16, no. 2 (1973): 9.

[5] Arthur M. Schlesinger Jr., *A Life in the Twentieth Century: Innocent Beginnings, 1917-1950* (New York: Houghton Mifflin, 2002), 200.

[6] Edward Said, *Representation of the Intellectual: The 1993 Reith Lectures* (New York: Vintage Books, 1996), 101–2.

[7] Heinrich Heine, *The Prose Writings of Heinrich Heine* (ed. by Havelock Ellis) (London: Walter Scott, 1887), 255–56.

[8] Yavor to E. Ginburg, February 10 and 22, 1960, GL-75682, ISA; R. Uqarat to Israel's Press Clipping Service, December 9, 1962, GL 7571/5, ISA; Israel's Press Clipping Service to A. Eban, November 11, 1962, GL 7571/5, ISA.

[9] Michael Freedman, interview with the author.

[10] Shabtai Teveth, "History vs. Biography," *Maariv*, July 21, 1987.

[11] The National Press Club, "NPC Luncheon with Abba Eban," May 27, 1994. Eban repeated this quip on many occasions, see for example "Address by the Honorable Abba Eban at the Fortieth Anniversary Convocation at Brandeis University," October 26, 1988, 4-30-1985-17a, LPA; "Address by Ambassador Eban at Iowa University's Lewitt Lecture, 1998," C-281/F-3356, AEA.

I: The Making of a Zionist Wunderkind

[1] David Vital, *A People Apart: A Political History of the Jews in Europe 1789–1939* (Oxford: Oxford University Press, 2001); Ben C. Pinchuk, "Jewish Discourse and the *Shtetl*," *Jewish History* 15, no. 2 (2001): 169–79. Only a small number of Jews—normally the highly educated or the very skilled—were permitted to reside outside the Pale.

[2] John D. Klier and Shlomo Lambroza, eds., *Pogroms: Anti-Jewish Violence in Modern Russian History* (Cambridge: Cambridge University Press, 1992).

[3] "Joniskis," File no. 73296, BH.

[4] Aleck Goldberg, *Profile of a Community: South African Jewry* (Johannesburg: Rabbi Aloy Foundation Trust, 2002), 5.

[5] Marcia Gitlin, *The Vision Amazing: The Story of South African Zionism* (Johannesburg: Menorah Book Club, 1950), 18.

[6] Robert St. John, *Eban* (New York: Doubleday, 1972), 4; Oliver Sacks, *Uncle Tungsten: Memories of a Chemical Boyhood* (New York: Knopf, 2001), 171.

[7] United Kingdom, 1911 Census, NA.

[8] "Abba Eban's Father," *South African Jewish Times*, September 10, 1980.

[9] "Abba Eban's Father"; St. John, *Eban*, 6.

[10] St. John, *Eban*, 7.

[11] Emanuel Shimoni, interview with the author.

[12] Abba Eban, *An Autobiography* (New York: Random House, 1977), 4.

[13] St. John, *Eban*, 8.

[14] St. John, *Eban*, 8; "Abba Eban's Father"; Eban, *An Autobiography*, 4.

[15] For a concise account on the historiography of the Balfour Declaration, including revisionist interpretations of events leading up to the declaration and British motives, see Avi Shlaim, "The Balfour Declaration and Its Consequences," in *Yet More Adventures with Britannia: Personalities, Politics and Culture in Britain*, ed. William Roger Louis (London: Tauris, 2005), 251–70; James Renton, "Flawed Foundations: The Balfour Declaration and the Palestine Mandate," in *Britain, Palestine and Empire: The Mandate Years*, ed. Rory Miller (Farnham, England: Ashgate, 2010), 15–37.

[16] Charles Webster, *The Art and Practice of Diplomacy* (New York: Barnes and Noble, 1962), 114.

[17] "The Great Dilemma That Is Palestine," *New York Times*, September 1, 1946; Keith Jeffery, *MI6: The History of the Secret Intelligence Service, 1909–1949* (London: Bloomsbury, 2010), 132–33.

[18] St. John, *Eban*, 9.

[19] Oliver Sacks, interview with the author.

[20] St. John, *Eban*, 10.

[21] "Belfast's Legacy to Israel," *Belfast Telegraph*, November 20, 2002.

[22] Suzy Eban, *A Sense of Purpose: Recollections* (London: Orion, 2008), 96.

[23] St. John, *Eban*, 15.

[24] "A Remembrance of Abba Eban," *Charlie Rose*, November 18, 2002, PBS, http://www.youtube.com/watch?v=_9OISlPyGAQ.

[25] Eban, *An Autobiography*, 6.

[26] Abba Eban, TV interview, *Erev Hadash*, May 8, 1987, 4–30–1987–43C, LPA; "Mother Tells of Abba (Eban)," *Yediot Ahronot*, February 21, 1964.

[27] Eban, *A Sense of Purpose*, 100–101; Jonathan and Rita Lynn, interview with the author.

[28] Raphael Eban, interview with the author; "Mother Tells of Abba (Eban)."
[29] St. John, *Eban*, 31–37.
[30] "Mother Tells of Abba (Eban)"; St. John, *Eban*, 30–31.
[31] Abba Eban, *Personal Witness: Israel through My Eyes* (New York: Putnam's, 1992), 18.
[32] St. John, *Eban*, 34.

II: At the Cradle of British Oratory

[1] Aubrey initially studied for the Classical Tripos, as the honors bachelor of arts degree is known at Cambridge, and was awarded a first class pass for part I in 1936. Thereafter he switched to study for the Oriental Languages Tripos and was awarded a first class pass both for part I, specializing in Hebrew and Aramaic, in 1937 and part II, specializing in Hebrew, in 1938. UA Graduati 12/72, Exam.L.50–2, CAM; Eban, *An Autobiography*, 15–17; "The Universities," *Observer*, June 5, 1938.
[2] C-150/F-1603, C-150/F-1605, AEA.
[3] Martin Garrett, *Cambridge: A Cultural and Literary History* (Oxford: Signal, 2004), 84–85.
[4] Percy Cradock, *Recollections of the Cambridge Union 1815–1939* (Cambridge: Bowes and Bowes), 166.
[5] T. E. B. Howarth, *Cambridge between Two Wars* (London: Collins, 1978).
[6] John Twigg, *A History of Queens' College, Cambridge 1448–1986* (Woodbridge, England: Boydell, 1987), 348.
[7] Stephen Parkinson, *Arena of Ambition: A History of the Cambridge Union* (London: Icon, 2009).
[8] "That 'New Boy' in Israel's Foreign Office," *New York Times*, April 17, 1966; St. John, *Eban*, 49; Eban, *An Autobiography*, 21.
[9] Schlesinger, *A Life in the Twentieth Century* (Ohel-Shem Auditorium in Tel-Aviv), 200.
[10] "Cambridge Union Society, Lent Term 1938, First Debate, 18 January 1938," C-148/F-1580, AEA.
[11] "Debate in the Cambridge Union, April 26, 1939," C-148/F-1579, AEA.
[12] "The Union Society," *The Cambridge Review*, April 29, 1938, 362; "Union Still Anti-Isolationist," *The Granta*, May 4, 1938, 384; C-297/F-3561, AEA.
[13] Oliver Sacks, interview with the author.
[14] St. John, *Eban*, 72.
[15] Ibid.
[16] Laurence Fowler and Helen Fowler, *Cambridge Commemorated: An Anthology of University Life* (Cambridge: Cambridge University Press, 1984), 341.
[17] Eban, *An Autobiography*, 18.

[18] Memorandum, "The Arab Question": Evidence of Lieutenant-Colonel Sir Mark Sykes, Bart., M.P., December 16, 1915, CAB 24/1/51, 1915, NA.

[19] Howard M. Sachar, *A History of Israel from the Rise of Zionism to Our Time* (New York: Knopf, 2010), 167–201.

[20] Palestine Royal Commission Report, Cmd 5479 (London, July 1937), 510–11, NA.

[21] Sachar, *A History of Israel from the Rise of Zionism to Our Time*, 204–7.

[22] Eban, *An Autobiography*, 25.

[23] David Ben-Gurion, "Chaim Weizmann—Champion of the Jewish People," in *Chaim Weizmann: Statesman of the Jewish Renaissance—The Weizmann Centenary 1874–1974*, eds. Dan Leon and Yehuda Adin (Jerusalem: Zionist Library, 1974), 25.

[24] Abba Eban, "Leadership without Precedent," in Leon and Adin, eds., *Chaim Weizmann*, 25.

[25] Cabinet Committee Minutes, April 20, 1939, CAB 24/285, NA.

[26] "General Situation: Arab and Jewish Claims," 1939, FO 371/23221, NA.

[27] Martin Gilbert, *Israel: A History* (New York: Morrow, 1998), 98–99.

[28] Norman Rose, *Chaim Weizmann: A Biography* (New York: Viking, 1986), 353–55.

[29] St. John, *Eban*, 75.

[30] "Weizmann to the Master of Pembroke College, Cambridge, December 18, 1939," in *The Letters and Papers of Chaim Weizmann*, vol. 9, *January 1939–June 1940*, ed. Norman Rose (New Brunswick, NJ: Transaction, 1979), 210.

[31] St. John, *Eban*, 83–84.

III: Aldershot, Cairo, Jerusalem

[1] St. John, *Eban*, 85.

[2] Eban, *An Autobiography*, 33.

[3] Ernest S. Turner, *The Phoney War on the Home Front* (London: Joseph, 1961), 9.

[4] Ibid., 11–24.

[5] St. John, *Eban*, 93–94; Eban, *An Autobiography*, 34.

[6] Eban, *An Autobiography*, 34.

[7] Alan Moorehead, *Desert War: The North African Campaign, 1940–1943* (London: Hamilton, 1965), 4.

[8] St. John, *Eban*, 102.

[9] For more on the cooperation between the Jewish Agency and the SOE during the war, see Eldad Harouvi, "Reuven Zaslany (Shiloah) and the Covert Cooperation with British Intelligence during the Second World War," in *Intelligence for Peace: the Role of Intelligence in Times of Peace*, ed. Hesi Carmel (London:

Cass, 2002), 30–48; Tuvia Friling, *Arrows in the Dark: David Ben-Gurion, the Yishuv Leadership, and the Rescue Attempts during the Holocaust* (Madison: University of Wisconsin Press, 2003).

10 Telegram, June 10, 1942, HS 3/207, NA; SOE Cairo to SOE London, July 15, 1942, HS 3/207, NA; "G" to D.S.O. (A), December 10, 1942, HS 3/207, NA.

11 Mark Twain, *The Innocents Abroad* (London: Penguin, 2003, reprinted edition), 313, 335, 360.

12 Abba Eban, *My Country: The Story of Modern Israel* (New York: Random House, 1972), 283–84. In recent years this conventional view of Palestine as a desolate place until its rehabilitation by the Zionists has come under increased reevaluation; see Norman Finkelstein, *Image and Reality of the Israel-Palestine Conflict* (London: Verso, 2003); and Shlomo Ben-Ami, *Scars of War, Wounds of Peace* (London: Weidenfeld Nicolson, 2006).

13 Eban, *Personal Witness*, 41.

14 St. John, *Eban*, 114.

15 Eban, *A Sense of Purpose*, 80.

16 Ibid., St. John, *Eban,* 111–12.

17 Ibid.Eban, *A Sense of Purpose*, 81.

18 "Abba Eban's Wife, Suzy, Makes a Bittersweet Pilgrimage Home to a Transformed Cairo", *People* (23 April 1979), 30–32.

19 Eban, *A Sense of Purpose*, 91.

20 Abba Eban TV Biography Filmed Interviews, February 1997, C-291/F-3490, AEA; Memorandum, W. C. Wallace to L. R. Werts, "National Testimonial Committee for Ambassador Eban," March 24, 1959, Papers of James P. Mitchell, 1953–1961, Box 38, Secretary's Personal File – Confidential, Miscellaneous, EPL.

21 D/HX to AMX, "Lieut. A. S. Eban," April 2, 1943, 22666/A, NA.

22 St. John, *Eban*, 127; Walid Khalidi, "On Albert Hourani, the Arab Office, and the Anglo-American Committee of 1946," *Journal of Palestine Studies* 35, no. (2005): 60.

23 "The Foundation of the Middle East Centre for Arab Studies', MS268 MECAS documents 1944–1991, Special Collections, UEA.

24 "Note on Centre of Arab Studies in Middle East," MS268 MECAS documents 1944–1991, Special Collections, UEA.

25 Eban, *A Sense of Purpose,* 86–87.

26 Eban, *An Autobiography*, 54.

27 Eban, *Personal Witness*, 60.

28 Joseph Gorney, *The British Labour Movement and Zionism* (London: Routledge, 1983), 178–79.

29 "Spotlight on Palestine," *Economist*, November 11, 1944.

30 Rose, *Chaim Weizmann*, 395.

[31] "Shamir Defends Terrorist Past," *Times* (London), October 21, 1983.

[32] Bernard Wasserstein, "The Assassination of Lord Moyne," *Transactions of the Jewish Historical Society of England* 27 (1978–80), 76.

[33] "Assassination of Lord Moyne," House of Commons Debate, November 7, 1944, Hansard (London: Parliament of the United Kingdom), vol. 404, col. 1270.

[34] "Palestine (Terrorist Activities)," House of Commons Debate, November 17, 1944, Hansard, vol. 404, col. 2242.

[35] J. B. Bell, *Terror out of Zion: The Fight for Israeli Independence* (New Brunswick, NJ: Transaction, 1996).

IV: Choosing Allegiances

[1] "Mapai to Labour Party," *Davar*, July 29, 1945; "Zionist Satisfaction with Labour Victory," *Davar*, July 29, 1945.

[2] "Great Britain's Position in the Middle East," September 8, 1945, CAB 192/2, CP (45)156, NA; "Statement on Palestine by British Foreign Secretary Bevin," *New York Times*, November 13, 1945.

[3] "Security Conditions in Palestine," September 10, 1945, CAB 129/2, CP(45) 165, NA.

[4] "Letter by D. Ben-Gurion," London, October 1, 1945, *Political Documents of the Jewish Agency*, vol. 1, May 1945–December 1946 (Jerusalem: Hassifriya Haziyonit, 1996), 149–150; David A. Charters, *The British Army and Jewish Insurgency in Palestine, 1945–47* (Basingstoke: MacMillan, 1987), 43–52.

[5] Peter Weiler, "British Labour and the Cold War: The Foreign Policy of the Labour Governments, 1945-1951." *Journal of British Politics* 26, no. 1 (1987), 57.

[6] Allis Radosh and Ronald Radosh, *A Safe Haven: Harry S. Truman and the Founding of Israel* (New York: HarperCollins, 2009), 91–112; William R. Lewis, *The British Empire in the Middle East, 1945–1951: Arab Nationalism, The United States, and Postwar Imperialism* (New York: Oxford University Press, 1998), 428; Francis Williams, *Ernest Bevin: A Portrait of a Great Englishman* (London: Hutchinson, 1952), 260.

[7] Michael J. Cohen, "The Genesis of the Anglo-American Committee on Palestine, November 1945: A Case Study in the Assertion of American Hegemony," *Historical Journal* 22, no. 1 (1979), 185–207; Martin Jones, *Failure in Palestine: British and United States Policy after the Second World War* (London: Mansell, 1986), chaps. 2–3.

[8] Bell, *Terror out of Zion*, 140–75.

[9] Major Aubrey Eban, "Zionism and the Arab World: Memorandum presented in March 1946 to the Anglo-American Committee of Inquiry on Palestine in Jerusalem by the Jewish Agency for Palestine," October 1946, C-150/F-1608, AEA.

[10] Richard Crossman, *A Nation Reborn: A Personal Report on the Roles Played by Weizmann, Bevin and Ben-Gurion in the Story of Israel* (New York: Atheneum, 1960), 69.

[11] Alan Bullock, *Ernest Bevin: Foreign Secretary 1945–51* (New York: William Heinemann, 1983), 305.

[12] David Ben-Gurion to the Jewish Agency Executive in Jerusalem, October 8, 1945, S25/1495, CZA.

[13] Minutes of Cabinet Meeting, CAB 128/5 C.M. (46), June 29, 1946, NA.

[14] Greer Fay Cashman, "Abba Eban Is Memorialized—Friend, Statesman and Intellectual," *Jerusalem Post*, February 13, 2003.

[15] St. John, *Eban*, 143–147; Suzy Eban, interview with the author.

[16] Eban, *An Autobiography*, 62; Eban, *A Sense of Purpose*, 110; Thurston Clarke, *By Blood and Fire: Attack on the King David Hotel* (London: Hutchinson, 1981).

[17] R. D. Wilson, *Cordon and Search: With the 6th Airborne Division in Palestine* (Brompton, England: Gale and Polden, 1949), 70–71; David Schaary, "The Social Structure of the Cyprus Detention Camps: 1946–1949," *Studies in Zionism* 3, no. 2 (1982): 273–90; Dalia Offer, "Holocaust Survivors as Immigrants: The Case of Israel and the Cyprus Detainees," *Modern Judaism* 16, no. 1 (1996): 1–23; Arieh J. Kochavi, "The Displaced Persons' Problem and the Formulation of British Policy in Palestine," *Studies in Zionism* 10, no. 1 (1989): 31–48.

[18] Charters, *The British Army and Jewish Insurgency in Palestine, 1945–47*, 205.

[19] Bruce Hoffman, *The Failure of British Military Strategy within Palestine, 1939–1947* (Jerusalem: Bar-Ilan University Press, 1983), 30–31.

[20] "Palestine Outrages (Martial Law)," House of Commons Debate, 3 March 1947, Hansard, vol. 434, col. 35.

[21] Eddie Little and Eric Higgins, "A Nasty Outbreak: Anti-Jewish Disturbances in 1947," *Manchester Region History Review* 10 (1996): 57–61; Yehuda Avner, *The Prime Ministers: An Intimate Narrative of Israeli Leadership* (London: Toby, 2010), 5; Ned Temko, *To Win or Die: A Personal Portrait of Menachem Begin* (New York: Morrow, 1987), 102.

[22] Telegram, Eban to Zaslani, "Some Recent Conversations," December 1, 1947, S25/453, CZA; Norman Rose, ed., *Baffy: The Diaries of Blanche Dugdale, 1936–1947* (London: Vallentine, Mitchell, 1973), 242.

[23] Eban, *An Autobiography*, 63.

[24] St. John, *Eban*, 147, 150.

[25] Eban, *Personal Witness*, 73; Menachem Begin, *The Revolt: Story of the Irgun*, rev. ed. (Tel Aviv: Steimatzky, 1977), 296.

[26] "Fraternization Ban on British Troops Lifted in Holy Land," *Daily Times*, August 8, 1946.

[27] "Lives Remembered, Abba Eban," *Independent*, November 19, 2002.

[28] Eban, "Reflections on Policy and Diplomacy," unpublished paper, November 20, 1944, C-150/F-1612, AEA.

V: London, Palestine, New York

[1] Eban, *Personal Witness*, 77.
[2] St. John, *Eban, 152.*
[3] Rosette to Hirsch, November 14, 1946, KV2/2262, NA.
[4] Eban, *Personal Witness*, 80.
[5] Giora Goodman, "'Palestine's Best': The Jewish Agency's Press Relations, 1946–1947," *Israel Studies* 16, no. 3 (2011): 1–27.
[6] Alan Rosenthal, *Jerusalem, Take One! Memoirs of a Jewish Filmmaker* (Carbondale: Southern Illinois University Press, 2000), 149.
[7] Abba Eban, "Tragedy and Triumph," in *Chaim Weizmann: A Biography by Several Hands*, eds. Meyer W. Weisgal and Joel Carmichael (New York: Atheneum, 1969), 287–89.
[8] Minutes of Cabinet Meetings, January 7, 14, 15, 1947, CAB 129/16, PREM 8/627 (part 6), NA; Brook to Attlee, "Palestine," January 14, 1947, CAB 129/16, PREM 8/627 (part 6), NA.
[9] Conor C. O'Brien, *The Siege: The Saga of Israel and Zionism* (New York: Simon and Schuster, 1986), 270.
[10] Rose, *Baffy*, 241–42.
[11] Eban, *An Autobiography*, 67–68.
[12] Rose, *Baffy*, 242, emphasis in the original.
[13] Rose, *Baffy*, 244.
[14] Jewish Telegraphic Agency, "Weizmann, Ben-Gurion, Wise Call for Participation in London Parley; Silver Urges Boycott," December 17, 1946; Rose, *Chaim Weizmann*, 419–20; Eban, "Tragedy and Triumph," 292–93.
[15] Jewish Telegraphic Agency, "Ben Gurion Urges Congress to Avoid Action on Partition and on Joining London Parley," December 20, 1946.
[16] Robert St. John, *Ben-Gurion: The Biography of an Extraordinary Man* (New York: Doubleday, 1959), 116.
[17] Shabtai Teveth, *Ben-Gurion: The Burning Ground, 1886–1948* (Boston: Houghton Mifflin, 1987), 875; Michael Bar-Zohar, *Ben-Gurion* (London: Weidenfeld and Nicolson, 1978), 139.
[18] Rose, *Baffy*, 245.
[19] *Political Documents of the Jewish Agency*, vol. 2, *January–November 1947* (Jerusalem: Hassifriya Haziyonit, 1998): 21–22; Record of Conversation between Bevin and Silver at Waldorf-Astoria Hotel, November 14, 1946, PREM 8/627 (part 5), NA.
[20] Eban, *An Autobiography*, 67.

[21] *Political Documents of the Jewish Agency*, 2: 21–22.

[22] "Minutes of a Meeting of the Jewish Agency Executive in London," January 2, 1947, Z4/10400II, CZA.

[23] Eban, *An Autobiography*, 70; Minutes of Meeting, "E. Bevin and Others—Members of the Jewish Agency Executive," London, January 29, 1947, Z4 303/32, CZA.

[24] Minutes of Meeting, "E. Bevin and others—Members of the Jewish Agency Executive," London, January 29, S25/7567, CZA; Minutes of Meetings, February 3, 6, 10, 13, 1947, S25/7567 and S25/7568, CZA; "Jewish Delegation Meetings" and "Jewish Delegation Memoranda," *Conferences on Palestine 1946–47*, CAB 133/85, NA; The Chargé in the United Kingdom (Gallman) to the Secretary of State, January 30, 1947, 4 p.m. and 7 p.m., 1017–21, and the Consul General at Jerusalem (Pinkerton) to the Secretary of State, January 31, 1947, 1024–28, in *Foreign Relations of the United States* (hereafter *FRUS*), 1947, vol. 5 (Washington, DC: Government Printing Office, 1972).

[25] Debate on the Address, House of Commons Debate, November 12, 1946, Hansard, vol. 430, col. 25.

[26] Minutes of Cabinet Meeting, February 14, 1947, PREM 8/627 (part 6), NA.

[27] Palestine Conference (Government Policy), House of Commons Debate, February 18, 1947, Hansard, vol. 433, col. 718.

[28] No title, KV 2/1435/V1, no. 460, February 1947, NA.

[29] "Conversation with Abba Eban," *Davar*, November 27, 1987.

[30] George Weidenfeld, interview with the author; Dov Shiloah, interview with the author.

[31] Goldman to Locker, April 10, 1947, Z4/10388II, CZA; St. John, *Eban*, 161.

[32] Eban, *A Sense of Purpose*, 122–23.

VI: We Live on the Mistakes of the Arabs

[1] Nichol Grey, quoted in Eytan Haber, *Menachem Begin: The Legend and the Man* (New York: Delacorte, 1978), 191.

[2] Francis Williams, *A Prime Minister Remembers: The War and Post-War Memoirs of The Right Hon. Earl Attlee* (London: Heinemann, 1961), 182.

[3] Report by A. Eban, May 14, 1947, Z4/15230I, CZA.

[4] *Political Documents of the Jewish Agency*, 2: 368–69.

[5] United Nations Special Committee on Palestine, *Summary Report (August 31, 1947)* (London: His Majesty's Stationery Office, 1947).

[6] Eban, *Personal Witness*, 97–98; District Commissioner of Galilee's fortnightly report, July 3, 1947, CO 537/2280, NA.

[7] District Commissioner of Lydda fortnightly report, July 2, 1947, CO 537/2280, NA; District Commissioner of Galilee fortnightly report, July 3, 1947, CO 537/2280, NA.

[8] Bunche to Hoo, "Cartographers," June 9, 1947, Department Of Trusteeship, Representations, S-0504-009, DAG-05/01/01–09, UNA.

[9] Brian Urquhart, *Ralph Bunche: An American Odyssey* (New York: Norton, 1993), 142.

[10] Shertok to Hoo, "Special Committee on Palestine: Communication from the Jewish Agency for Palestine," June 15, 1947, S-0613, Box 3, File 3, Acc. Dag 13/300, Jewish Agency for Palestine 16/06/1947–13/07/1947, UNA; Peter Grose, *Israel in the Mind of America* (New York: Knopf, 1983), 233.

[11] United Nations Special Committee on Palestine, *Report to the General Assembly, Supplement No. 11*, document A/364, 2:5, UNISPAL; St. John, *Eban*, 163.

[12] UNSCOP Summary of Records, June 1947, vol. 6.11, MG30 E77, NAC.

[13] David Horowitz, *State in the Making* (New York: Knopf, 1953), 168–71; "Special Committee on Palestine—Verbatim Record of the Forty-Sixth Meeting (Private), August 27, 1947, Geneva, A366/2, CZA; Jorge García Granados, *The Birth of Israel: The Drama as I Saw It* (New York: Knopf, 1948), 81–84, 123.

[14] Horowitz, *State in the Making*, 170.

[15] United Nations Special Committee on Palestine, Summary Report, annex 4, 7–8, UNISPAL; United Nations Special Committee on Palestine, Summary Record of the Twenty-Third Meeting (Private), July 8, 1947, UNISPAL; St. John, *Eban*, 166–167; "A State Is Born in Palestine," *New York Times*, October 9, 2011; Jewish Telegraphic Agency, "U.N. Palestine Committee Tours Hebrew University; Sandstroem Praises Institution," June 29, 1947; Eytan to Shertok, Myerson, Eban, and Horowitz, June 30, 1947, S25/5983, CZA; Horowitz, *State in the Making,* 171.

[16] District Commissioner of Galilee's fortnightly report, July 3, 1947, CO 537/2280, NA; Eytan to Shertok, Horowitz, Eban, and Toff, July 2, 1947, S25/5983, CZA.

[17] Meyer Weisgal, *Meyer Weisgal . . . So Far: An Autobiography* (Jerusalem: Weidenfeld and Nicolson, 1971), 189–90 (in Hebrew)..

[18] United Nations General Assembly, Official Records of the General Assembly, Second Session, Supplement No. 11, Volume III, Annex A (Oral Evidence Presented at Public Meetings, Verbatim the Twenty-First Meeting (Public), Held at the YMCA Building, Jerusalem, Tuesday, July 8, 1947, at 9 a.m., UNISPAL.

[19] Horowitz, *State in the Making*, 177.

[20] "Notes on Discussion with Dr. Weizmann, July 14," Department of Trusteeship, UN Special Committee on Palestine Notes on discussions, S-0504-009, DAG-05/01/01–09, UNA.

[21] Eban, *Personal Witness*, 101.

[22] "Ben-Gurion Tough, Able," *Miami Daily News*, May 10, 1951.

[23] Aubrey Eban, "The United Nations and the Palestine Question," *World Affairs* 2, no. 2 (1948): 132.

[24] Report by Haifa District Commissioner, August 5, 1947, CO 537/2280, NA.

[25] United Nations Special Committee on Palestine, Summary Record of the Thirty-Seventh Meeting (Private), held at the YMCA Building, Jerusalem, Saturday, July 19, 1947, at 12:30 p.m., UNISPAL; Aviva Halamish, *The Exodus Affair: Holocaust Survivors and the Struggle for Palestine* (Syracuse, NY: Syracuse University Press, 1998), 141–42.

[26] St. John, *Eban*, 168.

[27] "Palestine Telegraphic Service," July 24, 1947, FO 371/61903, NA.

[28] United Nations Special Committee on Palestine, Verbatim Record of the Thirty-Eighth Meeting (Public), Held at the Ministry of Foreign Affairs; Beirut, Lebanon, on Tuesday July 22, 1947, at 11 a.m., UNISPAL.

[29] Eban, "Arab Boycott," C-0112/F-1197, AEA.

[30] Eban, "Report on a Visit to London—August 5th to 9th," S25/5969, CZA.

[31] Ibid.

[32] García Granados, *The Birth of Israel*, 233.

[33] Horowitz, *State in the Making*, 184–86; "Meeting of Eban and Horowitz with Sandstrom," August 1, 1947, FM-2270/1, ISA; Meeting of Eban and Horowitz with Bunche, August 3, 1947, S25/5970, CZA; "Report by A. Eban," August 4, 1947, FM-2266/38, ISA; Meeting of Shertok and Eban with the Yugoslav Delegation, August 4, 1947, FM-2270/1, ISA.

[34] Urquhart, *Ralph Bunche*, 146–48.

[35] UNSCOP Verbatim Records, 2/6, 46th and 47th Meetings, vol. 6.14, MG30 E77, NAC.

[36] Ibid.; García Granados, *The Birth of Israel*, 52, 244–45.

[37] United Nations Special Committee on Palestine, *Report to the General Assembly by the United Nations Special Committee on Palestine, August 31, 1947* (New York: United Nations, 1947), 73.

[38] Ibid., 87.

[39] Ibid., 89, 97.

[40] Urquhart, *Ralph Bunche*, 148–50.

[41] Consul General in Jerusalem (Macatee) to the Secretary of State, September 2, 1947, in *FRUS*, 1947, vol. 5, 1144.

[42] St. John, *Eban*, 174.

[43] Meeting of A. Eban and D. Horowitz with Abdul Rahman Azzam Pasha, September 15, 1947, FM-2266/38, ISA; Horowitz, *State in the Making*, 233–34.

[44] "Half a Loaf," *Jerusalem Post*, November 28, 1997.

[45] Ad Hoc Committee on the Palestine Question, Round-up Covering the Period 23 September to 25 November 1947, November 26, 1947, GA/PAL/88, UNISPAL.

[46] Ibid.; Horowitz, *State in the Making*, 300.

[47] Dan Kurzman, *Genesis 1948: The First Arab-Israeli War* (London: Vallentine Mitchell, 1972), 18. The British too, of course, had been spying on the Jewish

Agency for years through various methods. Communications to and from the agency's offices in London, Jerusalem, New York, and Washington were regularly intercepted, and, according to Alexander Kellar, a British counterintelligence officer in the Middle East, with some degree of success: "These operations have been producing valuable results. We have obtained not only a great deal of background information which, taken in conjunction with material from other sources, has expanded our knowledge of the personalities connected with the Agency, but also many intercepts of political interest which we pass regularly to the Colonial Office." No title, KV 2/1435/V1, no. 158, December 20, 1945, NA.

[48] Robert J. Donovan, *Conflict and Crisis: The Presidency of Harry S. Truman, 1945–1948* (New York: Norton, 1977), 322.

[49] Harry S. Truman, *Memoirs by Harry S. Truman*, vol. 2, *Years of Trial and Hope* (New York: Doubleday, 1956), 158.

[50] Dan Kurzman, *Genesis 1948,* 18–20; García Granados, *The Birth of Israel*, 263–64; Eliezer Tauber, *Personal Policy Making: Canada's Role in the Adoption of the Palestine Partition Resolution* (Westport, CT: Greenwood, 2002), 102; E. Epstein to Members of the Jewish Agency Executive, July 11, 1947, FM-179/15, ISA; L. H. Foulds (British Legation, Manila) to Bevin, December 5, 1947, CO 537/2351, NA; UK Delegation to the United Nations to Foreign Office, October 11, 1947, FO 371/61948, NA.

[51] United Nations General Assembly, 128th Plenary Session, November 29, 1947, A/PV, 128, UNISPAL; "Partition Approved by More Than 2/3: 33 Vote Yes, 13 No, 10 Abstain," *Palestine Post*, November 30, 1947; Moshe Sharett, *At the Threshold of Statehood* (Tel Aviv: Am-Oved, 1958), 150–52 (in Hebrew); Eban, *A Sense of Purpose*, pp. 132-133. The representative of Siam (Thailand) was absent from the vote following a coup d'état in his country three weeks earlier.

VII: L'homme du Jour

[1] Eban, *Personal Witness*, 124.

[2] *Daily Worker*, December 31, 1947; Sidney Sugarman, *The Unrelenting Conflict: Britain, Balfour, and Betrayal* (Sussex, England: Book Guild, 2000), 244–45.

[3] Consul General in Jerusalem (Macatee) to the Secretary of State, December 31, 1947, in *FRUS*, 1947, vol. 5, 1322.

[4] "Preliminary Report on the Security Situation in Palestine," April 6, 1948. Folder 5, Box 5, Collection 364, UCLA.

[5] The Chargé in Syria (Memminger) to the Secretary of State, November 30, 1947, 1292; The Ambassador in Egypt (Tuck) to the Secretary of State, December 3, 1947, 1295; The Consul General in Jerusalem (Macatee) to the Secretary of State, December 31, 1947, 1324–25, all in *FRUS*, 1947, vol. 5.

[6] Remarks by Creech Jones on the Chicago University Roundtable, February 22, 1948, CO 733/486/1, NA.

[7] Kurzman, *Genesis 1948*, 91–92.

[8] Truman to Jacobson, February 27, 1948, Correspondence—Harry S. Truman, 1948–1952, Correspondence File, Jacobson Papers, TPL.

[9] Eddie Jacobson, "Two Presidents and a Haberdasher," *American Jewish Archives Journal* 20 (1968): 5–7; Abba Eban, *Diplomacy for the Next Century* (New Haven, CT: Yale University Press, 1998), 4.

[10] "At War with the Experts," *Decision: The Conflicts of Harry S. Truman* (TV series), MP80-5, TPL.

[11] Eban, *An Autobiography*, 103–14; Jonathan Daniels, *The Man of Independence* (Philadelphia: Lippincott, 1950), 318.

[12] Eban, *An Autobiography*, 106, 108.

[13] Ibid., 108–9.

[14] "That Witty Young Man from Israel," *Saturday Evening Post*, October 20, 1951.

[15] St. John, *Eban*, 196–97.

[16] Sachar, *A History of Israel*, 310.

[17] CIA Memo, "Probable Enemies, Allies, and Neutrals in the Event of War before 1953," April 5, 1949, Intelligence Memoranda—December 1948–December 1949, Central Intelligence Agency File, Staff Member and Office Files; National Security Council Files, Papers of Harry S. Truman, TPL.

[18] *Fifty Years War* (TV series), Abba Eban Oral History, 2/15, LHA.

[19] Three days later the Soviet Union followed suit with a de jure recognition of Israel—the stronger form of diplomatic recognition, as it applied to the legal basis of the Jewish state and not merely to the exercise of political authority in the territory. Truman granted de jure recognition of Israel in January 1949 following the swearing-in of the country's first government. The British withheld de jure recognition of Israel until April 1950. See Philip Marshall Brown, "The Recognition of Israel," *American Journal of International Law* 42 (1948): 620.

[20] St. John, *Eban*, 200–202.

[21] "Sharett's Address at a Meeting of the Heads of Divisions in the Ministry of Foreign Affairs, May 25, 1949," in *Documents on the Foreign Policy of Israel* (hereafter *DFPI*), vol. 4 (Jerusalem: Israel Ministry of Foreign Affairs, 1986), 67.

[22] "Sihot," *Maariv*, March 29, 1954.

[23] State of Israel, *Yalkut Hapirsumim*, March 25, 1954; "Ministers and Names," *Hed Hamizrach*, April 13, 1949.

[24] "That Witty Young Man from Israel."

[25] Kenneth W. Stein, "A Historiographic Review of Literature on the Origins of the Arab-Israeli Conflict," *American Historical Review*, 96, no. 5 (1991): 1450–65;

Benny Morris, The Birth of the Palestinian Refugee Problem, 1947-1949 (Cambridge: Cambridge University Press, 1989).

[26] Chaim Herzog, *The Arab-Israeli Wars: War and Peace in the Middle East from the 1948 War of Independence to the Present* (Barnsley, England: Frontline, 2010), 49–75.

[27] Saadia Touval, *The Peace Brokers: Mediators in the Arab-Israeli Conflict* (Princeton, NJ: Princeton University Press, 1982), 24–27.

[28] Eban, *An Autobiography*, 119.

[29] Abba Eban, *Voice of Israel* (New York: Horizon, 1957), 13; Eban, *Personal Witness*, 159.

[30] Telegram, Haifa to Foreign Office, September 18, 1948, FO 371/68696, NA.

[31] Ralph Bunche's Handwritten Notes, July 30, 1948, Folder 3, Box 6, Collection 364, UCLA.

[32] Eban, *Voice of Israel*, 14–21.

[33] Touval, *The Peace Brokers*, 31–37.

[34] Telegram, Jerusalem to Foreign Office, September 17, 1948, FO 371/68696, NA; "The Assassination of Count Bernadotte," Folder 3, Box 7, Collection 364, UCLA.

[35] Eban, *Personal Witness*, 63.

[36] Bell, *Terror Out of Zion*, 335–40.

[37] American Jewish Committee, *American Jewish Year Book* (Philadelphia: Jewish Publication Society of America, 1950), 51: 383.

[38] Herzog, *The Arab-Israeli Wars*, 97–105.

[39] Touval, *The Peace Brokers*, 65–69.

[40] Shertok to Lie, "Application of Israel for Admission to Membership in the United Nations," December 2, 1948, UN General Assembly A/752, UNISPAL; "The Acting Chairman of United States Delegation at Paris (Dulles) to the Secretary of State," November 29, 1948, in *FRUS*, 1948, vol. 5, pt. 2 (Washington, DC: Government Printing Office, 1976), 1635–36.

[41] Alvarez to Lie, "Application of Israel for Membership in the United Nations," March 9, 1948, UN General Assembly A/818, UNISPAL.

[42] Philip Quarles, "Abba Eban Pushes Israel's Application for U.N. Membership," *Annotations: The NEH Preservation Project*, WNYC, September 19, 2012, http://www.wnyc.org/story/215675-abba-eban/.

[43] Eban, *Voice of Israel*, 22–36; Two Hundred and Seventh Plenary Meeting of the General Assembly, Summary Records of Meetings, April 5–May 18, 1949, A/PV.207, UNISPAL.

[44] "Abba Eban Pushes Israel's Application."

[45] "Israel Wins a Seat in U.N. by 37–12 Vote," *New York Times*, May 12, 1949.

[46] "Eban: 24 Hours before the Vote There Was No Majority for Internationalization," *Maariv*, December 16, 1949.

[47] J. G. McDonald to D. Ben-Gurion, in *FRUS* 1949, vol. 6 (Washington, DC: Government Printing Office, 1977), 1072–74.

[48] A. Eban to W. Eytan, June 8, 1949, in DFPI, vol. 4, 101–104.

[49] Ben-Gurion Diary, entry for July 14, 1949, BGA.

[50] A. Eban to W. Eytan, June 8, 1949, in DFPI, vol. 4, 106–7.

[51] M. Sharett to J. G. McDonald, June 8, 1949, in DFPI, vol. 4, 107–11; Memorandum by the Department of State to the President, June 10, 1949, in *FRUS*, 1949, vol. 6, 1110.

[52] A. Eban to M. Sharett, June 16 and 22, 1949, in *DFPI*, vol. 4, 137–38.

[53] United Nations General Assembly, "Palestine Proposals for a Permanent International Regime for The Jerusalem Area: Communication from the United Nations Conciliation Commission for Palestine to the Secretary-General Transmitting the Text of a Draft Instrument, Fourth Session, September 12, 1949," A/973, UNISPAL; "Sharett: Jerusalem Vote is Black Day for UN," *Al Hamishmar*, December 11, 1949; "Introduction", in DFPI, vol. 4, 19–20.

[54] "Table Talk," *Observer*, March 5, 1950.

[55] M. Sharett to W. Eytan, December 10, 1949, in *DFPI*, vol. 4, 694; A. Eban to W. Eytan, December 13, 1949, in *DFPI*, vol. 4, 711; "Notes on an Interview with John Reedman," Folder 13, Box 2, Collection 364, UCLA.

[56] Eban, *An Autobiography*, 146.

[57] A. Eban to W. Eytan, December 15, 1949, in *DFPI*, vol. 4, 727.

[58] "A Remembrance of Abba Eban," *Charlie Rose*; "Britain Helping Arabs Make War," *Palestine Post*, November 5, 1948.

[59] "The Successful Choice: Abba Eban," *Maariv*, September 12, 1948.

[60] "On This and That," *Hed Hamizrach*, January 7, 1949.

[61] "Israel's Representative at the UN," *Davar,* June 17, 1948.

VIII: He Looks Remarkably Like a Wise Owl

[1] Eban, *A Sense of Purpose*, 145; St. John, *Eban*, 230.

[2] Eban, *Personal Witness*, 203–4; St. John, *Eban*, 232.

[3] Eban, *An Autobiography,* 151–52.

[4] Eban, *A Sense of Purpose*, 148–49; St. John, *Eban*, 249.

[5] St. John, *Eban*, 275.

[6] Ibid., 269, 274–75; 279–80.

[7] Eban, *Diplomacy for the Next Century*, 2.

[8] Ibid., 1–2.

[9] "That Witty Young Man From Israel."

[10] Ibid.

[11] Ibid., St. John, *Eban*, 504.

[12] St. John, *Eban*, 595.

[13] Various newspaper clippings, unidentified, March 11–April 24, 1959, C-164/F-

1768, AEA.

[14] L. R. Werts to W. C. Wallace, "National Testimonial Committee for Ambassador Eban," March 24, 1959, Papers of James Mitchell, Box 38, Secretary's Personal File, EPL.

[15] Eban, "If I Forget Thee, O Jerusalem," in *Voice of Israel*, 37–51.

[16] Abba Eban, "The Arab Refugees: A Speech before the Ad Hoc Committee of the Seventh Regular Session of the General Assembly of the United Nations," October 30, 1952, 5964/1–FM, ISA.

[17] "Eban Collapses after Vote," *Daily Mail*, May 19, 1951; "Security Council Orders Stop of Huleh Works," *Davar*, May 20, 1951; "Israeli Delegate in UN Recovered," *New York Times*, May 21, 1951.

[18] L. Shultz to A. Eban, June 1, 1951, 4/A427, CZA.

[19] A. Eban to L. Shultz, June 11, 1951. 4/A427, CZA.

[20] L. Shultz to A. Eban, September 17, 1951, 4/A427, CZA.

[21] Eli Eban, interview with the author; Suzy Eban, interview with author; "Eban's Baby Daughter Dies," *New York Times*, January 16, 1953; Eban, *An Autobiography*, 171.

[22] A. Eban to M. Sharett, August 5, 1954; C-260/F-3094, AEA.

[23] St. John, *Eban*, 279; "Daughter to Abba Eban," *New York Times*, December 14, 1954.

[24] St. John, *Eban*, 281–82.

[25] "Spokesman of a Nation," *Bamahane*, August 27, 1958.

[26] Suzy Eban, interview with the author; Elinor Burkett, *Golda* (New York: HarperCollins, 2008), 66–67.

[27] D. Ben-Gurion to A. Eban, January 2, 1951, in DFPI, vol. 6, (Jerusalem: Israel Ministry of Foreign Affairs, 1991), 3.

[28] Walter Eytan, *The First Ten Years* (New York: Simon and Schuster, 1958), 139.

[29] Uri Bialer, *Between East and West: Israel's Foreign Policy Orientation 1948–1956* (Cambridge: Cambridge University Press, 1990), 206–7.

[30] Address by M. Sharett at a Political Consultation at the Ministry of Foreign Affairs, July 13–14, 1949, in *DFPI*, vol. 4, 222–26.

[31] Consultation at the Ministry of Foreign Affairs, January 31, 1950, in *DFPI*, vol. 5 (Jerusalem: Israel Ministry of Foreign Affairs, 1988), 82–83.

[32] Ibid., 83.

[33] M. Keren to W. Eytan, May 31, 1950, in *DFPI*, vol. 5, 368–71.

[34] Editorial Note, in *DFPI*, vol. 5, 419.

[35] M. Keren to the United States Division, July 3, 1950, in *DFPI*, vol. 5, 421–22.

[36] The Ambassador in Israel (McDonald) to the Secretary of State, August 1, 1950, in *FRUS*, 1950, vol. 5 (Washington, DC: Government Printing Office, 1978), 961.

[37] St. John, *Eban*, 261.

[38] "The Question of Korea", *Yearbook of the United Nations* (New York: United Nations, 1951), 211; "International Organizations Summary of Activities: General Assembly," *International Organization* 5, no. 2 (1951): 313–15.

[39] Gideon Rafael, *Destination Peace: Three Decades of Israeli Foreign Policy* (New York: Stein and Day, 1981), 27; "The United Nations during 1950." *Yearbook of the United Nations* (New York: United Nations, 1950), 9–10.

[40] Editorial Note, in *DFPI*, vol. 5, 451; A. Lourie and G. Rafael to M. Sharett, August 2, 1950, in *DFPI*, vol. 5, 456.

[41] M. Keren to the United States Division, August 17, 1950, in *DFPI*, vol. 5, 481–82.

[42] A. Eban to W. Eytan, October 10, 1950, in *DFPI*, vol. 5, 579.

[43] A. Eban to H. E. Gaston, September 18, 1950, in *DFPI*, vol. 5, 543–44; O. Gass to E. Kaplan, October 16, 1950, in *DFPI*, vol. 5, 592n1.

[44] Bialer, *Between East and West*, 200–202.

[45] Zvi Ganin, *An Uneasy Relationship: American Jewish Leadership and Israel, 1948–1957* (Syracuse, NY: Syracuse University Press, 2005), 184.

[46] Isaac Alteras, *Eisenhower and Israel: U.S.-Israeli Relations, 1953–1960* (Gainesville: University Press of Florida, 1993).

[47] St. John, *Eban*, 265–66.

[48] M. Sharett to W. Eytan, April 11, 1953, in *DFPI*, vol. 8 (Jerusalem: Israel Ministry of Foreign Affairs, 1995), 283; M. Sharett to Ben-Gurion, April 11, 1953, in *DFPI*, vol. 8, 294.

[49] Yossi Melman and Dan Raviv, *Friends in Deed: Inside the U.S.-Israel Alliance* (New York: Hyperion, 1994), 71.

[50] Alteras, *Eisenhower and Israel*, 35.

[51] Memorandum of Conversation, May 14, 1953, in *FRUS*, 1952–54, vol. 9 (Washington, DC: Government Printing Office, 1986), 39.

[52] Visit of Secretary of State John Foster Dulles, May 1953, FM-2414/29, ISA.

[53] A. Eban to M. Sharett, n.d., A245/631, CZA; Memorandum of Conversation, 26 October 1954, in *FRUS*, 1952–54, vol. 9, 1676.

[54] Paul Charles Merkley, *American Presidents, Religion, and Israel* (Westport, CT: Praeger, 2004), 34–35.

[55] Alteras, *Eisenhower and Israel*, 86; Minor to Department of State, July 11, 1953, Russell to Department of State, July 11, 1953, Department of State Press Release, July 11, 1953, in *FRUS*, 1952–54, vol. 9, 1254–56.

[56] A. Eban to M. Sharett, September 22, 1953, V. Bennike to M. Sharett, September 23, 1953, D. Ben-Gurion: Diary Note, September 23, 1953, in *DFPI*, vol. 8, 672–77. For a detailed account of the crisis, see Abraham Ben-Zvi, *The United States and Israel: The Limits of the Special Relationship* (New York: Columbia University Press, 1993), 29–48.

[57] The Acting Secretary of State to the Embassy in Israel, September 19, 1953, in

FRUS, 1952–54, vol. 9, 1317.

[58] Memorandum of Conversation, September 25, 1953, in *FRUS*, 1952–54, vol. 9, 1320–25.

[59] Memorandum of Conversation, October 8, 1953, in *FRUS*, 1952–54, vol. 9, 1340–44.

[60] A. Eban to M. Sharett, September 24, 1953, in *DFPI*, vol. 8, 695.

[61] A. Eban to M. Sharett, September 26, 1953, in *DFPI*, vol. 8, 697–98. See Sharett's response to Eban three days later, 703–7.

[62] A. Eban (New York) to the United States Division, October 15, 1953, in *DFPI*, vol. 8, 753–54.

[63] W. Eytan to A. Eban, September 20, 1953, in *DFPI*, vol. 8, 665; "Israel Was Elected to One of General Assembly's Vice Presidencies," *Davar*, September 17, 1953. In 2005 Dan Gillerman became the second Israeli ambassador to be elected vice president, and seven years later Ron Prosor followed suit.

[64] Aide-Memoire from the Government of Israel to the Government of the United States, June 12, 1953, in *DFPI*, vol. 8, 473; United States Mission to the United Nations, "Palestine in the Security Council," April 13, 1954, Subject Files of the Office of the United Nations Political and Security Affairs, 1945–1957, Palestine—Memos of Conversation 1954–1955, Box 21, RG 59, NARA.

[65] Editorial Note, in *DFPI*, vol. 8, 412–13; K. Helm to F. Evans, November 12, 1953, FO 371/104745, NA.

[66] Rafael to the Israel Embassy in Washington, October 14, 1953, in *DFPI*, vol. 8, 747; Benny Morris, *Israel's Border Wars 1949–1956: Arab Infiltration, Israeli Retaliation, and the Countdown to the Suez War* (New York: Oxford University Press, 1993), 244–45.

[67] Morris, *Israel's Border Wars*, 246–47; The Chargé in Jordan (Seelye) to the Department of State, October 15, 1953, in *FRUS*, 1952–54, vol. 9, 1358–59; Avi Shlaim, *The Iron Wall: Israel and the Arab World* (London: Penguin, 2000), 90–91.

[68] "Attack by Israeli Forces," Press Release 572, *U.S. State Department Bulletin*, October 18, 1953, 552; Verbatim Record of the Press and Radio News Conference of the Secretary of State, Washington, October 20, 1953, in FRUS, 1952–54, vol. 9, 1369–71.

[69] Ganin, *An Uneasy Relationship*, 191.

[70] Note from Sir Francis Evans to M. Sharett, October 16, 1953, in *DFPI*, vol. 8, 756–57; E. Elath to M. Sharett, October 16, 1953, in *DFPI*, vol. 8, 757–59; "Israel Condemned in U.N. for Raid on Qibya: Sir Gladwyn Jebb Alleges Incident a Threat to Security," *Manchester Guardian*, November 10, 1953.

[71] E. Elath to W. Eytan, November 5, 1953, in *DFPI*, vol. 8, companion vol., 407.

[72] F. Evans to K. Helm, December 1, 1953, FO 371/104745, NA.

[73] Moshe Sharett, *Personal Diary*, ed. Yaacov Sharett (Tel Aviv: Maariv, 1978), entry for October 14, 1953.

[74] Rafael, *Destination Peace*, 34–35; Sharett, *Personal Diary*, entry for October 17, 1953.

[75] A. Eban to Gideon Rafael, 15 October 1953, in *DFPI*, vol. 8, 756; Eban, *An Autobiography*, 173; Eban, *Personal Witness,* 233.

[76] G. Rafael to W. Eytan, November 28, 1953, in *DFPI*, vol. 8, companion vol., 455; H. Berger to the Ministry of Foreign Affairs, October 17, 1953, in *DFPI*, vol. 8, 762; D. Hacohen to M. Sharett, October 16, 1953, in *DFPI*, vol. 8, 759.

[77] F. Evans to K. Helm, December 1, 1953, FO 371/104745, NA.

[78] Government Debate on Suspension of Work Near the Benot-Yaacov Bridge and the Qibya Operation, October 18, 1953, in *DFPI*, vol. 8, companion vol., 368–71; Sharett, *Personal Diary*, entry for October 18, 1953; The Prime Minister's Statement on the Qibya Action, Broadcast over the Radio on October 19, 1953, in *DFPI*, vol. 8, companion vol., 374–76.

[79] Sharett, *Personal Diary*, entry for November 11, 1953; A. Eban to M. Sharett, November 10, 1953, in *DFPI*, vol. 8, companion vol., 410–11.

[80] Government Debate on Suspension of Work Near the Benot-Yaacov Bridge and the Qibya Operation, October 18, 1953, in *DFPI*, vol. 8, companion vol., 368–71.

[81] A. Eban to M. Sharett, October 21, 1953, FM-2331/2, ISA.

[82] A. Eban to M. Sharett, October 23, 1953, in *DFPI*, vol. 8, 801; Sharett, *Personal Diary*, entry for October 24, 1956.

[83] A. Eban to M. Sharett, October 23, 1953, in *DFPI*, vol. 8, 801; A. Eban to M. Sharett, October 24, 1953, in *DFPI*, vol. 8, 807–8; Israel Embassy in Washington to the United States Division, October 26, 1953, in *DFPI*, vol. 8, 812–13.

[84] United Nations Security Council Resolution 100, October 27, 1953, in *FRUS*, 1952–54, vol. 9, 1389–90; Department of State Press Release, October 28, 1953, in *FRUS*, 1952–54, vol. 9, 1390–91.

[85] A. Eban to M. Sharett, October 17, 1953, in *DFPI*, vol. 8, 762.

[86] Rafael, *Destination Peace*, 34.

[87] Statements by Israel and Jordan, *Yearbook of the United Nations* (New York: United Nations, 1953), 219.

[88] Ibid.

[89] United Nations Security Council Resolution 101, November 24, 1953, in *FRUS*, 1952–54, vol. 9, 1436–37; "Security Council Censures Israel, 9–0, for Kibya Raid," *New York Times*, November 25, 1953.

[90] Sharett, *Personal Diary*, entry for November 29, 1953; Memorandum of Conversation, November 20, 1953, in *FRUS*, 1952–54, vol. 9, 1430.

[91] A. Eban to M. Sharett, November 26, 1953, in *DFPI*, vol. 8, companion vol., 9

[92] Ibid.

[93] "Profile: Moshe Sharett," *Observer*, March 2, 1952.

[94] Abba Eban, "Nationalism and Internationalism in the Middle East," February 21, 1952, A255/121, CZA.

[95] Michael Brecher, *The Foreign Policy System of Israel: Setting, Images, Process* (London: Oxford University Press, 1972), 328, 255, 269.

[96] Avi Shlaim, "Interview with Abba Eban, 11 March 1976," *Israel Studies* 8, no. 1 (2003): 155.

[97] Sharett, *Personal Diary*, entry for October 13, 1953.

[98] Brecher, *The Foreign Policy System of Israel*, 289, emphasis in the original.

[99] Neil Caplan, "'Oom-Shmoom' Revisited: Israeli Attitudes towards the UN and the Great Powers, 1948–1960," in *Global Politics: Essays in Honour of David Vital*, ed. Abraham Ben-Zvi and Aharon Klieman (London: Cass, 1991), 188, emphasis in the original. On this subject, see Avi Shlaim, "Conflicting Approaches to Israel's Relations with the Arabs: Ben-Gurion and Sharett, 1953–1956," *Middle East Journal* 37, no. 2 (1983): 180–201; Gabriel Sheffer, "Sharett, Ben-Gurion and the 1956 War of Choice," *State, Government and International Relations* 27 (1988): 1–28; and Yaacov Bar-Siman-Tov, "Ben-Gurion and Sharett: Conflict Management and Great Power Constraints in Israeli Foreign Policy," *Middle Eastern Studies* 24, no. 3 (1988): 330–56.

[100] St. John, *Eban*, 286, emphasis in the original.

[101] Eban, *An Autobiography*, 199; "Questions Concerning the Middle East," *Yearbook of the United Nations* (New York: United Nations, 1956), 3–4. On Operation Kinneret, see Morris, *Israel's Border Wars*, 364–69; and Shlaim, *The Iron Wall*, 149–55.

[102] A. Eban to Foreign Ministry, December 13, 1955, FM-2212/2, ISA.

[103] T. G. Fraser, *The Arab-Israeli Conflict* (Basingstoke, England: Palgrave, 2004), 61–63.

[104] St. John, *Eban*, 288.

IX: Suez

[1] Constantinople Convention Respecting the Free Navigation of the Suez Canal, October 29, 1888, Article 1, 688th Meeting of the Security Council, March 13, 1955, S/PV.688, UNISPAL.

[2] UN Security Council Resolution S/2322, September 1, 1951, UNISPAL.

[3] Alteras, *Eisenhower and Israel*, 112–13; "The Palestine Question," *Yearbook of the United Nations* (New York: United Nations, 1954), 62–66, 70–72.

[4] Telegram from the Department of State to the Embassy in Jordan, October 2, 1955, in *FRUS*, 1955–57, vol. 14 (Washington, DC: Government Printing Office, 1989), 540–41.

[5] Sharett, *Personal Diary*, entries from May 27, 1956 to June 13, 1956; Rafael,

Destination Peace, 55–58; Michael Bar-Zohar, *Yaacov Herzog: A Biography* (London: Halban, 2005), 125–27.

[6] A. Eban to M. Sharett, June 11, 1956, A245/198, CZA.

[7] M. Sharett to A. Eban, June 14, 1956, A245/198, CZA.

[8] R. Shiloah to M. Sharett, July 19, 1956, A245/198, CZA. On the political events surrounding Sharett's resignation, see Gabriel Sheffer, *Moshe Sharett: Biography of a Political Moderate* (Oxford: Oxford University Press, 1996), 862–84.

[9] Golda Meir, *My Life* (Jerusalem: Steimatzky, 1975), 242.

[10] Burkett, *Golda*, 182.

[11] Sharett, *Personal Diary*, entry for November 2, 1953.

[12] Eban, *Personal Witness*, 251.

[13] Ilan Troen, "The Protocol of Sèvres: British/French/Israeli Collusion against Egypt, 1956," *Israel Studies* 1, no. 2 (1996): 122–39; Avi Shlaim, "The Protocol of Sèvres: Anatomy of a War Plot," *International Affairs* 73, no. 3 (1997): 509–30.

[14] St. John, *Ben-Gurion*, 296–98.

[15] St. John, *Eban*, 303; "Special Watch Report of the Intelligence Advisory Committee," October 28, 1956, in *FRUS*, 1955–57, vol. 16 (Washington, DC: Government Printing Office, 1990), 798–9; "Message from President Eisenhower to Prime Minister Ben Gurion," October 28, 1956, in *FRUS*, 1955–57, vol. 16, 801.

[16] Memorandum of Conversation, October 28, 1956, in *FRUS*, 1955–57, vol. 16, 808–10.

[17] Memorandum of Telephone Conversation between the President and Secretary of State, October 28, 1956, in *FRUS*, 1955–57, vol. 16, 810–11.

[18] Telegram from the Embassy in Israel to the Department of State, October 28–29, 1956, *FRUS*, 1955–57, vol. 16, 810–12; "U.S.-Israeli Ties Badly Strained," *New York Times*, October 31, 1956.

[19] Text of Statement Made on October 30, 1956 in the House of Commons by Sir Anthony Eden, UN Document S/3711, UNISPAL.

[20] Anthony Nutting, *No End of a Lesson: The Story of Suez* (London: Constable, 1967), 113.

[21] Alteras, *Eisenhower and Israel*, 229.

[22] A. Eban to D. Ben-Gurion, October 29, 1956, FM-2213/11, ISA.

[23] Ministry of Foreign Affairs to the Israel Missions Abroad, October 31, 1956, FM-2401/13, ISA.

[24] Memorandum of Conversation, Secretary Dulles' Office, October 31, 1956, in *FRUS*, 1955–57, vol. 16, 891–93.

[25] "Questions Concerning the Middle East", *Yearbook of the United Nations* (New York: United Nations, 1956), 27–28.

[26] St. John, *Eban*, 308, 321. Eban put audience figures at seventy million; see Eban,

Personal Witness, 270–71.

[27] Eban, "Embattled, Blockaded, Besieged," in *Voice of Israel*, 219–20.

[28] Ibid., 228–29.

[29] Ibid., 228.

[30] St. John, *Eban*, 310; "Israel's Chief Orator," *New York Times*, June 21, 1967; H. B. Swope to A. Eban, November 2, 1956, C-297/F-3571, AEA; Esther Herlitz, interview with the author.

[31] Eban, *Personal Witness*, 271–72.

[32] General Assembly Resolution 997 (ES-I), November 2, 1956, UNISPAL.

[33] In 1957 Pearson won the Nobel Peace Prize for his vision in establishing UNEF.

[34] Eban, *Personal Witness*, 279.

[35] "Tough in 6 Languages," *New York Times*, February 14, 1957.

[36] A. Eban to D. Ben-Gurion, November 7, 1956, in *DFPI*, vol. 12 (Jerusalem: Israel Ministry of Foreign Affairs, 2009), 89.

[37] "Questions Concerning the Middle East," *Yearbook of the United Nations* (New York: United Nations, 1956), 33–34.

[38] Message from President Eisenhower to Prime Minister D. Ben-Gurion, November 7, 1956, in *DFPI*, vol. 12, 84–85.

[39] Oles M. Smolansky, "Moscow and the Suez Crisis, 1956: A Reappraisal," *Political Science Quarterly* 80, no. 4 (1965): 589.

[40] Michael Brecher, *Decisions in Israel's Foreign Policy* (London: Oxford University Press, 1974), 288.

[41] Eban, *Personal Witness*, 277–78.

[42] D. Ben-Gurion to A. Eban, January 13, 1957, in *DFPI*, vol. 12, 390. According to Mapai's secretary-general, Giora Yoseftal, just weeks before the outbreak of the Suez Crisis Ben-Gurion was seeking candidates to replace Eban in New York and Washington. See Sharett, *Personal Diary*, entry for October 13, 1956.

[43] United Nations General Assembly, First Emergency Special Session, annexes, Document A/3320, 8 November 1956, UNISPAL.

[44] United Nations General Assembly, Resolution 1120 (XI), A/RES/1120 (XI), November 24, 1956, UNISPAL.

[45] Brian Urquhart, *Hammarskjold* (New York: Norton, 1994), 203.

[46] "Israeli Withdrawal from Sinai," January 5, 1957, Folder 7, Box 12, Collection 364, UCLA; M. Kidron to J. Herzog, January 6, 1957, in *DFPI*, vol. 12, 349–51; A. Eban to the Prime Minister, January 6, 1957, in *DFPI*, vol. 12, 352–53.

[47] "Israeli Withdrawal from Sinai."

[48] Brian Urquhart, interview with the author; Meeting between Eban, Hammarskjöld and Bunche, January 14, 1957, Folder 7, Box 12, Collection 364, UCLA.

[49] United Nations General Assembly Resolution 1123 (XI), January 19 1957, UNISPAL; "UN, in 74–2 Vote, Renews Call for Israeli Withdrawal, U.S. Votes

with Soviets," *New York Times*, January 20, 1957.

[50] Message from President Eisenhower to Prime Minister Ben-Gurion, February 3, 1957, in *FRUS*, 1955–57, vol. 17 (Washington, DC: Government Printing Office, 1990), 82–84.

[51] A. Eban, "The Political Campaign in the United Nations and the United States following the Sinai Campaign, October 1956–March 1957," G-7276/3, ISA.

[52] Ben-Zvi, *The United States and Israel*, 70.

[53] Abba Eban, "Analysis of our Situation to 12.2.57," FM-2219/18, ISA.

[54] "Eban-Dulles Meeting," February 11, 1957, FM-2219/18, ISA; Memorandum of Conversation, "Questions Relating to the Israeli Withdrawal from Gaza and the Straits of Aqaba"; Aide-Memoire from the Department of State to the Israeli Embassy; Memorandum of Conversation, all from February 11, 1957, in *FRUS*, 1955–57, vol. 16, 125–36.

[55] Eban to Ben-Gurion, February 12, 1957, FM-2219/18, ISA.

[56] On February 4 Jacob Blaustein, one of the leaders in American Jewry who had direct access to Ben-Gurion, reported to Bunche from Jerusalem that Eban "has been sending to Jerusalem far too optimistic reports about the line Washington will take and despite all evidence to the contrary believes that sanctions are not possible on the grounds that Washington will not go along." Moreover, Blaustein reported, it seemed that Meir "[would] not permit Eban to give accurate accounts." Bunche to Hammarskjöld, February 4, 1957, Folder 8, Box 12, Collection 364, UCLA.

[57] Ben-Gurion to Eban, February 16, 1957, FM-2219/18, ISA.

[58] Shiloah to Herzog, "Eban-Dulles Meeting," February 17, 1953, FM-2219/18, ISA.

[59] Memorandum of Conversation, February 17, 1957, in *FRUS*, 1955–57, vol. 17, 189–94.

[60] A. Eban to J. Herzog, February 19, 1957, in *DFPI*, vol. 12, 591–93; "President Eisenhower Steps up the Pressure on Israel, February 20, 1957, in *DFPI*, vol. 12, 600–601.

[61] Eban's naming of Algeria may not have been inadvertent. In June 1962 Israel offered technical assistance to the emerging state of Algeria, and in the following month, immediately after Algeria gained independence, Israel granted full recognition to the Arab state. But the new Algerian government refused to reciprocate the Israeli gesture, claiming that its attitude toward Israel was "exactly like that of the other Arab states. . . . Palestine is an Arab country occupied by Israel and therefore Israel is a state we cannot recognize." See "Algiers Rebuffs Israeli Aid Offer," *New York Times*, July 14, 1962.

[62] Eban-Dulles Meeting, February 24, 1957, FM-2219/18, ISA; Memorandum of Conversation, February 24, 1957, in *FRUS*, 1955–57, vol. 17, 254–67.

[63] J. Herzog to A. Eban, February 25, 1957, in *DFPI*, vol. 12, 636–37.

[64] A. Eban to J. Herzog, February 26, 1957, in *DFPI*, vol. 12, 641–42.

[65] D. Ben-Gurion to A. Eban, February 26, 1957, in *DFPI*, vol. 12, 642; J. Herzog to A. Eban, February 25, 1957, in *DFPI*, vol. 12, 636n1. See also Memorandum of Telephone Conversation between Secretary of State and the Minister of the Israeli Embassy (Shiloah), February 25, 1957, in *FRUS*, 1955–57, vol. 17, 271–72 and note 2.

[66] Joseph Lash, *Dag Hammarskjöld: Custodian of the Brushfire Peace* (New York: Doubleday, 1961), 106–7.

[67] Memorandum of Conversation, February 26, 1957, in *FRUS*, 1955–57, vol. 17, 295–98; Memorandum by the Secretary of State, February 26, 1957, in *FRUS*, 1955–57, vol. 17, 298–99; A. Eban to D. Ben-Gurion, February 27, 1957, in *DFPI*, vol. 12, 647n2; Mordechai Gazit, *Israeli Diplomacy and the Quest for Peace* (London: Cass, 2002), 163–65.

[68] "The French Initiative," February 26, 1957, FM 2219/18, ISA.

[69] Joseph Heller, *Israel and the Cold War, 1948–1967* (Sde Boker: Ben-Gurion Heritage Institute, 2010), 212–13 (in Hebrew); Memorandum of Conversation, March 1, 1957, in *FRUS*, 1955–57, vol. 17, 332–36; "3 Key Mideast Decisions," *New York Times*, March 1, 1957.

[70] R. Shiloah to J. Herzog, March 2, 1957, in *DFPI*, vol. 12, 672. See also J. Herzog to A. Eban, March 2, 1957; A. Eban to J. Herzog, March 2, 1957, in *DFPI*, vol. 12, 669–70; Message from President Eisenhower to Prime Minister D. Ben-Gurion, March 2, 1957, in *DFPI*, vol. 12, 671; A. Eban to D. Ben-Gurion, March 2, 1957, in *DFPI*, vol. 12, 673–74; A. Eban to the Ministry of Foreign Affairs, March 2, 1957, in *DFPI*, vol. 12, 675; and "The Government's Final Decision on Withdrawal, despite the Danger to the Unity of the Coalition," March 1–5, 1957, in *DFPI*, vol. 12, 675–76.

[71] Message from President Eisenhower to Prime Minister D. Ben-Gurion, March 15, 1957, in *DFPI*, vol. 12, 740.

[72] Ralph Bunche's handwritten notes, Folder 4, Box 13, Collection 364, UCLA.

[73] Michael Brecher, "Eban and Israeli Foreign Policy: Diplomacy, War, and Disengagement," in *The Diplomats 1939–1979*, eds. Gordon A. Craig and Francis L. Loewenheim (Princeton, NJ: Princeton University Press, 1994), 400.

[74] "The Eban Phenomenon," *Jewish Observer and Middle East Review*, August 9, 1956.

[75] "Eban Transfer Denied," *New York Times*, March 30, 1957.

[76] Rafael, *Destination Peace*, 66.

X: There's Nobody Like Our Abba

[1] "The Eban Phenomenon."

[2] Seven Arts Feature Syndicate, "Off the Record," May 16, 1957; Jewish Telegraphic Agency, "The Statesman," *New York Times*, May 17, 1957; "The Man

on the Rostrum," *New York Times*, May 5, 1957; St. John, *Eban*, 320–21.

[3] Meir Ben-Horin, "The Tide of Nationalism by Abba Eban," *Jewish Social Studies* 22, no. 2 (1960): 113–14; Abba Eban, *The Tide of Nationalism* (New York: Horizon, 1959).

[4] Abba Eban, "The Outlook for Peace in the Middle East," *Proceedings of the Academy of Political Science* 26, no. 3 (1957): 122–23.

[5] Solomon Zeitlin, "Are Judaism and Christianity Fossil Religions?" *Jewish Quarterly Review* 47 (1956): 187–95; Eban, "The Toynbee Heresy," in *The Voice of Israel*, 165–86; "The Man on the Rostrum," *New York Times*, May 5, 1957; William H. McNeill, *Arnold J. Toynbee: A Life* (Oxford: Oxford University Press, 1989), 330n38. The final blow to Toynbee was delivered six years later by Israel's ambassador to Canada, Yaacov Herzog, who through a series of well-publicized public debates killed off Toynbee's reputation.

[6] "Mike Wallace Interview with Abba Eban," April 12, 1958, C-SPAN, http://www.c-span.org/video/?288935-1/mike-wallace-interview-abba-eban; M. Shafran to A. Eban, April 14, 1958, C-0004/F-0046, AEA.

[7] Ephraim Kishon, "Diplomatic Language," *Jerusalem Post*, Autumn 1958, C-244/F-2989, AEA.

[8] Eban, *An Autobiography*, 187.

[9] *Washington Post*, quoted in *The National Testimonial Committee for Ambassador Abba Eban*, C-0003/F-0030, AEA.

[10] A. Eban to J. Kimche, July 27, 1960, GL-7602/16, ISA.

[11] Eban, *An Autobiography*, 160.

[12] Ibid., 161.

[13] Isaiah L. Kenen, *Israel's Defense Line: Her Friends and Foes in Washington* (Buffalo, NY: Prometheus, 1981), 66–80.

[14] Ibid., 80–86; Dov Waxman, "The Pro-Israel Lobby in the United States," in *Israel and the United States: Six Decades of US-Israeli Relations*, ed. Robert O. Freedman (Boulder, CO: Westview, 2012), 85.

[15] Eban, *A Sense of Purpose*, 150–51.

[16] A. Eban to M. Leavitt, February 19, 1953, #729188, NY AR194554/4/82 /995, JDC.

[17] Eban, *A Sense of Purpose*, 151.

[18] Isaac Alteras, "Eisenhower, American Jewry, and Israel," *American Jewish Archives* 37 (1985): 262; Kenen, *Israel's Defense Line*, 111.

[19] Kenen, *Israel's Defense Line*, 107–10. Six years later the State Department viewed AIPAC as "an extremist Zionist lobbying organization . . . [its chairman] Rabbi Bernstein has a distorted and biased outlook on [Near East] history which he is prone to unleash on public occasions." See R. Davies to R. Hare, "Appointment with Rabbi Bernstein and I. L. Kenen of the American-Israel Public Affairs Committee," October 6, 1965, Bureau of Near Eastern and South Asian

Affairs, Office of the Country Director for Israel and Arab-Israeli Affairs, Records Relating to Israel, 1964–66 (5271 150–69–30–05), Box 9, RG 59, NARA.

[20] H. Freed to I. L. Kenen, March 19, 1959, C-003/F-0025, AEA.

[21] P. Shuster to A. Eban, January 23, 1959, C-003/F-0026, AEA.

[22] B. Eaton to A. Eban, June 13, 1958, C-003/F-0026, AEA.

[23] J. Simons to A. Eban, January 31, 1959, C-003/F-0026, AEA.

[24] M. Isaacs to A. Eban, March 11, 1956, C-004/F-0047, AEA.

[25] S. Theille to A. Eban, March 11, 1956, C-004/F-0047, AEA.

[26] "That Witty Young Man from Israel."

[27] A. Eban to Editor of *New York Herald Tribune*, July 23, 1957, C-260/F-3094, AEA.

[28] A. Eban to M. Dayan, June 23, 1958, C-003/F-0036, AEA.

[29] Ibid.; M. Dayan to A. Eban, July 2, 1958, C-003/F-0036, AEA.

[30] Burkett, *Golda*, 238.

[31] A. Eban to E. Livne, March 28, 1952, C-0001/F-0008, AEA.

[32] A. Eban to prime minister's office, August 10, 1957, C-003/F-0036, AEA.

[33] T. Kollek to A. Eban, May 13, 1957, P-648/22, ISA.

[34] "Eban's Position to Be Determined at Meeting with Ben-Gurion Today," *Maariv*, November 3, 1958.

[35] Weisgal, *Meyer Weisgal . . . So Far*, 275–76; A. Eban to N. Shadmi, December 18, 1959, GL-7568/1, ISA.

[36] D. Ben-Gurion to A. Eban, March 1, 1959, C-0154/F-1665, AEA.

[37] National Testimonial Committee for Ambassador Abba Eban, "Mission: 1948–1959, Ambassador Abba Eban of Israel," C-0003/F-0030, AEA.

[38] "Ambassador Eban's Appearances, Farewell Tour," April 2, 1959, C-0004/F-0048, AEA; H. Greenstein to A. Eban March 9, 1959, C-003/F-0028, AEA; KKL5/25906, CZA.

[39] A. Yoffe to M. Shalev, May 15, 1959, FM-3105/18, ISA; "Israel's Chief Orator," *New York Times*, June 21, 1967.

[40] "Israel's Ambassador," *Washington Post*, March 7, 1959.

[41] L. Spivak to A. Eban, May 15, 1959, C-0004–F/0048, AEA.

XI: Into the Fray

[1] "Abba Eban Returns Tomorrow Evening," *Davar*, July 1, 1959; A. Eban to G. Avner, February 27, 1959, C-003/F-0036, AEA.

[2] A. Eban to M. Weisgal, September 14, 1959, GL 7568/1, ISA.

[3] A. Eban to D. Pines, September 16, and A. Eban to M. Assaf, September 29, 1959, GL-7568/1, ISA; A. Eban to M. Assaf, September 9, 1960, GL-7571/3,

ISA; M. Assaf to A. Eban, September 23, 1960, GL-7571/3, ISA.

[4] A. Eban to U. Gordon, July 15, 1959, GL-7568/1, ISA.

[5] E. Nevet to M. Tal, September 22, 1959, GL-7568/1, ISA.

[6] A. Eban to I. Navon, March 13, 1959, C-003/F-0036, AEA.

[7] Shlomo Nakdimon, interview with the author.

[8] "Proletarian in a Cadillac," *Herut*, October 2, 1959.

[9] Ben-Gurion Diary, entry for November 2, 1958, BGA; Yosef Almogi, *Total Commitment* (Jerusalem: Edanim, 1980), 177 (in Hebrew).

[10] Eban, *A Sense of Purpose*, 186; "Abba Eban Learned Spanish on Airplane," *Maariv*, August 12, 1962; Uzi Baram, interview with the author.

[11] "Abba Eban against William Shakespeare," *Maariv*, March 28, 1962; "Social Aspects of Israeli Education," *Guardian*, April 24, 1963; "That 'New Boy' in Israel's Foreign Office," *New York Times*, April 17, 1966; Yossi Sarid, interview with the author.

[12] Brecher, *The Foreign Policy System of Israel*, 223; "Eban Stands Out in Israel Politics," *New York Times*, December 13, 1964; Marvin Kalb, interview with the author.

[13] D. Ochert to J. Cohn, October 5, 1962, GL-7571/5, ISA.

[14] A. Eban to Lord Rothschild, June 29, 1960, GL-7568/2, ISA; A. Eban to J. Rubens, June 16, 1962, GL-7568/2, ISA; "First Golf Links Opened in Israel," *New York Times*, January 10, 1961.

[15] Brecher, *The Foreign Policy System of Israel*, 328.

[16] "Mapai Central Committee Approved Candidates List for Knesset," *Davar*, September 7, 1959; Minutes of Meeting, Mapai Arranging Committee, November 22, 1959, 2–11–1959–99, LPA.

[17] A. Eban to L. F. Rushbrook Williams, December 23, 1959, GL-7568/1, ISA.

[18] "From Metula to Eilat," *Maariv*, January 1, 1960.

[19] "Will G. Meir Retire?" *Maariv*, June 16, 1958.

[20] "From Metula to Eilat," *Maariv*, March 20 1959; "Eban's Position to be determined at Meeting with Ben-Gurion Today," *Maariv*, November 3, 1958.

[21] Eban to Shiloah, February 3, 1959, C-205/F-2226, AEA.

[22] "Sharett Refuses, G. Meir Retires, Aranne Resigns, Namir Departs," *Maariv*, November 12, 1959.

[23] A. Eban to D. Ben-Gurion, n.d., 4–30–1987–45, LPA.

[24] Ben-Gurion Diary, entries for November 10 and December 2, 1959, BGA.

[25] Ben-Gurion Diary, entry for December 10, 1959, BGA.

[26] "Internal Intrigues among Mapai Leadership Hamper Government Formation," *Herut*, November 29, 1959.

[27] St. John, *Eban*, 362.

[28] "Argentine Removal Reported," *New York Times*, May 28, 1960; Eban, *Personal Witness*, 312–13.

[29] Ben-Gurion Diary, entries for November 11, November 29, and December 1,

1959, BGA; "Kor'im-Kotvim," *Maariv*, August 4, 1960; "Hatur Hashmini," *Herut*, July 25, 1960; "B.G. Offered Education Portfolio to Eban," *Maariv*, July 17, 1960.

[30] "Interview of the Week with Abba Eban," *Maariv*, June 17, 1960.

[31] Weizmann Institute of Science, "Mr. Eban Elected to American Academy," press release, May 12, 1960, GL-7571/3, ISA.

[32] "Hatur Hashmini," *Herut*, July 25, 1960.

[33] "Abba Eban Loses Both Worlds," *Herut*, January 12, 1961.

[34] Eban wrote to Weisgal, "The Party acknowledged my honourable battle scars by putting me on the list ahead of M. D. and S. P. and the other potential redeemers of Israel"; see A. Eban to M. Weisgal, September 14, 1959, GL-7568/1, ISA.

[35] A. Eban to B. Raeburn, December 30, 1960, GL-7571/3, ISA.

[36] Esther Herlitz, interview with the author.

[37] Weisgal, *Meyer Weisgal . . . So Far*, 276–77.

[38] Abba Eban, interview with David Susskind, *Open End*, March 14, 1965, C-149/F-1596, AEA.

[39] Weizmann Institute of Science, Progress Report, 1960, 2/74/25, WIA.

[40] "The Statesmen and the Scientists: First Meeting," *Davar*, August 19, 1960; "Science and New States: Israel Calls a Conference," *Guardian*, February 13, 1960.

[41] "Abba Eban," *Davar*, January 21, 1966; St. John, *Eban*, 387–88.

[42] "New Plans for Education in Israel: An Interview with Mr. Abba Eban," n.d., DDI/7340, CZA; A. Eban to J. Kimche, July 27, 1960, GL-7602/16, ISA.

[43] "Secondary Schools Reopen Today," *Davar*, April 30, 1961; "30,000 Pupils Return to School Today," *Herut*, April 30, 1961; Meron Medzini, interview with the author.

[44] St. John, *Eban*, 372.

[45] "Education Minister: Less Shakespeare and More English Teaching," *Davar*, July 12, 1961; "Abba Eban against William Shakespeare."

[46] "Abba Eban Admits: The Israeli People Are Divided into Two Peoples," *Herut*, July 13, 1961; "Closing the Gap," *Davar*, April 8, 1965.

[47] Meeting of Mapai's Central Committee, May 25, 1961, 2–23–1961–81, LPA; "Minister Comes and Minister Goes," *Maariv*, June 26, 1963.

[48] Jewish Telegraphic Agency, "Israeli Cabinet Discusses Educational TV; Ben-Gurion Opposes Plan," November 19, 1962; Eban, interview with David Susskind.

[49] Section 691, January 28, 1964, GL-1427/7, ISA; "Summary," March 16, 1964, GL-1427/8, ISA.

[50] St. John, *Eban*, 381.

[51] Jewish Telegraphic Agency, "Knesset Again Postpones Voting on Educational Television Project," January 16, 1963.

[52] "The Teachers Asked: No to Aranne!," *Maariv*, June 23, 1963.

[53] Ben-Gurion Diary, entry for August 30, 1961, BGA; Tzvi Tzameret, "Zalman Aranne and the Education System," in *The Second Decade, 1958–1968*, ed. Tzvi Tzameret and Hannah Yablonka (Jerusalem: Yad Ben-Zvi, 2000), 73–74 (in Hebrew); Eban, *Personal Witness*, 314.

[54] Ian Black and Benny Morris, *Israel's Secret Wars: A History of Israel's Intelligence Service* (Reading, England: Futura, 1991), 111–13.

[55] Rafael, *Destination Peace*, 37.

[56] Natan Yanay, *Rift at the Top* (Tel Aviv: Levin-Epstein, 1969, in Hebrew); Hagai Eshed, *Who Gave the Order? The Mishap, The Lavon Affair and Ben-Gurion's Resignation* (Jerusalem: Keter, 1982, in Hebrew); Shabtai Teveth, *Ben-Gurion's Spy: The Story of the Political Scandal That Shaped Modern Israel* (New York: Columbia University Press, 1996).

[57] Michal Sapir, *Hayesh Hagadol: A Biography of Pinchas Sapir* (Tel Aviv: Miskal, 2011, in Hebrew), 245–46, 589.

[58] Sharett, *Personal Diary*, entry for January 14, 1955.

[59] Ibid., entry for January 12, 1955.

[60] Rafael, *Destination Peace*, 41; Sharett, *Personal Diary*, entry for January 14, 1955.

[61] Patrick Tyler, *Fortress Israel: The Inside Story of the Military Elite Who Run the Country—And Why They Can't Make Peace* (London: Portobello, 2012), 56–63; Shlomo Nakdimon, interview with the author.

[62] Michael Bar-Zohar, *Shimon Peres: The Biography* (New York: Random House, 2007), 237.

[63] Ephraim Kahana, *Historical Dictionary of Israeli Intelligence* (Lanham, MD: Scarecrow, 2006), 66–67; Stuart Farson and Mark Phythian, *Commissions of Inquiry and National Security: Comparative Approaches* (Santa Barbara, CA: ABC-CLIO, 2011), 164–65.

[64] Yanay, *Rift at the Top*; Eshed, *Who Gave the Order?*; Teveth, *Ben-Gurion's Spy*.

[65] Sapir, *Hayesh Hagadol*, 589–90.

[66] Sachar, *A History of Israel*, 543–46.

[67] Burkett, *Golda*, 210.

[68] "Abba Eban," *Davar*, August 15, 1963.

[69] Yanay, *Rift at the Top*, 116.

[70] Eban, *My Country*, 184–86; Leslie Stein, *The Making of Modern Israel 1948–1967* (Cambridge: Polity, 2009), 217–26.

[71] Sapir, *Hayesh Hagadol*, 592; L. Eshkol to Y. Ben-Zvi, November 2, 1961, N-56/1, ISA; Amnon Lammfrom and Hagai Tsoref, eds., *Levi Eshkol: The Third Prime Minister, Selected Documents 1896–1969* (Jerusalem: Israel State Archive, 2002), 369–71.

[72] Shlomo Aronson, *David Ben-Gurion and the Jewish Renaissance* (New York:

Cambridge University Press, 2011), 303–4; Stein, *The Making of Modern Israel,* 225–26.

[73] *Maariv*, "Levi Eshkol," June 28, 1963; Yossi Goldstein, *Eshkol: A Biography* (Jerusalem: Keter, 2003), 496–99 (in Hebrew).

[74] Eban to Stevenson, September 1, 1963, FM-4321/1, ISA.

[75] Eli Evans, *The Lonely Days Were Sundays: Reflections of a Jewish Southerner* (Jackson: University Press of Mississippi, 1993), 239; St. John, *Eban*, 267.

[76] Yanay, *Rift at the Top*, 108–110.

[77] Eban, *Personal Witness*, 320.

[78] Eban, *An Autobiography*, 298; St. John, *Eban*, 399.

[79] "The Government in the Country—and Abroad," *Maariv*, June 6, 1964.

[80] "Abba Eban—The Latest Victim of Wrath," *Herut*, December 11, 1964; "All Bridges between Eshkol and B.G. Burnt," *Maariv*, December 13, 1964; "A. Eban Calls to Draw Line over Unimportant Arguments," *Davar*, June 27, 1965.

[81] Goldstein, *Eshkol,* 465–67; "Moshe Dayan Resigned," *Maariv*, November 4, 1964; "Dayan: Need to Stop De-Ben-Gurionism," *Davar*, November 5, 1964.

[82] Goldstein, *Eshkol,* 486–88; Danny Hadari, *Israel Galili: A Biography* (Tel Aviv: Hakibutz Hameuchad, 2011), 428–48 (in Hebrew).

[83] Sheffer, *Moshe Sharett*, 1016–18; Meron Medzini, *Golda: A Political Biography* (Tel Aviv: Miskal, 2008), 398–400 (in Hebrew); Burkett, *Golda*, 214–15; "Sharett at Mapai Conference," *Herut*, February 18, 1965; "Mapai Conference," *Maariv*, February 19, 1965; "The Tenth Conference of Mapai," *Davar*, February 19, 1965.

[84] "Rafi's Founders Expelled Themselves from the Party," *Maariv*, July 25, 1965; "Shimon Peres Disqualifies Ministers Too," *Maariv*, May 27, 1965.

[85] "Eban: Rafi the Most Unfortunate Phenomenon in Last 10 Years," *Davar*, November 2, 1965; "An Interview with Shimon Peres," *Davar*, January 13, 1967; Yechiam Weitz, "Levi Eshkol," in Tzameret and Yablonka, eds., *The Second Decade*, 185; Yanay, *Rift at the Top*, 278–79.

[86] "Another Honorary Doctorate to A. Eban," *Davar*, July 22, 1965.

[87] Abba Eban, "Reality and Vision in the Middle East: An Israeli View," *Foreign Affairs* 43, no. 4 (1965): 632–33.

[88] Ibid., 634.

[89] Ibid., 637–38.

[90] Ben-Gurion to Eban, June 27, 1965, C-234/F-2923, AEA; "The Tragedy of Old Age," *Maariv*, July 4, 1965; "The Temptations of the Deputy Prime Minsiter," *Herut*, July 9, 1965.

[91] Eban, *An Autobiography*, 301–2; Jewish Telegraphic Agency, "Eshkol Scores Victory in National Elections in Israel; Thanks Nation," November 4, 1965; "The Israeli Voter Turned Away from Activism," *Maariv*, March 8, 1966.

[92] "A. Eban Likely to Succeed G. Meir as Foreign Minister," *Davar*, November

4, 1965; "Eshkol Hospitalized Due to Weakness and Fatigue," *Davar*, December 5, 1965.

XII: Der Klug Na'ar

1 St. John, *Eban*, 399.

2 Eli Eban, interview with the author; "Eban between Travels," *Maariv*, February 27, 1967; "A. Eban on His Trip," *Davar*, March 1, 1967.

3 Eli Eban, interview with the author; Raphael Eban, interview with the author; St. John, *Eban*, 489.

4 "Israeli Talks of Tashkent Type," *New York Times*, January 25, 1966; "Tashkent, Paris and Jerusalem," *Davar*, February 8, 1966; "Israel Sees Danger in Arms Race," *Guardian*, February 16, 1966; Jewish Telegraphic Agency, "Eban Tells Knesset Peace Is Not Essential for Israel's Survival," March 24, 1966; Moshe Gat, *Britain and the Conflict in the Middle East, 1964–1967: The Coming of the Six-Day War* (Westport, CT: Praeger, 2003), 142–145.

5 "Peace Offensive," *Maariv*, February 1, 1966; W. W. Rostow to Johnson, November 15, 1966, in *FRUS*, 1964–68, vol. 18 (Washington, DC: Government Printing Office, 2000), 660; W. Komer to M. Bundy, January 21, 1966, in *FRUS*, 1964–68, vol. 18, 537.

6 E. Lawson to D. Bergus, April 11, 1957, "Correspondence with Tel Aviv," Bureau of Near Eastern and South Asian Affairs, Records Relating to Lebanon and Israel, 1954–1958, Box 4, RG 59, NARA.

7 Eban, *Personal Witness*, 336–37.

8 Eban, *An Autobiography*, 303; Immanuel Shimoni, Nitza Pinnes, Rachel Gordon, Shlomo Nakdimon, Dan Margalit, and Dov Shiloah, interviews with the author.

9 "Stone Age Man," *Observer*, February 13, 1966.

10 "Visit of Mr. Abba Eban, Foreign Minister of Israel, 16–24 February," January 19, 1968, FCO 17/471, NA.

11 "Eshkol: Israel Will Not Launch Preemptive War," *Davar*, January 13, 1966.

12 "Paris Interested in Eban Visit," *Maariv*, January 30, 1966.

13 "An Interview with Mr. Eban," *New Outlook* 9, no. 6 (1966): 17–18; Jewish Telegraphic Agency, "Eban Returns to Israel; Brings Strong Assurances from President Johnson," February 18, 1966; "*Jeune Afrique*: A. Eban Could Outline Way towards Coexistence," *Davar*, February 8, 1966.

14 Eban, *Personal Witness*, 340–45.

15 "People Who Became 'Problems,'" *Maariv*, February 4, 1966; "Overhaul in the Foreign Ministry," *Davar*, March 18, 1966; "Mideast Bureau in the Foreign Ministry," *Davar*, April 4, 1966; "Eban's Meeting with Foreign Ministry Employees", January 23, 1966, GL-7593/3, ISA; "Abba Eban's First One Hundred Days," *Davar*, April 24, 1966.

[16] Abba Eban, *"Not Backward to Belligerency but Forward to Peace": Text of the Address by Israel's Foreign Minister, Mr. Abba Eban, in the United Nations Security Council on 6 June 1967* (New York: Israel Information Services, 1967).

[17] Shlomo Nakdimon, Michael Bar-Zohar, Meron Medzini, Yehuda Avner, and Immanuel Shimoni, interviews with the author; Avner, *The Prime Ministers*, 142.

[18] Eitan Haber, *Today War Will Break Out: The Reminiscences of Brig. Gen. Israel Lior* (Jerusalem: Edanim, 1987), 120–21 (in Hebrew); "That 'New Boy' in Israel's Foreign Office."

[19] Bar-Zohar, *Yaacov Herzog*, 137, 288–90, 312–13; Esther Herlitz, interview with the author; Meron Medzini, interview with the author. According to Bar-Zohar, acquaintances of Eban and Herzog explained the latter's personal animosity toward Eban as a function of a latent rivalry between two similar individuals with two different career paths: "They both sprang from the same Anglo-Saxon background, both were talented diplomats and brilliant speakers, both were at home in the intricacies of international politics, but Eban had risen in the hierarchy to the position of Foreign Minister and deputy Prime Minister, while Herzog's abilities had not been given their full scope." See Bar-Zohar, *Yaacov Herzog*, 311–12.

[20] Avner, *The Prime Ministers*, 110–11; "Israel's Twilight Peace," *Guardian*, November 18, 1966; Eban, *Personal Witness*, 346, 380.

[21] Some of the earliest accounts of the war include Michael Bar-Zohar, *The Longest Month* (Tel Aviv: Levin Epstein, 1968, in Hebrew), and its English translation *Embassies in Crisis: Diplomats and Demagogues behind the Six-Day War* (Englewood Cliffs, NJ: Prentice Hall, 1970); David Kimche and Dan Bawly, *The Sandstorm: The Arab-Israeli War of June 1967: Prelude and Aftermath* (London: Secker and Warburg, 1968); Walter Laqueur, *The Road to Jerusalem: The Origins of the Arab-Israeli Conflict, 1967* (New York: Columbia University Press, 1968); and Shabtai Teveth, *The Tanks of Tamuz* (London: Sphere, 1969). Some later studies attempted to dispel the myth of Israel being "poor little David" against the mighty Arab Goliath, or to assign Israel a larger portion of the blame for the war, while others contended that Syrian and Egyptian provocations left Israel no choice but to launch a preemptive strike. See, for example, L. Carl Brown, "Origins of the Crisis," in *The Six-Day War: A Retrospective*, ed. Richard B. Parker (Gainesville: University Press of Florida, 1996), 13–73; Moshe Gat, "Nasser and the Six Day War, 5 June 1967: A Premeditated Strategy or Inexorable Drift to War?" *Israel Affairs* 11, no. 2 (2005): 608–35; W. Roger Louis and Avi Shlaim, eds., *The 1967 Arab-Israeli War: Origins and Consequences* (Cambridge: Cambridge University Press, 2012); Michael Oren, *Six Days of War: June 1967 and the Making of the Modern Middle East* (Oxford: Oxford University Press, 2002); Tom Segev, *1967: Israel, the War, and the Year That Transformed the Middle East* (New York: Metropolitan, 2005); Isabella

Ginor and Gideon Remez, *Foxbats over Dimona: The Soviets' Nuclear Gamble in the Six-Day War* (New Haven, CT: Yale University Press, 2007); and Ronald Popp, "Stumbling Decidedly into the Six-Day War," *Middle East Journal* 60, no. 2 (2007), 281–309.

[22] Eban, *Personal Witness*, 346; Brecher, *Decisions in Israel's Foreign Policy*, 355–56.

[23] W. Rostow to President Johnson, December 12, 1966, in *FRUS*, 1964–68, vol. 18, 713; Clea Lutz Bunch, "Strike at Samu: Jordan, Israel, the United States, and the Origins of the Six-Day War," *Diplomatic History* 32, no. 1 (2008): 55–76; Moshe Shemesh, "The IDF Raid on Samu: The Turning-Point in Jordan's Relations with Israel and the West Bank Palestinians," *Israel Studies* 7, no. 1 (2002): 139–67; "Eshkol: We Hope Lesson is Learnt by Damascus Rulers," *Davar*, November 14, 1966; "The Source of Trouble: Still Damascus," *Maariv*, November 15, 1966; "The Operation in Jordan—A Warning to Damascus," *Maariv*, November 16, 1966; "London Asked: Why Didn't You Attack Syria?" *Maariv*, November 17, 1966.

[24] W. Barbour to Department of State, November 22, 1966, in *FRUS*, 1964–68, vol. 18, 681–83.

[25] Minutes of Meeting, Foreign Affairs and Defense Committee, December 20, 1966, A-8161/4, ISA; Haber, *Today War Will Break Out,* 106–7; Abba Eban on *Meet the Press*, December 11, 1966, C-0013/F-0124, AEA; "Israeli Policy Defended," *New York Times*, December 7, 1966.

[26] Zaki Shalom, *The Role of US Diplomacy in the Lead-up to the Six-Day War: Balancing Moral Commitments and National Interests* (Brighton, England: Sussex Academic, 2011), 62–66; Ami Gluska, *The Israeli Military and the Origins of the 1967 War: Government, Armed Forces and Defence Policy 1963–1967* (London: Routledge, 2007), 101–3.

[27] Telegram, Embassy in Tel Aviv to State Department, May 18, 1967, Folder 1, National Security Files (hereafter NSF), Country File Israel, Box 140, LBJ.

[28] Mordechai Bar-On, "The Generals' 'Revolt': Civil-Military Relations in Israel on the Eve of the Six Day War," *Middle Eastern Studies* 48, no. 1 (2012): 39.

[29] Referring to the outcome of the war, the Soviet agent added, "This grand design, which envisaged a long war in the Middle East, misfired because the Arabs failed completely and the Israeli blitzkrieg was so decisive. Faced with this situation the Soviets had no alternative but to back down as quickly and gracefully as possible so as not to appear the villains of the conflict." CIA to White House Situation Room, "Soviet Official's Comments on Soviet Policy on the Middle Eastern War," June 8, 1967, Fiche no. 280, Doc. No. 00047, LBJ.

[30] "Public Statements by Israeli leaders, May 1967," Folder 3, Box 23, Collection 364, UCLA; Oren, *Six Days of War*, 52.

[31] Eban, *An Autobiography*, 319.

[32] Rafael, *Destination Peace*, 136–37.

[33] Eban, *"Not Backward to Belligerency but Forward to Peace"*; Brecher, *Decisions in Israel's Foreign Policy*, 363–64; Brian Urquhart, interview with the author; Foreign Ministry to Delegation at UN, May 21, 1967, FM-4085/6, ISA; Abba Eban interview, ABC, June 2, 1967, C-252/F-3028, AEC.

[34] Barbour to State Department, May 21, 1967 (Telegram no. 3692), Central Files 1967–69, POL ARAB-ISR, RG 59, NARA; Kathleen Christison, *Perceptions of Palestine: Their Influence on U.S. Middle East Policy* (Berkeley: University of California Press, 2001), 109–10; Telegram from the Department of State to the Embassy in Tel Aviv, May 17, 1967, in *FRUS*, 1964–68, vol. 19 (Washington, DC: Government Printing Office, 2004), 10–11.

[35] Harold Saunders, "The President in the Middle East Crisis May 12–June 19, 1967," NSF, National Security Council History, Box 17, LBJ.

[36] Eban, *Personal Witness*, 364–65.

[37] Bar-Zohar, *The Longest Month*, 82–83; Moshe Bitan, *Political Diary 1967–1970* (Tel Aviv: Olam Hadash, 2014), 40–41 (in Hebrew); Moshe Raviv, *Israel at Fifty: Five Decades of Struggle for Peace* (London: Weidenfeld and Nicolson, 1998), 82–83; Eban, *Personal Witness*, 366–67.

[38] Bar-Zohar, *The Longest Month*, 83–87; St. John, *Eban*, 417–18; Eban, *Personal Witness,* 368–69; Oren, *Six Days of War*, 89–90.

[39] Meir was undergoing cancer treatment at the time and was unfit to travel in any case; Burkett, *Golda*, 219–20.

[40] Report from the Israeli Embassy in France to Foreign Ministry, May 22–23, 1967, FM-4084/2, ISA; Bitan, *Political Diary*, 41; Bar-Zohar, *Embassies in Crisis*, 87–88.

[41] Eban's Report to Foreign Ministry, May 24, 1967, FM-2080/5, ISA; Israeli Embassy in France to Foreign Ministry, May 24, 1967, FM-4084/2, ISA; Bar-Zohar, *Embassies in Crisis,* 91–96; Eban, *Personal Witness*, 373–75.

[42] Report from the Israeli Embassy in Britain to the Foreign Ministry, May 23–24, 1967, A-7920/1, ISA; Record of Conversation between Wilson and Eban, May 24, 1967, PREM 13/1618, NA; St. John, *Eban*, 424–26.

[43] Embassy in Israel to the Department of State, May 25, 1967, in *FRUS*, 1964–68, vol. 19, 108–9; Gideon Rafael Oral History, January 29, 1997, 2/36, The Fifty Years War, LHA; Eban, *Personal Witness*, 382–83; Zaki Shalom, *Diplomacy in the Shadow of War: Myth and Reality in Advance of the Six-Day War* (Tel Aviv: Ministry of Defence Publishing House, 2007), 299–304 (in Hebrew).

[44] Segev, *1967*, 257–59; Yitzhak Rabin, *The Rabin Memoirs* (Berkeley: University of California Press, 1996), 87–88.

[45] Gideon Rafael Oral History; Eugene Rostow Oral History, 9/21, The Fifty Years War, LHA; Eban, *An Autobiography*, 352.

[46] Memorandum of Conversation, May 25 1967, NSF, National Security Council History, Box 17, LBJ; Memorandum of Conversation between Undersecretary Rostow and Foreign Minister Eban, Thursday, May 25, 1967, NSF, National Security Council History, Box 17, LBJ; Bar-Zohar, *Embassies in Crisis*, 110–14.

[47] Eban, *Personal Witness*, 383.

[48] Saunders, "The President in the Middle East Crisis"; Memorandum for the Record, "Walt Rostow's Recollections of June 5, 1967, NSF, National Security Council History, Box 18, LBJ; Eban's Memorandum on a Conversation with Rusk, May 26, 1967, FM-5937/30, ISA; Bar Zohar, *Embassies in Crisis*, 116.

[49] Memorandum of Conversation, "Dangers of Arab-Israeli War," May 26, 1967 (handwritten notes taken by Saunders), NSF, National Security Council History, Box 17, LBJ. The CIA estimated that even if Egypt did strike first, Israel could "defend successfully against simultaneous Arab attacks on all fronts . . . or hold on to any three fronts while mounting successfully a major offensive on the fourth." CIA Office of Current Intelligence, "Overall Arab and Israeli Military Capabilities," May 23, 1967, in *FRUS*, 1964–68, vol. 19, 73–74; See also White House Memorandum of Conversation, May 26, 1967, NSF, Country File Middle East Crisis II, Box 106, LBJ.

[50] Eban to the Prime Minister's Office, May 26, 1967, FM-5937/30, ISA; Rusk to Johnson, "Your Conversation with the Israeli Foreign Minister," May 26, 1967, NSF, Memos to the President, Box 16, LBJ.

[51] Israeli Embassy to the Foreign Ministry, May 26, 1967, FM-5937/30, ISA; Walt Rostow Oral History, 8/22, LHA; William B. Quandt, "Lyndon Johnson and the June 1967 War: What Color Was the Light?" *Middle East Journal* 46, no. 2 (1992): 198–228; Steven L. Spiegel, *The Other Arab-Israeli Conflict: Making America's Middle East Policy from Truman to Reagan* (Chicago: University of Chicago Press, 1986), 142; Eban, *Personal Witness*, 386–87.

[52] Notes of a Meeting with President Johnson and A. Eban, May 26, 1967, A-7919/1 and FM-5937/30, ISA; Memorandum of Conversation, May 26, 1967, in *FRUS*, 1964–68, vol. 19, 140–46; Washington Embassy to Foreign Office, May 25, 1967, FCO 17/483, NA.

[53] Harold Saunders, interview with the author; Joseph Sisco Oral History, 8/26, The Fifty Years War, LHA.

[54] Notes of a Meeting with President Johnson and A. Eban, May 26, 1967, A-7919/1 and FM-5937/30, ISA; Memorandum of Conversation, May 26, 1967, in *FRUS*, 1964–68, vol. 19, 140–46; Eban, *Personal Witness*, 388–91, 398, emphasis added.

[55] Memorandum of Conversation, May 26, 1967, in *FRUS*, 1964–68, vol. 19, 140–46.

[56] Evron to Foreign Ministry, May 26, 1967, FM 5937/30, ISA.

[57] Board of National Estimates, "Military Capabilities of Israel and the Arab States," May 26, 1967, in *FRUS*, 1964–68, vol. 19, 138–39; J. L. Freshwater [pseud.], "Policy and Intelligence: The Arab-Israeli War," *Studies in Intelligence* 13, no. 1 (1969): 6.

[58] Segev, *1967*, 267; Eban, *An Autobiography*, 359; Michael Oren, "Did Israel Want the Six Day War?" *Azure* 7 (1999): 67.

[59] Quandt, "Lyndon Johnson and the June 1967 War," 214; Washington Embassy to Foreign Office, May 25, 1967, FCO 17/483, NA.

[60] President's Daily Diary, 4/16/67–6/30/67, Box 11: Daily Diary May 16–31, 1967 (26 May 1967), LBJ.

[61] Bar Zohar, *Embassies in Crisis*, 126–27, 132–33.

[62] *Maariv*, May 28, 1967.

[63] Protocol of Government of Israel Meeting, May 28, 1967, A-8164/4, ISA; Shalom, *Diplomacy in the Shadow of War*, 348–49; Bar-Zohar, *Embassies in Crisis*, 136–37.

[64] Michael Bar-Zohar, interview with the author; Moshe Gilboa, *Six Years, Six Days: Origins and History of the Six-Day War* (Tel Aviv: Am Oved, 1968), 154; Bitan, *Political Diary*, 299–305; *Jerusalem Post*, December 8, 1968; *Maariv*, November 17 and 25, 1968, and December 10 and 11, 1968, A-7070/8, ISA.

[65] Levi Eshkol Papers, Meeting of the Cabinet, May 27, 1967, A-7920/4, ISA; Meeting of Israeli Government, 28 May, 1967, A-8164/4, ISA; Johnson to Eshkol, May 27, 1967, NSF, National Security Council History, Box 17, LBJ; Bar Zohar, *Embassies in Crisis*, 137–38; Eban, *Personal Witness*, 406–7.

[66] Bar-Zohar, *Embassies in Crisis*, 78–79; "The Test," *Maariv*, May 26, 1967; "Britain's Chief Rabbi Proposes Poll Tax on World Jewry," *Maariv*, May 31, 1967.

[67] Segev, *1967*, 249–51; Goldstein, *Eshkol*, 551; Haber, *Today War Will Break Out*, 159–61; *Haaretz*, May 29, 1967.

[68] Eban, *Personal Witness*, 399–400; Ahron Bregman and Jihan El-Tahri, *The Fifty Years War: Israel and the Arabs* (London: Penguin, 1998), 77; Tamar Liebes, "Acoustic Space: The Role of Radio in Israeli Collective History," *Jewish History* 20, no. 1 (2006): 76.

[69] Bar-On, "The Generals' "Revolt," 33–50; Gluska, *The Israeli Military*; Haber, *Today War Will Break Out*, 194–98; Tyler, *Fortress Israel*, 160–90.

[70] Segev, *1967*, 307–19; Goldstein, *Eshkol*, 550–63; Haber, *Today War Will Break Out*, 177–85; "Eshkol in a Shelved 1968 Interview: 'There is Dayan who is a man and there is Dayan who is Abu-Gilda,'" *Yediot Ahronot*, March 23, 1969.

[71] Diplomatic Note from the Israeli Ambassador (Harman) to Secretary of State Rusk, May 30, 1967, NSF, Country File Middle East Crisis II, LBJ; Bar-Zohar, *Embassies in Crisis*, 160.

[72] Memorandum from the President's Special Assistant (Rostow) to President Johnson, May 31, 1967, in *FRUS*, 1964–68, vol. 19, 201–2; Letter from President Johnson to Prime Minister Eshkol, June 3, 1967, NSF, Country File Middle East Crisis III, LBJ.

[73] John Kimche, *Palestine or Israel: The Untold Story of Why We Failed, 1917–1923; 1967–1973* (London: Secker and Warburg, 1973), 257–58; Amos Gilboa, *Mr. Intelligence: Ahrale Yariv* (Tel Aviv: Miskal, 2013), 282–83 (in Hebrew).

[74] Segev, *1967*, 329.

[75] Compare Amit's own account of the faithful meeting in Parker, ed., *The Six-Day War: A Retrospective*, 136–52, and in his autobiography, Meir Amit, *Head On* (Tel Aviv: Hed Artzi, 1999, in Hebrew), with the account of the meeting in Patrick Tyler, *A World of Trouble: The White House and the Middle East—from the Cold War to the War on Terror* (New York: Farrar, Straus and Giroux, 2010), 94–95, which notes that Amit's version "is so at variance with the facts that it raises the question of whether the Mossad chief fabricated his most prominent account, published in Hebrew, to justify the pre-emptive war decision for domestic Israeli audience."

[76] Helms to Johnson, "Memorandum for the President," June 2, 1967, National Security Archive, http://www2.gwu.edu/~nsarchiv/NSAEBB/NSAEBB265/19670602.pdf.

[77] Oren, *Six Days of War*, 147.

[78] W.W. to the President, June 2, 1967, NSF, National Security Council History, Middle East Crisis, May 12–June 19, 1967, Box 18, LBJ.

[79] William B. Quandt, *Decade of Decisions: American Policy toward the Arab–Israeli Conflict, 1967–1976* (Berkeley: University of California Press, 1977), 57; Eban, *An Autobiography*, 384–85.

[80] Herzog, *The Arab-Israeli Wars*, 149, 154–55, 167–69, 185–87; "Eban Says Israel Would Act Alone," *New York Times*, May 31, 1967; Oren, "Did Israel Want the Six Day War?", 72; St. John, *Eban*, 441–42; Eban, *Personal Witness*, 401–2; Eban, *My Country*, 215–16.

[81] Michael Brecher, *Decisions in Crisis: Israel, 1967 and 1973* (Berkeley: University of California Press, 1980), 157; Oren, *Six Days of War*, 149–52.

[82] Memorandum from the Deputy Assistant Secretary of Defense for International Security Affairs (Hoopes) to Secretary of Defense McNamara, "Middle East Situation," June 2, 1967, in *FRUS*, 1964–68, vol. 19, 259–62; Office of the Executive Secretariat, Middle East Crisis files, 1967, Maritime Declaration—Cables [May 31–June 15, 1967], Box 2, RG 59, NARA; Memorandum from Rostow to Johnson, June 4, 1967, NSF, Country File Middle East Crisis III, LBJ.

[83] Eban, *An Autobiography*, 384–85, 394; Bar-Zohar, *Embassies in Crisis,* 157; St. John, *Eban*, 443–45; Yitzhak Rabin, *Service Diary* (Tel Aviv: Maariv, 1979), 179 (in Hebrew).

[84] Haber, *Today War Will Break Out*, 204–12.

[85] Brecher, *Decisions in Crisis*, 163–64; Haber, *Today War Will Break Out*, 215–18; Segev, *1967*, 332–34; Letter from President Johnson to Prime Minister Eshkol, June 3, 1967, in *FRUS*, 1964–68, vol. 19, 262–64.

[86] Haber, *Today War Will Break Out*, 219.

[87] Brecher, *Decisions in Crisis*, 166–68; Segev, *1967*, 335–37; Bar-Zohar, *Embassies in Crisis*, 190–91.

XIII: A Very Foreign Foreign Minister

[1] Moshe Dayan, *Story of My Life* (London: Weidenfeld and Nicolson, 1976), 350–81; Herzog, *The Arab-Israeli Wars*, 151–91; Rabin, *The Rabin Memoirs*, 100–118; Ahron Bregman, *Israel's Wars: A History since 1947* (London: Routledge, 2010), 84–91; Kenneth M. Pollack, "Air Power in the Six-Day War," *Journal of Strategic Studies* 28, no. 3 (2005): 471–503.

[2] Suzy Eban, interview with the author.

[3] Eban, *Personal Witness*, 412–13.

[4] Raviv, *Israel at Fifty*, 132–33; Rafael, *Destination Peace*, 158–61; St. John, *Eban*, 451–56.

[5] "TV: Spotlight on Crisis," *New York Times*, June 7, 1967.

[6] Eban, *"Not Backward to Belligerency but Forward to Peace"*; Brian Urquhart, interview with the author; St. John, *Eban*, 457–59.

[7] Eban, "*Not Backward to Belligerency but Forward to Peace.*"

[8] "TV: Spotlight on Crisis"; "Meeting of Foreign Minister Abba Eban with President L. B. Johnson," October 24, 1967, FM-6853/3, ISA.

[9] St. John, *Eban,* 459–60.

[10] "Israeli Storm Warning," *New York Times*, June 14, 1967; "The Cry Is: No Retreat!," *New York Times*, June 18, 1967; "A. Eban to Head Israeli Delegation to UN Emergency Delegation," *Davar*, June 16, 1967; "Israel Ready to Defy UN," *Observer*, June 18, 1967; St. John, *Eban*, 463–64; Rafael, *Destination Peace*, 171–72.

[11] "Transcript of President Johnson's Address to Educators on U.S. Foreign Policy," *New York Times*, June 20, 1967; "President Johnson on Middle East," June 20, 1967, FM-6853/2, ISA.

[12] United Nations General Assembly, Fifth Emergency Special Session, June 19, 1967, A/PV.1526, UNISPAL.

[13] Emanuel Shimoni, interview with the author; "Kosygin Will Speak First at the UN General Assembly," *Maariv*, June 19, 1967.

[14] "Israel's Chief Orator," *New York Times*, June 21, 1967.

[15] United Nations General Assembly, Fifth Emergency Special Session; "Debate Is Sharp," *New York Times*, June 20, 1967; "TV: Some Familiar Lines," *New*

York Times, June 20, 1967; "Eban: The Russian Proposals—Recipe to Renewed Hostilities," *Maariv*, June 20, 1967; St. John, *Eban*, 465–67; Emanuel Shimoni, interview with the author; Rafael, *Destination Peace*, 174–75.

16 United Nations General Assembly, Fifth Emergency Session, 1527th meeting, June 20, 1967, UNISPAL; "Stalemate in UN General Assembly," *Maariv*, June 21; "Interview with Gideon Rafael," *Maariv*, August 4, 1967.

17 - Avi Raz, "The Generous Peace Offer That Was Never Offered: The Israeli Cabinet Resolution of June 19, 1967", Diplomatic History 37, no. 1 (2013): 85-108.

18 Telegram from the Mission to the United Nations to the Department of State, June 22, 1967, in *FRUS*, 1964–68, vol. 19, 532–34; Caradon to Foreign Office, June 21, 1967, FCO 17/251, NA; Tekoah to Diplomatic Missions, June 26, 1967, A-7920/8, ISA; Eban to Eshkol, June 29, 1967, A-7920/8, ISA; Minutes of Cabinet meetings of June 26 and 27, A-8164/11, ISA.

19 United Nations General Assembly Resolution 2253, July 4, 1967, *Yearbook of the United Nations* (New York: United Nations, 1967), 223; Rafael, *Destination Peace*, 178–79; "UN Rebuffs Russia on Israel," *Guardian*, July 5, 1967.

20 Minutes of Two Meetings of the Israeli Government, June 19, 1967, A-8164/9, ISA; Telegram from the Mission to the United Nations to the Department of State, June 22, 1967, in *FRUS*, 1964–68, vol. 19, 532–34; Yoram Meital, "The Khartoum Conference and Egyptian Policy after the 1967 War: A Reexamination," *Middle East Journal* 54, no. 1 (2000): 64–82; Avi Raz, *The Bride and the Dowry: Israel, Jordan and the Palestinians in the Aftermath of the June 1967 War* (London: Yale University Press, 2012), 136–38; Theodor Meron to Adi Yafeh, September 18, 1967, A-7921/3, ISA.

21 Eban to Levavi, September 24, 1967, FM-4088/8, ISA; Gershom Gorenberg, *The Accidental Empire: Israel and the Birth of the Settlements, 1967, 1977* (New York: Times Books, 2006), 119.

22 U. Gordon to M. Gazit, "The 'From Territories' Formula in Resolution 242," March 3, 1971, 5257/2–FM, ISA; Security Council Official Records, S/PV.1381, November 20, 1967, and S/PV.1382, November 21, 1967, UNISPAL; Lord Caradon, Arthur J. Goldberg, Mohamed H. El-Zayyat, and Abba Eban, *U.N. Security Council Resolution 242: A Case Study in Diplomatic Ambiguity* (Washington, DC: Institute for the Study of Diplomacy, Georgetown University, 1981); Arthur Lall, *The UN and the Middle East Crisis, 1967* (New York: Columbia University Press, 1968), 253–54; Sydney D. Bailey, *The Making of Resolution 242* (Dordrecht, Netherlands: Nijhoff, 1985), 143–61.

23 Eban, *Personal Witness*, 450.

24 *Haaretz*, July 24, 1967; "'Eban Must Go' Shouts Growing Number of Israelis," *Montreal Gazette*, June 27, 1967; "Sketches of Chief Negotiators," *New York Times*, December 21, 1973.

XIV: The Harbinger of a Vacuous Diplomacy

1 Abba Eban, *The New Diplomacy: International Affairs in the Modern Age* (New York: Random House, 1983), 222–24.

2 Abba Eban, "Reflections on June 5," FM-5933/3, ISA; Gorenberg, *The Accidental Empire*, 83–84.

3 Levi Eshkol, quoted in Shlomo Gazit, *The Carrot and the Stick: Israel's Policy in Judea and Samaria, 1967–1969* (Washington, DC: B'nai Brith Books, 1995), 135.

4 Minutes of two meetings of the Israeli Government, June 18, 1967, A-8164/7, ISA; Foreign Minister's Office to Argov, May 18, 1969, FM-5257/2, ISA; Raz, *The Bride and the Dowry*, 40–43; Raviv, *Israel at Fifty*, 139; Rafael, *Destination Peace*, 169–71; St. John, *Eban*, 465.

5 Minutes of Meeting of Mapai Secretariat, September 15, 1967, 2–24–1967–91, LPA.

6 Minutes of Meeting, May 29, 1967, A-7921/4, ISA; Minutes of Meeting of Mapai Secretariat, September 14, 1967, 2–24–1967–91, LPA.

7 "Goldberg to State Department, "Israeli Views on the Middle East," September 23, 1967, Central Files 1967–69, POL S27 ARAB-ISR, RG 59, NARA.

8 Labor Party's Conference, August 4, 1968, 2–021–1969–95, LPA; "The Oral Law," 2–23–1969–98, LPA; Yossi Beilin, *The Price of Unity: The Labour Party until the Yom Kippur War* (Tel Aviv: Revivim, 1985), 57 (in Hebrew); Jewish Telegraphic Agency, "Labor Party Leaders, Dayan Reach Agreement on Party Platform, Rafi Demands," August 18, 1969.

9 Minutes of Meetings of Mapai Secretariat, September 14, 1967, 2–24–1967–91, and January 2, 1968, 2–24–1968–92, LPA; Address by Abba Eban to the National Press Club, Washington, DC, October 24, 1967, FM-5932/2, ISA.

10 Minutes of Meeting of Mapai Secretariat, September 14, 1967, 2–24–1967–91, LPA.

11 Eban's Address before the Assembly of the Council of Europe, Strasbourg, September 27, 1967, C-252/F-3026, AEA.

12 "An Interview with Abba Eban," *Haaretz*, February 2, 1968; "The June 4 Map Reminds us of Auschwitz," *Yediot Ahronot*, January 28, 1969; Suzy Eban, TV interview on *Roim Olam*, Channel 1, July 17, 2010; Suzy Eban, radio interview on *Hakol Diburim*, Reshet Bet, July 18, 2010.

13 "An Interview with Abba Eban."

14 "Reservation from the Foreign Minister," *Davar*, February 8, 1968; Minutes of Mapai Party Meetings on February 13, 1968, 2–11–1968–153, and April 4, 2–24–1968–93A, LPA.

15 McPherson to Johnson, May 27, 1968, NSF, Country File Israel, Box 141, Folder 7, LBJ.

[16] Barbour to Rusk, May 19, 1968, NSF, Country File Israel, Box 141, Folder 5, LBJ.

[17] Harold Saunders, Memo for the Record, May 20, 1968, NSF, Country File Israel, Box 141, Folder 8, LBJ.

[18] "Mr. Eshkol and Mr. Eban," January 19, 1968, FCO 17/471, NA.

[19] Atherton to Battle, "Effect of U.S. Policy on Israeli Cabinet Decisions," December 15, 1967, POL 27, Arab/Israel Disputes 1968, Bureau of Near Eastern and South Asian Affairs, Office of Israel and Arab-Israel Affairs, Box 21, RG 59, NARA.

[20] Abba Eban, "Reflections on June 5," FM-5933/3, ISA.

[21] "Interview with Abba Eban," *Bamahane*, 1968, in C-13/F:119-125, AEA; Minutes of Meeting of the Central Committee of the Labor Party, May 15, 1969, A-4235/1, ISA; Minutes of Meeting of Senior Staff at the Foreign Ministry, January 20, 1970, FM-5254/4, ISA.

[22] Minutes of Meeting of Mapai Secretariat, April 21, 1968, 2–24–1968–93B, LPA.

[23] Press Conference with Abba Eban, Marski Hotel, Helsinki, May 15, 1968, FM-5932/3, ISA.

[24] Jewish Telegraphic Agency, "Latest Eshkol-Dayan Incident 'Closed'; Rafi Bids for Merger with Mapai," December 19, 1967.

[25] "Arab Opinion Poll: Secondary Analysis," *Davar*, October 4, 1968; "Dayan's Popularity Soaring," *Maariv*, January 20, 1969; Stackhouse to Atherton, June 6, 1968, POL 15, 1 October 1968, Bureau of Near Eastern and South Asian Affairs, Office of Israel and Arab-Israel Affairs, Box 19, RG 59, NARA.

[26] "If I Wanted to Be a Prime Minister I Would Have Had to Be Reborn," *Maariv*, February 7, 1969.

[27] "Report on Jarring Talks, December 1967–September 1968," November 4, 1968, C-283/F-3382, AEA; Touval, *The Peace Brokers*, 135–64.

[28] Memorandum of Conversation, June 23, 1968, in *FRUS*, 1964–68, vol. 20 (Washington, DC: Government Printing Office, 2001), 385–87; "Jarring Sees No Point in Mission if There Is No Substantial Progress in the Coming Weeks," *Maariv*, October 6, 1968; "The Government Approved 'the Explicit and the Implicit' in A. Eban's Speech Today at the UN General Assembly," *Maariv*, October 8, 1968.

[29] Abba Eban, Statement to the General Assembly, October 8, 1968, C-19/F-179, AEA; "Israel Presents Peace Proposal: Offers Pullout," *New York Times*, October 9, 1968; "Eban Presents at Assembly Nine-Point Peace Plan," *Davar*, October 9, 1968.

[30] "A Survey of Press, Radio and TV Reactions to Foreign Minister Abba Eban's Speech at the United Nations General Assembly on October 8th, 1968," C-19/F-179, AEA.

[31] "Israel Presents Peace Proposal"; "Israeli Assails Eban Peace Plan," *New York*

Times, October 14, 1968; Jewish Telegraphic Agency, "Arab Press Cold to Eban's Nine-Point Peace Program," October 11, 1968; "Cairo Response to Eban's Address Clarified: No Change in Egyptian Position," *Maariv*, October 10, 1968; "Begin Will Argue at Cabinet Meeting: Eban Deviated from Decisions in Assembly Address," *Maariv*, October 11, 1968; "Jarring Mission: Press Conference with the Foreign Minister," November 11, 1968, C-12/F-118, AEA.

32 "A Debate in Israel," *New York Times*, November 11, 1968; Minutes of Meeting of Mapai Secretariat, August 1, 1968, 2–24–1968–94A, LPA; "Report on Jarring Talks, December 1967–September 1968," November 4, 1968, C-283/F-3382, AEA; "Jarring Mission: Press Conference with the Foreign Minister,"; Avi Raz, interview with the author.

33 Eric Rouleau, "Hawks and Doves in Israel's Foreign Policy," *The World Today*, December 1968, 500; Avi Shlaim, interview with the author.

34 Eban, *An Autobiography*, 454; Rafael, *Destination Peace*, 193.

35 Memorandum of Conversation, June 23, 1968, in *FRUS*, 1964–68, vol. 20, 385–87; Eban Meeting with Danish Foreign Minister, Poul Hartling, May 22, 1968, FCO 17/616, NA.

36 Minutes of Meeting of Mapai Secretariat, April 4, 1968, 2–24–1968–93A, LPA; Rouleau, "Hawks and Doves in Israel's Foreign Policy," 500.

37 Bar-Zohar, *Yaacov Herzog*, 306–7.

38 Beilin, *The Price of Unity*, 50–51.

39 Avi Shlaim, *Lion of Jordan: The Life of King Hussein in War and Peace* (New York: Vintage, 2007), 671–72.

40 For more on these secret talks, see Yaacov Herzog's diary, A-4511/4, ISA; Shlaim, *Lion of Jordan*, 281–314; Raz, *The Bride and the Dowry*, 245–61; Moshe Zak, *King Hussein Makes Peace: Thirty Years of Secret Talks* (Ramat-Gan, Israel: Bar-Ilan University Press, 1996), 146–72 (in Hebrew); Eban, *Personal Witness*, 496–99.

41 Shlaim, *Lion of Jordan*, 293; Bar-Zohar, *Yaacov Herzog*, 315.

42 Bar-Zohar, *Yaacov Herzog*, 326–28.

43 Ibid., 335–36.

44 Gorenberg, *The Accidental Empire*, 165.

45 "Who steps In?" *Daily Mail*, February 27, 1969; "If I Wanted to Be a Prime Minister."

46 Meron Medzini, interview with the author; Brecher, *The Foreign Policy System of Israel*, 302–11; Beilin, *The Price of Unity*, 52–53; Shlaim, *The Iron Wall*, 283–89; "Labor Bureau Chose G. Meir—Begins Today Interparty Negotiations to Form Government," *Maariv*, March 4, 1969; "The President Begins Consultations—Before Asking G. Meir to Form Government," *Maariv*, March 9, 1969; "G. Meir Presents Her Government," *Maariv*, March 17, 1969.

47 Nixon to Haldeman, Ehrlichman, and Kissinger, March 2, 1970, NSC Files, Box

341, Subject Files, HAK/President Memos 1969–1970, Nixon Presidential Material Staff (hereafter NPMS), NARA.

[48] "The President's News Conference," January 27, 1969, *Public Papers of the Presidents* (Washington, DC: Government Printing Office, 1969): 18; Rogers to Nixon, "The General Situation: Need for Movement," March 12, 1969, NSC Files, Country Files Middle East, Israel, Box 604, Folder 1, NPMS, NARA. In essence the four-power talks were dictated by the two-power talks between the United States and the Soviet Union; on these talks, see Memorandum from Kissinger to Nixon, March 30, 1969, 109–17; Memorandum from Saunders to Kissinger, April 18, 1969, 13–38; Memorandum from Saunders to Kissinger, May 10, 1969, 154–55; Memorandum from Saunders to Kissinger, June 20, 1969, 184–88; Memorandum of Conversation, June 2, 1970, 484–484, and Memorandum of Conversation, July 23, 1970, 569–572, all in *FRUS*, 1969–76, vol. 12 (Washington, DC: Government Printing Office, 2006); Boaz Vanetik and Zaki Shalom, *The Nixon Administration and the Middle East Peace Process, 1969–1973: From the Rogers Plan to the Outbreak of the Yom Kippur War* (Eastbourne, England: Sussex Academic, 2013), 28–53. The Americans gradually came to view the four-power talks as "essentially a peripheral activity that could make no useful contribution to the on-going peace efforts. . . . [They] were doomed to failure from the start as the perceptions of the participants of the role they could play differed in certain fundamental respects." See "The Four Power Talks," POL 3, Four Power Talks, Bureau of Near Eastern and South Asian Affairs, Office of Israel and Arab-Israel Affairs, Records Relating to Israel and Arab-Israeli Affairs, 1951–1976, Box 17, RG 59, NARA.

[49] Rabin, *The Rabin Memoirs*, 149; Eban's Talks in State, March 13, 1969, Memorandum of Conversation (Eban, Rabin, Argov, Kissinger, Saunders), and Memorandum of Conversation (The President, Sisco, Kissinger, Mosbacher, Saunders, Eban, Rabin, Argov), March 17, 1969, NSC Files, Country Files—Middle East, Israel, Box 604, NPMS, NARA.

[50] Rogers to Nixon, "Your Meeting with Israeli Foreign Minister Abba Eban—Friday, March 14," March 12, 1969, NSC Files, Country Files—Middle East, Israel, Box 604, Folder 1, NPMS, NARA.

[51] Memorandum of Conversation (Eban, Rabin, Kissinger, Saunders), December 16, 1969, NSC Files, Country Files—Middle East, Israel, Box 605, Folder 1A, NPMS, NARA; Meir, *My Life*, 321; Brecher, *Decisions in Israel's Foreign Policy*, 485–86.

[52] "The Four Power Talks," POL 3, Four Power Talks, Bureau of Near Eastern and South Asian Affairs, Office of Israel and Arab-Israel Affairs, Records Relating to Israel and Arab-Israeli Affairs, 1951–1976, Box 17, RG 59, NARA; David A. Korn, "US-Soviet Negotiations of 1969 and the Rogers Plan," *Middle East Journal* 44, no. 1 (1990): 37–50.

[53] A few months after the failure of the Rogers Plan, John Freeman, the British ambassador to Washington at the time, reported back to London on the Kissinger takeover: "The Arab/Israel dispute was for a long time handled by the State Department without much intervention (or even close interest) on the part of the White House. Sometime during the summer, the president (or his advisers) began to question the Department's unsupervised handling of a situation which was growing increasingly dangerous and was increasingly affecting US-USSR relations. The White House moved in. Important decisions concerning Arab/Israel [*sic*] are now taken in the White House, and the State Department is fairly closely tied by presidential rulings. . . . Sisco is still a key figure. But he is no longer a free-booter. He must now get clearance, not only from Rogers . . . but from Kissinger or the President." Freeman to Greenhill, "The White House and the State Department," October 28, 1970, PREM 15/2231, NA. On relations between Kissinger and Rogers and the inner workings of the Nixon administration's foreign policy, see Asaf Siniver, *Nixon, Kissinger and U.S. Foreign Policy Making: The Machinery of Crisis* (New York: Cambridge University Press, 2008); William Bundy, *A Tangled Web: The Making of Foreign Policy in the Nixon Administration* (New York: Hill and Wang, 1998); Robert Dallek, *Nixon and Kissinger: Partners in Power* (New York: HarperCollins, 2007).

[54] Eban to Rabin, February 4, 1970, A-4239/10, ISA.

[55] "The Foreign Ministry Can be Good," *Davar*, August 6, 1971.

[56] Meron Medzini, interview with the author.

[57] H. H. Stackhouse, "Mrs. Meir–Dayan Relationship," December 4, 1969, POL 15, Government 1969, Bureau of Near Eastern and South Asian Affairs, Office of Israel and Arab-Israel Affairs, Box 19, RG 59, NARA.

[58] Memorandum for the Record, "Conversation with Moshe Meisels," May 8, 1969, POL 27, Arab/Israel Disputes 1968, Bureau of Near Eastern and South Asian Affairs, Office of Israel and Arab-Israel Affairs, Box 21, RG 59, NARA; Sapir, *Hayesh Hagadol,* 615; Moshe Meisels, *From Ben-Gurion to Rabin* (Tel Aviv: Yaron Golan, 2000), 58 (in Hebrew).

[59] "Haba Bator," *Al Hamishmar*, September 17, 1969; Dan Margalit, Shlomo Nakdimon, and Meron Medzini, interviews with the author; Eban, *Personal Witness*, 476–77.

[60] "Hasbara", A-4178/12, ISA; St. John, *Eban*, 483–84; Jewish Telegraphic Agency, "Mrs. Meir Announces Ministry of Information Will Remain with Foreign Ministry," March 9, 1970; "Foreign Ministry Fiercely Objects to Higher Hasbara Authority," *Davar*, December 7, 1969; "The Problem: Who Is in Charge of Hasbara?" *Maariv*, January 4, 1970; "'Wars of the Jews' over Hasbara ministry," *Davar*, February 20, 1970.

[61] "Israel's Self-Inflicted Wounds," *New York Times*, April 24, 1977; Bitan, *Political Diary*, 156–57; Meisels, *From Ben-Gurion to Peres*, 63.

[62] Eban, *Personal Witness*, 567.

[63] Shlomo Nakdimon, Meron Medzini, and Michael Bar-Zohar, interviews with the author; Minutes of Meeting between Gideon Rafael and Rabin, December 14, 1970, C-205/F-2228, AEA; A-7061/4, ISA.

[64] Bitan, *Political Diary*, 105–6, 110–11, 369–86; Moshe Raviv, Immanuel Shimoni, and Eytan Bentsur, interviews with the author; "Internal Israeli Politics," January 28, 1969, POL 12, Political Parties, General 1969, Bureau of Near Eastern and South Asian Affairs, Office of Israel and Arab-Israel Affairs, Box 19, RG 59, NARA; "Abba Eban: Impulsive but Controlled Decision-Making," *Yediot Ahronot*, September 5, 1969. In 1970 Bitan left the foreign ministry over his objections to how it was run by Eban and Raphael. Ironically, Rabin himself, who described Bitan as his only friend in the foreign ministry, warned him that his excessive sharing with others of his personal qualms with Eban and Rafael would be his downfall; Bitan, *Political Diary*, 298–99.

[65] Henry Kissinger, *White House Years* (London: Phoenix, 1977), 359, 355, 389–90. In his memoirs Rabin insisted that the idea to bypass Eban—and his American counterpart William Rogers—was Nixon's, and the inevitable result was the souring of relations between himself and Eban. "[If] that suggests a lack of confidence in Rogers by Nixon and in Eban by Golda that's hardly my fault, is it?" Rabin explained to Menachem Begin in December 1969. "The trouble is, I'm caught in the middle, and have to take the brunt of Eban's umbrage." See Yitzhak Rabin, *Service Diary*, 257–58; Avner, *The Prime Ministers*, 188. The Americans were, of course, aware of the Eban-Rabin rivalry, which sometimes manifested itself in Eban's insistence on excluding Rabin from his official talks with Kissinger. On one such occasion Harold Saunders of the National Security Council reminded Kissinger of "Rabin's sensitivity to being asked to wait outside while you talk with Eban since there is an active rivalry there." Saunders to Kissinger, "Your Breakfast with Foreign Minister Eban," December 15, 1969, NSC Files, Country Files—Middle East, Israel, Box 605, Folder 1A, NPMS, NARA.

[66] Rabin to Dinitz, March 31, 1971, A-7244/2, ISA; Dinitz to Rabin, April 2, 1971, A-7244/2, ISA.

[67] Rabin to Dinitz, March 10, 1971, A-7244/2, ISA. Following a sensitive meeting with Sisco in October 1972, Rabin wrote to Dinitz: "I ask again in every possible way not to transmit Sisco's report to the foreign ministry and the foreign minister." A couple of weeks later, after Rabin filled Eban on his latest conversation with Kissinger, he found the story in the pages of the *Washington Star*. Kissinger angrily demanded from Rabin "clarifications" and threatened to sever the backchannel as it became clear that Eban was the source of the story. Rabin to Dinitz, October 20, 1972, A-7061/5, ISA; Rabin to Dinitz, November 1, 1972, A-7550/3, ISA, respectively.

[68] Bitan, *Political Diary*, 184–85.

[69] Interview with Abba Eban, *Ot*, May 27, 1971.

[70] Rabin to Foreign Ministry (Eyes Only to Eban), October 31, 1971, A-7073/1, ISA; Shlomo Nakdimon, interview with the author; "The Dismissal That Never Was," *Sof Hashavua*, November 1, 2013.

[71] Eban, *Personal Witness*, 485–86; Rafael, *Destination Peace*, 215; Jewish Telegraphic Agency, "Mrs. Meir Denies Cabinet Rift over Eban's Proposal for Israel's Peace Initiative," February 13, 1970; "Who Will Do the Hasbara?" *Maariv*, February 13, 1970; Dan Margalit, Suzy Eban, and Eli Eban, interviews with the author.

XV: Against the National Style

[1] Dima Adamsky, "The "Seventh Day" of the Six Day War: The Soviet Intervention in the War of Attrition (1969–1970)," in Yaacov Roi and Boris Morozov, eds., *The Soviet Union and the June 1967 Six Day War* (Redwood City, CA: Stanford University Press, 2008), 198–250; Zeev Maoz, *Defending the Holy Land: A Critical Analysis of Israel's Security and Foreign Policy* (Ann Arbor: University of Michigan Press, 2006), 126–29; Jewish Telegraphic Agency, "Israel Government Announces Officially Russian Pilots Are Flying Egyptian Jets," April 30, 1970.

[2] Touval, *The Peace Brokers*, 171–75; William B. Quandt, *Peace Process: American Diplomacy and the Arab-Israeli Conflict since 1967* (Washington, DC: Brookings Institution, 2001), 73–76; Kissinger, *White House Years*, 576–90; Jewish Telegraphic Agency, "Gahal Quits Cabinet; Begin Charges U.S. Plan Makes Israel Another Czechoslovakia," August 5, 1970; Brecher, *Decisions in Israel's Foreign Policy*, 489–96; "How to Accept Nixon's Dispatch and Reject the Rogers Plan," *Maariv*, July 31, 1970.

[3] "The Four Power Talks," POL 3, Four Power Talks, Bureau of Near Eastern and South Asian Affairs, Office of Israel and Arab-Israel Affairs, Records Relating to Israel and Arab-Israeli Affairs, 1951–1976, Box 17, RG 59, NARA; Maoz, *Defending the Holy Land*, 129–30; Rafael, *Destination Peace*, 230–31.

[4] Richard Nixon, *RN: The Memoirs of Richard Nixon* (New York: Simon and Schuster, 1978), 483.

[5] On the Jordanian, Israeli, and American actions during the crisis, see Shlaim, *Lion of Jordan*, 315–45; Zak, *King Hussein Makes Peace*, 120–30; Siniver, *Nixon, Kissinger*, 115–47; see also *FRUS*, 1969–76, vol. 24 (Washington, DC: Government Printing Office, 2004), docs. 199–334.

[6] Anwar Sadat, *In Search of Identity* (London: HarperCollins, 1978), 215; Kissinger, *White House Years*, 1276–77; Rabin, *Service Diary*, 325–26.

[7] USUN to Department of State, November 16, 1970, POL 27–14 ARAB-ISR,

1970–73, Subject-Numeric File, RG 59, NARA; Moorer to Secretary of Defense, "Combat Aircraft Sales to Israel," November 30, 1971, Richard Nixon Foundation; Mordechai Gazit, *Israeli Diplomacy and the Quest for Peace* (London: Routledge, 2002), 206–209.

[8] Gideon Rafael to Yosef Tekoah, March 23, 1970, A-4239/10, ISA.

[9] "Dr. Jarring's Note of 8 February 1971," FM-5253/1, ISA; Touval, *The Peace Brokers*, 157; Quandt, *Peace Process*, 88–89.

[10] Gazit, *Israeli Diplomacy and the Quest for Peace*, 94–95; Moshe Gat, *In Search of a Peace Settlement: Egypt and Israel between the Wars, 1967–1973* (Basingstoke, England: Palgrave, 2012), 142–46; Rafael, *Destination Peace*, 253–55.

[11] Mordechai Gazit, "Egypt and Israel—Was There a Peace Opportunity Missed in 1971?" *Journal of Contemporary History* 32, no. 1 (1997): 97–115; Jewish Telegraphic Agency, "Israel Seen Giving Serious Consideration to Sadat Proposal to Reopen Suez Canal," February 8, 1971.

[12] Minutes of Meeting of Labor Party's Central Committee, February 11, 1971, A-4235/2, ISA.

[13] Maoz, *Defending the Holly Land*, 412–13; Medzini, *Golda,* 500–501; Beilin, *The Price of Unity*, 119–120; Jewish Telegraphic Agency, "Eban Denies Israel Rejects Sadat's Canal Plan; Offers Three Proposals for Peace," February 11, 1971; Eban, *Personal Witness*, 501–2.

[14] Beilin, *The Price of Unity*, 89, 123–24.

[15] Gazit to Eban, December 6, 1971, A-7114/1, ISA; Rabin to the Foreign Ministry, July 31, 1972, FM-5253/1, ISA.

[16] Gazit to Tekoah, January 16, 1972, FM-5253/1, ISA.

[17] "UN Spokesman: Jarring Dissociated Nazi Links in 1937," *Davar*, May 14, 1972; "Swedish Newspaper Charges Jarring Was Once Member of Nazi Party, UN Spokesman Rejects Charge as Trivial," May 16, 1972.

[18] Kimche to Gazit, "Gunnar Jarring," June 19, 1972, FM-5253/1, ISA; Veron to Foreign Ministry, May 20, 1972, FM-5253/1, ISA.

[19] Jewish Telegraphic Agency, "Israel Has Conducted No Independent Probe on Reports That Jarring Was a Member of a Pro-Nazi Party," May 31, 1972.

[20] Maroz to Veron, May 18, 1972, FM-5253/1, ISA.

[21] Kimche to Gazit, "Gunnar Jarring," June 19, 1972, FM-5253/1, ISA; Veron to Foreign Ministry, May 20, 1972, FM-5253/1, ISA.

[22] Tekoah to Foreign Ministry, July 10, 1972, FM-5253/1, ISA.

[23] Eban to New York and Washington, July 14, FM-1972, 5253/1, ISA; Jewish Telegraphic Agency, "Israelis Remain Sceptical Jarring Back at UN on Mission; Egypt Adamant on Withdrawal," August 3, 1972.

[24] Minutes of Labour Party Secretariat, November 23, 1972, C-120/F-1303, AEA.

[25] Eban, "The National Style," 6-9.

[26] Minutes of Meeting of Labor Party, September 21 and November 9, 1972, 2–024–1972, LPA; Minutes of Meeting of Labor Party, April 12, 1973, 2–024–1973, LPA.

[27] "Increased Activity – in Allon Plan Boundaries," *Davar*, August 17, 1973; "Moshe Dayan's 'Secure Borders,'" *Maariv*, August 24, 1973; Shlomo Nakdimon, *Low Probability: A Narrative of the Dramatic Story preceding the Yom Kippur War and of the Fateful Events which Followed* (Tel Aviv: Revivim, 1982), 39–42 (in Hebrew).

[28] Minutes of Meeting of Labor Secretariat, September 3, 1973, 2–024–1973, LPA.

[29] Hadari, *Israel Galili,* 526–31; Tel Aviv Embassy to Department of State, "Labor Party Policy on Occupied Territories," August 29, 1973, Public Library of US Diplomacy, [https://www.wikileaks.org/plusd/cables/1973TELAV06812_b.html]; Tel Aviv Embassy to Department of State, "Eban's Comment on the Occupied Territories," September 14, 1973, Public Library of US Diplomacy, [www.wikileaks.org/plusd/cables /1973TELAV06812_b.html]; Rafael, *Destination Peace*, 283; "The Galili Document and the Allon Plan," *Davar*, August 19, 1973; "Moshe Dayan's Secure Borders,"; "American Diplomatic Initiative Is Welcomed," *Davar*, September 26, 1973.

[30] Nakdimon, *Low Probability*, 45.

[31] Eban to Meir, "Kissinger and Galili Document," October 5, 1973, A-7049–53, ISA.

XVI: A Superfluous and Disgruntled Foreign Minister

[1] Ephraim Kahana, "Early Warning versus Concept: The Case of the Yom Kippur War, 1973," *Intelligence and National Security* 17, no. 2 (2002), 81–104; Uri Bar-Joseph, *The Watchman Fell Asleep: The Surprise of Yom Kippur and Its Sources* (Albany: State University of New York Press, 2005); Yigal Kipnis, *1973, The Way to War* (Or Yehuda: Kinneret, Zmora-Bitan, Dvir, 2012, in Hebrew).

[2] Memo, NSC Staff, "Indications of Arab Intentions to Initiate Hostilities," May 1973, HAK Office Files, Rabin/Kissinger (Dinitz) 1973 Jan–July, Box 135, NPMS, NARA.

[3] Minutes of Meeting, May, 12, 1973, Folder 4, Country Files—Middle East, NSC Files HAK Office, Box 135, NPMS, NARA.

[4] Quandt to Scowcroft, "Arab-Israeli Tensions," October 6, 1973, 1973 War (Middle East) Oct. 6 1973 File No. 1, NSF, NPMS, NARA.

[5] Sadat, *In Search of Identity*, 215.

[6] Siniver, *Nixon, Kissinger*, 189–91.

[7] Kissinger, *Years of Upheaval*, 220–21.

[8] "The Battle is Now Inevitable," *Newsweek*, April 9, 1973.

[9] "Foreign Minister Eban's Appearance before Members of the House Middle East Subcommittee May 10," May 11, 1973, Bureau of Near Eastern and South Asian Affairs, Office of Israel and Arab-Israel Affairs, Records Relating to Israel and Arab-Israel Affairs, Box 6, RG 59, NARA.

[10] "Rabin: The Slow Road to Peace," *Maariv*, July 13, 1973; Nakdimon, *Low Probability*, 36.

[11] Yoram Meital, "The October War and Egypt's Multiple Crossings"; Asaf Siniver, "U.S. Foreign Policy and the Kissinger Stratagem," in *The Yom Kippur War: Politics, Diplomacy, Legacy*, ed. Asaf Siniver (New York: Oxford University Press, 2013), 85–99; Ahron Bregman, "Ashraf Marwan and Israel's Intelligence Failure," in Siniver, ed., *The Yom Kippur War*, 195–208.

[12] Dayan, *Story of My Life*, 474–75; Herzog, *The Arab-Israeli Wars*, 227–42, 287–89.

[13] Matti Golan, *The Secret Conversations of Henry Kissinger* (New York: Quadrangle, 1976), 42–43.

[14] Gazit to Dinitz, October 7, 1973, A-4996/3, ISA; Dinitz to Gazit, October 9, 1973, A-4996/3, ISA.

[15] "All of Dinitz's Wonders," *Maariv*, May 22, 1987.

[16] Eban, *Personal Witness*, 524–25; Nakdimon, *Low Probability*, 97–98.

[17] Galili to Eban, October 6, 1973, F-6857/5; ISA.

[18] Kissinger Telcons, Chronological File, Box 22, NPMS, NARA; Henry Kissinger, *Crisis: The Anatomy of Two Major Foreign Policy Crises* (New York: Simon and Schuster, 2003), 15–26.

[19] Golan, *The Secret Conversations of Henry Kissinger*, 51.

[20] Kissinger Telcons, Chronological File, Box 22, NPMS, NARA.

[21] "Statement to the General Assembly by Foreign Minister Eban, 8 October 1973," Israel Ministry of Foreign Affairs [http://www.mfa.gov.il/mfa/foreignpolicy/mfadocuments/yearbook1/pages/4%20statement%20to%20the%20general%20assembly%20by%20foreign%20min.aspx].

[22] "The Situation in the Middle East," *Yearbook of the United Nations* (New York: United Nations, 1973), 194–96, 210–21.

[23] Gazit to Dinitz, October 9, 1973 (1040 and 1100), A-4996/3, ISA; Dinitz to Gazit, October 9, 1973, A-4996/3, ISA.

[24] Prime Minister to Foreign Minister, October 11, 1973, FM-6857/5, ISA.

[25] Shalev to Gazit, October 13, 1973, FM-6857/5, ISA.

[26] Memorandum of Conversation, *FRUS*, 1969–76, vol. 25 (Washington, DC: Government Printing Office, 2011), 482–86; William B. Quandt, interview with the author; Siniver, *Kissinger, Nixon*, 199–203.

[27] Melman and Raviv, *Friends in Deed*, 163.

[28] Gazit to Dinitz, October 14, 1973, A-4996/4, ISA.

[29] Dinitz to Prime Minister, October 18, 1973, A-7250/8, ISA.

[30] Dinitz to Gazit, October 19, 1973, A-7047/13, ISA.

[31] Shalev to Gazit, October 18, 1973, A-7250/8, ISA.

[32] Prime Minister to Foreign Minister, October 18, 1973, FM-6875/5, ISA; Golan, *The Secret Conversations of Henry Kissinger*, 72.

[33] Eban to Dinitz, October 19, 1973, A-4996/5, ISA; Dinitz to Gazit, October 20, 1973, A-4996/5, ISA; Gazit to Dinitz, October 21, 1973, A-4996/5, ISA.

[34] Dinitz to Gazit, October 19, 1973, 7047/13–A, ISA; Shalev to Bentsur, October 30, 1973, FM-6860/12, ISA; Eytan Bentsur, Meron Medzini, and Shlomo Nakdimon, interviews with the author; Nakdimon, *Low Probability*, 206–8, 212–13.

[35] Siniver, *Kissinger, Nixon*, 205–17; Galia Golan, "The Soviet Union and the October War," in Siniver, ed., *The Yom Kippur War*, 101–18.

[36] Tel Aviv Embassy to Secretary of State, "Eban Calls for Israeli Policy Reassessment," November 28, 1973, NSC Files, Country Files—Middle East, Israel Box 611, Folder 1, NPMS, NARA; Kissinger, *Years of Upheaval*, 560.

[37] Tel Aviv Embassy to Secretary of State, "Eban Calls for Israeli Policy Reassessment"

[38] Ibid.

[39] Gazit to Dinitz, November 16, 1973, A-4996/6, ISA.

[40] Rosen to Eban, December 6, 1973, FM-5201/16, ISA; Foreign Ministry to Paris and Geneva, December 10, 1973, FM-5201/12, ISA; Romem to Shak, December 23, 1973, FM-5201/12, ISA; Kenneth W. Stein, *Heroic Diplomacy: Sadat, Kissinger, Carter, Begin, and the Quest for Arab-Israeli Peace* (New York: Routledge, 1999), 122; "The Information War in Geneva," *Haaretz*, December 12, 1973.

[41] Golan, *The Secret Conversations of Henry Kissinger*, 124–25.

[42] The Geneva Press Conference, FM-860/13, ISA; "'Table War': Eban Threatened to Leave," *Jerusalem Post*, December 23, 1973; Stein, *Heroic Diplomacy*, 142–43.

[43] "Verbatim Record of Opening Meeting, Peace Conference on the Middle East, PCME/PV.1," December 21, 1973, FM-4783/6, ISA.

[44] Ibid.

[45] Myron J. Aronoff, *Power and Ritual in the Israel Labor Party: A Study in Political Anthropology* (London: Sharp, 1993), 144–51; Nakdimon, *Low Probability*, 262–63; Golan, *The Secret Conversations of Henry Kissinger*, 124–25, 132; Jewish Telegraphic Agency, "Labor Party Circles Demand Dayan be Excluded from Next Cabinet," January 14, 1974.

[46] Nakdimon, *Low Probability*, 13.

XVII: Dismissal

[1] Sapir, *Hayesh Hagadol*, 636–37; Eban, *Personal Witness*, 565; Meron Medzini, interview with the author; Yossi Sarid, interview with the author; "Abba Eban Sees Himself as Candidate for Premiership," *Yediot Ahronot*, June 25, 1976.

[2] Meisels, *From Ben-Gurion to Peres*, 138–39; "The Unfinished Battle of Pinchas Sapir," *Maariv*, April 26, 1974; Sapir, *Hayesh Hagadol*, 636–37.

[3] "I Was Wrong Not to Compete against Rabin and Peres for the Premiership," *Yediot Ahronot*, July 1, 1988.

[4] Rabin, *Service Diary*, 420–22; Meisels, *From Ben-Gurion to Peres*, 66.

[5] Minutes of Meeting, Labor Party, May 25, 1974, 2–25–1974–61, LPA.

[6] Ibid.; Meron Medzini, interview with the author; Rabin, *Service Diary*, 421–22; Meisels, *From Ben-Gurion to Peres*, 138–39; "Yigal Allon Explains," *Maariv*, June 6, 1974; Eli Evans, "Abba Eban: Campaigning at Columbia," *New York*, December 16, 1974, 8.

[7] Minutes of Meeting, Labor Party, May 28, 1974, 2–25–1974–61, LPA.

[8] Ibid.

[9] Eban, *A Sense of Purpose*, 314.

[10] Rafael, *Destination Peace*, 318.

[11] Abba Eban, "'Obsequious Deference' to the PLO," *New York Times*, November 7, 1974; Minutes of Meeting of Labor Party Meeting, August 5, 1979, 2–025–1979–86b, LPA.

[12] Evans, "Abba Eban: Campaigning at Columbia"; "Abba Eban in Academia: Another Arab-Israeli War Not Inevitable," *Philadelphia Inquirer*, December 1, 1974; "Notes on People," *New York Times*, June 28, 1974.

[13] Evans, "Abba Eban: Campaigning at Columbia."

[14] "Alignment and Labor Bodies Will Discuss Eban's Criticism," *Davar*, May 12, 1975; "Effort to Prevent an Alignment Quarrel Tonight over Eban's Statements," *Davar*, May 13, 1975; Jewish Telegraphic Agency, "Furore Rages in Israel over Eban's Charge That Israel Was to Blame for Breakdown of Talks," May 12, 1975; Jewish Telegraphic Agency, "Rabin Lashes Out at Eban for Making 'Irresponsible' Statements," May 13, 1975.

[15] "Eban: 1976 is a Year for Initiative," *Jerusalem Post*, November 21, 1975.

[16] "The Strange 'Alliance' between Dayan and Eban," *Yediot Ahronot*, June 25, 1976.

[17] "Where Do We Go from Here? Interview with Abba Eban," *New Outlook*, September 1975, 10.

[18] Hal Saunders, interview with the author.

[19] Philip Gillon, "Where Now Abba?" *Jerusalem Post*, July 2, 1976.

[20] Aronoff, *Power and Ritual in the Israel Labor Party*, 167–68; Tyler, *Fortress Israel*, 259–60; Jewish Telegraphic Agency, "No-Confidence Motion for Alleged

Sabbath Desecration Defeated by a Vote of 55–48 with 9 Abstentions," December 15, 1976.

[21] Tel Aviv Embassy to Department of State, "Cabinet Crisis: The Rabin-Peres Rivalry," December 27, 1976, Public Library of US Diplomacy, [https://search.wikileaks.org/plusd/cables/1976TELAV08651_b.html]; Tel Aviv Embassy to Department of State, "Eban Formally Announces His Candidacy," January 25, 1977, Public Library of US Diplomacy, [https://search.wikileaks.org/plusd/cables /1977TELAV00565_c.html]; "Eban Removes Candidacy in Support of Peres," *Davar*, February 4, 1977; "Peres Is Unopposed as Allon Bows Out," *New York Times*, April 10, 1977.

[22] Nadav Safran, *Israel: The Embattled Ally* (Cambridge, MA: Harvard University Press, 1980), 196–98; Jewish Telegraphic Agency, "Rabin Resigns Following Probe into Illegal Bank Accounts Held by Him and His Wife in Washington," April 8, 1977.

[23] "Eban Holds Active Account at City Bank in New York," *Davar*, April 24, 1977; "Eban's Foreign Accounts Permit Still Not Found," *Davar*, April 25 1977; "Eban Asked to Cancel His Appearances," *Haaretz*, April 26, 1977.

[24] Shlomo Nakdimon, Yossi Sarid, and Yaacov Ahimeir, interviews with the author; "Eban, the Writer, Discusses No. 3: 'To Live or Perish,'" *New York Times*, March 25, 1969.

[25] "Lt. General Hearsay and Eban's Account," *Davar*, April 25, 1977; "Eban's Foreign Accounts Permit Still Not Found," *Davar*, April 25 1977; Jewish Telegraphic Agency, "Eban Explains to Treasury Official Nature of His Bank Accounts in N.Y.," April 25, 1977; "Eban Dollars Make News," *Jewish Chronicle*, April 29, 1977; "Abba Eban's Dollar Account," *Ha'Olam Ha'Ze*, April 27, 1977; Jewish Telegraphic Agency, "Former Finance Ministry Official Confirms Eban Was Granted Permit to Maintain Bank Account in N.Y.," April 27, 1977.

[26] "Opposing Recommendations—Lenient and Severe—Submitted in Eban's Foreign Currency Affair," *Davar*, May 29, 1977.

[27] "Attorney General Did Not Find Grounds for Proceedings over Eban's Foreign Bank Accounts," *Davar*, July 7, 1977; "Eban Won't Be Prosecuted under Currency Laws," *New York Times*, July 7, 1977; "Report," *Maariv*, June 27, 1986.

[28] "Voice of Israel," *Newsweek*, January 23, 1978; "The Eloquent Diplomat," *New York Times*, December 18, 1977.

[29] Ben Halpern, "Room at the Top?" *Commentary*, May 1978, 72–76; "Abba Eban on Himself," *Haaretz*, March 5, 1978.

[30] Abba Eban, *An Autobiography* (Tel Aviv: Steimatzky, 1977), 602 (in Hebrew).

[31] Eban's Lecture on "The Arab-Israeli Conflict," Peace Seminar at the Van Leer Jerusalem Foundation, May 29, 1973, C-290/F-3463-348, AEA.

[32] The 139th Session of the 9th Knesset, July 26, 1978, Knesset Minutes, KA.

[33] "Masach Ishi," C-0197/F-2124, AEA.

[34] "Personal File," C-0141/F-1507, AEA; "Eban Will Cry Out—for $3,500," *Ha'Olam Ha'Ze*, September 21, 1977.

[35] Yossi Sarid, Dan Margalit, Yaacov Ahimeir, and Uri Raday, interviews with the author; Zvi Israeli, *Mr Speaker, Knesset in Crisis!* (Jerusalem: Carmel, 1988), 144, 164–65, 168 (in Hebrew).

[36] "Kshishim Ve'Masheu," *NRG Maariv*, October 3, 2005 ,[http://www.nrg.co.il/online/1/ART/991/780.html]

[37] "Eban Discusses Rumor about Cairo Ambassadorship," *New York Times*, April 30, 1979.

[38] Avi Shlaim, "The Likud in Power: The Historiography of Revisionist Zionism," *Israel Studies* 1, no. 2 (1996): 254–55.

[39] Noam Chomsky, *Fateful Triangle: The United States, Israel and the Palestinians* (Cambridge, MA: South End, 1999), 227–28; Anita Shapira, *Israel: A History* (London: Orion, 2012), 380; Shlaim, "The Likud in Power," 255; "Interview with MK Abba Eban," *Maariv*, August 6, 1982.

[40] Ronald Reagan, *An American Life: The Autobiography* (New York: Simon and Schuster, 1990), 419.

[41] Chomsky, *Fateful Triangle*, 224–28; "Labor Objects Entry to Beirut," *Maariv*, August 6, 1982.

[42] Abba Eban, "Introduction," in *The Beirut Massacre: The Complete Kahan Commission Report* (New York: Karz-Cohl, 1983), viii–xiv; Thomas Friedman, *From Beirut to Jerusalem* (New York: HarperCollins, 1988), 156–66; Tyler, *Fortress Israel*, 309–15.

[43] "Tragic Thinking," *Maariv*, October 6, 1982.

[44] *The Beirut Massacre*, 103–5; "Sharon Will Stay in Israeli Cabinet; Duties Uncertain," *New York Times*, February 14, 1983.

[45] The 171st Session of the 10th Knesset, February 7, 1983, Knesset Minutes, KA.

[46] "Big disgrace . . . Like the Vietnam War," *Hadashot*, December 28, 1984.

[47] "Eban Joins US Blast," *Jewish Chronicle*, April 8, 1983.

[48] "Sharon: Abba Eban in US Blamed the Government for 500 Casualties," *Yediot Ahronot*, May 24, 1983.

[49] Eban, "Introduction," in *The Beirut Massacre*, xiii.

[50] "February 1997," C-272/F-3261, AEA; "Abba Eban on Diplomacy," *New York Times*, October 31, 1993; Eban interview, *Charlie Rose*, November 21, 1991, PBS.

[51] "Rolls-Royce of the Diplomatic Circuit," *Guardian*, March 7, 1984.

[52] "Master of the New Diplomacy," *Observer*, February 27, 1984.

[53] Eli Evans, interview with the author; Rudy Cohen, interview with the author; "Heritage," C-205/F-2331, AEA; "Newspaper Clippings," C-0038/F-361, AEA; Rosenthal, *Jerusalem, Take One!* 235–59; "Religious Arrogance versus Imperishable Truths," *Jewish Chronicle*, February 22, 1985; "TV Review: 'Civilization and the Jews' Series on Channel 13," *New York Times*, October 1, 1984.

[54] "First Four Places Allocated Immediately—The Problems Started from Fifth Place Down," *Yediot Ahronot*, May 25, 1984; Yossi Beilin, interview with the author; Micha Harish, interview with the author.

[55] Eban to Peres, May 16, 1984, C-121/F-1315, AEA.

[56] "First Four Places Allocated Immediately."

[57] "Eban: Either Foreign Minister—Or Out," *Israel Shelanu*, May 25, 1984.

[58] Dan Korn, *Time in Gray: The National Unity Governments 1984–1990* (Tel Aviv: Zmora Bitan, 1994), 120–21 (in Hebrew).

[59] "Big Disgrace . . . Like the Vietnam War."

[60] Yaacov Ahimeir, interview with the author; Uzi Baram, interview with the author; "Only Eban's Humor Saved the Knesset's First Day," *Davar*, September 4, 1984; "Eban to Shulamit Aloni: 'Your Proposal is Very Tempting,'" *Maariv*, September 4, 1984; "Politics, Personality Keep Eban Out," *Canadian Jewish News*, November 8, 1984.

[61] Uri Raday, interview with the author.

[62] The 5th Session of the 11th Knesset, September 12, 1984, Knesset Minutes, KA.

[63] Uri Radai, interview with the author; Yossi Sarid, interview with the author.

XVIII: How Terrible Is This Place

[1] David Schoenbaum, *The United States and the State of Israel* (New York: Oxford University Press, 1993), 314–19; Melman and Raviv, *Friends in Deed*, 283–87; Black and Morris, *Israel's Secret Wars*, 416–422.

[2] Ehud Olmert, interview with the author; Micha Harish, interview with the author.

[3] "Eban vs. Rotenstreich," *Yediot Ahronot*, May 25, 1987; "Bucking a Bum Rap and Anguish," *Jerusalem Post*, June 2, 1987.

[4] "All of Dinitz's Wonders."

[5] Ehud Olmert, Micha Harish, and Uri Raday, interviews with the author.

[6] "The Eban Commission's Recommendations," *Hatzofe*, May 25, 1987; "Eban Feared Set for Anti-Climax," *Jerusalem Post*, May 26, 1987.

[7] TV interview with Abba Eban, *Erev Hadash*, May 8, 1987, Israeli Educational Television, 4–30–1987–43C, LPA.

[8] "Difficulties in Drafting Eban report," *Maariv*, May 8, 1987.

[9] Uri Raday, interview with the author; "'Eban Commission' Locked in Police Facility to Finalise Recommendations over 'Pollard Affair,'" *Hatzofe*, May 25, 1987; "Likud MK Will Share Room with Labor MK," *Hadashot*, May 25, 1987; "60 Hours of Group Dynamics," *Yediot Ahronot*, May 29, 1987.

[10] Ehud Olmert, Micha Harish, and Uri Raday, interviews with the author; "Burg Replied in Writing to the Questions of the 'Eban Commission,'" *Hatzofe*, May

25, 1987; "60 Hours of Group Dynamics," *Yediot Ahronot*, May 29, 1987; "Eban's Neurim," *Haaretz*, May 29, 1987.

[11] "Report of the Subcommittee for Intelligence and Secret Services on Jonathan Pollard," May 26, 1987, KA; "The Full Eban Report," *Maariv*, May 28, 1987; Jewish Telegraphic Agency, "Inner Cabinet Adopts Report Blaming Entire Cabinet for Pollard Affair," May 28, 1987.

[12] "Spy Case Reports Seen Changing Little in Israel," *Washington Post*, May 27, 1987; William Safire, "Three Outrages," *New York Times*, May 28, 1987; "Israeli Cabinet Accepts Spy Blame," *New York Times*, May 28, 1987.

[13] Uzi Baram, interview with the author; Yaron Deckel, interview with the author.

[14] Protocol of Meeting of the Central Committee of the Labor Party, May 28, 1987, 2–23–1987–131A, LPA; "Rabin: Eban Gave a Hand to Likud Campaign," *Haaretz*, May 29, 1987.

[15] "Party Flays Eban for Pollard Report: Peres, Rabin Lead Labor's Attack on Israeli Elder Statement," *Washington Post*, May 29, 1987; Uzi Baram, interview with the author.

[16] "Eban: I Was Insulted," *Yediot Ahronot*, June 2, 1987.

[17] "Bucking a Bum Rap and Anguish"; "Eban Hits Back at 'Strident' Peres," *Jerusalem Post,* May 31, 1987.

[18] "July Poll: Peres Still Leads," *Maariv*, July 26, 1987; "Peres—42 per cent, Shamir—9 per cent," *Maariv*, January 30, 1985.

[19] Uzi Baram, interview with the author; Yitzhak Herzog, interview with the author.

[20] Yossi Beilin, interview with the author.

[21] "Eban in '87: On Fringe of politics."

[22] Abba Eban, "Shamir's No. 1 Problem," *New York Times*, November 9, 1986.

[23] "After 30 Years in the Knesset," *Haaretz*, June 16, 1988.

[24] Yossi Beilin, Micha Harish, Uzi Baram, and Yaron Deckel, interviews with the author.

[25] Yossi Sarid, interview with the author; "Interview with Shevach Weiss," *Maariv*, June 24, 1988; Eban, *A Sense of Purpose*, 330–37.

[26] "Eban Retired from Race," *Maariv*, June 16, 1988; Yossi Beilin, interview with the author; Yitzhak Herzog, interview with the author.

[27] Suzy Eban, interview with the author; Yaacov Ahimeir, interview with the author.

XIX: Will I Be Remembered?

[1] "Upheaval in Labor: 18 MKs Ousted from Knesset list," *Haaretz*, June 16, 1988.

[2] "Eban on the Sidelines," *Los Angeles Times*, June 17, 1988.

[3] "A True Statesman," *Miami Herald*, June 17, 1988.

[4] "Suzy, We're Leaving," *Maariv*, June 17, 1988; "Peres in a Letter to Abba

Eban," *Maariv*, June 19, 1988; "Abba Eban: Not Right That They Are Elected and I Will Carry the Flag," *Maariv*, June 24, 1988.

5 "Abba Eban: Not Right That They Are Elected and I Will Carry the Flag"; "After 30 Years in the Knesset."

6 "Eban Decision Could Hurt Labour," *Jerusalem Post*, August 14, 1988.

7 Eban to Baram, July 25, 1988, C-205/F-2225, AEA.

8 "Eban Blasts Political Primitivism," *Jerusalem Post*, November 8, 1988.

9 "The Issues That Won't Go Away," *Jerusalem Post*, November 11, 1988.

10 "The 'Partner' Fantasy," *Jerusalem Post*, July 14, 1989.

11 "Israel, Hardly the Monaco of the Middle East," *New York Times*, January 2, 1989.

12 "Peres Should Have Offered to Step Down!," *Ha'Olam Ha'Ze*, April 18, 1989.

13 The 32nd Session of the 12th Knesset, February 7, 1989, Knesset Minutes, KA; "I Didn't Consult with Peres So I Wouldn't Get a Negative Answer!," *Ha'Olam Ha'Ze,* February 8, 1989; "Israel's Eban Urges Talks with Arabs," *Los Angeles Times*, February 1, 1989; "Eban Will Manage without a Passport," *Maariv*, December 29, 1991.

14 "Peres Should Have Offered to Step Down!"

15 "All the World's His Stage," *Jerusalem Post*, November 13, 1992; Eban, *A Sense of Purpose*, 346–47; "I Am Not Flattered by the Comparison to Bibi," *Yediot Ahronot*, November 29, 1991.

16 "I Am Not Flattered by the Comparison to Bibi."

17 "Chronicle," *New York Times*, June 6, 1990; "Abba Eban, 'The Voice of Israel,' dies at 87," *Haaretz*, November 18, 2002; "Abba Eban Appeals to the U.S.: Don't Leave Us in the Middle of the Road," *Yediot New York*, June 15, 1990; "Missing Eban," *Israel Shelanu*, May 7, 1990.

18 "Israel's Cicero," *Financial Times*, February 22, 1993.

19 Abba Eban, "Israeli Diplomacy in the 1990s: Speech at the Dedication of the Abba Eban Centre at the Hebrew University," November 19, 1992, C-292/F-3513, AEA.

20 Stephen Trachtenberg, Mike Freedman, and Nathan Brown, interviews with the author; Trachtenberg to Eban, May 28, 1993, C-293/F-3522, AEA; "Abba's Travels for Peace," *Jewish Chronicle*, December 10, 1993.

21 "Just Not David Levy," *Al Hasharon*, June 4, 1999.

22 "Peace and Life, or War and Death," *Los Angeles Times*, September 3, 1993.

23 "Bibi," 1996 (undated draft), C-015/F-1628, AEA.

24 "A Reluctant Realist," *New York Times Book Review*, March 28, 1998.

25 Eban, *Diplomacy for the Next Century*,15, 38, 122.

26 Ibid., 161.

27 "Abba Eban Will Not Arrive to Accept Award," *Maariv-Zman Hasharon*, April 20, 2001.

[28] Eban, *A Sense of Purpose*, 346–47; Suzy Eban, Eli Eban, Yael Student, and Oliver Sacks, interviews with the author.

[29] Eban, *A Sense of Purpose*, 347–48; "End of a Legend," *Yediot Ahronot*, November 18, 2002; "Special Session in Memory of Former Minister and MK Abba Eban," 13th Session of the 16th Knesset, March 12, 2003, Knesset Minutes, KA; "President Katzav: The Whole World Listened to Abba Eban," *Haaretz*, November 18, 2002.

XX: Legacy

[1] Potter Stewart, quoted in Stephen J. Stedman, *Peacemaking in Civil War: International Mediation in Zimbabwe, 1974–1980* (Boulder, CO: Lynne Rienner, 1991), 240.

[2] Richard Hofstadter, *Anti-Intellectualism in American Life* (London: Jonathan Cape, 1962), 7.

[3] Arnold M. Eisen, "Israel at 50: An American Jewish Perspective," *American Jewish Yearbook* (1998), 54.

[4] Peter Y. Medding, *Mapai in Israel: Political Organisation and Government in a New Society* (Cambridge: Cambridge University Press, 1972), 59–60; Bernard D. Weinryb, "The Lost Generation in Israel," *Middle East Journal* 7, no. 4 (1953): 415–29; Julie Ebel, "Eyeless in Gaza: Some Reflections on Teaching Early English Literature in Israel," *College English* 34, no. 4 (1973): 549.

[5] Micha Kirshner, *The Israelis* (Or Yehuda: Hed Arzi, 1997, in Hebrew).

[6] Eban, quoted in Ron Adam, ed., *Abba Eban: A Statesman and a Diplomat* (Jerusalem: Ministry of Foreign Affairs, 2003), 138.

[7] Eban, "The National Style"; Tel Aviv Embassy to Secretary of State, "Eban Calls for Israeli Policy Reassessment," November 28, 1973, NSC Files, Country Files—Middle East, Israel Box, 611, NPMS, NARA.

[8] The Abba Eban You Didn't Know," *Maariv*, November 18, 2002.

Sources

Archives and Databases

AEA	Abba Eban Archives at the Abba Eban Centre for Israeli Diplomacy, Hebrew University of Jerusalem.
BGA	David Ben-Gurion Archives, Sde Boker, Israel.
BH	Beit Hatfutsot, Tel Aviv.
CAM	Cambridge University Student Records, Cambridge.
CZA	Central Zionist Archives, Jerusalem.
EPL	Dwight D. Eisenhower Presidential Library, Abilene, Kansas.
ISA	Israel State Archives, Jerusalem.
JDC	American Jewish Joint Distribution Committee Archives, New York.
LBJ	Lyndon B. Johnson Presidential Library, Austin, Texas.
LHA	Liddell Hart Centre for Military Archives, King's College London.
LPA	Israel Labor Party Archives, Beit Berl, Israel.
KA	Knesset Archive, Jerusalem.
NA	National Archives, London
NAC	National Archives of Canada, Ottawa, Ontario.
NARA	US National Archives and Records Administration, College Park, Maryland.
TPL	Harry S. Truman Presidential Library, Independence, Missouri.
UCLA	Charles E. Young Research Library, Department of Special Collections, University of California–Los Angeles.
UEA	University of Exeter Archives, Exeter, England.
UNA	United Nations Archives, New York.
UNISPAL	United Nations Information System on the Question of Palestine
WIA	Weizmann Institute of Science Archives, Rehovot, Israel.

Official Government Collections

Department of Public Information, United Nations. *Yearbook of the United Nations*, 1950, 1951, 1953, 1956, 1967, 1973. New York: United Nations.

House of Commons. Hansard (verbatim report of proceedings). London: Parliament of the United Kingdom.

Israel Ministry of Foreign Affairs. *Documents on the Foreign Policy of Israel* (*DFPI*). Vol. 4, May–December 1949 (1986); vol. 5, 1950 (1988); vol. 6, 1951 (1991); vol. 8,

1953 (1995); vol. 8, 1953, companion vol. (1953); vol. 12, 1956 (2009). Jerusalem: Israel Ministry of Foreign Affairs.

Jewish Agency. *Political Documents of the Jewish Agency*. Vol. 1, May 1945–December 1946 (1998); vol. 2, January–November 1947 (1998). Jerusalem: Hassifriya Haziyonit.

United Nations General Assembly. Official Records of the General Assembly. New York: United Nations.

U.S. Department of State. *State Department Bulletin*, 1952–59.

U.S. Department of State, Office of the Historian. *Foreign Relations of the United States* (FRUS). 1947, vol. 5 (1972); 1948, vol. 5, pt. 2 (1976); 1949, vol. 6 (1977); 1950, vol. 5 (1978); 1952–54, vol. 9 (1986); 1955–57, vol. 14 (1989); 1955–57, vol. 16 (1990); 1955–57, vol. 17 (1990); 1964–68, vol. 18 (2000); 1964–68, vol. 19 (2004); 1964–68, vol. 20 (2001); 1969–76, vol. 12 (2006); 1969–76, vol. 24 (2004); 1969–76, vol. 25 (2010). Washington, DC: Government Printing Office.

Interviews

Interviewee	*Pertinent Position*	*Date and Place*
Ahimeir, Yaacov	Broadcaster	July 29, 2010, Jerusalem
Avner, Yehuda	Adviser to Prime Minister Levi Eshkol	December 6, 2011, Jerusalem
Bar-Zohar, Michael	Member, Israel Labor Party	July 27, 2010, Tel Aviv
Baram, Uzi	Member, Israel Labor Party	July 26, 2010, Tel Aviv
Beilin, Yossi	Member, Israel Labor Party	September 8, 2014, Tel Aviv
Bentsur, Eytan	Abba Eban's private secretary	June, 6, 2010, Tel Aviv
Brown, Nathan	Professor, George Washington University	February, 18, 2010, by phone
Cohen, Rudy	Producer, *Heritage* TV series	June 9, 2010, Tel Aviv
Deckel, Yaron	Broadcaster	July 17, 2010, Tel Aviv
Eban, Eli	Abba Eban's son	December 7, 2011, Hertzliya, Israel
Eban, Raphael	Abba Eban's brother	July 7, 2010, London
Eban, Suzy	Abba Eban's wife	March 17, 2010, Hertzliya, Israel
Evans, Eli	President, Revson Foundation	February 22, 2010, New York
Freedman, Michael	Professor, George Washington University	February 16, 2010, Washington, DC
Gordon, Rachel	Abba Eban's secretary	July 27, 2010, Tel Aviv
Harish, Micha	Member, Israel Labor Party	September 9, 2014, Ramat-Gan, Israel
Herzog, Yitzhak	Abba Eban's nephew	June 3, 2010, Tel Aviv
Kalb, Marvin	Journalist	February 17, 2010, Washington, DC
Lynn, Jonathan	Abba Eban's nephew	September 24, 2010, London
Lynn, Rita	Jonathan Lynn's wife	September 24, 2010, London
Medzini, Meron	Director, Israel Government Press Office	May 27, 2013, Jerusalem

Margalit, Dan	Broadcaster	July 26, 2010, Tel Aviv
Nakdimon, Shlomo	Journalist	July 26, 2010, Tel Aviv
Olmert, Ehud	Member, Israel Likud Party	September 8, 2014, Tel Aviv
Pines, Nitza	Abba Eban's secretary	December 5, 2011, Tel Aviv
Quandt, William B.	Member, U.S. National Security Council	August 26, 2004, Charlottesville, Virginia
Raday, Uri	Manager, Knesset Foreign Affairs and Defense Committee	July 28, 2010, Jerusalem
Raviv, Moshe	Abba Eban's political secretary	May 12, 2009, Hertzliya, Israel
Raz, Avi	Fellow, University of Oxford	October 8, 2010, Oxford
Sacks, Oliver	Abba Eban's cousin	February 23, 2010, New York
Sarid, Yossi	Member, Israel Labor Party	July 28, 2010, Tel Aviv
Saunders, Harold	Member, U.S. National Security Council	February 17, 2010, Washington, DC
Shiloah, Dov	Reuven Shiloah's son	October 24, 2012, Ra'anana, Israel
Shlaim, Avi	Professor, University of Oxford	October 8, 2010, Oxford
Shimoni, Emanuel	Abba Eban's chief of bureau	October 9, 2011, Nordia, Israel
Student, Yael	Assistant to the Ebans	July 25, 2010, Hertzliya, Israel
Trachtenberg, Stephen	President, George Washington University	February 17, 2010, Washington, DC
Urquhart, Brian	Under-Secretary-General of the United Nations	February 24, 2010, New York
Weidenfeld, George	Publisher	February 24, 2012, London

Books and Articles

Adam, Ron, ed. *Abba Eban: A Statesman and a Diplomat*. Jerusalem: Ministry of Foreign Affairs, 2003.

Adamsky, Dima. "The 'Seventh Day' of the Six Day War: The Soviet Intervention in the War of Attrition (1969–1970)." In *The Soviet Union and the June 1967 Six Day War*, edited by Yaacov Roi and Boris Morozov, 198–250. Stanford, CA: Stanford University Press, 2008.

Almogi, Yosef. *Total Commitment*. Jerusalem: Edanim, 1980. In Hebrew.

Alteras, Isaac. "Eisenhower, American Jewry, and Israel." *American Jewish Archives* 37 (1985): 258–74.

———. *Eisenhower and Israel: U.S.-Israeli Relations, 1953–1960*. Gainesville: University Press of Florida, 1993.

American Jewish Committee. *American Jewish Yearbook*. Vol. 51. Philadelphia: Jewish Publication Society of America, 1950.

Amit, Meir. *Head On*. Tel Aviv: Hed Artzi, 1999. In Hebrew.

Aronoff, Myron J. *Power and Ritual in the Israel Labor Party: A Study in Political Anthropology*. London: Sharp, 1993.

Aronson, Shlomo. *David Ben-Gurion and the Jewish Renaissance*. New York: Cambridge University Press, 2011.

Avner, Yehuda. *The Prime Ministers: An Intimate Narrative of Israeli Leadership*. London: Toby, 2010.

Bailey, Sydney D. *The Making of Resolution 242*. Dordrecht, Netherlands: Nijhoff, 1985.

Bar-Joseph, Uri. *The Watchman Fell Asleep: The Surprise of Yom Kippur and Its Sources*. Albany: State University of New York Press, 2005.

Bar-On, Mordechai. "The Generals' 'Revolt': Civil-Military Relations in Israel on the Eve of the Six Day War." *Middle Eastern Studies* 48, no. 1 (2012): 33–50.

Bar-Siman-Tov, Yaacov. "Ben-Gurion and Sharett: Conflict Management and Great Power Constraints in Israeli Foreign Policy." Middle Eastern Studies 24, no. 3 (1988): 330–56.

Bar-Zohar, Michael. *Ben-Gurion*. London: Weidenfeld and Nicolson, 1978.

———. *Embassies in Crisis: Diplomats and Demagogues behind the Six-Day War*. Englewood Cliffs, NJ: Prentice Hall, 1970.

———. *The Longest Month*. Tel Aviv: Levin Epstein, 1968. In Hebrew.

———. *Shimon Peres: The Biography*. New York: Random House, 2007.

———. *Yaacov Herzog: A Biography*. London: Halban, 2005.

Beilin, Yossi. *The Price of Unity: The Labour Party until the Yom Kippur War*. Tel Aviv: Revivim, 1985. In Hebrew.

Bell, J. B. *Terror out of Zion: The Fight for Israeli Independence*. New Brunswick, NJ: Transaction, 1996.

Ben-Ami, Shlomo. *Scars of War, Wounds of Peace*. London: Weidenfeld and Nicolson, 2006.

Ben-Gurion, David. "Chaim Weizmann—Champion of the Jewish People." In *Chaim Weizmann: Statesman of the Jewish Renaissance—The Weizmann Centenary 1874–1974*, edited by Dan Leon and Yehuda Adin, 11–20. Jerusalem: Zionist Library, 1974.

Ben-Horin, Meir. "The Tide of Nationalism by Abba Eban." *Jewish Social Studies* 22, no. 2 (1960): 113–14.

Ben-Zvi, Abraham. *The United States: The Limits of the Special Relationship*. New York: Columbia University Press, 1993.

Bialer, Uri. *Between East and West: Israel's Foreign Policy Orientation 1948–1956*. Cambridge: Cambridge University Press, 1990.

Bitan, Moshe. *Political Diary 1967–1970.* Tel Aviv: Olam Hadash, 2014. In Hebrew.

Black, Ian, and Benny Morris. *Israel's Secret Wars: A History of Israel's Intelligence Service*. Reading, England: Futura, 1991.

Brecher, Michael. *Decisions in Crisis: Israel, 1967 and 1973*. Berkeley: University of California Press, 1980.

———. *Decisions in Israel's Foreign Policy*. London: Oxford University Press, 1974.

———. "Eban and Israeli Foreign Policy: Diplomacy, War, and Disengagement." In *The Diplomats 1939–1979*, edited by Gordon A. Craig and Francis L. Loewenheim, 398-435. Princeton, NJ: Princeton University Press, 1994.

———. *The Foreign Policy System of Israel: Setting, Images, Process*. London: Oxford University Press, 1972.

Bregman, Ahron. "Ashraf Marwan and Israel's Intelligence Failure." In *The Yom Kippur War: Politics, Diplomacy, Legacy*, edited by Asaf Siniver, 195–208. New York: Oxford University Press, 2013.

———. *Israel's Wars: A History since 1947*. London: Routledge, 2010.

Bregman, Ahron, and Jihan El-Tahri. *The Fifty Years War: Israel and the Arabs*. London: Penguin, 1998.

Brown, L. Carl. "Origins of the Crisis." In *The Six-Day War: A Retrospective*, edited by Richard B. Parker, 13–73. Gainesville: University Press of Florida, 1996.

Brown, Philip Marshall. "The Recognition of Israel." *American Journal of International Law* 42 (1948): 620–27.

Bullock, Alan. *Ernest Bevin: Foreign Secretary 1945–51*. New York: Heinemann, 1983.

Burkett, Elinor. *Golda*. New York: HarperCollins, 2008.

Caplan, Neil. "'Oom-Shmoom' Revisited: Israeli Attitudes towards the UN and the Great Powers, 1948–1960." In *Global Politics: Essays in Honour of David Vital*, edited by Abraham Ben-Zvi and Aharon Klieman, 167–99. London: Cass, 1991.

Caradon, Lord, Arthur J. Goldberg, Mohamed H. El-Zayyat, and Abba Eban. *U.N. Security Council Resolution 242: A Case Study in Diplomatic Ambiguity*. Washington, DC: Institute for the Study of Diplomacy, Georgetown University, 1981.

Charters, David A. *The British Army and Jewish Insurgency in Palestine, 1945–47*. Basingstoke, England: Macmillan, 1987.

Chomsky, Noam. *Fateful Triangle: The United States, Israel and the Palestinians*. Cambridge, MA: South End, 1999.

Christison, Kathleen. *Perceptions of Palestine: Their Influence on U.S. Middle East Policy*. Berkeley: University of California Press, 2001.

Clarke, Thurston. *By Blood and Fire: Attack on the King David Hotel*. London: Hutchinson, 1981.

Cohen, Michael J. "The Genesis of the Anglo-American Committee on Palestine, November 1945: A Case Study in the Assertion of American Hegemony." *Historical Journal* 22, no. 1 (1979): 185–207.

Cradock, Percy. *Recollections of the Cambridge Union 1815–1939*. Cambridge: Bowes and Bowes.

Crossman, Richard. *A Nation Reborn: A Personal Report on the Roles Played by Weizmann, Bevin and Ben-Gurion in the Story of Israel*. New York: Atheneum, 1960.

Dayan, Moshe. *Story of My Life*. London: Weidenfeld and Nicolson, 1976.

Donovan, Robert J. *Conflict and Crisis: The Presidency of Harry S. Truman, 1945–1948*. New York: Norton, 1977.

Eban, Abba. *An Autobiography*. New York: Random House, 1977.

———. *An Autobiography*. Tel Aviv: Steimatzky, 1977. In Hebrew.

———. *Diplomacy for the Next Century*. New Haven, CT: Yale University Press, 1998.

———. "An Interview with Mr. Eban: Israel's Foreign Minister Reviews His First Year in Office and Outlines the Policies by Which He Hopes to Work." *New Outlook* 9, no. 6 (1966): 11–20.

———. *My Country: The Story of Modern Israel*. New York: Random House, 1972.

———. "The National Style." *New Outlook* 16, no. 3 (1973): 6–9.

———. *The New Diplomacy: International Affairs in the Modern Age*. New York: Random House, 1983.

———. *"Not Backward to Belligerency but Forward to Peace": Text of the Address by Israel's Foreign Minister, Mr. Abba Eban, in the United Nations Security Council on 6 June 1967*. New York: Israel Information Services, 1967.

———. "The Outlook for Peace in the Middle East." *Proceedings of the Academy of Political Science* 26, no. 3 (1957): 111–26.

———. *Personal Witness: Israel through My Eyes*. New York: Putnam's, 1992.

———. "Reality and Vision in the Middle East: An Israeli View." *Foreign Affairs* 43, no. 4 (1965): 626–38.

———. *The Tide of Nationalism*. New York: Horizon, 1959.

———. "Tragedy and Triumph." In *Chaim Weizmann: A Biography by Several Hands*, edited by Meyer W. Weisgal and Joel Carmichael, 249–313. New York: Atheneum, 1969.

———. *Voice of Israel*. New York: Horizon, 1957.

Eban, Aubrey. "The United Nations and the Palestine Question." *World Affairs* 2, no. 2 (1948): 124–35.

Eban, Suzy. *A Sense of Purpose: Recollections by Suzy Eban*. London: Orion, 2008.

Ebel, Julie. "Eyeless in Gaza: Some Reflections on Teaching Early English Literature in Israel." *College English* 34, no. 4 (1973): 537–50.

Eisen, Arnold M. "Israel at 50: An American Jewish Perspective." In *American Jewish Yearbook* (1998), 47–71 (Philadelphia: Jewish Publication Society of America, 1998.

Eshed, Hagai. *Who Gave the Order? The Mishap, The Lavon Affair and Ben-Gurion's Resignation*. Jerusalem: Keter, 1982. In Hebrew.

Evans, Eli. *The Lonely Days Were Sundays: Reflections of a Jewish Southerner*. Jackson: University Press of Mississippi, 1993.

Eytan, Walter. *The First Ten Years*. New York: Simon and Schuster, 1958.

Farson, Stuart, and Mark Phythian. *Commissions of Inquiry and National Security: Comparative Approaches*. Santa Barbara, CA: ABC-CLIO, 2011.

Finkelstein, Norman. *Image and Reality of the Israel-Palestine Conflict*. London: Verso, 2003.

Fowler, Laurence, and Helen Fowler. *Cambridge Commemorated: An Anthology of University Life*. Cambridge: Cambridge University Press, 1984.

Fraser, T. G. *The Arab-Israeli Conflict*. Basingstoke, England: Palgrave, 2004.

Freshwater, J. L [pseud.]. "Policy and Intelligence: The Arab-Israeli War." *Studies in Intelligence* 13, no. 1 (1969): 1–8.

Friedman, Thomas. *From Beirut to Jerusalem*. New York: HarperCollins, 1988.

Friling, Tuvia. *Arrows in the Dark: David Ben-Gurion, the Yishuv Leadership, and the Rescue Attempts during the Holocaust*. Madison: University of Wisconsin Press, 2003.

Ganin, Zvi. *An Uneasy Relationship: American Jewish Leadership and Israel, 1948–1957*. Syracuse, NY: Syracuse University Press, 2005.

García Granados, Jorge. *The Birth of Israel: The Drama as I Saw It*. New York: Knopf, 1948.

Garrett, Martin. *Cambridge: A Cultural and Literary History*. Oxford: Signal, 2004.

Gat, Moshe. *Britain and the Conflict in the Middle East, 1964–1967: The Coming of the Six-Day War*. Westport, CT: Praeger, 2003.

———. *In Search of a Peace Settlement: Egypt and Israel between the Wars, 1967–1973*. Basingstoke, England: Palgrave, 2012.

———. "Nasser and the Six Day War, 5 June 1967: A Premeditated Strategy or Inexorable Drift to War?" *Israel Affairs* 11, no. 2 (2005): 608–35.

Gazit, Mordechai. "Egypt and Israel—Was There a Peace Opportunity Missed in 1971?" *Journal of Contemporary History* 32, no. 1 (1997): 97–115.

———. *Israeli Diplomacy and the Quest for Peace*. London: Cass, 2002.

Gazit, Shlomo. *The Carrot and the Stick: Israel's Policy in Judea and Samaria, 1967–1969*. Washington, DC: B'nai Brith Books, 1995.

Gilbert, Martin. *Israel: A History*. New York: Morrow, 1998.

Gilboa, Amos. *Mr. Intelligence—Ahrale Yariv*. Tel Aviv: Miskal, 2013. In Hebrew.

Gilboa, Moshe. *Six Years, Six Days: Origins and History of the Six-Day War*. Tel Aviv: Am Oved, 1968.

Ginor, Isabella, and Gideon Remez. *Foxbats over Dimona: The Soviets' Nuclear Gamble in the Six-Day War*. New Haven, CT: Yale University Press, 2007.

Gitlin, Marcia. *The Vision Amazing: The Story of South African Zionism*. Johannesburg: Menorah Book Club, 1950.

Gluska, Ami. *The Israeli Military and the Origins of the 1967 War: Government, Armed Forces and Defence Policy 1963–1967*. London: Routledge, 2007.

Golan, Galia. "The Soviet Union and the October War." In *The Yom Kippur War: Politics, Diplomacy, Legacy*, edited by Asaf Siniver, 101–18. New York: Oxford University Press, 2013.

Golan, Matti. *The Secret Conversations of Henry Kissinger*. New York: Quadrangle, 1976.

Goldberg, Aleck. *Profile of a Community: South African Jewry*. Johannesburg: Rabbi Aloy Foundation Trust, 2002.

Goldstein, Yossi. *Eshkol: Biography*. Jerusalem: Keter, 2003. In Hebrew.

Goodman, Giora. "'Palestine's Best': The Jewish Agency's Press Relations, 1946–1947." *Israel Studies* 16, no. 3 (2011): 1–27.

Gorenberg, Gershom. *The Accidental Empire: Israel and the Birth of the Settlements, 1967, 1977*. New York: Times Books, 2006.

Gorney, Joseph. *The British Labour Movement and Zionism*. London: Routledge, 1983.

Grose, Peter. *Israel in the Mind of America*. New York: Knopf, 1983.

Haber, Eitan. *Menachem Begin: The Legend and the Man*. New York: Delacorte, 1978.

———. *Today War Will Break Out: The Reminiscences of Brig. Gen. Israel Lior*. Jerusalem: Edanim, 1987. In Hebrew.

Hadari, Danny. *Israel Galili: A Biography.* Tel Aviv: Hakibutz Hameuchad, 2011. In Hebrew.

Halamish, Aviva. *The Exodus Affair: Holocaust Survivors and the Struggle for Palestine*. Syracuse, NY: Syracuse University Press, 1998.

Harouvi, Eldad. "Reuven Zaslany (Shiloah) and the Covert Cooperation with British Intelligence during the Second World War." In *Intelligence for Peace: the Role of Intelligence in Times of Peace*, edited by Hesi Carmel, 30–48. London: Cass, 2002.

Heine, Heinrich. *The Prose Writings of Heinrich Heine*. Edited by Havelock Ellis. London: Scott, 1887.

Heller, Joseph. *Israel and the Cold War, 1948–1967*. Sde Boker: Ben-Gurion Heritage Institute, 2010. In Hebrew.

Herzog, Chaim. *The Arab-Israeli Wars: War and Peace in the Middle East from the 1948 War of Independence to the Present*. Barnsley, England: Frontline, 2010.

Hoffman, Bruce. *The Failure of British Military Strategy Within Palestine, 1939–1947*. Jerusalem: Bar-Ilan University Press, 1983.

Hoffman, Stanley. "Ralph Bunche: A Man of the World, but Never at Home." *Foreign Affairs* 74, no. 1 (1995): 177–78.

Hofstadter, Richard. *Anti-Intellectualism in American Life*. London: Cape, 1962.

Horowitz, David. *State in the Making*. New York: Knopf, 1953.

Howarth, T. E. B. *Cambridge between Two Wars*. London: Collins, 1978.

International Organization. "International Organization's Summary of Activities: General Assembly." 5:2 (1951): 313–27.

Israeli, Zvi. *Mr Speaker, Knesset in Crisis!* Jerusalem: Carmel, 1988. In Hebrew.

Jacobson, Eddie. "Two Presidents and a Haberdasher—1948." *American Jewish Archives Journal* 20 (April 1968): 3–15.

Jeffery, Keith. *MI6: The History of the Secret Intelligence Service, 1909–1949*. London: Bloomsbury, 2010.

Jones, Martin. *Failure in Palestine: British and United States Policy after the Second World War*. London: Mansell, 1986.

Kahana, Ephraim. “Early Warning versus Concept: The Case of the Yom Kippur War, 1973.” *Intelligence and National Security* 17, no. 2 (2002): 81–104.

———. *Historical Dictionary of Israeli Intelligence*. Lanham, MD: Scarecrow, 2006.

Kenen, Isaiah L. *Israel's Defense Line: Her Friends and Foes in Washington*. Buffalo, NY: Prometheus, 1981.

Kochavi, Arieh J. “The Displaced Persons' Problem and the Formulation of British Policy in Palestine.” *Studies in Zionism* 10, no. 1 (1989): 31–48.

Khalidi, Walid. “On Albert Hourani, the Arab Office, and the Anglo-American Committee of 1946.” *Journal of Palestine Studies* 35, no. 1 (2005): 60–79.

Kimche, David, and Dan Bawly. *The Sandstorm: The Arab-Israeli War of June 1967—Prelude and Aftermath*. London: Secker and Warburg, 1968.

Kimche, John. *Palestine or Israel: The Untold Story of Why We Failed, 1917–1923; 1967–1973*. London: Secker and Warburg, 1973.

Kipnis, Yigal. *1973, The Way to War*. Or Yehuda, Israel: Kinneret, Zmora-Bitan, Dvir, 2012. In Hebrew.

Kirshner, Micha. *The Israelis*. Or Yehuda, Israel: Hed Arzi, 1997. In Hebrew.

Kissinger, Henry. *Crisis: The Anatomy of Two Major Foreign Policy Crises*. New York: Simon and Schuster, 2003.

———. *White House Years*. London: Phoenix, 1977.

———. *Years of Upheaval*. Boston: Little, Brown, 1983.

Klier, D. John, and Shlomo Lambroza, eds. *Pogroms: Anti-Jewish Violence in Modern Russian History*. Cambridge: Cambridge University Press, 1992.

Korn, Dan. *Time in Gray: The National Unity Governments 1984–1990*. Tel Aviv: Zmora Bitan, 1994. In Hebrew.

Korn, David A. “US-Soviet Negotiations of 1969 and the Rogers Plan.” *Middle East Journal* 44, no. 1 (1990): 37–50.

Kurzman, Dan. *Genesis 1948: The First Arab-Israeli War*. London: Vallentine Mitchell, 1972.

Lall, Arthur. *The UN and the Middle East Crisis, 1967*. New York: Columbia University Press, 1968.

Lammfrom, Amnon, and Hagai Tsoref, eds. *Levi Eshkol: The Third Prime Minister, Selected Documents 1896–1969*. Jerusalem: Israel State Archive, 2002.

Laqueur, Walter. *The Road to Jerusalem: The Origins of the Arab-Israeli Conflict, 1967*. New York: Columbia University Press, 1968.

Lash, Joseph P. *Dag Hammarskjöld: Custodian of the Brushfire Peace*. New York: Doubleday, 1961.

Liebes, Tamar. “Acoustic Space: The Role of Radio in Israeli Collective History.” *Jewish History* 20, no. 1 (2006): 69–90.

Lewis, William R. *The British Empire in the Middle East, 1945–1951: Arab Nationalism, The United States, and Postwar Imperialism*. New York: Oxford University Press, 1998.

Little, Eddie, and Eric Higgins. “A Nasty Outbreak: Anti-Jewish Disturbances in 1947.” *Manchester Region History Review* 10 (1996): 57–61.

Louis, W. Roger, and Avi Shlaim, eds. *The 1967 Arab-Israeli War: Origins and Consequences*. Cambridge: Cambridge University Press, 2012.

Maoz, Zeev. *Defending the Holy Land: A Critical Analysis of Israel's Security and Foreign Policy.* Ann Arbor: University of Michigan Press, 2006.

McNeill, William H. *Arnold J. Toynbee: A Life*. Oxford: Oxford University Press, 1989.

Medding, Peter Y. *Mapai in Israel: Political Organisation and Government in a New Society*. Cambridge: Cambridge University Press, 1972.

Medzini, Meron. *Golda: A Political Biography*. Tel Aviv: Miskal, 2008. In Hebrew.

Meir, Golda. *My Life*. Jerusalem: Steimatzky, 1975.

Meisels, Moshe. *From Ben-Gurion to Rabin*. Tel Aviv: Yaron Golan, 2000. In Hebrew.

Meital, Yoram. "The Khartoum Conference and Egyptian Policy after the 1967 War: A Reexamination." *Middle East Journal* 54, no. 1 (2000): 64–82.

———. "The October War and Egypt's Multiple Crossings." In *The Yom Kippur War: Politics, Diplomacy, Legacy*, edited by Asaf Siniver, 85–99. New York: Oxford University Press, 2013.

Melman, Yossi, and Dan Raviv. *Friends In Deed: Inside the U.S.-Israel Alliance.* New York: Hyperion, 1994.

Merkley, Paul Charles. *American Presidents, Religion, and Israel.* Westport, CT: Praeger, 2004.

Moorehead, Alan. *Desert War: The North African Campaign, 1940–1943.* London: Hamilton, 1965.

Morris, Benny. *The Birth of the Palestinian Refugee Problem, 1947-1949*. Cambridge: Cambridge University Press, 1989.

———. *Israel's Border Wars 1949–1956: Arab Infiltration, Israeli Retaliation, and the Countdown to the Suez War*. New York: Oxford University Press, 1993.

Nakdimon, Shlomo. *Low Probability: A Narrative of the Dramatic Story Preceding the Yom Kippur War and of the Fateful Events Which Followed.* Tel Aviv: Revivim, 1982. In Hebrew.

Nixon, Richard. *RN: The Memoirs of Richard Nixon.* New York: Simon and Schuster, 1978.

Nutting, Anthony. *No End of a Lesson: The Story of Suez*. London: Constable, 1967.

O'Brien, Conor C. *The Siege: The Saga of Israel and Zionism*. New York: Simon and Schuster, 1986.

Offer, Dalia. "Holocaust Survivors as Immigrants: The Case of Israel and the Cyprus Detainees." *Modern Judaism* 16, no. 1 (1996): 1–23.

Oren, Michael. "Did Israel Want the Six Day War?" *Azure* 7 (1999): 47–86.

———. *Six Days of War: June 1967 and the Making of the Modern Middle East.* Oxford: Oxford University Press, 2002.

Parker, Richard B., ed., *The Six-Day War: A Retrospective*. Gainesville: University Press of Florida, 1996.

Parkinson, Stephen. *Arena of Ambition: A History of the Cambridge Union*. London: Icon, 2009.

Pollack, Kenneth M. "Air Power in the Six-Day War." *Journal of Strategic Studies* 28, no. 3 (2005): 471–503.

Popp, Ronald. "Stumbling Decidedly into the Six-Day War." *Middle East Journal* 60, no. 2 (2007): 281–309.

Pinchuk, Ben C. "Jewish Discourse and the *Shtetl*." *Jewish History* 15, no. 2 (2001): 169–79.

Quandt, William B. *Decade of Decisions: American Policy toward the Arab-Israeli Conflict, 1967–1976,* Berkeley: University of California Press, 1977.

———. "Lyndon Johnson and the June 1967 War: What Color Was the Light?" *Middle East Journal* 46, no. 2 (1992): 198–228.

———. *Peace Process: American Diplomacy and the Arab-Israeli Conflict since 1967*. Washington, DC: Brookings Institution Press, 2001.

Rabin, Yitzhak. *Service Diary*. Tel Aviv: Ma'ariv, 1979. In Hebrew.

———. *The Rabin Memoirs*. Berkeley: University of California Press, 1996.

Radosh, Allis, and Ronald Radosh. *A Safe Haven: Harry S. Truman and the Founding of Israel*. New York: HarperCollins, 2009.

Rafael, Gideon. *Destination Peace: Three Decades of Israeli Foreign Policy*. New York: Stein and Day, 1981.

Raviv, Moshe. *Israel at Fifty: Five Decades of Struggle for Peace.* London: Weidenfeld and Nicolson, 1998.

Raz, Avi. *The Bride and the Dowry: Israel, Jordan and the Palestinians in the Aftermath of the June 1967 War*. London: Yale University Press, 2012.

———. "The Generous Peace Offer That Was Never Offered: The Israeli Cabinet Resolution of June 19, 1967." *Diplomatic History* 37, no. 1 (2013): 85–108.

Reagan, Ronald. *An American Life: The Autobiography*. New York: Simon and Schuster, 1990.

Renton, James. "Flawed Foundations: The Balfour Declaration and the Palestine Mandate." In *Britain, Palestine and Empire: The Mandate Years*, edited by Rory Miller, 15-39. Farnham, England: Ashgate, 2010.

Rose, Norman, ed. *Baffy: The Diaries of Blanche Dugdale, 1936–1947*. London: Vallentine, Mitchell and Co., 1973.

———. *Chaim Weizmann: A Biography*. New York: Viking, 1986.

———, ed. *The Letters and Papers of Chaim Weizmann*, vol. 19, *January 1939–June 1940*. New Brunswick, NJ: Transaction, 1979.

Rosenthal, Alan. *Jerusalem, Take One! Memoirs of a Jewish Filmmaker*. Carbondale: Southern Illinois University Press, 2000.

Rouleau, Eric. "Hawks and Doves in Israel's Foreign Policy." *The World Today*, December 1968, 496–503.

Sachar, Howard M. *A History of Israel from the Rise of Zionism to Our Time*. New York: Knopf, 2010.

Sacks, Oliver. *Uncle Tungsten: Memories of a Chemical Boyhood*. New York: Knopf, 2001.

Sadat, Anwar. *In Search of Identity*. London: Collins, 1978.

Safran, Nadav. *Israel: The Embattled Ally*. Cambridge, MA: Harvard University Press, 1980.

Said, Edward. *Representation of the Intellectual: The 1993 Reith Lectures*. New York: Vintage, 1996.

Sapir, Michal. *Hayesh Hagadol: A Biography of Pinchas Sapir.* Tel Aviv: Miskal, 2011. In Hebrew.

Schaary, David. "The Social Structure of the Cyprus Detention Camps: 1946–1949." *Studies in Zionism* 3, no. 2 (1982): 273–90.

Schlesinger, Arthur M., Jr. *A Life in the Twentieth Century: Innocent Beginnings, 1917–1950*. New York: Houghton Mifflin, 2002.

Schoenbaum, David. *The United States and the State of Israel*. New York: Oxford University Press, 1993.

Segev, Tom. *1967: Israel, the War, and the Year that Transformed the Middle East.* New York: Metropolitan, 2005.

Shalom, Zaki. *Diplomacy in the Shadow of War: Myth and Reality in Advance of the Six-Day War*. Tel Aviv: Ministry of Defence Publishing House, 2007. In Hebrew.

———. *The Role of US Diplomacy in the Lead-up to the Six-Day War: Balancing Moral Commitments and National Interests*. Brighton, England: Sussex Academic, 2011.

Shapira, Anita. *Israel: A History.* London: Orion, 2012.

Sharett, Moshe. *At the Threshold of Statehood.* Tel Aviv: Am-Oved, 1958. In Hebrew.

———. *Personal Diary*. Edited by Yaacov Sharett. Tel Aviv: Maariv, 1978. In Hebrew.

Sheffer, Gabriel. *Moshe Sharett: Biography of a Political Moderate.* Oxford: Oxford University Press, 1996.

———. "Sharett, Ben-Gurion and the 1956 War of Choice." *State, Government and International Relations* 27 (1988): 1–28.

Shlaim, Avi. "The Balfour Declaration and Its Consequences." In *Yet More Adventures with Britannia: Personalities, Politics and Culture in Britain*, edited by W. R. Louis, 251–70. London: Tauris, 2005.

———. "Conflicting Approaches to Israel's Relations with the Arabs: Ben-Gurion and Sharett, 1953–1956." *Middle East Journal* 37, no. 2 (1983): 180–201.

———. "Interview with Abba Eban, 11 March 1976." *Israel Studies* 8, no. 1 (2003): 153–77.

———. *The Iron Wall: Israel and the Arab World.* London: Penguin, 2000.

———. "The Likud in Power: The Historiography of Revisionist Zionism." *Israel Studies* 1, no. 2 (1996): 254–55.

———. *Lion of Jordan: The Life of King Hussein in War and Peace*. New York: Vintage, 2007.

———. "The Protocol of Sèvres: Anatomy of a War Plot." *International Affairs* 73, no. 3 (1997): 509–30.

Siniver, Asaf. *Nixon, Kissinger, and U.S. Foreign Policy Making: The Machinery of Crisis*. New York: Cambridge University Press, 2008.

———. "U.S. Foreign Policy and the Kissinger Stratagem." In *The Yom Kippur War: Politics, Diplomacy, Legacy*, edited by Asaf Siniver, 85–99. New York: Oxford University Press, 2013.

Smolansky, Oles M. "Moscow and the Suez Crisis, 1956: A Reappraisal." *Political Science Quarterly* 80, no. 4 (1965): 581–604.

Spiegel, Steven L. *The Other Arab-Israeli Conflict: Making America's Middle East Policy from Truman to Reagan*. Chicago: University of Chicago Press, 1986.

St. John, Robert. *Ben-Gurion: The Biography of an Extraordinary Man*. New York: Doubleday, 1959.

———. *Eban*. New York: Doubleday, 1972.

State of Israel, *Yalkut Hapirsumim* (Portfolio of Notifications). Jerusalem: State of Israel, 1954.

Stedman, Stephen J. *Peacemaking in Civil War: International Mediation in Zimbabwe, 1974–1980*. Boulder, CO: Lynne Rienner, 1991.

Stein, Kenneth W. *Heroic Diplomacy: Sadat, Kissinger, Carter, Begin, and the Quest for Arab-Israeli Peace*. New York: Routledge, 1999.

———. "A Historiographic Review of Literature on the Origins of the Arab-Israeli Conflict." *American Historical Review* 96, no. 5 (1991): 1450–65.

Stein, Leslie. *The Making of Modern Israel 1948–1967*. Cambridge: Polity, 2009.

Sugarman, Sidney. *The Unrelenting Conflict: Britain, Balfour, and Betrayal*. Sussex, England: Book Guild, 2000.

Tauber, Eliezer. *Personal Policy Making: Canada's Role in the Adoption of the Palestine Partition Resolution*. Westport, CT: Greenwood, 2002.

Temko, Ned. *To Win or Die: A Personal Portrait of Menachem Begin*. New York: Morrow, 1987.

Teveth, Shabtai. *Ben-Gurion: The Burning Ground, 1886–1948*. Boston: Houghton Mifflin, 1987.

———. *Ben-Gurion's Spy: The Story of the Political Scandal That Shaped Modern Israel*. New York: Columbia University Press, 1996.

———. *The Tanks of Tamuz*. London: Sphere, 1969.

Touval, Saadia. *The Peace Brokers: Mediators in the Arab-Israeli Conflict*. Princeton, NJ: Princeton University Press, 1982.

Troen, Ilan. "The Protocol of Sèvres: British/French/Israeli Collusion against Egypt, 1956." *Israel Studies* 1, no. 2 (1996): 122–39.

Truman, Harry S. *Memoirs by Harry S. Truman, vol. 2: Years of Trial and Hope*. New York: Doubleday, 1956.

Turner, Ernest S. *The Phoney War on the Home Front*. London: Joseph, 1961.

Twain, Mark. *The Innocents Abroad*. Reprint ed. London: Penguin, 2003.

Twigg, John. *A History of Queens' College, Cambridge 1448–1986*. Woodbridge, England: Boydell, 1987.

Tyler, Patrick. *Fortress Israel: The Inside Story of the Military Elite Who Run the Country—And Why They Can't Make Peace*. London: Portobello, 2012.

Tzameret, Tzvi. "Zalman Arrane and the Education System." In *The Second Decade, 1958–1968*, edited by Tzvi Tzameret and Hannah Yablonka, 61-78. Jerusalem: Yad Ben-Zvi, 2000. In Hebrew.

United Nations Special Committee on Palestine. *Summary Report (August 31, 1947)*. London: His Majesty's Stationery Office, 1947.

———. *Report to the General Assembly, Supplement No. 11*. Document A/364. New York: United Nations, 1947.

Urquhart, Brian. *Hammarskjold*. New York: Norton, 1994.

———. *Ralph Bunche: An American Odyssey*. New York: Norton, 1993.

Vanetik, Boaz, and Zaki Shalom, *The Nixon Administration and the Middle East Peace Process, 1969–1973: From the Rogers Plan to the Outbreak of the Yom Kippur War*. Eastbourne, England: Sussex Academic, 2013.

Vital, David. *A People Apart: A Political History of the Jews in Europe 1789–1939*. New York: Oxford University Press, 2001.

Wasserstein, Bernard. "The Assassination of Lord Moyne." *Transactions of the Jewish Historical Society of England* 27 (1978–80): 72–83.

Waxman, Dov. "The Pro-Israel Lobby in the United States." In *Israel and the United States: Six Decades of US-Israeli Relations*, edited by Robert O. Freedman, 79–99. Boulder, CO: Westview, 2012.

Webster, Charles. *The Art and Practice of Diplomacy*. New York: Barnes and Noble, 1962.

Weiler, Peter. "British Labour and the Cold War: The Foreign Policy of the Labour Governments, 1945–1951." *Journal of British Politics* 26, no. 1 (1987): 54–82.

Weinryb, Bernard D. "The Lost Generation in Israel." *Middle East Journal* 7, no. 4 (1953): 415–29.

Weisgal, Meyer. *Meyer Weisgal . . . So Far*. Jerusalem: Weidenfeld and Nicolson, 1971. In Hebrew.

Wilson, R. D. *Cordon and Search: With the 6th Airborne Division in Palestine*. Brompton, England: Gale and Polden, 1949.

Williams, Francis. *Ernest Bevin: A Portrait of a Great Englishman*. London: Hutchinson, 1952.

———. *A Prime Minister Remembers: The War and Post-War Memoirs of the Right Hon. Earl Attlee*. London: Heinemann, 1961.

Yanay, Natan. *Rift at the Top*. Tel Aviv: Levin-Epstein, 1969. In Hebrew.

Zak, Moshe. *King Hussein Makes Peace: Thirty Years of Secret Talks*. Ramat-Gan, Israel: Bar-Ilan University Press, 1996. In Hebrew.

Zeitlin, Solomon. "Are Judaism and Christianity Fossil Religions?" *Jewish Quarterly Review*, 47 (1956): 187–95.

Index

Elazar, David 238, 248, 309